SVPPLEMENTVM
FESTIVVM

Studies in Honor of
Paul Oskar Kristeller

Paul Oskar Kristeller
Berlin ca. 1925

NACHMITTAG DES LEBENS

Ich stand am Fenster eines Nachmittags
Und sah die Sonne hoch im Himmel schweben,
Tief prägte sich ihr Bild dem Aug' und Geiste ein.
Da wandt' ich mich hinweg und blieb verloren
In Tätigkeit und mancherlei Gedanken.
Als ich mich wiederum besann, trat ich ans Fenster
Und dachte sie am gleichen Ort zu finden:
Der Platz war leer, die Sonne sank bereits
Zum Untergang und grüsste mich im Scheiden.

Paul Oskar Kristeller
Iter Italicum I (1965)

Paul Oskar Kristeller
New York 1980

medieval & renaissance
texts & studies

VOLUME 49

SVPPLEMENTVM
FESTIVVM

Studies in Honor of
Paul Oskar Kristeller

edited by

| JAMES | JOHN | FREDERICK |
| HANKINS | MONFASANI | PURNELL, JR. |

Medieval & Renaissance Texts & Studies
Binghamton, New York
1987

Library of Congress Cataloging-in-Publication Data

Supplementum festivum.

(Medieval & Renaissance texts & studies ; 49)
Bibliography: p.
Includes index.
1. Philosophy, Renaissance. 2. Humanism. 3. Ficino, Marsilio,
1433-1499. 4. Kristeller, Paul Oskar, 1905-   .
I. Kristeller, Paul Oskar, 1905-   . II. Hankins, James.
III. Monfasani, John.   IV. Purnell, Jr. Frederick.   V. Series:
Medieval & Renaissance texts & studies ; v. 49.
B775.S85   1987   190   87-18422
ISBN 0-86698-033-4 (alk. paper)

This book is set in Bembo typeface,
smythe-sewn and printed on
acid-free paper to library specifications.
It will not fade, tear, or crumble.

Printed in the United States of America

Tabula Gratulatoria

The following individuals and institutions have generously contributed towards the publication of this volume:

The Renaissance Society of America
State University of New York at Binghamton

The Medieval and Renaissance Program
    Barnard College
Prof. Aldo S. Bernardo
Prof. Jo Anne G. Bernstein
Prof. Gene A. Brucker
Dr. Curt F. Bühler
Prof. F. Edward Cranz
Prof. and Mrs. Mario A. DiCesare
Prof. Elizabeth Story Donno
Dr. John Dooley
Prof. Deno Geanakoplos
Prof. Neal Ward Gilbert
Dr. Phyllis Goodhart Gordan
Prof. Gordon Griffiths
Prof. James Gutmann
Mr. and Mrs. Frank W. Hankins, Jr.
Prof. Richard Harrier
Dr. Rudolf Hirsch
Hill Monastic Manuscript Library
The Hon. Hubert Howard
Prof. Georg N. Knauer
Dr. Elfriede R. Knauer
Prof. Jill Kraye
Mr. George Labalme, Jr.
Prof. Patricia H. Labalme
Prof. Rensselaer W. Lee
Prof. Walther Ludwig
Prof. Stuart MacClintock

Prof. Edward P. Mahoney
Prof. Herbert S. Matsen
Dr. Mary E. Milham
Prof. James V. Mirollo
Prof. John W. O'Malley
Mr. Richard Pachella
Prof. Martin Pine
Prof. David Pingree
Prof. Emil Polak
Prof. Sesto Prete
Prof. Ennio Rao
Prof. Eugene F. Rice, Jr.
Miss Marjorie A. Riley
Prof. Paul Rosenfeld
Mr. Bernard M. Rosenthal
Prof. Peter Rudnytsky
Prof. Paul Gerhard Schmidt
Dr. Susan Field Senneff
Prof. Herman Shapiro
Prof. Nancy Siraisi
Prof. Craig Hugh Smyth
Prof. Friedrich Solmsen
Prof. Robert Somerville
Prof. Joseph R. Strayer
Prof. Leonardo Tarán
Prof. Morimichi Watanabe
Prof. Ronald G. Witt
Dr. T. C. Price Zimmermann

CONTENTS

CONTENTS

PREFACE

In 1975, on the occasion of his seventieth birthday, Paul Oskar Kristeller was presented with three volumes of essays, published in three different countries, to honor him for his extraordinary contributions to philosophical, historical, and literary scholarship. In 1980, Kristeller's Italian friends, some of whom had been his first students more than forty years earlier at the Scuola Normale Superiore in Pisa, honored him with yet a fourth volume. Even for eminent scholars the gift of a Festschrift is an exceptional honor; that four such volumes have appeared, containing the works of seventy-two European and American contributors, is striking evidence of the great impact Kristeller has had on the scholarship of his time, as well as a tribute to the unique esteem he enjoys in the international academic community. So why now a fifth volume? The answer is simple. While the four earlier volumes were in preparation, Professor Kristeller trained and influenced a new generation of students and continually enlarged the circle of his friends and admirers. Hence, on the occasion of his eightieth birthday, these friends and disciples by means of the present volume wish in their turn to pay homage to an inspiring teacher and a generous friend, and in so doing to contribute in their own measure to the scholarly tradition he has transmitted to them.

The first time one of the editors spoke to Professor Kristeller he was surprised to hear him characterize an elderly scholar—or so he seemed to the young student at the time—as one of the "younger men" in the field. In the spirit of Kristeller's expansive view of youth, the editors did not invite participation in the volume on the basis of age; rather, they sought out those who might now consider themselves in some sense Kristeller's disciples, yet whose careers were not sufficiently advanced when the earlier Festschriften were planned for them to have been included in those volumes. Because of other commitments and the shortage of time, not all those invited were able to join the enterprise, but the response of those who could was most gratifying, both in terms of the number and the quality of the studies contributed.

As testimony to the breadth of Professor Kristeller's scholarly interests and influence, the essays in this volume have intentionally not been confined to any single theme or period, but are arranged chronologically. The majority, to be sure, deal with Renaissance humanism and philosophy, reflecting Kristeller's long association with those subjects, and there is a solid core of articles dealing with Renaissance Platonism. It is particularly appropriate that one of the latter was contributed by the grandson of Giovanni Gentile, the distinguished Italian scholar who offered support and encouragement to Professor Kristeller when he began his research on Marsilio Ficino more than fifty years ago. But the range of interests reflected in the contributions extends far beyond these limits, involving topics as diverse as medieval canon law, the philosophy of history, and art patronage, and embracing a period extending from the eleventh to the seventeenth centuries. The breadth of this diversity well reflects the many areas of research in which Professor Kristeller's writing and teaching have proven influential. In spite of his belief in the distinct character of the Renaissance as an historical period, Professor Kristeller has always stressed the close ties between medieval and early modern cultural and intellectual history. In his own historical method he has emphasized the close study of primary sources, both printed and manuscript, and this approach is well represented in the present volume. Indeed, the editors have encouraged contributors to provide the textual basis for their researches where feasible, and they have responded with a wide range of newly edited and previously unpublished source materials.

Over and above the specific ways in which Professor Kristeller's advice and assistance have influenced the work of the many scholars here represented, he has provided us all with something more. His steadfast dedication to an ongoing tradition of humanistic studies in the face of contrary trends in Western culture has afforded us a sense of continuity with his and prior generations of scholars which we will carry with us always. It is our hope that the present volume will serve as a sign of our conviction that that tradition will be carried on.

The editors have received aid from many quarters in bringing this volume to completion. Cynthia M. Pyle first proposed the volume and helped in the initial stages. Eugene F. Rice, Jr. has given sage counsel at various points in the enterprise; James Beck and F. Edward Cranz kindly served as editorial consultants; Mario A. Di Cesare and the staff at Medieval & Renaissance Texts & Studies have been unfailingly helpful. We are deeply indebted to Richard Pachella for undertaking the labor of providing a bibliography of Professor Kristeller's writings from 1975 to 1985, which brings up to date the earlier bibliography of Edward P. Mahoney in *Philosophy and Humanism: Renaissance Essays in Honor of Paul Oskar Kristeller,* (1976). Gladys Passoa and Joan Lesnoy of the Department of Philosophy, Queens College, kindly assisted in manuscript preparation and correspondence. We are grateful most of all to the many friends of Professor Kristeller who contributed so generously to defray the costs of publication. Their names, printed at the head of this volume, are a further witness to the affection we all share for our beloved teacher and friend.

December, 1986

The PUBLICATIONS of
PAUL OSKAR KRISTELLER
For the Years 1975–1985

T HE PRESENT BIBLIOGRAPHY forms a sequel to Edward P. Mahoney's
"Bibliography of the Publications of Paul Oskar Kristeller for the
Years 1929–1974," which appeared in *Philosophy and Humanism: Renaissance Essays in Honor of Paul Oskar Kristeller* (Leiden: E. J. Brill, and New
York: Columbia University Press, 1976), at 543–89. With the exception
of the list of Festschriften at the end, its plan is the same as that of the
earlier work, and continues its numbering. All editions of Professor Kristeller's own books, pamphlets, and articles are dealt with in detail, but books
and periodicals containing what Professor Kristeller deems to be "minor"
contributions are fully described only for first editions. Later imprints and
editions are usually noted briefly, except where they have some particular
significance or may be mistaken for first imprints. Editors and translators
have been noted in all cases where their names were available.

The descriptive method is based upon that adopted by the American
Library Association and used for catalogue cards printed and distributed
in the United States by the Library of Congress. I have modified the Library
of Congress usage, as did Professor Mahoney, to ignore blanks and leaves
containing only advertisements. Descriptions are based on multiple copies
of the books and pamphlets themselves, with notes drawn from information supplied internally by publishers as well as by other sources, particularly the author himself.

Major Publications

1975

150 "The Latin Poems of Giovanni Pico della Mirandola: A Supplementary Note," in *Poetry and Poetics from Ancient Greece to the Renaissance: Studies in Honor of James Hutton.* Cornell Studies in Classical Philology, 38. Edited by G. M. Kirkwood. Ithaca, N.Y.: Cornell University Press, 1975, 185–206.

151 "Methods of Research in Renaissance Manuscripts," *Manuscripta* 19 (1975), 3–14. See also no. 154.

152 (Editor). Ludwig Bertalot, *Studien zum italienischen und deutschen Humanismus.* 2 vols. Rome: Edizioni di storia e letteratura, 1975. xII, 434 and xI, 470 pp. I, p. vII–x: Vorrede. II, p. 449–70: Zusätze.

153 "Le mythe de l'athéisme de la Renaissance et la tradition française de la libre pensée," in *Bibliothèque d'humanisme et Renaissance* 37 (1975), 337–48. French translation of Mahoney 124, which had been revised and enlarged from Mahoney 46.

154 No. 151 above, reprinted in *Visible Language* 9:3 (1975), 263–75.

155 "Petrarca, der Humanismus und die Scholastik," in *Petrarca.* Wege der Forschung, 353. Edited by August Buck. Darmstadt: Wissenschaftliche Buchgesellschaft, 1975. German translation of Mahoney 55 by Günter Memmert.

1976

156 *Huit philosophes de la Renaissance italienne.* Translated by Anne Denis. Travaux d'histoire ethico-politique, 30. Geneva: Librairie Droz, 1976. 165 pp. French translation of Mahoney 101.

157 *Humanismus und Renaissance, II: Philosophie, Bildung und Kunst.* Edited by Eckhard Kessler and translated by Renate Schweyen-Ott. Humanistische Bibliothek, Reihe 1, Band 22. Munich: Wilhelm Fink, 1976. 346 pp.

The twelve chapters of this book have appeared earlier, mostly in

English, but also in Italian and German. Ch. I–IX (pp. 9–206) = Mahoney 104; Ch. X (pp. 207–22) = Mahoney 45; Ch. XI (pp. 223–43) = Mahoney 74 as revised in Mahoney 146; Ch. XII (pp. 244–64) = Mahoney 127. The footnotes are grouped together (pp. 265–319). Kessler's "Bibliographie Paul Oskar Kristeller" (pp. 320–24) is only selective; Mahoney's "Bibliography of the Publications of Paul Oskar Kristeller for the Years 1929–1974" was not yet available. The "Sachregister" and "Namenregister" (pp. 325–33, 334–46) serve both this volume and Mahoney 149. In his "Vorrede," dated August 27, 1975, Professor Kristeller indicated where the different chapters had appeared previously.

158 "Il codice Plimpton 187 della Columbia University Library e gli scritti di Lauro Quirini sulla nobiltà," in *Miscellanea marciana di studi bessarionei.* Medioevo e umanesimo, 24. Padua: Editrice Antenore, 1976, 201–11.

159 (Associate Editor). Union académique internationale, *Catalogus translationum et commentariorum: Mediaeval and Renaissance Latin Translations and Commentaries; Annotated Lists and Guides,* vol. 3. Edited by F. Edward Cranz. Washington, D.C.: Catholic University of America Press, 1976. xvi, 486 pp. See especially articles on Persius (written with F. Edward Cranz and Dorothy Robathan, 201–312); addenda to Aristarchus (written with F. Edward Cranz, 412–13); Autolycus (413); Stephanus Byzantius (written with Aubrey Diller, 431); Juvenalis (written with F. Edward Cranz, 432–45). See also Mahoney 70 and 138.

160 "L'état présent des études sur Marsile Ficin," in *Platon et Aristote à la Renaissance: XVIe Colloque international de Tours.* De Pétrarque à Descartes, 32. Paris: Vrin, 1976, 59–77.

161 "The Search for Medieval and Renaissance Manuscripts," *Proceedings of the American Philosophical Society* 120:5 (1976), 307–10.

162 "Giovanni Pico della Mirandola and His Latin Poems: A New Manuscript," *Manuscripta* 20 (1976), 154–62. This periodical issue also bears the title *Science, Medicine and the University: 1200–1550: Essays in Honor of Pearl Kibre, Part II.* Edited by Nancy Siraisi and Luke Demaitre.

163 "The Historical Position of Johannes Scottus Eriugena," in *Latin Script and Letters, A.D. 400–900: Festschrift Presented to Ludwig Bieler*

On the Occasion of His 70th Birthday. Edited by John J. O'Meara and B. Naumann. Leiden: E. J. Brill, 1976, 156–64.

164   "Bartholomaeus, Musandinus and Maurus of Salerno and Other Early Commentators of the 'Articella', With a Tentative List of Texts and Manuscripts," *Italia medioevale e umanistica* 19 (1976), 57–87.

165   "Tasks and Problems of Manuscript Research," in *Codicologia I: Théories et principes.* Edited by A. Gruys and J. P. Gumbert. Leiden: E. J. Brill, 1976, 84–90. This article is based on a lecture given in the seminars of Professor Sesto Prete (Fordham University) and of Professor Hugo Friedrich (Freiburg-im-Breisgau).

1977

166   Mahoney 93 and 123 reprinted. London: The Warburg Institute, and Leiden: E. J. Brill, 1977.

167   "Medieval and Renaissance Studies: Reflections of a Scholar," in *Speculum* 52:1 (1977), 1–4.

168   *Runessansu no Shiso [Renaissance Thought].* Translated by Morimichi Watanabe. Tokyo: University of Tokyo Press, 1977. xi, 211, 19 pp. Japanese translation of Mahoney 80.

169   "Introduzione," preceding "Tre trattati di Lauro Quirini sulla nobiltà . . . a cura di Konrad Krautter, con la collaborazione . . . di Helmut Roob," in *Lauro Quirini umanista.* Edited by Vittore Branca. Florence: Leo S. Olschki, 1977, 21–42.

170   "Firenze no Academia Platonica," in *Gendai Shiso* 5:7 (1977), 198–209. Japanese version of Mahoney 68. Translated by Hideo Katayama.

171   *Il sistema moderno delle arti.* Biblioteca di Architettura, Saggi e Documenti, 5. An unauthorized publication, edited by Paolo Bagni and translated by David Drudi, with a commentary by Bagni. Florence: Uniedit, 1977. xxiii, 83 pp. (including 7 plates). Italian translation of Mahoney 43.

172   "Philosophy and Medicine in Medieval and Renaissance Italy," in *Organism, Medicine and Metaphysics: Essays in Honor of Hans Jonas.* Philosophy and Medicine, 7. Edited by Stuart F. Spicker. Dordrecht and Boston: D. Reidel, 1978, 29–40.

173 *Concetti rinascimentali dell'uomo e altri saggi.* Translated by Simonetta Salvestroni. Florence: La Nuova Italia, 1978. 333 pp. Italian version of Mahoney 142, Ch. 1–3 and 6; and of Mahoney 104, Ch. 3 and 7–9.

174 "The First Printed Edition of Plato's Works and the Date of Its Publication (1484)," in *Science and History: Studies in Honor of Edward Rosen.* Studia Copernicana, 16. Wroclaw: Ossolineum, 1978, 25–35.

1979

175 Mahoney 59, reprinted in *Storia della civiltà veneziana*, vol. 2. Florence: Sansoni, 1979, 79–92.

176 "Between the Italian Renaissance and the French Enlightenment: Gabriel Naudé as an Editor," *Renaissance Quarterly* 32:1 (1979), 41–72.

177 "The Modern System of the Arts," in *Art and Philosophy.* Second Edition. Edited by W. E. Kenwick. New York: St. Martin's Press, 1979, 7–33. Mahoney 43, abridged and without notes.

178 "Il rinascimento nella storia del pensiero filosofico," in *Il Rinascimento: Interpretazioni e problemi.* Dedicated to Eugenio Garin. Bari: Laterza, 1979, 149–79. See no. 228.

179 "Cattani da Diacetto, Francesco," *Dizionario biografico degli italiani* 22 (1979), 507–9.

180 *Renaissance Thought and Its Sources.* Edited by Michael Mooney. New York: Columbia University Press, 1979. xiv, 347 pp. For this volume, Professor Kristeller added a new "Introduction" (1–14) and a final "Part Five: Philosophy and Rhetoric From Antiquity to the Renaissance" (211–59, 312–27). Part One (15–81, 201–72) = Mahoney 54; Part Two (83–133, 272–97) = Mahoney 24 and 117; Part Three (135–63, 297–306) = Mahoney 142, Ch. 4–5; Part Four (165–208, 306–12) = Mahoney 142, Ch. 1–3. The three essays of Part Five were originally delivered at a University of Colorado Faculty Colloquium in Boulder, November 27–29, 1975.

181 "Die Stellung der Ethik im Denken der Renaissance," *Quellen und Forschungen aus italienischen Archiven und Bibliotheken* 59 (1979),

273–95. Based on an address given at the Deutsches Historisches Institut in Rome, June 5, 1978.

1980

182   Mahoney 149 and no. 157 reprinted in a 2–volume paperback edition. Uni-Taschenbücher, 914 and 915. Munich: Wilhelm Fink, 1980.

183   Mahoney 104 reprinted as *Renaissance Thought and the Arts*. Princeton, N.J.: Princeton University Press, 1980. With a new preface, pp. VII–X.

184   *Szellemi áramlatok a reneszánszban.* Gyorsuló idö. Edited by Zachar Szofia and translated by Takács Ferenc. Budapest: Magvetö Kodó, 1980. 173 pp. Hungarian version of Mahoney 54.

185   (Associate Editor). Union académique internationale. *Catalogus translationum et commentariorum: Mediaeval and Renaissance Latin Translations and Commentaries; Annotated Lists and Guides,* vol. 4. Edited by F. Edward Cranz. Washington, D.C.: Catholic University of America Press, 1980. XXII, 524 pp. This volume includes a reprint of the preface to vol. 1, (XIII–XVIII), Mahoney 70.

186   "Thomas More as a Renaissance Humanist," *Moreana* 17 (1980), 5–22.

187   "Learned Women of Early Modern Italy: Humanists and University Scholars," in *Beyond Their Sex: Learned Women of the European Past*. Edited by Patricia H. Labalme. New York: New York University Press, 1980, 91–116.

188   "L'etica nel pensiero del rinascimento," *Il Veltro* 24 (1980), 245–61. Italian version of no. 181.

189   "Philosophie und Gelehrsamkeit," *Heidelberger Jahrbücher* 24 (1980), 35–45. This lecture was delivered at Heidelberg University, November 28, 1979, on the occasion of Professor Kristeller's doctoral jubilee.

190   *La Scuola Medica di Salerno secondo ricerche e scoperte recenti.* Quaderni del Centro di Studi e documentazione della Scuola Medica Salernitana, 5. Salerno: TMS—Mutualipassi, 1980. 16 pp.

1981

191 No. 180 reprinted in a paperback edition. New York: Columbia University Press, 1981.

192 *In memoria di Giorgio Radetti: Fonti antiche e rinascimentali dell'* Etica dello Spinoza: *Conferenza tenuta il 24 novembre 1979 al Circolo della cultura e delle arti di Trieste.* Trieste: Tipografia-Litografia "Moderna", 1981. 19 pp. See no. 220.

193 "Historical Scholarship and Philosophical Thought," *Minerva* 18:2 (1980), 313–23. An English version of no. 189, actually published in 1981.

194 *Studien zur Geschichte der Rhetorik und zum Begriff des Menschen in der Renaissance.* Gratia, Bamberger Schriften zur Renaissance-forschung, 9. Edited by Dieter Wuttke and translated by Renate Jochum. Göttingen: Gratia-Verlag (Stephan Fuessel), 1981. 149 pp. German version of no. 180, Parts Five and Four.

195 "Niccolò Perotti ed i suoi contributi alla storia dell' Umanesimo," *Res publica litterarum* 4 (1981), 7–25.

196 *Marsilio Ficino letterato e le glosse attribuite a lui nel codice Caetani di Dante.* Quaderni della Fondazione Camillo Caetani, 3. Rome: Città nuova, 1981. 77 pp. (including 3 plates). With a preface by the Hon. Hubert Howard and appendices by Albinia de la Mare and Augusto Campana. This paper is based on a lecture delivered at Rome, November 15, 1979, under the auspices of the Fondazione and its president, the Hon. Hubert Howard.

197 "Un opuscolo sconosciuto di Cencio de' Rustici dedicato a Bornio da Sala: La traduzione del dialogo *De virtute* attribuito a Platone," in *Miscellanea Augusto Campana*, vol. I. Medioevo e Umanesimo, 44. Padua: Editrice Antenore, 1981, 355–76 (including 7 plates, numbered 9–15).

198 *Retorica e filosofia dall' antichità al rinascimento.* Saggi Bibliopolis, 6. Translated by Antonio Gargano. Naples: Bibliopolis, 1981. 102 pp. Italian translation in paperback of no. 180, Part Five.

1982

199 "Thomas Morus als Humanist," in *Thomas Morus als Humanist. Zwei Essays*. Edited by Dieter Wüttke. Bamberg: H. Kaiser, 1982, 9–37. (The other essay is by Hans Maier.) German version of no. 186.

200 *Handschriftenforschung und Geistesgeschichte der italienischen Renaissance*. Akademie der Wissenschaften und der Literatur, Mainz, Abhandlungen der Geistes- und Sozialwissenschaftlichen Klasse, (9:)7. Wiesbaden: Franz Steiner, 1982. 31 pp.

201 "The Renaissance in the History of Philosophical Thought," in *The Renaissance, Essays in Interpretation*. Dedicated to Eugenio Garin. London and New York: Methuen, 1982, 127–52. English version of no. 178.

202 "Neue Quellen zur Salernitaner Medizin des 12. Jahrhunderts," in *Medizin im mittelalterlichen Abendland*. Edited by Gerhard Baader and Gundolf Keil. Darmstadt: Wissenschaftliche Buchgesellschaft, 1982, 191–208. German translation of Mahoney 62 by Christine Porzer.

203 "Un documento ignoto per la biografia di Poggio Bracciolini," in *Poggio Bracciolini 1380–1980*. Florence: Sansoni, 1982, 261–63.

204 "Filosofia ed erudizione," *Il Veltro* 26:1–2 (1982), 49–62. Italian translation of no. 189 by Luciano Tosti, with summaries in Italian, French, English, German, and Spanish.

205 "Humanizm i Scholastycyzm we Wloskim Renesansie," *Pamietnik Literaski* 73:1–2 (1982), 237–67. Polish translation of Mahoney 24 by G. Cendrowska.

206 *El pensamiento Renacentista y sus fuentes*. Translated by Federico Patan Lopez. Mexico City: Fondo de Cultura Económica, 1982. 366 pp. Spanish version of no. 180.

207 "I codici umanistici posseduti dalle biblioteche dell' Italia Meridionale e di Brindisi," *Monumenta Apuliae ac Japygiae* 2 (1982), 7–14.

1983

208 "'Creativity' and 'Tradition'," *Journal of the History of Ideas* 44 (1983), 105–13.

209 "Aristotelismo e sincretismo nel pensiero di Pietro Pomponazzi,"
    in *Aristotelismo Veneto e scienza moderna: Atti del 25° anno accademico
    del Centro per la Storia della tradizione aristotelica nel Veneto,* vol. 2.
    Saggi e testi, 18–19. Edited by L. Olivieri. Padua: Editrice Ante-
    nore, 1983, 1077–99. This was the closing lecture at the Padua Con-
    ference, March 8, 1982.

210 No. 210, printed as a separate pamphlet, with preface by Ezio Ri-
    ondato. Padua: Antenore, 1983. 23 pp.

211 "Marsilio Ficino as a Man of Letters and the Glosses Attributed to
    Him in the Caetani Codex of Dante," *Renaissance Quarterly* 36:1
    (1983), 1–47 (including 3 plates). With appendices by Albinia de
    la Mare and Augusto Campana. English translation of no. 196. Pub-
    lished with a subsidy from the Fondazione Camillo Caetani, Rome.

212 "Petrarcas Stellung in der Geschichte der Gelehrsamkeit," in *Italien
    und die Romania in Humanismus und Renaissance: Festschrift für Erich
    Loos.* Edited by Klaus W. Hempfer and Enrico Straub. Weisbaden:
    Steiner, 1983, 102–21.

213 "Rhetoric in Medieval and Renaissance Culture," in *Renaissance Elo-
    quence, Studies in the Theory and Practice of Renaissance Rhetoric.* Edit-
    ed by James J. Murphy. Berkeley, Los Angeles, and London:
    University of California Press, 1983, 1–19.

214 "Professional Opportunities and Intellectual Tradition in Medieval
    and Renaissance Europe," in *Proceedings of the Symposium on Slavic
    Cultures: Bulgarian Contributions to Slavic Culture.* Sofia: Sofia Press,
    1983, 162–67.

215 *Iter Italicum: A Finding List of Uncatalogued or Incompletely Catalogued
    Humanistic Manuscripts of the Renaissance in Italian and Other Libraries.*
    Vol. III: *Accedunt Alia Itinera I, Australia to Germany.* London: The
    Warburg Institute, and Leiden: E. J. Brill, 1983. xxxix, 747 pp.
    See Mahoney 93 and 123.

216 "Marsilio Ficino e Venezia," in *Miscellanea di studi in onore di Vittore
    Branca.* Vol. III, pt. 2: *Umanesimo e Rinascimento a Firenze e a Vene-
    zia.* Florence: Leo S. Olschki, 1983, 475–92.

217 "Rinascimento," in *Dizionario degli Istituti di perfezione.* Edited by G.
    Pelliccia and G. Rocca. Vol. 7. Rome: Edizioni Paoline, 1983, cols.
    1773–88. Edited and translated from Mahoney 131 by L. Giovannini.

218   "Il pensiero del rinascimento: Problemi e ricerche," *Annali della Scuola
      Normale Superiore di Pisa, Classe di lettere e filosofia, ser. III,* 13:4 (1983),
      1007–23.

1984

Mahoney 60 reprinted. Rome: Edizioni di storia e letteratura, 1984.
"Stoic and Neoplatonic Sources of Spinoza's *Ethics,*" *History of European Ideas* 5 (1984), 1–15. Based on a lecture given at the University
of Haifa, March 22, 1982, and at the Institute for Advanced Studies
of the Hebrew University, Jerusalem, March 28, 1982. An Italian
version, no. 192, was published in memory of Giorgio Radetti by
the Circolo della Cultura e delle Arti di Trieste in 1981; see no. 192.
"La cultura umanistica a Roma nel Quattrocento," in *Umanesimo
a Roma nel Quattrocento: Atti del Convegno . . . New York, 1–4 dicembre
1981.* Edited by P. Brezzi and Maristella de Panizza Lorch. Rome:
Istituto di Studi Romani, and New York: Barnard College, 1984,
323–32.
"Latein und Vulgärsprache im Italien des 14. und 15. Jahrhunderts,"
Deutsches Dante Jahrbuch 59 (1984), 7–35.
"Creatività e tradizione," *Il Veltro* 28:1–2 (1984), 17–29. Italian trans-
lation of no. 208 by Paola Pavanini.
(Associate Editor). Union acadèmique internationale, *Catalogus trans-
lationum et commentariorum: Mediaeval and Renaissance Latin Transla-
tions and Commentaries; Annotated Lists and Guides,* vol. 5. Edited by
F. Edward Cranz. Washington, D. C.: Catholic University of
America Press, 1984. xxi, 427 pp. This volume includes a reprint
of the preface to vol. 1 (xi–xvi), Mahoney 70.
"The Lachmann Method: Merits and Limitations," *Text: Transac-
tions of the Society for Textual Scholarship* 1 (1981), 11–20. Actually
published in 1984.
"Vita attiva e vita contemplativa in un brano inedito di Bornio da
Sala e in S. Tommaso d'Aquino," in *Essere e libertà: Studi in onore
di Cornelio Fabro.* Perugia: Università degli Studi, 1984, 211–24.

1985

227   "Scopi e problemi della ricerca di manoscritti," in *La critica del testo*. Edited by Alfredo Stussi. Bologna: Il Mulino, 1985, 119–28. Italian translation of Mahoney 90.

228   *Humanizm i filosofia*. Edited by L. Szczucki. Warsaw: Polska Akademia Nauk, Instytut Filozofii i Socjologii, 1985. 189 pp. Polish translations of Mahoney 54 (ch. 1), 24, 81 and of no. 178.

229   "The Editing of Fifteenth-Century Texts: Tasks and Problems," *Italian Culture* 4 (1983, [published 1985]), 115–22.

230   "Latin and Vernacular in Fourteenth- and Fifteenth-Century Italy," *Journal of the Rocky Mountain Medieval and Renaissance Association* 6 (1985), 105–26. English version of no. 222 with minor additions.

231   "Jewish Contributions to Italian Renaissance Culture," *Italia* (Jerusalem: The Hebrew University) 4 (1985), 7–20.

232   Mahoney 129 reprinted in a paperback edition. Mexico City: Fondo de Cultura Económica, 1985.

233   "Marsilio Ficino and the Roman Curia," in *Roma humanistica: studia in honorem revdi. adm. dni. dni. Iosaei Ruysschaert*. Humanistica Lovaniensia, 34A. Edited by Jozef IJsewijn. Leuven: Leuven University Press, 1985, 83–98.

234   "Philosophy and Its Historiography," *Journal of Philosophy* 82:11 (1985), 618–25.

235   "The Active and the Contemplative Life in Renaissance Humanism," in *Arbeit, Musse, Meditation: Betrachtungen zur "Vita activa" und "Vita contemplativa"*. Edited by Brian Vickers. Zürich: Verlag der Fachvereine, 1985, 133–52.

236   *Studies in Renaissance Thought and Letters*, vol. II. Storia e Letteratura, 166. Rome: Edizioni di Storia e Letteratura, 1985. xvi, 635 pp. This volume, continuing the first volume (Mahoney 60, 1956), contains various previously published articles, some of which are here revised. The following list indicates the chapter number in the volume and the entry number of the article in this bibliographic series. Ch. I (pp. 3–23) = Mahoney 79; Ch. II (pp. 25–48) = Mahoney 86; Ch. III (pp. 49–63) = Mahoney 89; Ch. IV (pp.

65–91) = Mahoney 140; Ch. V (pp. 93–110) = Mahoney 71; Ch. VI (pp. 111–27) = Mahoney 114; Ch. VII (pp. 129–33) = Mahoney 217; Ch. VIII (pp. 135–46) = Mahoney 57; Ch. IX (pp. 147–65) = Mahoney 85; Ch. XI (pp. 185–205) = no. 187; Ch. XII (pp. 209–16) = Mahoney 44; Ch. XIII (pp. 217–38) = Mahoney 55; Ch. XIV (pp. 239–57) = no. 197; Ch. XV (pp. 259–63) = Mahoney 112; Ch. XVI (pp. 265–80) = Mahoney 105; Ch. XVII (pp. 281–300) = Mahoney 113; Ch. XVIII (pp. 301–19) = no. 195; Ch. XIX (pp. 321–39) = no. 169; Ch. XX (pp. 341–83) = Mahoney 100; Ch. XXI (pp. 385–402) = Mahoney 58; Ch. XXII (pp. 403–5) = Mahoney 143; Ch. XXIII (pp. 407–42) = Mahoney 98; Ch. XXIV (pp. 443–56) = Mahoney 132; Ch. XXV (pp. 457–64) = Mahoney 137; Ch. XXVI (pp. 465–72) = Mahoney 78; Ch. XXVII (pp. 473–89) = no. 186. Ch. X (pp. 167–84), though based on no. 181, is unpublished. At the end, the following new pieces are added: Addenda et Corrigenda to the preceding chapters (pp. 493–503); Appendix I: Additional Remarks on the Life and Letters of Bartolomeo Facio (pp. 507–29); Appendix II: Frater Antonius Bergensis and His Treatise on the Dignity of Man (pp. 531–60); Appendix III: Notes on Decembrio's Writings (pp. 561–65); Appendix IV: Decembrio's Treatise on Immortality (pp. 567–84); Appendix V: Erasmus, His Relations to Italy and His Platonism (pp. 585–87). The separate Indexes of Manuscripts and Rare Books, of Incipits, and of Names (pp. 589–635) were compiled by Bruno Blumenfeld.

"Una lettera inedita di Erasmo a Hutten conservata a Firenze," in *Tradizione classica e letteratura umanistica. Per Alessandro Perosa.* Edited by Roberto Cardini, Eugenio Garin, Lucia Cesarini Martinelli, and Giovanni Pascucci. Vol. 2. Rome: Bulzoni, 1985, 629–41.

Minor Publications

1964

221   (Co-author). "Report of the Renaissance Society of America on the State of the Humanities," in *Report of the Commission on the Humanities*. New York: American Council of Learned Societies, 1964, 207–13.

1965

222   No. 221 reprinted in *Congressional Record: Proceedings and Debates of the 89th Congress, First Session* (121:) 3, 1 (January 4–27, 1965), 237–39 (as Exhibit 2).

223   "Letter to Representative Frank Thompson, Jr., of New Jersey (February 18, 1965)," in U.S. House of Representatives, 89th Congress, First Session, Committee on Education and Labor, Special Subcommittee on Labor, *Hearings On Bills HR 334, HR 2043, HR 3617, and Other Related Bills, to Establish a National Foundation of the Arts and Humanities* (February 24, also March 22–24, 1965), 402.

1973

224   Excerpts in *Problemi e scrittori della letteratura italiana* Vol. 1: *Dalle origini all' umanesimo.* Edited by Aldo Giudici and Giovanni Bruni. Turin: Paravia 1973. VIII, 998 pp. "Obiezioni al Burdach e al Toffanin" (670–71); "Umanesimo pagano e Umanesimo Cristiano: L'Umanesimo e la Scolastica" (671); "Carattere e significato della scoperta dei classici" (676–77). These excerpts are drawn from Mahoney 139. See also no. 250.

1975

225   Review of Plotinus, *Opera.* Vol. III: *Enneas VI.* Edited by Paul Henry
and Hans-Rudolf Schwyzer. Paris: Desclée de Brouwer, Brussels:
L'Edition Universelle, and Leiden: E. J. Brill, 1973, in *Journal of
Philosophy* 72 (1975), 21–22.

226   "Letter to the Editors," *New York Review of Books* 22:4 (March
20, 1975), 34. Professor Kristeller's letter reacts to Lord Kenneth
Clark's Dec. 12, 1974 review of Leonardo da Vinci, *The Madrid
Codices.* Edited and translated by Ladislao Reti. 5 vols. New York:
McGraw-Hill, 1974. This is a facsimile edition of two codices in
Madrid's Biblioteca Nacional, nos. 8936 and 8937. See Mahoney 207.

227   "The Humanities as Scholarship and a Branch of Knowledge," in
The Philosophy of the Curriculum: The Need for General Education.
Edited by Sidney Hook, Paul Kurtz and Miro Todorovich. Buffa-
lo, N.Y.: Prometheus Books, 1975, 217–20.

228   Review of Angelo Poliziano, *Miscellaneorum centuria secunda.* Edited by Vittore Branca and Manlio Pastore Stocchi. 4 vols. Florence:
Fratelli Alinari, 1972, in *Renaissance Quarterly* 28:1 (1975), 64–66.

229   "Methods of Research in Renaissance Manuscripts," *Manuscripta*
19 (1975), 77–78. An abstract of no. 151.

230   "Preface," in Marsilio Ficino, *The Letters,* vol. 1. Translated from
the Latin by Members of the Language Department of the School
of Economic Science. London: Shepheard-Walwyn, 1975, 17–18.

231   Letter to Maria Rosa Lida de Malkiel of December 12, 1952, excerpted by Maria Rosa Lida de Malkiel, in Spanish, in *La tradición
clasica en España.* Edited by Y. Malkiel. Barcelona: Editorial Ariel,
1975, 397.

1976

232   Review of *Il Notariato a Perugia: Mostra documentaria e iconografica
per il XVI. Congresso Nazionale del Notariato (Perugia, maggio–luglio
1967).* Edited by Roberto Abbondanza. Rome: Consiglio Nazionale

Notariato, distributed by Volumnia Editrice, Perugia, 1973, in *Renaissance Quarterly* 29:1 (1976), 75.

233   "Preface," in Armand L. De Gaetano, *Giambattista Gelli and the Florentine Academy. The Rebellion Against Latin.* Florence: Leo S. Olschki, 1976, VII–VIII.

234   Review of *Catalogue of Books and Manuscripts in the Harvard College Library, Department of Printing and Graphic Arts.* Part 2, Ruth Mortimer, comp.: *Italian 16th Century Books.* Cambridge, Mass.: Harvard University Press (Belknap), 1974, in *Renaissance Quarterly* 29:3 (1976), 421–22.

235   "Liberal Education and Western Humanism," *Seminar Reports of the Columbia University Program of General Education in the Humanities* 5:1 (1976), 15–26.

236   "Ernest Addison Moody," *Speculum* 51 (1976), 577–78.

237   Review of Helmut Kuhn, *Liebe, Geschichte eines Begriffs.* Munich: Kosel, 1975, in *Journal of Philosophy* 73 (1976), 877–78.

238   Letter to Giuseppe Prezzolini of 1964, in Giuseppe Prezzolini, "La Casa Italiana di Columbia University," *L'Osservatore politico letterario* 22:4 (1976), 65–93 (at 74–75).

1977

239   "Foreword," in René Descartes, *The Essential Writings.* Translated by John J. Blom. New York: Harper and Row, 1977, IX–X.

1978

240   "Humanism," *Minerva* 16:4 (1978), 586–95.

241   "Presentation," in Bartolomeo Facio, *Invective in Laurentium Vallam.* Edited by Ennio J. Rao. Naples: Società Editrice Napoletana, 1978, 5–6.

1979

242   "Etienne Gilson, (1884–1978)," *The American Philosophical Society, Year Book 1978* (Philadelphia: The American Philosophical Society, 1979), 77–80.

243   Review of Walter Ullmann, *Medieval Foundations of Renaissance Humanism.* Ithaca, N.Y.: Cornell University Press, 1977, in *Speculum* 54:2 (1979), 436–38.

244   Review of Anthony R. A. Hobson, *Apollo and Pegasus: An Enquiry Into the Formation and Dispersal of a Renaissance Library.* Amsterdam: Gérard Th. Van Heusden, 1975, in *Renaissance Quarterly* 32:4 (1979), 588–90.

1980

245   Review of Philip Merlan, *Kleine philosophische Schriften.* Collectanea, 20. Edited by Franciszka Merlan. Hildesheim and New York: Georg Olms, 1976, in *Journal of Philosophy* 77 (1980), 52–54.

246   "Joseph L. Blau: In Appreciation," in *History, Religion and Spiritual Democracy: Essays in Honor of Joseph L. Blau.* Edited by Maurice Wohlgelertner. New York: Columbia University Press, 1980, XX–XXI.

247   Review of Günter Abel, *Stoizismus und frühe Neuzeit.* Berlin and New York: Walter de Gruyter, 1978, in *Renaissance Quarterly* 33:2 (1980), 235–36.

248   Review of Franz Josef Worstbrock, *Deutsche Antikerezeption, 1450–1550.* Teil 1: *Verzeichnis der deutschen Uebersetzungen antiker Autoren, mit einer Bibliografie der Uebersetzer.* Veröffentlichungen zur Humanismusforschung. Boppard-am-Rhein: Harald Boldt Verlag, 1976, in *Renaissance Quarterly* 33:3 (1980), 419–20.

249   Note on Csaba Csapodi and Klara Csapodi-Gárdonyi, *Bibliotheca Corviniana: The Library of King Matthias Corvinus of Hungary.* Second Edition. New York: Frederick A. Praeger, 1978, in *Renaissance Quarterly* 33:4 (1980), 507.

1981

250 No. 224 reprinted. Turin: Paravia, 1981.

251 Review of Wladyslaw Tatarkiewicz, *A History of Six Ideas: An Essay in Aesthetics.* Translated by Christopher Kasparek. Warsaw: PWN (Polish Scientific Publishers), and The Hague: Martinus Nijhoff, 1980, in *Journal of Philosophy* 78 (1981), 56–58.

252 "Comment: In Defense of the Humanities," *Humanities Report* (Washington, D.C.: American Association for the Advancement of the Humanities) 3:5 (1981), 2–3.

253 "Randall and the History of Philosophy," *Journal of the History of Ideas* 42 (1981), 489–91.

254 "Contemplation in Plotinus and Marsilio Ficino," *Notes and Commentary* (Dallas) 3 (Fall 1981), 4. Abstract of a lecture given at the University of Dallas Center for Contemplative Studies on February 3, 1981.

255 "Un esperimento riuscito," *Annali della pubblica istruzione* 27 (1981), 465–67. This article describes the Scuola di Studi Superiori of the Istituto Italiano per gli Studi Filosofici at Naples.

256 Two untitled speeches given at Pisa, October 27, 1968, on receiving the Premio Internazionale Galileo Galilei, in *Studiosi stranieri della civiltà italiana.* Edited by Tristano Bolelli. Pisa: Lischi e Figli, 1981, 42–49. The first speech (42–48) is Professor Kristeller's judgment on his own life. The second, a shorter talk (48–49), was given at the luncheon-presentation of the Premio Internazionale Galileo Galilei.

257 "John H. Randall, Jr.," *Renaissance Quarterly* 34:2 (1981), 298–99.

258 "Preface," in Marion L. Kuntz, *Guillaume Postel, Prophet of the Restitution of All Things: His Life and Thought.* International Archives of the History of Ideas, 98. The Hague: Martinus Nijhoff, 1981, ix–x.

259 "Foreword," in Concetta Carestia Greenfield, *Humanist and Scholastic Poetics, 1250–1500.* Lewisburg, Pa.: Bucknell University Press, 1981, 9–10.

260 "Philosophy and Learning," in *Bridges and Boundaries in the Humanities, Arts and Social Sciences: Proceedings of the Columbia University General Education Seminar* 9 (1980–81), 37–42. A lecture abstract.

1982

261 "Il 2° anno della Scuola di Studi Superiori: Platone in Italia," *Il Mattino* (Naples), anno 91 (16 Jan. 1982), 3.

262 "The Humanities and Humanism," *Humanities Report* (Washington, D.C.: American Association for the Advancement of the Humanities) 4:1 (1982), 17–18.

263 No. 262 reprinted in *Community* (Collegeville, Minn.: St. John's University) (Feb. 18, 1982), 1 and 3.

264 "Tribute to the Renaissance Centre in Tours," in Centre d'Etudes Supérieures de la Renaissance, *Rétrospective et prospective.* Tours: Centre d'Etudes Supérieures de la Renaissance, 1982, 52–54.

265 "Man and His Universe in Medieval and Renaissance Philosophy," in *L'homme et son univers au Moyen Age: Septième congrès international de philosophie médiévale, Louvain-la-Neuve et Leuven ... 1982.* Résumés des communications, 2. Louvain-la-Neuve: Editions de l'Institut Supérieur de Philosophie, 1982, 14. An abstract of the lecture delivered at this conference. [This lecture has now appeared under the same title in *L'Homme et son univers au Moyen Age: Actes du Septième congrès international de philosophie médiévale, 30 août – 4 septembre* 1982, vol. 1. Edited by Christian Wenin. Philosophes médiévaux, 26. Louvain-la-Neuve: Editions de l'Institut supérieur de philosophie, 1986, 77–91. -*Ed.*]

266 Review of Domenico Maffei, *Giuristi medievali e falsificazioni editoriali del primo Cinquecento: Iacopo di Belviso in Provenza?* Frankfurt: Klostermann, 1979, in *Renaissance Quarterly* 35:2 (1982), 273–74.

267 "Punto di riferimento," *Il Mattino* (Naples), anno 91 (20 nov. 1982), 11. An interview on Benedetto Croce for the thirtieth anniversary of his death, held with Dott. Antonio Gargano.

1983

268 "Testimonianza," in Giuseppe Prezzolini, *Ricordi, saggi e testimonianze.* Edited by Margherita Marchione. Prato: Cassa di Risparmi e Depositi, 1983, 115–16.

269   Review of Walter Berschin, *Griechisch-Lateinisches Mittelalter von Hieronymus zu Nikolaus von Kues.* Bern and Munich: Francke, 1980, in *Speculum* 58 (1983), 147–49.

270   Review of Giuseppe Billanovich, *La tradizione del testo di Livio e le origini dell' umanesimo.* Vol. 1: *Tradizione e fortuna di Livio tra medioevo e umanesimo.* Studi sul Petrarca, 9. Vol. 2: *Il Livio del Petrarca e del Valla (British Library Harleian 2493 riprodotto integralmente).* Studi sul Petrarca, 11. Padua: Antenore, 1981, in *Renaissance Quarterly* 36:1 (1983), 78–79.

271   Review of William G. Craven, *Giovanni Pico della Mirandola, Symbol of His Age.* Geneva: Droz, 1981, in *Journal of Modern History* 55 (1983), 756–58.

272   Review of Philippe Renouard, *Imprimeurs et libraires parisiens du XVIe siècle. Fascicule Breyer.* Edited by Geneviève Deblock and Geneviève Guilleminot. Paris: Bibliothèque Nationale, 1982, in *Renaissance Quarterly* 36:4 (1983), 587–88.

1984

273   "Latein und Vulgärsprache im Italien des 14. und 15. Jahrhunderts," *Mitteilungsblatt der Deutschen Dante-Gesellschaft E.V.* (Juni 1984), 11–12. A lecture summary. See Major Publications, no. 222.

274   "Wallace K. Ferguson: A Tribute," *Renaissance Quarterly* 37:4 (1984), 675–76.

1985

275   Review of Anthony Grafton, *Joseph Scaliger: A Study in the History of Classical Scholarship.* Vol. 1: *Textual Criticism and Exegesis.* Oxford: Clarendon Press, 1984, in *American Scholar* 54 (1985), 428–30.

276   Draft of a Report of the Renaissance Society of America, in *A Report to the Congress of the United States on the State of the Humanities and the Reauthorization of the National Endowment for the Humanities.* New York: American Council of Learned Societies, 1985, 218–22.

277   "Rensselaer W. Lee," *Renaissance Quarterly* 38:1 (1985), 190–91.

278 "Vorrede," in Ludwig Bertalot, *Initia humanistica Latina.* Band I, *Poesie.* Edited by U. Jaitner-Hahner. Tübingen: Max Niemeyer, 1985, VII–XI.

Festschriften

1 *Itinerarium Italicum, The Profile of the Italian Renaissance in the Mirror of its European Transformations: Dedicated to Paul Oskar Kristeller on the Occasion of his 70th birthday.* Studies in Medieval and Reformation Thought, 14. Edited by Heiko A. Oberman with Thomas A. Brady, Jr. Leiden: E. J. Brill, 1975. XXVIII, 471 pp. The contributors are Heiko A. Oberman, William J. Bouwsma, Myron P. Gilmore, Sem Dresden, Jozef IJsewijn, Denis Hay, and Lewis W. Spitz.

2 *Philosophy and Humanism: Renaissance Essays in Honor of Paul Oskar Kristeller.* Edited by Edward P. Mahoney. Leiden: E. J. Brill, and New York: Columbia University Press, 1976. xxv, 624 pp. The contributors are Eugene F. Rice, Jr., Donald R. Kelley, Richard H. Popkin, Richard Lemay, Martin Pine, F. Edward Cranz, Josef Soudek, Edward P. Mahoney, Joan Kelly-Gadol, Charles Trinkaus, Maristella de Panizza Lorch, Neil W. Gilbert, Malcolm Brown, John H. Randall, Jr., William F. Edwards, C. Doris Hellman, Edward Rosen, W. T. H. Jackson, John Charles Nelson, George B. Parks, Richard Harrier, Helene Wieruszowski, Morimichi Watanabe, Raymond de Roover, Julius Kirshner, John Mundy, Charles B. Schmitt, Guido Kisch, Patricia H. Labalme, Felix Gilbert, Herbert S. Matsen, and Theodore E. James. This volume also includes Edward P. Mahoney's "Bibliography of the Publications of Paul Oskar Kristeller for the Years 1929–1974" (543–89).

3 *Cultural Aspects of the Italian Renaissance: Essays in Honour of Paul Oskar Kristeller.* Edited by Cecil H. Clough. Manchester: Manchester University Press, and New York: Alfred F. Zambelli, 1976. XI, 555 pp. (with 12 pages of plates). The contributors are A. H. McDonald, Anthony Luttrell, John Larner, Cecil H. Clough, D. S. Chambers, Frances A. Yates, A. F. C. Ryder, A. V. Antonovics, Albinia de la Mare, M. E. Mallett, Nicolai Rubinstein, S. A. Jayawardene, Charles B. Schmitt, Philip McNair, D. M. Bueno

de Mesquita, Paul Lawrence Rose, Martin Kemp, C. Malcolm Brown, Walter H. Kemp, Dennis E. Rhodes, C. P. Brand, John Sparrow, T. C. Price Zimmermann, Roger Jacob, J. R. Hale, C. E. Wright, and Anthony Hobson. Margaret Anne Clough provided the Index of Manuscripts and Alison Quinn the General Index.

4   *Umanesimo e Rinascimento: Studi offerti a Paul Oskar Kristeller.* Florence: Leo S. Olschki, 1980. 173 pp. The contributors are Vittore Branca, Arsenio Frugoni, Eugenio Garin, Vito R. Giustiniani, Scevola Mariotti, Alessandro Perosa, and Cesare Vasoli.

RICHARD PACHELLA

ABBREVIATIONS

ASF = Archivio di Stato, Florence.

BAV = Biblioteca Apostolica Vaticana, Vatican City.

Bibl. = Biblioteca, Bibliothèque, Bibliothek.

Bibl. Laur. = Biblioteca Laurenziana, Florence.

BL = British Library, London.

BN = Biblioteca Nazionale, Bibliothèque Nationale.

CSEL = *Corpus scriptorum ecclesiasticorum Latinorum* (Vienna, 1866 to date).

CTC = *Catalogus translationum et commentariorum: Mediaeval and Renaissance Latin Translations and Commentaries*, eds. V. Brown, F. Edward Cranz, and P. O. Kristeller (Washington, D. C., 1960 to date).

DBI = *Dizionario biografico degli italiani* (Rome, 1960 to date).

DHGE = *Dictionnaire d'histoire et de géographie ecclésiastiques* (Paris, 1912 to date).

DSAM = *Dictionnaire de spiritualité, ascétique et mystique* (Paris, 1932 to date).

DTC = *Dictionnaire de théologie catholique*, 15 vols. (Paris, 1908-50).

Eubel = C. Eubel, *Hierarchia catholica Medii Aevi*, 6 vols. (Regensburg, 1901-58).

Guarino, *Epistolario* = *Epistolario di Guarino Veronese*, ed. R. Sabbadini, 3 vols. Miscellanea di storia veneta, 8, 9, and 14 (Venice, 1915-19).

GW = *Gesamtkatalog der Wiegendrucke* (Leipzig, 1925 to date).

Hain = L. Hain, *Repertorium bibliographicum, in quo libri omnes ab arte typographica inventa usque ad annum M. D. typis expressi ordine alphabetico recensentur*, 2 vols. in 4 (Stuttgart and Paris, 1826-38).

IMU = *Italia medioevale e umanistica* (Padua, 1958 to date).

JWCI = *Journal of the Warburg and Courtauld Institutes* (London, 1937 to date).

Kristeller, *Iter* = P. O. Kristeller, *Iter Italicum: A Finding List of Uncatalogued or Incompletely Catalogued Humanistic Manuscripts of the Renaissance in Italian and Other Libraries*, 3 vols. to date (London and Leiden, 1963-83).

Kristeller, *Studies* = P.O. Kristeller, *Studies in Renaissance Thought and Letters* (Rome, 1956).

Kristeller, *Supplementum* = P. O. Kristeller, *Supplementum Ficinianum: Marsilii Ficini Florentini philosophi Platonici opuscula inedita et dispersa*, 2 vols. (Florence, 1937).

MGH = *Monumenta Germaniae historica* (Berlin, 1877 to date).

PG = J. P. Migne, *Patrologiae cursus completus. Series Graeca*, 161 vols. (Paris, 1857-66).

PL = J. P. Migne, *Patrologiae cursus completus. Series Latina*, 221 vols. (Paris, 1844-64).

RQ = *Renaissance Quarterly* (New York, 1947 to date).

Salutati, *Epistolario* = *Epistolario di Coluccio Salutati*, ed. F. Novati, 4 vols., Fonti per la storia d'Italia, 15-18 (Rome, 1891-1911).

ST = *Studi e Testi* (Vatican City, 1900 to date).

THE CORRESPONDENCE OF
POPE PASCHAL II
AND GUIDO OF VIENNE
1111–1116

THE LETTERS EXCHANGED between Pope Paschal II and his legate, Guido, archbishop of Vienne, which are the subject of this paper, survive without any, or with only incomplete, dating formulae.[1] This is a serious lacuna because these letters are important evidence for the opposition within the church to Paschal's policies with regard to investiture and regalia. These connected issues arose during the Gregorian reform in the second half of the eleventh century, when the papacy began first to limit and then to abolish the customary investiture of bishops and abbots with the temporalities of their sees by kings and other lay nobles.[2] Pope Urban II, Paschal's predecessor, couched the prohibition for laymen to invest clergy in particularly strong terms at the council of Clermont in 1095, forbidding not only investiture but also homage.[3] Paschal II (1099–1118) reaf-

---

1. P. Jaffé, *Regesta pontificum romanorum*, 2nd rev. ed., 2 vols. (Leipzig, 1885 and 1888; repr. Graz, 1956). The letters under discussion are catalogued as JL 6313 ("Actionem concilii"), JL 6330 ("Cum alicuius"), and JL 6325 ("Si constantiam").

2. For the process see now R. Schieffer, *Die Entstehung des päpstlichen Investiturverbots für den deutschen König. MGH Schriften*, 28 (Stuttgart, 1981). The book contains a full bibliography. A brief and excellent introduction are the relevant chapters by F. Kempf in *Handbook of Church History*, ed. H. Jedin and J. Dolan, 3: *The Church in the Age of Feudalism*, tr. A. Biggs (New York and London, 1969) part 2, chapters 42–45, with outstanding bibliographies.

3. C.14: "Interdictum est ne reges vel aliqui principes aliquam investituram de honoribus ec-

firmed both these prohibitions at the Lateran council of 1102.[4] In April 1111, however, Paschal, who had been captured and imprisoned with his entourage by Henry V of Germany, turned around and granted Henry the right of investiture with ring and staff, the customary symbols, in return for his own liberty and that of the curia.[5] This privilege proved unacceptable to the church as a whole and after bitter struggles was revoked by the Lateran council of 1112. In the final analysis the authority of the council overrode that of the pope, who merely consented.[6] In brief, this is the context for the letters under discussion. Fixing their date, however, not only will reveal how the line of argument developed, but also will provide a more accurate date for the anonymous *Disputatio vel defensio Paschalis papae,* one of the few theoretical discussions of the investiture problem, and the only one from the later years of Paschal's pontificate.[7]

The treatise was discovered together with two letters of Paschal II in a twelfth-century manuscript, Naples, BN, MS V. C. 46, by Wilhelm Schum, who published his findings in 1877.[8] Because of the poor condition of the last folio, Schum (who, as he noted apologetically, was pressed for time when he copied the texts) remained uncertain about some of his

clesiasticis faciant"; c.15: "Ne episcopus vel sacerdos regi vel alicui laico in manibus ligiam fidelitatem faciat." The texts are quoted from the critical edition by R. Somerville, *The Councils of Urban II,* 1: *Decreta Claromontensia* (Amsterdam, 1972), 77, 78. See also *ibid.,* 145, nos. 18 and 19 for related transmissions.

4. See JL 5908: "Qua de re in synodo nuper apud Lateranense consistorium celebrata patrum nostrorum decreta renovavimus, sancientes et interdicentes, ne quisquam omnino clericus hominium faciat laico aut de manu laici ecclesias vel ecclesiastica dona suscipiat." A discussion is found in my *The Early Councils of Pope Paschal II, 1100–1110* (Toronto, 1978), 17–20.

5. *MGH Constitutiones et acta publica (Legum sectio IV),* 1, ed. L. Weiland, 144ff., no. 96 (cited below as *MGH Const.* 1).

6. The best partial edition of the 1112 council is that by Weiland, *ibid.,* 570–74, nos. 399 and 400. The long version of the minutes has to be read in *Le Liber Pontificalis,* ed. L. Duchesne, 2 (Paris, 1892; repr. 1955), 369–371. For the discussion of some of the problems see my "Opposition to Pope Paschal II," *Annuarium Historiae Conciliorum,* 10 (1978):82–98.

7. *Disputatio vel defensio Paschalis papae,* ed. E. Sackur, *MGH, Libelli de lite,* 2 (1892):658–666, on the basis of Schum's publication. (See the following note.)

8. W. Schum, "Kaiser Heinrich V. und Papst Paschalis II. im Jahre 1112," *Jahrbücher der Königlichen Akademie gemeinnütziger Wissenschaften zu Erfurt,* n.s., 8 (1877): 189–318. Cf. the remarks by G. Meyer von Knonau, *Jahrbücher des deutschen Reiches unter Heinrich IV. und Heinrich V.,* 6 (Leipzig, 1907), Exkurs I, 387 with note 58. See in general the penetrating discussion by R. L. Benson, *The Bishop-Elect. A Study in Medieval Ecclesiastical Office* (Princeton, 1968), esp. 203–250; and M. J. Wilks, "Ecclesiastica and Regalia: Papal Investiture Policy from the Council of Guastalla to the First Lateran Council, 1106–1123," *Studies in Church History,* 7 (Cambridge, 1971): 69–85.

readings in the treatise and the letters to Guido of Vienne and Girard, archbishop of Angoulême. Sackur, with the help of Bethmann and Waitz, emended the treatise, but paid no attention to the letters. A visit to Naples showed that the letters are still sufficiently legible to permit a check of Schum's readings and a confirmation of most of his suggestions.[9] Of particular interest in the present context is Paschal's letter to Guido. The body of the texts reads as follows:

> Actionem concilii quod nuper Laterani domino presente egimus ab eis qui interfuerunt scire plenius poteris. Nos autem predecessorum nostrorum statuta sequentes precipue domni Gregorii VII et Urbani secundi quod dampnaverunt dampnavimus, quod firmaverunt firmavimus, quod statuerunt statuimus. Comisse tibi legationis officium vivaciter exequaris et ad amorem Dei et ecclesie periclitantis quorum poteris corda solicites.[10]

The textual correspondences between the letter (JL 6313) and the extant *acta* from the council held in the Lateran from March 18 to 23, 1112, leave no doubt that it is this synod to which the text specifically refers. The *actio* of the council also mentioned in JL 6313 is a reference to the formal document (*carta*) solemnly ratified by this assembly.[11] Under the circumstances, it is difficult to explain why the letter which was published and dated by Schum more than a hundred years ago is so often disregarded, Meyer von Knonau being the exception that confirms the rule.[12] The reason, perhaps, is the uncertainty regarding the text as well as a certain confusion caused by the manuscript transmission of the document known as *Actio concilii*. As it happens, it is often accompanied by a different letter of Paschal to Guido of Vienne as well as by a letter of Guido and the council of Vienne to the pontiff.[13] JL 6313 is not a part of this group of material.

9. I am indebted to Mr. Rolf Krause, Rome, who confirmed my readings of the manuscript.
10. Cf. Schum, "Kaiser Heinrich V," 278f.
11. See *ibid.*, 279 note 1 and compare the complete text of the letter as given here with *MGH Const.* 1, no. 399, 571ff. A relevant portion of the text is cited below, note 26.
12. Knonau, *Jahrbücher*, 6:235.
13. Manuscripts with the combination of *Actio concilii* and the letters are Paris, BN, MS lat. 10402, ff. 70v–72v; Boso's *Vita Paschalis* (ed. Duchesne, *Liber Pontificalis* 2:369–376) and the numerous MSS of the *Liber Censuum* which incorporate Boso's compilation. The original manuscript of the *Liber Censuum*, BAV, MS Vat. lat. 8486, does not contain the *Vita*; see the *Le Liber Censu-*

Paschal II had particular difficulties in reasserting his authority in France and imperial Burgundy during the years 1111 to 1116. Guido of Vienne coordinated and perhaps stirred up opposition to the pontiff, even after the Lateran council of 1112. The revocation of the April 1111 privilege in the *Actio concilii* was the result of a compromise by the assembly. In exchange for Paschal's reconfirmation of the validity of the prohibitions of his predecessors Gregory VII and Urban II, Paschal was permitted to refrain from personally excommunicating Henry V. Paschal thus did not violate the oath which he had sworn in the camp of the king just outside of Rome on April 11, 1111.[14] Archbishop Guido of Vienne, however, and his supporters were not satisfied with this outcome of the Lateran council of March 1112, of which they had been informed by Paschal's letter "Actionem concilii" (JL 6313) quoted earlier, as well as by participants. The pontiff therefore instructed Guido to hold a council at Vienne to discuss the problems.[15] Whatever Guido's motives, whether he was animated by reforming zeal or dynastic ambitions as has recently been suggested,[16] the council's discussions concluded on September 16, 1112, with the signing of a solemn letter to the pontiff threatening him with the withdrawal of obedience by the French, unless he sent an open letter con-

---

um de l'Eglise Romaine, ed. P. Fabre and L. Duchesne, "Introduction" [Paris, 1910], 32 with a *stemma codicum*. Fabre and Duchesne prove that not Vat. lat. 8486 but Florence, Bibl. Riccardiana, MS 228, where the *Vitae* were first added, was the source for all other extant copies. This codex is described *ibid.*, 18–24 and 28f. The texts are also found in BAV, MS Ottob. lat. 3057 (*Liber Censuum*, 2:135–137), and in a "vetus liber" which was edited by François Juret (1553–1626) in his edition of the works of Ivo of Chartres, reprinted by J. P. Migne, *PL*, vols. 161–162. I have consulted the 1647 edition of Juret's work in the Biblioteca Apostolica Vaticana (signature: R. I. I 307: *D. Ivonis Carnotensis episcopi opera omnia in duas partes distributa*, . . . Parisiis, apud Laurentium Cottereau, Via Iacobaea sub signo Montis Carmeli. 1647). The text of the *Actio concilii* and the letters is found in vol. 2:194–196, as part of the commentary for Ivo's epistle no. 238. It has not been possible to identify Juret's manuscript. I suspect that my present list of manuscripts is still incomplete.

14. *MGH Const.* 1, 142f., nos. 91 and esp. 92: ". . . et penitus in personam regis Heinrici nunquam anathema ponet. . . ."

15. We do not know how Paschal made this request. No such letter from 1112 has survived. That the synod at Vienne was convened by Guido in accordance with the wishes of Paschal is made clear by the synod's letter to the pontiff. It begins: "Sancte pietatis vestre mandata sequentes apud Viennam convenimus. . . ." The letter is quoted on the basis of Duchesne's edition, *Liber Pontificalis* 2:373f. The material for the synod of Vienne is collected in Mansi, *Amplissima collectio*, 21:cols. 73–78. For a full citation see note 17 below.

16. See the astute article by M. Stroll, "New Perspectives on the Struggle between Guy of Vienne and Henry V," *Archivum Historiae Pontificiae*, 18 (1980):97–115, with further bibliographical references for Guido-Calixtus II.

firming the excommunication of Henry V by name. Such an excommunication had been pronounced by the assembled fathers at Vienne on their
own initiative. Paschal's expected letter was to be circulated, the pope
was informed, in order to rally forces in opposition to Henry V. Since
Paschal was to promise all involved *remissio peccatorum suorum*, Guido seems
to have thought in military terms.[17] Paschal sent the requested confirmation immediately, JL 6330, a sure sign of the vulnerability[18] under which
he seems to have labored into the winter.[19] The letter, however, probably pleased Guido and his supporters very little, for it certainly did not
urge a crusade against Henry by promising a *remissio peccatorum* to Guido's supporters, nor did Paschal repeat the excommunication of Henry
V. He merely confirmed the decisions of the synod of Vienne in very general
terms: ". . . Deo gratias referimus, et quae statuta sunt ibi rata suscipimus
et confirmamus, et cooperante Domino Deo illibata permanere censemus."
Guido and his circle did not circulate Paschal's reply. Instead, they apparently circulated the decisions of the council they had held at Vienne with
an inscription which attributed these to the pontiff himself.[20]

17. See G. D. Mansi, *Sacrorum conciliorum nova et amplissima collectio* . . . , 21 (Venice, 1775),
coll. 75f. for the text of the letter from the synod of Vienne with dating clause. After requesting
papal confirmation for the decisions and excommunication at Vienne, the council added: ". . .
Cuius confirmationis argumentum per apertas nobis litteras significare dignemini; quas etiam, ut
gaudium nostrum sit plenum, alter alteri destinare possimus. Et quoniam principum terrae pars
maxima, et universi fere populi multitudo in hac re nobiscum sentit: in remissionem peccatorum
suorum omnibus iniungatis ut, si necesse fuerit, auxilium nobis et patriae unanimiter ferant. . . .
Si vero . . . assertiones praedictas roborare nolueritis: propitius sit nobis Deus, quia nos a vestra
subjectione et obedientia repelletis." See also note 15 above.
18. JL 6330. The short letter is found *ibid.*, col. 76, with the date: "Data Laterani XIII. Kal.
Novembris." Since the text refers explicitly to the council of Vienne, the date is Oct. 20, 1112.
The letter from Vienne (see note 17 above) accordingly took about four weeks to reach the pontiff
in Rome. See R. Elze, "Über die Leistungsfähigkeit von Gesandtschaften und Boten im 11. Jahrhundert" in: *Histoire comparée de l'administration*. Francia, Beihefte, 9 (Munich, 1980):3–10.
19. A further letter of the pontiff from the same period, November 1, 1112, looks suspiciously
like another effort to conciliate Guido. It is addressed to Archbishop William of Besançon and
confirms Guido's decision in favor of the clergy of St. Jean in Besançon. Paschal gave the oppo-
nent of St. Jean, St. Etienne of Besançon, only five days to present its case—in the event they
should appear in Rome—before he confirmed Guido's decision. Paschal did eventually revise his
decision when St. Etienne was able to prove its case and requested Guido to hold a council to
review his earlier decision. The letter to William of Besançon is published by W. Wiederhold,
Papsturkunden in Frankreich. Gesellschaft der Wissenschaften Göttingen, Nachrichten (Göttingen,
1906), 1:26f., no. 6. Paschal's relevant letters from 1115 are JL 6456, JL 6467 and JL 6365. Further bibliography is found in the article by Stroll; see note 16 above.
20. This seems indicated by the canonical *Collection in Ten Parts* which contains as 3.7.7. the
following text: "Paschalis .II. Guidoni Viennensi archiepiscopo. Investituram episcopatuum, ab-

The sequence of events so far appears unassailable. The confirmation of Schum's readings in the Naples codex provided a starting point for the chronological arrangement of the texts surrounding the councils of Vienne and of the Lateran in 1112, and especially for the papal letters JL 6313 ("Actionem concilii") and JL 6330 ("Cum alicuius"). All of the material is linked by dates as well as cross-references and fits in smoothly with the political circumstances prevalent in Rome as well as in Burgundy.[21] The only item not preserved as far as we know—perhaps it was an oral message delivered by the returning participants from the Lateran council—is Paschal's request to Guido to hold a council at Vienne.[22] Problems are created, however, by another letter of Paschal II, JL 6325 ("Si constantiam"), which is also addressed to Guido of Vienne and also refers to the events of the spring of 1111. Furthermore, "Si constantiam" happens to be frequently transmitted in the manuscripts together with the letter to Paschal II from the synod of Vienne requesting his confirmation of the decrees.[23] JL 6325 is undated and transmitted with few exceptions in a collection of various unrelated items from the pontificate of Paschal II that are also largely undated and undatable. They were probably collected by Cardinal Boso and are euphemistically called the *Vita Paschalis*.[24] It is easy, therefore, to connect the letter JL 6325 with the synod of Vienne of 1112 and to attribute it to that year as well. The letter exhorts Guido to stand fast in the face of adversity and reminds him that he, Guido, a member of the Church, could hardly expect a better fate,

batiarum et omnium rerum ecclesiasticarum de manu laica sancte Romane ecclesie auctoritatem sequentes heresim esse iudicamus." It corresponds to c.1 from the council of Vienne (= Mansi, *Amplissima collectio,* 21:col. 74). For the *Collection in Ten Parts* see P. Fournier and G. LeBras, *Histoire des collections canoniques en occident,* 2 (Paris, 1932; repr. Aalen, 1972), 296–306. See also my "Decrees and Decretals of Paschal II," *Bulletin of Medieval Canon Law,* n.s. 10 (1980):15–30, at 29.

21. For Burgundy see Stroll, "New Perspectives," (note 16 above); for Rome see Knonau, *Jahrbücher* 6:231–248 and C. Servatius, *Paschalis II. (1099–1118).* Päpste und Papsttum, 9 (Stuttgart, 1982), 309–325, all with further references. The article by P. R. McKeon, "The Lateran Council of 1112, the Heresy of Lay Investiture, and the Excommunication of Henry V," *Medievalia et Humanistica,* 17 (1966):3–12, is somewhat misleading because of some misunderstandings.

22. JL 6456 (= Migne *PL* 163, col. 334f.), probably from 1115, also instructs Guido to hold a council, but its purpose is to review the case of the Besançon churches St. Jean and St. Etienne. It should not be confused with the council at Vienne in 1112. See also the references given in note 19 above.

23. This is the letter discussed and quoted in notes 15 and 17 above.

24. The text of JL 6325 is found in Migne, *PL* 163, col. 292 and *Liber Pontificalis* 2:373 and elsewhere as indicated by Jaffé-Loewenfeld. For the manuscripts see above note 13.

considering what had happened to its head.[25] In conclusion Paschal adds a ringing denunciation of his agreements with Henry V at Ponte Mammolo in 1111 and reaffirms the decisions of his predecessors, especially of Gregory VII and Urban II, as well as of conciliar decrees:

> ... Que cognoscere postulasti sunt hec: Scripta que in tentoriis, in quibus cum multitudine clericorum et civium Urbis et totius provincie custodiebamur, pro libertate Ecclesie, pro absolutione captivorum omnium et pro excidio quod Ecclesie, Urbi et universe provincie superincubante undique gladio imminere videbatur, de electione seu de investituris personarum facta sunt, ... ego canonica censura cassa omnino et irrita iudico, et anathemate et sub dampnatione perpetuo permanere decerno, ut nullius umquam auctoritatis sint et nullius bone memorie. Ea vero que ... predecessores nostri et precipue felicis memorie dompnus Gregorius et Urbanus de hiis prohibuerunt, dampnaverunt, statuerunt et firmaverunt, ego prohibeo, dampno, constituo et confirmo. ..." (*Liber Pontificalis* 2, 373, lines 14–23)

Despite similarities to the papal profession of faith of March 1112, the differences are noticeable.[26] Nevertheless, scholars, including Jaffé and Loewenfeld, never hesitated to follow the arguments of Wilhelm von Giesebrecht, who suggested in 1877 that JL 6325 had been written several months after the Lateran synod of 1112. Giesebrecht clinched the argument with a reference to the letter dispatched to Paschal from the synod of Vienne: "Es [JL 6325] ist dasselbe, welches Guido in seinem Bericht über die Synode von Vienne an den Papst erwähnt."[27] Guido indeed referred to a letter from Paschal which he had received, but this letter is

---

25. JL 6325: "... Si enim in viridi ligno sic factum est quid fiet in aliis? Si in capite sic perpetratum est, quid fiet in membris? ..." These references to the suffering of Christ refer by implication to Paschal's capture by Henry V and his troops in February 1111.

26. In addition to the text quoted above see especially *MGH Const.* 1, 571: "Actio concilii contra heresim de investitura. ... Amplector omnem divinam scripturam, scilicet ... et decreta sanctorum patrum Romanorum pontificum, et precipue decreta domni mei pape Gregorii et beate memorie pape Urbani. Que ipsi laudaverunt, laudo; que ipsi tenuerunt, teneo; que confirmaverunt, confirmo; que dampnaverunt, dampno; que reppulerunt, repello; que interdixerunt, interdico; que prohibuerunt, prohibeo in omnibus et per omnia, et in his semper perseverabo. ..."

27. W. von Giesebrecht, *Geschichte der deutschen Kaiserzeit*, 4th rev. ed., 3/2 (Anmerkungen), (Braunschweig, 1877), 1201; for pp. 830–833 cited in the text see vol. 3/1.

the letter which was published by Schum from the Naples codex in 1877 and was, one assumes, still unknown to Giesebrecht.[28] It is, of course, impossible to exclude entirely the possibility that Paschal wrote twice to Guido confirming the decisions of the Lateran synod, provided that all else were equal.[29]

But this is not the case. In March 1116 Paschal held another council at the Lateran.[30] Among the extant sources are two chronicle accounts. The fuller account is found in the chronicle of Ekkehard of Aura, a very reliable source which covers the entire six days of the synod, March 6 to March 11, and is presumably based on a synodal protocol which is no longer extant.[31] Ekkehard included speeches by the pontiff as well as excerpts from the sometimes acrimonious discussions among the participants, sometimes verbatim and sometimes only in paraphrase. The textual correspondences between Paschal's letter JL 6325 ("Si constantiam") and Ekkehard's account from the council are so close that the question of its date has to be settled in favor of 1116:

> ... Postquam Dominus ... me [Paschal] populumque Romanum tradidit in manus regis ... huiusmodi mala cupiebam avertere ... et quod feci, pro liberatione populi Dei feci. ... Illud autem malum scriptum, quod in tentoriis factum est, quod pro pravitate sui Pravilegium dicitur, condempno sub perpetuo anathemate, ut nullius umquam sit bone memorie. ... (Ekkehard, pp. 318, 320)

The concluding statement of Paschal's letter to Guido that repeats the 1112 references to Gregory VII and Urban II is only indirectly reflected in Ekkehard's account, but we have at least proof that this repetition oc-

28. Schum's article (see note 8 above) appeared in the same year as Giesebrecht's revised edition (see the preceding note).

29. It should be noted that neither JL 6313 (the text is quoted above) nor JL 6325 (see note 24 above) instruct Guido to assemble what was to become the council of Vienne.

30. For the Lateran council of 1116 see Mansi, *Amplissima collectio,* 21 (Venice, 1776), col. 145–152, for the basic sources, as well as C.-J. von Hefele and H. LeClercq, *Histoire des conciles,* 5/1 (Paris, 1912), 553–559; Knonau, *Jahrbücher,* 6:350–356 with further references; Servatius, *Paschalis II.,* 330–332 and my "Paschal II and the Roman Primacy," *Archivum Historiae Pontificiae,* 16 (1978):67–92, esp. 83ff.

31. The chronicle of Ekkehard of Aura is critically edited by F.-J. Schmale and I. Schmale-Ott, *Frutolfs und Ekkehards Chroniken und die Anonyme Kaiserchronik.* Freiherr vom Stein-Gedächtnisausgabe, 15 (Darmstadt, 1972), 318–324, and 319 note 8.

curred.[32] The chronicle also mentions that Guido of Vienne had once again avoided the journey to Rome, and that he had sent emissaries with a letter supporting Cardinal Cono's request for a formal recognition by Paschal of the various legatine excommunications of Henry V, thus providing an explanation for the phrase: "Que cognoscere postulasti sunt hec . . ." in JL 6325.[33] Finally, even the second independent chronicle account of the 1116 council, although incomplete, shows obvious connections between the discussions of 1116 and Paschal's letter "Si constantiam" to Guido of Vienne.[34] The conclusion that this epistle belongs to the year 1116 and is a report from the second of Paschal's major councils which dealt with the problem of the privilege of 1111 seems indeed appropriate.

It is certainly helpful to be able to read the extant letters exchanged between Pope Paschal II and his legate, Archbishop Guido of Vienne, in the correct chronological sequence: JL 6313 ("Actionem concilii") sent after the Lateran synod of 1112, JL 6330 ("Cum alicuius") confirming the decisions of the council of Vienne of September 16, 1112, and JL 6325 ("Si constantiam") reporting from the Lateran council of March 1116. The sequence mirrors the tensions within the church with regard to lay investiture and shows how the pontiff reasserted his authority by 1116.[35] But the significance of the established chronology extends further than that. An anonymous treatise, *Disputatio vel defensio Paschalis papae*, has been dated by both its editors to 1112, either before or after the September synod of Vienne.[36] The more recent editor, Ernst Sackur, argued for a date just prior to this synod, a suggestion tentatively approved by Carl Mirbt in his standard work.[37] The disagreement reflects the uncertain nature of this text which scholars have been unable to explain.[38] The *Defen-*

---

32. ". . . Pravilegium investiture, quod in tentoriis concessisse videbatur, obliterare volens, iterans sententiam pape Gregorii VII. investituram ecclesiasticarum rerum a laica manu rursus excommunicavit. . . ." (Ekkehard, *ibid.*, 322).

33. *Ibid.*, 323–324, line 4.

34. Gerhoch of Reichersberg, *Opusculum de edificio dei*, ed. E. Sackur. MGH *Libelli de lite*, 3 (Hanover, 1897), at 190–191n.

35. Blumenthal, "Paschal II and the Roman Primacy," as in note 30 above. See in general G. M. Cantarella, *Ecclesiologia e politica nel papato di Pasquale II* (Rome, 1982).

36. *Disputatio vel defensio Paschalis papae*, ed. by W. Schum (see note 8 above) and by E. Sackur, MGH *Libelli de lite*, 2 (Hanover, 1892), 658–666. See esp. the introduction, 658 and note 5.

37. *Die Publizistik im Zeitalter Gregors VII* (Leipzig, 1894), 78.

38. The best discussion of the tract is found in A. Becker, *Studien zum Investiturproblem in Frankreich*

sio appears to reply to complaints raised in a lost letter or tract— presumably of French origin—against the perceived intention of Paschal to excommunicate Henry V. Such an excommunication is said to be unacceptable because it would force the pontiff to break his solemn oath of 1111 never to excommunicate the emperor.[39] The *Defensio* argues the contrary, somewhat speciously perhaps, but the main thrust of the reply is to show beyond a shadow of a doubt that kings had no right to lay investiture and that the 1111 privilege, known since the 1112 synod as "pravilegium," had no validity because it was extorted by force. It is particularly worth noting that the author relies on canon law as well as Roman law for support. The *Defensio*, as transmitted in the only extant manuscript, Naples, BN, MS V. C. 46, which also contains Paschal's letter JL 6313, makes yet a third point, probably in order to keep the doors open for further negotiations. After reasserting his opposition to lay investiture as currently practiced because of the use of ring and staff as symbols in the ceremony, the author continues:

> . . . Sicut enim in aecclesia pastoralis virga est necessaria . . . sic in domibus regum et imperatorum illud insigne sceptrum, quod est imperialis vel regalis virga, qua regitur patria, ducatus, comitatus, et cetera regalia distribuuntur iura. Si ergo dixerit [imperator] quod per virgam pontificalem et anulum sua tantum regalia velit conferre, aut sceptrum regale deserat, aut per illud regalia sua conferat. . . . (*MGH Lib. lit.* 2, 666)

This argument is striking. First of all it is close to the position of the canonist Ivo of Chartres. Secondly, the eventual settlement of the quarrel over investitures under Calixtus II, who was none other than Guido of Vienne, by the agreements of Worms in 1122/1123 was accomplished precisely because of the adoption of the royal scepter as investiture symbol.[40] It is well known that the negotiations between pope and king dur-

---

(Saarbrücken, 1955), 158f. Servatius, *Paschalis II,* refers only once to the *Disputatio* without discussing the work (at 289).

39. ". . . Nunc transeamus ad ea que nobis proposuistis: Paschalem nec dici nec haberi posse apostolicum, si excommunicaverit regem Henricum. . . ." (*Disputatio,* 663, lines 38f.)

40. See *MGH Const.* l, 159ff., no. 107f., to be supplemented with the edition of the papal documents in A. Hofmeister, *Das Wormser Konkordat,* ed. with a new preface by R. Schmidt (Darmstadt, 1962), 84, paragraph 3: "Electus autem regalia per sceptrum a te recipiat et, quae ex his iure tibi debet, faciat." For a discussion see P. Classen, "Das Wormser Konkordat in der deut-

ing the pontificate of Paschal II largely prepared the way for the concordat of Worms,[41] but there is no other witness apart from the *Defensio Paschalis* that Paschal's advisers, if not he himself, actually had come to accept the idea of investiture with regalia through the royal scepter by the end of the reign. The account of the Lateran council of 1116 by Ekkehard includes references to negotiations with an embassy sent by Emperor Henry V.[42] They have always been a puzzle and nothing is known about their substance.[43] Could it be that the statement quoted from the *Defensio* is an indication of the tendencies during these negotiations? I think that the answer is a qualified yes. The reason is that the treatise includes a long excerpt from Paschal's letter JL 6325 ("Si constantiam").[44] Barring interpolation which can be neither proven nor disproven, the *Disputatio vel defensio Paschalis papae* will have to be dated 1116 to 1118 instead of 1112. The treatise contains no hint that Paschal's death (January 21, 1118) had already occurred. Rather, the author defends this pontiff's policies and identifies himself fully with him. Further evidence would be desirable, but as long as there is no proof to the contrary the *Disputatio* may be considered a most welcome addition to the very meagre information that has been preserved for the last two years of Paschal's pontificate.

UTA-RENATE BLUMENTHAL

schen Verfassungsgeschichte," *Investiturstreit und Reichsverfassung.* Vorträge und Forschungen, 17 (Sigmaringen, 1973), 411–460.

41. See esp. E. Bernheim, *Das Wormser Konkordat und seine Vorurkunden.* Untersuchungen zur deutschen Staats- und Rechtsgeschichte, Alte Folge, 81 (Breslau, 1906) and the material cited in the preceding note.

42. Ekkehard, 320: ". . . Quinta feria papa in concilio non sedit multis et maxime regis negotiis per domnum Cluniacensem, Iohannem Caitanum et Petrum Leonis et Urbis prefectum ceterosque illius partis fautores impeditus. . . ."

43. See recently Servatius, *Paschalis II,* 331–335.

44. *Disputatio,* ed. Sackur, 661, lines 2–10. The derivation of the text from JL 6325 is indicated by the editor.

THE INVOCATION OF
H E L L
IN THIRTEENTH—CENTURY
P A R I S

U NDERSTANDING THE PROCESS of doctrinal dissemination in thirteenth-century Europe is a more complex task than is generally supposed.[1] Theoretical models implying that doctrine is applied "from the top down" or that religious ideas permeate a community "from the grass roots up" are oversimplifications. They are misleading because they assume a hieratic model in which religious authority is assigned the top and popular belief the bottom, with either end (depending on the model) a passive, Aristotelian matter receiving its form from the other. In fact, no single explanatory formula will suffice. The religious community of thirteenth-century Europe cannot be divided simply into a "clergy" and a "laity." The clergy

In this place, traditionally devoted to acknowledgements, I would like to express my heartfelt appreciation for all that Paul Oskar Kristeller has given me. He showed me how one actually performs the tasks of critical scholarship. From the time he assured me that the scholarly skills I desire to possess are, after all, "acquired traits," his example of curiosity, precision, and humanity has been a continuing inspiration.

For their help in various stages of preparing this article I wish also to thank Jonathan Beck, JoAnne Bernstein, Alfred Büchler, Thomas Izbicki, Stephan Kuttner, Kathryn Larch, Guy Lobrichon, Hilary Martin, and Nikki Matz.

1. On the subject of hell in general see M. Carrouges et al., *L'Enfer* (Paris, 1950); K. Kohler, *Heaven and Hell in Comparative Religion* (New York, 1923); S. Brandon, *The Judgment of the Dead* (New York, 1967); F. Heer, *Abschied von Höllen und Himmeln* (Munich, 1970); G. Panneton,*Enfer* (Paris, 1956); M. Landau, *Hölle und Fegefeuer in Volksglaube, Dichtung, und Kirchenlehre* (Heidel-

was a complex body whose members performed quite specialized functions, and the laity could include the king, the court, guild members, laborers, beggars—men and women varying widely in sophistication.

It is not possible to describe the religious ideas of the laity except indirectly, by inference from clerical activities. Nonetheless, we may characterize the approaches of various clerical groups and categorize their functions roughly as follows: (1) popes defined dogma, (2) theologians explained papal declarations, systematized and defended the teachings of the church, (3) encyclopedists compiled manuals for preachers containing the conclusions of the theologians, and (4) preachers interacted directly with the laity.

To be sure, many individuals exercised more than one of these functions. Innocent III studied (and possibly taught) theology before becoming pope. Many theologians were active at the pulpit as well as the lectern. Nonetheless, we may fruitfully distinguish these functions and characterize the treatment of important themes when each is being addressed, provided we do not lose sight of the versatility of many individual churchmen.

It might appear that I have listed these specialists in decreasing order of authority or in increasing order of proximity to the laity, but that is precisely the type of presupposition I hope this article will help to dispel. We shall see that although the popes would naturally seem to cap this system, they are in some ways closer than the theologians to the preachers and to the laity. Similarly, the preachers did not always use manuals as the compilers would seem to have intended. Rather, preachers were very selective and sometimes relied less on given literary sources than on a certain "feel" for their audience.

For the purpose of exposition we must consider each group of specialists in isolation. And for reasons of space, we must let individuals represent

berg, 1909); H. Patch, *The Other World According to Descriptions in Medieval Literature* (Cambridge, Mass., 1950); D. Owen, *The Vision of Hell: Infernal Journeys in Medieval French Literature* (Edinburgh, 1970); J. Delumeau, *Le péché et la peur. La culpabilisation en Occident. XIIIe–XVIIIe siècles* (Paris, 1983); R. Hughes, *Heaven and Hell in Western Art* (New York, 1968); Y. Christe, *La vision de Matthieu. Origines et développement d'une image de la Seconde Parousie*. Bibliothèque des cahiers archéologiques, 10 (Paris, 1973); E. DuBruck, "The Devil and Hell in Medieval French Drama," *Romania* 100.2 [398] (1979): 165–79; G. de Don, "Structures et significations de l'imagerie médiévale de l'enfer," *Cahiers de civilisation médiévale* 22 (1979): 363–72; J. Le Goff, *La naissance du Purgatoire* (Paris, 1981), English tr. by A. Goldhammer, *The Birth of Purgatory* (Chicago, 1984); M. Himmelfarb, *Tours of Hell: An Apocalyptic Form in Jewish and Christian Literature* (Philadelphia, 1983).

particular activities. Yet by analyzing various emphases in the invocation of hell by persons performing the functions identified above, it will become clear that the interactions of those groups and their functions are numerous and diverse.

To explore these suggestions more carefully, it is valuable to limit the area of investigation. Thus we shall focus upon the concept of hell (and, where necessary, upon the related questions of penance and purgatory) within the temporal and geographical limits of thirteenth-century Paris. That the concept of hell, so fundamental to eschatology and discipline, and the region of Paris, court of a great king, home of a thriving mercantile community, and seat of what was then Europe's foremost school of theology, should constitute a significant "test case" for investigating the methods of doctrinal dissemination should not be open to serious question. In the rest of this paper, therefore, we shall consider the theme of hell as providing an example of how religious ideas were disseminated within thirteenth-century Paris.

Before beginning to analyze the paths of communication within this religious community, it is necessary to mention two influences that affected it, that charged its atmosphere. First is the decree *Omnis utriusque sexus* issued by the Fourth Lateran Council under Pope Innocent III in 1215 requiring that "every believer of either sex ... faithfully confess all sins alone to his priest at least once a year."[2] The requirement of annual confession moved the church's penitential institutions to the fore in its relationship with the laity and made confession one of the primary actions urged by preachers on their audiences.[3] Second is the rise of the Franciscans and Dominicans, who, during the thirteenth century, evolved into influential orders with rights to preach, hear confession, impose penance in all but a few reserved cases, and offer to their benefactors burial within the precincts of their friaries.[4] Leaving aside the vicissitudes of the gradual

2. "Omnis utriusque sexus fidelis . . . omnia sua solus peccata confiteatur fideliter saltem semel in anno proprio sacerdoti. . . ." J. Alberigo, J. Dossetti, P. Joannou eds., *Conciliorum Oecumenicorum Decreta* (Bologna, 1973), 245. This is canon 21 of Lateran IV; cf. *Liber Extra* 5. 38. 12, *Corpus Juris Canonici*, ed. A. Friedberg, 2 vols. (Leipzig, 1879), 2: 887.

3. R. Rusconi, "De la prédication à la confession: transmission et contrôle de modèles de comportement au XIIIᵉ siècle" in *Faire croire. Modalités de la diffusion et de la réception des messages religieux du XIIᵉ au XVᵉ siècle* (Rome,1981), 67–85 at 68–70.

4. P. Mandonnet, *Saint Dominique, l'idée, l'homme et l'oeuvre*, 2nd ed., 2 vols. (Paris, 1937). See also: J. Moorman, *A History of the Franciscan Order* (Oxford, 1968); W.Hinnebusch, *The History of the Dominican Order*, 2 vols. (New York, 1966–73).

endowment of the mendicants with these rights and their rivalry with
the traditional clergy,[5] we need only note that it was these orders which
occupied, at most of its crucial intersections, the network of communications we shall examine here.[6]

Now we may turn to the invocation of hell by the first group of
specialists.

I

The Popes

Papal declarations on hell were made in 1215, 1254, and 1274. In the
creed *Firmiter credimus* promulgated at the Fourth Lateran Council in 1215,
Innocent III did not explicitly mention hell, but his allusion to it is clear:
at the end of time, Christ will return to judge the living and the dead
according to their merits or demerits ("secundum merita sua, sive bona
fuerint sive mala") so that those who have done good "will receive eternal glory with Christ" and those who have done evil "will receive eternal
punishment with the devil."[7] This explanation implies a weighing or
counting of both good and evil deeds, with a greater weight or number
of merits being sufficient for salvation. Prior release from the evil deeds
is not considered here to affect one's fate. In the Creed of Lateran IV,

5. Moorman, 125, note 1. Add: K. Schleyer, *Anfänge des Gallikanismus im 13. Jht. Der Wider-
stand des französischen Klerus gegen die Privilegierung der Bettelorden.* Historisch Studien, 314 (Berlin,
1937); M. M. Dufeil, *Guillaume de Saint-Amour et la polémique universitaire parisienne, 1250–1259*
(Paris, 1972); Y. Congar, "Aspects ecclésiologiques de la querelle entre mendiants et séculiers
. . . ," *Archives d'histoire doctrinale et littéraire du moyen âge,* 28 (1961): 35–151.

6. See for example J. Le Goff, "Ordres mendiants et urbanisation dans la France médiévale,"
Annales, E.S.C., 25 (1970): 924–46; Rusconi, "De la prédication"; and idem "I Francescani e la
confessione nel secolo XIII," *Francescanesimo e vita religiosa dei laici nel '200. Atti del'VIII Convegno
Internazionale, Assisi, 16–18 ottobre, 1980* (Assisi, 1981), 253–309; Z. Zafarana, "La Predicazione
francescana," *ibid.,* 205–250; M. H. Vicaire, *Dominique et ses prêcheurs,* 2nd ed. (Paris, 1979), esp.
chap. 6; L. Bataillon, "La predicazione dei religiosi mendicanti del secolo XIII nell'Italia Centrale," *Mélanges de l'École française de Rome. Moyen Age et Temps Modernes* 89.2 (1977): 691–94;
R. & M. Rouse, *Preachers, Florilegia, and Sermons* (Toronto, 1979), esp. chap. 2.

7. "Venturus in fine saeculi iudicare vivos et mortuos, et redditurus singulis secundum opera
sua, tam reprobis quam electis. Qui omnes cum suis propriis corporibus resurgent, quae nunc
gestant, ut recipiant secundum merita sua, sive bona fuerint sive mala, illi cum diabolo poenam
perpetuam et isti cum Christo gloriam sempiternam." J. Alberigo et al., p. 230.

therefore, hell is portrayed as one of two possible destinations for the soul after the divine judgment at the end of time.

In 1254 Innocent IV described the basis of judgment somewhat differently: "If anyone should die in mortal sin without penance, ... he will be tormented forever by the flames of eternal Gehenna."[8] As compared to Innocent III's statement, Innocent IV's implies that judgment depends not on a balancing of good versus evil deeds, but upon the condition of being or not being in mortal sin and, further, if it does not actually equate them, it links the absence of penance to the state of mortal sin.

The term "paenitentia" is difficult to interpret. It may refer to the sacrament in all its parts (contritio, confessio, satisfactio); it may stand as a synonym for satisfaction; or it may be used loosely as a synonym for paenitudo and mean a generic remorse in the sense of repentance. To understand Innocent IV's usage we must return to the context of the statement itself. In his letter Sub catholicae professione of March 6, 1254, from which our text is drawn, Innocent IV reviews the differences between the Roman and the Greek churches. He discusses each of the sacraments in turn. On the subject of penance he first describes the fate of souls who die "having undertaken penance, but not completed it, or who die without mortal sin, but with venial and tiny ones," and he proceeds to make the first papal definition of purgatory by naming the place where such sins are purged.[9] He then concludes: "By that transitory fire, sins which have not been previously remitted through penance—not criminal or capital ones, of course, but small and minute ones—are purged. For these (small and minute sins) continue to weigh down the soul even after death, if they have not been absolved in life."[10] Thus, where mortal sin is concerned, undertaking penance gains admission to purgatory and escape from hell.

---

8. "Si quis autem absque paenitentia in peccato mortali decedit, hic procul dubio aeternae gehennae ardoribus perpetuo cruciatur." Innocent IV, Sub catholicae professione, March 6, 1254: J. D. Mansi, Sacrorum Conciliorum nova et amplissima collectio, 23 (Venice, 1779): 582. Cf. H. Denzinger & A. Schönmetzer, Enchiridion Symbolorum, ed. 24 (Barcelona, 1967), no. 839, 272.

9. "... animas illorum, qui, suscepta paenitentia, ea non peracta, vel qui sine mortali peccato, cum venialibus tamen et minutis decedunt, purgari post mortem, et posse suffragiis Ecclesie adiuvari. Nos ... illum [locum] quidem ... 'Purgatorium' nominantes volumus, quod de cetero apud ipsos [Graecos] isto nomine appelletur." Ibid.

10. "Illo enim transitorio igne peccata, utique non tamen criminalia seu capitalia, quae prius per paenitentiam non fuere remissa, sed parva et minuta purgantur, quae post mortem etiam gravant, si in vita non fuerint relaxata." Ibid. Note that Denzinger omits the non before fuerint relaxata, following the Bullarum Diplomatum et Privilegiorum Sanctorum Romanorum Pontificum, ed. A.

In another context we find a similar opinion. Innocent IV was a great canonist, author of an *Apparatus* or *Commentary on the Five Books of Decretals,* which he continued to revise until his death in 1254.[11] The *Decretals* contain the text of the canon *Omnis utriusque sexus,* by which Innocent III, at the Fourth Lateran Council in 1215, required annual confession of every Catholic. In his treatment of this canon, when he reaches the word "confess" (*confiteri*), Innocent IV treats the sacrament of penance by subdividing it into the usual three parts.[12] Later, in the same discussion, treating the word "annual" (*semel in anno*), he says of one in mortal sin, "That sinner, once he has bound himself in sin, will never be absolved by God unless he is first absolved by a priest."[13]

Thus it is in the strict sense of the sacrament of penance that Innocent IV's declaration should be read: In contrast to those who, having been in mortal sin, had begun penance but died before completing it and will be able to do so in purgatory, are those who died in mortal sin, never availing themselves of the sacrament of penance, without which there is no absolution, who will be tormented forever in hell.

Innocent IV's linkage of hell to the absence of penance is not so much a decisive theological change, in which a new doctrine "replaces" an older one, as it is a change in emphasis.[14] Whereas the balancing of one's merits and demerits takes place, according to Lateran IV, at the Last Judgment, annual confession is an occurrence regulated by the clergy under the direc-

---

Tomassetti, 24 vols. (Turin, 1857–72) 2: 582. Cf. J. Le Goff, *La naissance du Purgatoire,* 379–80 (283–84). References to the English translation follow in parentheses.

11. S. Kuttner, "Die Konstitutionen des ersten allgemeinen Konzils von Lyon," *Studia et documenta historiae et iuris,* 6 (Rome, 1940): 70–131, reprinted in idem, *Medieval Councils, Decretals, and Collections of Canon Law. Selected Essays* (London, 1980), no. XI, 114.

12. Innocentius IV, *Super Libros Quinque Decretalium* (Frankfurt, 1570; repr. 1968) in 5.38.12, *confiteri:* "Contritio necessaria est cuilibet peccatori" (f. 544vb). On confession: "Nisi confiteatur, si tempus haberet confitendi, nihil sibi valeat praecedens contritio" (f. 545ra). "Satisfactio fit per solutionem poenae impositae pro peccato, puta quia poenitentiam iniunctam plene facit. . . ." (f. 545ra).

13. *Ibid.,* ad verb. *semel:* "Nunquam absolvetur a Deo iste peccator, postquam se ligavit peccato, nisi prius absolvatur a presbytero."

14. Innocent IV's declaration is not an innovation but a reinforcement of existing notions. In Gratian's *Decretum* we find the statement, "fit enim veniale per confessionem quod criminale erat in operatione," *De Pen.* d.1 c.88 (Friedberg 1: 1188); and Peter Lombard in his *Sentences,* IV 17.1.6 (Grottaferrata, 1981, vol. 2: 344) quotes Ambrose, *De Paradiso* 14, n.71 (*PL* 14: 310D; *CSEL,* 32.2: 321): "Non potest quisquam iustificari a peccato, nisi fuerit peccatum ante confessus." Gratian (*ibid.* c. 74) and the Lombard (*ibid.* n.8) again quote Ambrose (*ibid.*): "Venialis est culpa, quam sequitur professio delictorum." The weighing of souls is frequently depicted in medieval art.

tion of the papacy. Thus Innocent IV's renewed stress on penance as indicative of the state of the soul at death accords better with the requirement of annual confession. It is this strict connection that was to become, as we shall see, a common theme of thirteenth-century Parisian preachers.

Unlike the pronouncement of Innocent III, which assigns judgment to the end of time, that of Innocent IV does not specify when the sentence in hell is to begin. On the eternal reward, however, Innocent IV stated: "The souls of the little ones dying after the bath of baptism and of adults [dying] in charity, who are held neither by sin nor to any satisfaction for it, pass across to the eternal fatherland immediately."[15] Although dealing explicitly only with the saved, this statement suggests a tendency to collapse eschatological time, to begin to focus more on the moment of individual judgment at death than upon the universal judgment at the end of time.

This growing attention to the individual's death constitutes the second development in papal pronouncements on hell. It was extended to the damned with the declaration that infernal torments begin immediately upon the death of a sinner. In 1274, in the profession of faith composed by the Second Council of Lyons under Gregory X for the Byzantine Emperor Michael Palaeologus, the imbalance we noticed in Innocent IV's statement is rectified. Hell is said to begin immediately at death, just like purgatory and heaven. Those dying in charity (i.e. in the state of grace) but "before they shall have satisfied by the due fruits of penance" their sins of commission and omission, will be purged after death. Those who have incurred no fault, or having been purged in this life, are received immediately into heaven. "But the souls of those who die in mortal sin or only with original [sin, we assert] descend immediately into hell, though to be punished with unequal punishments."[16]

Gregory X thus perfected the second development by specifying the immediate commencement of post-mortem punishment as well as reward.

15. *Sub catholicae professione,* in Mansi, 23: 582: "Animae vero parvulorum post baptismi lavacrum, et adultorum etiam in caritate decedentium, qui nec peccato, nec ad satisfactionem aliquam pro ipso tenentur, ad patriam protinus transvolant sempiternam."

16. Tomassetti (see note 10 above), 14: 26: "Quod si vere poenitentes in caritate decesserint, antequam dignis poenitentiae fructibus de commissis satisfecerint et omissis: eorum animas poenis purgatoriis, hoc est catharteriis, . . . post mortem purgari. . . . Illorum autem animas, qui in mortali peccato vel cum solo originali decedunt, mox in infernum descendere, poenis tamen disparibus puniendas."

This is not to say that Innocent IV or Gregory X initiated these beliefs or declared them dogmatically out of thin air. Jacques Le Goff has shown how gradual the process was that led to Innocent IV's definition of purgatory.[17] Belief in the individual judgment, taking place immediately after death, implicit in Luke 16, 23, also has a hoary past.[18] The significance of the telescoping of eschatological time is that, upon papal authority, it emphasizes aspects of the Catholic tradition which make more vivid, because more present, the consequences of the individual's moral and sacramental actions.

To recapitulate, we may now combine the two developments we have identified in papal pronouncements on hell. Between 1215 and 1274 papal declarations concerning hell moved the beginning of one's sentence from the general resurrection at the end of time to the moment of an individual's death. Meanwhile the criterion for a successful passage through the divine scrutiny shifted from a comparison of good versus evil deeds in general, to the accomplishment (or at least the undertaking) of a specific sequence of actions, those composing the sacrament of penance. As we shall see, the papal tendency to associate hell with confession and penance will become characteristic of Parisian preachers too. It does not seem rash to propose that this trend in authoritative, papal pronouncements supported the practice of annual confession mandated by Lateran IV and that those very active preachers, the mendicants, the very people charged with supplementing the labors of priests and bishops in administering penitential discipline, should find these themes congenial.

II

Theologians

Whereas in papal declarations dogma is simply asserted, the task of the theologian is to show a doctrine's conformity to Scripture, other authorities, and reason. Then it had to be classified among other doctrines, defined,

---

17. Note that Le Goff's discussion of the background to Innocent IV's definition of Purgatory requires seven chapters.

18. A. Suelzer, "Judgment, Divine (In the Bible)," *New Catholic Encyclopedia*, 8 (1967): 26–30. J. H. Wright, "Judgment, Divine (In Theology)," *ibid.*, 30–40.

subdivided, and explicated in detail. Where hell is concerned, thirteenth-century theologians sought first to prove its existence, then demonstrate its eternity, and explain the justice of damnation.

An example of such a theologian is William of Auvergne, who taught theology at the University of Paris and was bishop of that city from 1228 to 1249.[19] William's arguments for the existence of hell may be paraphrased as follows. Just as a place of happiness exists for the blessed, so there should be a place of misery for the damned.[20] Every castle has a dungeon, every city has a jail, thus the earth, which is the city of God, should have a "place . . . set aside for exercising divine justice . . . and this is the place which the three common laws [Christianity, Islam, Judaism] understand to be hell."[21] Further, William argued that the pains of hell are not to be imputed to a malicious God and dismissed as unjust. He admits that God is one cause (the efficient cause) of damnation, but only because He provides the punishments. It is the sinners' evil deeds, William insists, that are the material factor in their punishment.[22] Moreover, that punishment may justly be eternal because, in addition to the sin, the sinner has added impenitence and contumacy. And since the penalty should last as long as the injury, it is clear that, in the case of an impenitent, it is just for the punishment to be eternal.[23]

Thomas Aquinas proved the existence of hell with the same argument

19. See my "Theology between Heresy and Folklore: William of Auvergne on Punishment after Death," *Studies in Medieval and Renaissance History*, 5 (1982): 5–44. The ideas about to be sketched here are treated more fully in my "Esoteric Theology: William of Auvergne on the Fires of Hell and Purgatory," *Speculum* 57 (1982): 509–31.

20. "Cum locum habeat certum et proprium vera foelicitas earum, necesse est verum et proprium locum habere veram miseriam [animarum humanarum]." Guilielmus Alvernus, *Opera Omnia*, 2 vols. (1674, rpt. Frankfurt, 1963), *De Universo*, p. 663 (673)a B. Cf. "Cum locum proprium et determinatum habeant remunerationes eius et praemia perennes et perennia, necesse est ut locum habeant proprium vindictae eiusdem perpetuae." *Ibid.* b A.

21. "Universum seu mundum civitatem esse Dei altissimi . . . quare necesse est hanc civitatem locum habere . . . appropriatum exercendae divinae iustitiae . . . quem infernum intelligunt tres leges communes." *Ibid.*

22. "Iustitia Dei causa est damnationis eorum utique *efficiens*. . . . Mala vero eorum merita causa sunt quasi *materialis* perditionis ipsorum. . . ." *De Legibus*, 59b B.

23. "Qui addit super peccatum impoenitentiam, seu contumaciam, addit de iure et poenam. Et iustissime quantum durat in unoquoque Dei iniuria, tantum in eodem durat et poena. Quia igitur existentes in inferno super peccata sua etiam addunt impoenitentiam et contumaciam, nunquam poenitentes nec unquam poenitere volentes, quia semper durat in eis Dei iniuria, id est, peccatum; quare semper merito durat et eis poena. . . ." *De Legibus*, 61a C. These are but two arguments from an extremely dense passage that runs from p. 57 to p. 64b.

he used for its justice. He posited a right order in which the individual is subject to God's will. Sinning is an act of insubordination which breaks the bond of charity that had united the sinner to God.[24] As long as that order is subverted, that bond broken, punishment is deserved. An impenitent is in rebellion forever, hence his punishment must last forever.[25]

In addition to demonstrating the existence and justice of eternal damnation, theologians had to describe the nature of hell itself. In this task they proved to be very circumspect. They displayed a certain repugnance for detailed concern with the physical characteristics of the place—a concern they probably regarded as over-literal or superstitious. They avoided the graphic descriptions found in vernacular literature and popular preaching. Parisian theologians of the thirteenth century sought to prevent popular religion from confusing or contaminating the rational exposition of doctrine. One way they did that was to de-emphasize the corporeal aspects of hell and to stress instead the spiritual effects of its torments on the damned.

William of Auvergne was one of those theologians who opposed popular exaggerations of hell's physical torments and showed a pronounced disdain for the material details of infernal punishment. Consequently, William's speculations on the physical character of hell were purely logical:

> Because the highest place [in the universe] has been declared to be that of the true felicity [of human souls], it is fitting that the lowest be the proper place for the true misery of the same. Now there ought not to be less distance between their true felicity and their true misery than between the places suited to their conditions. But between

24. "Quidquid contra ordinem aliquem insurgit, consequens est ut ab ipso ordine, vel principe ordinis, deprimatur. Cum autem peccatum sit actus inordinatus, manifestum est quod quicumque peccat, contra aliquem ordinem agit. Et ideo ab ipso ordine consequens est quod deprimatur. Quae quidem depressio poena est." Thomas Aquinas, *Summa Theologiae*, 2 q.87 a.1 (*Opera Omnia*, Rome, 1892), 7: 121. For references to the *Summa Theologiae*, I follow the practice of the editors of the *Index Thomisticus*, dividing the whole into four parts of which the first and second parts of Part Two are parts 2 and 3 respectively. Thus ST2 refers to the *Summa Theologiae*, First Part of the Second Part.

25. "Manente autem causa, manet effectus. Unde quandiu perversitas ordinis remanet, necesse est quod remaneat reatus poenae. . . . Si per peccatum corrumpatur principium ordinis quo voluntas hominis subditur Deo, erit inordinatio, quantum est de se, irreparabilis, etsi reparari possit virtute divina. Principium autem huius ordinis est ultimus finis, cui homo inhaeret per caritatem. Et ideo quaecumque peccata avertunt a Deo, caritatem auferentia, quantum est de se, inducunt reatum aeternae poenae." *Ibid.* a.3; p. 123.

highest and the lowest there exists the greatest distance not only
in space, but also in a multiplicity of contrary dispositions, such as
highness and lowness, breadth and narrowness, brightness and darkness, stability and restlessness, and many others. Moreover, the lowest
point of the body of the universe is the center of the earth. . . .[26]

Thus William's description of hell does not go beyond the abstract. He
contrasts hell to heaven by means of a reverse analogy.

In the same mode, William deduced that, just as the blessed are far
removed from any evil, and every aspect of heaven increases their glory,

so necessarily, those given over to misery must not only be far from
all goods that might be able to temper or alleviate or diminish their
misery, but indeed they must be afflicted by all evils, so that nothing in hell may detract from their torments.[27]

Within these logical constructions, no mention has yet been made of
hell's fire. Indeed William so emphasized the psychological qualities of
hell, that he considered hellfire as a kind of "spiritual form"[28] and that
it functions like an image in a nightmare.[29] Yet immediately below, William contends that this fire "corporeally and truly torments the bodies
of these people and their souls too," because otherwise "the God of truth"
would have to resort to "the lies of dreams."[30] The reason for William's

---

26. "Quia igitur locus supremus declaratus est locus esse verae foelicitatis ipsarum, conveniens
est ut locus infimus sit locus proprius verae miseriae earundem. Non enim debet esse minor distantia inter veram foelicitatem illarum et veram miseriam illarum, quam inter loca congruentia huiusmodi statibus ipsarum. Maxima autem distantia non solum localis est inter supremum et infimum,
sed etiam multiplicium contrariarum dispositionum: quales sunt supremitas et infimitas, amplitudo et angustia, luminositas et tenebrositas, stabilitas et inquietudo, et multa alia. Infimum autem
universi corporis medium terrae est. . . ." *De Universo,* 663 (673)a B–C.

27. "Necesse est miseriae addictos non solum longe esse ab omnibus bonis, quae miseriam huiusmodi vel temperare, vel lenire, vel minuere possint, sed etiam affligi omnibus malis, ut nihil
in inferno vacet a tormento eorum." *Ibid.* 663 (673)b C.

28. See my "Esoteric Theology," 512–15. William says: "Quia igitur ipsa anima substantia
spiritualis est, in ea impossibile est formam aliquam corporalem esse. Quapropter necesse est tormentum istud . . . formam spiritualem esse." *De Universo,* 681b B.

29. "Manifestum est de somniantibus, quoniam interdum somniant se ardere et esse in igne
et cruciantur intolerabiliter, tanquam in veritate ardeant. Quare quoniam veritas et substantia ignis apud eos non est, sed sola species ignis (vel in fantasia, vel imaginatione eorum est), manifestum
est eos cruciatum huiusmodi ardoris a sola specie ignis pati." *Ibid.* 682a F–G. Thomas Aquinas
rejects this view in *Quaestiones de Anima,* q. 21, responsio 8, ed. J. Robb. Pontifical Institute
of Medieval Studies, Studies and Texts, 14 (Toronto, 1968): 270.

30. "Corporaliter et vere torqueat corpora animarum hujusmodi et etiam animas ipsas. Am-

sudden shift in attitude appears in his next statement: "The idea of only dreaming of the flames would not sufficiently deter men from vice and sins, since very few are able to understand that souls are able to be tormented by dreams or by the imagination of tortures."[31] William retreated from his psychological interpretation because, if spread abroad, it might diminish the deterrent effect of hell and would therefore not be suitable for preaching.[32] Thus William introduces a functional distinction into his teaching. He divides theory for his theology students from what will deter people from sinning. William's tacit distinction offers support for the method I have adopted of categorizing authors by their purposes, audiences, and rhetoric.

Thomas Aquinas did not distinguish an esoteric from an exoteric view of infernal torments, but he certainly agreed that hell serves to deter men from evil through fear of punishment.[33] Thomas did not deny the physical reality of infernal torments, but, like William, he refrained from treating them in detail. Building upon his view of sin as insubordination, Thomas looked at damnation as a restoration of order. Failure to achieve a final order would be impossible. Without damnation, sin would remain unpunished. Thus: "God leaves nothing in disorder, therefore he never releases from fault without punishment."[34] The deadline for the establishment of

---

plius. Cum ipse sit Deus veritatis et veritas, non decet magnificentiam gloriae ipsius ut utatur mendaciis somniorum. *De Universo*, 682b E.

31. "Modus somniandi tantum ardores non satis deterreret homines a vitiis et peccatis, cum paucissimi intelligere possint animas posse, vel somniis vel suppliciorum imaginationibus cruciari." *Ibid.*, 682b E.

32. Jacques Le Goff disagrees with this interpretation. With all due respect to a historian whose work has consistently been a stimulus and whose personal encouragement I deeply appreciate, I must observe that his discussion omits William's statement quoted in note 28. He believes that William really meant to say "Since fire is effective when it exists only in men's imagination, . . . it is even more effective when it is real." (p. 330; p. 245). William was no stranger to the *a fortiori* argument, but he did not use this particular one. Moreover, truncating the sentence "Et corporaliter et vere torqueat corpora animarum huiusmodi et etiam animas ipsas" to obtain the phrase "corpora animarum," does not resolve the problem. (In the English translation [p. 245] the repetition of "corpora animarum" is removed.) First, it does not strengthen William's statement ("torqueat corpora . . . et animas ipsas"). Second, it underlines one side of the contradiction without doing justice to the other.

33. "Aeternae poenae reproborum a Deo inflictae sunt medicinales his qui consideratione poenarum abstinent a peccatis," ST2 q.87 a.3 ad 2. Cf. *Summa Contra Gentiles* III, cap. 144: "Nihil igitur prohibet . . . ut ex perpetue poene timore homines peccare desistant." *Opera Omnia* 14 (Rome, 1926): 430, line 42b.

34. "Deus nihil inordinatum relinquit, ideo nunquam culpam sine poena dimittit." *Scriptum*

perfect order is the end of time, Judgment Day. At the sound of the trumpet will come the separation of good from evil, pure from impure.

> At the end of the world, fire and the other elements will be divided. Whatever is in them that is beautiful and clear will remain up above for the glory of the saints. Whatever is in them that is sordid and injurious will descend into hell for the punishment of the damned . . . , who will not suffer only from the punishment of fire. For it is just that those who have offended the Creator should be punished by the whole of creation."[35]

The question then arises as to how the soul, a spiritual substance, can suffer from the imposition of these material things, to which, by its nature, it is superior. To the best of my knowledge, Thomas' fullest discussion of this issue concerns not the resurrected spiritual body that is recomposed after the Last Judgment, but instead examines how fire can harm the soul separated from the body, between an individual's death and the general resurrection. We shall see that the principles involved are closely related.

In his discussion, Thomas distinguishes those hurts perceived through the senses from those which arise from the soul's interior perception of opposition to the will.[36] The separated soul cannot suffer from the corporeal fire of hell in the first way because it is spiritual and free in principle from the order of corporeal things.[37] In hell, however, it is bound "by divine power" (*virtute divina*) to fire, a lower, corporeal substance;[38]

---

super Sententiis M. Petri Lombardi, Lib. 4, d.21 q.1 a.2 ad 3; eds. R. Mandonnet and M. Moos, 4 vols. (Paris, 1924–47), 4:1056.

35. "In fine mundi ignis dividetur et alia elementa; et quidquid est in eis pulchrum et clarum remanebit superius ad gloriam beatorum; quod vero est in eis faeculentum et poenosum descendet in infernum ad poenam damnatorum; et ita faex totius creaturae in infernum colligetur, et erit damnatis in poenam, et non solum patientur poenam ignis. Iustum est enim ut qui Creatorem offenderunt, ab omni creatura puniantur. . . ." *Quodl.* 8 q.8 a.18; *Opera Omnia*, 25 vols. (Parma, 1852–73) 9: 583–4. Thomas is quoting Saint Basil, *Homil.*, in Ps. 28, n.6. Cf. Basil's Homil. VI *in Hexaem.*, n.3.

36. "Nam passio quae est secundum alterationem a contrario infert afflictionem et poenam secundum sensibilem dolorem. . . . Sed secunda passio non infert poenam secundum dolorem sensibilem sed secundum interiorem tristitiam, quae oritur in homine vel in animali ex hoc quod aliquid interiori aliqua vi apprehenditur ut repugnans voluntati vel cuicumque appetitui." *Quaestiones de Anima*, q. 21, responsio; *ed. cit.*, 270.

37. "Secundum igitur primum modum passionis anima non potest pati poenam ab igne corporeo. . . . Anima enim et quaelibet incorporalis substantia, quantum est de sua natura, non est obligata alicui loco sed transcendit totum ordinem corporalium." *Ibid.*

38. "Et per hunc modum animae . . . alligantur virtute divina in sui poenam corporeo igni. . . .

and this happens "against its nature and is contrary to its natural appetite."[39] Thus the fire of hell afflicts the soul with "interior sadness . . . when it considers that what was born to be united in fruition with God, is now subjected to the lowest things . . . to corporeal things . . . in the lowest and most abject place."[40]

Yet, despite the disgust which infects the hell-bound soul, Thomas insists, "the greatest affliction of the damned will be from the fact that they will be separated from God."[41] For Thomas, then, the psychological impact of damnation outweighs any physical torments of hell as a place. Consequently he has little patience for details such as its fire, ice, smoke, noise, stench and other characteristics that intrigued others. Indeed, in one place he seems to belittle "certain thinkers [perhaps including William?], who devote their attention to the damnation of the reprobate" and who insist "that no evil can be lacking for [the damned]."[42] Nonetheless Thomas too employed similar axioms in working out specific questions. As an example, consider his response to the question "Whether, after Judgment Day, the damned see the glory of the elect."[43] In setting up his answer, Thomas invokes the saying "after the Day of Judgment no affliction will be subtracted from the damned."[44] We cannot be sure that Thomas accepts this premise as his own until we consider his answer. First he distinguishes the glory of the saints as it is enjoyed by the saints from the way it is seen by the damned who, before Judgment Day, have knowledge but no experience of it. But after that moment, "they will be wholly removed from the company of the saints, as befits those who will attain the height of misery (*summum miseriae*) and who therefore are not considered worthy even of the company of the saints [and so they will not see the glory of the saints], for he who sees has a certain company with that which he sees."[45] Since the damned attain the height of misery after

Et sic verum est quod ignis ille, in quantum virtute divina detinet animam alligatam, agit in animam ut instrumentum divinae iustitiae." *Ibid.*, 270–71.

39. "Quod ergo alligetur alicui et determinetur ad aliquem locum per quandam necessitatem est contra eius naturam et contrarium appetitui naturali." *Ibid.*, 270.

40. ". . . interiori tristitia affligitur; . . . cum considerat se infimis rebus subdi quae nata fuit Deo per fruitionem uniri . . . rebus corporalibus . . . et infimo et abiectissimo loco." *Ibid.*, 271.

41. "Maxima igitur afflictio damnatorum erit ex eo quod a Deo separabuntur." *Ibid.*

42. "Quidam enim, attendentes damnationem reproborum, ut nihil eis mali deesset . . ." *Quodlibeta* 7, a.12; p. 562.

43. "Utrum damnati post diem iudicii videant gloriam sanctorum." *Quodl.* 8, a.16; *Ibid.*, p. 583a.

44. "Post diem iudicii nulla afflictio a damnatis subtrahetur" *Ibid.*

45. "Tunc erunt penitus a sanctorum consortio alienati, ut qui ad summum iam miseriae per-

the end of time, Thomas must explain how deprivation of the sight of the saints' bliss will increase, indeed consummate, their unhappiness. After all, if seeing the punishment of the damned is part of the happiness of the saved, who thus enjoy the justice of God, why should not the damned see the glory of the blessed as part of their punishment?[46] "To see the glory of the saints would bring some bit of perfection, from which, after Judgment Day, the damned will be excluded."[47] But this lack will actually heighten their suffering because

> the damned in hell after Judgment Day will remember the glory of the saints, which they saw before and during the judgment. They will know that [the saints] are in the greatest glory, although they may not see the blessed themselves or their glory, and so they will be tormented by envy. Thus the affliction [envy] which is in them now when they have such vision will remain when the vision is removed. And from this they will grieve even more, recognizing that they are considered unworthy even to see the saints.[48]

Maxima gloria versus *summum miseriae*, spiritual freedom versus corporeal constraint, these are the poles around which Thomas constructs his treatment of hell. Privation of all perfection, omnipresence of all affliction, continuation (and intensification after the Last Judgment) of envy and all other spiritual vices, the removal of all relief, these are the abstractions in which the theologians deal.[49] William and Thomas have provided two samples of the discourse produced by theologians. Yet before moving to another type of writer, we should note one more source, not the product of individual genius and possibly thereby unrepresentative of a class of

venerunt, et ideo nec etiam sanctorum consortio digni habebuntur: nam videns aliquod consortium habet cum eo quod videt." *Ibid.*

46. Here I adapt argument 1: "De perfectione gloriae sanctorum est ut videant miseriam damnatorum. . . . Ergo de perfectione miseriae damnatorum est ut videant gloriam sanctorum. . . ." *Ibid.*

47. "Videre sanctorum gloriam aliquid perfectionis importat, qua post diem iudicii damnati privabuntur." *Ibid.*

48. "Damnati in inferno existentes post diem iudicii memores erunt gloriae sanctorum, quam ante iudicium et in iudicio viderunt; et sic cognoscent eos esse in maxima gloria, quamvis non videant ipsos beatos, nec eorum gloriam; et ita invidia torquebuntur; et sic afflictio quae est in eis nunc ex tali visione, manebit visione sublata: de quo etiam magis dolebunt videntes se etiam visione sanctorum indignos reputatos." *Ibid.*

49. *Ibid.*, a.17 & a.18; p. 583b.

thinkers, but the product of a committee. Thomas died in 1274 before he was able to complete his magisterial *Summa Theologiae*. Among the subjects he did not treat there is eschatology. Headed primarily by Reginald of Piperno, a group of Thomas' secretaries compiled material largely, but not exclusively, from Thomas' other writings to fill in the missing portions. These are now found in the Supplement to Part III of the *Summa Theologiae*.[50] As we turn to this source we expect to find not so much the ripest fruits of Thomas's teaching, as evidence for a certain consensus about the nature of, and procedures prevalent in, theological discourse as understood by those in his immediate circle.

Like their master, his continuators refrained from describing the physical reality of hell in any detail. They preferred simply to give a rule of thumb: "Hell will be such that everything in it will contribute to the maximum unhappiness of the damned."[51] We find another example of reasoning by reverse analogy: "Just as on account of the perfect beatitude of the saints, nothing will apply to them that is not a source of joy; so nothing will apply to the damned that is not a matter and cause of sadness. Nor could anything which pertains to unhappiness be lacking them, so that their misery may be consummate."[52]

The compilers apply the rule of the maximum misery of the damned — already articulated by William and Thomas himself — to each question that arises. In Question 97 they discuss the corporeal torments and in Question 98 the psychological anguish of the damned. Thus it is asked whether the damned will be able to see. The conclusion follows the principle named above: "There will be light and darkness in whatever proportion most tends to the misery of the damned."[53] The same is true of their memory.

They will remember the evil they did, for which they are damned,

---

50. J. Weisheipl, *Friar Thomas d'Aquino. His Life, Thought, and Work* (Garden City, N.Y., 1974), 339, 362. Even using the *Index Thomisticus,* I find the following statements from the *Supplement* nowhere else in Thomas' work. I must therefore assume that Thomas' continuators contributed some text of their own composition.

51. "Dispositio inferni erit talis quod maxime miseriae damnatorum competet. . . . ST4 Supp. q.97 a.4; p. 241.

52. "Sicut propter perfectam sanctorum beatitudinem nihil erit in eis quod non sit gaudii materia, ita nihil erit in damnatis quod non sit eis materia et causa tristitiae; nec aliquid quod ad tristitiam possit pertinere, deerit, ut sit eorum miseria consummata." *Ibid.,* q.98 a.7; p. 246.

53. "Sunt ibi lux et tenebra prout maxime spectant ad miseriam damnatorum." *Ibid.,* q.97 a.4; p. 241.

and the good that they loved which they lost. They will be tormented by both types of memories. They will be tormented also by the fact that they will see that the knowledge which they had of speculative things was imperfect and by the fact that they have let slip the highest perfection of it [speculative, intelligible knowledge], which they were [theoretically] able to obtain.[54]

Torment through reflection upon error is clearly a suffering of the intellect, not the body. Yet the objection is raised that "the damned are in greater suffering than any of this world. But in this world, when someone is situated in the greatest torments, he is unable to consider any intelligible conclusions apart from the suffering he is experiencing. Therefore those in hell will be much less able to do so."[55] This question amounts to asking whether the physical sufferings of hell will be so great as to overwhelm the soul completely and leave it without any ability to consider intelligible conclusions, and, by implication, without any consciousness of the rationale behind its suffering. Thomas' followers have no doubt that "however much the body may be afflicted, the soul will always consider most lucidly those things which are able to be a cause of anguish for it."[56]

Thomas' continuators, therefore, confirm the characterization of theological discourse we derived from our brief consideration of William of Auvergne and Thomas himself. In thirteenth-century Paris, theologians described hell in abstract terms by deducing conclusions from principles (particularly that of maximum suffering). Equally important, they emphasized not so much the physical characteristics of the place as the psychological condition of the damned.

54. "Considerabunt enim et mala quae gesserunt, ex quibus damnati sunt, et bona dilecta, quae amiserunt, et ex utroque torquebuntur. Similiter etiam torquebuntur de hoc quod considerabunt notitiam quam de rebus speculabilibus habuerunt imperfectam esse, et amisisse summam eius perfectionem, quam poterant adipisci." *Ibid.,* q.98 a.7; p. 246a.

55. "Damnati sunt in maioribus poenis quam sint aliquae poenae huius mundi. Sed in hoc mundo, dum aliquis est in maximis tormentis constitutus, non potest considerare aliquas intelligibiles conclusiones, abstractus a poenis quas patitur. Ergo multo minus in inferno." *Ibid.,* q.98 a.7 obj.2; p. 246a.

56. "Quantumcumque corpus affligatur, tamen anima semper considerabit lucidissime illa quae ei poterunt esse causa maeroris." *Ibid.,* q.98 a.7 ad 2; p. 246b.

III

The Compilers

While the theologians gave considerably more attention to the justice of damnation and to the psychology of hell than to its physical makeup, the case is far different for the authors of preachers' manuals.[57] Of these I have chosen as an example the Dominican Stephen of Bourbon, compiler of the extensive *Treatise on Different Preachable Matters,* an encyclopedic compendium of theological conclusions, biblical quotations arranged by subject, and illustrative sermon-stories called *exempla.* Born around 1180, Stephen studied at the University of Paris and was one of the first to join the Dominican order after Dominic's envoys reached the university city in 1217. By 1223 he was associated with the Dominican house in Lyon. From about 1235 he was active as an inquisitor and travelled extensively in that function in southern France. Around 1250 he began to compile his famous treatise. He died in 1261 before completing the fifth part of his projected seven-part work.[58] To locate Stephen chronologically, we may observe that he was at Paris during the time that William of Auvergne was teaching there and that he wrote just after William's death and at the beginning of Thomas' teaching career (though I posit no personal contact in either case). His death comes a dozen years before the transcription of the manuscript of sermons we shall consider. From Stephen's own compilation, only selected sermon-stories have ever been published.[59]

57. R. & M. Rouse, (note 6 above) esp. chap. 1 for a review of aids to study in the later Middle Ages (twelfth-fourteenth centuries). C. Delcorno, *La predicazione nell'età comunale* (Florence, 1974), 10–19 and bibliography at 52–3. J-L. Bataillon, "Les instruments de travail des prédicateurs au XIIIe siècle" in G. Hasenohr & J. Longère, eds., *Culture et travail intellectuel dans l'Occident médiéval* (Paris, 1981), 197–209. In the same collection see also R. Rouse, "L'évolution des attitudes envers l'autorité écrite: le développement des instruments de travail au XIIIe siècle," 115–144. J. Longère, *La prédication médiévale* (Paris, 1983), chap. 7, "Instruments de travail des prédicateurs," 177–202.

58. A. Lecoy de la Marche, *Anecdotes historiques . . . d'Etienne de Bourbon* (Paris, 1877), ii–xi; J.-C. Schmitt, *Le Saint Lévrier* (Paris, 1979), 23–5.

59. We are indebted to Lecoy de la Marche for what is available so far. His publication of isolated exempla, however, obscures any view of the work as a whole. A complete edition based

Universally considered the best manuscript, Paris, BN, lat. 15970, shows that Stephen's treatise is composed like a law code, divided into books, each book divided into titles, and these into chapters. Each book is devoted to one of the seven gifts of the Holy Spirit, a popular method of organization among the scholastics. Each chapter begins with a statement of the material it will treat and announces the number of articles it will contain. Not every article is treated exactly the same, but a typical discussion consists of a general statement explaining why that article comes within its particular title. Then follows a bit of mnemonic verse to introduce many of the key terms that will recur in later discussion. Scriptural references follow, then theological proofs "by reason," capped by authoritative *sententiae* or maxims from the Church Fathers. Only then does Stephen provide (usually) between two and four exempla to illustrate each point. It is vital to observe how useful the outlines were to Stephen's Dominican brothers in the composition of sermons.

The multitude of exempla have made Stephen's compilation famous, but because they are so carefully integrated into this theological framework, it is best to regard the work as fulfilling two separate functions, first, that of an encyclopedia of doctrine, a summary of theology, second, that of a collection of sermon-stories.

In Book I, "On Fear," Title IV, "On the Fear of Hell," has nine chapters, each having from nine to twelve articles, each of which in turn contain several biblical references and/or exempla. An outline showing the subject matter of each article is sufficient to demonstrate that, although the psychological effects of hell are far from neglected, there is an attention to the physical components of hell that is almost entirely lacking in the writing of the theologians. (For the sake of the outline I occasionally paraphrase rather than translate the Latin literally.)[60]

---

on Paris, BN, MS lat. 15970 is in progress: Part II by D. Ogilvie-David, *Positions de thèse de l'Ecole des chartes* (Paris, 1978), 133–136 and Part III by J. Berlioz, *ibid.,* (Paris, 1977), 25–33. To the best of my knowledge, these theses themselves are not generally available.

60. Please see Appendix.

On the Fear of Hell

I. Existence and location of hell.

II. The nature of the place. Hell is: (1) [deep]; (2) dark; (3) fiery; (4) intemperate, whence it is called Avernus, as if to say without the moderated temperature of spring (a-vernum, without spring). There will be there a disproportion of qualities. There will be no tempering there, but all [conditions] will rage in the highest degree. That is, fire will be of the most intense heat, cold and stench and the other evils will also be at their peak. [Further, hell is:] (5) horrible; (6) dry and barren; (7) foul and dirty; (8) pungent and poisonous; (9) tumultuous; (10) concealed and forgotten; (11) smoky and full of sorrow; (12) dangerous, whence it is called the Pit (Baratrum), after its narrow (arta) width, because its mouth is wide as an entrance, but narrow as an exit, like the snare of the devil.

III. Twelve things that aggravate the pains of hell. Hell's pains are: (1) eternal; (2) bitter; (3) diverse; (4) immense; (5) continuous; (6) generalized, inside and out, in soul and (after the Judgment) body, and in all members simultaneously; (7) in conformity to the blame; (8) inescapable; (9) fearful; (10) useless (as contrasted to this present suffering, which can be useful for three things, namely, to purify sinners, to diminish or annul future suffering, and to acquire and augment [future] rewards. The future Purgatory is valid for the first two, although it confers no merit, but the suffering of hell is useful for nothing.); (11) horrible company; (12) poverty and the lack of all goods.

IV. On the deformity of the demons. Note their (1) horribleness and ugliness; (2) cruelty; (3) aggressiveness and eagerness; (4) strengh and power; (5) speed; (6) zeal, shrewdness, and versatility in doing harm; (7) deviousness and falsity; (8) weight.

V. Miseries afflicting the soul: (1) the perturbation of never-failing fear; (2) the confusion of the inevitable shame when all sins will be revealed by the Lord; (3) the intensity of grief and sorrow; (4) distress that is always present; (5) the burning of hatred and the bitterness of anger, sadness, and rage (here is the worm which will not die—Isaiah 66, 24); (6) absence from God's mind (for God will consign them to oblivion); (7) the grief of desperation; (8) disturbance or remorse of a heart which knows itself; (9) the blinding of reason; (10) the consumption [of the heart by] envy and malice; (11) boredom with life [after death] and the desire for death [without consciousness]; (12) memory of past goods and the lack of them forever.

VI. The twelve miseries afflicting the bodies of the wicked after the Judgment: (1) ugliness; (2) weakness, or the impossibility of resisting [demons and the elements]; (3) infirmities of all kinds; (4) uselessness and powerlessness (for their limbs will be useless and unable to do anything); (5) rot; (6) stink; (7) corrosiveness and liability to being eaten; (8) a diversity of scourges, for the bodies of the damned will be thrashed, trampled, kicked, and split apart by the sword; (9) weight; (10) absence of nourishment and lack of clothes (there will be poverty); (11) immense wailing; (12) submissiveness and sensitivity. (Above all there will be an unfailing supply of things to be suffered and felt. And this corruption or putrefaction will not remove their ability to feel, as happens in a withered limb, but instead sensitivity will be heightened as in leprosy or the boils of Egypt.)

VII. The aggravation of the penalty from consideration of the anger of God, whom they have implacably offended. . . . There are twelve reasons the anger of God will seem most serious to the damned: (1) He will cast them away from Himself and His own and His company as excommunicated and accursed persons; (2) He will cast them into the lake of His anger; (3) He will hurl their sins against them; (4) the Father of Mercies will not seem to have sympathy for them, nor will He ever extract them from the fire; (5) since He will turn them over to demons, indeed demons who will torture them; (6) it will seem to them that God and the heavenly court rejoice at their woes since God will ridicule, deride, and mock them; (7) He will never hear their cries or pleas; (8) He will not listen to the prayers of their servants for their salvation, nor will he hold pleasing or proper the offerings and gifts made for them either by themselves or by others, nor will He allow their redemption; (9) in order to increase their pain, He will reimpose their bodies upon them so that they may be punished in body and soul; (10) He will direct, encourage, and augment their pains and torments; (11) He will rouse all His creatures and His saints against them and will equip and lead [His company] to punish them; (12) because He will eternally close the door of His kingdom and will deprive them of the vision of His glory.

VIII. Awareness of goods not enjoyed: (1) the eternal good, i.e., the vision of God; (2) the company of the saints; (3) the help of the Lord, since God will no longer offer them mercy; (4) the help, suffrages, and favor of the saints and the merits of the good they have done, from which they could have received great reward in eternal glory had their sins not prevented it; (5) the suffrages of the church, which are not valid for release from eternal punishment; (6) holy places are useless, indeed unsuitable for them (it does them no good, but rather harm, to be buried in holy places); (7) present goods; (8) the time for penance, and of gaining and meriting mercy; (9) the loss of oneself; (10) one's friends; (11) hope; (12) charity.

IX. Benefits of meditating upon hell: (1) it dries out the flesh and its pleasures; (2) in temptation it preserves one from sin and defeats and overcomes the devil; (3) it turns and recalls one from sin; (4) it incites one to great weeping, as there is a nearness to fire and smoke; (5) it mitigates present suffering; (6) it offers solace to the saints, for it shows them the punishment of the wicked;

(7) it perturbs the demons; (8) it changes present delights into bitterness; (9) it augments even more the torments for those who are not converted; (10) it calls one to the contempt of self and of the world; (11) it shows that God is of the highest justice and supremely to be feared; (12) it causes one to maintain the good and persevere.

Thus Stephen has reviewed 91 characteristics of hell, each representing a detail in a vision of eternal horror. Every particular is supported by a reference to Scripture and finally illustrated by one or more exempla.

Before examining the exempla, let us consider for a moment the purpose for which they were intended. An exemplum is a short, edifying story from which a moral might be drawn. In a well-constructed sermon that moral would reinforce the preacher's main theme. In the preface to his *Sermones Vulgares* of about 1200, James of Vitry (d. 1240) urged using the exemplum specifically to reach the unlettered. He said:

> We ought to turn our skill to the edification of the uncultivated and the instruction of the country folk. To them we should more frequently present corporeal and palpable and such-like subjects which they know by experience. For they are moved more by external examples than by [quoted] authorities or profound propositions.[61]

Moreover, the exempla will "excite and arouse the laity," keep them awake, and recall their wandering attention.[62]

Stephen of Bourbon also regarded the exemplum as particularly suited to the needs of the uneducated, because they "refine the coarseness of simple persons and they present and impress [the truth] with an easier and more durable tenacity upon the memory."[63] Developing James of Vitry's notion that preachers should stress the corporeal or palpable, Stephen cited

61. "Convertere debemus ingenium nostrum ad aedificationem rudium et agrestium eruditionem, quibus quasi corporalia et palpabilia et talia que per experientiam norunt frequentius sunt proponenda. Magis enim moventur exterioribus exemplis quam auctoritatibus vel profundis sententiis." Prologue to the *Sermones Vulgares* from Paris, BN, MS lat. 17509 fol. 2v, quoted in T. Crane, *The Exempla . . . of Jacques de Vitry* (repr., New York, 1971), xli, note.

62. "Exempla ad laicorum excitationem et recreationem sunt interserenda." Cf. below: " . . . non solum ad aedificationem, sed ad recreationem, maxime quando fatigati et tedio affecti incipiunt dormitare . . . omnes incitati sunt et innovati ad audiendum." Crane, xlii, note.

63. " . . . exempla, que maxime erudiunt simplicium hominum ruditatem, et faciliorem et longiorem ingerunt et imprimunt in memoria tenacitatem." Paris, BN, MS lat. 15970, fol. 137v; ed. Lecoy, 4.

Christ Himself as both a user of exempla and as an illustration of a Truth given material form.

> Jesus Christ taught first in deeds rather than words and He rendered the subtlety of His preaching and doctrine weighty, as though corporeal and visible, by arming and dressing it with diverse comparisons, parables, miracles, and exempla so that His doctrine might be more quickly grasped, more easily learned, more forcibly retained in the memory, and more efficaciously put into action.[64]

Thus for Stephen, exempla "incorporate" truth as Christ incarnated the Word, and the use of exempla illustrates the doctrine of Christ even as it commemorates His act of teaching. We can hardly overestimate, then, the force Stephen and his fellow compilers and preachers attributed to this particular literary form.[65]

In his *Treatise on Different Preachable Matters,* Stephen distributed his exempla according to the framework outlined above. Thus we must read each exemplum first at the most literal level, for example to show that hell is dark or fiery, and then at the moral level.

Of the over 200 exempla on hell, most are taken from older literature. Some come from sources that go back to late antiquity, like the *Vision of St. Paul,* the *Lives of the Fathers,* or the *Dialogues* of Gregory the Great. Others are drawn from slightly earlier thirteenth-century compilations, like those of James of Vitry or Caesarius of Heisterbach. Even though the vast majority of these exempla were drawn from traditional monastic sources,[66] they were calculated, as we have learned, to appeal to the tastes, experience, and imagination of the laity.

---

64. "Christus Ihesus primo docuit factis quam verbis et subtilitatem predicationis et doctrine grossam quasi corpoream et visibilem reddidit, muniens et vestiens eam diversis similitudinibus, parabolis, miraculis et exemplis, ut eius doctrina citius caperetur, facilius cognosceretur, fortius in memoria retineretur et efficatius opere adimpletur." *Ibid.*

65. On exempla in general, in addition to the works cited in note 57, above, see: C. Bremond, J. Le Goff, J.-C. Schmitt, *L'exemplum*. Typologie des sources du moyen âge occidental, 40 (Turnhout, 1982); F. C. Tubach, *Index Exemplorum: A Handbook of Medieval Religious Tales*. FF Communications, 204 (Helsinki, 1969); C. Delcorno, *L'exemplum nella predicazione volgare di Giordano di Pisa* (Venice, 1972); B. McGuire, "The Cistercians and the Rise of the Exemplum in Early Thirteenth-Century France: A Re-evaluation of Paris, BN, MS lat. 15912," *Classica et Mediaevalia* 34 (1983): 214–267; R. Rusconi, *Predicazione e vita religiosa nella società italiana* (Torino, 1981), 124.

66. An important category of exceptions to this statement is the number of exempla collected by Stephen himself on his travels. I draw from one of these exempla below. Jean-Claude Schmitt's,

A first category consists of exempla which describe the types of punishment consequent to particular forms of wickedness. Perhaps the most direct is one that Stephen has taken, as he tells us, from the *Vision of St. Paul:*

> In a certain book, which is entitled the *Vision of Saint Paul,* it is said that he [St. Paul] saw in hell black women covered with pitch and sulphur and dragons and serpents tormenting and rebuking them and saying, "At least now acknowledge your sins." And they had fiery horns and snakes and vipers around their necks sucking and racking them. These were the voluptuous women who killed their own children [i.e. licentious women guilty of abortion or infanticide].[67]

One unidentified vision is cited to show that hell is noisy, chaotic, and filled with cacophony. It reports the fate of those who engage in usury. A certain usurer "buried in flames" sees the soul of his son arrive to join him in hell. Each blames the other for his own damnation:

> "Accursed be the hour, my son, in which I produced you, and accursed be you because on account of you I did evil, and so I am tormented here." For his part, the son replied that it should be the father who is accursed and the hour in which he became his father, because the father had taught him to lend at interest and had be-

---

Le Saint Lévrier, cited above, note 58, pursues in "exemplary" fashion the consequences of Stephen's activity as inquisitor/ethnographer.

67. In the following notes from Stephen of Bourbon I have collated the oldest manuscript, Paris, BN, lat. 15970, which belonged to the Sorbonne (siglum S) against a younger manuscript, Paris, BN, lat. 14598, which belonged to Saint Victor (siglum V). The readings will be those of S unless V is indicated. Some of Stephen's exempla may also be found in Vincentius Bellovacensis, *Speculum Quadruplex sive Speculum Maius. 2. Speculum Morale* (Douai, 1624; repr. Graz, 1964), abbreviated as Vin.

"In quodam libro qui intitulatur 'Visio Pauli' dicitur quod vidit in inferno mulieres nigras indutas pice et sulphure et drachones et serpentes torquentes eas et increpantes et dicentes 'Agnoscite nunc saltem peccatum vestrum'. Et habebant cornua ignita et serpentes et vipere circa colla earum eas suggentes et torquentes. Hee fuerant luxuriose et necatrices puerorum [suorum V]." S, f. 147rb; V. f. 15ra; Vin. 816 E. Cf. T. Silverstein, *Visio Sancti Pauli* (London, 1935) Redactions I, Para. 7, p. 154; II, Para. 10, p. 157; III, Para. 13, pp. 176–9; V, lines 7–16, p. 199; VII, lines 19–23, p. 204; VIII, lines 21–25, p. 211. For Redaction IV, which Silverstein regards as the most widespread and influential, see H. Brandes, *Visio S. Pauli: Ein Beitrag zur Visionsliteratur.* Gesellschaft für deutsche Philologie, 5 (Halle, 1885): p. 77. In the *Archives d'histoire doctrinale et litteraire du moyen-âge* 26 (1959): 199–248, Silverstein published other variants and Redactions IX and X. See pp. 228, Para. 7; 232, Para. 13; 237, Para. 10; 241, Para. 7; 246, Para. 13.

Considering the antiquity of many exempla in Stephen's treatment of hell, the analysis by Himmelfarb (above, note 1) of Jewish and Christian apocalyptic literature, which isolates individual motifs in visions of punishment after death, should prove a particularly valuable guide.

queathed him the property of others, and so he [the son] too will be tortured forever.[68]

One can imagine the dreadful racket endured by the damned, subject to interminable family squabbles!

Usurers were particularly likely to involve their kin in evil, as we see from the following story, classified as illustrating the horrible company one finds in hell. Stephen tells us that his account is based on a sermon preached by a certain Franciscan named William of Poitiers or of Poitou, but which was told to Stephen by the men of a certain town. That Stephen should learn this clerical tale from laymen helps to underline the immediacy and effectiveness of the exemplum as a rhetorical strategy. The following is a superb example of Franciscan preaching. The story does not merely describe extreme suffering, but also opposes illicit enterprise while describing the justice of hell, where unequal torments are distributed according to degree of guilt.

A certain man had a vision of the future punishments and among other things: He saw a man lying at the base of a blazing flame and from his side grew a tall tree from whose branches men were hung, and they were most bitterly and variously tormented by the fire that proceeded from the base. The one who lay at the bottom was tortured most of all. When the one who saw this asked his guide what sort of man this was, the guide responded: "The one who lies at the bottom was the beginning of the generation of all these, and he was a poor man, but he became prosperous by usury. The others are those who proceeded from him, and they are punished either because they were imitators of the paternal evil or because they did not give back what had been acquired through usury. But the first is tormented more than the others by seeing those who came into this punishment through him, and because the pain accumulated for all of them is upon him."[69]

68. "Unde dicitur quod quidam vidit in inferno quemdam usurarium sepultum in flammis. Et cum anima filii mortui deportaretur ibi, pater hoc videns eiulando clamabat, 'Maladicta sit hora, fili, in qua te genui, et tu sis maladictus quia propter te feci mala, propter que hic crucior!' E contra filius respondebat [patri V] eum maledictum esse et horam maledictam in qua fuerat factus pater suus, quia ipse docuerat eum fenerari et alienum ei reliquerat, propter que in perpetuum torqueretur." S, f. 147va; V, f. 15ra–b; Vin. 818 A.

69. "Item audivi fratrem Guillelmum Pictavum [sic] de ordine fratrum minorum hoc predicasse in quadam villa ab hominibus illius ville, quod quidam in quadam visione futurorum malorum

The three preceding exempla illustrate that type of exemplum which portrays an infernal punishment as the result of a given sin.

A second category of exempla shows how reflection on hell promotes endurance in ascetic discipline or perseverance in the good. From the *Lives of the Fathers,* Stephen relates how

> a certain [young hermit] asked an old one what he should do because boredom was making it impossible for him to remain in his cell. The old [hermit] replied that if he thought about the worms and other pains of hell, and he would peacefully put up with having here [in this life] worms even up to his neck.[70]

In a similar case recorded about 800 years later by a Cistercian historian relating the beginnings of his Order, the youth does not seek help on his own, but receives it in a vision of his mother. A novice in the Cistercian order finds the discipline too hard to bear and seeks to leave. His mother appears to him in his cell and begs him to remain in the order, otherwise he would probably end up in hell. The son complains: "what order can be as hard as this one?" (In Vincent of Beauvais, this complaint is: "this order is as hard as hell.") The mother asks if he would like to sample a tiny torment from hell. He hears a horrible grunting of pigs, louder than thunder. And it seems that the sky is splitting apart and falling on his head. Would he like a sample of heaven? He hears voices of such great sweetness and smoothness that they surpass all the harmony of music. Then his mother says: "If you wish to escape the torments of

---

[majorum *S, Lecoy*] vidit inter alia unum hominem in ymo flammarum prostratum, de cuius utero alta arbor procedebat, in cuius ramis homines suspensi erant et a flamma ab imo procedente diversimode et acerrime torquebantur. Et ille qui in fundo iacebat magis inter illos torquebatur.

"Et cum quereret ille qui hoc videbat a ductore suo cuiusmodi esset homo, ait illi: 'Ille qui iacet in imo fuit principium generationis omnium istorum et fuit pauper et per usuras ascendit. Alii sunt qui processerunt ab eo et torquentur vel quia fuerunt imitatores paterni sceleris vel quia adquisita per usuram non restituerunt. Primus autem super alios torquetur, videndo eos qui per eum in hoc tormentum venerunt, vel quia pro omnibus ei pena accumulatur.' " S, f. 150va; V, f. 19va–b; Lecoy, no. 17, p. 25.

70. "Quidam quesivit a quodam sene quid faceret quia per accidia non poterat morari in cella sua. Iste respondit quod si cogitaret de vermibus et penis inferni, si haberet ibi usque ad collum vermes, pacifice sustineret." S, f. 147rb; V, f. 15ra; Vin. 816 E. *Paterica armeniaca* VII, 19, Ba, ed. L. Leloir (*Corpus Scriptorum Christianorum Orientalium,* vols. 353, 361, 371, 379 = *Subsidia,* vols. 42, 43, 47, 51, Louvain, 1974–76) vol. 43, p. 154. Cf. *Verba Seniorum interprete Pelagio* VII, 28, in *PL* 73: 900 C.

hell and obtain the joys of heaven, remain in the religious life you have begun." The son firmly promised her this and did it.[71]

Sometimes the person undergoing temptation had to seek a physical stimulus to remind himself of hell. From the *Lives of the Fathers* Stephen recounts the tale about the youths who hired a prostitute to lead an anchorite into sin. She gained entrance to his cell under the pretext of seeking shelter. Once inside, she lay down naked next to the fire.

Greatly disturbed, the hermit fled to the back of the cell to his prayers. As he felt carnal desire rising, he immersed his fingers in the flame of a lamp saying within himself, "Woe is me if I sin with this woman. How will I be able to bear the fire of hell when I cannot bear this one?" And all night long, whenever temptation rose within him, he did this until he had almost completely burned his hand. But when the youths forced their way in, they found the wretched woman dead and they found the hermit with his hands burned. And by the hermit's prayers, God revived the woman, who said she had seen extending from the highest heaven to the earth a flame into which she deserved to be thrown.[72]

71. "Legi in quodam libro de initiis ordinis Cisterciensis quod cum de novo incepisset ordo Cisterciensis quidam intravit ibi et cum diu temptatus fuisset ibi de exitu proponebat [probabit S] exire. Cui [apparuerunt V] semel et secundo pater suus et mater sua dissuadentes exitum. Item cum tertio vellet omnino exire, apparuit ei mater multum tristis et querens quare vellet hoc. Qui cum diceret quod non posset sustinere asperitatem ordinis, quesivit mater quomodo posset sustinere infernum aut eius minimum tormentum.

"Et cum ille diceret, 'Quis ordo tante duritie [Vin.: quod ordo erat tante duritie ac inferno]? cuius vigilie quasi perpetue, silentium amarum, lectus ferreus, cibus insipidus, etc.?' intulit mater, 'Vis experiri unum modicum inferni tormentum?' Ita cum ille diceret, 'Volo,' audivit tam horribilem porcorum grunnitum quod nulli tonitruum possent ei comparari. Et videbatur ei quod celum scinderetur et quod caderet super caput eius. Et cum per timore clamaret et deficeret, confortavit eum mater et cessavit sonitus ille. Item mater ad eum, 'Vis audire unum minimum paradisi gaudium?' Dixit quod sic. Et tunc audivit voces tante dulcedinis et suavitatis quod superabant omnem dulcedinem musicorum. Et tunc mater ad eum: 'Si vis evadere tormenta inferni et adipisci gaudia paradisi, persevera in incepto.' Tunc ille firmiter hoc ei promisit et complevit." S, f. 147va; V, f. 15rb; Vin. 818 B. C. (I have not located a Cistercian source for this tale.)

72. "In Vitis Patrum legitur quod quidam iuvenes miserunt meretricem quamdam ad quemdam solitarium que asserebat eis quod faceret eum peccare secum. Que venit ad cellam eius dicens se esse errabundam, supplicans ut intromitteret eam intra domum suam, ne extra moriretur frigore vel occideretur a bestiis. Quod fecit ad ultimum motus pietate. Et cum illa multum sollicitaret eum, se nudans ad ignem et verbis similiter et signis, et ille fugeret ad interiora celle ad orationem, sentiens motus surgere carnales [carnales *om.* S], comburebat digitos suos ad lucernam dicens intra se, 'Miser, si cum ista peccavero. Ignem inferni quomodo sustinere potero qui hunc sustinere non

The two categories of exempla we have considered do not cover all the types in Stephen of Bourbon's treatise, but they represent a substantial portion, especially within the section on hell. The first group threatens punishment for proscribed behavior, the second encourages perseverance in the good or ascetic life in general. Neither encourages any particular behavior or action such as confession. That is because most of them derive from older sources and were conceived prior to the obligation of annual confession mandated in 1215.[73]

I do not wish to imply that no exemplum prior to 1215 seeks to encourage repentance in general or, specifically, confession. In fact, Stephen himself includes one obvious exception drawn from the *Dialogues* of Gregory the Great. By contrasting Stephen's paraphrase to Gregory's original version, we may highlight Stephen's own techniques and prepare ourselves for the sermons we are about to take up in which penance figures very prominently.

The tales related by Gregory the Great in his *Dialogues* refer to repentance with some frequency. In Gregory's exemplum concerning a monk who pretended to fast while eating covertly, the absence of repentance provides a dramatic highlight. Ill to the point of death, the monk revealed his secret and described his capture by a dragon from hell.

> "His tail is now coiled around my feet and knees and, with his head to my mouth, he is stealing the breath of life from me." Saying this he immediately died and was not expected even by repenting to be able to free himself from the dragon he had seen. For clearly it was for the sole benefit of the bystanders that he, who had marked out and could not escape the enemy to whom he was delivered, had seen [the dragon].[74]

possum?' Et hoc fecit totiens in nocte quotiens insurgebat temptatio usque quo manum quasi totam sibi combussit. Iuvenes autem irruentes invenerunt [inveniunt V] illam miseram mor⟨tu⟩am et heremitam habentem manus combustas. Ad cuius preces eam dominus suscitavit; que dicebat quod viderat flammam a summo celo usque ad terram durantem in qua debebat proici." S, f. 149vb; V, f. 18va–b; *Paterica Armeniaca* V 24R; vol. 43: 106–7. Cf. *Verba Seniorum interprete Pelagio* 5: 37; *PL* 73: 883–4.

73. See an important exception analyzed by J. Berlioz, " 'Quand dire c'est faire dire.' Exempla et confession chez Etienne de Bourbon," in *Faire croire*, 299–335 at 301, but note that this exemplum comes from another section of Stephen's work and does not refer to hell.

74. "Nam cum se ieiunare cum fratribus demonstraret, occulte manducare consueverat. . . . Qui cum iam essit [*sic*] in fine, fratres ad se omnes, qui monasterio inerant, congregari fecit. . . . Quibus ipse adflictus et tremens conpulsus est prodere, cui hosti traditus cogebatur exire. Nam dixit:

Stephen of Bourbon paraphrases this story in a section devoted to the deformity of hell's demons and particularly to their cruelty. He points to Gregory's exemplum concerning

> the gluttonous monk who seemed very religious and abstinent, but who ate in secret. At the end he proclaimed this [and cried out] that as a dragon the devil had absorbed his soul and that he had already entwined himself around his feet and his knees and with his mouth in his mouth was sucking out his soul. Saying this, he died.[75]

In a section devoted to demons, there is no room in Stephen's analysis for the monk's lack of repentance. (One might observe that the speed of the dragon's operation adds here to his cruelty by depriving the monk of his last chance to do penance.) Acting as a compiler, Stephen omits even vital details from his source partly because they would confuse the classification he is using and partly because he saw his role as isolating, not combining, themes for preaching.[76]

Thus the needs of the compiler acting as such may also partly explain the relative absence of specific recommendations for virtuous behavior in Stephen's discussion of hell. Even considering the restrictions of the genre employed by Stephen, hell, in his compilation of exempla, is presented

'Quando me vobiscum ieiunare credebatis, occulte comedebam. Et nunc ecce ad devorandum draconi sum traditus, qui cauda sua mea genua pedesque conlegavit, caput viro [sic] suum intra meum os mittens, spiritum meum ebibens abstrahit.' Quibus dictis statim defunctus est, adque ut paenitendo liberari potuissit [sic] a dracone quem viderat, expectatus non est. Quod nimirum constat quia ad solam utilitatem audientium viderit, qui eum hostem cui traditus fuerat et innotuit et non evasit." Gregorius Magnus, *Dialogi* 4, 40, ed. V. Moricca (Rome, 1924), 295. Moricca preserves the dialectical orthography of his manuscripts.

75. "In dyal. xl. exemplum de . . . monacho guloso qui videbatur valde religiosus et abstinens, sed commedebat in occulto. Qui in fine hoc clamavit, et quod dyabolus absorberat animam eius ut dracho et quod pedes eius et genua iam ligaverat et animam eius absorbebat, os suum habens in ore suo. Hoc dicens mortuus est." S, f. 151ra; V, f. 20ra.

76. It is logically possible that the simple avowal of his secret vice might constitute a sign of remorse, an informal confession, and the beginning of penance, yet neither author allows much room for this interpretation either explicitly or by classification. Gregory speaks of benefits to the bystanders; Stephen is more interested in the dragon.

It is true that in Part Three of his treatise Stephen provides a series of exempla on confession. They tend in general to emphasize confession as an escape from the devil, rather than from hell itself. (See Berlioz, above, note 73.) This difference is actually quite considerable, since the devil actively pursues the sinner (indeed tempts him or her into sin) in this life, whereas hell awaits one either at the end of life or the end of time. In the terms of the sampling presented here, the point to be made is that where Stephen describes hell he does not discuss confession and vice versa. The situation is quite different for the active preachers of Paris in the 1270s.

as a sanction against sin and a stimulus to a traditional, ascetic virtue. The Parisian preachers of the generation after Stephen took a different direction. They treated hell as a goad to confession.

IV

Preachers

The manuals and the exempla they contain served to prepare preachers to address the laity. But what did the preachers actually say? Normally this question would be nearly impossible to answer, but fortunately in the Bibliothèque Nationale at Paris there exists a manuscript of 219 sermons recorded as delivered during the academic or liturgical year 1272–73. At that time a Sorbonne theologian named Peter of Limoges commissioned a group of students or assistants to attend churches and record sermons as they were preached. He thus composed a manuscript, BN, lat. 16481, which is virtually unique for the thirteenth century. For nearly all these 219 sermons we know the name of the preacher, the name of the church, and the date of the sermon. The sermons were recorded in Latin but we know from internal evidence that they were delivered in French. Of all the literature we have considered so far, only these sermons were so tailored to the people as to be delivered orally and, indeed, in the vernacular.[77]

Like the theologians, the preachers also sought to prove the justice of damnation. Usually there was no formal demonstration; the point was made by means of an exemplum or extended simile.[78] For example, the Dominican Daniel of Paris preaching at St. Gervais on the Feast of the Trinity, June 4, 1273, drew upon the notion of one's freedom to choose one's own friends. If you choose wrong, your associates may use you for their own profit and lead you to crime, the king's gallows, and the gibbet of hell. But the company indicated by the Apostle seeks your benefit.

77. See N. Bériou, "La prédication au béguinage de Paris pendant l'année liturgique 1272–1273," *Recherches augustiniennes* 13 (1978): 105–229 for an extensive account of this manuscript and its continuation, Paris, BN, lat. 16482. For the use of French, see p. 114, note 35. Also, in the MS, see "li estorbelions d'enfer" f. 41rb.

78. For an examination of that aspect of the exemplum which depends more on the development of a simile than on the use of narrative, see F. Knapp, *Similitudo. Stil- und Erzählfunktion von Vergleich und Exempel in der lateinischen, französischen und deutschen Großepik des Hochmittelalters.* Philologica Germanica, 2 (Stuttgart, 1975): 41–107.

Therefore choose the company of the Trinity, which you can find in any church and which brings consolation against the cares of the flesh, the world, and the devil.[79] That hell is the just punishment of those who refuse the choice prescribed by biblical authority is clear. Here hell is a punishment for disobedience.

The image of evil returned for evil done was employed by an unnamed Dominican on the Feast of St. Nicholas, Dec. 6, 1272, at St. Lefroy. The friar describes the Second Coming and explains the justice of the fact that some will be condemned. In his exemplum he leaves implicit a theme we have seen developed by William of Auvergne, and which was very common, that sins are an injury to Christ. Thus damnation was presented as vengeance. Christ in judgment, he says, is like a knight who has sustained many wounds, but pulls the sword out of him and uses it to wreak vengeance.[80] He will make wounds that never heal.[81] This theme is underlined when the preacher specifies that Christ will come to the Judgment fully armed with the nails and equipment of His passion.[82] And those who injured him, even though they were created in his image, will be condemned, for "who will be able to look upon Him when He throws His very own image into the fire of hell?"[83]

Clearly the preachers were concerned to illustrate the justice of damna-

---

79. "Sed multo meliorem adhuc societatem optat nobis apostolus cum dixit quod tota trinitas sit nobiscum. . . . Sunt enim multum societates que non sunt multe bone nec secure, . . . [sed] qui faciunt se suspendi per societatem et qui faciunt luxurias et huiusmodi propter societatem. Unde sepe suspenduntur ad gibetum regis, et inde sepe vadunt ad gibetum inferni. Sed predicta societas [i.e. trinitas] est ita secura et ita fidelis quod de tua societate non querit *suam* utilitatem sed *tuam* tantum. . . . Et quantumcumque grave vellum [*sic*] habeas, vel contra carnem, vel contra [mundus *corrected to*:] mundum, vel contra diabolum, vade ad ecclesiam et voca patrem et filium et spiritum sanctum et consolatio tibi accurret in quacumque tribulatione sis." Paris, BN, MS lat. 16481, no. 160, f. 281rb–281va.

80. "Quia modo peccatores iostant [*joust*] contra dominum, et militant per blasphemias ipsum iterum plus quam Iudei dilaniantes unde conqueritur dominus, 'foderunt manus meas et pedes meas,' [Ps. 21, 17] etc. Sed scitis qui[d] est bonus miles quandoque multum patitur, sed in fine extrahit gladium et circumcirca [*sic*] se totum ponit ad gladium. Sic dominus hic omnia turpia sibi dicta in se et facta in membris suis, scil. pauperibus, omnia patienter sustinet, sed in fine, scil. in iudicio, totum mittet ad gladium. In Deut. [32, 41] 'si acuero ut fulgur gladium meum et arripuerit iudicium manus mea'." *Ibid.*, no. 33, f. 37va.

81. "Tantum ictum percutiam quod nunquam plaga in perpetuum sanabitur. Et quis poterit hoc videre? Unde propheta, 'Quis poterit stare ad videndum eum?' [Cf. 1 Reg. 6, 20], scil. quando tales ictus percutiet, quos omnes cerurgici de mundo non possent sanare." *Ibid.*

82. "Videbunt eum venientem contra se . . . totum armatum clavis et armaturis sue passionis. . . ." *Ibid.* f. 37vb.

83. "Quis poterit eum respicere quando suam propriam ymaginem proiciet in ignem inferni." *Ibid.,* f. 37va.

tion, though their techniques for showing it were more vivid and direct than those of the theologians. In the process, even in these few quotations on justice, they were able to display numerous infernal punishments: bad company, hanging, unhealable wounds, and there were many more. But the preachers never used more than a few of the compilers' details at one time. They seem to have believed that their audience would recognize a reference to hell through allusion to only one or two of its characteristics. It is not this selectivity alone that distinguishes the preachers from the theologians and the compilers. The preachers also stand out for their consistent emphasis on one theme above all. When they refer to hell, they nearly always continue to make the point that sinners can escape hell through the sacrament of penance.

In thirteenth-century Paris, preachers invoked hell to provoke penance. Whereas writers in all the other literary genres we have examined acknowledged that hell inspires fear and could, in general, promote conversion to, or perseverance in, the good life, these sermons actually preached show that the sermon was intended as a stimulus to a specific behavior, namely, confession. Indeed the sermon we have just considered, even with the attention it gives to the justice of damnation for sinners, can recommend only the remedy of confession against the "confusion of the damned and the turpitude of . . . sinners. . . . He who performs this faithfully will never be confounded."[84] Thus when we find the clergy in direct contact with the laity, we see them working to inspire contrition and to encourage confession. This emphasis on confession accords with the legislation of the Fourth Lateran Council in 1215 and Innocent IV's declaration of 1254.

Before proceeding to consider the rhetorical strategies used to promote penance, we should take a moment to consider penance in general. Since at least the twelfth century, theologians divided the sacrament of penance into three parts: contrition, confession, and satisfaction. Contrition is the internal feeling which makes the sinner hate his sins and seek freedom from them. Confession is the individual, private admission of all one's sins to an ordained minister of the church. Satisfaction is evidence of a truly amended life and takes five forms: fasting, prayer, endowing masses,

---

84. "Veniet [Christus] cum magno comitatu . . . ad videndum confusionem dampnatorum et turpitudinem peccatorum illorum. . . . Ideo non video nisi unicum consilium, scil. quod cooperirent peccata sua hic, et firmarent in archa sub clave confessionis. Et qui sic fideliter fecerit nunquam confundetur." *Ibid.* f. 37rb.

giving alms, and making restitution of ill-gotten gains.[85] The last three of these involved money payment to churches, and it was in this area that competition, though concealed, was fierce.[86] The sermons in BN, MS lat. 16481 are ample proof of this conflict. The sermons were preached by seculars, Dominicans, and Franciscans and yet they all insist on one theme: to escape hell you must confess. The thirteenth-century clergy was competing for penitents. Aside from the genuine conviction that confession was good for the soul and the legitimate pride in belonging to a group perceived as actively helping people, the cash from endowed masses and alms and the restitution of ill-gotten goods (and eventually, burial rights and bequests) were valuable additions to the otherwise fixed revenues of any religious house.[87]

What we shall see in the following accounts of selected sermons actually preached is the variety of techniques employed to stimulate the fear of hell and indicate the path of safety through the confessional.

85. E. Amann, "Pénitence," *DTC* 12.1 (1933): 894–994; E. Vacandard, "Confession," *ibid.* 3 (1908): 894–926; B. Poschmann, *Penance and the Anointing of the Sick* (Freiburg & London, 1964), esp. chap. 3; P. Anciaux, *La théologie du sacrement de pénitence au XIIᵉ siècle* (Louvain, 1949); J.-Ch. Payen, "La pénitence dans le context culturel des XIIᵉ et XIIIᵉ siècles. Dès doctrines contritionnistes aux pénitentiels vernaculaires," *Revue des sciences philosophiques et théologiques*, 61 (1977): 399–428.

86. Restitution was theoretically paid not to the church, but to the offended party; and alms were only administered by the church. In these cases the benefit to the church was only indirect in that its utility as an institution was enhanced. The three occasions for cash payments to the church become confused, however, when the holder of unjustly obtained goods cannot find the person from whom he obtained them. Since restitution is then impossible, Raymund of Peñaforte (who compiled the collection of canon law given out by Gregory IX in 1234, the *Decretals*) recommended that the sum "cum auctoritate Ecclesiae erogetur in pias causas pro anima illius, cuius res fuit . . . quia . . . in hoc gessit utiliter negotium illius (*Summa de Poenitentia*, 2, 5, 22, [Rome, 1603], p. 193). The same principle is invoked at 2, 7, 16; p. 241b–242a. T. Tentler, *Sin and Confession on the Eve of the Reformation* (Princeton, 1977), 340–43, omits mention of Raymund's coverage of this option. In a stricter passage, Raymund insists on complete restitution, denying otherwise the offender any audience with the confessor and Christian burial. "And this is done to frighten them (*ad terrorem*)." Raymund 2, 5, 2; p. 167b. That is where hell comes in.

87. This conclusion follows not only from the competition implicit in these texts, but also from the century-long conflict between seculars and regulars cited above in note 5. Church revenues are outlined in a theoretical way by G. Le Bras, *Institutions ecclésiastiques de la Chrétienté médiévale*, 2 vols. Histoire de l'Église, 12 (Paris, 1959–1964) 2: 251–61. Documentation for an actual case is furnished by Toulouse: M. Castaign-Sirard, "Donations toulousaines du Xᵉ au XIIIᵉ siècles," *Annales du Midi*, an. 1957, 27–64; J. H. Mundy, "Charity and Social Work in Toulouse, 1100–1250," *Traditio*, 22 (1966): 203–287; and M.-H. Vicaire, "Le Financement des Jacobins de Toulouse," in *Dominique et ses Prêcheurs*, 307–339. For a survey of the legal consilia concerning this rivalry well into the fourteenth century, see T. Izbicki, "The Problem of Canonical Portion in the Later Middle Ages: the Application of *Super Cathedram*," to be published in the Acts of the Seventh International Congress of Medieval Canon Law, Cambridge, 1984.

John of Meth, a Franciscan, preaching in the Champeaux, the open area that became Les Halles, on the Feast of the Conversion of St. Paul, January 25, 1273, showed confession as the escape from damnation in three different ways.

1. The sinner is justly damned if he does not confess a mortal sin. For he is like a man who has two mortal wounds and shows only one to the doctor. That man will die for concealing the other.[88]

2. Penance avoids the confusion of the damned on Judgment Day. Their sins, written on their breasts, will become visible to all. But sins may be erased by penance so they will not be seen on That Day. Therefore repent. "Without doing penance, we cannot avoid the pains of hell."[89]

3. "If a man were condemned to be hung, . . . he would gladly go overseas (to the Holy Land) or to Saint James (of Compostella) to avoid that punishment. Now when a sinner commits a mortal sin, he is already sentenced to be hung on the gibbet of hell unless he afterwards does penance and confesses. And that is what the Lord Himself said through the prophet, "Unless you do penance, you will all perish" (cf. Luke 13, 5). And truly good people are those who have well considered how they will be punished in hell and how great a multitude of gibbets and of persons hanging will be there. No penance here would be more serious for one because on the Day of Judgment, as we read, the whole world will turn into fire and flames, the mountains and the hills and the heavens and the earth and all that we see [will burn]. And in the end all that fire in [all] parts of the world will gather itself together and will fall all into one heap, all at once, down into hell upon the sinners. . . . And so, to avoid that punishment we should do penance."[90]

88. "Si hic esset unus homo qui haberet duas plagas mortales, et unam ostenderet medico et alteram et forte periculosiorem absconderet, ne medicus vel cyrurgicus eam videret, nullo modo eum sanare posset. . . . Sic peccator ita bene dampnatur pro uno solo peccato mortali, si ipsum retineat. . . ." Paris, BN, MS lat. 16481, no. 69, f. 99rb.

89. "Per penitentiam possumus vitare confusionem quam dampnati habebunt in die iudicii pro peccatis suis, quia confusio erit ibi tanta quod quilibet sua peccata et enormitates habebit scripta in pectore, ita quod quilibet videbit aperte, sed per penitentiam delentur, ne ibi videantur. Unde penitemini ut deleantur peccata vestra. . . . Sine penitentia facienda, non possumus vitare penas inferni." Ibid., f., 99v a–b.

90. "Si unus homo esset iudicatus ad suspendendum, . . . libenter iret ultra mare vel ad Sanctum Jacobum ut posset evitare illam penam. Et ideo quando unus peccator facit unum peccatum mortale, ipse iam est adiudicatus ad essendum suspensus ad gibetum inferni nisi inde peniteat et confiteatur. Et hoc est quod dicit ipse dominus per prophetam, 'Nisi penitenciam egeritis, omnes

A sinner may intend to amend his life and do penance, but delay in actually beginning until it is too late. The consequences are severe, as Friar John of Varziaco (Varzy) suggested to those present in the royal chapel on the Feast of Mary Magdalene, July 22, 1273. Here the justice of damnation is illustrated by means of a parallel with princely justice. In this case a prince offers a condemned thief the grace of choosing the tree from which he is to be hanged. When, after a long time, the thief has passed over many trees, the prince throws him into a great fire.[91] "Thus many wish to be hung on the tree of penance that they choose, but can find none which pleases them. Therefore the Lord says concerning them that they should be placed in the fire of hell (or at least purgatory)."[92]

The folly of withholding sins from a confessor in the hope of concealing them forever is a theme illustrated twice in one sermon by the Dominican Giles of Liège (or of Orp, near Namur) at St. Gervais, on the fifth Sunday after Easter, May 14, 1273. In both cases, the failure to confess leads to hell.

> It would be a great source of shame for someone if he were arrested in the act of stealing and led to death and hung on the gibbet with his booty displayed next to him. But that is what will happen to sinners on the Day of Judgment because then their sins will be made known and will be, as it were, tied to them when they are sent to the gallows of hell. Thus the villainies of their sins, which they secretly

peribitis' (cf. Luke 13, 5). Et vere bone gentes qui respicerent bene quomodo in inferno tormentabuntur et quanta multitudo gibetorum ibi erit et suspensorum. Nulla penitentia hic esset ei gravius, quia in die iudicii, ut legimus, totus mundus ardebit ad ignem et flammam et montes et colles et celum et terra[m] et omnia que videmus. Et in fine totus ille ignis ardebit, mundi partibus se congregabit, et cadet totus in unum montem simul inferius in infernum super peccatores. . . . Sic ergo ad vitandum illam penam oportet nos facere penitentiam. . . ." *Ibid.*, f. 99vb.

91. "Sepe contigit illud quod dicitur de quodam latrone cui dixit quidam dominus, 'Tu suspenderis, sed tantum fiet tibi de gratia quod tu eliges arborem ad quam malueris suspendi.' Et ductus ad nemus, dum quererent homines ab eo, 'Vis suspendi ad istam arborem?' dixit quod non. Et sic de aliis, ita quod nullam invenit ad quam vellet suspendi. Reduxerunt eum ad dominum, qui hoc audito dixit, 'Ponetis ipsum in unum magnum ignem et comburetur." *Ibid.*, no. 171, f. 288vb–289ra. [Note that no. 169 begins at 288rb, line 3 from the bottom; heading omitted. No. 170 begins at f. 288va and no. 171 *ibid*, line 10 from the bottom, badly smudged.]

92. "Sic multi bene volunt suspendi ad arborem penitentie quam volunt, sed nullam possunt invenire que sibi placeat. Et ideo de ipsis dixit dominus ut ponantur in igne inferni, vel saltem purgatorii." *Ibid.*, f. 289ra. The reference to purgatory is logical here, because the story implies the presence of contrition or some other aspect of the desire to initiate penance. If penance is actually undertaken (even if not finished) purgatory is expected; if not, hell.

concealed in their hearts and never wished to reveal through confession, will then appear openly to all.[93]

In a second simile, Giles warns against the dangers of relapse, which increases the guilt of the impenitent.

If there were someone here who had a phial filled with poison out of which he wished to poison the king, and he were caught, and pardoned the misdeed, and yet he were to take up the phial again and seek a second time to kill the king; and if he were found and that phial seized, the man would be worthy of death. Thus it is with the sinner, because while the sinner is in mortal sin, he has a phial in his breast full of poison, that is, sin, which is a deadly poison, with which, in so far as he is able, he wishes to kill Christ. But when [that phial] is found and exposed through confession, then all is forgiven him. Therefore he ought to watch himself lest he take it up again, which would be more serious than before. And the Lord frequently punishes such people without mercy and catches them in their sin and thus they are condemned. And therefore we ought to let go entirely of that damned phial (sin).[94]

Not all the preachers recorded in Peter of Limoges's collection were obscure friars. Indeed the manuscript includes three sermons by Saint Bonaventure, the General of the Franciscan Order. In the one which concerns us, delivered at the Beguines on the Feast of Saint Mark, April 25, 1273, Bonaventure combines the themes of sins becoming invisible, damnation as the defeat of evil, and confession as the decisive act. He urged

93. "Magnus pudor esset alicui si caperetur in furto suo et duceretur ad mortem et patibulum suo furto ligato iuxta ipsum. Sic erit peccatoribus in die iudicii, quia peccata sua tunc aperta erunt et ligabuntur quasi cum ipsis quando mittentur in patibulum inferni. Unde latrocinia peccatorum suorum, que latenter servaverant in corde suo, nec unquam voluerunt revelare per confessionem, tunc apparebunt manifeste coram omnibus." *Ibid.*, no. 141, f. 242vb.

94. "Si esset hic aliquis qui haberet unam pixidem plenam veneno de quo vellet impotionare regem, *et len la li trouat, et li perdonat on le mefait,* et ipse recaperet eam et vellet iterum regem interficere. Si invenitur saisitus illa pixide, ipse esset dignus morte. Sed sic est peccator, quia dum peccator est in peccato mortali, ipse habet unam pixidem in sinu suo plenam veneno, scilicet peccato, quod est venenum mortiferum, de quo quantum in se est, vult interficere Christum. Sed quando inventa est et revelata per confessionem, tunc totum ei est indultum, et ideo debet sibi cavere ne eam recapiat, quid gravius esset quam prius. Et tales dominus sepe sine misericordia punit et capit in peccato suo et sic condempna⟨n⟩tur. Et ideo debemus omnino dimmittere istam maledictam pixidem. . . ." *Ibid.* f. 242rb–va.

his audience by saying God did not order men to confess to angels, who have no idea what sin is, but rather to a man who does understand. Thus there is no reason to be embarrassed to confess.[95] Indeed, the ultimate embarrassment comes from failing to confess.

Elaborating upon an idea drawn from Anselm of Canterbury's *Liber de Similitudinibus,* Bonaventure inverts the logic we have seen developed so far. Rather than confession deleting all memory of sins, those of both the damned and the saved will be made visible in eternity.

> Neither the Magdalene nor Saint Peter will suffer shame on Judgment Day nor in Paradise because of their sins. Instead, [their sins] will be signs of great honor for them and even of honor for God, because in this [i.e., their sins being overcome], the Lord will be glorified and praised forever. Thus joy will be yours because you will have escaped danger, and praise and glory will be God's because He will always be praised for it.[96]

Then Bonaventure develops the image with a comparison and a conclusion that are his own and which, in spite of the opposite premises used, fit neatly into the pattern we have established, tying the invocation of hell to the promotion of penance.

---

95. "Si dominus statuisset quod cum angelo confitemur, . . . qui nescit quid sit peccatum, nec in se sentit motum peccati. Sed dominus voluit quod confiterer uni homini qui forefecit aliquid. . . . Ideo non fugiat homo vel erubescat pro uno modico pudoris. . . ." *Ibid.,* f. 240ra.

96. "Magdalena nec Petrus habebunt pudorem in die iudicii, nec in paradiso de suis peccatis. Sed ista signa erunt eis ad magnum honorem et etiam ad honorem dei, quia in hoc glorificabitur dominus et laudabitur in eternum. Unde tuum erit gaudium de hoc quod effugisti periculum et dei erit laus et gloria, quia ipse semper de hoc laudabit⟨ur⟩." *Ibid.,* f. 240r a–b. Bonaventure introduces this fascinating passage with a reference to Anselm, as follows: "Anselmus in *Libro de Similitudinibus* querit unam demandam [*sic*], utrum omnes homines sciant omnia nostra peccata in futuro. Arguit sic: cur ergo confessus sum si peccata mea videbuntur et scientur? Respondet quod Magdalena nec Petrus . . ." etc. But in chapter 40 of the cited work (*PL* 159: 636), the question is posed: "Quid est hoc? Peccata quae feci, scient omnes? Ad hoc ea confessus sum ut delerentur et obliviscerentur, ut nulli amplius panderentur." The reply follows a logic similar to that of Bonaventure. Peter and Mary Magdalene are named, but Anselm refers simply to Christ as a powerful healer ("Sapientia medici qui te sanavit . . . magnificabitur") and the brother who has manfully struggled out of a chasm ("Magnificabit in te . . . vim atque constantiam quibus enitens voraginem tanti mali viriliter evasisti"). There are no knights, warriors, or scars, no parallel to the stigmata, to confession, or the confusion of the damned. Bonaventure's would appear to be a thirteenth-century reworking of Anselm's idea. On the nature of this anonymous compilation of Anselm's sayings, see R. W. Southern, *Saint Anselm and His Biographer* (Cambridge, 1963), 221–226. Peter Lombard also touches upon this theme at 4.43.6; 2: 513–14.

And you see that knights do not blush to bear the scars of wounds dealt them in a tournament, for they are signs of probity, and you see that they have not faded away or hid themselves. Do you not think that the Lord is able to cause the stigmata of his passion not to appear? No one, I believe, doubts that He could, and since you rightly believe [it is appropriate that the stigmata be visible], it is also appropriate for the sins of the elect. But [the visibility of sins] will serve the honor of God and of the elect who have conquered them through holy confession and penance and good works and [the visibility of sins] will serve to cause great shame for the damned, who will then be embarrassed in front of the whole world because they did not wish to confess in front of one man alone. Therefore do not let a little shame block your mouths from confession.[97]

These references to gallows, knights, wounds, fire, and royal justice are evidence that preachers were following James of Vitry's suggestion that they make their points with reference to familiar objects of which the unlettered have direct experience. We have seen how these vivid images are arrayed within one particular context: hell as the consequence of dying unconfessed. This connection between hell and penance distinguishes the sermons actually preached from the theological manual and the exempla we have discussed. Rather than seeing hell in the manner of the theologians (and more particularly after the style of the desert fathers) as a deterrent to evil, the preachers used it as a stimulus to good.

In conclusion we may return to our opening theme and consider how the network of doctrinal dissemination employed by the thirteenth-century church and sampled through our study of hell as it was invoked in Paris might be described as a system. Working as the authoritative heads, the popes determined those affirmations requisite to orthodox belief. The popes increasingly emphasized the time of the individual's death as the point

97. "Sicut videtis quod isti milites non erubescunt portare cicatrices vulnerum sibi factorum in torneamento quia sunt signa probitatis, et quod non se muceaverint vel absconderint. Nonne putatis vos quod dominus posset facere quod non apparerent stimata sue passionis? Nullus verum, ut credo, dubitat, cum bene credatis quod sic oportet, sic et de peccatis electorum. Sed hoc erit ad honorem dei et electorum, qui ista vicerunt per sanctam confessionem et penitentiam et bona opera, et ad faciendum magnum pudorem dampnatis, qui confusionem habebunt tunc coram toto mundo de hoc quod non voluerunt confiteri coram uno solo. Non ergo modicum pudoris obstruat vobis ora confessionis." Paris, BN, MS lat. 16481, f. 240rb.

when reward or punishment begins and declared failure to perform penance as indicative of the state of mortal sin.

Theologians, as the most highly specialized, erudite members of the community, articulated the premises of the faith, debated the limits of their implications, and ordered them systematically. Because they worked with premises, they were responsible for the application of reason to religious ideas in general. They rejected elements incompatible with their own categories, whether these challenges came from Greek philosophy, rival religions, or the popular beliefs of their own people. To resist uncritical acceptance of popular notions which they felt threatened rational (or at least systematic) exposition, they preferred to describe the psychology of hell rather than encourage morbid fascination with graphic description of its physical composition. In general, they defended hell as an expression of divine justice and studied its psychological effect on the damned. They were careful, however, not to let hell become so much of an abstraction that it would lose its force as a deterrent to evil.

Whereas theologians trained teachers and preachers in the schools, the reference books provided by the compilers were intended to assure a certain standard of learning also among the rank and file of preachers who had left the university. In his encyclopedic manual for preachers, Stephen of Bourbon adopted the conclusions of theology, but used them as a framework over which to spread more than 2000 sermon-stories, classified by subject. All this added detail, distrusted and scorned by theologians, was presumably intended as an aid to preachers in their function as direct link between the ecclesiastical organization and the lay audience. There were, however, two obstacles: theology was written and it was in Latin. Its content needed to be pronounced out loud and in the vernacular. The act of translating also involved interpretation for a less sophisticated audience. By its very nature, the exemplum was supposed to bridge this difference in levels of education. Stephen's exempla, however, were, in the majority, drawn from a traditional literature that invoked hell to encourage perseverance in virtue and in the ascetic, religious life. Thus, the treatment of hell in Stephen's manual did not fully meet the needs of preachers, one of whose principal concerns was to stimulate confession.

From the sermons we have studied, we have observed that preachers were very selective in their references to hell. An allusion to fire or gallows or to the Last Judgment was sufficient to inspire the fear of hell, and having invoked this threat, preachers immediately advocated confession as the pathway to safety. Thus the preachers of 1272–73 departed from the ethical, ascetic thrust of Stephen's compilation to emphasize the direct link between hell and confession. In so doing they adopted the penitential context of papal invocations of hell. Using the compilers only selectively, but still agreeing with James of Vitry's advice to tell the story in terms familiar to the unlettered, the preachers carried the popes' message to the people.

ALAN E. BERNSTEIN

APPENDIX

Stephanus de Borbone

Tractatus de diversis materiis predicabilibus

Paris, BN, lat. 15970 (originally from the Sorbonne) = S.
Paris, BN, lat. 14598 (originally from St. Victor) = V.

Quartus titulus prime partis De inferno.

I. Quod infernus sit et ubi sit (S 145vb–146rb; V 12vb–13rb).

II. De qualitate et conditione loci infernalis: (1) [profundus]; (2) tenebrosus; (3) igneus; (4) intemperatus (unde dicitur Avernus, quasi sine vernancia temperamenti, quia erit ibi qualitatum inequalitas, quia nulla temperies erit ibi, sed omnia sevient et quasi in summo gradu, scil., ignis ardore vehementissimus, frigus et fetor et alia mala quasi in summo erunt); (5) horridus; (6) aridus et penuriosus; (7) fetidus et immundus; (8) asper et venenosus; (9) tumultuosus; (10) occultus et obliviosus; (11) fumosus [et luctuosus *add.* V]; (12) periculosus (unde dicitur baratrum quasi latitudo arta quia introitus eius latus est ad ingrediendum, artus autem ad egrediendum, ut nassa dyaboli). (S 146rb–148ra; V 13va–16ra).

III. De qualitate pene seu supplicii inferni quod aggravant xii: (1) supplicii eternitas; (2) ipsius pene acerbitas; (3) diversitas; (4) immensitas; (5) continuitas; (6) generalitas (qu⟨i⟩a est intus et extra in anima et corpore post iudicium et in omnibus membris); (7) pene conformitas (scil., pene culpe respondentis); (8)

egrediendi impossibilitas (id est ineffugabilitas); (9) timiditas; (10) aggravans est pene inutilitas (Ista presens pena potest esse utilis ad tria, scil., ad peccatorum purgationem, ad future pene diminutionem vel adnullationem, et ad premii augmentationem et acquisitionem. Purgatoria futura ad prima duo valet, sed non habet meritum, sed pena inferni ad nichil est utilis.); (11) horribilis societas; (12) paupertas et defectus omnium bonorum (S 148ra–150va; V 16rb–19vb).

IV. De demonum deformitate: (1) eorum horribilitas et deformitas; (2) crudelitas; (3) procacitas et aviditas; (4) fortitudo et potestas; (5) velocitas; (6) nocendi studiositas et sagacitas et diversitas; (7) malignitas et falsitas; (8) ponderositas (S 150vb–151rb; V 19vb–20vb).

V. De qualitate ipsorum dampnatorum in anima: (1) perturbatio indeficientis timoris; (2) confusio inevitabilis pudoris quando nudabuntur omnia peccata a domino; (3) vehementia doloris et meroris; (4) assiduitas laboris; (5) corrosio odii et rancoris ire tristitie et furoris (hic est vermis qui non morietur); (6) oblivio dei (deus enim tradet eos oblivioni); (7) infelicitas desperationis; (8) infestatio sive remorsio cordis sibi conscii; (9) excecatio rationis; (10) tabefactio invidie sive livoris; (11) tedium vite et desiderium mortis; (12) memoria bonorum preteritorum et eorum defectus universalis (S 151va–152rb; V 20vb–21vb).

VI. De xii conditionibus seu miseriis corporum malorum post iudicium: (1) corporum deformitas; (2) impossibilitas ad resistendum seu debilitas; (3) omnimoda infirmitas; (4) impossibilia (sic) et inutilitas (erunt ei inutilia et impossibilia membra ad aliquid agendum); (5) putribilitas; (6) feditas; (7) corrosibilitas et devorabilitas; (8) flagellorum diversitas (erunt enim corpora dampnatorum flagellata attrita et conculcata et comminuta gladio); (9) ponderositas; (10) alimentorum et vestimentorum vacuitas et nuditas (erit ibi indigentia); (11) planctus immensitas; (12) passibilitas et sensibilitas. (Erunt enim passibilia et sensibilia super omnia et indeficientia. Ipsa enim corruptio vel putrefactio non auferet eis sensibilitatem ut fit de membro putrido, sed potius augebit ut lepra et ulcera Egypti.) (S 152rb–152vb; V 21vb–23ra.)

VII. De pene aggravatione dampnatorum que est ex consideratione iracundie dei, quem implacabiliter offenderunt. . . . XII cause sunt propter quas videbitur gravissima ira dei dampnatis: (1) quia eos tamquam maledictos et excommunicatos vere a se et a suis et suo consortio abiciet; (2) in lacum ire sue eos proiciet; (3) peccata eorum eis obiciet; (4) pater misericordiarum eis non videbitur condolere nec eos de igne in perpetuum extrahet, (5) cum demonibus, immo demonibus ad torquendum eos, tradet; (6) videbitur eis quod de malis eorum deus et celestis curia gaudeant cum eos deus irrideat subsannet et rideat; (7) clamores aut preces in perpetuum non audiet; (8) preces servorum pro eorum salute non exaudiet nec ipsorum nec aliorum pro eis oblationes et munera accepta vel grata habebit, nec eorum redemptionem accipiet; (9) ad eorum penam cumulandam corpora eorum eis restituet ut puniantur in corpore et anima; (10) eorum penas et tormenta ministret, foveat, et augeat; (11) omnes creaturas suas et sanctos suos contra eos commoveat et ad puniendum eos armet et secum adducat, (12) quia portam regni sui [eis V] eternaliter claudat et eos visione glorie sue privet (S 152vb–153ra; V 23ra–b).

VIII. De pene aggravatione ex consideratione amissi boni vel non habiti: (1) carentia eterni boni, scil., visionis dei; (2) privatio consortii sanctorum; (3) privatio divini adiutorii, quia de cetero non miserebitur eorum deus; (4) privatio adiutorii et suffragii et beneficii sanctorum et meritorum bonorum que fecerunt, de quibus potuissent habuisse magnam remunerationem in gloria eterna nisi peccata eorum impedivissent; (5) amissio suffragiorum ecclesiasticorum, que ad minus non valebunt quantum ad pene eterne liberationem; (6) inutilitas, immo incommoditas, locorum sacrorum (non eis valet hoc, quod in locis sacris sepeliuntur, immo videtur obesse); (7) dolor de amissione presentium bonorum; (8) temporis amissio penitendi et misericordiam consequendi et promerendi; (9) sui ipsius amissio quam plangunt; (10) amicorum suorum recordatio et perditio; (11) defectus spei; (12) defectus caritatis (S 153ra–154va; V 23rb–25rb).

IX. De xii effectibus meditationis pene infernalis: (1) quia carnem et eius voluptatem desiccat, (2) a peccato in [et S] temptatione servat et dyabolum vincit et superat; (3) convertit et a peccato revocat; (4) hominem ad magnum fletum concitat, ut hic ignis et fumi propinquitas [propinquitatis V]; (5) presentem penam mitigat; (6) sanctis solatium prestat dum malorum vindictam indicat eis; (7) demones perturbat; (8) presentes delectationes in amaritudinem conmutat; (9) maius tormentum accumulat eis qui non convertuntur; (10) hominem ad contemptum sui et mundi provocat; (11) ostendit deum summe iustitie et summe timendum; (12) in bono custodit et perseverare facit (S 154va–156ra; V 25rb–27rb).

THE EARLIEST CATALOGS LOCATING
MANUSCRIPTS
IN MORE THAN ONE
LIBRARY
A Short Review

PROFESSOR PAUL OSKAR KRISTELLER has provided scholars with the two most useful bibliographical tools for locating medieval and Renaissance Latin manuscripts, his *Latin Manuscript Books Before 1600, a List of the Printed Catalogues and Unpublished Inventories of Extant Collections,* a third edition of which was published in 1965, and his *Iter Italicum* (London, 1963 to date), which lists uncataloged and partially cataloged humanistic manuscripts throughout the world. In "Section B" of *Latin Manuscript Books* is a list of "works describing manuscripts of more than one city" (pp. 11–67), which shows that a considerable amount of previous effort went into compiling bibliographical works of more than purely local interest. The earliest work cited there was printed in 1600, Thomas James's *Ecloga Oxonio-Cantabrigiensis,* which lists manuscripts in the college libraries in Oxford and Cambridge and in the university library at Cambridge. James had some predecessors, however, as there are a few medieval examples of catalogs of manuscripts in more than one city. There are also three known medieval catalogs of manuscripts in different libraries within the same city. The collections listed in these early catalogs have, of course, long since been dispersed, but the catalogs are worthy of study in their own right. Indeed, several of them have been studied extensively. A few have been published, and some are now being edited for publication.

In the Middle Ages libraries increased their stock of books largely by having scribes make copies of books borrowed for that purpose. Books were generally borrowed from the nearest available source. So it was useful to know what books were in the nearby libraries. The catalogs of other libraries were therefore also borrowed and copied. Usually the lists of books in other libraries were appended to the catalog of the borrowing library. Although a number of such composite catalogs must have been compiled, only three are known to exist today. A fourth is known from two seventeenth-century descriptions of it. The first three of these composite catalogs were produced in France, and the last and largest, at least insofar as what has survived, was made in Germany. They range in date from the eleventh century to the middle of the fourteenth century.

In the early fourteenth century a new type of finding aid for locating books in several libraries was devised, the union catalog. The earliest union catalogs were, with one exception, incorporated into bio-bibliographies, a type of reference tool which was quite popular in the Middle Ages. These union catalogs were, therefore, unlike modern union catalogs, and they may have served a somewhat different function. They did not evolve from the composite catalogs. The composite catalogs may also have served one or more purposes other than locating books, but it is difficult to say what the original compilers intended. Whatever their original purpose, however, these early composite and union catalogs nevertheless did serve to indicate what manuscripts were to be found in several libraries. They thus facilitated inter-library borrowing, and they must have been quite useful to students, scholars, and preachers.[1]

The earliest known composite catalog was drawn up at the abbey of St. Arnoul in Metz in the eleventh century. Besides listing the manuscripts in its own library, it also included lists of manuscripts in the abbeys of St. Symphorien and St. Vincent in the same town.[2] This catalog is now MS 221 in the Public Library of Metz.

The second of the composite catalogs is one of manuscripts in libraries in Normandy made ca. 1210–1240, probably by monks of the abbey of Savigny-le-Vieux. Unfortunately, this catalog cannot now be found, but

---

1. A. Derolez, *Catalogues de bibliothèques*. Typologie des sources du moyen âge occidental, 31 (Turnhout, 1970), 45–47; K. Christ, *The Handbook of Medieval Library History*, rev. A. Kern, tr. T. M. Otto (Metuchen, N. J., 1984), 43–44.

2. T. Gottlieb, *Über mittelalterliche Bibliotheken* (Leipzig, 1890), 52–53.

it is known from two seventeenth-century descriptions of it. The counselor Du Molinet saw it in 1678 and said that it was compiled in 1240 and that it listed the titles of over a thousand works. Julien Bellaise saw it in 1687 and described it in a letter to Mabillon as a quarto volume compiled in 1210 containing an inventory of the large number of manuscripts then at Savigny as well as catalogs of other libraries in the province, among them those of Mont Saint-Michel, Caen, Bec, and Jumièges.[3]

Another composite catalog was compiled at the Sorbonne in the last third of the thirteenth century. Of this but one leaf has survived as part of the binding of another manuscript, and it was mutilated by the binder. It is now in the Bibliothèque Nationale, Paris (MS lat. 16203, ff. 71v–72r), and it contains part of a catalog of manuscripts in the library of Ste. Geneviève followed by part of the catalog of St. Germain-des-Prés. The catalogs were copied onto one side of a large sheet of vellum which was probably meant to be mounted on the wall or perhaps affixed to a book chest.[4]

The last composite catalog was compiled in Regensburg in 1347, and it lists manuscripts in the Benedictine monastery of St. Emmeram, where it was compiled, and in five other libraries in the area, i.e., those of the Benedictine monasteries of Prüfening and Prühl and of the houses of the Dominicans, Franciscans, and Augustinians. The manuscript of this composite catalog is now in the Bayerische Staatsbibliothek, Munich (MS Clm 14397, ff. 1r–19v).[5]

The first known union catalog was compiled in the early fourteenth century at Greyfriars, Oxford.[6] The original manuscript of this catalog

---

3. A. Besson, *Medieval Classification and Cataloguing: Classification Practices and Cataloguing Methods in France from the 12th. to the 15th. Centuries* (Biggleswade, 1980), 59; L. Delisle, *Le cabinet des manuscrits de la Bibliothèque Impériale* (Paris, 1868), 1: 527–531; G. Nortier, *Les Bibliothèques médiévales des abbayes bénédictines de Normandie . . .* (Paris, 1971), 46.

4. R. H. Rouse, "The Early Library of the Sorbonne [Part II]," *Scriptorium*, 21 (1968): 69–71; Besson, 59–62.

5. C. E. Ineichen-Eder, ed., *Mittelalterliche Bibliothekskataloge Deutschlands und der Schweiz*. 4.1. *Bistümer Passau und Regensburg* (Munich, 1977), 152–161, 400–403, 427–439, 445–446, 455–459, 469–470; Gottlieb, nos. 161–162, 171–174; J. A. Schmeller, "Über Büchercataloge des XV. und früherer Jahrhunderte. (Fortsetzung.)," *Serapeum*, 2 (1841): 256–271.

6. W. R. Jones, "Franciscan Education and Monastic Libraries: Some Documents," *Traditio*, 30 (1974): 435–445; E. A. Savage, "Cooperative Bibliography in the Thirteenth and Fifteenth Centuries," in his *Special Librarianship in General Libraries and Other Papers* (London, 1939), 285–298, which was originally published as "Notes on the Early Monastic Libraries of Scotland, with an Account of the *Registrum Librorum Angliae* and of the *Catalogus Scriptorum Ecclesiae* of John Boston

has not survived, but there are three fifteenth-century copies: one in the Tanner collection of the Bodleian Library, Oxford (MS Tanner 165, ff. 103r–120v), one at Cambridge University (MS Peterhouse 169), and one at the British Library, London (Royal MS 3 D i, ff. 106, 110, 108, 109, 107, 111, 112, 233, 234; the folios were bound out of sequence). There is also an abbreviated seventeenth-century transcript of the Tanner manuscript made by Henry Wharton and now in the library of Lambeth Palace (MS 594). The catalog is known by the title *Registrum Angliae de libris doctorum et auctorum veterum* or sometimes *Registrum librorum Angliae.* It begins with a numbered list of one hundred and eighty-three English, Scottish, and Welsh monasteries arranged according to the eight custodies of the English Franciscan province (but note that there are no mendicant houses listed): London, Salisbury, Oxford, Cambridge, Bristol, Worcester, York, and Newcastle, which emcompassed Scotland. Following the list of monasteries is a list of some ninety-eight ancient and medieval authors arranged in what seems to be random order, and after each author is a list of his works, often with their incipits. The total number of works listed is 1,412, and they are mainly scriptural, patristic, and doctrinal. Following the titles are numbers referring to the list of monasteries, thus indicating which monasteries held which titles. This remarkable work, the first real union catalog known to have been devised, throws much light on libraries and the spread of learning in early fourteenth-century England.

Another work that incorporates a union catalog is the *Tabula septem custodiarum super bibliam,* and this was also probably compiled by the Oxford Greyfriars. Professor Richard H. Rouse and Dr. Mary A. Rouse describe it as "a concordance to the incidental passages in the writings of the Fathers, arranged according to the text of the scriptures."[7] They list nine manuscripts containing the *Tabula.* According to Profesor W. R. Jones, the *Tabula* retained the same numbered list of monasteries as the *Registrum.*[8]

of the Abbey of Bury St Edmunds," *Publications of the Edinburgh Bibliographical Society,* 14 (1928): 1–7; D. M. Norris, *A History of Cataloguing and Cataloguing Methods 1100–1850* (London, 1939), 30–33; R. H. Rouse and M. A. Rouse, *Preachers, Florilegia and Sermons: Studies in the Manipulus florum of Thomas of Ireland* (Toronto, 1979), 24–25.

　　7. See Rouse and Rouse, 18–19.
　　8. See. W. R. Jones, 437.

The last of the known union catalogs compiled in England was the work of Henry Kirkestede, librarian of the Benedictine monastery of Bury St. Edmunds in East Anglia. Kirkestede held the position of librarian there probably in the third quarter of the fourteenth century. His catalog has the title *Catalogus scriptorum ecclesiae,* and survives only in a seventeenth-century copy in the Cambridge University Library (MS Add. 3470). The British Library has a garbled quotation from it (MS Add. 4787, ff. 132r–133r). A shortened version was printed in Thomas Tanner's *Bibliotheca Britannico-Hibernica* (London, 1748), pp. xvii–xli. The *Catalogus* was long thought to have been compiled by a John Boston of Bury, but Professor Rouse has shown that Boston was merely a ghost created by John Bale.[9]

Kirkestede's *Catalogus* was based in part on the Franciscan *Registrum,* and he used the same system of numbers for recording the location of manuscripts. Also, the majority of his locations are taken from the *Registrum*. He increased the number of authors from less than a hundred to six hundred and seventy-four, largely from the early *de viris illustribus* literature, and added more ancient Latin authors.[10] He also increased the number of libraries by eight, seven of which were in East Anglia. Kirkestede very often provided short biographical sketches of the authors, and he usually gave the incipits as well as the explicits of their works. For his greatly expanded list of authors he made much use of the *Manipulus Florum* of Thomas of Ireland.[11] This was an early fourteenth-century work which contained some six thousand extracts from patristic and other theological writers as an aid for preparing sermons. The extracts were culled from books in the library of the Sorbonne where Thomas was then studying. Kirkestede also used many other compilations in drawing up his list of authors and titles, among them the works of Gennadius, Isidore of Seville, and Vincent of Beauvais. According to Professor Rouse, the great value of Kirkestede's *Catalogus* lies in

> what it tells us about the content and distribution of medieval scholarly writing in fourteenth-century English monasteries. In a number of instances the *Catalogus* is the oldest or the most significant authority

9. R. H. Rouse, "Bostonus Buriensis and the Author of the *Catalogus Scriptorum Ecclesiae,*" *Speculum,* 41 (1966): 471-499.
10. R. A. B. Mynors, "The Latin Classics Known to Boston of Bury," in *Fritz Saxl, 1890–1948: A Volume of Memorial Essays from his Friends in England,* ed. D. J. Gordon (London, 1957), 199–217.
11. See Rouse and Rouse, 220–222.

for the attribution of a work to a certain author. In other instances it preserves information about works which no longer exist. In addition the *Catalogus* provides a picture of the contents of at least twenty-six monastic libraries, since it is a union catalogue; and for several of these libraries it provides the only surviving information.[12]

The *Catalogus* was used by John Bale for his *Scriptorum illustrium maioris Brytanniae catalogus,* and Bale, in turn, was used as a source by latter compilers of biographical and bibliographical works. Like the *Registrum,* the *Catalogus* has been much studied but never published. Both of these highly important works are now being edited by Professor Rouse and his wife, Dr. Mary A. Rouse.

Several bio-bibliographies with union catalogs were made in the Low Countries and the neighboring Rhine region between 1470 and 1540, all of them in monasteries having some connection with the Windesheim Congregation, one of the centers of the Modern Devotion. Only two of these are now extant, a fragment compiled in Cologne ca. 1470–1478 and a large register compiled ca. 1532–1538 in the monastery of Rooklooster (Red Cloister) a few miles east of Brussels.

The fragment, which is know as the Basel Fragment because it is now in the library of Basel University (MS F VI 53) or the Cologne Register because of its origin, consists of twenty-eight pages which were evidently extracted from a larger work. It contains the beginnings of a bio-bibliography of mainly theological authors arranged alphabetically, and in the margins following each title are letters, syllables, words, signs, and numbers indicating which libraries owned the titles. Unfortunately, the manuscript lacks the list of monasteries with the key to the sigla. It is possible, however, to understand a number of them. Manuscripts from the Windesheim monastery in Cologne have a special sign, and other monasteries in the city are designated by the letters *Co* for *Coloniae* followed by the name of the monastery. Not all of the libraries listed were monastic; a few were even private collections. Some printed books were also included.

The text is written mainly in one hand, but numerous additions were made in a variety of hands. Space was left for more additions, and Hermann Knaus has suggested that this manuscript was circulated among a

---

12. See Rouse, "Bostonus Buriensis," 472.

group of libraries so that the librarians of each could add sigla for titles of manuscripts in their own libraries or new authors and titles.[13]

The works of Jerome and Augustine loom large as each of their sermons and letters is listed separately, arranged alphabetically and numbered. The compiler drew his list of authors and titles from a variety of sources, the chief of which was the *Manipulus Florum* of Thomas of Ireland, which, as noted above, was also one of the chief sources used by Henry of Kirkestede.[14] The *Manipulus Florum* reflects the holdings of the Sorbonne in 1308. As the Cologne Register was one of the sources of the Rooklooster Register compiled in the 1530's, it served as a link in a bibliographical chain extending from the early fourteenth century to the early sixteenth century.

The Rooklooster Register is the last and most extensive of the early bio-bibliographies with a union catalog. It was most probably compiled by Antonius Geens (d. 1543) ca. 1532–1538 in the Augustinian monastery of Rooklooster near Brussels, and it is now in the Oesterreichische Nationalbibliothek in Vienna (MS Series nova 12899). It is so vast and complicated that so far the task of editing it has proved too overwhelming for those who have contemplated it.[15] A preliminary edition, however, is being prepared by Frans Hendrickx and P. Verdeyen under the auspices of the Ruysbroec Society in Antwerp.

13. H. Knaus, "Ein rheinischer Gesamtkatalog des 15. Jahrhunderts," *Gutenberg Jahrbuch,* an. 1976, 509–519. See also P. Lehmann, "Alte Vorläufer des Gesamtkatalogs," in *Festschrift Georg Leyh* (Leipzig, 1937), 69–81, reprinted in his *Erforschung des Mittelalters,* 4 (Stuttgart, 1961), 172–183.
14. See Rouse and Rouse, 222–224.
15. F. Hendrickx, "Die Kartäuserautoren und -Bibliotheken nach dem Register des Rooklosters bei Brüssel," *Cistercienser Chronik,* 87, n. s. 147 (1980–1981): 6–10; for other recent works on the Rooklooster Register see P. F. J. Obbema, "The Rooklooster Register Evaluated," *Quaerendo,* 7 (1977), 326–353; W. Smeyers, "Domus sancti Pauli in Rubeavalle (Rooklooster, Oudergem)," in *Monasticon Windeshemense.* Part 1. *Belgien,* eds. W. Kohl, E. Persoons, and A. G. Weiler (= *Archives et bibliothèques de Belgique,* Numéro spécial 16 [1976]), 109–130; W. Lourdaux, "Het boekenbezit en het boekengebruik bij de moderne devoten," in *Contributions à l'histoire des bibliothèques et de la lecture aux Pays-Bas avant 1600* (= *Archives et bibliothèques de Belgique,* Numéro spécial 11 [1974]), 247–325, especially 299–325; A. Gruijs, "Fragment d'un catalogue ancien de Groenendael ayant servi à la composition du répertoire collectif de Rougecloître (Paris, Mazarine, MS. 4095^A, et Vienne, Oe. N. B., MS. 9373)," in *Varia Codicologica: Essays Presented to G. I. Lieftinck,* eds. J. P. Gumbert and M. J. M. DeHaan, 1 (Amsterdam, 1972), 75–86; R. Lievens, "De lijst der Dietse boeken van Rooklooster," *Tijdschrift voor Nederlandse taal- en letterkunde,* 86 (1970): 234–239; W. Lourdaux and E. Persoons, "De bibliotheken en scriptoria van de Zuiderlandse kloosters van het kapittel van Windesheim. Een bibliografische inleiding," *Archives et bibliothèques de Belgique,* 37 (1966): 61–74, especially 71–74; and P. J. H. Vermeeren, "Op zoek naar de librije van Rooklooster," *Het Boek,* 35 (1961–1962), 134–173 (English summary, 171–173).

The Rooklooster Register functioned as a catalog of the Rooklooster monastery library, a union catalog of eighty-nine libraries in Belgium, The Netherlands, and the Lower Rhine region, and a bio-bibliography of over two thousand authors. It also listed many anonymous works, and in this it differed from its predecessors. The register begins with a prologue and two lists of sigla with their explanations. Then there is a catalog of some seven hundred and eighty volumes in the Rooklooster library (ff. 26r–41v). This is followed by the extensive bio-bibliography arranged in alphabetical order (ff. 42r–363v). Incipits are given for many titles, but explicits are very rarely provided. Sigla in the margins indicate in what libraries the texts listed may be found. Following this is a list of lives or legends of the saints arranged more or less alphabetically by name of the saint (ff. 384r–409r). Many of these works are anonymous. The register concludes with an alphabetical list of other anonymous works (ff. 410r–436r).

The Rooklooster Register is based on two earlier registers, the Cologne Register and the register of St. Martin's monastery in Louvain. The latter was in turn based on the register of a monastery in Gaesdonck, Germany, just south of the Dutch border and between the Maas and Rhine rivers. The St. Martin's register is now lost. The register of Gaesdonck is not even mentioned in the literature, but its existence has been inferred by Dr. Pieter F. J. Obbema after a careful analysis of the contents of the Rooklooster Register.[16] The compiler of the Rooklooster Register borrowed extensively from the bio-bibliographies of Jerome, Isidore, Gennadius, and Tritheim, among others. Indeed, he incorporated the whole of Tritheim's *De scriptoribus ecclesiasticis,* which was printed in Basel in 1494. He also used some manuscript catalogs of libraries, such as those of Mariënborn near Arnhem, Mariënhage near Eindhoven, and St. Catherine's in Nijmegen.

Though now lost, the register of St. Martin's monastery in Louvain was an important and frequently cited one. It was referred to until after the beginning of the eighteenth century as a source for tracing manuscripts.[17] The compiler was Gerardus Roelants (d. 1490), and it

16. See Obbema, 342–350.

17. See Obbema, 333. For other recent works on the register of St. Martin's see W. Lourdaux and M. Haverals, *Bibliotheca Vallis Sancti Martini in Lovanio. Bijdrage tot de studie van het geestesleven en de Nederlanden (15de–18th C.)* Symbolae Facultatis Litterarum et Philosophiae Lovaniensis, Ser-

probably dates from shortly before his death. It recorded the contents of about a hundred libraries in the area, and it was no doubt very similar to the other Windesheim catalogs, being a catalog of St. Martin's library, a union catalog, and a bibliography of the world's literature compiled from all available sources. Very likely it included incunabula. As mentioned above, it was based in part on the register of Gaesdonck, and it served as the basis for the Rooklooster Register.

Dr. Obbema mentions the possible existence of one other Windesheim register, but it is known only from a passing reference to it in a letter from Willem van Gheershoven, canon of Groenendaal, written in 1525 to a colleague in Louvain.[18]

Some of these early bio-bibliographies with union catalogs, then, were remarkable bibliographical tools for their time. They listed the writings of large numbers of authors and located manuscripts containing these texts in a good many libraries. The compilers demonstrated considerable industry and breadth of learning. These qualities are also evident in the many works of Professor Paul Oskar Kristeller, not least in his *Latin Manuscript Books* and *Iter Italicum,* the vademecums of all students of the Middle Ages and Renaissance.

PHILIP J. WEIMERSKIRCH

ies A, vol. 8. 2 vols. (Louvain, 1978–1982); idem, "Domus Sancti Martini in Lovanio (Sint Maartensdal, Löwen)," in *Monasticon Windeshemense,* 141–160; and W. Lourdaux, "Inleiding tot de studie van de handschriften van Sint-Maarten te Leuven," in *Sources de l'histoire religieuse de la Belgique, moyen âge et temps modernes. Actes du Colloque de Bruxelles 30 nov.–2 déc. 1967* (= *Bibliothèque de la revue d'histoire ecclésiastique,* 47 [1968]): 154–163.

18. See Obbema, 338.

TWO HUMANIST ANNOTATORS OF
VIRGIL
COLUCCIO SALUTATI
and
GIOVANNI TORTELLI

AN OLDER MANUSCRIPT WITNESS that remains to be explored by editors and students of Virgil's poems is Basel, Öffentliche Bibliothek der Universität F II 23 (described only recently in a printed catalogue by B. Munk Olsen, *L'étude des auteurs classiques latins aux XIe et XIIe siècles* 2 [Paris, 1985], 702). The codex, which is of moderate size (259 x 165 mm., with 33–34 long lines in a written space of 200 x 98 mm.), was copied (*teste* B. Bischoff) in the first half of the eleventh century, probably in northern Italy, by several scribes who wrote a more or less similar Caroline hand. It consists of 201 numbered folios now arranged in a fifteenth-century binding according to the schema I + 1^8 + 1^9 + 22^8 + 1^6 + 1, and

We would like to express our indebtedness and gratitude to the following: Professor Paul Oskar Kristeller, from whose unpublished volume of the *Iter italicum* we obtained the shelf mark of the manuscript which is the subject of this article; Dr. Martin Steinmann, who informed us of the manuscript's connection with Salutati and Tortelli and gave much assistance in various ways; Dr. A. C. de la Mare, who shared with us her palaeographical knowledge of humanistic hands; the Öffentliche Bibliothek der Universität, Basel for permission to publish photographs of the manuscript.

V. Brown examined the codex *in situ* and is responsible for the introduction (pp. 65–66) and the section on Tortelli (part II, pp. 91–148); C. Kallendorf is the author of the section on Salutati (part I, pp. 66–91). Each of us has incurred individual debts which will be acknowledged in the appropriate places.

contains the following: ff. 1r–14v *Eclogues*, ff. 14v–48r *Georgics*, ff. 48r–200v *Aeneid*.

Apart from its antiquity (and this must be relative in any case since other witnesses, even excluding papyrus fragments, survive from as early as the fourth or fifth century AD), MS F II 23 is notable for the number and variety of interlinear and marginal glosses entered by contemporary and later hands. Every page exhibits at least some annotation, and there are many instances where the text is surrounded on all four sides by notes so closely packed that it is difficult to discern where a verse begins or ends. Two of the later glossators were particularly assiduous and have thus left more than enough examples of their activity to enable us to distinguish with ease (usually) their respective interventions. Palaeographical and codicological evidence establishes that these zealous annotators are Coluccio Salutati (1331–1406) and Giovanni Tortelli (ca. 1400–1466), and in the present article we shall explore the nature and extent of their interest in Virgil.

I

Coluccio Salutati

For Coluccio Salutati, Chancellor of Florence from 1375 to 1406 and the acknowledged leader of Italian humanism after the deaths of Petrarca and Boccaccio, Virgil occupied a special place as "princeps poetarum."[1] Salutati quoted extensively from Virgil's poetry throughout his scholarly career and made that poetry a focal point of his critical theory, but a thorough analysis of these points has been hampered by the difficulties modern scholars have had in finding his personal copy of his favorite Roman poet. In 1977, A. C. de la Mare attributed Paris Bibl. nat. lat. 7942 (containing the *Eclogues, Georgics,* and *Aeneid*) to Salutati, but because the

---

1. B. L. Ullman, *The Humanism of Coluccio Salutati.* Medioevo e Umanesimo, 4 (Padua, 1963), 254 lists some of the flattering epithets Salutati gave to Virgil; this one is found in his *Epistolario,* 3:491. Though inclined to consider Virgil the best of all poets, Salutati vacillated in his judgment and spent much of his life trying to reconcile his admiration for Virgil among the ancients and Petrarca among the moderns; see Ullman, *Humanism,* 240–41 and R. P. Oliver, "Coluccio Salutati's Criticism of Petrarch," *Italica,* 16 (1939): 49–57.

manuscript was copied very late (ca. 1400) and contains virtually no notes, it offers little beyond a confirmation of Salutati's continued interest in Virgil. Now, however, with the recent discovery in the Universitätsbib-liothek at Basel of MS F II 23 (hereafter called 'B'), a manuscript of Virgil owned by Salutati and so extensively annotated by him as to constitute a real commentary, a thorough analysis of Salutati's Virgil studies is pos-sible.[2] Accordingly, I shall begin by examining the Basel manuscript to determine as precisely as possible when Salutati scholiated it and which aspects of Virgil's poetry interested him at that time; in presenting this analysis, I have transcribed and edited a number of representative mar-ginalia. Then, after discussing Virgil's place in Salutati's later works, I shall show how his careful study of the Basel manuscript provided an es-sential foundation for the critical treatment of Salutati's "optimus poetarum."[3]

The Basel manuscript has a number of features characteristic of Salutati ownership, among the most obvious being his pressmark in the upper right corner of f. 1r, an Arabic numeral (here "248"), followed by "carte" (written out), followed by the number of leaves in Roman numerals (here "clxxxxviii").[4] It is a little harder to say when Salutati bought this manuscript. In 1378, he wrote to Giuliano Zonarini in Bologna and asked his correspondent to buy a copy of Virgil for him there. We do not know for sure what came of this, but since we learn of the request in the same letter in which we discover that Zonarini considered Virgil a "vates men-tificus," it seems unlikely that the Basel manuscript came to Salutati from

2. There has been as yet no full-scale study of Salutati's treatment of Virgil. V. Zabughin, *Ver-gilio nel Rinascimento italiano da Dante a Torquato Tasso,* 2 vols. (Bologna, 1921–23) touches on a few of the most basic points (1:117–19), but R. Sabbadini's study of Renaissance allegorizations of Virgil, "Sull' allegoria dei poeti, specialmente di Vergilio," in *Storia del Ciceronianismo e di altre questioni letterarie nell' età della Rinascenza* (Turin, 1885), 103–11 does not mention Salutati at all. Virgil comes up in the longer discussion of Salutati's views on poetry, of course, but the interest here has up to now been focused elsewhere; see note 21, below. Twenty years ago Ullman wrote that "no manuscript of his [Virgil's] has survived" among codices known to have been in Saluta-ti's library (*Humanism,* 254). The attribution of Paris Bibl. nat. lat. 7942 to Salutati was made by A. C. de la Mare in "Humanistic Script: The First Ten Years," in *Das Verhältnis der Humanisten zum Buch,* ed. Fritz Krafft and Dieter Wuttke. Deutsche Forschungsgemeinschaft, Kommission für Humanismusforschung, Mitteilung, 4 (Boppard, 1977), 89–90, note 3. The identification of the Basel manuscript was announced by M. Steinmann, "Die humanistische Schrift und die An-fänge des Humanismus in Basel," *Archiv für Diplomatik,* 22 (1976): 389 and notes 24a, 24b.

3. *De laboribus Herculis,* ed. B. L. Ullman, 2 vols. (Zurich, 1951), 1:329.

4. Ullman, *Humanism,* 129–30 and A. C. de la Mare, *The Handwriting of Italian Humanists* (Ox-ford, 1973), 32.

this source.[5] The other obvious possibility focuses on a note found near the end of Florence, Bibl. Laur. MS Fies. 176, a Priscian once owned by Salutati and extensively annotated by him. The note has been erased, but Ullman read under ultraviolet light:

> Iste liber prisciani est s(er) Coluccii c(on)d(am) pieri coluccii d(e) Stignano not(ar)ii que(m) ip(s)e emit i(n) t(er)ra S(ancte) Marie in mo(n)tis a d(omina) (?) p(er)uccia c(on)d(am) (?) s(er) Landi p(er)ucci de d(i)c(t)o loco *cu(m) sc(ri)ptis V(ir)gilii* lucani (et) poete oratii p(ro) fl(o)r(enis) IIII sp(ecie) MCCCLV Ind(ictione) VIIII die XXIII Octubr(is).[6] (italics mine)

If the Basel manuscript was part of this purchase, it would join the Priscian as one of Salutati's oldest books, obtained well before he left the Valdinievole for "greener pastures."[7] But is this possible?

One way to approach the question is to examine the marginalia themselves to determine whether the kinds of information they contain and the handwriting in which they are written can be dated; the earlier the marginalia, the more probable the 1355 purchase date becomes. Examination of other manuscripts owned and annotated by Salutati shows that longer notes with philological and textual observations tend to be early, while the "indexing notes" frequently associated with Salutati are comparatively late, not before the 1380s.[8] The notes in the Basel manuscript are of the former type. Salutati's hand also changed over the course of time. The indexing notes are generally written in a large, firm hand which gives way in some manuscripts to a thin, shaky script like that a very old man might have used. The hand in the Virgil manuscript does not bear close comparison with these indexing notes. In fact, we might say that, rather than the lighter, better spaced appearance and slender, ele-

---

5. Ullman, *Humanism,* 254; the criticism of Virgil is found near the beginning of the letter to Zonarini, *Epistolario,* 1:300.

6. F. 217r, transcribed in *Humanism,* 167.

7. The importance of this early purchase for the intellectual development of the young Salutati has been described elsewhere: *ibid.,* 44–45 and in the standard biographical treatment, R. G. Witt, *Hercules at the Crossroads: The Life, Works, and Thought of Coluccio Salutati.* Duke Monographs in Medieval and Renaissance Studies, 6 (Durham, NC, 1983), 54. We also know that Salutati was interested enough in Virgil to attend the lectures delivered by Zanobi da Strada, a friend and admirer of Petrarca, and that these lectures were given in 1351 or 1352, just before Salutati bought a text of this poetry; *ibid.,* 53 and *De laboribus Herculis,* 2:483–86.

8. De la Mare, *Handwriting,* 33.

gant ascenders and descenders often found in Salutati's late hand, the marginalia of the Basel manuscript preserve a clearer "semi-Gothic" appearance typical of Salutati's earlier writing.[9] The letters are small and rather closely spaced, ascenders and descenders are fairly short, the ascender on the uncial *d* leans toward the horizontal, and fusion of letters is pronounced (see Plate I). Everything so far suggests that these marginalia were entered before 1380.

In fact, a comparison of this manuscript with the Priscian is instructive. Both manuscripts contain two markers which de la Mare finds typical of Salutati's earliest annotations, those tending to predate 1370: a small, neat pointing hand, inclined a bit at the wrist and with only four fingers showing, and a bracket formed by two wavy lines which precedes many of the notes.[10] What is more, a number of the notes in the Basel manuscript contain features typical of Salutati's chancery cursive, with looped ascenders—especially on the *d*—being prominent (see Plate II for an example). These features tend to disappear in Salutati's later marginalia; in fact, as Petrucci points out, Salutati even purged the looped ascenders from the chancery documents written in his last years. These cursive features are also found scattered among the notes to the Priscian.[11] Although material such as this is often difficult to evaluate, the evidence here clearly suggests that Salutati had read this manuscript and made notes in it before, say, becoming Chancellor of Florence in 1375, and a careful examination of these notes produces no reason to rule out a 1355 purchase date.

When we turn to the marginalia themselves, we quickly discover that a great many of them are extracts from Servius, whom Salutati later called one of the "commentatores antiquitate et autoritate nobilissimi," the "commentatorum optimus."[12] This should not necessarily surprise us given the popularity of Servius in fourteenth-century Italy—the text of Virgil in

9. *Ibid.*, 34–35, 38; *Il protocollo notarile di Coluccio Salutati (1372–73)*, ed. A. Petrucci (Milan, 1963), 33–34, 36–37; and B. L. Ullman, *The Origin and Development of Humanistic Script*. Storia e letteratura, 79 (Rome, 1960), 11–15.

10. *Handwriting*, 33–34.

11. *Il protocollo*, 27, 43–45. All of these features may be found on f. 53r of the Priscian manuscript.

12. *De laboribus Herculis*, 1:191 and 1:153. To my knowledge, a complete text of Servius has not survived among Salutati's books. While his hopes for obtaining a Servius from Carlo Malatesta in 1401 were dashed (*Epistolario*, 3:533, 539; cf. Ullman, *Humanism*, 251), Salutati must have also had access to a more complete version than the extracts in the Basel manuscript, since the extensive quotations from Servius in *De laboribus Herculis* are not restricted to what is quoted in the Basel manuscript.

Instaurant acies uulcani stirpe creatu̅
Coeculus & ueniens marsos montib; umbro;
Dardanides con̅ furit anxiris enie sinistra
Et totu̅ clipei ferro detererat orbem
Dixerat ille aliqd magnu̅ - uiq; ad fore uerbo
Credidera̅ - coloq; animus fortasse ferebat
Canitiesq; sibi . & longos miserat Annos;
Targit exultans ostra fulgentib; armis
Siluicole fauno dryope que nympha crearat
Obuius ardenti sese obtulit ille reducta
Lorica clypeiq; ingens onus impedit hasta;
Tu caput orantis neqeqa̅ &multa parantis
Dicere detu̅rbat terre truncu̅q; tepentem
Puoluens sup hec inimico pectore fatur;
Astie ne metuende iaceato optima mat'
Conde humi patriaque en̅ erabit mebra sepulchro;
Altrib; liq; re feris uel gurgite mersum
Unda feret piscesq; impasti uulnera la̅bent;
Protin̅ antaeu̅ & licam p̅ma agmina turni
Pseqtur fortiq; numa fuluu̅q; camertem
Magnanimo uolscente satu̅ ditissim̅ agri
Qfuit ausonidu̅ & tacitis regnauit amico lis;
Aegeon qualis centu̅ cui brachia dicunt
Centenasq; man̅ quinquaginta oribz ignē
Pectorib;q; arsisse iouis cu̅ fulmina totra
Tot paribz streperet clypeis tot stringeret enses;
Sic toto eneas deseuit inequore uictor
Utsemel intepuit mucro qui ecce tripha
Quadriiuges inequos aduersaq; pectora tendit
Atq; ille longe gradiente & dira frente
Ut uidere metu uorsi retroq; ruentes
Effunduntq; duce rapiuntq; adlitora curr;
Interea biuugis infert se lucagus albis

incidit atque uiam clipei molita per oras;

Tandem etiam magno strinxit de corpore Turni,

huc turn ferro praefixum robur acuto

in Pallanta diu librans iacit atque ita fa[tur],

aspice num mage sit nostrum penetrabile telum

Dixerat et clipeum tot ferri terga tot aeris

cum pellis totiens obeat circumdata tauri.

uibranti cuspis medium transuerberat ictu

loricaeque moras et pectus perforat ingens,

illeque rapit calidum frustra de uulnere telum

una eademque uia sanguis animusque secuntur.

corruit in uulnus sonitum super arma dedere,

et terram hostilem moriens petit ore cruento

Quem Turnus super adsistens

Arcades haec inquit memores mea dicta referte

Euandro: qualem meruit Pallanta remitto.

quisquis honos tumuli quidquid solamen humandi est

largior. haud illi stabit Aenea paruo

hospitia et laeuo pressit pede talia fatus

Exanimem rapiens immania pondera baltei

impressumque nefas una sub nocte iugali

Caesa manus iuuenum foede thalamique cruenti,

quae Clonus Eurytides multo caelauerat auro

Quo nunc Turnus ouat spolio gaudetque potitus.

Nescia mens hominum fati sortisque futurae

et seruare modum rebus sublata secundis

Turno tempus erit magno cum optauerit emptum

intactum Pallanta et cum spolia ista diemque

Oderit at socii multo gemitu lacrimisque

Impositum scuto referunt Pallanta frequentes

O dolor atque decus magnum rediture parenti,

haec te prima dies bello dedit haec eadem aufert,

cum tamen ingentis Rutulorum linquis aceruos;

Plate II. Basel, Öffentliche Bibliothek der Universität, MS F II 23, f. 166r.

the famous Ambrosian codex of Petrarca, we recall, is surrounded by Servius' commentary[13]—but it may at first prove a little disappointing for the reader who approaches the Basel manuscript in hopes of finding observations as original and imaginative as those of Petrarca. However, when we recall that the range of Servius' commentary runs from grammatical and stylistic observations to allegorical interpretations and information on ancient life and customs, it seems reasonable to assume that what Salutati chose to extract from Servius should tell us a great deal about which aspects of Virgilian poetry interested him at this comparatively early stage of his scholarly career. These trends should be confirmed by those marginalia which do not come directly from Servius.

For purposes of analysis, it will be easiest to separate Salutati's notes into categories. One group draws from Greek and Roman mythology to identify people and explain peculiarities of phrasing in Virgil's text. Thus Salutati reminds himself that Tithonus, the brother of Laomedon and lover of Aurora, was changed into a cicada (on *Georg*. 1.447, f. 21v; the note is taken from Serv. on *Aen*. 4.585 and also appears on f. 93r),[14] and that the god of the woodlands whom the Romans called "Silvanus" was called "Pan" by the Greeks (on *Aen*. 8.600, f. 144v). Often the mythological material goes beyond mere identification to help explicate the text of the poem. Why did Virgil describe Lycia as "hiberna" and Delos as "materna"? Salutati observes that

> constat Apolinem VI. mensibus hyemalibus apud Pat⟨a⟩ram Licie civitatem dare responsa, unde 'Patareus' Apollo dicitur, et VI estivis apud Delum, ubi nutritus fuit et ob hoc dicit 'maternam.' (Serv. on *Aen*. 4.143–44, f. 85v)

13. On Petrarca's Ambrosian codex, see M. L. Lord, "Petrarch and Vergil's First *Eclogue:* The Codex Ambrosianus," *Harvard Studies in Classical Philology,* 86 (1982): 253–76; P. de Nolhac, *Pétrarque et l'humanisme,* 2 vols., 2nd ed. (Paris, 1907), 1:140–61; and A. Ratti, "Ancora del celebre codice manoscritto delle opere di Virgilio già di Francesco Petrarca ed ora della Biblioteca Ambrosiana," in *Francesco Petrarca e la Lombardia* (Milan, 1904), 217–42. Servius maintained his popularity into the next century as well; G. Mambelli's census in *Gli annali delle edizioni virgiliane* (Florence, 1954) indicates an *editio princeps* of 1470, with almost half of the editions of Virgil published before 1500 being accompanied by Servius' commentary.

14. Actually, Tithonus was Laomedon's son. In order to avoid overburdening the notes, the folio citations for Salutati's notes from the Basel manuscript, the line references for Virgil's poetry (keyed to the 1969 Oxford Classical Text edition of R. A. B. Mynors), and references to Servius (when applicable) will be incorporated into the text. I have, of course, supplied punctuation and capitalization for Salutati's marginalia.

The annotator's interest in mythological detail also leads him now and again to confuse issues that Virgil had left clear; for example, he glosses Virgil's reference to the fifty heads of the Hydra with "quam quidam volunt quinquaginta habere capita, alii tria, alii vero novem" (Serv. on *Aen.* 6.575, f. 117r).

When Salutati glosses Cyllene as a mountain in Arcadia where Maia gave birth to Mercury (Serv. on *Aen.* 7.139, f. 137r), his interest in mythology has led him to another category in his note-taking: geographical identification. Salutati's well-known antiquarian interests are already evident when he writes, "*Butroti urbem*, id est Butrotium, ut fontem Timavi. Haec civitas est in Epiro, cuius pars est Caonia, que ante 'Molosia' dicta est" (Serv. on *Aen.* 3.293, f. 76v). These antiquarian interests in geography were reinforced by feelings of patriotism when he read about Italy, feelings drawn from his training in Roman law and the belief in the authority of a Roman Emperor ruling over the same Italy through which Aeneas had once travelled.[15] Thus it seemed worthwhile for Salutati to annotate very carefully sections of the catalogue of Latin troops in *Aeneid* 7, to identify the city Nursia, the mountain Massico and the river Volturnus, the Auruncan and Oscan peoples (Serv. on *Aen.* 7.715–30, f. 133v).

These feelings of patriotism led in turn to an interest in ancient history, which appears primarily in a small group of notes on the parade of Roman heroes at the end of *Aeneid* 6. Thus Salutati uses Servius to distinguish Cato the Censor, the warrior and historian mentioned in *Aen.* 6.841, from Cato Uticensis, and he draws on Servius again to explain the reference to Cossus in the same line by noting that he won the *spolia opima* against "Laertes Gallicus Columnus" (i.e., Lars Tolumnius of Veii, f. 121v). The note on *Aen.* 6.842 clarifies both family relationships and key elements of Roman history:

> *quis Gracci*. Gracos seditiosos constat fuisse, nobiles tamen genere, namque per Corneliam nepotes Africani Scipionis fuerunt. Ergo Scipiones dicit 'Grachi genus.' Duo autem fuerunt, maior Africanus, Emilianus minor, qui obsidione Cartaginis ab Italia revocavit Anibalem. (Serv., f. 121v)

In the same way, "tertiaque arma" at line 859 draws forth a note

---

15. The ideas on patriotism which appear in Salutati's early letters are discussed in Witt, *Hercules at the Crossroads*, 73–77.

distinguishing the three kinds of *spolia opima* and explaining that Marcellus' *spolia opima* had been preceded by similar honors given to Romulus and Cossus (Serv., f. 121v).

Another category of marginalia uses information about ancient life and customs to explicate Virgil's text. For instance, some of the men in this same parade of Roman heroes wear oak crowns; Salutati explains that these are the soldiers "qui in bello civem liberassent," then names and explains the "corone murales" and "corone agonales" (Serv. on *Aen.* 6.772, f. 120r). When Virgil described Amata's frenzied wanderings in *Aeneid* 7, he compared her movements to those of a "turbo," which Salutati glosses as "lignum rotundum ludi puerilis quod agitatur flagello, scilicet trochus" (on *Aen.* 7.378, f. 128r). Shortly afterwards, Amata tells the Latin matrons to join her revels, to loosen their headbands and follow her; these "victe crinales," writes Salutati, "erant solarum matronarum, nam meretricibus non dabantur" (Serv. on *Aen.* 7.403, f. 128v). Many of these notes, such as the references to how oracles predict the future (Serv. on *Aen.* 3.444, f. 79r) and to feasting on festival days (Serv. on *Aen.* 7.135–36, f. 124v), center on ancient religious rites and festivals.

While each of these categories contains an important group of notes, the vast majority of Salutati's marginalia fall into one of three other groups. Quite a number of notes define and explain individual words from Virgil's text. Some of these definitions function as simple dictionary entries: thus we learn that "exorsa" means "incepta" (on *Aen.* 10.111, f. 160v), "fulvum" is "rubeum vel rufum vel splendidum" (on *Aen.* 10.562, f. 167r), and "flere est cum voce lacrimari" (Serv. on *Aen.* 11.59, f. 173v). Sometimes the note rejects one possible meaning as inappropriate to the context; thus Sabinus in *Aeneid* 7 is described as "vitisator," that is, "non inventor vitis, sed qui vitis genus Italis populis demonstravit" (Serv. on *Aen.* 7.179, f. 125r). At other times Salutati is attracted to an unusual derivation, as when he notes that Carthage "lingua Penorum 'nova civitas' dicitur" (Serv. on *Aen.* 1.366, f. 53v), while elsewhere he glosses rare words with primarily technical applications: the "caetra" to which Virgil refers in *Aen.* 7.732, for example, appears as "scetra" in Salutati's marginalia and is defined as a "scutum de corio, quo utuntur Afri et Spani" (Serv. on *Aen.* 7.732, f. 133v). Other notes address the problem of common words used in somewhat uncommon ways. At the funeral games for Anchises, Aeneas can be called "pater" in the sense "paternum habens iudicium vel equale" (on *Aen*. 5.424, f. 101v); Camilla's love of spoils is "feminine" because it is "impatienti et ⟨in⟩rationabili" (Serv. on *Aen*. 11.782, f. 184v).

The second of these large groups of notes consists of paraphrases, re-wordings of difficult passages designed to simplify and clarify their content. In its simplest form, one of these notes recasts Virgil's poetic word order into something more like ordinary prose; such notes are introduced by "ordo est." As an example, let us consider *Aen*. 2.604–6 as it stands in the Basel manuscript, then as Salutati recasts it:

> ... omnem, quae nunc obducta tuenti
> Mortales hebetat visus tibi, et humida circum
> Caligat, nubem eripiam.
>   Ordo est: 'omnem tibi nubem eripiam, que humida
> circum caligat et mortales hebetat visus tuenti.'
> (Serv., f. 69r)

More commonly, these notes change Virgil's wording slightly, expanding a bit and explaining the literal sense of what stands in the text. A variety of introductory tags appear. For instance, "scilicet planetas in quibus fatorum ratio continetur ..." explains why Dido prays to the "conscia fati sidera" (Serv. on *Aen*. 4.519, f. 91v, although Servius introduces the passage with "id est"). "Id est" is perhaps the most obvious sign of a paraphrase, and occurs often in Salutati's notes; an example appears where the she-wolf who suckled Romulus and Remus is shown carved on Aeneas' new armor and is said to "procubuisse, id est, prima parte se inclinasse, ut inclinatione corporis ubera preberet infantibus" (Serv. on *Aen*. 8.631, f. 145r). "Sensus est" introduces Salutati's effort to bring the two terms of an epic simile closer together: "Sensus est, ille Mezentius est actus velut aper qui est actus de altis montibus morsu canum ..." (on *Aen*. 10.707ff., f. 169r). This kind of note takes another form at *Aen*. 10.233 in a speech by one of the sea goddesses whom Cybele created when she changed Aeneas' ships to nymphs. Cymodoce says that they left Aeneas "invite, quasi dicat 'malueramus tibi servire quam in numero nimpharum conputari'" (Serv., f. 162r); this introductory tag sometimes appears in the form "ac si diceret" (cf. Serv. on *Aen*. 1.241, f. 51v).

A third large group of notes also concentrates on explicating Virgil's text, but moves beyond paraphrase to answer questions that might be raised by a careful reading of the poem. For example, one might wonder why a hero like Aeneas is described as "pulcherrimus" at the beginning of the famous hunting scene in *Aeneid* 4; Salutati explains that Virgil, "quia amat, ideo ei dat pulcritudinem, licet Ascanio magis conveniat" (Serv. on *Aen.* 4.141, f. 85v). Later in the same book, Dido regrets her involvement with Aeneas and wishes that she had remained a chaste widow "more fere"; since the point of this reference is not immediately obvious, Salutati turns to Servius and finds that "Plinius in Naturali Ystoria dicit lincas post amissos coniuges aliis non iungi" (Serv. on *Aen.* 4.551, f. 92r). Lest one wonder how Beroe persuades the Trojan women to burn their ships in *Aen.* 5.621ff., Salutati explains that "Troiane matrone cognoscebant illam Beroem nobilem esse et dignam audiri" (f. 104v). Why does the Sibyl announce the god's presence twice at *Aen.* 6.46? "Bis dixit 'deus' ad ostendendum quod deus erat presens" (f. 109r). A modern reader may not find all these explanations convincing, but they do show an honest effort to grapple with the meaning of an admittedly difficult text.

If we search for a common focus to Salutati's observations, we discover that those notes which define individual words, paraphrase difficult passages, and answer questions raised by the text — most of what Salutati wrote, in other words — all function to clarify the literal meaning of the text, to make the difficulties of Virgil's Latin less perplexing. On occasion the smaller groups of notes, those dealing with mythological references, geographical identifications, historical background, and ancient life and customs, might drift a little farther from the text, but the *raison d'être* for each note remains the same: to clarify what Virgil wrote. This may at first seem to belabor the obvious — after all, what else is a commentary supposed to do? Nevertheless, comparison to Petrarca's Ambrosian codex of Virgil brings out an interesting contrast. Many of Petrarca's notes would fit just as easily into the Basel manuscript, but quite a number of others move away from the literal meaning of the text into allegory.[16] Indeed, as J. IJsewijn has observed, such allegorical interpretations occur frequently in humanist commentaries until the early fifteenth century, and allegorical notes still appear in the commentaries of Cristoforo Landino, one of Virgil's

---

16. A good discussion of this point may be found in Lord, "Petrarch and Vergil's First *Eclogue*," 260–61; as J. Brink, "Simone Martini, Francesco Petrarca, and the Humanistic Program of the Virgil Frontispiece," *Mediaevalia,* 3 (1977): 83–91, points out, the famous miniatures at the beginning of the Ambrosian codex reflect this same tendency to allegorize the Virgilian corpus. Petrarca's allegorical interpretation of the *Aeneid* is presented at some length in *Seniles* 4.5.

most important critics in late Quattrocento Italy.[17] What is more, the commentary of Servius on which many of Salutati's notes are based has many allegorical observations that would have been easy to adapt.[18] Thus we must ask ourselves the next logical question: contrary to what we might expect, is Salutati in fact not interested in allegorizing Virgil?

Our analysis of Salutati's notes in the Basel manuscript also leads to one other question. While almost all of the marginalia focus on explicating the literal meaning of Virgil's text, there is one small group of notes that we have not yet considered: those in which Salutati identifies the figures of speech Virgil uses. On *Aen.* 1.412, f. 54r, for example, Salutati draws from Servius and writes, "temesis [*sic*] est, et hoc fit quandocumque secto sermone aliquid interponitur, et hoc fit in conpositis." Similarly, Salutati points out examples of hypallage (Serv. on *Aen.* 5.480, f. 102v), sarcasm (Serv. on *Aen.* 10.557, f.167r and Serv. on *Aen.* 12.359, f.192r), periphrasis (Serv. on *Aen.* 4.254, f.87v), and so forth. There are quite a number of "comparatio" tags spread throughout the manuscript which are probably in Salutati's hand as well (e.g. ff. 84r, 90v, 129v, 192r); it is worth noting that the same figure is isolated repeatedly in the manuscript of Seneca copied and annotated by Salutati shortly afterward (London, British Library, MS Add. 11987).[19] What is it about the figures of speech that draws Salutati's interest to them and away from the literal sense of the text?

To put questions like these into perspective, we must leave the Basel manuscript for a while and examine Virgil's place in Salutati's later scholarly writings. Here our attention is drawn to the letter collection, which cites Virgil more than any other ancient writer except Cicero, and to the *De laboribus Herculis*, which ostensibly focuses on Seneca but actually treats Virgil just as extensively. However, I have also surveyed Salutati's other scholarly writings and shall cite them when appropriate.[20] Fortunately,

17. "Laurentius Vallas 'Sprachliche Kommentare'," in *Der Kommentar in der Renaissance,* ed. A. Buck and O. Herding (Boppard am Rhein, 1975), 97 and my "Cristoforo Landino's *Aeneid* and the Humanist Critical Tradition," *RQ,* 36 (1983): 520–21.

18. J. W. Jones, Jr. has studied this matter and found 183 allegorical notes in Servius' commentary; see his "An Analysis of the Allegorical Interpretations in the Servian Commentary on the *Aeneid,*" (Diss., University of North Carolina, 1959), with findings summarized in his "Allegorical Interpretation in Servius," *Classical Journal,* 56 (1961): 220–21.

19. Salutati's interest in this figure is noted by Witt, *Hercules at the Crossroads,* 56. The manuscript is described by Ullman, *Humanism,* 197 and dated by Petrucci, *Il protocollo,* 33–34.

20. A good, brief description of Salutati's works may be found in Ullman, *Humanism,* 19–36; discussion of these works is integrated into Salutati's political and intellectual development in Witt,

in these later works, Salutati's remarks about Virgil appear in the context of a broader consideration of poetry in general, which allows us to organize and interpret a host of scattered observations on the *Eclogues*, *Georgics*, and *Aeneid*.

The *De laboribus Herculis*, which presents a long moral allegory based on Seneca's *Hercules*, contains Salutati's clearest definition of the poet.[21] Beginning with Cato's famous description of the orator, Salutati fashions the following definition:

> Est igitur poeta vir optimus laudandi vituperandique peritus, metrico figurativoque sermone sub alicuius narrationis misterio vera recondens.[22]

This deceptively simple statement, which as Ullman notes succeeds in uniting the classical *rhetor*, Averroes' paraphrase of Aristotle's *Poetics*, and the Christianized notion of literary allegory,[23] can be divided into three parts, which involve the character of the poet, the content of his poetry, and the nature of literary language. Each of these parts in turn leads us to Virgil.

The first phrase in the definition, which requires the poet to be a man of the highest moral character, presents the fewest obstacles to interpretation. The Ciceronian rhetorical tradition requires the perfect orator to

---

Hercules at the Crossroads. A thorough bibliography on Salutati has been prepared by D. De Rosa, "Cenni bibliografici relativi a Coluccio Salutati," in *Atti del Convegno su Coluccio Salutati* (Buggiano, 1981), 47–62.

21. Much of the discussion of Salutati's literary criticism has focused on a famous series of letters spanning the last thirty years of his life, in which he defended poetry against various attacks by Giuliano Zonarini, Giovanni da San Miniato, Giovanni Dominici, and Pellegrino Zambeccari. These letters are published in the *Epistolario*, 1:298–307, 321–29; 3:285–308; 4:170–240; additional commentary is supplied by B. L. Ullman, "Observations on Novati's Edition of Salutati's Letters," in his *Studies in the Italian Renaissance* (Rome, 1955), 215–16, 232, 237. Ullman, *Humanism*, 53–58 presents a clear summary of the correspondence and of the issues involved, as does J. Cinquino, "Coluccio Salutati, Defender of Poetry," *Italica*, 26 (1949): 131–35. The following discussion takes due account of these letters, but by starting with the definition of poetry in *De laboribus Herculis*, I have reached a somewhat different set of conclusions; cf. C. C. Greenfield, *Humanist and Scholastic Poetics, 1250–1500* (Lewisburg, PA, 1981), 129–63, and D. Aguzzi-Barbagli, "Dante e la poetica di Coluccio Salutati," *Italica*, 42 (1965): 108–31.

22. *De laboribus Herculis*, 1:63; cf. Quintilian, *Inst.* 12.1.1. The *De laboribus Herculis* exists in two forms, the first of which is a long letter to Giovanni da Siena that was presumably abandoned at Giovanni's death in 1383 to allow a more comprehensive, less personal analysis. This second edition, however, was also not finished; see Ullman, *Humanism*, 21–26.

23. *Ibid.*, 26.

possess soundness of character as well as technical skill,[24] and Salutati is simply transferring the association from rhetoric to poetry. The emphasis on the character of the poet is in fact required by the general failure of fourteenth-century criticism to distinguish between the ethical soundness of a poem and its author's soundness of character.[25] Only a virtuous man, in other words, can write a virtuous poem.

In the *De laboribus Herculis*, Salutati claims that Virgil was exemplary in character, lifestyle, and speech. Unfortunately, the ancient lives of Virgil allude to certain libidinous tendencies which Salutati had to consider.[26] Of the two explanations he offers, one involves a recognition that ethical standards change along with the times, and that any sexual failings on Virgil's part are the fault of his age, which accepted activities that no Christian can countenance. However, Virgil was known to the writers of the past as "Parthenias." From this Salutati concludes that his sexual conduct was probably above reproach, so that one can simply reject the charges against him. Of the two possible explanations, Salutati vastly prefers the latter.[27]

24. See J. Seigel, *Rhetoric and Philosophy in Renaissance Humanism: The Union of Eloquence and Wisdom, Petrarch to Valla* (Princeton, 1968), 3–30, and H. H. Gray, "Renaissance Humanism: The Pursuit of Eloquence," *Journal of the History of Ideas,* 24 (1963): 498.

25. There are occasional suggestions of an aesthetic stance in early humanist literature. In his *De studiis et litteris,* for example, Bruni's description of the encounter between Dido and Aeneas takes the first step toward distinguishing the poem *qua* poem from the ethical standards of reality: "Equidem, si quando Didonis Aeneaeque amores apud Virgilium lego, ingenium poetae admirari soleo, rem autem ipsam, quia fictam esse scio, nequaquam attendere. Quod idem mihi accidit in aliis fictionibus poetarum, animum certe non movent, quia fabulosas et aliud pro alio significantes intellego" (*Leonardo Bruni Aretino. Humanistisch-philosophische Schriften,* ed. H. Baron [Leipzig, 1928; repr. Wiesbaden, 1969], 18). Spingarn focuses on this distinction between the "res ipsa" and its fictional presentation as "a distinct attempt at the aesthetic appreciation of literature" (*A History of Literary Criticism in the Renaissance* [New York, 1899], 7). The recognition of a "fiction" that can be simultaneously condemned in the ethics of everyday life and praised on artistic grounds could also sever the tie between the character of the poet and the ethical content of the poem, but the reference to allegory at the end of Bruni's statement ("aliud pro alio significantes") might just as well suggest a purification of *Aeneid,* Book 4, through moral allegory. And in any event, Spingarn is forced to admit that this passage contains "isolated sentiments" (*ibid.*).

26. As the preface to Servius' commentary puts it, Virgil was upright in character but labored under only one shortcoming, that he was "inpatiens libidinis" (*Servianorum in Vergilii carmina commentariorum,* ed. E. K. Rand et al. [Lancaster, PA, 1946], 1).

27. *De laboribus Herculis,* 1:64–65. Interest in Virgil's life continued with the later humanists; see, for example, L. Valmaggi, "La biografia di Virgilio attribuita al grammatico Elio Donato," *Rivista di filologia e d' istruzione classica,* 14 (1886): 1–106. Salutati had access to the lives of Donatus and Servius, but the early Renaissance also saw the discovery of Probus' life and a fourteenth century compilation by Sicco Polenton, which appears in *Scriptorum illustrium latinae linguae libri*

The second part of Salutati's definition emphasizes the poet's "skill in praise and blame." This statement rests on a long-standing association between poetry and epideictic rhetoric, which presents guidelines for the praise or rebuke of men, events, and institutions.[28] As the orator praises virtue and rebukes vice in his speeches, so the poet builds the same moral foundation for his writing. For Salutati, this association is authorized by the great critics of antiquity; Aristotle, for example,

> inquit enim in ipsius libelli [the *Poetics*] fronte omne poema esse oratio-nem vituperationis aut laudis. Carpunt equidem nostri poete vitiosos et vitia, celebrant autem cum virtuosis honesta laudatione virtutes; ut ab illis deterreant genus omne mortalium, ad has autem splendore commendationis alliciant et invitent.[29]

This interpretation of Aristotle, which is based on Averroes' paraphrase and is standard for the Middle Ages,[30] builds on the notion of the poet

---

XVIII, ed. B. L. Ullman (Rome, 1928), 73–90. See R. Sabbadini, *Le scoperte dei codici latini e greci ne' secoli XIV e XV*, 2 vols. (Florence, 1905; repr. Florence, 1967), 1:132–33.

28. The general role of epideictic rhetoric in literary theory and practice is explored in detail by O. B. Hardison in *The Enduring Monument: A Study of the Idea of Praise in Renaissance Literary Theory and Practice* (Chapel Hill, NC, 1962). For an interesting extension of this approach, see A. P. McCormick, "Freedom of Speech in Early Renaissance Florence: Salutati's 'Questio est coram Decemviris', " *Rinascimento*, n.s., 19 (1979): 235–40, where the question of what to do with those who compose or recite a famous poem against someone else turns in part on the use of praise and blame in a civic setting.

29. *De laboribus Herculis*, 1:10; cf. Aristotle, *Poetics* 4; 1448b. Salutati also considers Aristotle and the praise and blame topic in his letter to Giovanni da San Miniato, *Epistolario*, 4:196–97.

30. The *Poetics* was widely used in Italian literary criticism of the sixteenth century, when it was translated into Latin (1498) and Italian (1549) and furnished with a commentary in Latin (1548); see W. K. Wimsatt, Jr. and C. Brooks, *Literary Criticism: A Short History* (New York, 1969), 156. The text was known to earlier humanists, but was not much used. Poliziano, for example, owned a Greek text (now Florence, Bibl. Laur., MS LX,14), but he seems to have acquired it late in life, and it certainly failed to have any decisive effect on his critical thinking; see R. Sabbadini, *Il metodo degli umanisti* (Florence, 1922), 71–74 and A. Buck, *Italienische Dichtungslehren vom Mittelalter bis zum Ausgang der Renaissance* (Tübingen, 1952), 144. Some knowledge of the *Poetics* also appears in the writings of Guarino da Verona (*Epistolario*, 1:505 and 2:461) and Lorenzo Valla (*Historiarum Ferdinandi Regis Aragoniae libri tres*, in *Opera omnia*, ed. E. Garin, 2 vols. [Turin, 1962], 2:5). That Salutati took such an interest in Aristotle is thus a matter of some importance. His understanding of the *Poetics*, of course, is not that of modern scholars. William of Moerbeke had translated the *Poetics* ca. 1278, but his translation enjoyed little circulation, surviving in only two manuscripts. Rather, the Middle Ages knew the work primarily from Averroes' paraphrase, which Hermannus Alemannus translated into Latin in 1256. Salutati used this translation (*Epistolario*, 3:225–26), which had been heavily moralized and thus harmonized well with his theories about poetry. This moralized Aristotle remained popular even after the Greek text was printed in 1508, and it was in fact the first version of the *Poetics* to be published in

as *vir optimus*: as a virtuous man himself, the poet distinguishes good from evil in order to stimulate ethical progress in others. For Salutati, Horace said essentially the same thing in the *Ars poetica*:

> Nam et Flaccus inquit: 'Aut prodesse volunt aut delectare poete.' Prodest quidem reprehensor vitiis obvians sed non immediate delectat. Delectat vero commendans sed non statim et immediate prodest. Principaliter igitur utilitati vituperatio correspondet, delectationi laus, licet secundario prosit hec, et illa delectet.[31]

This is Horace filtered through epideictic rhetoric, so that profit and delight become enmeshed with praise and blame in an effort to make poetry a tool for ethical instruction.

Salutati turns to Virgil with this premise in mind. Using the figure of the explorer scout, he scrutinizes Virgil's poetry to see what he could find there that pertains to virtuous living.[32] He discovers that Aeneas embodies the four cardinal virtues of wisdom, courage, temperance, and justice, and that Virgil wrote the poem to praise these things.[33] We may wonder whether the incident with Dido redounds to Aeneas' credit, and Salutati admits that the liaison itself is not commendable. But when Aeneas leaves Dido behind, he prevails over carnal temptation and his own passion, which must be present for virtue to exist. Thus Virgil even arranged this scene so that Aeneas could be praised for continence.[34] In this way Virgil's praise of virtue presents lessons that are applicable to the life of the reader. As Salutati wrote to Iodoco Marchese di Moravia, the *Aeneid* can teach a prince enough about virtuous ruling so that he will outshine all other governors.[35] Thus Virgil makes Aeneas a model for us to imitate in our own lives.[36]

---

the Renaissance (1481); see *Classical and Medieval Literary Criticism*, ed. A. Preminger, O. B. Hardison, Jr. and K. Kerrane (New York, 1974), 341–48 and W. F. Boggess, "Averrois Cordubensis Commentarium Medium in Aristotelis Poetriam," (Diss., University of North Carolina, 1965), iv–lii.

31. *De laboribus Herculis*, 1:68; Salutati also treats this rhetoricized Horace in his letters to Pellegrino Zambeccari, *Epistolario*, 2:289 and to Giovanni Dominici, *Epistolario*, 4:231.

32. *Epistolario*, 1:304.

33. *Ibid.*, 3:233.

34. *Ibid.*, 3:233, 235.

35. *Ibid.*, 2:430–31. In arguing that hereditary kingship is better than elective as part of a short piece on monarchy, Salutati cites *Aen.* 12.435 ("Disce, puer, virtutem ex me . . .") to show how a king can rouse his offspring to virtue (B. L. Ullman, "Coluccio Salutati on Monarchy," in *Mélanges Eugène Tisserant*, 7 vols. [Vatican City, 1964], 5:402).

36. For example, in his copy of Seneca's *De beneficiis*, now Florence, Bibl. Laur., MS LXXVI,36,

Making Aeneas a repository of praiseworthy virtues does not, however, exhaust the moralizing zeal that Salutati turns toward Virgil. Long sections of the poem, such as the opening storm scene or the encounter with the Harpies, seem largely irrelevant to Salutati's overriding moral and rhetorical preoccupation. On the literal level this may be true, but the third part of Salutati's definition shows that almost any scene can offer ethical insights.

The final section of this definition turns to the way in which the virtuous poet praises virtue and condemns vice. Up to this point, as Salutati himself admits, poetry is indistinguishable from rhetoric.[37] But the uniqueness of poetry lies in the language it uses. Salutati describes the poet as one "metrico figurativoque sermone sub alicuius narrationis misterio vera recondens."[38] A poem must be written in meter, Salutati explains, but meter by itself will not make a composition into a poem. Turning to Aristotle once again, he insists that the poet's language must also be "figurative." What he means here is best explained in his own words:

> Alterum autem quod summe iocundum reperias in poetis est illa mirabilis tum verborum, tum rerum, tum etiam gestorum concinna mutatio, quod quidem ad poetam videmus peculiariter pertinere. Omnes enim translationes atque metaphore, comparationes et similitudines, et quicquid verborum aut rerum, orationum et negociorum videmus in aliud commutari poeticum est.[39]

Poetic language, that is, relies heavily on the figures of speech to attain its own special stylistic elegance, which sets it apart from rhetoric and from all other forms of communication.

For Salutati, Virgil's stylistic achievements are unequalled by any other poet.[40] When he defends poets against the charges lodged against them

Salutati wrote, "Vicit Eneas patrem ipse" (f. 13v) as an example of *pietas* toward a parent, an example which the reader can in turn apply to his own affairs.

37. *De laboribus Herculis,* 1:14–15; cf. *Epistolario,* 3:493. In his review of Ullman, *Humanism,* and Petrucci, *Il protocollo,* R. Fubini notes that in Salutati's thought, poetry and oratory alternate as an all-embracing discipline which encompasses knowledge of all things (*Rivista storica italiana,* 77 [1965]: 965–75).

38. See also the letter to Giovanni de' Pierleoni, *Epistolario,* 3:494: "Sermocinalis scientie pars est poetica, cuius proprium est metrico dicendi genere figuratoque sermone in cortice verborum unum ostendere et aliud sumendo res aut verba pro rebus aliis atque verbis medullitus importare."

39. *De laboribus Herculis,* 1:10; cf. Aristotle, *Poetics* 4; 1448b.

40. *Epistolario,* 1:301–2. Admiration for Virgil's style was, of course, a commonplace among

by Carlo Malatesta, who had pulled down a statue of Mantua's favorite son, Salutati praises Virgil for his embellishment ("ornatus"), maxims ("sententiae"), loftiness of speech ("verborum altitudo"), variation ("varietas"), and melodiousness ("musica melodia").[41] In fact, Virgil demonstrates his skill as a poet in the very first line of the *Aeneid*, for "arma virumque" replaces "virum armatum" by hendiadys, and "arma" in turn is understood as "bellum" by metonymy.[42] What is more, Salutati transfers his appreciation of Virgilian style to his own writing by quoting well-turned phrases as opportunity allows; *Aen.* 1.335 ("Haud equidem tali me dignor honore"), for instance, graces eight different passages in the *Epistolario*.[43]

The presence of meter and figurative language, however, is not the sole distinguishing feature of poetic language. According to Salutati, the poet uses this rhetorically heightened verse to "conceal true things under the secrecy of another narrative." Poetic language moves the imagination by means of allegory, through which what is understood differs from what is said.[44] Salutati's explanation of poetic allegory rests on the traditional fourfold distinction, which he explains in a letter to a certain unknown Giovanni:

> Eleva mentem igitur, mi Iohannes, et poesim quasi de quadam altissima dicendi sublimitate mirare, que modum omnem elocutionis ornatumque transcendens, litterali quadam iocunditate sensibus humanis alludens, figmentum aliquod pro inclusa veritate pretendit aut tropologice narrationis mysterio mores edocet vel quasi sursum

the humanists. Petrarca, for example, recognized two princes of Latin eloquence, Cicero in prose and Virgil in verse (*Fam.* 12.3.104), and this judgment can be traced back to Quintilian (*Inst.* 10.1.85–86, 105). See also *Fam.* 22.10.31–33 and 24.11.1, and *Rerum memorandarum* 2.16.

41. *Epistolario*, 3:291. This incident, which aroused considerable commentary in humanist circles, is described by Novati in his introductory note to the letter (*ibid.*, 3:285ff.); see also Vergerio's reaction to the incident in the *Epistolario di Pier Paolo Vergerio*, ed. L. Smith (Rome, 1934), 123ff.

42. *De laboribus Herculis*, 1:10–11.

43. *Epistolario*, 1:64, 157, 228; 3:457, 481; 4:13, 46, 161.

44. *De laboribus Herculis*, 1:69–70. Salutati's definitions and descriptions of poetry are not always so complete as the one from *De laboribus Herculis* that we have been looking at. It is worth noting that his abbreviated analyses tend to focus on allegory and the nature of poetic language, as in the letter to Giovanni Dominici (*Epistolario*, 4:233–34): "Est igitur poetica sermocinalis quedam ars atque facultas, et, ut supra dixi, bilinguis; exterius unum exhibens, aliud autem intrinseca ratione significans; semper in figura loquens ac sepenumero versibus alligans, si quid refert."

ducens anagogice dictionis oraculo statum eterne felicitatis, dum aliud videtur innuere, prefigurat.[45]

Salutati then illustrates the various levels of allegory through reference to the *Aeneid*. Aeneas' encounter with Turnus at *Aen*. 10.636–60, for example, conflicts with a more reliable account of the battles in Latium, but Virgil uses the discrepancy to present a hidden meaning on the first allegorical level. The scene where Aeneas takes control of his ship from the drowned steersman Palinurus can be interpreted morally, so that we learn how reason guides the will to proper ethical action. Finally, Virgil uses the Elysian fields and Aeneas' journey to Latium as anagogical prefigurations of our heavenly felicity.[46]

Each type of allegory, as it pertains to Virgil's poetry, calls for some additional comment. Salutati is less interested in the first level of allegory than in the other two, but he does consider instances in which the literal sense of a passage hides something which is not applicable to ethics or to Christian salvation. Not only Virgil, but Juvenal, Cicero, Ovid, Statius, Lucan, and Homer all use the god Jupiter to represent a star, air, fire, celestial influence, and both natural and supernatural agents.[47] The same passage, of course, can be interpreted on more than one level, so that Salutati includes a traditional association of Charon and time along with a moral allegory of the same passage.[48] Allegory is especially useful in salvaging poetic passages which conflict with "historical truth." In this way Virgil is exonerated for associating Dido and Aeneas, whom Salutati's historical sources placed in different generations.[49]

45. *Epistolario*, 3:230. This scheme, which appears in Dante's epistle to Can Grande, remained popular with early humanists such as Boccaccio (*Genealogie deorum gentilium*, ed. V. Romano, 2 vols. [Bari, 1951], 1:19 and *Il comento di Giovanni Boccaccio sopra la Commedia*, ed. G. Milanesi, 2 vols. [Florence, 1863], 1:153–54).

46. *Epistolario*, 3:230–31.

47. *De laboribus Herculis*, 1:87–106.

48. *Ibid.*, 2:536–38. Boccaccio also associates Charon with time (*Comento*, 1.93), as had Fulgentius (*Expositio Vergilianae continentiae*, in *Opera*, ed. R. Helm [Leipzig, 1898], 98) and Bernardus Silvestris (*The Commentary on the First Six Books of the Aeneid Commonly Attributed to Bernardus Silvestris*, ed. J. W. Jones and E. F. Jones [Lincoln, NE, 1977], 77).

49. *De laboribus Herculis*, 1:86. A marginal note to Florence, Bibl. Laur., San Marco MS 328, Salutati's copy of Macrobius' *Saturnalia*, protests that the story of Dido's lasciviousness is false: "continentissima fuit Dido" (f. 76v; cf. *Sat*. 5.17.4). The matter of the "historical Dido" was of some concern to the early humanists. Boccaccio, for example, presents the "true" version of Justinus (*Epitoma* 18.6.9) in his *Genealogie* (2.60), *De casibus illustrium virorum* (facsimile reproduction of the Paris 1520 edition, with an introduction by L. B. Hall [Gainesville, FL, 1962], 58),

Through anagogy, literature can supplement the Bible as a source for Christian teaching. According to Salutati, Scripture is a more certain guide to salvation than secular letters, but even the pagan poets present useful religious sentiments:

> Nec negaverim, cum in harum rerum fluxarum societatem venerimus, satius esse recta via ad eterna per sacrarum litterarum studia pergere, quam per poetarum flexus et devia pervenire. Sed quoniam utroque calle, si quis recte graditur, ad illum finem quem appetimus devenitur, quanvis ille sit preeligendus, non tamen iste negligendus est. . . . In quibus [poetarum carminibus] plerumque videtur aut sub allegoriarum mysterio aut in ipso verborum propatulo certissime veritatis divinus spiritus resonare.[50]

In his letters to Giuliano Zonarini, Salutati emphasizes Virgil's value for the Christian. Not only is the reference to the return of the ages in *Ecl.* 4.6–7 compatible with Christianity, but *Aen.* 1.664 shows the unity of Father and Son, and Book 6 of the *Aeneid* provides invaluable insight into the fate of the soul after death.[51] Salutati wavers as to whether or not Virgil and the other pagan poets perceived these truths by divine inspiration,[52] but the importance of his anagogical interpretation remains undiminished in either case.

and *De claris mulieribus* (in *Forty-Six Lives Translated . . . by Henry Parker, Lord Morley*, ed. H. G. Wright. Early English Text Society Edition [London, 1943], 6).

50. *Epistolario*, 1:323–24. This was a favorite theme with Salutati, who repeated it in several places: *Epistolario*, 1:302–3; 3:539–41; 4:200 and *De laboribus Herculis*, 1:82–83; see A. von Martin, *Mittelalterliche Welt- und Lebensanschauung im Spiegel der Schriften Coluccio Salutatis* (Munich, 1913), 142–52.

51. *Epistolario*, 1:303, 325–26. In this way, even Aeneas' graceful compliment to Dido in *Aen.* 1.603–5 ("Di tibi, si qua pios respectant numina, si quid/Usquam iustitiae est et mens sibi conscia recti,/Praemia digna ferant") can direct Salutati to God as the source of justice and glory (*Epistolario*, 2:427). On the letter to Zonarini, see A. von Martin, *Coluccio Salutati und das humanistische Lebensideal: Ein Kapitel aus der Genesis der Renaissance* (Leipzig, 1916; repr. Hildesheim, 1973), 223–26.

52. In considering how closely the underworld of the pagan poets parallels that described by Scripture, Salutati attributes passages like *Aeneid* 6 to divine inspiration in his *De laboribus Herculis* (2:461), and he takes the same position in the letters to Zonarini. However, in the letters to Giovanni da San Miniato and to Giovanni Dominici, Salutati drew closer to a position held by Petrarca and Boccaccio, that such religious truths as the pagan poets attained were accessible to natural reason without direct inspiration. This is the position developed by R. G. Witt in "Coluccio Salutati and the Conception of the *Poeta Theologus* in the Fourteenth Century," *RQ,* 30 (1977): 538–39; see also Martin, *Coluccio Salutati,* 64–66. On the poet as theologian in early Italian humanism, see Buck, *Italienische Dichtungslehren,* 67–87 and K. Vossler, *Poetische Theorien in der italienischen Frührenaissance* (Berlin, 1900), 29, 56.

Salutati's interest in the allegory of the *Aeneid*, however, centers on the moral level. He cites Fulgentius' *Expositio Virgilianae continentiae* and explains that the mystical sense of the poem teaches us about the Platonic descent of the spirit into the body and about the six ages of man.[53] When Aeneas and his men delight in the empty scenes ("pictura inanis") of Troy (*Aen.* 1.464), they stand for the state of infancy, in which we take pleasure in pictures and images rather than the thing itself. The second book in turn represents childhood, the third adolescence, the fourth young manhood, the fifth maturity, and the sixth old age.[54]

Though this scheme serves to focus critical attention onto the poem as a vehicle for discussing ethical philosophy, Salutati does not rely on it directly in most of his moral allegory.[55] He was a moralist *par excellence*, however, and he overlooks nothing from the *Aeneid* that could possibly offer edifying instruction. In the *De laboribus Herculis*, for example, Troy under Priam presents a model of luxurious living and the fate that overtakes men who choose this lifestyle. The Harpies stand for avarice, and Misenus should be understood as the act and habit of irascibility, which must be left behind and buried by anyone striving for proper understanding of virtue and vice. The affair with Dido, when interpreted morally, shows what happens when the will is temporarily seduced by the sensual appetite and rebels against the rule of reason.[56]

For Salutati, however, the allegorical content of the first five books is only a prologue to the ethical treasure contained in Book 6, the account of Aeneas' descent to the underworld. Citing Zanobi da Strada, the *De*

53. *De laboribus Herculis,* 1:12. Salutati's manuscript of the *Expositio* survives as BAV, MS Vat. lat. 3110; see Ullman, *Humanism,* 228–29.

54. *Epistolario,* 3:232–38.

55. He does return to Fulgentius' scheme now and again; in *De laboribus Herculis,* 1:351–52, for example, the seven stags that Aeneas kills after landing at Carthage (*Aen.* 1.180ff.) represent the seven years of infancy.

56. On Troy, 1:252; on the Harpies, 1:237–38; on Misenus, 2:578–82; and on *Aeneid* 4, 1:103–6. We should not assume that Salutati's moral allegory is all original. The association of the Harpies with avarice, for example, is found in Fulgentius (*Mythologiae,* in *Opera,* ed. R. Helm [Leipzig, 1898], 124), the third Vatican mythographer (in *Scriptores rerum mythicarum latini tres Romae nuper reperti,* ed. G. Bode [Celle, 1834], 1.173), Bernardus Silvestris (*Commentary,* 74–75), and Boccaccio (*Genealogie,* 2:529–30). Salutati was familiar with each of these authors, so that his discussion of the Harpies should be seen as traditional. See Ullman, *Humanism,* 219–20, 228–29, and 237–38; the introduction to Jones' edition of Bernardus Silvestris' *Commentary,* xviii–xix; and G. Padoan, "Tradizione e fortuna del commento all' 'Eneide' di Bernardo Silvestre," *IMU,* 3 (1960): 234–36. Salutati's moral allegory as a whole depends on a tradition like this, although the task of tracing the history of each allegorical association would lead us far astray from Salutati's Virgil criticism.

laboribus Herculis interprets the *descensus ad inferos* in four ways: the descent of the rational soul into the body, the use of magic in sacrifices and invocation of spirits, the rejection of spiritual values in favor of earthly desires (the "descensus vitiosus"), and a contemplative study of the frailties of temporal life in order to attain a better understanding of virtue (the "descensus moralis et virtuosus").[57] Salutati associates Aeneas with the "descensus virtuosus." The good, he explains, can be approached through pleasure (the Epicureans), virtue (the Stoics), or expediency (the masses), and the poets have selected different underworld descents to represent each philosophical approach. Orpheus' descent hides the teachings of the Epicureans, Theseus and Pirithous are associated with the followers of expediency, and Hercules and Aeneas represent the Stoic quest for uprightness and virtue.[58] What is more, the virtuous descent can be made by actually fighting with vice, as Hercules did, or by contemplating temporal affairs, the path that Aeneas chose.[59]

Each stage of Aeneas' trip through the underworld thus prefigures some treasure of moral allegory that can be referred to this interpretation of the *descensus ad inferos*. Aeneas' right to enter Avernus (the foulness of temporal affairs), for example, is guaranteed by the Golden Bough, which stands for virtue, or wealth, or the wisdom by which we come to ethical understanding.[60] The personified labors and afflictions in the vestibule of hell are the inevitable attendants at the union of spirit and body.[61] The rivers of hell can also be referred to this union, so that Lethe represents forgetfulness of the spirit's former life, Phlegethon the ardors of passion, Acheron the sins for which we repent, Cocytus whatever drives us to tears and grief, and Styx that which arouses hatred.[62] At the same time, the rivers stand for our bodily humors,[63] or for the process by which we

---

57. 2:483–86. Salutati's first treatment of the *descensus* included a fifth category, "qui fit per anime damnationem, sicut nostra sanctissima fide instruimur et tenemus"; see Ullman's edition, 2:600. This explanation of the *descensus ad inferos* parallels that of Bernardus Silvestris (*Commentary*, 30).

58. *De laboribus Herculis*, 2:487–89.

59. *Ibid.*, 2.622–23. The *De laboribus Herculis* ostensibly focuses on how Hercules, a perfect and virtuous man ("homo quidem perfectus et virtuosus," 1.336), fights with and overcomes vice; see, for example, 1.336–42, on the Cacus episode.

60. *Ibid.*, 1:11; 2:573–77.

61. *Ibid.*, 1:181.

62. *Ibid.*, 2:529–30. Salutati is quoting Macrobius, *Somn. Scip.* 1.10.9–15 here; his copy of the text is now Florence, Bibl. Laur., MS LXXVII,6.

63. *De laboribus Herculis*, 2:535–36.

long for something, decide to do it, and then repent and grieve for what we have done.[64] Charon the boatman represents freedom of the will,[65] and Cerberus stands for the bodily needs of food, drink, and sleep, through which pleasure sometimes seduces the will to rebel against reason.[66] When Aeneas' path forks, with one branch going to Elysium and the other to Tartarus, Salutati sees a graphic depiction of the choice that every man must make between virtue and vice.[67] The punishments assigned to the Great Sinners, he feels, make that choice easier for us to make.[68]

When we consider Salutati's definition of the poet and the application of his poetic principles to the works of Virgil, we see that there is a dominant emphasis in his criticism. The first part of the definition requires the poet to be of sound character, a test which Virgil as Salutati knew him could be made to pass. This requirement is linked to the second part of the definition, in which the poem is said to praise virtue and condemn vice, because Salutati could not separate the moral content of a poem from the character of the man who wrote it. By this standard as well, Virgil is an excellent poet, since the *Aeneid* in particular describes a hero who served Salutati as the very model of virtuous living. The third part of the definition focuses on poetic language, which draws freely on the figures of speech and relies on allegory, especially at the moral level, to carry through the goals of the rhetoric of praise and blame. In other words, the scholarly works written by Salutati after he placed his marginalia in B approach the Virgilian corpus with the expectation that poetry should praise virtue and condemn vice, an expectation which, as I have shown elsewhere, was a dominant trend in the literary criticism of the early Italian Renaissance.[69]

---

64. *Ibid.*, 2:554–55.
65. *Ibid.*, 2:556–57, 563–69.
66. *Ibid.*, 2:539–40, 606.
67. *Ibid.*, 1:182, 213–14; cf. *De seculo et religione*, ed. B. L. Ullman (Florence, 1957), 63–64.
68. *De laboribus Herculis*, 2:530. Salutati relies here again on Macrobius, *Somn. Scip.* 1.10.9–15.
69. "The Rhetorical Criticism of Literature in Early Italian Humanism from Boccaccio to Landino," *Rhetorica*, 1 (1983): 33–52. On the rhetorical aspect of humanist literary criticism in general, see Buck, *Italienische Dichtungslehren*, 54–67, 143–44; C. Trabalza, *La critica letteraria dai primordi dell' umanesimo all' età nostra* (Milan, 1913–15), 3–6, 19–20; and Vossler, *Poetische Theorien*, 78–80. It is important to note that, although Salutati's ideas about the relationship between wisdom and eloquence in general were somewhat unstable, his conception of rhetoricized poetry as it focused around praise and blame goes beyond the simplistic equation of rhetoric and style which still appears in some discussions of humanist poetics; see J. Lindhardt, *Rhetor, Poeta, Historicus: Studien*

Thus Salutati's special interest in Virgil began when as a relatively young man he entered his marginal notes in B, and this interest continued in one form or another to his death in 1406. As we might expect, there are a number of places where Salutati's analysis remained more or less constant throughout his scholarly career. For example, his discussion of the nature of poetry in *De laboribus Herculis* emphasizes the importance of the figures of speech, which he illustrates from Virgil's poetry at some length[70] in much the same way as he had identified some examples of the figures in his Virgil manuscript. In several other places we can see Salutati return years, even decades, later to a line whose meaning he had first struggled with in the Basel manuscript. Thus a letter to Leonardo Bruni on the formation of names quotes *Aen.* 6.842–43,[71] for which Salutati had prepared a long note in the Basel manuscript (Serv., f. 121v) giving historical information on the Scipiades and providing the erudition necessary to construct his later argument on patronymics. In a discussion of Theseus and Pirithous' descent to Hades, Salutati quotes *Aen.* 4.698–99 and explains the customs at religious sacrifices,[72] an interest which also appears in the marginal note to the same line in the Basel manuscript (Serv., f. 94v). Perhaps the best example here focuses on *Aen.* 4.436, a line which Conington considers "the most difficult in Virgil."[73] In Salutati's text it reads "Quam mihi cum dederis cumulatam morte remittam," and the Basel manuscript has a long note designed to settle on precisely what the line means (Serv., f. 90v). Once he feels comfortable with this, Salutati is ready to quote and paraphrase the line, which appears in six different letters written over a twenty-eight year period.[74]

Despite a number of instances like these, however, there is a basic and fundamental difference between Salutati's approach to Virgil in the Basel manuscript and that taken in his later criticism: the marginalia for the most part focus on the literal meaning of the text, while Salutati's later interest centers on allegory and the rhetorical figures as a means to praise virtue and condemn vice. For example, at *Aen.* 8.431 in the Basel

über rhetorische Erkenntnis und Lebensanschauung im italienischen Renaissancehumanismus (Leiden, 1979), 117–39, and Seigel, *Rhetoric and Philosophy*, 63–98.

70. 1:10–12.
71. *Epistolario,* 4:151.
72. *De laboribus Herculis,* 2:518.
73. Quoted by R. G. Austin, *P. Vergili Maronis Aeneidos Liber Quartus* (Oxford, 1966), 131.
74. The letters in which this line is used appear in *Epistolario,* 1:49, 320; 3:162, 220, 388; 4:265.

manuscript, Salutati glosses a passage on thunder and lightning as "per 'sonitum' tonitrua ostendit, per 'metum' fulgora" (f. 142r). In a passage about the battle of the gods and giants in *De laboribus Herculis*, Salutati writes that the poets speak about thunderbolts on three levels. The first is "secundum propriam naturam fulminum," in support of which Salutati quotes the same verse from the *Aeneid* followed by the same explanation, identical in wording except that now he follows Servius precisely, so that "fulgetras" replaces "fulgora." However, thunderbolts also allow for interpretation "secundum speculationem seu vitam contemplativam" and "secundum vitam moralem,"[75] leading Salutati to continue this discussion in terms of moral allegory. There is no shortage of similar examples from which to draw. If we turn to the story of Hercules and Cacus in the Basel manuscript, at *Aen.* 8.205 Salutati writes that Cacus "pro ingenti scelere furis nomen posuit" (Serv., f. 138v); in *De laboribus Herculis*, he writes "fur autem dicitur Cacus et furtim rapuisse tauros."[76] However, the latter passage continues by associating Cacus' furtive manner with "mala complexio," which he represents in the allegorical interpretation of the myth being developed here. Thus the marginalia in the Basel manuscript explicate the literal level of Virgil's story, which Salutati considers a "hystoria . . . dimissa, que et varia et obscura est," while the same material serves in the *De laboribus Herculis* to develop an allegory involving Hercules as "homo . . . perfectus et virtuosus" and Cacus as his moral enemy.[77] Similarly, the note on the Hydra in B is concerned with how many heads the creature had (Serv. on *Aen.* 6.575–76, f. 117r), while discussion of the same lines in *De laboribus Herculis* functions to allegorize the Hydra as a "calidissima sophysta."[78]

We must be careful not to draw the lines of demarcation too sharply here. In part because Salutati's later discussions of Virgil cannot neglect the literal meaning of the text as the beginning place for allegory, and in part because an interest in the figures of speech stayed with him through most of his life, we can find some passages from Virgil whose treatment in *De laboribus Herculis* or the *Epistolario* is very similar to what Salutati

75. 2:433.
76. 1:338.
77. The comment on the literal level of the story is found at 1:336; the allegorization of Hercules is found *ibid.*
78. 1:197–98.

had said in the marginalia to the Basel manuscript. Nevertheless, these similarities—and they are relatively few— should not blind us to the more fundamental point, that we look to the Basel manuscript in vain for that interest in praise of virtue and condemnation of vice which gives Salutati's scholarly writings on Virgil their distinctive cast. While we might begin to explain this difference by noting that the probing freedom of a letter or a discursive interpretation of the Hercules myth might be more suitable to a treatment of moral philosophy, allegory, and epideictic rhetoric than marginalia to a classical text, this does not by itself explain why Salutati passed over the allegorical notes in Servius' commentary to Virgil or why his notes are free of the allegory found in other humanist commentaries. The explanation for this discrepancy is also in part chronological. As a relatively young man, Salutati was content to work out the meaning of a difficult Latin text, proceeding slowly and thoroughly in an effort to digest the literal content of the poetry. With the basic points under control and a growing scholarly reputation, Salutati was able to develop his ideas about poetry at greater length. As he did so, it is no surprise to find him returning to a favorite text of his youth and building onto what he had done before. The interpretation of Virgil as a guide to virtuous living and master of allegory could not have developed without the careful study reflected in the margins of Basel MS F II 23, so that this manuscript provides us with a rare glimpse of some very important scholarly activity of the fourteenth century in its early, formative state.[79]

II

Giovanni Tortelli

The hand of Giovanni Tortelli is easily recognizable in the more than 500 marginal and interlinear notes entered in B by a single scholar who wrote a distinctive humanistic cursive. Characteristic features such as *e*

79. I would like to thank the Newberry Library and the University of North Carolina, Chapel Hill for supporting the initial research on which this study is based, and Texas A&M University's College of Liberal Arts for supporting my examination of Salutati manuscripts in Florence during the summer of 1984. I am also grateful to Professor Ronald G. Witt of Duke University, who was kind enough to read an earlier draft of this study.

with a slightly enlarged loop, short *t*, *h* and *m* with final strokes swinging below the base-line (see our Plate III) serve to identify the glossator as the humanist who was also the author of the encyclopedic *De orthographia*. This vast work of erudition survives in an autograph copy (BAV, Vat. lat. 1478), which furnishes a sure basis of comparison.[80] Two more autographs of Tortelli which will be relevant to our purpose contain a group of extracts from Latin classical and late antique authors and a Greek grammar, now respectively Basel, Öffentliche Bibliothek der Universität MSS E I i l, ff. 355r–417v and F VIII 3.[81]

In the fifteenth century Virgil retained his customary position as the preeminent poet of ancient Rome, and so it is not surprising that Tortelli, like Salutati in the fourteenth century, had a keen interest in this revered author and hence that he, like Salutati, would gloss zealously a manuscript of Virgil's works. What is unusual, however, is the coincidence that Tortelli annotated the codex once belonging to Salutati and also the fact that his annotations differ radically in character from those of Salutati. How and when did Tortelli come to have access to B, and what prompted him to adopt a different approach towards Virgil?

To the first question only a hypothetical, but very likely, answer can be given. In a letter written at Florence and dated 1 March 1438, Salutato Salutati reports the return from Constantinople of "Messer Giovanni d'Arezzo, el quale fu maestro di Coluccio ... cogli imbasiciadori del concilio di Basilea."[82] The "Messer Giovanni d'Arezzo" is our Giovanni Tortelli, who was born near Arezzo, and the "Coluccio" is, of course, the son of Salutato Salutati and grandson of the famous Coluccio Salutati whose name he had. This tutorship of the young Coluccio (born in 1417) must have taken place at some time during Tortelli's stay in Florence (1433–35) and certainly before the latter's departure for the East in the spring of

---

80. G. Mercati was the first to recognize that Tortelli is also the scribe of BAV, MS Vat. lat. 1978 (the dedication copy); cf. his *Scritti di Isidoro il cardinal Ruteno*, ST 46 (Rome, 1926), 82, note 4. For a reproduction of MS Vat. lat. 1978, see M. Regoliosi, "Nuove ricerche intorno a Giovanni Tortelli," *IMU*, 12 (1969): pls. 13.1 (f. 1r, detail) and 18 (ff. 61r, 256r, details); in the same article she also publishes facsimiles from other autographs of Tortelli.

81. MS E I i l has been studied by O. Besomi, "Un nuovo autografo di Giovanni Tortelli: uno schedario di umanista," *IMU*, 13 (1970): 95–137 and pls. 2 (f. 391, detail), 3 (f. 356r, details), 4 (f. 356v, detail), 5 (f. 374r, detail); for MS F VIII 3 see M. Cortesi, "Il 'Vocabularium' greco di Giovanni Tortelli," *ibid.*, 22 (1979): 450–83 and pls. 6 (details of ff. 141r and 153r) and 7 (details of ff. 164v and 278r).

82. *Epistolario*, 4:555.

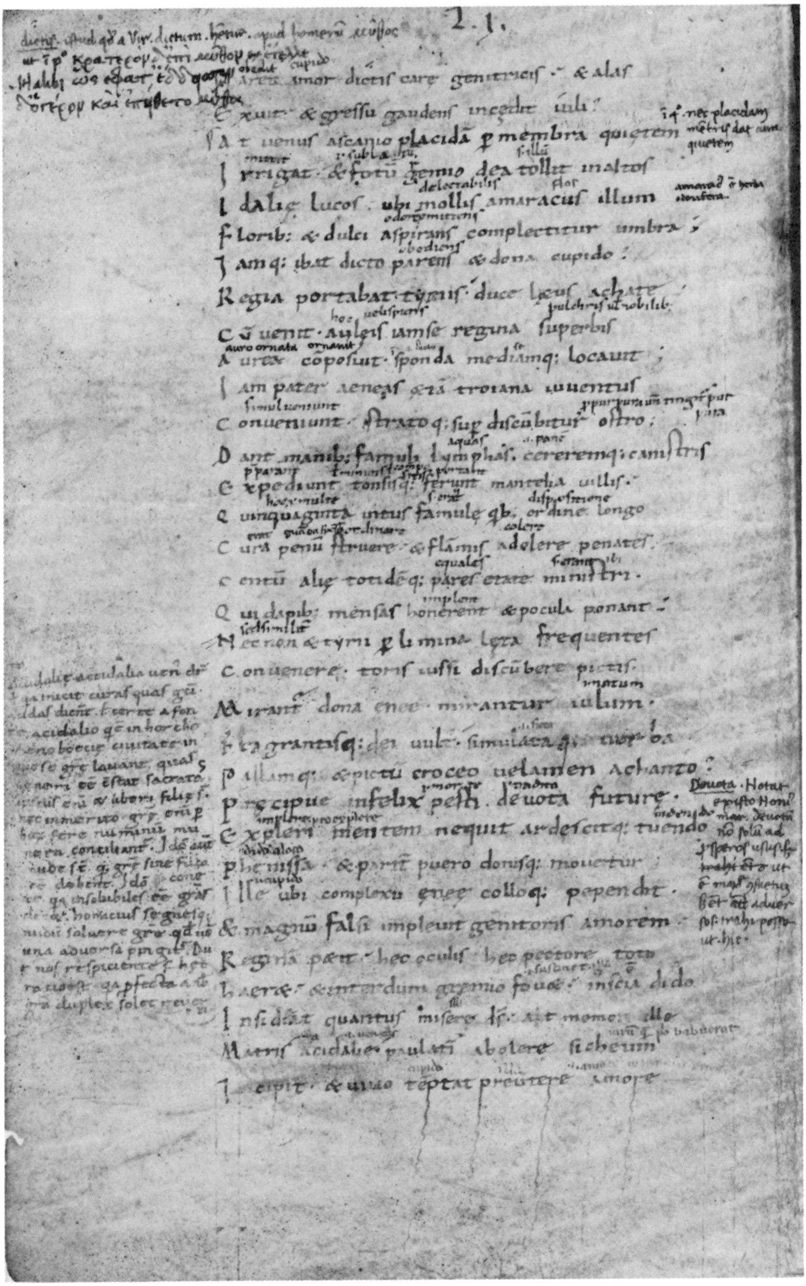

Ares amor dictis care genetricis et alas

exuit et gressu gaudens incedit iuli

At Venus Ascanio placidam per membra quietem

inrigat et fotu gremio dea tollit in altos

Idaliae lucos ubi mollis amaracus illum

floribus et dulci aspirans complectitur umbra;

Iamque ibat dicto parens et dona cupido

Regia portabat tyriis duce laetus achate

Cum venit aulaeis iamse regina superbis

Aurea composuit sponda mediamque locauit;

Iam pater aeneas et iam troiana iuuentus

Conueniunt stratoque super discumbitur ostro;

Dant manibus famuli lymphas cereremque canistris

Expediunt tonsisque ferunt mantelia uillis;

Quinquaginta intus famulae quibus ordine longo

Cura penum struere et flammis adolere penatis;

Centum aliae totidemque pares aetate ministri

Qui dapibus mensas onerent et pocula ponant;

Nec non et tyrii per limina laeta frequentes

Conuenere; toris iussi discumbere pictis;

Mirantur dona enee mirantur iulum

flagrantisque dei uultus simulataque uerba

Et pallamque et pictu croceo uelamen acantho;

Praecipue infelix pesti deuota futurae

Expleri mentem nequit ardescitque tuendo

Phenissa et pariter puero donisque mouetur;

Ille ubi complexu enee colloque pependit;

Et magnum falsi impleuit genitoris amorem

Reginam petit; hec oculis hec pectore totu

haeret et interdum gremio fouet inscia dido

Insideat quantus misero deus; at memor ille

Matris acidaliae paulatim abolere sicheum

Incipit et uiuo temptat praeuertere amore

Plate III. Basel, Öffentliche Bibliothek der Universität, MS F II 23, f. 58v.

1435 to study Greek. His connection with members of the Salutati family was clearly brief, but, even so, Tortelli gained their affection.[83] In keeping with Virgil's constant popularity as a school author, his poems were almost certain to be studied by a young pupil, and here it may be suggested that B remained in the Salutati family because of the traditionally high regard for Virgil and was used at the appropriate time for the instruction of Coluccio's grandson.[84] Moreover, given the apparently warm relationship between Tortelli and his employer, we may also venture the supposition that he could have been presented with the manuscript as a mark of esteem when this employment ceased.

While this hypothesis would explain quite simply why Tortelli had access to the codex, it cannot be confirmed by such helpful evidence as an ex-libris, for seemingly he did not insert any kind of *nota possessoris*. As it is, Tortelli's annotations constitute the sole evidence for his association with the codex. The manuscript does exhibit, however, three ex-libris in other hands whose contents do suggest that Tortelli at one time may actually have owned this copy of Virgil:

(1) on f. 201v, written upside-down, "Al nome di dio adj V di giugno 1437. Io. mainardo deglubaldinj da firenze ./ comfesso auere [. . .] allo expettabile huomo messer giouannj daraugia al [. . .] inbasciadore del santo concilio ./ questo presente libro per pregi[. . .] tredici e qualj Io o riceuutj e per sua chiareza o fattj quest⟨o⟩;"

(2) on f. Iv, in a fifteenth-century hand, "Iste liber est conuentus Basiliensis ordinis praedicatorum;"

(3) on f. Iv, just below (2), "Nunc autem Bibliothecae Academiae Basiliensis .1.5.59."

If we consider these points in order, it is clear from (1) that the manuscript was in Constantinople in 1437, and "messer giovannj daraugia" is presumably Giovanni da Ragusa, O. P. (ca. 1390–1443), who is well-known for his activities in connection with the Councils of Pavia and Basel, and who spent two years in Constantinople (23/24 September 1435–2

---

83. *Ibid.*: "el sopra detto messer Giovanni è tenuto valentissimo huomo . . . e perchè egli è huomo vertuoso ed è co signore che sso vi vuole bene e desso è grande nostro amicho, vi priegho quando lui verrà a Ferrara, voi lo vicitate, mostrandogli voi l' amiate per nostro amore quanto vostro fratello etc."

84. If the Virgil manuscript did remain in the family after Salutati's death, it was one of the few books to do so; for the disposal of Salutati's library by his sons see Ullman, *Humanism,* 137, 278–80.

November 1437) in an effort to unite the Latin and Greek Churches. He was also an ardent book collector, and, to judge from (1), took the opportunity in Constantinople to obtain from the trader Giovanni Mainardo Ubaldini[85] what is now our manuscript B. In accordance with the terms of Giovanni da Ragusa's will, his books went after his death to the Dominican convent at Basel, and this explains the ex-libris in (2). In the sixteenth century the convent was secularized and abandoned for a long time (1525–59), and the manuscripts were finally deposited in the University Library, as noted in (3).[86]

Giovanni da Ragusa also acquired three manuscripts that had undoubtedly belonged to Tortelli and are now at Basel: E III 4 (Thucydides, in Greek, with an ex-libris of Tortelli dated 3 June 1435, when he was already in Constantinople); E I i 1, ff. 355r–417v and F VIII 3, both mentioned above as autographs of Tortelli. Although the presence of the Virgil manuscript in Constantinople could perhaps be explained by supposing that the book was brought from Florence by Giovanni Mainardo Ubaldini, purchased in Constantinople by Giovanni da Ragusa, and annotated by Tortelli either before or after the sale, this does not seem especially plausible. At the very least we may object that Latin books were not likely to be offered for sale in the East (unless in this case our trader just happened to have the book among his wares, but this demands still more faith in coincidence); we may also wonder why Tortelli would have chosen in Constantinople to annotate a Latin text, and so fully at that, instead of doing something more specifically Greek (like the Greek grammar [Basel MS F VIII 3], which he composed while in Constantinople).[87] I think fewer difficulties accompany the hypothesis that Tortelli, former tutor to a young member of the Salutati family, took with him to Constantinople the elder Salutati's

85. Giovanni Mainardo Ubaldini was also the intermediary through whom money was paid to the Turks in 1454 for the release of Ubertino Pusculo; cf. C. de' Rosmini, *Vita e disciplina di Guarino Veronese e de' suoi discepoli,* 3 vols. (Brescia, 1806), 3:172 and 177–78, note 10.

86. For Giovanni da Ragusa's library and its history see A. Vernet, "Les manuscrits grecs de Jean de Raguse (+ 1443)," *Basler Zeitschrift für Geschichte und Altertumskunde,* 61 (1961): 75–108, with the older bibliography.

87. Steinmann, "Die humanistische Schrift" (above, note 2), 389 and note 24a suggests that Tortelli had access to the codex only while he was in Constantinople and that he annotated it there: "Anmerkungen Tortellis trägt auch ein Vergilcodex [= F II 23]. . . . Johannes von Ragusa hatte ihn am 5. Juni 1437 in Konstantinopel von dem Florentiner Kaufmann Mainardo degli Ubaldini erworben und dann wohl an Tortelli weitergeliehen. Tortellis Bemerkungen finden sich nur in den früheren Teilen des Bandes. Das lässt sich am besten damit erklären, dass ihm das Buch nur

copy of Virgil which he had already annotated, just as he must have taken the collection of extracts now in MS E I i l which he had compiled before leaving Italy.[88] The remaining travels of both the Virgil codex and the extracts are logical in view of their connection with Giovanni da Ragusa, particularly since Tortelli himself, so far as we know, was never in Basel. A possible reason behind Tortelli's disposal of the Virgil in Constantinople will be considered below.

Let us consider now the question of the character of Tortelli's annotations to the text of Virgil. First their extent: he begins on f. 1r, where he quotes Virgil, *Aen.* 4.171 to explain the use of *meditaris* in *Ecl.* 1.2, and his last entry is on f. 109r, where he illustrates the meaning of *furto* in *Aen.* 6.24 by a citation of *Georg.* 4.346. The more than 500 other notes in his hand between ff. 1r and 109r cover every *Eclogue* and every book of the *Georgics* and *Aeneid* with the exception of the eighth *Eclogue* and the fifth book of the *Aeneid*, which he did not gloss at all. The difference between his annotations and those of Salutati is simply this: while Salutati, as shown above, relies almost exclusively on Servius to supply mythological and geographical information about the Virgilian text, Tortelli's interest is relentlessly philological. He investigates the meaning and etymology of words, their metrical position in the line, and occurrences of the same or similar words and phrases elsewhere not only in Virgil but also in grammatical and other classical authors. Even Servius, whom he cites (by my count) thirty-one times, is used chiefly for this purpose, and it is clear that Tortelli's concerns are not for the same topics that attracted Salutati.

Such a marked shift of emphasis is owing, I think, to Tortelli's previous experience as a pupil himself under Vittorino da Feltre sometime between 1423 (when Vittorino came to Mantua) and 1433 (when we know that Tortelli was in Florence). A principal goal of this very influential educator

---

während der knapp fünf Monate bis zur Abreise des Johannes von Ragusa zur Verfügung gestanden hat." This explanation, however, does not take into account Tortelli's previous connection with the Salutati family or demonstrate why Tortelli would have occupied himself with Latin studies in Constantinople. The fact that Tortelli neglected to annotate the last six books of the *Aeneid* cannot be used as a measure of time, for usually the first six books of this work had more appeal and were annotated much more often than the last six.

88. After exploring various possibilities, Besomi concludes on the basis of watermarks and contents that Tortelli must have been still in Italy when he assembled the extracts in MS E I i l ("Un nuovo autografo," 124); also see below, pp. 115, 118.

was the attainment by his students of that thorough knowledge of Greek and Latin which was so essential for writing and speaking. In teaching ancient literature (which his pupils would attempt only after they had mastered grammar) he proceeded thus:

> Cicero and Vergil, to speak first of Latin writers, were naturally the corner-stones. Passages from both authors were from the first committed to memory as the basis of style, and as aids to vocabulary, and to prosody. With them Vittorino coupled Lucan and Ovid. But before prescribing a piece for recitation he took the greatest care in the explanation and rendering of the selected passage. His method in "reading" an author is described as follows. He dealt, first of all, with "verba," i.e. the exact meaning of each individual word and its construction in the sentence: that led up to the second part of the lesson, the exposition of "genus dicendi" or style; and this includes "ordo," "nexus," and "rhythmus verborum," as characteristic of the individual writer. Then the passage was further explained under "descriptio locorum," or allusions, and under "affectus personarum," or characters. All these points were illustrated from other passages of the same, or of another, author.... The matter thus given out was taken down by each member of the class, who formed, each for himself, his own written vocabulary, and collected examples of syntax and of prosody. The reverence of Vittorino for Vergil was characteristic of his age, and of his city.[89]

Vittorino's method, then, was philological for the most part, with literary interpretation as a secondary function. Tortelli's annotations in B put into practice (for the instruction of the young Coluccio?) nearly all of his own teacher's general prescriptions: a "basic" author like Virgil is chosen; certain words are singled out for explanation through citation of the same word in another passage from Virgil or a different author; phrases consisting of the same or similar words are located elsewhere in Virgil or other poets; finally, the authors chosen to illustrate explanations of words and phrases are among those recommended by Vittorino, namely, Cicero,

---

89. W. H. Woodward, *Vittorino da Feltre and Other Humanist Educators,* (Cambridge, 1897; repr. New York, 1963), 45–46. Regoliosi, "Nuove ricerche," 133–34 was the first to detect Tortelli's connection with Vittorino.

Homer, Livy, Lucan, Ovid, Pliny the Elder, Quintilian, Seneca, Valerius Maximus.[90] There is not much evidence in B for the literary interpretation of Virgil by Tortelli, but, if the codex and his annotations therein were used for teaching purposes, with the help of Salutati's notes he could have conveyed this aspect of textual study through oral observations, as Vittorino did.

While it would be tedious to discuss individually Tortelli's entries in B, it is important to examine them at least in a general way, for they are clear examples of the kind of training associated with Vittorino that equipped Tortelli in large measure to compose the *De orthographia*.[91] For the sake of completeness here as well as convenient comparison with the *De orthographia*, indices of Tortelli's lemmata and parallels in B are given at the end of this article, and it will be appropriate to treat now the annotations under the same headings, first in themselves and then with reference to the extracts in Basel MS E I i 1 and finally in connection with the *De orthographia*. Virgilian parallels, however, are considered with lemmata, since this is more convenient.[92]

---

90. *Ibid.*, 46–48.

91. Vittorino's insistence that his pupils learn Latin from the writings of the ancients themselves is novel; students of his contemporary Guarino Veronese used instead mnemonic verses and lexicons (A. T. Grafton and L. Jardine, "Humanism and the School of Guarino: A Problem of Evaluation," *Past & Present*, 96 [1982]: 62 ff.). There were, of course, other factors that aided Tortelli in the writing of the *De orthographia*, such as the rediscovery of the grammatical works of Probus, Diomedes, Charisius and others, and he acknowledges this indebtedness in the dedicatory epistle. W. K. Percival, "Changes in the Approach to Language," in *The Cambridge History of Later Medieval Philosophy*, (Cambridge, 1982), 812 leaves the impression that the reemergence of these writings was solely responsible for the *De orthographia;* but it should also be noted that Virgil, Cicero, and other authors whose works Tortelli would have studied under Vittorino figure much more prominently in the *De orthographia* than do the grammatical writers just named.

For Vittorino's own treatise dealing with Latin orthography cf. A. Casacci, "Un trattatello di Vittorino da Feltre sull' ortografia latina," *Atti del Reale Istituto Veneto di Scienze, Lettere ed Arti*, 86.2 (1926–27): 911–45 and R. Sabbadini, "L'Ortografia latina di Vittorino da Feltre e la scuola padovana," *Rendiconti della R. Accademia Nazionale dei Lincei, Classe di scienze morali, storiche e filologiche*, ser. 6, 4 (1928): 209–21. Negligible indeed is the influence which this brief composition seems to have had on Tortelli at least in the case of his annotations in B: Vittorino's sources are chiefly medieval and he cites Virgil only once (*Georg.* 1.165, a passage not quoted by Tortelli); of the words specifically mentioned by Vittorino, only slightly more than a dozen function as lemmata in B (they are, from Casacci's edition, *agger, Bacchus, carbasus, discrimen, erro, ferrum, hedera, hiems, honor, littus, Phoebus, scaena, stratus*) and Tortelli often uses a spelling different from that recommended by his teacher.

92. In the discussion that follows and also in the indices, I have taken the "lemma" to be the word(s) in the text of Virgil that appears also in the parallel; in a few instances the parallel contains a synonym instead of the exact same word. When the lemma consists of more than one

1. Lemmata and Virgilian parallels in B

If the sheer number of glosses added by Tortelli to each of the three works in B is any sort of trustworthy indication, the attention that he devoted to each of the works in B varies considerably. By my count he annotated from the *Eclogues* 60 separate lemmata that represent every *Eclogue* except the eighth, with the third *Eclogue* supplying the largest number of lemmata (12). Of the 127 lemmata which he annotated from the *Georgics*, books 1–4 furnish respectively 44, 29, 28, and 26 lemmata. From the *Aeneid* Tortelli quarried more lemmata than from the *Eclogues* and *Georgics* combined: a total of 212, which may be broken down into 54, 39, 76, 42 and 1 lemmata from books 1–4 and 6 respectively. His method of annotation is the same throughout the manuscript and usually consists of a short introductory phrase, with the name of the author and work (e.g., "Vir. IIII. Geor." or "Item 3° Eney." or "Item in 4°"), followed by a quotation that contains the lemma in a similar or different context. The lemma, if expressly noted by Tortelli (and for the most part it is not and must be ascertained from the context), precedes the name of the author and work. Virgil's own writings were by far Tortelli's favorite sources for parallels; he drew upon the *Eclogues*, *Georgics* and *Aeneid* 45 times to illustrate a word in the *Eclogues*, 40 times for the *Georgics* and 238 times in the case of the *Aeneid*.[93]

What motivated Tortelli to select a particular word for glossing in such a fashion? Evidence in this regard is scanty since he hardly ever inserts observations of his own, but I have found nineteen instances in which he gives a "personal" remark on the text:[94]

---

word, I cite them as a unit for the sake of clarity and hence do not include any intervening words in the text. I have also ignored the enclitics "-que" and "-ue" in the consideration of metrical position. Unless otherwise indicated, lemmata have the "classical" spelling for purpose of easy reference.

93. Tortelli's effort to explain Virgil by using Virgil himself is consonant with Valla's own tenets; cf. IJsewijn, "Laurentius Vallas 'Sprachliche Kommentare'" (above, note 17), 95–96: "Valla berücksichtigte sehr genau, welchen Text er vor sich hatte. Poesie ist keine Prosa; vereinzelte Fälle haben wenig oder gar keine Beweiskraft; bestimmte Schriftsteller haben einen sehr charakteristischen Sprachgebrauch oder einen eigenen Stil, dessen Merkmale nicht als allgemeingültig angesehen werden dürfen."

94. This list may not be exhaustive; as indicated above, the annotations of both Salutati and Tortelli often fill all the available blank space on a folio, and there is the possibility that a particularly brief "personal" comment could have escaped my attention.

(a) at *Ecl.* 2.21 *errant* (f. 2v), he comments, after citing parallels from Servius and *Georg.* 2.283, that the lemma has also the sense of "habitant" as in *Aen.* 3.644;

(b) at *Ecl.* 2.43 *iam pridem* (f. 2v), he notes "Iam pridem quod longo tempore, ad minus ultra diem, ut hic" and then cites as an example a short passage from the *De finibus* of Cicero;

(c) at *Ecl.* 3.18 *excipere* (f. 3v), he cites *Aen.* 4.114 as a parallel, notes then "Alibi ponitur pro cognouit" and follows this with a parallel from *Aen.* 4.297;

(d) at *Ecl.* 3.68 *parta* (f. 4r), he writes "*parta* idest pro parata" and adduces *Aen.* 3.495 as a parallel;

(e) at *Ecl.* 5.36 *mandauimus* (f. 6v), he understands "idest commisimus" and cites *Georg.* 1.223–224, which contains the synonym;

(f) at *Ecl.* 6.16 *procul* (f. 7v), he observes "alibi longe" as in *Georg.* 3.212–213;

(g) at *Ecl.* 10.57 *saltus* (f. 14r), he cites Varro, *De ling. lat.* 5.6.36 for two explanations of this word and remarks that in *Georg.* 3.143 "secundam significationem expressit Virgilius";

(h) at *Georg.* 1.149 *Dodona* (f. 17r), after citing Ovid, *Meta.* 13.716 ("Vocalemque sua terra [*sic*] dodonida quercu"), he digresses briefly and notes "In hac etiam fiebant ornatissima uasa querna" before citing *Aen.* 3.465–466;

(i) at *Aen.* 1.45 *turbine* (f. 48v), he notes "Turbine pro uertigine quadam positum" in *Aen.* 3.572–573;

(j) at *Aen.* 1.111 *urget* (f. 49v), his superscript note is very personal ("credo bene dicatur comprimit"), and the parallel from *Aen.* 3.578–579 is placed in the margin;

(k) at *Aen.* 1.123 *imbrem* (f. 49v), he remarks "imbrem pro quacumque aqua" as in *Georg.* 4.114–115 which he adduces as a parallel, and then adds "etiam pro tempestuosa pluuia" as in the parallel *Georg.* 1.333;

(l) at *Aen.* 1.484 *exanimumque* (f. 55r), he finds a synonym in *exsangue* ("Alio loco dixit exangue in secundo huius . . . [= *Aen.* 2.542–543]);

(m) at *Aen.* 1.574 (f. 56v), he observes "discrimine pro periculo positum" and cites *Aen.* 3.629 as an example of this other meaning;

(n) at *Aen.* 1.671 *Iunonia* (f. 58r), he adds superscript "quia carthago edificata erat sub iunonis nomine";

(o) at *Aen.* 1.698 *aurea* (f. 58v), he adds superscript "auro ornata ornauit";

(p) at *Aen.* 3.271 *Sameque* (f. 76r), he is not content with Servius' comment on this word (see pp. 111, 114 below) and cites testimonia from six other authors;

(q) at *Aen.* 3.579 *urgeri* (f. 81r), he gives a shortened version ("credo comprimi") of the observation in (j) above and cites *Aen.* 1.111 as a parallel;

(r) at *Aen.* 3.629 *discrimine* (f. 81v), he comments "alibi pro differentia ut in primo ..." (= *Aen.* 1.574), thus repeating the distinction made in (m) above;

(s) at *Aen.* 4.183 (*subrigit*) *auris* (f. 86r), he is seemingly remarking on a different form of a poetic expression when he observes "Alio usus est modo primo Eney. (= *Aen.* 1.152) 'silent arrectisque auribus astant'."

Brief though his own interventions are, they are telling nonetheless since they make it clear that Tortelli was primarily interested in determining the meanings of words through a comparison of their use elsewhere by Virgil and other authors. The same interest is evident in the numerous Virgilian parallels cited without a personal remark from Tortelli, as shown by the lists given below. Additional contexts for the Virgilian quotations selected seem to involve as well similarity of metrical position and reoccurrence of identical phrases in Virgil's own works or in later authors. We need hardly mention that all these points are in harmony with Vittorino's own method.

In keeping with the broad character of Tortelli's goals, lemmata themselves are varied. They represent the eight parts of speech and are descriptive, though admittedly not to an equal degree, of all topics that a teacher could be expected to discuss with regard to the *Eclogues, Georgics,* and *Aeneid* (e.g., rural life, natural phenomena, naval scenes, battle scenes, personal emotions, religious practices, grammatical points, etc.). The lemma prompting the largest number of parallels is *Sameque* (*Aen.* 3.271, f. 76r), which is illustrated by seven quotations, yet Tortelli as a general rule does not have many lemmata with "geographical" connotations; the only other examples are *Abydi* (*Georg.* 1.207, f. 17v), *Aegaeo* (*Aen.* 3.74, f. 73r), *Caystri* (*Georg.* 1.384, f. 20v), *Cnosiaque* (*Georg.* 1.222, f. 18r), *Cyllenius*

(*Georg.* 1.337 [f. 19v], *Aen.* 4.252 [f. 87r]), *Dodona* (*Georg.* 1.149, f. 17r), *Grynei* (*Ecl.* 6.72, f. 8v), *Gryneus* (*Aen.* 4.345, f. 89r), *Hydaspes* (*Georg.* 4.211, f. 42v), *Ithacus* (*Aen.* 2.122, f. 62r), *Leucatae* (*Aen.* 3.274, f. 76r), *Lyaeum* (*Aen.* 1.686, f. 58r), *Mygdonides* (*Aen.* 2.342, f. 65v), *Olympi* (*Ecl.* 5.56, f. 6v), *Olympo* (*Georg.* 1.450, f. 21v), *Pangaea* (*Georg.* 4.462, f. 46r), *Simoentis* (*Aen.* 1.618 [f. 57r], 3.302 [f. 76v]), *Tanaimque* (*Georg.* 4.517, f. 47r), *Thymbraee* (*Aen.* 3.85, f. 73v), *Thymbraeus* (*Georg.* 4.323, f. 44r), and *Tigrim* (*Ecl.* 1.62, f. 1v). Nor does he single out for comment names of personages: I have noted *Amphion* (*Ecl.* 2.24, f. 2v), *Aquilone* (*Georg.* 1.460, f. 21v), *Aquilonibus* (*Georg.* 2.334, f. 27v), *Arcturum* (*Georg.* 1.68, f. 15v), *Aurora* (*Aen.* 3.521, f. 80r), *Celaeno* (*Aen.* 3.245, f. 76r), *Indigetes* (*Georg.* 1.498, f. 22r), *Orion* (*Aen.* 4.52, f. 84r), *Pan* (*Georg.* 3.392, f. 36v), *Parcae* (*Ecl.* 4.47, f. 5v), *Phoebo* (*Aen.* 3.251, f. 76r), and *Volcano* (*Georg.* 1.295 [f. 19r], *Aen.* 2.311 [f. 65r]).

These specific types of lemmata form part of the largest general class, which, quite simply, embraces lemmata that consist of single words. Under this heading it may be observed that, in order to establish the meaning of a word, Tortelli often gives as a parallel another instance from a succeeding *Eclogue* or book of the *Georgics* and *Aeneid*, and then, when annotating this later occurrence in B, he uses the earlier appearance as a parallel, thus in effect setting up a system of cross-references. Such a practice, besides having the obvious pedagogical advantage of repetition, frequently exhibits the lemma, which may occupy the identical metrical position, in a different case or tense or as another word derived from the same root, and so reinforces grammatical and syntactical principles as well as quantity and poetic usage. The following list includes, apart from the proper names cited in the preceding paragraph, single-word lemmata which have this cross-reference function, with the asterisk signalling identical metrical position:

aggeribus (*Aen.* 2.496, f. 68r) and *aggerat* (*Aen.* 4.197, f. 86v)
alnos (*Georg.* 1.136, f. 16v) and *alnus* (*Georg.* 2.451, f. 29r)
ancora (*Aen.* 1.169, f. 50v) and *ancora* (*Aen.* 3.277, f. 76v)
arrectisque (*Aen.* 1.152, f. 50r) and *arrectaeque* (*Aen.* 4.280, f. 87v)
auribus (*Aen.* 1.152, f. 50r) and *auris* (*Aen.* 4.183, f. 86r)
auulsaque (*Aen.* 3.575, f. 81r) and *uulsis* (*Aen.* 3.650, f. 82r)
carmen (*Ecl.* 5.42, f. 6v) and *carmine* (*Aen.* 3.286–287, f. 76v)
cautes (*Aen.* 3.534 [f. 80r], 3.699 [f. 82v]) and *cautibus* (*Aen.* 4.366, f. 89r)

*chelydris (Georg. 2.214, f. 25v) and *chelydros (Georg. 3.415, f. 37r)

*crepitantibus (Georg. 1.85, f. 16r), *crepitantia (Georg. 4.151, f. 41v) and
  *crepitans (Georg. 1.449 [f. 21v], Aen. 3.70 [f. 73r])

*discrimine (Aen. 1.574, f. 56v) and *discrimine (Aen. 3.629, f. 81v)

*examina (Ecl. 7.13, f. 8v) and *examine (Georg. 4.139, f. 41v)

excipere (Ecl. 3.18, f. 3v) and excepit (Aen. 4.114, f. 85r)

exiguus (Georg. 1.181, f. 17r) and exiguus (Georg. 4.295, f. 43v)

extunderet (Georg. 1.133, f. 16v) and extuderat (Georg. 4.328, f. 44r)

fingitque (Georg. 2.407, f. 28v) and fingens (Aen. 4.148, f. 85v)

*glomerant (Georg. 1.323, f. 19v) and *glomeratque (Georg. 2.311,
  f. 27r)

*horrea (Georg. 1.49, f. 15r) and *horrea (Georg. 2.518, f. 30r)

ieiuna (Georg. 2.212, f. 25v) and ieiuna (Georg. 3.493, f. 38r)

ignibus (Aen. 1.90, f. 49r) and ignes (Aen. 3.199, f. 75r)

immane (Aen. 1.110, f. 49v) and immania (Aen. 3.583, f. 81r)

*intentique (Aen. 2.1, f. 59v) and *intentis (Aen. 3.716, f. 83r)

*inuia (Aen. 1.537, f. 56r) and *auia (Aen. 2.736, f. 71r)

lambere (Aen. 2.684, f. 70v) and lambit (Aen. 3.574, f. 81r)

laticis (Georg. 2.192, f. 25v) and laticum (Aen. 1.736, f. 59r)

luci (Georg. 1.209, f. 17v) and luce (Aen. 4.186, f. 86r)

lustra (Georg. 2.471, f. 29v) and lustra (Aen. 3.647, f. 82r)

*magalia (Aen. 1.421, f. 54r) and *magalia (Aen. 4.259, f. 87)

mugire (Aen. 3.92, f. 73v) and immugiit (Aen. 3.674, f. 82v)

nitens (Aen. 2.380, f. 66r) and nitens (Aen. 4.252, f. 87r)

obuerterit (Georg. 2.271, f. 26v) and obuertimus (Aen. 3.549, f. 80v)

opima (Aen. 2.782, f. 72r) and opimis (Aen. 3.224, f. 75v)

*passis (Aen. 1.480, f. 55r) and *passis (Aen. 3.263, f. 76r)

pernix (Georg. 3.93, f. 32r) and pernicibus (Aen. 4.180, f. 86r)

petit (Ecl. 3.64, f. 4r) and petit (Georg. 2.505, f. 30r)

*pone (Aen. 2.208, f. 63v) and *pone (Aen. 2.725, f. 71r)

*quidue (Aen. 1.9, f. 48r) and *quid (Aen. 1.518, f. 55v)

*reclusit (Georg. 4.52, f. 40r) and *recludit (Aen. 1.358, f. 53v)

retexit (Aen. 1.356, f. 53r) and retexerit (Aen. 4.119, f. 85r)

rimantur (Georg. 1.384, f. 20v) and rimantur (Georg. 3.534, f. 38v)

ruptis (Georg. 1.472, f. 21v) and ruptis (Aen. 3.580, f. 81r)

saliente (Ecl. 5.47, f. 6v) and salientem (Georg. 3.460, f. 37v)

*saucius (Aen. 2.223, f. 63v) and *saucia (Aen. 4.1, f. 83r)

*stratis (Aen. 3.176, f. 74v) and *strato (Aen. 3.513, f. 80r)

stringunt (Ecl. 9.61, f. 13r), stringere (Georg. 1.305, f. 19r) and stringe (Georg.
  2.368, f. 28r)

sulpura (*Georg.* 3.449, f. 37v) and *sulpure* (*Aen.* 2.698, f. 70v)
terebrare (*Aen.* 2.38, f. 60r) and *terebramus* (*Aen.* 3.635, f. 81v)
torquet (*Aen.* 4.269, f. 87v) and *torquet* (*Aen.* 4.482, f. 91r)
torsit (*Georg.* 4.529, f. 47v) and *contorsit* (*Aen.* 3.562, f. 80v)
trahit (*Aen.* 2.321, f. 65r) and *trahebat* (*Aen.* 2.457, f. 67r)
ueniamque (*Aen.* 3.144, f. 74v) and *ueniam* (*Aen.* 4.50, f. 84r)
uersat (*Georg.* 3.258, f. 34v) and *uersat* (*Aen.* 4.286, f. 88r)
*uinitor (*Ecl.* 10.36, f. 14r) and **uinitor* (*Georg.* 2.417, f. 28v)
uiscera (*Aen.* 1.211, f. 51r) and *uisceribus* (*Aen.* 3.622, f. 81v)
ululantibus (*Georg.* 1.486, f. 22r) and *ulularunt* (*Aen.* 4.168, f. 86r)
urget (*Aen.* 1.111, f. 49v) and *urgeri* (*Aen.* 3.579, f. 81r)
uulgo (*Georg.* 1.476, f. 21v) and *uulgo* (*Georg.* 3.246, f. 34v).

This list now allows us to survey specific philological points which Tortelli was able to establish from his reading of Virgil. For example, the poet's use of adjectives: *saucius* and *saucia* describe respectively a bull wounded by an ax and Dido wounded by love, and so the word is said both of animals and human beings; *arrectisque* and *arrectaeque* signify the pricking-up of hair or ears; *immane* and *immania* are applied to rocks forming a ridge in the sea and to monsters in the forest, and *exiguus* to the size of a mouse and a place (hence to both inanimate and animate objects); *opima* and *opimis* characterize fields and feasts; *pernicibus* (*alis*) and *pernix* imply the speed of heavenly beings; past participles of *auello* and *uello* connote violence, one describing an eruption of Aetna and the other the food of the Cyclops; the present participle of *salio* depicts the flowing of blood or water; *passis* adds to the emotional impact of a scene when joined with *crinibus* of the suppliant Trojan women and *palmis* of Anchises who is making a sacrifice; the Carthaginian audience pays close attention to Aeneas both at the beginning (*intentique*) and end (*intentis*) of his story. Verbs express usually a single meaning or occur in passages with similar content. *Glomerant* and *glomeratque*, for instance, are part of the description of a storm, and *torquet* describes the literal and figurative turning of the heavens by Atlas and Jupiter; but *excipere* ("to snare" [a goat]) and *excepit* ("replied") illustrate different meanings of the same verb. As for nouns and pronouns, in both occurrences *carmen* (*-ine*) has the sense of "inscription" and *ueniam* that of "favor" from the gods, while *quid*, the initial word in both lines, is the equivalent of "cur" and introduces an indirect question. Doubtless the rarity of such a curious word as *magalia* explains why Tortelli adduces a parallel containing the same word ("huts" [of the Carthaginians]).

There are also, naturally, many times when Tortelli chooses a word that is not a proper name and illustrates it by a parallel, but does not gloss in turn this parallel by citing the line with the original lemma or another example. Such annotations serve the same purposes of grammar, syntax, meaning and quantity as those which function as cross-references. Since the equivalents supplied by the parallels are not immediately evident from the Index of Lemmata below, I give the following list of occurrences not found in any of the above lists (the first word is that cited in the Index of Lemmata, the second is that found in the parallel, and the asterisk denotes identical metrical position):

*agitabo (Georg. 3.18, f. 31r) — *agitet (Aen. 3.609)
*agmine (Aen. 2.212, f. 63v) — *agmine (Aen. 1.82)
*amborum (Ecl. 1.61, f. 1v) — *utroque (Georg. 3.33)
arguta (Ecl. 7.1, f. 8v) — argutumque (Georg. 3.80)
*aurea (Ecl. 3.71, f. 4r) — aurea (*Aen. 1.492; Ecl. 8.52)
cantando (Ecl. 3.25, f. 3v) — arando (Georg. 2.239) and habendo (Georg. 2.250)
*carbasus (Aen. 4.417, f. 90r) — *carbasus (Aen. 3.357)
carcere (Aen. 1.54, f. 48v) — carceribus (Georg. 1.512)
classem (Aen. 1.39, f. 48v) — classis (Aen. 3.300)
cogant (Aen. 4.289, f. 88r) — coge (Ecl. 3.20)
*culpam (Aen. 4.172, f. 86r) — *culpae (Aen. 4.19)
*discrimina (Aen. 1.204, f. 51r) — *discrimine (Aen. 3.629)
*erepte (Aen. 3.711, f. 83r) — *erepte (Aen. 3.476)
*excipit (Aen. 3.318, f. 77r) — *excepi (Aen. 4.374)
falces (Georg. 1.508, f. 22r) — falce (Ecl. 3.11)
*figere (Ecl. 2.29, f. 3v) — *figere (Georg. 1.308)
focus (Ecl. 7.49, f. 9r) — focos (Aen. 3.134)
*furto (Aen. 6.24, f. 109r) — *furta (Georg. 4.346)
hiems (Aen. 1.122, f. 49v) — hiemem (Georg. 3.470), hiememque (Aen. 3.195)
ilice (Ecl. 6.54, f. 8r) — ilice (Georg. 4.81)
*ingentem (Aen. 3.555, f. 80v) — *ingenti (Georg. 1.334)
*intiba (Georg. 1.120, f. 16v) — *intiba (Georg. 4.120)
laterum (Aen. 1.122, f. 49v) — latera (Georg. 3.523)
*laxis (Aen. 1.122, f. 49v) — *laxis (Georg. 2.364), laxant (Georg. 2.331)
liba (Ecl. 7.33, f. 9r) — liba (Georg. 2.394)
liber (Ecl. 10.67, f. 14v) — libro (Georg. 2.77)

limen (*Ecl.* 5.56, f. 7r) — *limen* (*Georg.* 3.317)

lustramurque (*Aen.* 3.279, f. 76v) — *lustrabimus* (*Ecl.* 5.75)

*meditaris (*Ecl.* 1.2, f. 1r) — **meditatur* (*Aen.* 4.171)

messor (*Ecl.* 3.42, f. 4r) — *messorem* (*Georg.* 1.316)

*nidis (*Georg.* 2.210, f. 25v) — **nidis* (*Georg.* 4.17)

noua (*Ecl.* 3.86, f. 4v) — *noua* (*Georg.* 4.357)

nox (*Aen* 3.147, f. 74v) — *nox* (*Aen.* 3.512)

optauitque (*Aen.* 3.109, f. 74r) — *optate* (*Aen.* 3.132)

paeniteat (*Ecl.* 2.34, f. 2v) — *paeniteat* (*Aen.* 1.549)

*paupere (*Aen.* 3.615, f. 81v) — **pauper* (*Aen.* 2.87)

*praecipitant (*Aen.* 4.251, f. 87r) — **praecipitat* (*Aen.* 2.9)

prora (*Aen.* 1.104, f. 49v) — *proras* (*Aen.* 3.532)

*puniceaeue (*Georg.* 3.372, f. 36v) — **puniceis* (*Ecl.* 5.17)

quam (*Aen.* 1.327, f. 53r) — *quam* (*Aen.* 4.11, 47)

*rudentis (*Aen.* 3.267, f. 76r) — **rudentis* (*Aen.* 3.682), **rudentem* (*Aen.* 3.561)

saeptis (*Ecl.* 1.33, f. 1r) — *saepta* (*Georg.* 4.159)

saltus (*Ecl.* 10.57, f. 14r) — *saltibus* (*Georg.* 3.143)

*sentibus (*Ecl.* 4.29, f. 5v) — **sentibus* (*Aen.* 2.379)

sertis (*Aen.* 4.202, f. 86v) — *sertisque* (*Aen.* 1.417)

*sidere (*Aen.* 4.309, f. 88r) — **sidere* (*Georg.* 1.1)

sinus (*Georg.* 4.420, f. 45v) — *sinus* (*Aen.* 2.23)

*spirisque (*Aen.* 2.217, f. 63v) — **spiram* (*Georg.* 2.154)

squalentibus (*Georg.* 4.91, f. 40v) — *squamis* (*Georg.* 4.93), *squalent* (*Georg.* 1.507)

*statio (*Aen.* 2.23, f. 59v) — **statio* (*Georg.* 4.421)

sua (*Ecl.* 1.37, f. 1v) — *sua* (*Aen.* 3.469)

subnixa (*Aen.* 3.402, f. 78r) — *subnixus* (*Aen.* 4.217)

*temo (*Georg.* 3.173, f. 33r) — **temo* (*Georg.* 1.171)

tenditque (*Aen.* 1.18, f. 48r) — *tendit* (*Aen.* 2.220)

torquet (*Aen.* 1.117, f. 49v) — *torquent* (*Aen.* 3.532)

*tranat (*Aen.* 4.245, f. 87r) — **tranant* (*Georg.* 3.270)

trudunt (*Aen.* 4.405, f. 90r) — *truditur* (*Georg.* 2.31), *trudit* (*Georg.* 2.335)

*turbine (*Aen.* 1.45, f. 48v) — **turbine* (*Aen.* 3.573)

uiae (*Georg.* 1.41, f. 15r) — *uia* (*Georg.* 2.22).

From this second list we may also infer that Tortelli was able to make a number of interesting observations. First, he might notice the different moods and tenses of *agito* and establish that *amborum* and *utroque* are synonyms. *Arguta* and *argutum* have different meanings when modifying respectively an ilex ("whispering") and head of a horse ("clean-cut"), while *torquet* and *torquent* both describe a ship's motion and *culpam* and *culpae* Dido's illicit love for Aeneas. In one instance *figere* concerns the killing of stags and in the other the killing of does. The tricks of the gods are associated with *furto* and *furta*. *Puniceaeue* and *puniceis* do possible double duty as indications of poetic usage since the nouns they modify (*pennae* and *rosetis*) are each at the end of the line. The parallels given for *rudentis* deserve notice, for Tortelli must have meant to show the difference in meaning between words made up of identical letters. This lemma and *rudentis* at *Aen.* 3.682 signify the sheets (of a ship), while *rudentem* (*Aen.* 3.561) is the present participle of *rudo* and conveys the image of the "groaning" prow of a ship. In the matter of grammar and syntax, *cantando* and its parallels illustrate the function of a gerund; the fact that the passive *lustramurque* is used in a middle sense probably accounts for its inclusion (the parallel *lustrabimus* reflects more "normal" usage). And so forth. Similar reasons could also be given to explain Tortelli's choice of the remaining lemmata in this list.

Finally, it is instructive to note that, when he points out occurrences of phrases which are identical or nearly so elsewhere in Virgil, he often uses the same cross-reference system mentioned above. As with single-word lemmata, the content of these phrases varies considerably, and their mere presence in the poet's works may be reason enough for his interest in them. In the following list are given all instances involving recurring Virgilian phrases cited by Tortelli as parallels, whether or not they constitute cross-references, and the asterisk denotes metrical position that corresponds wholly or partially:

*a sanguine Teucri (Aen. 1.235 [f. 51v], 4.230 [f. 87r])
*aere cauo (Aen. 3.240 [f. 75v], 286)
*aestus harenis (Aen. 1.107, f. 49v) and *aestu harenae (Aen. 3.557, f. 80v)
*agens telis (Aen. 1.191 [f. 50v], 4.71 [f. 84r])
*angusti Pelori (Aen. 3.411, f. 78v) and *angusta Pelori (Aen. 3.687)
*auditur fractos (Georg. 4.72, f. 40v) and *audimus fractasque (Aen. 3.556)
*aurae uocant (Aen. 3.356–357, f. 77v) and *uocat auras (Aen. 4.417)
*aurea subnectens (Aen. 1.492, f. 55v) and *aurea subnectit (Aen. 4.139, f. 85v)
*carchesia Bacchi (Georg. 4.380, f. 45r) and *carchesia Baccho (Aen. 5.77)
*comae et uox faucibus haesit (Aen. 2.774 [f. 71v], 4.280)
corpora curamus (Aen. 3.511, f. 80r) and corpora curant (Georg. 4.187)

ferro foedare (*Aen.* 2.55 [f. 60r], 3.241 [f. 75v])

fessos sopor artus (*Aen.* 3.511, f. 80r) and *fessosque sopor artus* (*Georg.* 4.190)

flamma medullis (*Georg.* 3.271, f. 34v) and *flamma medullas* (*Aen.* 4.66, f. 84r)

haud ac iussi faciunt (*Aen.* 3.236 [f. 75v], 561 [f. 80v])

horrida barba (*Aen.* 4.251, f. 87r) and *horrida barbis* (*Georg.* 3.366)

hortamur fari quo sanguine cretus (*Aen.* 2.74, f. 60v) and *fari quo sanguine cretus hortamur* (*Aen.* 3.608–609, f. 81v)

iacet insula (*Aen.* 3.692 [f. 82v], 104)

iam pridem (*Ecl.* 5.55, f. 2v; *Aen.* 2.647, f. 69v)

in numerum (*Ecl.* 6.27 [f. 7v]; *Georg.* 4.175 [f. 42r])

indicit honorem (*Aen.* 1.632, f. 57v) and *indicit honores* (*Aen.* 3.264, f. 76r)

ingentem farris aceruum populant (*Aen.* 4.402–403, f. 89v) and *populatque ingentem farris aceruum* (*Georg.* 1.185)

lacte distenta capellae (*Ecl.* 4.21, f. 5r) and *distentas lacte capellas* (*Ecl.* 7.3, f. 8v)

lapidosa corna (*Georg.* 2.34, f. 23r) and *lapidosaque corna* (*Aen.* 3.649, f. 82r)

litora myrtetis (*Georg.* 2.112, f. 24r) and *litora myrtos* (*Georg.* 4.124)

malis absumpsere (*Georg.* 3.268, f. 34v) and *malis absumere* (*Aen.* 3.257)

nec moritura crudeli funere (*Georg.* 3.263, f. 34v; *Aen.* 4.308, f. 88r)

nocturnique orgia Bacchi (*Georg.* 4.521, f. 47r) and *Baccho orgia nocturnusque* (*Aen.* 4.302–303, f. 88r)

opere feruet (*Aen.* 4.407, f. 90r) and *feruet opus* (*Aen.* 1.436)

ore solutos (*Georg.* 1.399, f. 20v) and *soluto oraque* (*Georg.* 2.386–387)

perfidus ille (*Aen.* 4.421, f. 90r; *Ecl.* 8.91)

Phoebeae lampadis (*Aen.* 3.637, f. 81v) and *Phoebea lampade* (*Aen.* 4.6)

placidam membra quietem (*Aen.* 1.691, f. 58v) and *placidam membris quietem* (*Aen.* 4.5)

pressabimus ubera (*Ecl.* 3.99, f. 4v) and *ubera pressat* (*Aen.* 3.642, f. 82r)

redimitus tempora (*Aen.* 3.81, f. 73v; *Georg.* 1.349)

silicis excuderet (*Georg.* 1.135, f. 16v) and *silici excudit* (*Aen.* 1.174, f. 50v)

Simoentis ad undam (*Aen.* 1.618 [f. 57r], 3.302 [f. 76v])

squameus spiram (*Georg.* 2.154, f. 24v) and *spirisque squamea* (*Aen.* 2.217–218, f. 63v)

tilia leuis (*Georg.* 1.173, f. 17r) and *tiliae leues* (*Georg.* 2.449, f. 29r)

trabe cauauit (*Aen.* 2.481, f. 67v) and *caua trabe* (*Aen.* 3.191, f. 75r)

uinoque sepultam (*Aen.* 2.265, f. 64v) and *uinoque sepultus* (*Aen.* 3.630, f. 81v)

uiuoque saxo (*Aen.* 1.167, f. 50v) and *uiuo saxo* (*Aen.* 3.688, f. 82v)

uox exaudita (*Georg.* 1.476, f. 21v) and *exaudiri uoces* (*Aen.* 4.460, f. 90v).

2. Non-Virgilian parallels in B

Of the 18 authors used by Tortelli to supply parallels to lemmata from the *Eclogues*, *Georgics* and *Aeneid*, 5 are poets (Homer, Lucan, Lucretius, Ovid, Seneca) and 13 are prose writers (Apuleius, ps.-Aristotle, Cicero, Livy, Macrobius, Nonius Marcellus, Pliny the Elder, Priscian, Quintilian, Servius, Solinus, Valerius Maximus, Varro). All but Lucretius, Macrobius, Nonius Marcellus, Servius and Solinus were used as school authors by his teacher, Vittorino da Feltre. In general, Tortelli's quotations from prose writers and other poets function in the same way with regard to meaning, metrical similarity, different grammatical forms, etc. as do the Virgilian parallels. Servius is, of course, almost always commenting on a passage in Virgil, while Nonius Marcellus and Priscian often do so.[95] Among the poets Ovid is the most fruitful source for parallels, and of the prose writers Nonius Marcellus claims that distinction.

The contributions of four of the poets can be dispatched quickly. Lucan and Lucretius are each cited once and for similar lemmata. At *Georg.* 4.291 (f. 43v), *(fecundat) harena* is compared to *(stagnares* [sic]*) harenas* of Lucan, *Bellum ciuile* 2.417, and the words occupy in both instances the fifth and sixth feet of the line. The use of *bibula* to modify *harena* (*Georg.* 1.114, f. 16r) is also found in Lucretius, *De rer. nat.* 2.376 (*bibulam harenam*), and the noun is the last word in each line. Likewise there is but a single citation from Seneca (*Troad.* 518 "gressus nefandos dux Cephalonum [*sic*] admouet"), and this in connection with Servius' equation of Same and Cephalonia (*Aen.* 3.271, f. 76r and see above, p. 101). At *Aen.* 1.689 (f. 58v) there are two citations from Homer (shown in Plate III), and here Tortelli is concerned to show that *dictis* is a translation of μῦθος ("istud quod a Virgilio dictum habetur apud Homerum μῦθος ut in primo: κρατερὸν δ' ἐπὶ μῦθον ἔτελλε [= *Iliad* 1.25, 379]. Item alibi ὡς ἔφατ', ἔδδεισσιν (sic) δ' ὁ γέρων καὶ ἐπείθετο μῦθος [*Iliad* 1.33, 24.571]'). These are the only instances of Greek parallels adduced by Tortelli, and, apart from a single Greek word in a quotation from Varro, *De ling. lat.* 5.6.36 at *Ecl.* 10.57 *saltus* (f. 14r),[96] the only specimens of his Greek hand. He does not even insert the Greek in the passages chosen from Macrobius'

95. This fact enables Tortelli to remain faithful to Vall's principle of explaining the poet by the poet (above, note 93).
96. Tortelli writes νῆμη instead of νὲμη.

works, noting merely "quaere ibi" at the place where the Greek should have been written. The paucity of Greek is surprising in the light of Valla's reference to Tortelli's zeal for Greek studies even before Tortelli's journey to Constantinople;[97] but any emphasis on Greek would have been, of course, unnecessary if he were teaching the young Coluccio who had made little or no progress in this subject.

Three of Ovid's poems supply Tortelli with twenty-seven parallels, some of which seem expressly designed to show his dependence on and imitation of Virgil. For example, in the single citation from the *Ars amatoria*, Ovid's description of a love-charm made from the forelock of a new-born foal (2.100 "datque quod a teneri fronte reuellit equi") resembles the love-charm prepared by Dido for Aeneas (*Aen*. 4.515, f. 91v "quaeritur et nascentis equi de fronte reuulsus"). The close relationship between the two poets is also evident in the *Metamorphoses* (cited twenty-five times), particularly in books 13 and 14 which deal with the wanderings of the Trojans. Hence Tortelli notes the verbal and metrical similarity evident when Aeneas and his men are received by Anius, king of Delos and priest of Apollo (*Aen*. 3.80, f. 73v "rex Anius, rex idem hominum Phoebique sacerdos," *Meta*. 13.632 "Anius quo rege homines, antistite Phoebus") and when they continue on their way after the encounter with the Harpies on the islands of the Strophades (*Aen*. 3.271, f. 76r "Dulichiumque Sameque et Neritos ardua saxis," *Meta*. 13.711–712 ". . . Dulichios portus Ithacamque Gamumque [*ut uid*.] Naritiasque [*sic*] domos"). Note as well that Perseus, in flying to the realm of Atlas, looks down and sees the lands below (*Meta*. 4.623–624 ". . . ex alto seductas aethere longe despectat terras") as does Jupiter when he looks down from heaven and sees the sufferings of Aeneas and his men (*Aen*. 1.223–224, f. 51r ". . . aethere summo despiciens . . . terrasque"). Other Ovidian parallels illustrate the meaning of single lemmata in Virgil and evoke similarities of poetic usage and concept whether or not the lemma is repeated in the parallel. As examples the following may be cited (the asterisk signals identical metrical position): Daphnis harnessed tigers to a chariot (*Ecl*. 5.29 *tigris*, f. 6r) and Bacchus lynxes (*Meta*. 4.24–25); the drunken Silenus is a *senex* (*Ecl*. 6.18, f. 7v) and a drunken *senex* follows Bacchus (*Meta*. 4.26); *temo* is part of the plough

97. In a letter addressed to Tortelli and dated by the editors to 1434–35 Valla writes: "Accepi te [i.e., Tortelli] mirifice deditum litteris grecis, quod mihi pergratum est;" cf. O. Besomi and M. Regoliosi, eds. *Laurentii Valle Epistole* (Padua, 1984), 149–50, no. 6.

(*Georg. 1.171, f. 17r) used by farmers and Apollo's chariot (*Meta. 2.107) driven by Phaethon; Proteus tries to escape Aristaeus by transforming himself into wondrous shapes (*Georg. 4.441 miracula, f. 46r) and Phaethon in his panic sees strange shapes in the air (*Meta. 2.193 miracula); present and perfect participles characterize the motion of snakes' tongues (Aen. 2.211 uibrantibus, f. 63v) and thunderbolts (Meta. 2.308 uibrataque); "tomorrow" is expressed by postera (dies . . .) Aurora in *Aen. 3.588–589 (f. 81r) and postera Aurora in *Meta. 4.81–82; Ascanius receives the gift of a cloak from Andromache before he leaves Troy (*Aen. 3.484 chlamydem, f. 79v) and from Anius before he leaves Delos (*Meta. 13.679–680). The one parallel from the Metamorphoses that does not fit into this familiar pattern is cited at Aen. 3.245 (f. 76r), where Tortelli observes that in Meta. 13.709–715 Aello and not Celaeno is the Harpy who frightens the Trojans. Finally, it may be noted that the quotation from Fasti 3.871 ("paene simul periit de [ut uid.] uult succurrere lapsae"), which Tortelli enters at Aen. 1.611 (f. 57r), is a rather curious illustration of this line. The lemma is given in the Index below as petit (corresponding to uult), but the point seems to be that, just as Aeneas grasps his comrades with his right and left hands, so Helle grasps the ram's horn with her left hand (Fasti 3.869–870); however, these lines are not cited by Tortelli.

To take now the prose writers. Seven of these supply each a single parallel. In his quest to determine the name and location of Same (Aen. 3.271, f. 76r), Tortelli cites as witnesses Apuleius (Florida), ps.-Aristotle (De mirabilibus auscultationibus), and Valerius Maximus, who disagree with Servius, In Aen. 3.271, but does not give the actual text from ps.-Aristotle and Valerius Maximus. A further geographical consideration prompts a paraphrase at Aen. 3.274 (f. 76r) from Livy, and here, seemingly for the first and only time in B, Tortelli glosses a note written by Coluccio Salutati. The word in this line that interests Salutati is Leucatae, and his entry ("Leucata mons est altissimus in promontorio epiri iuxta ambrachiam ciuitatem") is a faithful extract from Servius, In Aen. 3.274 Leucatae; ambrachiam in turn interests Tortelli, although this word does not occur in Aen. 3.274, and he identifies the city with help from Livy. Cicero, on the other hand, is cited for his use of iam pridem in De fin. 5.8.23, which, according to Tortelli, helps to explain the meaning of the same phrase in Ecl. 2.43 (f. 2v). A similar grammatical concern is responsible for the citations at Aen. 2.99 in uulgum ambiguas (f. 62r) of an "anonymous commentator," i.e., Servius, on Donatus ("Repperi in quodam antiquo grammatico super arte donati hunc textum debere legi 'in uulgum ambiguam' et uulgum generis esse femenini aliquando") and at *Georg*. 3.143 *pascunt* (f. 33r) of Quintilian, *Instit. orat*. 9.3.7 (to the effect that some verbs have both active and deponent forms).

The same geographical and grammatical interests may be offered as reasons for Tortelli's use of parallels from other prose authors whom he cites rather more often, namely, Pliny the Elder (twice), Priscian (4 times), Solinus (4 times) and Varro (15 times).

Pliny's *Natural History* and Solinus' *Collectanea rerum naturalium* supply, naturally, the geographical information. Both Pliny and Solinus are cited at *Georg*. 1.207 *Abydi* (f. 17v), but the passage selected to explain the city's location is taken from Solinus alone. Pliny is cited again, briefly, at *Aen*. 3.271 *Sameque* (f. 76r) for the fact that Cephalonia was formerly called Melaena. There are fairly lengthy quotations from Solinus on the subjects of *Ecl*. 2.24 *Amphion* (f. 2v), *Georg*. 4.211 *Hydaspes* (f. 42v) and *Aen*. 2.342 *Mygdonides* (f. 65v), and so Tortelli apparently found him a more congenial or more convenient author than Pliny.

Three works of Priscian provide grammatical reasons for the occurrence of certain puzzling words and forms in Virgil. The poet's seeming contravention of the rules of quantity when he begins *Aen*. 2.664 (f. 70r) with *hoc erat* is set straight in *Instit. gramm*. 12.25 where Priscian records the older practice of writing "hocce." *Aen*. 2.642 *una* (f. 69v), modifying the plural *excidia*, is shown in *De fig. num*. 25 to be acceptable usage, and the unusual meanings of *Aen*. 1.5 *quoque* (f. 48r) and *Aen*. 1.479 *interea* (f. 55r) are clarified in *Partit. XII uersuum Aen*. 7.142 and 11.199 respectively.

Books 5 and 7 of Varro's *De lingua latina* also serve Tortelli's philological interests in a number of ways. To explain Virgil's poetic meaning and usage, he consulted especially book 7 (11 quotations), which discusses rare and difficult words in the writings of the poets. The passages chosen from Varro help Tortelli to understand the meaning and origin of such "agricultural words" as *rura* (*Ecl*. 2.28, f. 2v [*De ling. lat*. 5.6.40]) and *saltus* (*Ecl*. 10.57, f. 14r [*De ling. lat*. 5.6.36]) and "sea words" like *ratibus* (*Ecl*. 4.32, f. 5v [*De ling. lat*. 7.2.23]), *aequora* (*Georg*. 1.206 [*De ling. lat*. 7.2.23]), *freta* (*Aen*. 1.607, 3.127, ff. 57r, 74r [*De ling. lat*. 7.2.22]). He solves the problem of the etymology of *agresti* (*Ecl*. 1.10, f. 1r) and *cornua* (*Georg*. 3.222, f. 34r) by citing parts of *De ling. lat*. 7.3.24 and 7.3.25 respectively. *De ling. lat*. 5.20.100 illustrates the difference between *Tigrim*

(*Ecl.* 1.62, f. 1v) and *tigris* (*Georg.* 4.510, f. 47r); the location and etymology of *Olympi* (*Ecl.* 5.56, f. 6v) and *Aegaeo* (*Aen.* 3.74, f. 73r) are dealt with in *De ling. lat.* 7.2.20 and 7.2.22. The ancient poets also shed light on the meanings of *canibus* (*Ecl.* 3.67, f. 4r [*De ling. lat.* 7.3.32]), *polumque* (*Aen.* 2.251, f. 64r [*De ling. lat.* 7.2.14]), and *infula* (*Aen.* 2.430, f. 67r [*De ling. lat.* 7.3.24]).

The forty-three quotations from the *De compendiosa doctrina* of Nonius Marcellus, the fourth-century lexicographer and grammarian, make this by far the prose work most frequently cited by Tortelli and further emphasize the goal of his investigation of Virgilian vocabulary. By far the most helpful discussion from his point of view, that is, the meaning of words in Virgil's poems, was book 6 "De inpropriis" ("On Words Used Metaphorically"), which he cites thirty-three times. Nonius' treatment of "De differentia similium significationum" in book 5 and "De numeris et casibus" in book 9, each cited three times, are a distant second. Tortelli uses Nonius' book 7 "De contrariis generibus uerborum" ("On Abnormal Verb-Forms") twice (at *Georg.* 3.81 *luxuriatque*, f. 32r and *Aen.* 2.145 *miserescimus*, f. 62v), book 10 "De mutatis coniugationibus" once (at *Georg.* 3.221 *lauit*, f. 34r) and book 12 "De doctorum indagine" once (at *Georg.* 1.203 *atque*, f. 17v). The lemmata which Tortelli chose to illustrate by reference to Nonius' compilation are extremely varied, as may be seen from the Index of Parallels below, and they are often the words on which Nonius himself is commenting.

We may now examine more closely Tortelli's use of Servius as compared with that of the earlier owner of B. It has been shown in Part I above that Salutati's numerous annotations are for the most part more or less faithful extracts from this unnamed commentator. Tortelli was clearly aware of the identity of Salutati's source, for occasionally he adds "Ser." by way of identification at the conclusion of the excerpt, as on ff. 17r, 20v, 24v, 25r–v. He himself used Servius too: I have found in Tortelli's hand 18, 6, and 6 quotations respectively from Servius' commentary on the *Aeneid*, *Eclogues* and *Georgics*. Obviously the relatively meager total of 30 at once suggests a different approach. This suspicion is confirmed by the fact that Tortelli's quotations are usually quite brief, so much so that in some instances he does not bother to identify his source.[98] Moreover, Salutati's use of Servius on geographical, mythographical,

---

98. Some examples are: at *Ecl.* 3.86 *noua* (f. 4v) Tortelli comments "Noua idest magna" (Servius, *In Ecl.* 3.86 " 'Noua carmina', magna, miranda"); at *Ecl.* 7.1 *arguta* (f. 8v) he adds supra-

historical, and anthropological points (see Part I above) did not influence Tortelli to do the same. By my count he drew on Servius a mere two times for geographical information, namely, at *Georg.* 4.517 *Tanaimque* (f. 47r) and *Aen.* 3.271 *Sameque* (f. 76r), and in the latter instance it is only to disagree with him. Apart from a brief quotation of Servius at *Georg.* 1.68 *Arcturum* (f. 15v) to provide astronomical identification, in nearly all the remaining instances Tortelli extracts from Servius' commentaries the meaning of various words, dispensing with "unnecessary" information that Servius might have supplied in the passage.[99] What might be termed "exceptions" (although they have to do with philological matters) are these: at *Aen.* 1.186 *Lyaeum* (f. 58r) he cites Servius on a stylistic matter ("Lyaeum pro Lyaeium dixit, figurate ponens principalitatem pro deriuatione"); at *Ecl.* 3.25 *cantando* (f. 3v) and *Georg.* 2.239 *arando* (f. 26r) he is interested in grammar and cites Servius, *In Aen.* 1.713 for the active and passive sense of the gerund.

The common focus of Salutati's annotations in B is summed up in Part I of this article as follows: ". . . all function to clarify the literal meaning of the text, to make the difficulties of Virgil's Latin less perplexing . . . the *raison d'être* for each note remains the same: to clarify what Virgil wrote." I would suggest that on the whole the major difference between the two annotators can be ascertained from their use of Servius: Tortelli, unlike Salutati, employed Servius not to establish *what* Virgil wrote but *how* he wrote. His interest in language and style need not have precluded explanations to the young Coluccio of the same topics that interested the grandfather, but such comments were already present in the codex and hence Tortelli was free to apply the new principles of his own teacher to the reading of Virgil.

It remains to treat the last of the prose authors from whom Tortelli drew parallels. This is Macrobius, who furnished Tortelli with three citations from his commentary on Cicero's *Somnium Scipionis* and sixteen citations from his *Saturnalia*. In Tortelli's fairly extensive quotations from these works is found a variety that is lacking elsewhere in his annotations in B. For example, astronomical information is the reason for the two passages from *In somn. Scip.* 1.15.12 and 1.18.14–15 at *Georg.* 2.478 *defectus solis*

script "sonora, aliter breuis . . ." (cf. Servius, *In Ecl.* 7.1 " 'arguta' autem modo canora, stridula; alibi 'argutum' breue significat"); at *Georg.* 1.41 *uiae* (f. 15r) he notes "uiae idest ratione" (Servius, *In Georg.* 1.41 " 'ignarosque uiae mecum' . . . aut mecum uiae, idest rationis").

99. Such as the geographical, mythological and historical information which interested Salutati.

(f. 29v) and *Georg.* 1.217 *candidus auratis* (f. 18r) respectively, while a cosmological detail is behind the citation of *In somn. Scip.* 1.17.15 at *Aen.* 1.47 *et soror et coniunx* (f. 48v). The motif most often found in the excerpts from the *Saturnalia* is, of course, the language used by Virgil, but with a slightly different twist. There are several categories: the citation adduced at *Ecl.* 10.52 *spelaea* (f. 14r), *Georg.* 4.179 *daedala* (f. 42r) and *Georg.* 4.462 *Pangaea* (f. 46r) is from *Sat.* 5.17.15 (or 15–16) and deals with Virgil's love of Greek and use of Greek words; regarding *Aen.* 1.42 *ignem* (f. 48v), 2.351 *excessere* (f. 65v) and 3.251 *Phoebo* (f. 76r) he cites *Sat.* 5.22.7–8, 11–14 to explain that the lines are actually imitations of Euripides and Aeschylus; certain words employed by Virgil (*Georg.* 1.85 *crepitantibus* [f. 16r], *Georg.* 2.462 *uomit undam* [f. 29v], *Aen.* 2.782 *agmine* [f. 72r]) had already been used in the same way by Ennius and Lucretius; the possible meanings that could be attached to *Ecl.* 6.17 *cantharus* (f. 7v) and *Aen.* 3.699 *proiectaque* (f. 82v) are given in *Sat.* 5.21.14–16 and 6.4.14–15 respectively. The remaining four citations from the *Saturnalia* deal with various matters, such as the division of time (*Aen.* 3.587 *nox intempesta*, f. 81r), practice of libation (*Aen.* 1.736 *mensam laticum libauit*, f. 59r), Sallust's reference to theatrical settings (*Georg.* 3.24 *scaena*, f. 31r) and the shape and use of *lituus* (*Georg.* 3.183 *lituosque*, f. 33v).

3. The relationship between B and MS E I i 1

Tortelli's autograph extracts from classical and late antique Latin authors in Basel, Öffentliche Bibliothek der Universität MS E I i 1 occupy ff. 355r–417v in a paper codex that otherwise preserves Giovanni da Ragusa's compilation of the "Gesta Concilii Basiliensis." In his wide-ranging discussion of these "schede," Besomi points out that the manuscript must have been acquired from Tortelli when both Giovanni da Ragusa and Tortelli were in Constantinople, hence sometime between 1435 and 1437; given the Latin contents of the extracts and the watermarks, he makes the very plausible suggestion that Tortelli assembled the extracts while still in Italy since his main purpose in coming to Constantinople was the study of Greek.[100] This, then, would place the extracts, like the annotations in B, early in Tortelli's career.

---

100. Besomi, "Un nuovo autografo," 124 and see above at note 88.

The extracts vary in character and fall into two divisions: ff. 355r–389r contain lemmata arranged in a roughly alphabetical order and illustrated by quotations from one or more authors; ff. 390r–417v are more homogeneous, comprising passages from Macrobius' *Saturnalia* (ff. 390v–398r) and Servius' commentaries on the *Aeneid* and *Georgics* (ff. 413r–415v).[101] Not only does Tortelli's method of citing an extract (e.g., "Vir. Geor. li. II" and "Idem eodem .li.," shown in Plate III of Besomi's study) correspond to what has been noted in B, but he cites some of the same authors whom he used to illustrate lemmata in B. Let us examine the latter similarity in more detail so as to resolve the question of a possible relationship between the two manuscripts.

First, Tortelli's extracts in MS E I i 1 number approximately 500, as do his annotations in B. Next, citations from Lucretius, Nonius Marcellus, Ovid (*Fasti, Metamorphoses*), Quintilian (*Institutio oratoria*), Solinus, Varro (*De lingua latina*), Virgil (*Aeneid, Eclogues, Georgics*), and, of course, Macrobius (*Saturnalia*) and Servius (commentaries on the *Aeneid* and *Georgics*) occur in both codices. Virgil is the most frequently cited author in the two manuscripts, and in both Tortelli quotes almost exclusively from the first six books of the *Aeneid* (in MS E I i 1 there is one citation from book 7), with special emphasis on books 1–3 and no quotations from book 5. The passages selected for quotation which are the same in both manuscripts are the following (lemmata, where present, and folio number are supplied):

MS E I i 1	B
Macrobius, *Sat.* 1.3.2–15	Macrobius, *Sat.* 1.3.15
dies (ff. 364v–365v)	*nox intempesta* (f. 81r)
——— 5.17.15–20 (f. 392v)	——— 5.17.15–16
	spelaea (f. 14r), *daedala* (f. 42r),
	Pangaea (f. 46r)
——— 5.21.14–16 (f. 393v)	——— 5.21.14–16 *cantharus* (f. 7v)
——— 5.22.7–15 (f. 393v)	——— 22.7, 8, 9–10, 11–14 *Pan*
	(f. 36v), *ignem* (f. 48v), *excessere*
	(f. 65v), *Phoebo* (f. 76r)
——— 6.4.8–5.4 (f. 394v)	——— 6.4.14–15 *proiectaque* (f.
	82v)

101. These are the divisions noted by Besomi, *ibid.*, 99 ff.

———— 6.7.9–8.8 (f. 396r)

Servius, *In Aen.* 1.686 (f. 414r)

———— 1.713 (f. 414v)

Varro, *De ling. lat.* 5.6.40 *pratum* (f. 379r)

Virgil, *Aen.* 2.21–23 *stationem* (f. 373r)

————, *Aen.* 2.223–224 *excussit* (f. 358v)

————, *Georg.* 1.184–185 *ferre* (f. 368v)

————, *Georg.* 4.521 *sacrum* (f. 372v)

———— 6.8.1 *lituosque* (f. 33v)

Servius, *In Aen.* 1.686 *laticis* (f. 25v), *Lyaeum* (f. 58r)

———— 1.713 *cantando* (f. 3v), *arando* (f. 26r)

Varro, *De ling. lat.* 5.6.40 *rura* (f. 3v)

Virgil, *Aen.* 2.23 *sinus* (f. 45v)

————, *Aen.* 2.223 *saucia* (f. 83r)

————, *Georg.* 1.185 *ingentem farris aceruum populant* (f. 89v)

————, *Georg.* 4.521 *Baccho orgia nocturnusque* (f. 88r).

Tortelli exhibits the same general philological concerns in MS E I i l that were evident in his annotations to the text of Virgil in B, and he uses the same authors in a similar way, even as regards the noticeable brevity of the passages from Servius. For MS E I i l Besomi describes Tortelli's procedure thus:

. . . il Tortelli ricava di preferenza dal testo di Macrobio notizie che riguardano l'antiquaria e l'etimologia di termini greci e latini. Sono pure riprese con una certa ampiezza informazioni di carattere scientifico, indicazioni di tipo letterario, stilistico e retorico, giudizi su autori antichi, notizie varie. . . . Al Tortelli interessa soprattutto l'interpretazione letterale data da Servio all'opera virgiliana, attraverso la quale il grammatico non considera solo le parole per determinarne il senso nel passo commentato, ma ne indica anche altri significati, precisando se il loro uso riveste un senso proprio o figurato. Pone meno attenzione, per contro, all'interpretazione letteraria del poema. . . . Si può così osservare che delle circa 180 schede che il Tortelli estrasse da Servio (per lo più molto brevi, di una sola o di poche righe), oltre un terzo riflette le spiegazioni che il commentatore dà per mettere a fuoco il senso proprio e il valore di ogni parola: commento lessicale che Servio costruisce per lo più con il confronto del termine con altri simili o dissimili, della stessa famiglia o con sinonimi. . . . Il contenuto delle schede [lemmata on ff. 359r–389r] è vario. Di molti termini viene semplicemente documentata la presenza in testi classici . . ., con particolare riferimento a Virgilio. In questi casi il Tortelli riproduce unicamente un verso o passi brevissimi. Qualche volta invece di un singolo termine indica più esempi che ne danno accezioni diverse. . . . Ma il nucleo più grosso dello schedario comprende voci di cui viene proposto il significato, sempre attraverso la citazione di testi classici, per lo più letterari o giuridici.[102]

There are, however, some differences. For one thing, of the 27 authors cited in MS E I i l, only 9 figure also in B, and only 13 quotations are common to both manuscripts. Then there is the emphasis in MS E I i l on juridical texts, a feature certainly lacking in B. In light of such striking facts, it is scarcely prudent to postulate one of the Basel codices as the source of the other and hence to declare that one is older than the other. What they both show is Tortelli's investigation of Latin authors for lexical and stylistic purposes; the extracts in MS E I i l are equally in keeping with the training that Tortelli received from Vittorino da Feltre. What we may affirm with some assurance, in view of Giovanni da Ragusa's book acquisitions at Constantinople, is that Tortelli by early 1435 must have worked on both MS E I i l and B. The two sets of annotations may be earlier; they may even be to some extent contemporary since they reflect similar interests on his part and the same lack of Greek citations (which is understandable if both sets of annotations were assembled in Italy).

4. The relationship between B and the *De orthographia*

In purpose and style Tortelli's glosses in B are remarkably close to the testimonia given for the spelling and meaning of words in his monumental *De orthographia*. This encyclopedic work is certainly later in date;[103] it establishes the Latin spelling of Greek words, and Tortelli expounds,

---

102. *Ibid.,* 105–106, 107–108, 112–13.
103. See L. Capoduro, "L'edizione romana del 'De orthographia' di Giovanni Tortelli (Hain 15563) e Adamo da Montaldo," in M. Miglio et al., eds. *Scrittura biblioteche e stampa a Roma nel Quattrocento. Atti del 2° seminario 6–8 maggio 1982. Littera antiqua* 3 (Vatican City, 1983), 39 and note 11 for the various dates proposed (between 1449 and 1453); she suggests that a copy was given to Pope Nicholas V, the dedicatee, towards the end of 1451.

first, general rules that apply to each letter of the alphabet and then gives an alphabetical list of Greek words taken over into Latin (this list constitutes over three quarters of the treatise). Every entry in the list contains an explicit statement of how the word should be spelled and what it means, followed by, usually, at least one quotation from an ancient author to support this spelling and meaning, and Tortelli often takes the opportunity to insert geographical, mythological, historical and antiquarian information. As a typical example we may cite from BAV, MS Vat. lat. 1978, the autograph copy of the *De orthographia*, the entry for *Anius* (f. 67v) (I have introduced modern capitalization and punctuation):

> Anius cum *i* latino scribitur. Rex fuit in Delo, dicente Virgilio li°
> Enei. II°: "Rex Anius, rex idem hominum Phoebique sacerdos," de
> quo Ouidius li° Metamorph. XIIII° plura scripsit. Hic filium habuit
> Andrum, a quo Andros insula in qua regnauit denominata fuit, ut
> ostendit Ouidius praefato loco.

It so happens that the line from Virgil (*Aen.* 3.80) is one which Tortelli chose to annotate in B (f. 73v) by a quotation from Ovid, *Meta.* 13.632–633, the lemma being "Anius" here as well. Even this single instance indicates that his entries in B are precisely the kind that could have served him well in the compilation of the *De orthographia*. But did, in fact, his annotations in B perform such a service? Before anyone postulates that Tortelli had this codex actually at hand while at work on the *De orthographia*, and is then obliged to explain how he retrieved the manuscript after disposing of it in Constantinople, it would be prudent to examine more closely the material (lemmata and quotations) common to both. For the character and extent of this evidence must determine the relationship between B and the *De orthographia*.

There is, unfortunately, no modern edition of the *De orthographia*, and none of the fifteenth- and sixteenth-century printings has an index of lemmata or authors.[104] In order to ascertain what are the shared features, I have scanned the whole of MS Vat. lat. 1978 (the autograph copy) and have indeed found words that function as whole or partial or slightly different lemmata both for the *De orthographia* and for Tortelli's notes in B. In the list that follows, the lemma is spelled as it appears in MS Vat.

---

104. For the printing history of the *De orthographia*, see M. D. Rinaldi, "Fortuna e diffusione del 'De orthographia'," *IMU*, 16 (1973): 200–243.

lat. 1978 and the folio number in parentheses signals its occurrence in that manuscript; the asterisk signifies Tortelli's use in both MS Vat. lat. 1978 and B of the same passage from Virgil or another author to illustrate the word:[105]

*Abydus (f. 44r)
Aegaeum (f. 48v)
*Amphion (f. 64r)
ancora (f. 67r)
*Anius (f. 67v)
Arcturus (f. 76r)
*Arion (f. 77v)
Bacchus (f. 7r)
*cantharus (f. 101r)
*Cayster (f. 98r)
Celeno (f. 106v)
chlamys (f. 120r)
*Cnosius (f. 120v)
coma (f. 122r)
*corymbus (f. 124r)
Cyllenius (f. 110v)
daedalus (f. 131r)
*Dodona (f. 149v)
errare (f. 161r)
*foedo (f. 143r)
*Gryneum (f. 171v)
hedera (f. 174v)
horreum (f. 198r)
hortor (f. 198r)
hululo (f. 199r)
Hydaspes (f. 182r)

hyems (f. 182r)
imber (f. 203v)
*indico (f. 39v)
*intyba (f. 204r)
Ithacus (f. 208r)
lituus (f. 218r)
Lyaeus (f. 213r)
*mapalia (f. 224v)
*Mygdonides (f. 233v)
myrtus (f. 236r)
nox (f. 249r)
Olympus (f. 244v)
orgia (f. 252r)
Orion (f. 252v)
Pangaeum (f. 259v)
Pelorus (f. 266r)
*Phoebus (f. 276v)
*scaena (f. 332v)
sidus (f. 339r)
*Simois (f. 342r)
*Tanais (f. 356r)
telum (f. 359r)
Teucer (f. 364v)
*Thymbreus (f. 367v)
traho (f. 200r)
uni, unae, una (f. 39r)
Vulcanus (f. 376v).

The total comes, by my count, to a shared 53 lemmata, of which 20 are illustrated by shared parallels. There are also approximately 50 instances where Tortelli introduces parallels found in B to illustrate

---

105. So far as I know, this list is exhaustive, but absolute certainty is impossible until the *De orthographia* is critically edited with indexes. As regards the words cited from B, I have sometimes given, for the sake of clarity, the nominative form when the word actually appears in another case (e.g., *Cahistri, Theucri*), but in every instance the relevant spelling is that of Tortelli.

words in the *De orthographia* that are different from the lemmata in B; e.g., *Georg.* 1.85 (lemma *crepitantibus*) is cited under the word *agricola* (f. 57r) and *Georg.* 2.192 (lemma *laticis*) under the word *patera* (f. 263r). Given the magnitude of the *De orthographia* and the large number of Tortelli's entries in B, the statistics are not necessarily overwhelming in favor of Tortelli's debt to B as a *direct* source for the *De orthographia*. The statistics demonstrate, certainly, that some of the same material can be found in both, and his attention to metrical position in B was undoubtedly very helpful when he came to assign quantity to vowels of individual words in the *De orthographia*; but the statistics also show that his interests had changed as regards the choice of words to be included in the *De orthographia*. At a conservative estimate, certainly more than half the words treated in the *De orthographia* are proper names, while the list just given includes all the Greek names which Tortelli glossed in B, and which comprise only a very small portion of the total lemmata in B. Although the *Eclogues*, *Georgics* and *Aeneid* offer many additional examples of Greek words taken over into Latin, particularly proper names, Tortelli simply preferred, in the case of B, to devote most of his attention to purely Latin words. Clearly, at this point in his career the problems discussed in the *De orthographia* had not yet begun to occupy him.

Further, it is instructive to compare Tortelli's spelling of Latinized Greek proper names in B with the authoritative version in the *De orthographia*. Some names have the same spelling in both: Amphion, Anius, Arcturus, Celeno, Dodona, Ithacus, Olympus, Orion, Pelorus. But different spellings for other names make up a slightly larger group, as may be seen from these variations:[106]

B	*De orthographia* (MS Vat. lat. 1978)
Abidos (f. 17v)	*Abydus* (f. 44r)
Bachus (ff. 47r, 88r)	*Bacchus* (f. 87r)
Cahister (f. 20v)	*Cayster* (f. 98r)
Cylen(n)ius (ff. 19v, 87r)	*Cyllenius* (f. 110v)
Egeum (f. 73r)	*Aegaeum* (f. 48v)
Gnosia (f. 18r)	*Cnosia* (f. 120v)
Grineus (ff. 8v, 89r)	*Gryneus* (f. 171v)

106. This list could be made longer by the inclusion from B of proper names that occur in the parallels cited by Tortelli but are not themselves lemmata. The types of variation, however, would remain the same.

Hidaspes (f. 42v)	*Hydaspes* (f. 182r)
Lyeium (f. 58r)	*Lyaeus* (f. 213r)
Migdonides (f. 65v)	*Mygdonides* (f. 233v)
Simeontis (ff. 57r, 76v)	*Simoentis* (f. 342r)
Theucri (ff. 51v, 87r)	*Teucer* (f. 364v)
Tymbree (ff. 44r, 73v)	*Thymbree* (f. 367v).

The same uncertainty regarding diphthongs, the insertion of aspirant *h*, and the use of *y* and *i* is also noticeable in lemmata that are not proper names in B. There Tortelli records, for example, "an*c*hora" (ff. 50v, 76v), "*c*lamidem" (ff. 79v, 85v), "cor*i*(mbis)" (f. 3v), "fedare" (ff. 60r, 75v), "int*i*ba" (f. 16v), "mirtos" (f. 24r), "scenisque" (f. 31r), "sydere" (f. 88r), but in the *De orthographia* he insists on "ancora" (f. 67r), "*c*hlamys" (f. 120r), "corymbus" (f. 124r), "foedo" (f. 143r), "intyba" (f. 204r), "myrtus" (f. 236r), "scaena" (f. 332v), "sidus" (f. 339r). On the other hand he also has the same spelling in both for some words that are not proper names, such as *cantharus, coma, horrea, hyems, lituus, nox,* etc.

The inconsistencies of spelling suggest, I think, that when Tortelli annotated B he had not yet done the advanced research on the spelling of Greek words in Latin that is evident in the *De orthographia*. And, it may be repeated, the choice of lemmata in B shows that the topic did not particularly attract him at this time. We do not know his reasons for disposing of the codex in Constantinople; the answer may be as simple as the fact that his interests could have changed during his stay in that city. Strictly speaking, he would not need to have had at hand the annotations in B while composing the *De orthographia*, for he did not insert them *en bloc* into the latter work; they could have been helpful in a general way, just as was, doubtless, the training he received from Vittorino da Feltre, who required his pupils to memorize what seem to us prodigiously large portions of ancient texts.[107] In any event, B is interesting for the light it sheds on the difference of textual method and purpose between Salutati, who was still wedded to the medieval grammatical tradition, and Tortelli, the representative of the new philological interests. In his own way, Tortelli was as zealous a scholar, but he has not been equally studied. Surely other manuscripts will come to light,

---

107. Woodward, *Vittorino da Feltre* (above, note 89), 45, note 3: "It is said that not a few of his pupils could before leaving school repeat the whole of Vergil, entire speeches, treatises and letters of Cicero, large parts of Livy, and the whole of Sallust."

like the codex briefly discussed in the Appendix, that will contain further
traces of his scholarly activity and perhaps will further illustrate the various
stages in his career.

VIRGINIA BROWN AND CRAIG KALLENDORF

APPENDIX

The recovery of Tortelli's library still remains a desideratum. As a small contribution, it may be pointed out that Oxford, Bodleian Library MS Auct. F.2.6,
a twelfth-century codex of the *Aeneid*, seems to have been at one time in Tortelli's
possession: he copied on f. 1v the twelve hexameters (*Anthol. lat.* C. 634) that
often precede the poem as *argumenta*, and he is the scribe of ff. 2r–10v (*Aen.*
1.1–2.104); there are also notes in his hand scattered throughout the margins
of the manuscript (the last entry seemingly on f. 91r at *Aen.* 12.451 with the
comment "Comparatio") and frequently he rewrote faded lines or words.[108]
Obviously, then, Tortelli did not restrict his study of Virgil to just B, a fact
already evident from the *De orthographia* where he quotes from all twelve books
of the *Aeneid* and not just from *Aeneid* 1–4 and 6 as in B.

In the Oxford manuscript Tortelli's notes are much briefer than his annotations in B, and of a different nature, consisting for the most part of the simple
marginal notation of figures of speech or words that are usually but not always
proper names (e.g., "apheresis," "Ortygia," "res"). The few exceptions are, as
in B, quotations or explanations illustrating a lemma (which I have supplied in
italics):[109]

(f. 11r) *Aen.* 2.131 *exitium* — Exitium dicitur eo quod prestet exitum rebus
humanis [cf. Varro, *De ling. lat.* 5.10.60].

---

108. I owe to Dr. A. C. de la Mare my knowledge of Tortelli's activity regarding this manuscript.
The codex is briefly described by F. Madan, *A Summary Catalogue of Western Manuscripts in the
Bodleian Library at Oxford,* 3 (Oxford, 1895), 17, no. 8855, and identified as the codex given to
Nicholas Heinsius by Ovidio Montalbani (1601–72), physician and professor of philosophy at Bolo-
gna. I have examined this manuscript only on microfilm.

109. Another humanistic hand has made occasional entries in MS Auct. F.2.6, and this list
comprises only those notes which can be attributed with some certainty to Tortelli. There may,
of course, be other notes which a personal inspection of the codex would reveal to be Tortelli's
as well, but they would have this same general character.

(f. 11r) *Aen.* 2.140 *effugia* — Effugium. Ovidius: "Aspiciunt oculis superi mortalia iustis" [*Meta.* 13.70].

(f. 24v) *Aen.* 4.35 *esto* — Esto: aduerbium concedentis [Servius, *In Aen.* 4.35]

(f. 71r) *Aen.* 10.145 *Capys* — Nota quod Capis Capuam condidit.

(f. 78v) *Aen.* 11.4 *Eoo* — Prima pars solis orientis.

None of these longer marginal notes appears in B, but they reflect a similar approach and interest. The single-word entries, however, indicate a special philological concern that is not at all prominent in B; to the best of my knowledge, in B Tortelli does not identify even one figure of speech, and it has already been observed that his annotations in B do not demonstrate by any means a definite bias for proper names of persons and places. The Oxford manuscript tells a different story: of the 86 instances in which Tortelli wrote a geographical or personal name in the margin, all but 13 (among them such decidedly "Latin" examples like "Anagnia", "Aventinus") appear in the *De orthographia*, which exhibits for these words, in 37 instances, also the Virgilian line(s) "annotated" in the Oxford codex; of the 12 figures of speech identified by Tortelli in the Oxford witness, all appear in the *De orthographia*. Often his spelling of these names and terms is not consistent; some examples are:

MS Auct. F.2.6	*De orthographia* (MS Vat. lat. 1978)
Achimenides (f. 23r)	*Achaemenides* (f. 44v)
Agillina (f. 53v)	*Agellina* (f. 54r)
Agregas (f. 23v)	*Acragas* (f. 46v)
Astianata (f. 22r)	*Astyanax* (f. 82r)
Calidonia (f. 50r)	*Calydonia* (f. 99v)
Hiacynthos (f. 19v)	*Zacynthos* (f. 378v)
ipalage (ff. 55v, 56r–v, 86v)	*hypallage* (f. 183v)
(h)iperbole (ff. 15v, 21r, 23v, 55r)	*hyperbole* (f. 183v)
synalimpha (f. 17v)	*synaloepha* (f. 342v)
syneresis (f. 50r)	*synaeresis* (f. 342r).

Tortelli's notes in MS Auct. F.2.6 deserve further study. They show the same variation in the use of diphthongs, *h*, and *i* for *y* evident in his annotations in B; this would seem to indicate that the Oxford manuscript was likewise in his possession prior to the compilation of the *De orthographia*. Exactly how early in his career it is impossible to determine at present, given the available evidence, but MS Auct. F.2.6 does seem more directly connected with the *De orthographia* than B. It may not be too wide of the mark to suggest that Tortelli studied

MS Auct. F.2.6 after his return from Constantinople and at a time when he was actually involved in the production of the *De orthographia*.[110]

INDICES

I

Index of Tortelli's Lemmata [111]

a sanguine Teucri (*Aen.* 1.235): *Aen.* 4.230–231
a sanguine Teucri (*Aen.* 4.230): *Aen.* 1.235
Abydi (*Georg.* 1.207): Solinus, *Coll. rer. mem.* 10.21; Pliny, *Hist. nat.* 4.11.49
adfare (*Aen.* 4.424): Nonius, *De comp. doct.* 463
adurat (*Georg.* 1.93): Servius, *In Georg.* 1.93
aedificant (*Aen.* 2.16): Nonius, *De comp. doct.* 452
Aegaeo (*Aen.* 3.74): Varro, *De ling. lat.* 7.2.22

---

110. This hypothesis is strengthened by evidence found in Tortelli's *epistolario* (BAV, MS Vat. lat. 3908, which comprises only letters addressed to him). Among his correspondents was Agostino Scanella, a close friend, who was a pupil of Niccolò Volpe at Bologna during the late 1440s. Scanella was studying and commenting on the *Aeneid* during this period, and repeatedly asked Tortelli to supply him with a manuscript of Virgil since his own was incomplete (e.g., ff. 21r, 22r, 24r and letter nos. 15, 16, 18 according to the inventory of M. Regoliosi, "Nuove ricerche intorno a Giovanni Tortelli," *IMU*, 9 [1966]: 137–38). Eventually Scanella received the desired manuscript, for he thanks Tortelli warmly in a letter dated 12 December (s.a.), Bologna and observes that Tortelli himself had copied the "first book": "... Virgilium ea die habui qua me orbatum tuo aspectu reliquisti. Qui tam gratus mihi extitit ut uerbis dicere nequeam, nam conspiciens ego librum primum manu tua scriptum nil gratius uidere potui cum et tuas litteras uiderem" (f. 30r, no. 27 [Regoliosi, *ibid.*, 139–40]). By 9 December 1450 Scanella was dead and his books had been sold by his teacher Volpe (f. 99r–v, no. 110 [Regoliosi, *ibid.*, 155–56]: Volpe's letter of this date to Tortelli). Hence 1450 is the *terminus post quem non*.
    I suggest that the codex of Virgil given by Tortelli to Scanella is now MS Auct. F.2.6 (in which Tortelli copied the first book of the *Aeneid*). This identification is all the more plausible in view of the Bolognese provenance mentioned in note 108 above. Tortelli may have been slow to send the manuscript to Scanella simply because first he had to recopy the opening folios; if he performed this task sometime during the 1440s (as seems likely), MS Auct. F.2.6 is definitely to be placed in the period after his return from Constantinople and before the completion of the *De orthographia* (sometime between 1449 and 1453, note 103 above).
    111. See above, note 92 for the principles according to which the lemmata are reported; "classical" spelling is used for the lemmata in both indices. Multiple parallels to lemmata are given in the order of occurrence in B.

aequora (*Georg.* 1.206): Varro, *De ling. lat.* 7.2.23

aere cauo (*Aen.* 3.240): *Aen.* 3.286

aestu harenae (*Aen.* 3.557): *Aen.* 1.106–107

aestus harenis (*Aen.* 1.107): *Aen.* 3.557

aethere summo despiciens terrasque (*Aen.* 1.223–224): Ovid, *Meta.* 4.623–624

agens telis (*Aen.* 1.191): *Aen.* 4.71–72

agens telis (*Aen.* 4.71): *Aen.* 1.191

aggerat (*Aen.* 4.197): *Aen.* 2.496

aggeribus (*Aen.* 2.496): *Aen.* 4.197

agitabo (*Georg.* 3.18): *Aen.* 3.609

agitauimus (*Aen.* 2.421): Servius, *In Aen.* 3.609

agmine (*Aen.* 2.212): Servius, *In Aen.* 2.212; *Aen.* 1.82

agmine (*Aen.* 2.782): Macrobius, *Sat.* 6.4.4

agresti (*Ecl.* 1.10): Varro, *De ling. lat.* 7.3.24

alnos (*Georg.* 1.136): *Georg.* 2.451

alnus (*Georg.* 2.451): *Georg.* 1.136

amborum (*Ecl.* 1.61): *Georg.* 3.33

Amphion (*Ecl.* 2.24): Solinus, *Coll. rer. mem.* 7.21

ancora (*Aen.* 1.169): *Aen.* 3.277

ancora (*Aen.* 3.277): *Aen.* 1.169

angusti Pelori (*Aen.* 3.411): *Aen.* 3.687

Anius rex idem hominum Phoebique sacerdos (*Aen.* 3.80): Ovid, *Meta.* 13.632–633

Aquilone (*Georg.* 1.460): *Georg.* 2.334

Aquilonibus (*Georg.* 2.334): *Georg.* 1.460

arando (*Georg.* 2.239): Servius, *In Aen.* 1.713

Arcturum (*Georg.* 1.68): Servius, *In Aen.* 3.516

ardua (*Georg.* 2.67): Ovid, *Meta.* 4.90; *Aen.* 3.619

arguta (*Ecl.* 7.1): Servius, *In Ecl.* 7.1; *Georg.* 3.79–80

arrectaeque (*Aen.* 4.280): *Aen.* 1.152

arrectisque (*Aen.* 1.152): *Aen.* 4.280

atque (*Georg.* 1.203): Nonius, *De comp. doct.* 530

audit (*Georg.* 1.514): Nonius, *De comp. doct.* 466

auditur fractos (*Georg.* 4.72): *Aen.* 3.555–556

auia (*Aen.* 2.736): *Aen.* 1.537

auidaeque (*Georg.* 2.375): Nonius, *De comp. doct.* 442

aurae uocant (*Aen.* 3.356–357): *Aen.* 4.417

aurea (*Ecl.* 3.71): Servius, *In Ecl.* 3.71; *Ecl.* 8.52–53; *Aen.* 1.492

aurea subnectens (*Aen.* 1.492): *Aen.* 4.139

aurea subnectit (*Aen.* 4.139): *Aen.* 1.492

auribus (*Aen.* 1.152): *Aen.* 4.183

auris (*Aen.* 4.183): *Aen.* 1.152
Aurora (*Aen.* 3.521): *Georg.* 1.447
auulsaque (*Aen.* 3.575): *Aen.* 3.650

Baccho orgia nocturnusque (*Aen.* 4.302–303): *Georg.* 4.521
biberunt (*Ecl.* 3.111): Nonius, *De comp. doct.* 453
bibula harena (*Georg.* 1.114): Lucretius, *De rer. nat.* 2.376

caelatum (*Ecl.* 3.37): *Aen.* 1.640–641; Servius, *In Aen.* 1.640
candidus auratis (*Georg.* 1.217): Macrobius, *In somn. Scip.* 1.18.14–15
canibus (*Ecl.* 3.67): Varro, *De ling. lat.* 7.3.32
cantando (*Ecl.* 3.25): Servius, *In Aen.* 1.713; *Georg.* 2.239; *Georg.* 2.250
cantharus (*Ecl.* 6.17): Macrobius, *Sat.* 5.21.14–16
carbasus (*Aen.* 4.417): *Aen.* 3.357
carcere (*Aen.* 1.54): *Georg.* 1.512
carchesia Bacchi (*Georg.* 4.380): *Aen.* 5.77
carmen (*Ecl.* 5.42): *Aen.* 3.286–287
carmine (*Aen.* 3.287): *Ecl.* 5.42
castris (*Georg.* 4.108): Servius, *In Aen.* 3.519
catulorum (*Georg.* 3.245): Nonius, *De comp. doct.* 457
caua trabe (*Aen.* 3.191): *Aen.* 2.480–482
cautes (*Aen.* 3.534): *Aen.* 3.699; *Aen.* 4.366
cautes (*Aen.* 3.699): *Aen.* 4.366
cautibus (*Aen.* 4.366): *Aen.* 3.699; *Aen.* 3.534
Caystri (*Georg.* 1.384): Ovid, *Meta.* 5.385–387
Celaeno (*Aen.* 3.245): Ovid, *Meta.* 13.709–715
chelydris (*Georg.* 2.214): *Georg.* 3.415
chelydros (*Georg.* 3.415): *Georg.* 2.214
chlamydem (*Aen.* 3.484): Ovid, *Meta.* 13.679–680
chlamydem limbo (*Aen.* 4.137): Ovid, *Meta.* 5.51
classem (*Aen.* 1.39): *Aen.* 3.300
Cnosiaque (*Georg.* 1.222): *Aen.* 3.115
cogant (*Aen.* 4.289): *Ecl.* 3.20
comae et uox faucibus haesit (*Aen.* 2.774): *Aen.* 4.280
compulerantque (*Ecl.* 7.2): Servius, *In Ecl.* 7.2
contorsit (*Aen.* 3.562): *Georg.* 4.529
cornua (*Georg.* 3.222): Varro, *De ling. lat.* 7.3.25
corpora curamus (*Aen.* 3.511): *Georg.* 4.187
crepitans (*Aen.* 3.70): *Georg.* 1.85
crepitans (*Georg.* 1.449): *Georg.* 1.85
crepitantia (*Georg.* 4.151): *Georg.* 1.85

crepitantibus (*Georg.* 1.85): *Georg.* 1.449; *Georg.* 2.540; *Georg.* 4.151; *Aen.* 3.69–70; Macrobius, *Sat.* 6.4.5

culpam (*Aen.* 4.172): *Aen.* 4.19

Cyllenius (*Aen.* 4.252): *Georg.* 1.337

Cyllenius (*Georg.* 1.337): *Aen.* 4.252

daedala (*Georg.* 4.179): Macrobius, *Sat.* 5.17.15

dapes (*Ecl.* 6.79): Nonius, *De comp. doct.* 461

dare lintea (*Aen.* 3.686): Ovid, *Meta.* 7.40

defectus solis (*Georg.* 2.478): Macrobius, *In somn. Scip.* 1.15.12

dente (*Georg.* 2.406): Nonius, *De comp. doct.* 462

deuota (*Aen.* 1.712): Nonius, *De comp. doct.* 460

dictis (*Aen.* 1.689): Homer, *Iliad* 1.25, 379; Homer, *Iliad* 1.33, 24.571

discrimina (*Aen.* 1.204): *Aen.* 3.629

discrimine (*Aen.* 1.574): *Aen.* 3.629

discrimine (*Aen.* 3.629): *Aen.* 1.574

distentas lacte capellas (*Ecl.* 7.3): *Ecl.* 4.21

Dodona (*Georg.* 1.149): Ovid, *Meta.* 13.716; *Aen.* 3.465–466

domos (*Georg.* 2.209): Nonius, *De comp. doct.* 461

dorsum (*Aen.* 1.110): Nonius, *De comp. doct.* 459

enixae (*Aen.* 3.327): Nonius, *De comp. doct.* 458

equi de fronte reuulsus (*Aen.* 4.515): Ovid, *Ars amat.* 2.99–100

erepte (*Aen.* 3.711): *Aen.* 3.476

errant (*Ecl.* 2.21): Servius, *In Ecl.* 2.21; *Georg.* 2.283; *Aen.* 3.644; *Ecl.* 6.64

eructans (*Aen.* 3.576): Servius, *In Aen.* 3.576

et soror et coniunx (*Aen.* 1.47): Macrobius, *In somn. Scip.* 1.17.15

examina (*Ecl.* 7.13): *Georg.* 4.139

examine (*Georg.* 4.139): *Ecl.* 7.13

exanimum (*Aen.* 1.484): *Aen.* 2.542–543

exaudiri uoces (*Aen.* 4.460): *Georg.* 1.476

excepit (*Aen.* 4.114): *Ecl.* 3.17–18

excessere (*Aen.* 2.351): Macrobius, *Sat.* 5.22.7

excipere (*Ecl.* 3.18): *Aen.* 4.114; *Aen.* 4.297; *Aen.* 4.373–374

excipit (*Aen.* 3.317–318): *Aen.* 4.373–374

exiguus (*Georg.* 1.181): *Georg.* 4.295–296

exiguus (*Georg.* 4.295): *Georg.* 1.181–182

explorare (*Aen.* 1.77): Servius, *In Aen.* 1.77

extuderat (*Georg.* 4.328): *Georg.* 1.133

extunderet (*Georg.* 1.133): *Georg.* 4.328

exuuiis (*Georg.* 3.437): Nonius, *De comp. doct.* 458

falces (*Georg.* 1.508): *Ecl.* 3.11
fari quo sanguine cretus hortamur (*Aen.* 3.608–609): *Aen.* 2.74–75
fastigia (*Georg.* 2.288): Nonius, *De comp. doct.* 463
fauilla (*Aen.* 3.573): Servius, *In Aen.* 3.573
ferro foedare (*Aen.* 2.55): *Aen.* 3.241
ferro foedare (*Aen.* 3.241): *Aen.* 2.55
feruere (*Georg.* 1.456): Nonius, *De comp. doct.* 464
fessos sopor artus (*Aen.* 3.511): *Georg.* 4.189–190
figere (*Ecl.* 2.29): *Georg.* 1.308
fingens (*Aen.* 4.148): *Georg.* 2.407
fingitque (*Georg.* 2.407): *Aen.* 4.148
flamma medullas (*Aen.* 4.66): *Georg.* 3.271
flamma medullis (*Georg.* 3.271): *Aen.* 4.66; *Aen.* 4.101
focus (*Ecl.* 7.49): *Aen.* 3.134
fractos (*Georg.* 4.72): *Aen.* 3.555–556
fremitu (*Georg.* 2.160): Nonius, *De comp. doct.* 447
freta (*Aen.* 1.607): Varro, *De ling. lat.* 7.2.22
freta (*Aen.* 3.127): Varro, *De ling. lat.* 7.2.22
fulmina (*Georg.* 1.329): Nonius, *De comp. doct.* 430
funda (*Georg.* 1.141): Ovid, *Meta.* 4.518
furta (*Georg.* 4.346): Nonius, *De comp. doct.* 453
furto (*Aen.* 6.24): *Georg.* 4.346

geminique (*Aen.* 1.162): Servius, *In Aen.* 1.162
glomerant (*Georg.* 1.323): *Georg.* 2.311; *Georg.* 4.79
glomeratque (*Georg.* 2.311): *Georg.* 1.323; *Georg.* 4.79
gradibusque (*Georg.* 3.191): *Aen.* 3.598
gradum (*Aen.* 3.598): *Georg.* 3.191
Grynei (*Ecl.* 6.72): *Aen.* 4.345
Gryneus (*Aen.* 4.345): *Ecl.* 6.72

harena (*Georg.* 4.291): Lucan, *Bell. ciu.* 2.416–417
haud ac iussi faciunt (*Aen.* 3.236): *Aen.* 3.561
haud ac iussi faciunt (*Aen.* 3.561): *Aen.* 3.236
hedera corymbos (*Ecl.* 3.39): Ovid, *Meta.* 3.664–665
hiems (*Aen.* 1.122): *Georg.* 3.470; *Aen.* 3.194–195
hoc (*Aen.* 2.664): Priscian, *Instit. gramm.* 12.25
horrea (*Georg.* 1.49): *Georg.* 2.518

horrea (*Georg.* 2.518): *Georg.* 1.49
horrida barba (*Aen.* 4.251): *Georg.* 3.366
hortamur fari quo sanguine cretus (*Aen.* 2.74): *Aen.* 3.608–609
Hydaspes (*Georg.* 4.211): Solinus, *Coll. rer. mem.* 38.4–5, 3

iacet insula (*Aen.* 3.692): *Aen.* 3.104
iam pridem (*Aen.* 2.647): *Ecl.* 5.55
iam pridem (*Ecl.* 2.43): Cicero, *De fin.* 5.8.23
iam pridem (*Ecl.* 5.55): *Aen.* 2.647
ieiuna (*Georg.* 2.212): *Georg.* 3.493
ieiuna (*Georg.* 3.493): *Georg.* 2.212
ignari (*Aen.* 1.198): Servius, *In Aen.* 1.198
ignem (*Aen.* 1.42): Macrobius, *Sat.* 5.22.8
ignes (*Aen.* 3.199): *Aen.* 1.90
ignibus (*Aen.* 1.90): *Aen.* 3.198–199
ilice (*Ecl.* 6.54): *Georg.* 4.81
imbrem (*Aen.* 1.123): *Georg.* 4.114–115; *Georg.* 1.333
imbris (*Georg.* 4.115): Nonius, *De comp. doct.* 459
immane (*Aen.* 1.110): *Aen.* 3.583–584; *Aen.* 4.199
immania (*Aen.* 3.583): *Aen.* 1.110
immugiit (*Aen.* 3.674): *Aen.* 3.92
in numerum (*Ecl.* 6.27): *Georg.* 4.174–175
in numerum (*Georg.* 4.175): *Ecl.* 6.27
in uulgum ambiguas (*Aen.* 2.99): Servius, *In Donatum* (ed. Keil, 4:431, 27–28)
indicit (*Aen.* 1.632): *Aen.* 3.264; *Aen.* 3.234–235
indicit honores (*Aen.* 3.264): *Aen.* 1.631–632
Indigetes (*Georg.* 1.498): Servius, *In Georg.* 1.498; Ovid, *Meta.* 14.605–608
infula (*Aen.* 2.430): Varro, *De ling. lat.* 7.3.24
ingentem (*Aen.* 3.555): *Georg.* 1.334
ingentem farris aceruum populant (*Aen.* 4.402–403): *Georg.* 1.185–186
insani (*Ecl.* 9.43): Nonius, *De comp. doct.* 465
insano (*Georg.* 1.481): Servius, *In Georg.* 1.481
intentique (*Aen.* 2.1): *Aen.* 3.716
intentis (*Aen.* 3.716): *Aen.* 2.1
interea (*Aen.* 1.479): Priscian, *Partit. XII versuum Aen.* 11.199
interfice (*Georg.* 4.330): Nonius, *De comp. doct.* 449
intiba (*Georg.* 1.120): *Georg.* 4.120
inuia (*Aen.* 1.537): *Aen.* 2.735–737; *Aen.* 4.151
Ithacus (*Aen.* 2.122): *Aen.* 3.272–273; *Aen.* 3.613–614

labellum (*Ecl.* 2.34): Nonius, *De comp. doct.* 449

lacte distenta capellae (*Ecl.* 4.21): *Ecl.* 7.3

lambere (*Aen.* 2.684): *Aen.* 3.574

lambit (*Aen.* 3.574): *Aen.* 2.682–684

lambrusca (*Ecl.* 5.7): Nonius, *De comp. doct.* 449

lapidosa corna (*Georg.* 2.34): *Aen.* 3.649–650

lapidosaque corna (*Aen.* 3.649): *Georg.* 2.33–34

laterum (*Aen.* 1.122): *Georg.* 3.523

laticis (*Georg.* 2.192): *Aen.* 1.736; *Aen.* 1.686; Servius, *In Aen.* 1.686

laticum (*Aen.* 1.736): *Georg.* 2.192

lauit (*Georg.* 3.221): Nonius, *De comp. doct.* 503–504

laxis (*Aen.* 1.122): *Georg.* 2.330–331; *Georg.* 2.363–364

Leucatae (*Aen.* 3.274): Livy, *A.U.C.* 38.4.2

liba (*Ecl.* 7.33): *Georg.* 2.394

liber (*Ecl.* 10.67): *Georg.* 2.77

limen (*Ecl.* 5.56): *Georg.* 3.317

litora myrtetis (*Georg.* 2.112): *Georg.* 4.124

lituosque (*Georg.* 3.183): Macrobius, *Sat.* 6.8.1

luce (*Aen.* 4.186): *Georg.* 1.209

luci (*Georg.* 1.209): *Aen.* 4.186

lustra (*Aen.* 3.647): *Aen.* 4.151; *Georg.* 2.471

lustra (*Georg.* 2.471): *Aen.* 3.646–647; *Aen.* 4.151

lustramurque (*Aen.* 3.279): *Ecl.* 5.74–75

luxuriatque (*Georg.* 3.81): Nonius, *De comp. doct.* 481

Lyaeum (*Aen.* 1.686): *Georg.* 2.229; Servius, *In Aen.* 1.686

maestumque timorem (*Aen.* 1.202): Servius, *In Aen.* 1.202

magalia (*Aen.* 1.421): *Aen.* 4.259

magalia (*Aen.* 4.259): *Aen.* 1.421

malis absumpsere (*Georg.* 3.268): *Aen.* 3.257

mandauimus (*Ecl.* 5.36): *Georg.* 1.223–224

meditaris (*Ecl.* 1.2): *Aen.* 4.171

mensam laticum libauit (*Aen.* 1.736): Macrobius, *Sat.* 3.11.3, 7

messor (*Ecl.* 3.42): *Georg.* 1.316–317

miracula (*Georg.* 4.441): Ovid, *Meta.* 2.193

miserescimus (*Aen.* 2.145): Nonius, *De comp. doct.* 472

mugire (*Aen.* 3.92): *Aen.* 3.674

murice (*Ecl.* 4.44): Servius, *In Ecl.* 4.44; Nonius, *De comp. doct.* 461–462

Mygdonides (*Aen.* 2.342): Solinus, *Coll. rer. mem.* 42.1

nec moritura crudeli funere (*Aen.* 4.308): *Georg.* 3.263

nec moritura crudeli funere (*Georg.* 3.263): *Aen.* 4.308
nidis (*Georg.* 2.210): *Georg.* 4.17
nidis (*Georg.* 4.17): Nonius, *De comp. doct.* 459
nitens (*Aen.* 2.380): *Aen.* 4.252
nitens (*Aen.* 4.252): *Aen.* 2.380
nitens (*Georg.* 3.172): *Aen.* 2.380; *Aen.* 4.252
niualis (*Georg.* 3.318): Ovid, *Meta.* 6.692
nocturnique orgia Bacchi (*Georg.* 4.521): *Aen.* 4.302–303
noua (*Ecl.* 3.86): Servius, *In Ecl.* 3.86; *Georg.* 4.357
nox (*Aen.* 3.147): *Aen.* 3.512
nox intempesta (*Aen.* 3.587): Macrobius, *Sat.* 1.3.15

obuerterit (*Georg.* 2.271): *Aen.* 3.549
obuertimus (*Aen.* 3.549): *Georg.* 2.270–271
oleo (*Georg.* 2.222): Nonius, *De comp. doct.* 500
Olympi (*Ecl.* 5.56): *Georg.* 1.450; Varro, *De ling. lat.* 7.2.20
Olympo (*Georg.* 1.450): *Ecl.* 5.56
opere feruet (*Aen.* 4.407): *Aen.* 1.436
opima (*Aen.* 2.782): *Aen.* 3.224
opimis (*Aen.* 3.224): *Aen.* 2.782
optauitque (*Aen.* 3.109): *Aen.* 3.132
opum (*Aen.* 1.14): Nonius, *De comp. doct.* 501
ore (*Aen.* 2.482): Nonius, *De comp. doct.* 459
ore solutos (*Georg.* 1.399): Servius, *In Georg.* 1.399; *Georg.* 2.386–387
Orion (*Aen.* 4.52): *Aen.* 3.517
os (*Georg.* 3.454): Nonius, *De comp. doct.* 459

paeniteat (*Ecl.* 2.34): *Aen.* 1.548–549
Pan (*Georg.* 3.392): Macrobius, *Sat.* 5.22.9–10
Pangaea (*Georg.* 4.462): Macrobius, *Sat.* 5.17.15–16
Parcae (*Ecl.* 4.47): *Aen.* 3.379–380
parta (*Ecl.* 3.68): *Aen.* 3.495
pascunt (*Georg.* 3.143): Quintilian, *Instit. orat.* 9.3.7
passis (*Aen.* 1.480): *Aen.* 3.263
passis (*Aen.* 3.263): *Aen.* 1.480
paupere (*Aen.* 3.614–615): *Aen.* 2.86–87
pecudum (*Georg.* 4.327): Nonius, *De comp. doct.* 460
perfidus ille (*Aen.* 4.421): *Ecl.* 8.91
pernicibus (*Aen.* 4.180): *Georg.* 3.93
pernix (*Georg.* 3.93): *Aen.* 4.180

petit (*Aen.* 1.611): Ovid, *Fasti* 3.871
petit (*Ecl.* 3.64): *Georg.* 2.505
petit (*Georg.* 2.505): *Ecl.* 3.64
Phoebeae lampadis (*Aen.* 3.637): *Aen.* 4.6
Phoebo (*Aen.* 3.251): Macrobius, *Sat.* 5.22.11–14
placidam membra quietem (*Aen.* 1.691): *Aen.* 4.5
polumque (*Aen.* 2.251): Varro, *De ling. lat.* 7.2.14
pone (*Aen.* 2.208): *Aen.* 2.725
pone (*Aen.* 2.725): *Aen.* 2.207–208
populatque ingentem farris aceruum (*Georg.* 1.185): *Aen.* 4.402–403
postera Aurora (*Aen.* 3.588–589): Ovid, *Meta.* 4.81–82
praecipitant (*Aen.* 4.251): *Aen.* 2.8–9
praepetis (*Aen.* 3.361): Ovid, *Meta.* 14.576–577
pressabimus ubera (*Ecl.* 3.99): *Aen.* 3.642
procacibus (*Aen.* 1.536): Nonius, *De comp. doct.* 460
procul (*Ecl.* 6.16): *Georg.* 3.212–213
proiectaque (*Aen.* 3.699): Macrobius, *Sat.* 6.4.14–15
prora (*Aen.* 1.104): *Aen.* 3.532
puniceaeue (*Georg.* 3.372): *Ecl.* 5.17

quam (*Aen.* 1.327): *Aen.* 4.47; *Aen.* 4.11
quid (*Aen.* 1.518): *Aen.* 1.9
quidue (*Aen.* 1.9): *Aen.* 1.518
quoque (*Aen.* 1.5): Priscian, *Partit. XII uersuum Aen.* 7.142

ratibus (*Ecl.* 4.32): Varro, *De ling. lat.* 7.2.23
recludit (*Aen.* 1.358): *Georg.* 4.51–52
reclusit (*Georg.* 4.52): *Aen.* 1.356; *Aen.* 1.358
redimitus tempora (*Aen.* 3.81): *Georg.* 1.349
retexerit (*Aen.* 4.119): *Aen.* 1.356–357
retexit (*Aen.* 1.356): *Aen.* 4.119
rimantur (*Georg.* 1.384): *Georg.* 3.534
rimantur (*Georg.* 3.534): *Georg.* 1.384
rudentis (*Aen.* 3.267): *Aen.* 3.561; *Aen.* 3.682
ruptis (*Aen.* 3.580): *Georg.* 1.472
ruptis (*Georg.* 1.472): *Aen.* 3.580
rura (*Ecl.* 2.28): Varro, *De ling. lat.* 5.6.40

saeptis (*Ecl.* 1.33): *Georg.* 4.158–160
saliente (*Ecl.* 5.47): *Georg.* 3.460

salientem (*Georg.* 3.460): *Ecl.* 5.47

saltus (*Ecl.* 10.57): Varro, *De ling. lat.* 5.6.36; *Georg.* 3.143

Sameque (*Aen.* 3.271): Servius, *In Aen.* 3.271; ps.- Aristotle, *De mirab. auscult.* 9 (831a19 ff.); Valerius Maximus, *Fact. et dict. mem.* 1.8, ext. 18; Pliny, *Hist. nat.* 4.12.54; Seneca, *Troad.* 518; Apuleius, *Flor.* 15; Ovid, *Meta.* 13.711–712

saucia (*Aen.* 4.1): *Aen.* 2.223

saucius (*Aen.* 2.223): *Aen.* 4.1

scaena (*Georg.* 3.24): Macrobius, *Sat.* 3.13.7

seminibus (*Georg.* 2.354): Nonius, *De comp. doct.* 457

senex (*Ecl.* 6.18): Ovid, *Meta.* 4.26–27

sentibus (*Ecl.* 4.29): *Aen.* 2.379

sertis (*Aen.* 4.202): *Aen.* 1.417

sidere (*Aen.* 4.309): *Georg.* 1.1

silici excudit (*Aen.* 1.174): *Georg.* 1.135

silicis excuderet (*Georg.* 1.135): *Aen.* 1.174

Simoentis ad undam (*Aen.* 1.618): *Aen.* 3.302

Simoentis ad undam (*Aen.* 3.302): *Aen.* 1.617–618

sinus (*Georg.* 4.420): *Aen.* 2.23

soles (*Aen.* 3.203): Nonius, *De comp. doct.* 502

spelaea (*Ecl.* 10.52): Macrobius, *Sat.* 5.17.15

spirisque squamea (*Aen.* 2.217): *Georg.* 2.153–154

squalentibus (*Georg.* 4.91): *Georg.* 4.93; *Georg.* 1.507; Ovid, *Meta.* 4.656

squameus spiram (*Georg.* 2.154): *Aen.* 2.216–219

stant (*Ecl.* 7.53): Servius, *In Aen.* 1.646

statio (*Aen.* 2.23): *Georg.* 4.421

stratis (*Aen.* 3.176): *Aen.* 3.513

strato (*Aen.* 3.513): *Aen.* 3.176

stringe (*Georg.* 2.368): *Ecl.* 9.60–61

stringere (*Georg.* 1.305): *Ecl.* 9.60–61

stringunt (*Ecl.* 9.61): *Georg.* 1.305; *Georg.* 2.367–368

sua (*Ecl.* 1.37): *Aen.* 3.469

subnixa (*Aen.* 3.402): *Aen.* 4.216–217

sulpura (*Georg.* 3.449): *Aen.* 2.698

sulpure (*Aen.* 2.698): *Georg.* 3.449

supplex (*Georg.* 4.534): Nonius, *De comp. doct.* 460

Tanaimque (*Georg.* 4.517): Servius, *In Georg.* 4.517

telorum (*Aen.* 2.468): Servius, *In Aen.* 2.468; Nonius, *De comp. doct.* 448–449

temo (*Georg.* 1.171): Ovid, *Meta.* 2.107–108

temo (*Georg.* 3.173): *Georg.* 1.171

tendit (*Aen.* 1.18): *Aen.* 2.220
terebramus (*Aen.* 3.635): *Aen.* 2.38
terebrare (*Aen.* 2.38): *Aen.* 3.635
tergo (*Georg.* 3.361): Nonius, *De comp. doct.* 459
Thymbraee (*Aen.* 3.85): *Georg.* 4.323
Thymbraeus (*Georg.* 4.323): *Aen.* 3.85
Tigrim (*Ecl.* 1.62): Varro, *De ling. lat.* 5.20.100
tigris (*Ecl.* 5.29): Ovid, *Meta.* 4.24–25, 3.666–668
tigris (*Georg.* 4.510): Varro, *De ling. lat.* 5.20.100
tilia leuis (*Georg.* 1.173): *Georg.* 2.449–450
tiliae leues (*Georg.* 2.449): *Georg.* 1.173
torquet (*Aen.* 1.117): *Aen.* 3.532
torquet (*Aen.* 4.269): *Aen.* 4.482
torquet (*Aen.* 4.482): *Aen.* 4.269
torsit (*Georg.* 4.529): *Aen.* 3.562; *Aen.* 4.220
trabe cauauit (*Aen.* 2.481): *Aen.* 3.191
trahebat (*Aen.* 2.457): *Aen.* 2.320–321
trahit (*Aen.* 2.321): *Aen.* 2.457
tranat (*Aen.* 4.245): *Georg.* 3.270
trudunt (*Aen.* 4.405): *Georg.* 2.31; *Georg.* 2.335
turbine (*Aen.* 1.45): *Aen.* 3.572–573

ubera pressat (*Aen.* 3.642): *Ecl.* 3.98–99
ueniam (*Aen.* 4.50): *Aen.* 3.144
ueniamque (*Aen.* 3.144): *Aen.* 4.50; *Aen.* 4.435
uersat (*Aen.* 4.286): *Georg.* 3.258
uersat (*Georg.* 3.258): *Aen.* 4.286
uerso cardine (*Aen.* 3.448): Ovid, *Meta.* 4.93
uestigia (*Aen.* 2.753): Nonius, *De comp. doct.* 464
uiae (*Georg.* 1.41): Servius, *In Georg.* 1.41; *Georg.* 2.22
uibrantibus (*Aen.* 2.211): Ovid, *Meta.* 2.308
uinitor (*Ecl.* 10.36): *Georg.* 2.417
uinitor (*Georg.* 2.417): *Ecl.* 10.36
uinoque sepultam (*Aen.* 2.265): *Aen.* 3.630
uinoque sepultus (*Aen.* 3.630): *Aen.* 2.265
uir (*Ecl.* 7.7): Nonius, *De comp. doct.* 464
uiscera (*Aen.* 1.211): *Aen.* 3.622; *Aen.* 3.575–576
uisceribus (*Aen.* 3.622): *Aen.* 1.211; *Aen.* 3.575
uiuo (*Aen.* 1.167): Nonius, *De comp. doct.* 456
uiuo saxo (*Aen.* 3.688): *Aen.* 1.167

uiuoque saxo (*Aen.* 1.167): *Aen.* 3.688
ululantibus (*Georg.* 1.486): *Aen.* 4.168
ulularunt (*Aen.* 4.168): *Georg.* 1.486
una (*Aen.* 2.642): Priscian, *De fig. num.* 25
Volcano (*Aen.* 2.311): *Georg.* 1.295
Volcano (*Georg.* 1.295): *Aen.* 2.310–312
uomit (*Georg.* 2.462): Macrobius, *Sat.* 6.4.3
uox exaudita (*Georg.* 1.476): *Aen.* 4.460
urgeri (*Aen.* 3.579): *Aen.* 1.111
urget (*Aen.* 1.111): *Aen.* 3.578–579
usque adeo (*Ecl.* 1.12): Ovid, *Meta.* 5.396
uulgo (*Georg.* 1.476): *Georg.* 3.246–247
uulgo (*Georg.* 3.246): *Georg.* 1.476
uulsis (*Aen.* 3.650): *Aen.* 3.575

II

Index of Tortelli's Parallels [112]

Apuleius, *Florida* 15: Sameque (*Aen.* 3.271)
ps.-Aristotle, *De mirabilibus auscultationibus* 9 (831a19 ff.): Sameque (*Aen.* 3.271)
Cicero, *De finibus* 5.8.23: iam pridem (*Ecl.* 2.43)
Homer, *Iliad* 1.25, 379: dictis (*Aen.* 1.689)
    1.33, 24.571: dictis (*Aen.* 1.689)
Livy, *Ab urbe condita* 38.4.2: Leucatae (*Aen.* 3.274)
Lucan, *Bellum ciuile* 2.416–417: harena (*Georg.* 4.291)
Lucretius, *De rerum natura* 2.376: bibula harena (*Georg.* 1.114)
Macrobius, *In somnium Scipionis* 1.15.12: defectus solis (*Georg.* 2.478)
    1.17.15: et soror et coniunx (*Aen.* 1.47)
    1.18.14–15: candidus auratis (*Georg.* 1.217)
Macrobius, *Saturnalia* 1.3.15: nox intempesta (*Aen.* 3.587)
    3.11.3, 7: mensam laticum libauit (*Aen.* 1.736)
    3.13.7: scaena (*Georg.* 3.24)
    5.17.15: spelaea (*Ecl.* 10.52)
    5.17.15: daedala (*Georg.* 4.179)
    5.17.15–16: Pangaea (*Georg.* 4.462)

112. In this index the parallel is given first; following the colon is the lemma illustrated.

5.21.14–16: cantharus (*Ecl.* 6.17)

5.22.7: excessere (*Aen.* 2.351)

5.22.8: ignem (*Aen.* 1.42)

5.22.9–10: Pan (*Georg.* 3.392)

5.22.11–14: Phoebo (*Aen.* 3.251)

6.4.3: uomit (*Georg.* 2.462)

6.4.4: agmine (*Aen.* 2.782)

6.4.5: crepitantibus (*Georg.* 1.85)

6.4.14–15: proiectaque (*Aen.* 3.699)

6.8.1: lituosque (*Georg.* 3.183)

Nonius Marcellus, *De compendiosa doctrina* 430: fulmina (*Georg.* 1.329)

442: auidaeque (*Georg.* 2.375)

447: fremitu (*Georg.* 2.160)

448–449: telorum (*Aen.* 2.468)

449: labellum (*Ecl.* 2.34)

449: lambrusca (*Ecl.* 5.7)

449: interfice (*Georg.* 4.330)

452: aedificant (*Aen.* 2.16)

453: biberunt (*Ecl.* 3.111)

453: furta (*Georg.* 4.346)

456: uiuo (*Aen.* 1.167)

457: seminibus (*Georg.* 2.354)

457: catulorum (*Georg.* 3.245)

458: enixae (*Aen.* 3.327)

458: exuuiis (*Georg.* 3.437)

459: dorsum (*Aen.* 1.110)

459: tergo (*Georg.* 3.361)

459: ore (*Aen.* 2.482)

459: os (*Georg.* 3.454)

459: nidis (*Georg.* 4.17)

459: imbris (*Georg.* 4.115)

460: deuota (*Aen.* 1.712)

460: procacibus (*Aen.* 1.536)

460: pecudum (*Georg.* 4.327)

460: supplex (*Georg.* 4.534)

461: dapes (*Ecl.* 6.79)

461: domos (*Georg.* 2.209)

461–462: murice (*Ecl.* 4.44)

462: dente (*Georg.* 2.406)

463: adfare (*Aen.* 4.424)

463: fastigia (*Georg.* 2.288)

464: uestigia (*Aen.* 2.753)
464: uir (*Ecl.* 7.7)
464: feruere (*Georg.* 1.456)
465: insani (*Ecl.* 9.43)
466: audit (*Georg.* 1.514)
472: miserescimus (*Aen.* 2.145)
481: luxuriatque (*Georg.* 3.81)
500: oleo (*Georg.* 2.222)
501: opum (*Aen.* 1.14)
502: soles (*Aen.* 3.203)
503–504: lauit (*Georg.* 3.221)
530: atque (*Georg.* 1.203)

Ovid, *Ars amatoria* 2.99–100: equi de fronte reuulsus (*Aen.* 4.515)
Fasti 3.871: petit (*Aen.* 1.611)
Metamorphoses 2.107–108: temo (*Georg.* 1.171)
2.193: miracula (*Georg.* 4.441)
2.308: uibrantibus (*Aen.* 2.211)
3.664–665: hedera corymbos (*Ecl.* 3.39)
3.666–668: tigris (*Ecl.* 5.29)
4.24–25: tigris (*Ecl.* 5.29)
4.26–27: senex (*Ecl.* 6.18)
4.81–82: postera Aurora (*Aen.* 3.588–589)
4.90: ardua (*Georg.* 2.67)
4.93: uerso cardine (*Aen.* 3.448)
4.518: funda (*Georg.* 1.141)
4.623–624: aethere summo despiciens terrasque (*Aen.* 1.223–224)
4.656: squalentibus (*Georg.* 4.91)
5.51: chlamydem limbo (*Aen.* 4.137)
5.385–387: Caystri (*Georg.* 1.384)
5.396: usque adeo (*Ecl.* 1.12)
6.692: niualis (*Georg.* 3.318)
7.40: dare lintea (*Aen.* 3.686)
13.632–633: Anius rex idem hominum Phoebique sacerdos (*Aen.* 3.80)
13.679–680: chlamydem (*Aen.* 3.484)
13.709–715: Celaeno (*Aen.* 3.245)
13.711–712: Sameque (*Aen.* 3.271)
13.716: Dodona (*Georg.* 1.149)
14.576–577: praepetis (*Aen.* 3.361)
14.605–608: Indigetes (*Georg.* 1.498)

Pliny, *Historia naturalis* 4.11.49: Abydi (*Georg.* 1.207)

4.12.54: Sameque (*Aen.* 3.271)

Priscian, *De figuris numerorum* 25: una (*Aen.* 2.642)

    Institutiones grammaticae 12.25: hoc (*Aen.* 2.664)

    Partitiones XII uersuum Aeneidos 7.142: quoque (*Aen.* 1.5)

                         11.199: interea (*Aen.* 1.479)

Quintilian, *Institutio oratoria* 9.3.7: pascunt (*Georg.* 3.143)

Seneca, *Troades* 518: Sameque (*Aen.* 3.271)

Servius, *In Aeneidem* 1.77: explorare (*Aen.* 1.77)

    1.162: geminique (*Aen.* 1.162)

    1.198: ignari (*Aen.* 1.198)

    1.202: maestumque timorem (*Aen.* 1.202)

    1.640: caelatum (*Ecl.* 3.37)

    1.646: stant (*Ecl.* 7.53)

    1.686: laticis (*Georg.* 2.192)

    1.686: Lyaeum (*Aen.* 1.686)

    1.713: cantando (*Ecl.* 3.25)

    1.713: arando (*Georg.* 2.239)

    2.212: agmine (*Aen.* 2.212)

    2.468: telorum (*Aen.* 2.468)

    3.271: Sameque (*Aen.* 3.271)

    3.516: Arcturum (*Georg.* 1.68)

    3.519: castris (*Georg.* 4.108)

    3.573: fauilla (*Aen.* 3.573)

    3.576: eructans (*Aen.* 3.576)

    3.609: agitauimus (*Aen.* 2.421)

Servius, *In Donatum* (ed. Keil, 4:431, 27–28): in uulgum ambiguas (*Aen.* 2.99)

Servius, *In Eclogas* 2.21: errant (*Ecl.* 2.21)

    3.71: aurea (*Ecl.* 3.71)

    3.86: noua (*Ecl.* 3.86)

    4.44: murice (*Ecl.* 4.44)

    7.1: arguta (*Ecl.* 7.1)

    7.2: compulerantque (*Ecl.* 7.2)

Servius, *In Georgica* 1.41: uiae (*Georg.* 1.41)

    1.93: adurat (*Georg.* 1.93)

    1.399: solutos (*Georg.* 1.399)

    1.481: insano (*Georg.* 1.481)

    1.498: Indigetes (*Georg.* 1.498)

    4.517: Tanaimque (*Georg.* 4.517)

Solinus, *Collectanea rerum memorabilium* 7.21: Amphion (*Ecl.* 2.24)

    10.21: Abydi (*Georg.* 1.207)

    38.4–5, 3: Hydaspes (*Georg.* 4.211)

    42.1: Mygdonides (*Aen.* 2.342)

Valerius Maximus, *Factorum et dictorum memorabilium liber* 1.8, ext. 18: Sameque
    (*Aen.* 3.271)

Varro, *De lingua latina* 5.6.36: saltus (*Ecl.* 10.57)

    5.6.40: rura (*Ecl.* 2.28)

    5.20.100: Tigrim (*Ecl.* 1.62)

    5.20.100: tigris (*Georg.* 4.510)

    7.2.14: polumque (*Aen.* 2.251)

    7.2.20: Olympi (*Ecl.* 5.56)

    7.2.22: Aegaeo (*Aen.* 3.74)

    7.2.22: freta (*Aen.* 1.607)

    7.2.22: freta (*Aen.* 3.127)

    7.2.23: ratibus (*Ecl.* 4.32)

    7.2.23: aequora (*Georg.* 1.206)

    7.3.24: infula (*Aen.* 2.430)

    7.3.24: agresti (*Ecl.* 1.10)

    7.3.25: cornua (*Georg.* 3.222)

    7.3.32: canibus (*Ecl.* 3.67)

Virgil, *Aeneid* 1.9: quid (*Aen.* 1.518)

    1.82: agmine (*Aen.* 2.212)

    1.90: ignes (*Aen.* 3.199)

    1.106–107: aestu harenae (*Aen.* 3.557)

    1.110: immania (*Aen.* 3.583)

    1.111: urgeri (*Aen.* 3.579)

    1.152: arrectaeque (*Aen.* 4.280)

    1.152: auris (*Aen.* 4.183)

    1.167: uiuo saxo (*Aen.* 3.688)

    1.169: ancora (*Aen.* 3.277)

    1.174: silicis excuderet (*Georg.* 1.135)

    1.191: agens telis (*Aen.* 4.71)

    1.211: uisceribus (*Aen.* 3.622)

    1.235: a sanguine Teucri (*Aen.* 4.230)

    1.356: reclusit (*Georg.* 4.52)

    1.356–357: retexerit (*Aen.* 4.119)

    1.358: reclusit (*Georg.* 4.52)

    1.417: sertis (*Aen.* 4.202)

    1.421: magalia (*Aen.* 4.259)

    1.436: opere feruet (*Aen.* 4.407)

1.480: passis (*Aen.* 3.263)
1.492: aurea (*Ecl.* 3.71)
1.492: aurea subnectit (*Aen.* 4.139)
1.518: quidue (*Aen.* 1.9)
1.537: auia (*Aen.* 2.736)
1.548–549: paeniteat (*Ecl.* 2.34)
1.574: discrimine (*Aen.* 3.629)
1.617–618: Simoentis ad undam (*Aen.* 3.302)
1.631–632: indicit honores (*Aen.* 3.264)
1.640–641: caelatum (*Ecl.* 3.37)
1.686: laticis (*Georg.* 2.192)
1.736: laticis (*Georg.* 2.192)
2.1: intentis (*Aen.* 3.716)
2.8–9: praecipitant (*Aen.* 4.251)
2.23: sinus (*Georg.* 4.420)
2.38: terebramus (*Aen.* 3.635)
2.55: ferro foedare (*Aen.* 3.241)
2.74–75: fari quo sanguine cretus hortamur (*Aen.* 3.608–609)
2.86–87: paupere (*Aen.* 3.614–615)
2.207–208: pone (*Aen.* 2.725)
2.216–219: squameus spiram (*Georg.* 2.154)
2.220: tendit (*Aen.* 1.18)
2.223: saucia (*Aen.* 4.1)
2.265: uinoque sepultus (*Aen.* 3.630)
2.310–312: Volcano (*Georg.* 1.295)
2.320–321: trahebat (*Aen.* 2.457)
2.379: sentibus (*Ecl.* 4.29)
2.380: nitens (*Georg.* 3.172)
2.380: nitens (*Aen.* 4.252)
2.457: trahit (*Aen.* 2.321)
2.480–482: caua trabe (*Aen.* 3.191)
2.496: aggerat (*Aen.* 4.197)
2.542–543: exanimum (*Aen.* 1.484)
2.647: iam pridem (*Ecl.* 5.55)
2.682–684: lambit (*Aen.* 3.574)
2.698: sulpura (*Georg.* 3.449)
2.725: pone (*Aen.* 2.208)
2.735–737: inuia (*Aen.* 1.537)
2.782: opimis (*Aen.* 3.224)
3.69–70: crepitantibus (*Georg.* 1.85)

3.85: Thymbraeus (*Georg.* 4.323)
3.92: immugiit (*Aen.* 3.674)
3.104: iacet insula (*Aen.* 3.692)
3.115: Cnosiaque (*Georg.* 1.222)
3.132: optauitque (*Aen.* 3.109)
3.134: focus (*Ecl.* 7.49)
3.144: ueniam (*Aen.* 4.50)
3.176: strato (*Aen.* 3.513)
3.191: trabe cauauit (*Aen.* 2.481)
3.194–195: hiems (*Aen.* 1.122)
3.198–199: ignibus (*Aen.* 1.90)
3.224: opima (*Aen.* 2.782)
3.234–235: indicit (*Aen.* 1.632)
3.236: haud ac iussi faciunt (*Aen.* 3.561)
3.241: ferro foedare (*Aen.* 2.55)
3.257: malis absumpsere (*Georg.* 3.268)
3.263: passis (*Aen.* 1.480)
3.264: indicit honorem (*Aen.* 1.632)
3.272–273: Ithacus (*Aen.* 2.122)
3.277: ancora (*Aen.* 1.169)
3.286: aere cauo (*Aen.* 3.240)
3.286–287: carmen (*Ecl.* 5.42)
3.300: classem (*Aen.* 1.39)
3.302: Simoentis ad undam (*Aen.* 1.618)
3.357: carbasus (*Aen.* 4.417)
3.379–380: Parcae (*Ecl.* 4.47)
3.465–466: Dodona (*Georg.* 1.149)
3.469: sua (*Ecl.* 1.37)
3.476: erepte (*Aen.* 3.711)
3.495: parta (*Ecl.* 3.68)
3.512: nox (*Aen.* 3.147)
3.513: stratis (*Aen.* 3.176)
3.517: Orion (*Aen.* 4.52)
3.532: prora (*Aen.* 1.104)
3.532: torquet (*Aen.* 1.117)
3.534: cautibus (*Aen.* 4.366)
3.549: obuerterit (*Georg.* 2.271)
3.555–556: auditur fractos (*Georg.* 4.72)
3.557: aestus harenis (*Aen.* 1.107)
3.561: haud ac iussi faciunt (*Aen.* 3.236)

3.561: rudentis (*Aen.* 3.267)
3.562: torsit (*Georg.* 4.529)
3.572–573: turbine (*Aen.* 1.45)
3.574: lambere (*Aen.* 2.684)
3.575: uisceribus (*Aen.* 3.622)
3.575–576: uiscera (*Aen.* 1.211)
3.578–579: urget (*Aen.* 1.111)
3.580: ruptis (*Georg.* 1.472)
3.583–584: immane (*Aen.* 1.110)
3.598: gradibusque (*Georg.* 3.191)
3.608–609: hortamur fari quo sanguine cretus (*Aen.* 2.74)
3.609: agitabo (*Georg.* 3.18)
3.613–614: Ithacus (*Aen.* 2.122)
3.619: ardua (*Georg.* 2.67)
3.622: uiscera (*Aen.* 1.211)
3.629: discrimina (*Aen.* 1.204)
3.629: discrimine (*Aen.* 1.574)
3.630: uinoque sepultam (*Aen.* 2.265)
3.635: terebrare (*Aen.* 2.38)
3.642: pressabimus ubera (*Ecl.* 3.99)
3.644: errant (*Ecl.* 2.21)
3.646–647: lustra (*Georg.* 2.471)
3.649–650: lapidosa corna (*Georg.* 2.34)
3.650: auulsaque (*Aen.* 3.575)
3.674: mugire (*Aen.* 3.92)
3.682: rudentis (*Aen.* 3.267)
3.687: angusti Pelori (*Aen.* 3.411)
3.688: uiuoque saxo (*Aen.* 1.167)
3.699: cautes (*Aen.* 3.534)
3.699: cautibus (*Aen.* 4.366)
3.716: intentique (*Aen.* 2.1)
4.1: saucius (*Aen.* 2.223)
4.5: placidam membra quietem (*Aen.* 1.691)
4.6: Phoebeae lampadis (*Aen.* 3.637)
4.11: quam (*Aen.* 1.327)
4.19: culpam (*Aen.* 4.172)
4.47: quam (*Aen.* 1.327)
4.50: ueniamque (*Aen.* 3.144)
4.66: flamma medullis (*Georg.* 3.271)
4.71–72: agens telis (*Aen.* 1.191)

4.101: flamma medullis (*Georg.* 3.271)

4.114: excipere (*Ecl.* 3.18)

4.119: retexit (*Aen.* 1.356)

4.139: aurea subnectens (*Aen.* 1.492)

4.148: fingitque (*Georg.* 2.407)

4.151: inuia (*Aen.* 1.537)

4.151: lustra (*Aen.* 3.647)

4.151: lustra (*Georg.* 2.471)

4.168: ululantibus (*Georg.* 1.486)

4.171: meditaris (*Ecl.* 1.2)

4.180: pernix (*Georg.* 3.93)

4.183: auribus (*Aen.* 1.152)

4.186: luci (*Georg.* 1.209)

4.197: aggeribus (*Aen.* 2.496)

4.199: immane (*Aen.* 1.110)

4.216–217: subnixa (*Aen.* 3.402)

4.220: torsit (*Georg.* 4.529)

4.230–231: a sanguine Teucri (*Aen.* 1.235)

4.252: Cyllenius (*Georg.* 1.337)

4.252: nitens (*Aen.* 2.380)

4.252: nitens (*Georg.* 3.172)

4.269: torquet (*Aen.* 4.482)

4.280: arrectisque (*Aen.* 1.152)

4.280: comae et uox faucibus haesit (*Aen.* 2.774)

4.286: uersat (*Georg.* 3.258)

4.297: excipere (*Ecl.* 3.18)

4.302–303: nocturnique orgia Bacchi (*Georg.* 4.521)

4.308: nec moritura crudeli funere (*Georg.* 3.263)

4.366: cautes (*Aen.* 3.534)

4.366: cautes (*Aen.* 3.699)

4.373–374: excipere (*Ecl.* 3.18)

4.373–374: excipit (*Aen.* 3.317–318)

4.402–403: populatque ingentem farris aceruum (*Georg.* 1.185)

4.417: aurae uocant (*Aen.* 3.356–357)

4.435: ueniamque (*Aen.* 3.144)

4.460: uox exaudita (*Georg.* 1.476)

4.482: torquet (*Aen.* 4.269)

5.77: carchesia Bacchi (*Georg.* 4.380)

Virgil, *Eclogues* 3.11: falces (*Georg.* 1.508)

3.17–18: excepit (*Aen.* 4.114)

3.20: cogant (*Aen.* 4.289)
3.64: petit (*Georg.* 2.505)
3.98–99: ubera pressat (*Aen.* 3.642)
4.21: distentas lacte capellas (*Ecl.* 7.3)
5.17: puniceaeue (*Georg.* 3.372)
5.42: carmine (*Aen.* 3.287)
5.47: salientem (*Georg.* 3.460)
5.55: iam pridem (*Aen.* 2.647)
5.56: Olympo (*Georg.* 1.450)
5.74–75: lustramurque (*Aen.* 3.279)
6.27: in numerum (*Georg.* 4.175)
6.64: errant (*Ecl.* 2.21)
6.72: Gryneus (*Aen.* 4.345)
7.3: lacte distenta capellae (*Ecl.* 4.21)
7.13: examine (*Georg.* 4.139)
8.52–53: aurea (*Ecl.* 3.71)
8.91: perfidus ille (*Aen.* 4.421)
9.60–61: stringere (*Georg.* 1.305)
9.60–61: stringe (*Georg.* 2.368)
10.36: uinitor (*Georg.* 2.417)
Virgil, *Georgics* 1.1: sidere (*Aen.* 4.309)
1.49: horrea (*Georg.* 2.518)
1.85: crepitans (*Aen.* 3.70)
1.85: crepitans (*Georg.* 1.449)
1.85: crepitantia (*Georg.* 4.151)
1.133: extuderat (*Georg.* 4.328)
1.135: silici excudit (*Aen.* 1.174)
1.136: alnus (*Georg.* 2.451)
1.171: temo (*Georg.* 3.173)
1.173: tiliae leues (*Georg.* 2.449)
1.181–182: exiguus (*Georg.* 4.295)
1.185–186: ingentem farris aceruum populant (*Aen.* 4.402–403)
1.209: luce (*Aen.* 4.186)
1.223–224: mandauimus (*Ecl.* 5.36)
1.295: Volcano (*Aen.* 2.311)
1.305: stringunt (*Ecl.* 9.61)
1.308: figere (*Ecl.* 2.29)
1.316–317: messor (*Ecl.* 3.42)
1.323: glomeratque (*Georg.* 2.311)
1.333: imbrem (*Aen.* 1.123)

1.334: ingentem (*Aen.* 3.555)

1.337: Cyllenius (*Aen.* 4.252)

1.349: redimitus tempora (*Aen.* 3.81)

1.384: rimantur (*Georg.* 3.534)

1.447: Aurora (*Aen.* 3.521)

1.449: crepitantibus (*Georg.* 1.85)

1.450: Olympi (*Ecl.* 5.56)

1.460: Aquilonibus (*Georg.* 2.334)

1.472: ruptis (*Aen.* 3.580)

1.476: exaudiri uoces (*Aen.* 4.460)

1.476: uulgo (*Georg.* 3.246)

1.486: ulularunt (*Aen.* 4.186)

1.507: squalentibus (*Georg.* 4.91)

1.512: carcere (*Aen.* 1.54)

2.22: uiae (*Georg.* 1.41)

2.31: trudunt (*Aen.* 4.405)

2.33–34: lapidosaque corna (*Aen.* 3.649)

2.77: liber (*Ecl.* 10.67)

2.153–154: spirisque squamea (*Aen.* 2.217)

2.192: laticum (*Aen.* 1.736)

2.212: ieiuna (*Georg.* 3.493)

2.214: chelydros (*Georg.* 3.415)

2.229: Lyaeum (*Aen.* 1.686)

2.239: cantando (*Ecl.* 3.25)

2.250: cantando (*Ecl.* 3.25)

2.270–271: obuertimus (*Aen.* 3.549)

2.283: errant (*Ecl.* 2.21)

2.311: glomerant (*Georg.* 1.323)

2.330–331: laxis (*Aen.* 1.122)

2.334: Aquilone (*Georg.* 1.460)

2.335: trudunt (*Aen.* 4.405)

2.363–364: laxis (*Aen.* 1.122)

2.367–368: stringunt (*Ecl.* 9.61)

2.386–387: ore solutos (*Georg.* 1.399)

2.394: liba (*Ecl.* 7.33)

2.407: fingens (*Aen.* 4.148)

2.417: uinitor (*Ecl.* 10.36)

2.449–450: tilia leuis (*Georg.* 1.173)

2.451: alnos (*Georg.* 1.136)

2.471: lustra (*Aen.* 3.647)

2.505: petit (*Ecl.* 3.64)
2.518: horrea (*Georg.* 1.49)
2.540: crepitantibus (*Georg.* 1.85)
3.33: amborum (*Ecl.* 1.61)
3.79–80: arguta (*Ecl.* 7.1)
3.93: pernicibus (*Aen.* 4.180)
3.143: saltus (*Ecl.* 10.57)
3.191: gradum (*Aen.* 3.598)
3.212–213: procul (*Ecl.* 6.16)
3.246–247: uulgo (*Georg.* 1.476)
3.258: uersat (*Aen.* 4.286)
3.263: nec moritura crudeli funere (*Aen.* 4.308)
3.270: tranat (*Aen.* 4.245)
3.271: flamma medullas (*Aen.* 4.66)
3.317: limen (*Ecl.* 5.56)
3.366: horrida barba (*Aen.* 4.251)
3.415: chelydris (*Georg.* 2.214)
3.449: sulpure (*Aen.* 2.698)
3.460: saliente (*Ecl.* 5.47)
3.470: hiems (*Aen.* 1.122)
3.493: ieiuna (*Georg.* 2.212)
3.523: laterum (*Aen.* 1.122)
3.534: rimantur (*Georg.* 1.384)
3.575: uulsis (*Aen.* 3.650)
4.17: nidis (*Georg.* 2.210)
4.51–52: recludit (*Aen.* 1.358)
4.79: glomerant (*Georg.* 1.323)
4.79: glomeratque (*Georg.* 2.311)
4.81: ilice (*Ecl.* 6.54)
4.93: squalentibus (*Georg.* 4.91)
4.114–115: imbrem (*Aen.* 1.123)
4.120: intiba (*Georg.* 1.120)
4.124: litora myrtetis (*Georg.* 2.112)
4.139: examina (*Ecl.* 7.13)
4.151: crepitantibus (*Georg.* 1.85)
4.158–160: saeptis (*Ecl.* 1.33)
4.174–175: in numerum (*Ecl.* 6.27)
4.187: corpora curamus (*Aen.* 3.511)
4.189–190: fessos sopor artus (*Aen.* 3.511)
4.259: magalia (*Aen.* 1.421)

4.295–296: exiguus (*Georg.* 1.181)
4.323: Thymbraee (*Aen.* 3.85)
4.328: extunderet (*Georg.* 1.133)
4.345: Grynei (*Ecl.* 6.72)
4.346: furto (*Aen.* 6.24)
4.357: noua (*Ecl.* 3.86)
4.421: statio (*Aen.* 2.23)
4.521: Baccho orgia nocturnusque (*Aen.* 4.302–303)
4.529: contorsit (*Aen.* 3.562)[113]

113. Research on my section of this article was funded in part by a grant from the Research Division of the National Endowment for the Humanities, an independent Federal agency, for the preparation of the article on Virgil for the *Catalogus translationum et commentariorum*, and I am happy to acknowledge this assistance.

A MANUSCRIPT OF PLATO'S
REPUBLIC IN THE TRANSLATION OF CHRYSOLORAS AND UBERTO DE— CEMBRIO WITH ANNOTATIONS OF GUARINO VERONESE (REG. LAT.1131)

I

Chrysoloras, Uberto Decembrio, and the Translation of the Republic

IT HAS BEEN GENERALLY ACKNOWLEDGED by students of Italian humanism that the translation of Plato's *Republic* into Latin during the first years of the fifteenth century was an event of some importance in the cultural history of the Renaissance.[1] The first of Plato's dialogues to be translated since the later thirteenth century, the *Republic* was brought into the Latin West, as it would appear, through a combination of Giangaleazzo Visconti's cultural politics and the Greek emigré Manuel Chrysoloras' educational zeal. Yet the version has presented scholars with a number of per-

---

1. See for instance E. Garin, "Ricerche sulle traduzioni di Platone nella prima metà del secolo XV," in *Medioevo e Rinascimento: Studi in onore di Bruno Nardi* (Florence, 1955), 1:341–374, and in many other works of this scholar, most recently in *Il ritorno dei filosofi antichi* (Naples, 1983), 37f. A complete listing of medieval and Renaissance translations of Plato with their histories is given in the present writer's *Latin Translations of Plato in the Renaissance* (Ph.D. diss., Columbia Univ., 1984); chapter 2 contains a detailed account of the genesis of the Chrysoloras-Decembrio translation and its influence; Appendix A gives a list of manuscripts; Uberto Decembrio's prologue to the translation is edited on pp. 339–345.

sistent questions. It has been a matter of dispute how much the finished translation owes to the help of Uberto Decembrio, who claims in a prologue attached to the work to have applied some literary polish to Manuel's rough word-for-word rendering. This claim has raised the further question why Chrysoloras should have made a literal version of the *Republic* when what is known of his teaching from his students Guarino Veronese, Cencio de' Rustici, and Leonardo Bruni indicates that he favored a freer style of translation which would preserve the literary effect of the original. Finally, there has been some doubt how accurately the translation represented the thought of Plato, though many scholars have preferred rather carelessly to assume that the possession of the new version did for the Greekless of the fifteenth century what Cornford or Shorey do for those of the twentieth. In what follows I shall attempt to cast some light on all three of these problems, and in so doing to suggest to the reader how little real understanding of Plato's thought could have been communicated by the new translation of the *Republic*.

The manuscript Reginensis latinus 1131 of the Vatican Library, one of ten manuscripts containing our translation of the *Republic*, gives some light on the first of the three problems mentioned above.[2] For it contains on the fly-leaf an angry note denying that Uberto Decembrio contributed to the translation in any way beyond that of serving as Manuel's scribe.

> The author of this proem, who for the sake of honor shall remain nameless, has in the manner of Aesop's crow transferred another's lustre to himself in an empty boast. For it is a known fact that the distinguished Manuel Chrysoloras of Constantinople, by whose efforts and generosity Greek learning has returned among us, turned

2. Saec. XV 1/4, 345 x 250 mm., II + 45 + I folios, arranged in four gatherings of ten folios each, and one gathering of 6 folios at the end. The text is written throughout in an Italian gothic hand, which same hand has added into the margins some of Uberto's annotations (see Hankins, *Latin Translations*, 87, note 62). Numerous marginalia have been added in the hand of Guarino Veronese, which are edited and discussed below. Four other hands also appear in the margins, three of them gothic cursive hands of the early fifteenth century and the fourth a humanistic cursive of the later fifteenth century, perhaps belonging to one of Guarino's sons, who severally inherited his manuscripts. The *argumentula* (edited in Hankins, *Latin Translations*, 345–347) have been added by the rubricator in Books VI–IX only; they are omitted from Books IV, V, and X, but added in one of the gothic cursive hands for Books I–III. The MS is described by Kristeller, *Iter*, 2:407. For indications of Guarino's ownership of the MS, see below, notes 4 and 61.

into Latin the divine volumes of Plato's *Republic* in his own words, with the aid of no mortal man. Yet this insignificant braggart, feeding like the drone he is on the labor of another, claims perfectly falsely to have fixed up Manuel's style, though all the world knows, and I am convinced, that his knowledge of Greek did not extend beyond the accents and syllables of the letters, and his Latin is inferior even to Manuel's. No one will deny, to be sure, that this fellow of whom I speak, this vainglorious maker of prologues, has indeed attached some efforts of his own to Manuel's: for Manuel dictated it, and he wrote down what was said, like a professional scribe. You then, whoever you be that transcribe this volume, by the immortal God and his son Jesus Christ, I beg, pray, and abjure you that you transcribe this epigram at the beginning of the work, lest you permit so impudent a fellow to despoil of his glory a most outstanding and learned man to whom Italian culture is highly indebted; or else that you omit the prologue itself which contains nothing but foolishness.[3]

The writer of this note can now be identified, thanks to Dr. Albinia de la Mare, as Guarino Veronese.[4] Such being the case, the testimony would seem to weigh heavily against Uberto's claim to have participated in the translation.[5] Guarino, after all, lived in Chrysoloras' house in Con-

---

3. The Latin text is given below in Appendix B. The note was previously printed by Gianvito Resta in his article, "Antonio Cassarino e le sue traduzioni di Plutarcho e Platone," *IMU*, 2 (1959): 207–283, at 255n., as that of an "anonimo quattrocentesco."

4. Identified upon request of the present author in a letter of 23 February 1983. The attribution to Guarino is further supported, if any support is needed, by the quotations from Aesop, one of Guarino's favorite authors, and the general circumstances, for which see below. Guarino used the phrase "ne fucorum instar alienos depasci labores" in a letter to Francesco Barbaro of 1414 (Guarino, *Epistolario*, 1:58). See also Appendix B, note 5.

5. For Uberto's claim, see below at note 15. By the end of his life, Chrysoloras' part in the translation seems to have been quite forgotten, as for example in the clumsy rhyming hexameters of Uberto's epitaph, preserved in the courtyard of Sant'Ambrogio, Milan:

Sorte nescis pariter stratis cum corpore membris
Hic locus ossa tenet Uberti inclusa Decembris.
Iste ducis Ligurum secreta peregit et urbis,
Platonice dederat translata uolumina turbis,
Argiue ac Latie linguarum dogmate fultus
Viglevani natus, famosa est urbe sepultus.
Non tamen extinxit seno mors omnia tello:
Terrea pars terre cessit, pars optima celo.

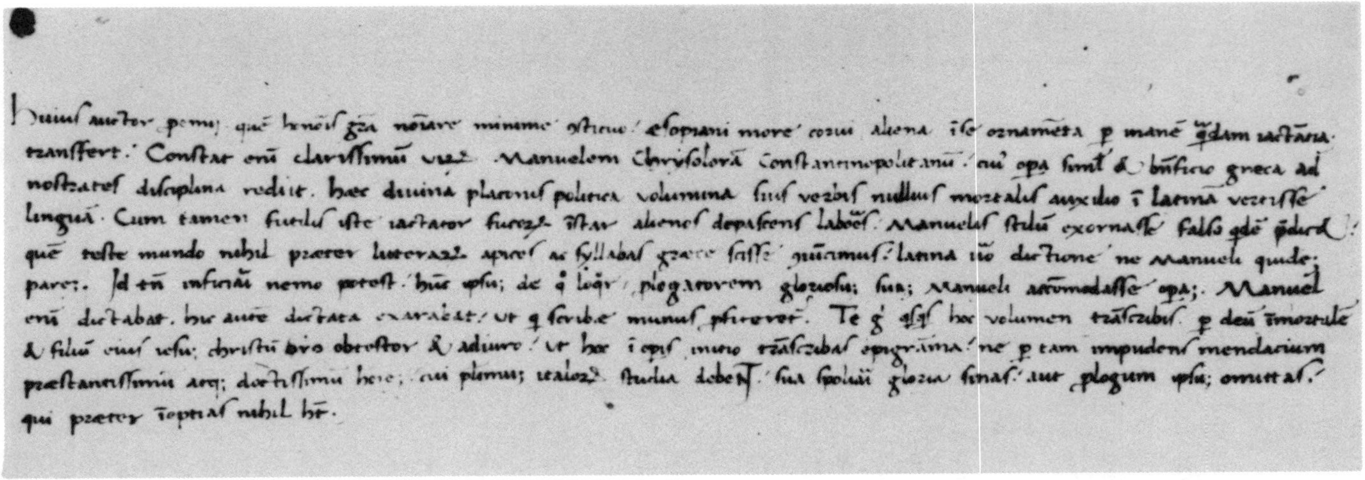

Plate 1. BAV, MS Reg. lat 1131, f. 1v, note by Guarino Veronese.

stantinople from 1403 until 1408 and maintained close relations with him until Manuel's death at Constance in 1415. That Guarino saw the new *Republic* and wrote his note between the composition of the prologue in the summer of 1402 and his departure for Constantinople in the spring of 1403 is possible, but not likely.[6] So Guarino would have had plenty of opportunities ask Chrysoloras himself about the manner in which the *Republic* had been translated. Yet we must not be too hasty. Guarino is known to have held a strong animus against the Decembrii, father and son, an animus which led him at times to say less than the truth about them. It was not true, as we shall see, that Uberto's Latin was inferior to Manuel's. Nor was it true that Pier Candido Decembrio's translation of the *Republic* was a simple transcript of the earlier version, as Guarino asserted some years later.[7] The Decembrii, as official representatives of Venice's historic enemies, the Visconti of Milan, harbored political affections that the sentimentally republican Guarino, who called Venice his second *patria*, found distasteful; these tensions occasionally surfaced, as in the affair of Francesco Carmagnola in 1428.[8] It may indeed be easily suspected that the *ineptiae* Guarino wanted to suppress in Uberto's prologue to the *Republic* included his praise of Giangaleazzo's contributions to culture and his suggestion that Plato's authority might be invoked against republican *libertas*: Guarino's own interpretation of Plato's politics was quite different.[9] Finally, it is undeniable that Chrysoloras' letter to Uberto of 1413 contains no hint that his affection for Uberto had diminished, such

His sons Pier Candido and Angelo as well often spoke as though the translation had been made by Uberto alone; see below, note 12.

6. For the dates, see Hankins, *Latin Translations*, 60f.

7. Florence, Bibl. Riccardiana, MS 827, f. 86v (Pier Candido to Angelo Decembrio): "Miror itaque dixisse Guarinum ut scribis cum traductionem meam obtulisses, se alios libros istos inspexisse nec ex traductione traductionem distinxisse." This was only one of a number of frictions between Pier Candido and Guarino. Earlier, Guarino or some member of his circle, with the usual contempt of the well-trained for the self-taught, expressed doubts that Decembrio could have genuinely learned Greek thus without a master; Decembrio defended himself by writing several letters exposing (with some justice) defects in the translations of Bruni, Jacopo Angeli da Scarperia, and even, diffidently, Guarino himself. Eventually he even was able to compose a letter in Greek and sent it to Guarino; Guarino returned it politely, covered with corrections. On all this see G. Resta, *Le epitomi di Plutarco nel Quattrocento* (Padua, 1962), 23f.

8. See M. Borsa, "Pier Candido Decembrio e l'umanesimo in Lombardia," *Archivio storico lombardo*, 20 (1893): 15f.

9. See the *Prologus*, edited in Hankins, *Latin Translations*, 339–345, lines 17–27 and 40–51. For Guarino's view of Plato's politics, see below, in the second part.

as we might expect if the latter had been helping himself to Chrysoloras' literary glory.[10]

Though these considerations must then induce a certain caution in accepting Guarino's account of the version's genesis, it is at the same time clear that it contains a seed of truth. It is indeed most unlikely that Uberto knew much Greek, as the striking incompetance of the Greek epigram he wrote for himself reveals.[11] It is probably significant as well that Manuel, though he corresponded with his other Italian students in Greek, corresponded with Uberto in Latin. The report in Borsa's study of Uberto that he translated "orations of Demosthenes, Lysias, and Plato" arises from

10. Chrysoloras addresses Uberto as "vir optime, frater amantissime," and the tone of the entire letter is cordial. The letter was edited by Sabbadini in *Classici e umanisti da codici Ambrosiani*. Fontes Ambrosiani, 2 (Florence, 1933): 85–87.

11. Preserved in the courtyard of Sant'Ambrogio, Milan, and copied by Pier Candido Decembrio into a family *zibaldone* (Milan, Bibl. Ambrosiana, MS B 123 sup., f. 79r:

ΕΛΕΗΣΟΝ ΜΕ Ο ΘΕΟΣ ΜΟΥ
ΕΙΣ ΧΕΙΡΑΣ ΣΟΥ ΠΑΡΑΘΗΣΟΜΑΙ ΤΟ ΠΝΕΥΜΑ ΜΟΥ
ΕΛΥΤΡΩΣΩ ΜΕ ΚΥΡΙΕ Ο ΤΗΕΟΣ ΤΗΣ ΑΛΗΘΗΣ
ΕΛΕΗΣΟΝ ΜΕ ΚΥΡΙΕ ΟΤΙ ΘΛΙΒΟΜΑΙ
ΕΓΩ ΔΕ ΕΠΙ ΣΟΙ ΚΥΡΙΕ ΗΛΠΙΣΑ
MCCCCoXXVII die veneris XXV aprilis.

———

3 ἀλειθηας (!) MS

There are but a few other known examples of Uberto's forays into Greek. There are numerous errors in the Greek words and phrases used in Uberto's own treatise *De re publica* [ca. 1420], which is preserved in a single manuscript, Milan, Bibl. Ambrosiana B 123 sup. But according to M. Ferrari, "Dalle antiche biblioteche domenicane a Milano: Codici superstiti nell' Ambrosiana," *Ricerche storiche sulla Chiesa ambrosiana*, 8 = *Archivio Ambrosiano*, 35 (1978–79): 185–186, the part of the manuscript containing the *De re publica* was written by Uberto's son Modesto, who may be responsible for the errors. P.O. Kristeller drew my attention to a colophon written by Uberto in a manuscript formerly at Strathfield Saye House, Reading, in the collection of the Duke of Wellington [s.n.]. A silverprint of this colophon from a film at the Bodleian Library was kindly supplied by Rev. P. Osmund Lewry, O.P.; I give an exact transcription of it below. It contains several grammatical errors and displays considerable uncertainty in spelling and accentuation:

Virgilius biblos dedit hos dulcore refertus
December calamo descriptos prebet Ubertus.
Εγράφη ἐν μεδϊολανω τῆς λϊγουρίας καὶ εθε [*canc.*] ετελειωθὴ ἔτει απὸ τῆς χ⟨ριστο⟩ῦ γεννισεως χιλιοστῷ τετρακοσιαστῷ δεκα επτὰ μηνος ἰοῦλίου εἴκοστὴ ὄντος τοῦ ϊγεμονος του μεδιολανοῦ Φιλιππου τῆς μαρήας τρϊτου. Θ⟨ε⟩ῶ τας χαρϊτας. αμϊν.

[This manuscript has recently been purchased by the Morgan Library in New York, according to a communication from P. O. Kristeller.]

a simple misreading of a source,[12] and it would in any case be difficult to explain why Uberto, if he had possessed such valuable knowledge, did not pass it on to any of the sons upon whom he so doted.[13] On the other hand, it seems that Chrysoloras' mastery of formal Latin prose style was equally limited. This even Guarino himself implies, when he says in his note that Uberto's Latin was inferior "*even* to Manuel's" ("ne Manueli quidem parem"). And the point is proved by Manuel's one surviving Latin work, the letter to Uberto, which is little attuned to the Muses of Latium. The kind of faults the letter exhibits — the use of the participle after a verb of speech, the unidiomatic double negative, the use of participles in place of gerundives in oblique cases — shows that Manuel was not free from the tendency of those learning a new language to import idioms and constructions from their own language directly and literally into the other. No doubt Manuel was perfectly competent in the diplomatic Latin of the Italian courts, but a formal Latin prose that could stand as an equal to his choice Attic Greek was evidently beyond his powers.

So then while our information does not perhaps permit us to settle definitively the question of Uberto's and Chrysoloras' respective roles in the translation of the *Republic*, it does allow us to make an informed guess which accords sufficiently well with the evidence. Chrysoloras, we may suppose, dictated to Uberto a literal and unidiomatic Latin translation from which Uberto afterwards removed the most obvious blemishes of grammar and style, but without consulting the Greek. This hypothesis steers between Uberto's boasts and Guarino's spite, and agrees with what is known of each party's philological competence. It also enables us to put a solution to another, more serious problem: the apparent contradiction that exists between Chrysoloras' theory of translation and his practice. Why, it has been asked, did Chrysoloras teach his students to translate *ad sententiam* rather than *ad verbum*, to prefer sense and literary grace to

12. M. Borsa, "Un umanista vigevanasco del sec. XIV," *Giornale ligustico*, 20 (1893): 110, who cites Angelo Decembrio's *De politia literaria libri VII* (Basel, 1562), 51 [= I, 8]. But the passage cited in fact claims only that Uberto translated the *Republic*: "Sic in eloquentiae genere Demosthenis et Lysiae Platonisque orationes et epistolae latinae factae sunt [by the translators of that time], praeter eius decem summi philosophi *De republica* libros, ut abs te, Veronense [!], saepe audivi, per Ubertum Decembrium translatos, huius Angeli nostri genitorem, qui Mediolanensium primus aetate nostra graecas litteras dicitur ex praeceptore Chrysolora didicisse." Angelo was doubtless thinking of Bruni's translations of Demosthenes and Plato's *Phaedrus*.

13. Pier Candido did not begin to learn Greek until the 1430s, after his father had died, as has been shown by Resta in *Le epitomi*, 23f.

a misguided loyalty to the letter, but himself produce a literal translation of the *Republic*?[14] The answer is clear: whatever literalism there was in Chrysoloras' original version was the result, not of some inconsistency in his principles, but of the limitations of his Latinity. Indeed, if we can believe Uberto's prologue, Chrysoloras knew and approved Uberto's efforts to improve the literary quality of his version precisely because he felt his rendering did not match the standards he had set elsewhere for literary translation. Because of the difference between the languages, Uberto says, Chrysoloras' word-for-word translation seemed to make Plato crude and cacophonous. Not wishing to have the eloquence of so great a man (Plato, not Chrysoloras) made unlovely in Latin, I thought it more seemly to follow the example of Calcidius and others in ordering the words to make them sounding, not departing from Plato's sense, but by taking away the inconcinnity of diction to sooth the reader's soul with vocalic melody. "*This my teacher bade me do, and approved when I had done it;* I made it my business, as far as I could, not to depart from Plato's words, except where it came out sounding badly; for although in Greek Plato's teaching is extremely melodious, in Latin (so great is the difference of words and sense), little or nothing sounds well [when literally translated from the Greek.]"[15] The principles of translation expressed here, however vaguely put, are in no way different from those expressed by Leonardo Bruni in his *De recta interpretatione* or by Cencio de' Rustici in his

---

14. Giuseppe Cammelli, in his study *I dotti bizantini e le origini dell'umanesimo, 1: Manuele Crisolora* (Florence, 1941), 124f., is troubled by this seeming contradiction, and advances the hypothesis that Chrysoloras used *ad verbum* translations in his teaching, but recommended a freer method in literary translations meant for publication. Resta, "Antonio Cassarino," 255, note 2, regards this as a "semplicistica soluzione" and rightly points out that there is no evidence that Chrysoloras used the *Republic* in his teaching, or even that he had other students beside Decembrio at Pavia

15. *Prologus in Platonis De republica libri decem . . . Uberti Decembris*, in Hankins, *Latin Translations*, 341–342: "Platonis tandem *De republica* translatio de graeco in Latinum per uirum insignem et praestantis ingenii Emanuelem Crisoluram de Constantinopoli meumque Graecae litterae famosissimum praeceptorem feliciter extitit consummata. Verum quia postmodum linguarum uarietate uerbum ex uerbo redditum nimis incultum ac dissonum uidebatur, ne ex hoc tanti uiri facundia Latinis incultior litteris redderetur, uisum est pulchrius atque uenustius, Calcidii et ceterorum exemplo ad consonantiam dictionibus collocatis, nec a Platonis mente discedere et lectoris animum sermonis inconcinnitate sublata, orationis qualicumque dulcedine consolari. Quod equidem in his uoluminibus, praeceptore meo iubente et postmodum adprobante, ad posse facere procuraui, nulla platonicis uerbis uarietate prorsus adhibita nisi in quantum plerumque nonnulla dissonantia uidebantur, quae licet in graeca forent sonantissima disciplina, latina tamen oratione, tantum uocabulorum disciplinaeque potest uarietas, nihil aut fere modicum personabant."

famous letter, both of which are generally supposed to preserve Chrysoloras' teaching on the art of translation.[16]

It is not however quite true to say, as some have said, that Chrysoloras' and Uberto's version of the *Republic* was unrelievedly *ad verbum*.
There are, to be sure, many literal passages such as the following, which
might be the work of one of the more liberal medieval translators like
Henricus Aristippus:

ἐπεὶ ὅτι γε ἡ τοῦ ἀγαθοῦ ἰδέα μέγιστον μάθημα, πολλάκις ἀκή-
κοας, ᾗ δὴ καὶ δίκαια καὶ τἆλλα προσχρησάμενα χρήσιμα καὶ ὠφέλι-
μα γίγνεται. καὶ νῦν σχεδὸν οἶσθ' ὅτι μέλλω τοῦτο λέγειν, καὶ πρὸς
τούτῳ ὅτι αὐτὴν οὐχ ἱκανῶς ἴσμεν. εἰ δὲ μὴ ἴσμεν, ἄνευ δὲ ταύτης.
εἰ ὅτι μάλιστα τἆλλα ἐπισταίμεθα, οἶσθ' ὅτι οὐδὲν ἡμῖν ὄφελος,
ὥσπερ οὐδ' εἰ κεκτήμεθά τι ἄνευ τοῦ ἀγαθοῦ. ἢ οἴει τι πλέον εἶναι
πᾶσαν κτῆσιν ἐκτῆσθαι, μὴ μέντοι ἀγαθήν; ἢ πάντα τἆλλα φρονεῖν
ἄνευ τοῦ ἀγαθοῦ, καλὸν δὲ καὶ ἀγαθὸν μηδὲν φρονεῖν; (Book VI,
505ᵃ2–ᵇ3)

Cum quod ydea boni est maxima disciplina pluries audiuisti qua
quidem iusta ac alia huiusmodi usa cum fuerit utilia fuit atque pro-
ficua, et nunc fere scis quod hoc sim futurus disserere cum hocque
quod ipsam *boni species* non sufficienter agnoscimus. Si uero ipsam
nescimus et sine ipsa alia quam maxime norimus, scito quod nulla
est nobis utilitas, sicut neque si sine bono aliquid possidemus. Aut
quid maius putas omnem, non tamen bonam, tenere possessionem,
uel omnia alia sine bono cognoscere, decorum uero et bonum nichil
sapere? (Reg. lat. 1131, f. 27v)

Here there are only minor transpositions in the word-order, one omission
(the εἰ in 505ᵃ6), and a relative clause in place of a participle, all of which
features appear commonly in medieval translations; the only non-medieval
feature is the silent gloss *boni species* in line 6. The affinity with the sublime
incomprehensibility of medieval translation is emphasized by the failure
to translate the idiom τι πλέον and by the use of *qua* in line 2, whose

16. For the references and a description of Chrysoloras' principles of translation, see Hankins,
Latin Translations, chapter 2. I have discussed Leonardo Bruni's translation theory in more detail
in an introduction to Bruni's treatise *On the Proper Way to Translate* in *The Humanism of Leonardo
Bruni*, trs. G. Griffiths, J. Hankins, and D. Thompson. Medieval and Renaissance Texts and Studies,
46 (Binghamton, NY, 1987).

antecedent, clear in the Greek, becomes ambiguous in Latin. But there are many other passages where the text is drastically paraphrased, short phrases omitted, and the word-order changed, to say nothing of mistakes and glosses.[17] This strange alternation of word-for-word translation with inaccurate paraphrase represents, we may suppose, the respective contributions of Chrysoloras and Decembrio. The supposition is lent color by both Resta's brief comparison and by the collations of the present author, which locate the majority of lexical and stylistic errors in the literal passages, while the parts rendered more loosely tend more frequently to display mistakes in grasping the sense of the Greek.

The reader will not be wrong if he has concluded by now that the translation of Chrysoloras and Decembrio was not one of the outstanding feats of fifteenth-century scholarship. For accuracy and felicity it does not bear comparison with the best coeval translations by Bruni or Guarino. But the worst of its sins is its inadequacy to the task of grasping and conveying the sense of Plato's doctrine. For most of the ten books this is merely a matter of omission, confusion, and error. But in the more difficult passages the translators ascend to positive misinformation and nonsense.

The end of Book VI of the *Republic* contains the most concentrated and vivid statement of the metaphysics and epistemology of Plato's middle period. Here is a typical example of Chrysoloras' and Decembrio's rendering, charitably punctuated.[18]

Καὶ αὐτὸ δὴ καλὸν καὶ αὐτὸ ἀγαθόν, καὶ οὕτω περὶ πάντων ἃ τότε ὡς πολλὰ ἐτίθεμεν, πάλιν αὖ κατ' ἰδέαν μίαν ἑκάστου ὡς μιᾶς οὔσης τιθέντες, "ὃ ἔστιν" ἕκαστον προσαγορεύομεν, καὶ τὰ μὲν δὴ ὁρᾶσθαί φαμεν, νοεῖσθαι δ' οὔ, τὰς δ' αὖ ἰδέας νοεῖσθαι μέν, ὁρᾶσθαι δ' οὔ. (507ᵇ5–10, from the simile of the Sun)

Et ipsum decorum igitur et bonum ipsum et sic de omnibus que tamquam plura *entia* ponebamus: an iterum secundum unam ydeam cui-

17. For an example see the passage from Book I collated and studied by Resta, "Antonio Cassarino," 263–268. Resta too remarks on the odd combination of paraphrase and literal translation, but without drawing any conclusions (p. 268): "In conclusione, la traduzione Crisolora-Decembrio, quando non compendia il testo greco, lo traduce *verbum ad verbum*, con improprietà lessicali e qualche tentativo di finezza stilistica."

18. I give the Greek text according to the readings of Burnet's 'W' family, a manuscript of which was evidently used by Chrysoloras for his translation. I will present the evidence for this in detail in a future publication. [See now Bottoni, p. 89f, cited below in note 28].

uslibet tamquam una existente ponentes ipsum quid est quodlibet
appellamus, et illa quidem uideri, intelligi autem non dicimus; ydeas
uero intelligi, uideri autem non utique? (*ibid.*, f. 28)

Here the translators, apparently reading ἄν for αὖ, have made the sentence interrogative; they take μιᾶς οὔσης as a genitive absolute instead
of appositively with ἑκάστου; they wrongly add the gloss *entia* after *plura*
where Plato clearly intends πολλὰ τὰ πράγματα, viz., the ontologically
dependent *visibilia*. The candid reader struggling through this might well
decide that Plato was a sort of Lockean empiricist.

A longer passage, this time from the Divided Line, I have postponed
to an appendix because of its length (App. A), but it too gives a good
sample of the difficulties an inquiring philosophical mind would have met
with when poring over the new translation. If not discomfited by the
two periods which do not parse, and several other constructions of doubtful
Latinity, if not confused by the four or five omissions of Greek words
and phrases,[19] the lexical and syntactical inaccuracies,[20] and the inept
conjectures,[21] it remains improbable that a reader could have successful-
ly grasped Plato's meaning in the face of the translators' unsuccessful attempts to gloss and interpret him. Of the seven or eight glosses in this
passage, six are inaccurate or wrong, and three of them seriously affect
the sense.[22] The unhypothesized first principle τὸ ἐπ' ἀρχὴν ἀνυπόθετον
cannot on any reasonable interpretation be equated with a *principium cuius
suppositio non existit*.[23] The glosses *ac superiora ... ac inferiora* seem to be
the detritus of some neoplatonizing assimilation of the hypothetical method
to the method of collection and division of the later dialogues; but the
weakness of the text (reading τμηθεῖσιν for μιμηθεῖσιν at 510[b]4) and the

19. Omissions: 510 b 2 ᾗ τμητέον, b 5 ζητεῖν, c 5 ἀδελφὰ καθ' ἑκάστην μέθοδον, c 7 περὶ
αὐτῶν, d 8 ἔνεκα, e 3 αὖ, 511 d 4 ἀλλ' οὐ νοῦν, d 8 γιγνόμενα.
20. The more significant errors are *basses et principia* for ἐπιβάσεις καὶ ὁρμάς ("steps and sallies")
which robs Plato's method of its dialectical character, as does also *demonstratio* for τὸ διαλέγεσθαι;
manifestat for ἅπτεται, and *disserere* for διορίζειν. *Concernare* is used indifferently for ἔοικε, εἰσιν
and ἴδοι, while at 511 b 3 *opineris* is used to translate μάνθανε, which shows the translators did
not understand the distinction Plato makes elsewhere between *opinio* and *scientia*. The most glaring syntactical error is the misplaced antecedent at 511 b 3-4, where *partem ... illud quod* is given
for τμῆμα ... τοῦτο οὖ.
21. Such as at 510 a 5 where the translators evidently read τι θείῳ for τιθει ᾧ or 510 b 7 where
they read ὥσπερ (*sicut*) for ὤνπερ.
22. See Appendix A. The glosses added by the translators are given in italics.
23. For various possible interpretations of this famous passage see R. Robinson, *Plato's Earlier
Dialectic*, 2nd edn. (Oxford, 1953), chapter 10.

inept conjecture ἂν εἰ (*ut videtur*) for ἄνευ would certainly prevent the reader from achieving so sophisticated (though wrong) an interpretation. His predicament would have been made even worse by the inconsistency in the use of technical vocabulary, as when ὑποθέσεις is translated alternately by *suppositiones* and *rationes*. It is no wonder that one frustrated reader wrote at 504[e] that "up to the end of Book VI I understand little or nothing."[24]

Two remarks are worth making, I believe, in the light of this brief examination of the Latin *Republic*. First, some *chiaroscuro* must be introduced into the portrayals of humanistic translation which currently solicit our credence. According to one view, humanistic translations are pretty but faithless, while medieval translations are like the satyr Marsyas, rough and shaggy without, but wise within.[25] Another view has it that the humanistic versions were an improvement generally speaking upon their medieval predecessors, superior in their mastery of Greek idiom and syntax as well as in the greater knowledge and understanding they display of the ancient world.[26] Of these views, the second has more truth. The best humanistic translations, such as those made by Guarino, by Francesco Filelfo, and by the mature Bruni, do indeed represent an advance in almost every respect upon the knowledge and technique of the earlier translators.[27] But we must distinguish between these translators and others, such as Rinuccio Aretino, Pier Candido Decembrio, and here, Chrysoloras and Uberto Decembrio, whose ministrations on behalf of the ancient authors were less effective, perhaps, than even those of some medieval translators. We must furthermore distinguish among genres: for while the superior knowledge of the Greek language and culture the humanists possessed enabled them to produce immediately excellent versions of Greek

24. Written into the margin of f. 27v in one of the unidentified gothic cursive hands: "Usque in finem libri huius sexti nihil intelligo aut parum. .d." The annotator also signs himself ".d." on f. 9r. Another glaring example of inconsistency in the rendering of technical vocabulary is at 505 b 2–3, where φρονεῖν is translated alternatively within the space of two lines by *cognoscere* and *sapere*.

25. The view, for instance, of Lynn Thorndike and Lorenzo Minio-Paluello; the latter's views are summarized conveniently in his article on William of Moerbeke in the *Dictionary of Scientific Biography* (New York, 1974), 10:435–436.

26. An opinion expressed a number of times by Paul Oskar Kristeller, most recently, I believe, in his "L'état présent des études sur Marsile Ficin," in *Platon et Aristote à la Renaissance: XVIe Colloque internationale de Tours* (Paris, 1976), 66.

27. See R. Sabbadini, "Del tradurre i classici antichi in Italia," *Atene e Roma*, 3 (July–August, 1900): 201–217.

literary works, the more technical works of Greek philosophy, science, and medicine required a professional expertise that the humanists did not at first possess, but which their medieval predecessors did. It was only later, when humanistic schooling was commonly combined with a university training in the professional disciplines, that translation of technical works emerged which were clearly superior to the medieval renderings, as in the case of many sixteenth-century medical translators and such philosophers as Ficino or Joachim Périon.

This leads to my second remark. It is not uncommon for those who represent the Italian humanists as philosophers to pretend that the wave of new translations of the Platonic dialogues in the early fifteenth century amounted to a renaissance of Platonism. But the slight understanding of Plato's thought displayed by the Chrysoloras-Decembrio translation of the *Republic* and by other humanistic translations[28] should stand as a warning that the view of Plato and his philosophy held by the humanists of the early Renaissance is likely to have little in common with the idealistic Plato of modern Germany and Italy or even the analytic Plato of the modern Anglo-Saxons. The only way to see Plato as the early fifteenth century saw him is to put away the Platos of modern scholarship and betake ourselves to the sources—the letters, treatises, prefaces, translations, biographies, and *libri annotati* of the early humanists—and to revivify for ourselves, as far as we may, the gowned and reverend figure with hoary beard and uplifted eye who so often adorns the folios of Renaissance manuscripts.

---

28. For the weaknesses of Pier Candido Decembrio and Antonio Cassarino in rendering the philosophical content of the *Republic*, see Hankins in *Latin Translations*, Chapter 3, and my article, "Some Remarks on the History and Character of Ficino's Translation of Plato," in *Marsilio Ficino e il ritorno di Platone, Studi e documenti*, 2 vols. (Florence, 1986), 1:287–304. For Leonardo Bruni's troubles in translating the *Nicomachean Ethics*, see Hankins in *The Humanism* and the literature cited there. [Addendum: Only after the present article was in press was I able to consult the excellent article of D. Bottoni, "I Decembrio e la traduzione della *Repubblica* di Platone: Dalle correzioni dell' autografo di Uberto alle integrazioni greche di Pier Candido," in *Vestigia. Studi in onore di Giuseppe Billanovich*, ed. R. Avesani et al. (Rome, 1984), 75–91. Bottoni argues that Ambrosiana MS B 123 sup. was the working copy used by Chrysoloras and Uberto as well as the exemplar for the rest of the manuscript tradition. His study of the variants confirms my view of the respective roles of Chrysoloras and Uberto in confecting the translation: he argues that Uberto's improvements in rendering the Greek were guided by Chrysoloras, while his independent interventions were mainly stylistic.]

II

Guarino and Plato

The first decades of the fifteenth century are a tantalizing period for the historian of the Platonic tradition. After the long famine of sources in the Aristotelian wilderness of the thirteenth and fourteenth centuries, after two hundred years wherein only a single dialogue of Plato was translated and scarcely a single real Platonist is to be found, there suddenly appears at the beginning of the Quattrocento a banquet of new documents to feast upon.[29] Manuscripts of Plato's works are brought in from the East, a dozen new translations are made, the dialogues are read, excerpted, and quoted. From Byzantium come scholars, some of whom are indeed Platonists, and all of whom have read Plato as a regular part of their literary education. With such an influx of new sources, the scholar must be very austere indeed who resists the temptation to conjure up in his mind a resurgence of Platonism among the early fifteenth-century humanists. Even so learned and acute a scholar as Eugenio Garin yields in some measure to this temptation when he tells us in *La cultura filosofica del rinascimento italiano* that the early fifteenth century saw a revival of Plato's political philosophy among the *uomini di stato* of the Italian city-states.[30] At Ferrara, Garin continues, this Platonism coalesces around the figure of Guarino Veronese, who wrote a life of 'his' Plato, who had studied with Chrysoloras, the translator of the *Republic*, and who had contacts with the Platonist Gemistus Pletho at the Council of Ferrara in 1438. For Garin it was Guarino who sowed the seeds of the Platonic school of Ferrara that sprang up in the late sixteenth century and is associated with the names of Francesco Patrizi and Tomasso Giannini.[31]

29. For a survey of medieval Platonism, see the present author's article "Plato in the Middle Ages," in *Dictionary of the Middle Ages*, ed. J. R. Strayer, 9 (1987): 694–704.

30. 2nd edn. (Florence, 1979), 415–416: "E quel 'platonismo' di cui s' è detto, che significa in certa misura il disegno della 'città felice' come 'città razionale', fu una cosa molto importante e molto seria," etc. The only real example of the influence of Plato's political philosophy in the early Quattrocento appears in Uberto Decembrio's *De re publica libri IV*, but even there the influence is extremely limited and superficial. I shall discuss this work more fully in my forthcoming book, *The Interpretation of Plato in the Early Italian Renaissance*.

31. *Ibid.*, 416–417: "A Ferrara Guarino, sembra, comincia la sua attività di dotto lavorando alla *Vita* di Platone, il suo Platone, il Platone novello . . . Ove Platone diventerà il filosofo di casa, quando per lunghi anni, sul cadere del Cinquecento, Francesco Patrizi terrà cattedra, proprio

Here however it might be well to recall the dictum of a great textual critic, that testimonies are not to be counted, but weighed. The resurgence of interest in Plato during the early fifteenth century can be readily accounted for by the general revival of all things classical, without resorting to the hypothesis of a specifically Platonic revival. Is there any hard evidence of Platonism, even a Platonic political philosophy, in the early Quattrocento? Platonism can of course mean many things, but minimally it must surely mean an understanding of some at least of Plato's doctrines, together with the arguments he advances for their acceptance. Can such an understanding of Plato be discovered in the works of Guarino Veronese?

Guarino was almost certainly introduced to Plato by his teacher, Manuel Chrysoloras, who seems to have read Plato with all of his Italian students, and whose style and doctrine he praised as ideal for furnishing the minds and the pens of young aristocrats.[32] That Guarino agreed with his teacher about the pedagogic value of Plato's works is shown from the reports of his own curriculum, which included readings from both Plato and Aristotle, though it remains a matter of doubt how frequently Guarino's students progressed far enough to reach the philosophic portion of the syllabus.[33] It is clear at least that Guarino himself kept up his acquaintance with Plato, for he acquired four Greek manuscripts of his works,[34] he compiled a

e solo di filosofia platonica, finché il lunghissimo insegnamento platonico del Giannini, a cui fu innalzato un monumento da vivo, concluderà il secolo XVI e aprirà il XVII. Chi amasse cosiffate 'figure', potrebbe a questo punto sottolineare come Guarino, iniziatore dell' Umanesimo ferrarese, devoto del Crisolora, da Crisolora facesse cominciare un'era nuova, da quel Crisolora che, venuto in Italia, aveva per prima cosa tradotto la *Repubblica* di Platone. Il Quattrocento sembra aprirsi al nuovo studio del greco su quel libro—il Rinascimento ferrarese sembra chiudersi, nel campo della storia del pensiero, sull' entusiasmo platonico del Patrizi." To Garin's list of Ferrarese students of Plato may be added Battista Panetti, who annotated a copy of Cassarino's translation of the *Republic*, now in Ferrara, Bibl. Comunale Ariostea, MS II 66 (see Kristeller, *Iter* 1:56). On Panetti, see A. Bargellesi Severi, "Due Carmelitani a Ferrara nel Rinascimento: Battista Panetti e Giovanni M. Verrati," *Carmelus*, 8 (1961): 63–131, and P.O. Kristeller, *Medieval Aspects of Renaissance Learning*, ed. E.P. Mahoney (Durham, N.C., 1974), 148.

32. On Chrysoloras' attitude to Plato, see Hankins, *Latin Translations*, 57f.

33. That Guarino read Plato and Aristotle as a part of the regular syllabus of studies is asserted by Sabbadini in his *Vita di Guarino Veronese* (Genoa, 1891), 37, who bases himself on the program of studies in Battista Guarino's later *De ordine docendi et studendi*, which is supposed to enshrine the teachings of his father. Doubts about how frequently Guarino's students actually read Plato and Aristotle are expressed by Anthony Grafton and Lisa Jardine in their article "Humanism and the School of Guarino: A Problem of Evaluation," *Past and Present* (August, 1982): 51–80.

34. H. Omont, "Les manuscrits grecs de Guarino," *Revue des bibliothèques* 2 (1982): 79–80,

rather detailed biography of him in 1430, and he quotes him directly a number of times in his letters.

The quotations from Plato in Guarino's *epistolario* give us some initial idea of the how and why of Guarino's Platonic reading. In a letter of 1416, Guarino advises his student Ugo to be satisfied with a certain stipend he has received even though he thinks it less than he deserves, since it is right to be generously minded even in the least matters. We should imitate Jove in this, he continues, who because of their holiness accepted the sacrifices of the Lacedaemonians much more readily than those of the other Greeks, even though the latter were more costly.[35] This illustration, which reminds one of Christ's parable of the widow's mite, he attributes to Plato, and it is in fact based on the ps.-Platonic *Alcibiades secundus* (148b9f.). But the pseudonymous author's purpose in employing that anecdote had in fact been to illustrate the famous Socratic equation of knowledge and virtue by showing that the gods always grant the prayers of the wise, who never pray but for what is good. Of this doctrine (which is not easily reconciled with Christianity) Guarino gives us no hint.

In another letter, this time to his patron, Leonello d'Este, Guarino recounts a conversation he had had with a certain Greek he met in 1438 during the Council of Ferrara-Florence. After greeting him, Guarino immediately launches into a praise of the pleasures of this life, not because he himself believed fully what he was saying, but in order to draw out the other's Platonic wisdom.[36] In response the Greek delivers a small oration (of which Guarino evidently approves) showing that life is only a

lists four manuscripts owned by Guarino's sons which probably belonged originally to Guarino: item 25, Platonis dialogi; item 39, Platonis nonnulla; item 46, Platonis multa; item 49, Platonis leges. Neither A. Diller in his article, "The Greek Codices of Palla Strozzi and Guarino Veronese," *JWCI*, 24 (1961): 313–321, nor I. Thompson, "Some Notes on the Contents of Guarino's Library," *RQ*, 29 (1976): 169–177, identify the present location of any of these manuscripts. Guarino mentions that he is studying Plato in a letter of 1431 written after his *Life of Plato* (Guarino, *Epistolario*, 2:173).

35. Guarino, *Epistolario*, 1:95: "Suscipe igitur hoc stipendium tuum, quod ne vile aut pusillum videatur, amplissimum certe in re minima velim animum contempleris, Iovem ipsum imitans qui, ut auctor est Plato, longe maius tenuia Lacedaemoniorum sacrificia quam reliquorum Graecorum sumptuossima suscipiebat. Quam ob rem? propter egregiam illorum in rebus divinis pietatem, cultum ac reverentiam."

36. *Ibid.*, 366–371 (367): "Plura praeter opinionem de industria quidem adieci, ut eum ad disserendum allicerem."

preparation for death, that one should not fear to die since death brings
an end to physical sensation and to the evils of this life, and that despite
the attractions of being dead, yet one ought not to commit suicide in
order to enjoy them. All this is in fact a rather shallow digest of the ps.-
Platonic dialogue *Axiochus*,[37] a work whose most remarkable feature
philosophically is the contradictory brew of Epicurus and Plato it contains: on the one hand, one should not fear death because sensation and
personal existence cease after death; on the other, one should not fear death
because the soul is immortal and shall enjoy heavenly delights hereafter.
In Guarino's version the contradiction is removed, either because Guarino
was consciously trying to Christianize Plato, or, more likely, because he
did not notice it. The result in either case is Plato *moralisé*: Plato by his
doctrine of immortality teaches us not to fear death; by his authority,
not to commit suicide. But we have no proof that Guarino understood
or was interested in Plato's proofs of the immortality of the soul, or his
arguments against suicide.[38]

Guarino's other citations from Plato are similarly disembodied. He quotes
Plato's praise of truth at *Laws* V, 730ᶜ in a passage of a letter condemning
flatterers; but Plato is speaking of fools and traitors.[39] The doctrine of
palingenesis is mentioned merely in elegant variation of the already-worn
trope of publishing as a transit from darkness to light.[40] He alludes to
the *Symposium* in order to invoke Plato's authority in favor of playing
decent and sober music at table, a testimony whose force would seem to
depend upon his correspondent's ignorance of that dialogue's riotous do-

37. The *Axiochus* was translated by Rinuccio Aretino between 1426 and 1431 and by Cencio
de' Rustici around 1436, but I have found no verbal parallels between their translations and Guarino's letters. He could easily, of course, have read it in Greek.

38. Guarino's purpose may well have been to illustrate the contention of St. Augustine (*Civ.
Dei* I, 22) that Plato prohibited suicide, against philistine contemporaries who quoted the story
in Cicero's *Tusculans* (I, 34, 84) of how Cleombrotus committed suicide after reading Plato's book
On the Immortality of the Soul (i.e., the *Phaedo*). Cardinal Guillaume Fillastre defended the same
point in a letter of transmission with Bruni's translation of the *Phaedo* (edited in Hankins, *Latin
Translations*, 327–329).

39. Guarino, *Epistolario*, 1:245: "Quod si veritas divinum ac celeste opus est et bonorum omnium deis ac mortalibus principium, ut inquit Plato, assentator diis atque hominibus hostis habendus est."

40. *Ibid.*, 2:582: "Qua de re tuo de paterna scriptione iudicio gratulor; scriptis vero meis perinde
ac ab inferis in lucem revolutis et ferme mihi ipsi incognitis nonnihil erubesco, quae post lethaeos
haustus ad superos instar platonicae illius παλιγγενεσίας Mercurius alter reuocasti."

ings, which partake less of the prim psaltery than of the Dionysiac flute.[41]

None of this will occasion surprise to anyone familiar with the use of sources and the general neglect of context in Renaissance literature. The ancients, who are presumed to be infinitely wise and good, are brought in to endorse an opinion, to point a moral, to show one's education, and to decorate one's prose. If some appearance of similarity between pagan and Christian doctrine can be plausibly alleged, so much the more fodder for one's rhetorical cannons, and so much the more evidence that the *studia humanitatis* can be safely utilized by Christians. But such a use of the Platonic dialogues as Guarino's does not license us to suppose that he had any grasp of their philosophical economy.

Nor does Guarino's *Life of Plato* give us any help. Guarino composed the *Life* in 1430 for Leonello d'Este's doctor, Filippo Pellicione, who had requested of him an account of the chronology of Plato's life.[42] Though the biography's chief formal debt is to Diogenes Laertius, it is not in fact, as Sabbadini claimed and Resta repeated, a loose compendium of Diogenes, for it demonstrably makes use of many other sources, including Apuleius, Aristophanes, Augustine, Cicero, Gellius, Pliny the Elder, Plutarch, Seneca, Servius, and Plato himself.[43] Despite this array of authorities, however, it cannot be compared in point of historiographical technique to the much more sophisticated and critical biography of Aristotle published the previous year by Leonardo Bruni.[44] Guarino chooses from among his authorities, but he does not criticize them; he clearly works according to the hagiographical principle that whatever should have been true, must have been true.[45] Thus he accepts such *mirabilia* as the stories of Plato's Apollonian birth and the prodigies that accompanied it, the story of bees making honey on his lips, of Socrates' prophetic dream about him, of his having been sold into slavery, of his having read the Jewish prophets during a sojourn in Egypt.

That Guarino was so credulous a biographer should not come as a great

---

41. *Ibid.*, 1:405: "Solebant vero maiores nostri non lascivientem, sed sobriam conviviis adhibere musicam, quocirca nullas fere festas apud prius saeculum epulas legis, quibus cantores ipsi non interfuissent . . . Platonis quoque *Symposium* inducta non caret psaltria."

42. See *ibid.*, 3:270.

43. Sabbadini, *La scuola e gli studi di Guarino Veronese* (Catania, 1896), 136; Resta, "Antonio Cassarino," 263.

44. See the present author's introduction to Bruni's *Vita Aristotelis* in *The Humanism*, Section VI.1.

45. I owe this characterization of hagiography to Eugene F. Rice.

surprise, for he was, after all, first and last a teacher: his choice of authorities is governed not so much by the desire to know the truth about the historical Plato as by the desire to edify and instruct his audience.[46] This is shown in the first instance by his omission of all anecdotes from Diogenes and elsewhere which might have cast discredit on Plato's character. As in Bruni's contemporary translations of the *Phaedrus* and the *Symposium*, all references to homosexuality are suppressed; the epigrams in Diogenes which purport to be the record of Plato's ἔρως for the boy Aster undergo a sex change:

ἀστέρας εἰσαθρεῖς 'Αστὴρ ἐμός· εἴθε γενοίμην
οὐρανός, ὡς πολλοῖς ὄμμασιν εἰς σὲ βλέπω.

ἀστὴρ πρὶν μὲν ἔλαμπες ἐνὶ ζωοῖσιν Ἑῷος,
νῦν δὲ θανὼν λάμπεις Ἕσπερος ἐν φθιμένοις.

Ardentes stellas luces mea Stella tueris
   Coelum utinam fierem te ut multo lumine cernam.

Stella prius superis fulgebas Lucifer;
   At nunc Hesperus, ah fulges manibus occiduus.[47]

And generally, in Guarino's desire to produce a model for emulation, he seems at times to have produced rather a *Laus* than a *Vita Platonis*.

More to the point is Guarino's omission of practically all matter relative to Plato's philosophy. The reports of Plato's doctrine which fill over fifty capitula of Diogenes' biography are reduced to a few moral and political maxims. Plato's doctrine of the community of women, children and goods, notorious from Aristotle's *Politics*, is passed over in silence, and of Plato's dialectic, metaphysics, epistemology, and natural philosophy there is no mention at all. Worse, the few moral and political doctrines Guarino does

46. Guarino's idea of the uses of history is revealed in the preface to his translation of the *Lives* of Pelopidas and Marcellus in Plutarch (*Epistolario*, 2:309): "Quantus autem historiarum et eorum hominum, quos prisci nobis annales signant, fructus legitur, ignotum esse debet nemini. Principio quid magis ad immortalitatem et ad res ex oblivionis morsibus vendicandas valet possetque quam rerum gestarum serios scriptis ad posteritatem prodita? Cuius ope hominum populorum nationum regum mores instituta consilia eventus in utramque partem proponuntur, unde virtus imitatione comparetur, cautius turpitudo fugiatur. Praeterea qui privati sunt vel ipsa antiquitatis peritia quae non parva prudentiae pars est, ad magistratus et imperia digniores evadunt," etc.

47. Diogenes Laertius III, 29 (= *Anth. Pal.* VII, 669–670); I quote Guarino's translation from f. CCCXXXIIv of the edition printed in Venice in 1516 (*Vitae Plutarchi Cheronei* . . .), hereinafter referred to as *Vitae*.

quote from Diogenes go chiefly to show that his own reading of Plato was not so perceptive as to arm him against Diogenes' misrepresentations of Plato's doctrines. It is hard to see how someone who had read the *Republic* with understanding could have copied without a murmur Diogenes' muddled report — drawn probably from some syncretistic Middle Platonic *placita* — that Plato believed corporeal and external goods instrumentally necessary for happiness.[48] Even Plato's most famous political *sententia aurea*, accurately recorded in Burley and many medieval collections of *auctoritates*, is given by Guarino in a garbled and innocuous form which he had apparently extracted, not from his reading of the *Republic*, but rather from Boethius' *Consolation of Philosophy*. Plato had said, "Unless either philosophers shall rule in our polities or those who are now called kings and rulers take up philosophy with a suitable understanding . . . there can be no lack of evils." Guarino writes instead: "Polities will be blessed if those who are preeminent in their government are either possessed of wisdom or are controlled by the desire for wisdom."[49] This trivialization of Plato's doctrine shows better than anything else how, in the case of some authors at least, Guarino for all his professed reverence of the ancient *auctoritates* was more interested in producing grist for his educational mill than in confronting receptively the thought of another man.

What purposes Plato might be made to serve in educating young aristocrats is shown by the material from Diogenes and other sources that Guarino chose to exhibit prominently in his biography. Plato, we read, was a model schoolboy who honored his teachers Dionysius *grammaticus* and Socrates, and excelled as much in literary as in physical culture. He

48. *Vitae*, f. CCCXXXIIIv: "Platonica est illa partitio: Bonorum quaedam animi, quaedam corporis, quaedam rerum externarum," etc. Cp. Diogenes Laertius III, 78. For Diogenes' source here, see M. Untersteiner, *Posidonio nei "placita" di Platone secondo Diogene Laerzio III* (Brescia, 1970); the ultimate source is of course Aristotle, *Eth. Nic.* I, 8 (1098 b).

49. Plato, *Rep.*, 473 e 11–c 5. *Uberto's version* (Reg. lat. 1131, f. 23va): "Si non, inquam, vel philosophi in urbibus principentur aut legittime et sufficienter philosophentur qui nunc reges et principes nuncupentur . . . non erit, amice Glauco, malicie requies civitatibus." *Guarino* (*Vitae*, f. CCCXXXVr): "Quam salubrem et illud est: beatissimas fore respublicas si qui earum gubernationi preessent, aut sapientia praediti essent, aut sapientie studio teneretur." Of the various ancient testimonia to the dictum (e.g., Cicero, *QFr.* 1.10, Apuleius, *De dog. Plat.* 2.257, Lactantius, *Div. inst.* 3.21), Guarino's version seems closest to Boethius' in *De cons. phil.* 1.4, as was pointed out to me by J. Monfasani. ("Atqui tu hanc sententiam Platonis ore sanxisti: beatas fore respublicas si eas vel studiosi sapientiae regerent vel earum rectores studere sapientiae contigisset.") But neither Boethius' nor any other ancient version of the dictum to my knowledge authorizes Guarino's suppression of Plato's subversive idea that those presently in power might better be replaced by philosophers. Guarino's position in the court of Leonello d'Este would of course have inhibited any such expressions of dissatisfaction with the political order.

loved to paint, was a *diligens naturae mimus*, and wrote tragedies, dithyrambs, and lyric poetry. His eloquence was so wonderful that Cicero said of him that if Jove should speak with human voice, he would speak in the voice of Plato. He was pious towards the gods, and the excellence of his philosophy, it is suggested, owed much to his having read the Hebrew prophets while in Egypt.[50] Most of all Guarino chose to emphasize, like Leonardo Bruni in the preface and argument to his translation of the *Letters*, the moral and political virtue of Plato, who, not content with mere words and argument, was thoroughly *engagé* in the task of bringing liberty to the Italian cities, thus increasing the reputation of philosophy among the human race.[51] In Guarino's telling, the emphases in Diogenes' anecdotes are subtly shifted, so that Plato appears a sort of civic humanist who was frequently called in to legislate for other cities, and whose *amor rei publicae* and reforming zeal towards his own city were frustrated only by the perverse conservatism of his people.

[Diogenes, after a report that Plato failed in his attempt to reform the Italian cities, omitted by Guarino:] At Athens Plato did not enter politics although his writings show he was a statesman. This was because the populace had grown used to other forms of government. Pamphila describes in the twenty-fifth book of her *Commentaries* how the Arcadians and Thebans when they were founding Megalopolis called him in as nomothete. But when

[Guarino:] I believe that many important men have wondered why Plato, who had a marvelous love of his commonwealth and no small desire to take part in governing it, appears to have ignored his responsibility to act as a counselor and administrator of his country. But in fact, though he displayed a singular love of country, he realized his efforts would be vain, since the city itself had already become accustomed in a nearly irrevocable way to laws

---

50. A story whose ultimate source is Justin Martyr, *Cohort. ad gent.*, 14, 15, but which Guarino probably knew from Ambrose, *apud* Augustine, *De doctr. Christ.* II, 107–9, or from Augustine, *Civ. Dei*, VIII, 11.

51. Diogenes (III, 21) has only: ἔνιοι δέ φασι καὶ κινδυνεῦσαι αὐτὸν ὡς ἀναπείθοντα Δίωνα καὶ Θεοδόταν ἐπὶ τῇ τῆς νήσου (scil. Σικελίας) ἐλευθερίᾳ. Guarino, drawing on Plato's *Letters*, has: "Utroque (*scil.* Dione et Theodota) igitur perinde ac consiliarium Platonem invocante, eo profectus est, eo proposito, ut ab Dionysio (*scil.* illo tyranno) civitatum Italicarum Sicularumque sibi subiectarum libertatem exoreret, quo philosophiae laudes et dignitatem non verbis tantum aut disputationibus, sed re ipsa et actione apud omne hominum genus compareret" (*Vitae*, f. CCCXXXIIIIr).

he learned that they were unwilling to have equality [of goods], he did not go. [Plutarch:] The Cyrenaeans called in Plato to give them written laws and to bring order to their state, but he refused, saying it was difficult to act as nomothete to the Cyrenaeans because they were so rich.[52]

that were foreign to his teaching, and the people were obstinately hardened against any new custom. At about the same time, when the Arcadians and Thebans were working together assiduously to attract colonists and inhabitants who might populate Megalopolis, they sent legates to beg Plato to come and bring order to their customs and laws. But when he recognized that they were averse to equality, he made no effort to do so, and this was right and just. For what sane doctor would prescribe the laws of health to a rebellious patient who refused to listen to his precepts? It seems that he felt the same about the Cyrenaeans, who, affluent with luxury and riches of every kind, had invited Plato in to instruct their city; this was the reply he made them: "It is difficult," he said, "to control with laws the citizens of Cyrene, made dissolute by their vast wealth." A weighty and mature judgment, as usual.[53]

52. [Diogenes, III, 23]: ἔνθα [scil. ᾿Αθηναῖς] πολιτείας μὲν οὐχ ἥψατο, καίτοι πολιτικὸς ὢν ἐξ ὧν γέγραφεν. αἴτιον δὲ τὸ ἤδη τὸν δῆμον ἄλλοις πολιτεύμασιν ἐνειθίσθαι. φησὶ δὲ Παμφίλη ἐν τῷ πέμπτῳ καὶ εἰκοστῷ τῶν Ὑπομνημάτων ὡς ᾿Αρκάδες καὶ Θηβαῖοι Μεγάλην πόλιν οἰκίζοντες παρεκάλουν αὐτὸν νομοθέτην. ὁ δὲ μαθὼν ἴσον ἔχειν οὐ θέλοντας οὐκ ἐπορεύθη. [Plutarch, Moralia, 779 d (Πρὸς ἡγεμόνα ἀπαίδευτον)]: Πλάτωνα Κυρηναῖοι παρεκάλουν νόμους τε γραψάμενον αὐτοῖς ἀπολιπεῖν καὶ διακοσμῆσαι τὴν πολιτείαν, ὁ δέ παρητήσατο φήσας χαλεπὸν εἶναι Κυρηναίοις νομοθετεῖν οὕτως εὐτυχοῦσιν.
53. Vitae, f. CCCXXXIIIIv: "Mirari plerosque et eos quidem graves viros arbitror quamobrem Plato quem mirificus reipublicae tenebat amor et eius gubernandae non parvum trahebat desiderium, administrandorum officiorum patriaeque consulendi curam abiecisse visus sit. Verumenim-

Plato was, in fine, the very model of the sort of man the humanists wanted to nurture in their schools: pious, virtuous, eloquent of tongue and pen, patriotic, and eager for reform.[54] Like his favorite author Aesop, Guarino has written a tale with a moral: He who would acquire Plato's fame, let him act with Plato's virtue.

But our best evidence of how and why Guarino read Plato appears in the annotated copy of the Latin *Republic* recently identified as his.[55] That codex contains 167 short annotations in his hand (App. B), almost all of them in Books II through V. That is to say, Guarino has annotated the passages of the *Republic* describing the foundation of the city, the education of the guardians, the censorship of the poets, the tripartite soul and the nature of the four virtues, the community of women, children and goods, the philosopher-kings, and the distinction between knowledge and opinion. He has omitted to annotate the disputations in Book I about the nature of justice, and the passages in Books VI–X which discuss the nature of the true philosopher, the form of the Good, the similes of the Sun, the Line, and the Cave, the historical morphology of states, the attack on poetry as *mimēsis*, and the myth of Er. In other words, his attention is focussed on the political, moral and educational doctrine of Plato, rather than on his dialectics, metaphysics, and epistemology.

Looking more closely at the notes, we observe that none of them are concerned to elucidate Plato's argumentation. There are few indeed that have anything to do with what we would call philosophy, apart from political maxims. In a few instances terminology is noted: *opinio* is distinguished from *scientia* (477^e8); the three faculties of the soul are noticed (440^e8); Plato's division of the soul into better and worse parts at 431^a3f.

vero quum is singularem patriae charitatem prae se ferret, inanem sui futuram operam animadvertit quia iam alienis ab institutione sua legibus et irrevocando ferme ritu civitas ipsa consueverat [consenuerat *edn.*] et alia consuetudine populus offirmatus induruerat. Interea quum Arcades et Thebani ad deducendos Megalopolim colonos et frequentes habitatores enixe conspirarent, Platonem per legatos obsecrarunt ut eo pergeret eam moribus ordinaturus et legibus. Quod, quum illos ab aequalitate abhorrentes cognovisset, facere neglexit, idque iure quidem ac merito. Nam quis medicus (modo mentis compos sit) rebelli ac nullis audienti praeceptis aegroto sanitatis leges indixit? Idem et in Cyrenaeos sensisse visus est, qui quum omni divitiarum genere et lautitia affluentes Platonem ad suae civitatis institutionem accerserent, hoc ab eo responsum retulerunt: difficilimum est, inquit, Cyrenaei cives amplissima fortuna dissolutos legibus continere. Graviter quidem et mature ut assolebat."

54. Bruni presents a similar portrait of Aristotle in his *Vita Aristotelis*; see the discussion of the present author in *The Humanism*, Section VI.1.

55. See above, at note 4.

is inaccurately linked with the scholastic and Aristotelian terms *ratio* and *appetitus sensitivus*. Guarino was evidently familiar with the *Politics* and *Economics*, for he remarks two instances where Aristotle's doctrine diverges from Plato's (457ᵃ6 and 457ᶜ10) with respect to female dress and the community of women and children. In one place he brings out into the margin a doctrine of natural science (436ᶜ8).

What does evidently interest Guarino is the contribution Plato's *Republic* can make to learning in the normal subjects of the *studia humanitatis*: grammar, rhetoric, history, poetry, and moral philosophy.[56] He notes frequently similes and exempla, unfamiliar words, information about mythology, Greek literature, and ancient customs; he identifies a testimonium of Hesiod and gives parallel passages from Vergil, Terence, Hesiod, and Aristotle. He remarks several places where Plato's teaching agrees with Christianity (379ᵈ4, 380ᶜ8, 380ᵈ1, 415ᵃ4).[57] Plato's educational theory too interests him closely, no doubt because of contemporary criticism of humanist educators for their reading of the pagan poets: Plato's teaching, read in a particular way, could provide the humanists with the high moral ground they needed to promote their studies.[58] Hence Guarino notes approvingly Plato's ban on amorous and impious poetry (378ᵃ1), and his view that the poets need to be censored in order that they not enervate the military virtue of the guardians (387ᵇ1); Plato's more virulent attack on poetry in Book X did not apparently engage his attention. He takes note too of Platonic *dicta* on the value of good role-models (395ᶜ), on the importance of early instruction (425ᵇ), on the qualifications of a teacher (467ᵈ), and in many places on the education of "knights" and "princes" (as Chrysoloras and he translate ἐπίκουροι and ἐπιστάται).

But what attracts the great majority of Guarino's marginal notes, as might be expected, are Plato's teachings on mores, ethics, and politics. He copies Plato's advice on eating and drinking, medicine, dress, joking, the proper age of marriage, and good behavior generally; he records his *sententiae* about the proper conduct of soldiers in warfare (469ᵈ6) and the

---

56. The meaning of the *studia humanitatis* has been discussed frequently by P.O. Kristeller, most recently in his *Renaissance Thought and Its Sources*, ed. M. Mooney (New York, 1979), 21f.

57. This was an especial concern of Bruni as well in the prefaces to his translations of the *Phaedo* and the *Gorgias*; see Hankins, *Latin Translations*, chapter 2.

58. On contemporary opposition to the reading of the poets, see G. Ronconi, *Le origini delle dispute umanistiche sulla poesia* (Rome, 1976) and the discussion of E. Garin, *L'educazione in Europa, 1400–1600*, 2nd edn. with corrections (Bari, 1976), 80f.

superiority of free men to lawyers (405^b). In politics, he notes what Plato says about the origins of war (373^{d}7), the suitability of aged judges (409^{b}4), the best size for a city (423^{c}2), the virtues of a good state (427^{e}6), especially its military virtue (429^{b}1), and the types of constitution (544^{c}1). He is interested in Plato's counsels for the good prince: how he is to regulate marriages (460^{a}2), when he is permitted to lie to his subjects for the sake of the public good (459^{c}8), how future princes may be recognized (413^{e}2), how he should control his appetites (389^{d}9), avoid drunkenness (403^{e}4), and refuse bribes (390^{d}7). He shows his disapproval of the community of women, children, and goods by opposing to it the authority of Aristotle's *Politics* (457^{c}10). In a particularly egregious example of selective reading he misrepresents Plato's views on the participation of women in public life (455^{a}9–^{c}4); elsewhere (434^{a}9), he appears to interpret Plato's tripartite scheme of classes as a device to prevent social climbing.

Annotations such as these, clearly, are not the mark of a mind that has come to grips in any profound way with Plato's thought. There is no sign of a critical testing of hypotheses, or even an attempt to elucidate systematically Plato's position on any key issue. It is noteworthy that Guarino makes no attempt to weigh the context of Plato's remarks, and this in a text whose interpretation notoriously requires close attention to irony and levels of seriousness. What Guarino was plainly doing was mining the text for suitable *dicta* for transferral into a commonplace-book, *dicta* which might afterwards be introduced in likely places to enliven his speech and his prose. This was a practice his son recommended in a treatise generally thought to preserve the elder Guarino's educational methods;[59] we have already seen its fruits earlier in our discussion of Guarino's letters.

It may be, however, that Guarino read the *Republic* with a particular purpose in mind, *viz.*, to help his student and life-long friend Francesco Barbaro in the composition of the latter's famous treatise *De re uxoria*. There is a good deal of circumstantial evidence that this was the case. Barbaro composed the treatise, dedicated to Lorenzo de' Medici, after his visit to Florence in the summer of 1415 and before Lorenzo's marriage in the spring of 1416. It is known that in composing it he worked closely

---

59. *De ordine docendi et studendi*, in W.H. Woodward, *Vittorino da Feltre and Other Humanist Educators* (Cambridge, 1897; repr. New York, 1963), 173. A number of the glosses are already labelled for future use, e.g., 374 c 6 *contra milites nostri temporis*, 389 d 9 *contra principes nostri temporis*, 434 a 9 *pro militibus et huiusmodi presidibus etatis nostre*, etc.

with Guarino, with whom he had lived and studied Greek for most of the previous year.[60] Guarino can be plausibly supposed to have possessed the Reginensis codex of the *Republic* at least by 1416, for in August of that year he wrote to Leonardo Giustiniani a letter from Padua apologizing for not being able to lend him the manuscript, which he had left behind in Venice.[61] Guarino's annotations cover approximately the same range of subjects dealt with in the *De re uxoria*. Finally, Guarino addresses him by name in one of the marginal glosses,[62] and several passages from the *Republic* appear in the *De re uxoria* which display verbal affinities with the translation of Chrysoloras and Decembrio.

If Barbaro did indeed use Guarino's annotated *Republic* in the preparation of his treatise, we are in an unusually good position to see both the beginning and the final result of a humanistic reading of a text. Although Barbaro read Greek with some facility, he will have welcomed the help afforded by Chrysoloras' translation in getting another Greek author under his belt. Probably he read most carefully those passages marked by his teacher. Later, in composing his treatise, when he wished to illustrate his belief that wives should be chosen for their prudence rather than for their wealth and station, he remembered what seemed a parallel case in

60. For these two sentences, see the introduction of A. Gnesotto to his edition of the *De re uxoria* in the *Atti e memorie della R. Accademia di scienze, lettere, ed arti in Padova*, ser. 2, 32 (1915–16), 9f.

61. Published by E. Lobel, "A Letter of Guarino and Other Things," in the *Bodleian Quarterly Record*, 5 (1926–29), 43–46, from Bodleian MS Bywater 38, formerly owned by Francesco Barbaro: Γουαρίνος ὁ Ὀυεροναῖος τῷ πεπαιδευμένῳ καὶ παναρίστῳ Λεονάρδῳ χαίρειν. . . . ἄρτι παρὰ σοῦ Μαφαῖος ὁ καλὸς τὴν τοῦ Πλάτωνος Πολιτείαν ᾔτησεν. ἐγὼ δὲ πάντα ἐξετάσας τὰ ἐνταῦθα βιβλία, αὐτὴν οὐχ εὑρίσκω. διὸ ἐν ταῖς ουενετίαις αὐτὴν καταλειπεῖν ἔγνων. οὐ γὰρ πάσας μετ' ἐμοῦ βίβλους ἐκεῖθεν ἤνεγκα. τίνι δὲ περὶ αὐτῆς γράφω, οὐκ οἶδα καλῶς, τὴν οἰκίαν ἔρημον καταλείψας. νῦν δυσχεραίνω, νῦν ἀγανακτῶ, νῦν βαρέως φέρω αὐτὴν οὐ κομίσαι δεῦρο ὅτι τῷ φιλτάτῳ μοῦ καὶ χαριεστάτῳ Λεονάρδῳ εὐχαριστεῖν οὐκ ἔξεστι. σὺ τοίνυν πράως τὴν ἀδυναμίαν μοῦ πρὸς τὸ παρὸν φέρε. εὐτύχει πολυχρόνιος, ἄνερ ἄριστε, καὶ μὲ τῷ φρονιμωτάτῳ καὶ βελτίστῳ Μάρκῳ ἀδέλφου παράδος ὁ φιλτατός σοι Βάρβαρος πλεῖστα σὲ χαίρειν εὔχεται. ἐκ τοῦ Παταβίου τῇ τοῦ Αὐγούστου πρώτῃ. (Spelling, punctuation, and accentuation regularized). P. Hochschild, in a note in *JWCI*, 17 (1955), 142–143, plausibly identifies the recipient of the letter as Leonardo Giustiniani, and dates the letter to the summer of 1416 when Guarino had taken refuge from the plague in Padua with Francesco Barbaro. Since the MS is spoken of as containing only the *Republic*, I venture to identify it with the Reginensis codex; the four Greek manuscripts of Plato owned by Guarino (see above, note 34) seem to have had different contents.

62. At 387 d 5. There is no other Francesco in Guarino's correspondence with whom this could reasonably be identified. The "Nota, Francisce," occurs in a passage where Plato condemns excessive display of grief at the death of friends; perhaps Francesco needed reminding of this after the death of his beloved friend and mentor Zaccaria Trevisan in 1414.

Plato, i.e., that magistrates should be chosen for their ability rather than their ambition. This *locus*, which Guarino had marked for him, he wove into his argument, probably from memory.[63] In another place he wanted to illustrate how *novi homines* always meet with disapproval from the upper classes; he remembered how Plato had compared his guardians to dogs who attacked strangers but loved those familiar to them.[64] Elsewhere he recorded Hesiod's view of the proper age for marriage, which Guarino had compared with Plato's opinion in a marginal note.[65]

Barbaro's use of Plato, like Guarino's, shows little interest in or grasp of Platonic philosophy—indeed, it is hard to imagine a work more foreign to the *Republic*'s social theory than the *De re uxoria*. This is a circumstance not necessarily to be deplored: classicists have for centuries read Plato for his literary grace and his charming vignettes of Athenian intellectual life, without troubling very much about his philosophy. Of course Guarino's way of reading Plato for his *doctrina* is two-dimensional, utilitarian, and (in consequence) frequently ahistorical, but it is not much different from the way he was read by teachers of the humanities for the next

63. *De re uxoria*, ed. Gnesotto, 36: "Plato, gravissimus philosophus, in iis libris quos divinitus *De re publica* scripsit, instituit ut praestantibus, non ambitiosis civibus magistratus tribuantur. Prospiciebat enim brevi paucos admodum decertaturos esse, si coronae nobilitate non bene merentes, sed cupidi pugiles donarentur. Quare publicam mercedem magistratibus ipse proposuit, ne rei familiaris incommodo ab officio rei publicae retraherentur. Sic nos in uxore prudentiam tanti faciemus. . . ." The Chrysoloras-Decembrio translation, at 347 c: "Propterea, inquam, neque pecuniarum neque honoris cupidine boni cupiunt principari. Non enim propter premium principantis palam pecuniam postulantes volunt mercenarii nuncupari, nec clam sumentes fures esse, neque propter honorem iterum cum ambitiosi protinus non asistant. Oportet igitur necessitatem illis et damnum incumbere quando cogantur aliquotiens principari. Ex quo convincitur evidenter sponte ad principatum accedere, non expectata necessitate, turpissimum reputari" (Reg. lat. 1131, f. 5rb). Barbaro seems to interpret this passage as though it meant, "good men (if not compensated properly) will suffer loss when they are compelled to take part in government; therefore Plato proposed public salaries for the rulers" (a reference probably to 416 e). This interpretation might easily be read into the sentence "Oportet . . . principari," if the context was not observed too closely. It could not be read into the Greek, since Plato clearly says, "Some compulsion or penalty must be imposed on them, if they are going to consent to hold office" (δεῖ δὴ αὐτοῖς ἀνάγκην προσεῖναι καὶ ζημίαν, εἰ μέλλουσιν ἐθέλειν ἄρχειν); Barbaro's reading of the passage therefore seems closer to the Latin mistranslation than to the Greek text.

64. *De re uxoria*, ed. Gnesotto, 43: "Canes, ut in veteri proverbio est, cum in alienos a tergo, a fronte, a lateribus asperi latrent ac saeviant, domesticis tamen tractabiles sunt." The Chrysoloras-Decembrio translation at 375 e 1: "Nosti etenim generosorum canum nativi moris existere ad consuetos ac notos quantum est possibile se gerere mansuetos, asperos vero ad ignotos videri. . . . Ignotum enim cum viderit etsi nil mali passus ab eo fuerit statim irascitur, notum vero quamquam ab eo nil fructus acceperit dilectione prosequitur" (Reg. lat. 1131, f. 9rb–va).

65. See Guarino's annotation at 460 e 4–7.

three centuries.[66] Certainly it is much preferable to the *morbus gallicus* that has infected academic reading of literature in recent decades.

Whatever the merits of Guarino's literary method, it is clear that it was not well-adapted to grasp critically or receptively the dialectical necessity of Plato's philosophical position. For Guarino, as for Decembrio, Bruni, and the other humanists of the early fifteenth century, Plato's philosophy was not a systematic exposition of the nature of the cosmos, man, and the state, but a collection of wise sayings and melodious maxims "suitable for use in schools" and for the furnishing of one's copybook. There is no evidence in any of Guarino's works that he either understood Plato's argumentation or that his thinking on any matter was perceptibly altered by his reading of the dialogues. If he was fascinated by "lo stato razionale" of Plato, he gives no sign of it. For a more sophisticated understanding of Plato's philosophy we must await the Plato-Aristotle controversy of mid-century and the work of Marsilio Ficino; in the early fifteenth century, such an understanding simply did not exist. This truth will distress only those who insist on maintaining that the humanists were genuine philosophers as well as men of letters, or worse, that the humanist movement was a kind of philosophical school. Such persons only do their historical subjects a disservice by attempting to construe their vague, disconnected and frequently contradictory remarks into something like a philosophy. Guarino, surely, would rather have been remembered as a great teacher than as a bad philosopher.

JAMES HANKINS

---

66. The twin emphasis on philology and morality is also typical, for instance, of the lectures at the Collège Royal in Paris during the sixteenth century; see the illuminating article by Grafton in volume 1 of *History of Universities* (1980).

APPENDIX A

Plato's "Divided Line" in the Latin Translation Of Manuel Chrysoloras and Uberto Decembrio

(Rep., Bk. VI, 509ᵈ6–511ᵉ5)

I give the text according to the autograph, Milan, Biblioteca Ambrosiana, MS B 123 sup., ff. 183v–184v (= A), together with the readings of Guarino's manuscript, Reg. lat. 1131, ff. 28va–29ra (= R). The Ambrosiana MS has marginal and interlinear corrections in the hand of Uberto, which I have indicated in the apparatus, and marginal notations in the hand of Pier Candido Decembrio, which I intend to edit on another occasion. The italicized words are glosses added by the translators. Capitalization and punctuation have been regularized in accordance with modern usage.

/ f. 183v / Sicut igitur lineam ad duas inequales sectam portiones cum acceperis, iterum utramque partem eadem ratione diviseris, et illam que visibilis generis et illam iterum que intelligibilis *reputatur*, tibique ad alterutrum claritas atque obscuritas orietur in visibili quidem imagines — dico vero ima-
5   gines: primum umbras, posteaque in aquis et in aliis aliqui speculantur, quecunque densa atque levia et lucida consistunt et omne huiusmodi si consideres.

    Ego, *inquit*, considero.

    Divino alterum igitur similatur animaliaque que apud nos extant et totum plantabile ac fabricabile genus ponas.

10   Pono, inquit.

    An et velis, / f. 184r / inquam, ipsum veritate et non *veritate* dicere separari, sicut opinabile ad scibile, sic simile cui simile uideatur.

    Valde, inquit.

Interlocutores passim indicantur in R, desunt autem in A.   5 aliqui] alii R
8 *vicem* τίθει ᾧ *legunt* τι θείῳ *interpretes, ut videtur*   11 ipsum *add. supra* Decembrius; *uterque* ueritate *ex* uera *corr. manu eiusdem*

Considera iterum igitur intelligibilis sectionem.

15 Quonam, inquit, modo?

Quo alterum ipsius, *inquam*, existit quod illis, videlicet que prius divisimus, tamquam imaginibus utens anima ex suppositione compellitur, non ad principium *ac superiora*, sed ad finem *ac inferiora* procedere; reliquum vero *est* quod ad principium cuius suppositio non existit ex suppositionibus pro-

20 greditur, ac sicut imaginibus per quas in illo altero ipsis speciebus per ipsas methodum faciens *utebatur*.

Hec, inquit, non sufficienter equidem intellexi.

Sed facilius, inquam, his predictis intelliges. Puto enim te scire quod qui geometriam, arismetricam et huiusmodi cogitant rationes, par et impar figu-

25 rasque angulorum trinas species et alia similia supponentes, hec quidem tamquam scientes et suppositionibus facientes nullam rationem neque sibi ipsis neque aliis dignum reddere putant, tamquam huiusmodi existentibus cuilibet manifestis. Ex his vero inchoantes iam reliqua disserentes ad illud finiunt cuius considerationem equidem antea posuerunt.

30 Valde equidem, inquit, hec nosco.

Visibilibus speciebus etiam coutuntur sermonesque de his, quamquam non de ipsis intelligentes, faciuntur, sed de illis *videlicet* quorum hec imagines concernuntur, de quadrato ipsomet ac diametro iudicantes, sed non de illo quem scribunt et alia consequenter. Hec equidem ipsa que fingunt atque describunt

35 quorum etiam umbre et in aquis imagines concernuntur tamquam imaginibus utentes, querunt illamet agnoscere que non aliter quam mente cernuntur.

Verum, inquit.

Hanc speciem igitur intelligibilis predicebam ad ipsius vero indagationem suppositionibus uti animam cohartari, non ad principia procedentem tamquam

40 supra ⟨sup⟩positiones progredi non potentem, illis vero imaginibus utentem que sunt ex inferioribus similata ac illis ad illa tamquam perspicue divisis et similiter opinatis.

Intelligo, inquit, te dicere quod in geometria et germanis illi artibus dici solet.

45 Reliquam igitur intelligibilis partem dicere me etiam opineris, illud quod

---

20 *vicem* ὥνπερ *legunt* ὥσπερ *interpretes*, ἄνευ *praetermisso*   23 his *add.*
in marg. Decembrius   32 de ipsis *add. in marg. Decembrius*; sed *add. idem supra*
33 -met *add in marg. Decembrius*   40 positiones *AR*, ὑποθέσεις *graece*

ipsa ratio demonstrandi potentia manifestat, suppositiones non principia
fabricans, sed vere suppositiones tamquam basses atque principia, ut usque ad
illud quod supponi non potest, ad principium ueniens uniuersi ac ipsum tan-
gens, iterumque tenens adherentibus*que* illi adherens *assidue*, sensibili prorsus
50   nullo utens, sed ipsis speciebus per ipsas ad ipsas atque ad speciem finiens
ad finem *usque* perveniat.

Intelligo, inquit, quamquam minime sufficienter *ut cuperem*. Videris enim
arduam michi rem proponere. Moliris tamen disserere partem entis atque intelligibilis quam a demonstrationis scientia speculamur illa esse clariorem que
55   ab *illis scientiis que* artes nuncupantur quibus suppositiones *pro* principiis *sug-
geruntur*, et mente quidem coguntur, non sensibus, quicumque ea viderint intueri. Quia vero non ad principium ascendentes sed ex suppositionibus speculantur, intellectum erga ipsa tibi habere non videntur, quamvis intelligibilia
cum principio concernantur. Mentem autem videris mihi geometricalium et
60   huiusmodi habitum appellare, tamquam mente inter opinionem et intellectum
huiusmodi consistente.

Sufficientissime me, inquam, *ut video*, percepisti, ac super istis quattuor
portionibus quattuor quasi quasdam anime dispositiones accipias: / f. 184v /
intellectum in primo, mentem in secundo, tertio vero fidem, ultimoque con-
65   jecturationem, ipsaque ordines analogice, quemadmodum illa in quibus ista
consistunt participant veritatis, sic ista participare concipiens claritatis.

Intelligo, inquit, et concedo et iuxta tua dicta dispono.

---

53 Molliris *mss.*   54 ad demonstrationes R: ὑπὸ τῆς τοῦ διαλέγεσθαι
ἐπιστήμης *graece*

Figura (f. 184v):

	¶Visibile		¶Intelligibile
¶Obscurum	¶Clarum	¶Obscurum	¶Clarum
Imagines	Quorum imagines	Quod ex suppositionibus principiis non ad principia sed ad finem procedit per imagines visibiles scilicet mathematichas.	Quod ex suppositionibus non principiis ad princium cuius non est suppositio sicut imaginibus per ipsas species procedit quam scientiam dialecticam uocat, methaphisicam existentem.

Coniecturatio	Fides	Mens	Intelligentia ac intellectus
Opinio ac opinabile _____		Scientia ac scibile _____	
Non veritas _____		Veritas _____	
Non veritas	Magis quodammodo veritas	Minus quodammodo veritas	Magis veritas

This diagram is probably based on a scholion in Chrysoloras' Greek manuscript, for it shows some affinity to the one edited by W. C. Greene in his *Scholia Platonica*;[1] a definite proof of this however will not be possible until the scholia of the "W" family are investigated more thoroughly. Yet even if it is a mere translation of a Greek scholion, that the translators chose to repeat it uncritically re-

---

1. (Haverford, 1938), 246. Greene gives the following scholion at 510b, which corresponds to a large degree with the entries under "Obscurum" and "Clarum" on the right-hand side of the line:

γ	δ
μαθηματική	διαλεκτική
ἐξ ὑποθέσεως	ἐξ ὑποθέσεως
ἐπὶ τέλος ἰοῦσα	ἐπ' ἀρχὴν ἰοῦσα ἀνυπόθετον
δι' αἰσθητῶν εἰκόνων	δι' αὐτῶν τῶν εἰδῶν
διάνοια	νοῦς

veals their lack of understanding of Platonic philosophy. The distinction posited in the main division of the Line between objects of thought and states of knowledge is obscured by the presence of *opinabile* and *scibile* among the states of knowledge. The scale of truth-values is equally unplatonic: it is doubtful whether Plato would have labelled the left side of the line simply as *non veritas*, since he allows in many places for a state of correct belief (ὀρθὴ δόξα), for instance at *Rep.* 506b. The mistaken reading at 510b7 of ὥσπερ for ὧνπερ (with the omission of ἄνευ) reappears in the far right-hand column of the diagram, with the result that dialectic is made to proceed by means of images, whereas Plato's point had been precisely the opposite. The translation of μετέχειν by *participare* and εἴδη by *species* was sanctioned by the medieval tradition, but the translation of διάνοια as *mens*, when νοῦς had been translated *intellectum*, is odd, and argues an ignorance of the Neoplatonic tradition of exegesis.[2] The remarkable rendering of πίστις by *fides* (which Ficino uses as well), and its clear labelling as a truth-value inferior to the philosopher's *intelligentia*, also suggests an absence of reflection: it is unlikely that Uberto and Chrysoloras (unlike Ficino) would have dared so boldly to reverse the values of medieval Christian philosophy if they had realized what they were doing.

APPENDIX B

Marginalia of Guarino Veronese in Reg. lat. 1131

Except for the first long note, all marginalia are preceded by a reference corresponding to the standard pagination of Plato's works, and a line number corresponding to Burnet's Oxford text of 1902; the folio number of the MS is given in parentheses following each note. In a few cases I have thought it helpful to give either the Greek text or the Latin version or both of the passage annotated by Guarino in square brackets preceding the note. Punctuation and capitalization have been modernized.

2. Ficino translates *cogitatio* and *intelligentia* respectively.

Huius auctor proemii, quem honoris gratia nominare minime constituo, aesopiani more corui aliena in se ornamenta per inanem quandam iactantiam transfert [cf. *Aesopica*, ed. Perry (Urbana, Ill., 1952), 482, Fab. gr. no. 398 = Apthonius 40]. Constat enim clarissimum virum Manuelem Chrysoloram Constantinopolitanum, cuius opera similiter et beneficio graeca ad nostrates disciplina rediit, haec diuina Platonis *Politica* volumina suis verbis nullius mortalis auxilio in Latinam vertisse linguam. Cum tamen futilis iste iactator, fucorum instar, alienos depascens labores [cf. *ibid.*, 573, Fab. lat. no. 504 = Phaedrus III, 13; vid. etiam ad n. 4 supra] Manuelis stilum exornasse falso quidem predicet, quem teste mundo nihil praeter litterarum apices ac syllabas graece scisse conuincimus, latina uero dictione ne Manueli quidem parem. Id tamen inficiari nemo potest, hunc ipsum de quo loquor prologatorem gloriosum suam Manueli accommodasse operam: Manuel enim dictabat, hic autem dictata exarabat ut qui scribae munus profiteretur. Te igitur, quisquis hoc volumen transcribis, per Deum immortalem et filium eius Iesum Christum oro, obtestor, et adiuro, ut hoc in operis initio transcribis epigramma, ne per tam inpudens mendacium praestantissimum atque doctissimum hominem, cui plurimum Italorum studia debent, sua spoliari gloria sinas, aut prologum ipsum omittas, qui praeter ineptias nihil habet. (f. 1v)

Bk. I]
347 c 2–3:   Non sponte principandum. (f. 5rb)

Bk. II]
357 b 4f.:   Nota hanc divisionem. (f. 6va)
359 e 2f.:   Mos pastorum. (f. 6vb)
362 b 1:   [versus ex *Septem* Aeschyli, ll. 592f.]:
                       Consilia gloriosa. (f. 7ra)
371 a 10:   Mercatores. (f. 8va)
371 d 4:   Revenditores. (f. 8vb)
371 e 1f.:   Mercenarii. (f. 8vb)
373 d 7f.:   Ortus bellorum. (f. 9ra)
374 c 6:   Contra milites nostri temporis. (f. 9ra)
374 e 6:   Optime. (f. 9rb)
375 a 9:   Ciuis qualis corpore. (f. 9rb)
375 b 7:   Ciuis animo iracundum. (f. 9rb)
375 c 1:   In suos mansuetus, in hostes difficilis. (f. 9rb)
375 e 2:   Generosi canes. (f. 9rb)
376 b 11:   Philosophi. (f. 9va)
376 c 4:   Ciuitatis custos fortis et irascibilis. (f. 9va)
376 e 6:   Erudiantur prius musica, deinde gymnastica. (f. 9va)

378 a 1:	Contra legentes amatoria carmina iuuenibus. (f. 9vb)
378 d 2:	Contra poetas. (f. 9vb)
379 c 4:	Deus non est causa mali. (f. 10ra)
379 d 3:	Dolia sortium. (f. 10ra)
380 c 8:	Deus solum causa bonorum. (f. 10ra)
380 d 1f.:	Quod deus non transformetur. (f. 10ra)
381 d 5:	Protheus. (f. 10rb)

Bk. III]

386 d 10:	Hebes. (f. 10vb)
387 b 1f.:	Pulchre. (f. 10vb)
387 d 5:	Nota, Francisce. (f. 10vb)
387 e 9:	Non plorandum. (f. 10vb)
388 a 6:	Achilles. (f. 11ra)
388 b 4:	Priamus. (f. 11ra)
388 c 7:	Sarpedon. (f. 11ra)
388 e 5:	Non frequenter ridendum. (f. 11ra)
389 b 7:	Quibus forte mentiri liceat. (f. 11ra)
389 d 1:	Puniendi mendaces. (f. 11ra)
389 d 9:	Contra principes nostri temporis. (f. 11ra)
390 d 7:	Bona institutio. (f. 11rb)
391 c 3:	Chiron. (f. 11rb)
395 b 8f.:	De libertate policie et liberalibus studiis. (f. 12ra)
395 c 3f.:	De consuetudine pulchre. (f. 12ra)
395 e 7f.:	Contra plerosque quos uocant facetos. (f. 12ra)
396 c 5:	Vnde historiarum et annalium fructus. (f. 12rb)
398 c 11:	Sermo Armonia ⟩ in cantu (f. 12va) Rithimus
398 e 6:	Ebrietas Molicies ⟩ (f. 12va) Ocium
401 c 6:	Simile. (f. 13ra)
402 b 9:	Musici. (f. 13rb)
402 e 5:	Voluptas insanos facit. (f. 13rb)
403 d 2:	Virtus corporis ab animo. (f. 13rb)
403 e 4:	Ebrietas in principe turpissima. (f. 13va)
404 b 4:	Gymnastica germana musice. (f. 13va)
404 c 1f.:	Carnes assate militares. (f. 13va)
404 c 6f.:	Abstinendum condimentis. (f. 13va)

504 a 1f.:	Medicorum officine. (f. 13va)
405 b 6f.:	Pulchre contra causidicos. (f. 13va)
406 a 7:	Herodicus. (f. 13vb)
406 c 1f.:	Quibus non conveniant medicine. (f. 13vb)
407 a 7:	Phocilides. (f. 14ra)
408 d 10f.:	Pro medicis. (f. 14rb)
409 b 4f.:	Senex iudex. (f. 14rb)
409 c 4:	Bonus. (f. 14rb)
409 c 5:	Sagax. (f. 14rb)
410 d 3f.:	Gymnastica agrestis, musica mollis. (f. 14va)
412 c 2–3:	Principes seniores. (f. 14vb)
412 c 12–13:	Quales custodes ciuitatis. (f. 14vb)
413 b 4:	Decepti. (f. 14vb)
413 b 9:	Violati. (f. 14vb)
413 c 1:	Incantati. (f. 14vb)
413 e 2f.:	Quis a puero princeps futurus agnoscitur. (f. 15ra)
415 a 4:	Deus artifex. (f. 15rb)
415 a 4f.:	Aurum reges. (f. 15rb)
415 a 6–7:	Ferrum agricole. (f. 15rb)
416 a 2–8:	Pulchre. (f. 15rb)

Bk. IV]

420 c 4f.:	Apta similitudo. (f. 15vb)
421 d 4f.:	Divicie. Paupertas. (f. 15vb)
423 c 2f.:	Mediocris ciuitas. (f. 16ra)
424 b 4:	Tutores ciuitatis. (f. 16rb)
424 e 5:	Legalis eruditio. (f. 16rb)
425 b 10–c 2:	Magna uis prime institutionis. (f. 16va)
425 c 10f.:	Plebeia commercia. (f. 16va)
426 a 1f.:	Passio egrotantium. (f. 16va)
426 b 3–4:	Non succensendum bene monentibus. (f. 16vb)
426 e 8:	Sectio ydre. (f. 16vb)
427 e 6–8:	Qualis ciuitas recte constituta. (f. 16vb)
428 a 8–b 1:	Scientia sapienter deliberatur. (f. 16vb)
428 c 9:	Agricultura. (f. 17ra)
428 c 11–d 3:	Quia sapiens et recti consilii est ciuitas propter custoditiu. [*scil.* custoditiuam scientiam]. (f. 17ra)
429 a 2:	[σοφίαν] Prudentia. (f. 17ra)
429 b 1–3:	Ciuitas uirilis dicitur a bellatoribus suis. (f. 17ra)
429 d 4f.:	Simile. (f. 17ra)

429 e 7–430 b 5:   Virilitas. (f. 17rb)

430 e b: Temperantia. (f. 17rb)

431 a 3f.:   [*At inquam hic sermo mihi uidetur ostendere quod equidem in homines anima quiddam melius (*) et quiddam peius (**) existit,
quandoque quod natura est optimum peiori dominet, tunc iudicabi-
mus suimet potentiorem existere, quando uero contrarium, con-
cernatur debiliorem ac immoderatum qui sic dispositus fuerit
iudicamus.*] (*) Ratio. (**) Appetitus sensitiuus.[1] (f.
17rb).

431 c 5–7:   Pauci quos equus amauit Juppiter aut ardens euexit ad ethera
uirtus. [Vergil, *Aen.* VI, 129–130]. (f. 17ra)

431 e 10–432 a 9:   Temperantia communis omnibus. (f. 17ra)

433 a 1–6:   Optimum etiam in uno quoque genere naturam ducem sequi. (f. 17ra)

433 a 9:   Justitia. (f. 17va)

433 e 3–4:   Jus imprimis perdiscendum principi. (f. 17vb)

434 a 9–b 7:   Nota. Pro militibus et huiusmodi presidibus etatis nostre.
(f. 17vb)

434 c 7–8:   Questuarii, Auxiliatiui, Custodes. (f. 18ra)

436 c 8–d 2:   Non idem mouetur et quiescit. (f. 18ra)

436 d 5:   Trochus. (f. 18ra)

438 a 3–4:   [... *cum omnes bona equidem natura desiderent*] Omnia bona
appetunt. (f. 18rb)

439 d 5, 8:   Rationabile. Appetibile. (f. 18va)

440 c 1f.:   Generosi animi non irasci inter iniuriandum. (f. 18vb)

440 d 4–6:   Auxiliatores canes, principes pastores. (f. 18vb)

440 e 8–441 a 3:   [λογιστικὸν καὶ ἐπιθυμητικὸν ... τὸ θυμοειδές:
rationabile et appetibile ... irascibile]:
Rationabile. Appetibile. Irascibile.[2] (f. 18vb)

443 a 2–3:   A quibus cauendum. (f. 19rb)

---

1. It is worth noting Guarino's use of Aristotelian terminology here and also at 438ᵃ3–4, where
the phrase "omnia bonum appetunt" recalls Grosseteste's translation of the *Eth. Nic.* I, 1 (1094
a) rather than Bruni's. Guarino also shows his familiarity with Aristotle's *Ethics* (frequently
read in the arts curriculum of Italian universities of this period) at 457ᵃ6f. and 457ᶜ10–ᵈ 3.
2. The translation *rationabile, irascibile, appetibile* for Plato's three functions or faculties of the
soul would seem to be closest to Apuleius (*De dog. Plat.* 1, 13 and 2, 24, ed. P. Thomas [Stutt-
gart, 1970], pp. 97, 127–9), who uses *ratio, irascentia*, and *appetibile*; rather than Calcidius,
who translates *rationabile, iracundia, cupiditas* (*Comm. in Tim.*, cap. 233, ed. Waszink, p. 247),
or William of Conches, who employs *sapientia, animositas*, and *concupiscentia* in his unpublished
commentary on Macrobius (quoted by Jeauneau, *Glosae super Platonem* [Paris, 1965], 75n.).
Uberto makes unacknowledged use of William's commentary in the opening lines of his *Prologus*.

445 c 4–7:   [Καὶ μήν, ἦν δ' ἐγώ, ὥσπερ ἀπὸ σκοπιᾶς μοι φαίνεται, ἐπειδὴ ἐνταῦθα ἀναβεβήκαμεν τοῦ λόγου, ἓν μὲν εἶναι εἶδος τῆς ἀρετῆς, ἄπειρα δὲ τῆς κακίας, τέτταρα δ' ἐν αὐτοῖς ἄττα ὧν καὶ ἄξιον ἐπιμνησθῆναι:

Atqui, inquam, tamquam e specula cum huc sermonis ascendimus mihi uidetur unicam speciem uirtutis, malicie autem innumeras ...]:

Vnica species uirtutis, malicie innumerae.[3] (f. 19va)

445 d 6:   Regnum. Aristocratia.[4] (f. 19va)

Bk. V]

455 a 9–b 2:   A ciuilibus muneribus abstineant mulieres. (f. 20va)

455 b 4f.:   Diuersitas ingeniorum. (f. 20va)

455 c 4–d 1:   Deterior conditio mulierum in omnibus. (f. 20va)

456 b 1–3:   Mulieres custodes. (f. 20vb)

456 b 8–10:   Custodes ciuitatum eruditi meliores. (f. 20vb)

457 a 6f.:   Ornatissimum generis uestis. Contra doctrinam Aristotelis secundo *Politicorum* et *Economicorum*. [*Pol.* II, 9, 1269 b 20; *ps.-Aristoteles, Oecon.* I, 1344 a 19f.] (f. 20vb)

457 c 10–d 3:   Nota. Hic de communione mulierum et filiorum quam pulchre et subtiliter reprobat Aristoteles secundo *Politicorum*. [*Pol.* II, 2–4, 1261 a f.] (f. 21ra)

457 e 7f.:   Contra eos qui ex stultis insani fiunt.[5] (f. 21ra)

458 b 9–c 4:   Parere. Imperare. (f. 21ra)

458 c 6f.:   Domus et commesatio communis. (f. 21ra)

458 e 3–4:   Sacre nuptiae. (f. 21rb)

459 a 10–11:   Ex optimis et fortissimis procreandum. (f. 21rb)

459 c 2–6:   Quibus etiam uiles medici sufficiant. (f. 21rb)

459 c 8–d 2:   Principibus aliquando rei publice gratia mentiri licet. (f. 21rb)

459 d 7f.:   Optimi cum optimis coheant. (f. 21rb)

459 e 5f.:   Sponsalia. (f. 21rb)

460 a 2f.:   Principes censores nuptiarum. (f. 21rb)

460 a 8–10:   Sortes. (f. 21rb)

460 b 1–5:   Munera constituenda a principibus. (f. 21rb)

460 b 7–10:   Liberi communes. (f. 21rb)

---

3. The translators again follow Apuleius and the late ancient tradition in their translation of ἀρετή and κακία as *virtus* and *malicia*, rather than *virtus* and *vitium* with Cicero. Bruni censured the use of *malicia* as a medieval barbarism some years later in his *Praefatio quaedam ad evidentiam novae translationis* Ethicorum *Aristotelis* (ed. Baron, p. 81).

4. Chrysoloras and Uberto translate βασιλεία with the phrase *imperium vel regnum*.

5. Terence, *Eun.* 2, 2, 23, also quoted by Guarino in his *Epistolario*, 1:245.

460 e 4–7:	Mulier xx anno nubat, uir autem xxx. Hesiodus autem dicit xv. [*Op. et Dies*, 698] (f. 21va)
462 c 7–8:	Hic nota quemadmodum se habet pars corporis ad corpus, ita et ciuis ad rempublicam. (f. 21vb)
464 b 8–c 3:	Milites custodie, non lucri causa mercenarii sint. (f. 22ra)
465 a 5–6:	Seniores preceptores iuuenum. (f. 22ra)
465 d 6:	Victoria. (f. 22rb)
466 a 2–6:	Vniuersa ciuitas felix finis policie. (f. 22rb)
466 c 2–3:	[γνώσεται τὸν Ἡσίοδον ὅτι τῷ ὄντι ἦν σοφὸς λέγων πλέον εἶναί πως ἥμισυ παντός]: νήπιοι ὅδ' ἴσασι ὅσω πλέον ἥμισυ παντός.⁶ (f. 22rb)
466 e 4f.:	De iis qui ad militiam instituuntur. (f. 22rb)
467 d 5–7:	Pedagogi prudentes et senes. (f. 22va)
467 e 2f.:	Adolescentes instruantur equitare. (f. 22va)
468 a 5–7:	Timidi opifices uel coloni fiant. (f. 22va)
468 a 9–10:	Viuentes capti hostibus relinquantur. (f. 22va)
468 b 2–5:	Quae humanitas strenuis ac probis debeatur. (f. 22va)
468 c 10:	Homerus. (f. 22va)
468 d 1f.:	Aiax honoratus. (f. 22vb)
468 d 7f.:	Boni plurimum honorandi. (f. 22vb)
468 e 4f.:	Strenue in bello morientes aurei generis demones efficiuntur. (f. 22vb)
469 b 8f.:	Indulgendum liberis etiam in bello. (f. 22vb)
469 d 6f.:	Non licet spoliare cadauera mortuorum. (f. 22vb)
469 d 9–e 2:	Apta similitudo. (f. 22vb)
469 e 7f.:	Spolia grecorum non referantur. (f. 22vb)
470 a 5–7:	Flammis et populationibus abstinendum. (f. 23ra)
470 d 8–e 2:	In seditione fruges rapere concessum. (f. 23ra)
471 a 9–12:	Pauci qui fuerint causa discordie plectendi, reliquas ignoscendum. (f. 23ra)
472 b 7f.:	Vir iustus nil differt a justitia. (f. 23rb)
473 c 11–e 5:	Beatas fore res publicas que regantur a sapientibus.⁷ (f. 23va)
474 d 7–9:	Aquilinitas regalis. (f. 23va)
474 e 1:	Nigri uiriles. (f. 23va)
474 e 2:	Albi deorum filii (f. 23va)
475 a 9:	Ambitiosi (f. 23vb)

6. Guarino has filled out the line from *Op. et Dies*, 40.
7. See above, note 49.

475 b 8-9:	Philosophus studiosus sapientie. (f. 23vb)
475 d 1f.:	Similes philosophis. (f. 23vb)
477 e 8-478 a 1:	Opinio. Scientia. (f. 24ra)
479 e 10f.:	Amare. (f. 24va)
480 a 6:	Philodoxus. (f. 24va)

Bk. VI] —

Bk. VII]

| 520 d 2-4: | Ambitio causa seditionis. (f. 30ra) |
| 526 c 10: | Geometria. (f. 31ra) |

Bk. VIII]

| 544 c 1f.: | Timarchia. Oligarchia. Democratia. Tyrannis. (f. 33va) |

Bk. IX] —

Bk. X] —

PSEUDO–DIONYSIUS
THE AREOPAGITE
IN MID–QUAT–
TROCENTO
ROME

F ROM THE NINTH CENTURY, when first Hilduinus and then John Scotus
  Eriugena translated him, through the twelfth century, when John Sarra-
cenus made a new rendering, through the thirteenth century when Robert
Grosseteste retranslated him, to the fifteenth century, when Ambrogio
Traversari and Marsilio Ficino each produced fresh versions of his writings,
Pseudo-Dionysius the Areopagite exercised an almost continuous influence
on the philosophical and theological literature of the Latin West.[1] Hence,
the Renaissance unmasking of the Dionysian corpus as apocryphal is more
than an episode in the history of scholarship.[2] It constitutes part of the
wider transformation of the Western intellectual tradition in modern times.

1. The literature on Pseudo-Dionysius in the Latin West is extensive. The handiest guides are
B. De Mottoni Faes, Il "Corpus Dionysiacum" nel Medioevo. Rassegna di studi 1900–1972 (Bologna,
1977); the articles by A. Combes, M. de Gandillac, and R. Marcel in "Denys L'Aréopagite (Le
Pseudo-)," DSAM, 3 (Paris, 1957): 286–449, at 318–410; and those by M. Cappuyns and R.
Aubert in "Le Pseudo-Aréopagite," DHGE 14 (Paris, 1960): 265–310 at 290ff. The medieval Latin translations of the Dionysian corpus are collected by P. Chevalier et al. in Dionysiaca. Recueil
donnant l'ensemble des traductions latines des ouvrages attribués au Denys de l'Aréopage, 2 vols. (Bruges,
1937–50). The best introduction to Pseudo-Dionysius remains R. Rocques, L'Univers dionysien.
Structure hiérarchique du monde selon le Pseudo-Denys (Paris, 1954).
2. In addition to the articles cited in the previous note see E. N. Tigerstedt, The Decline and
Fall of the Neoplatonic Interpretation of Plato. An Outline and Some Observations (Helsinki, 1974),
21ff.; and M. de Gandillac in the introduction to his edition of Oeuvres complètes du Pseudo-Denys
l'Areopagite (Paris, 1943), 17ff.

Canonical accounts of the story invariably begin with Lorenzo Valla
in the mid-fifteenth century and then jump to the controversy caused by
Erasmus some seventy years later, with perhaps some notice of scholars
such as Marsilio Ficino who defended Pseudo-Dionysius in the intervening period.[3] Yet Erasmus himself insisted that he was not the first in his
own time to question Dionysius' authenticity, claiming that the English
scholar William Grocyn had done the same in lectures at St. Paul's in
London some years earlier.[4] Likewise, Valla had asserted that he did not
stand alone in his generation, noting that "some" contemporary Greek
scholars (*quidam nostrae aetatis eruditissimi Graeci*) considered "Dionysius
the Areopagite" actually to have been Apollinaris (the fourth-century heretic).[5] The purpose of this paper is to explore the Roman context of Valla's attack on the authenticity of the Areopagite and to identify the "learned
Greeks" whom Valla cited.

As is incontrovertibly proved by the first redaction of his *Collatio Novi
Testamenti*, written in the early 1440s at the court of King Alfonso of
Naples, Valla had rejected the traditional belief in "Dionysius the
Areopagite" well before he left Naples for Rome in 1448.[6] Valla's argu-
ment in this first, Neapolitan redaction of the *Collatio* may be schema-
tized under four headings:

    1. The name "Areopagite" connotes not a *locus philosophorum*, but

---

3. Occasionally one sees mistaken references to a letter in defense of the Areopagite by Giovanni
Pico della Mirandola. As Tigerstedt, *The Decline*, 90, n. 234, pointed out, the letter is actually
by his nephew, Gianfrancesco Pico. For the *fortuna* of the letter see C. B. Schmitt, *Gianfrancesco
Pico della Mirandola (1469–1533) and His Critique of Aristotle* (The Hague, 1967), 195, no. 21.

4. Tigerstedt, *The Decline*, 29–30, who dates the lectures to 1501–1502 on the basis of a reference by Thomas More (see E. F. Rogers, ed., *The Correspondence of Sir Thomas More* [Princeton,
1947], 4). The two times Erasmus referred to Grocyn's denial of the Areopagite's authorship were
in the second edition of his New Testament (1519; see *Desiderii Erasmi Opera omnia*, 6 [Leiden,
1705; repr. Hildesheim, 1964]: 503, n. 50) and in his *Declarationes* of 1531 against the Sorbonne's
Censurae of the same year (*ibid.*, 9: 917).

5. "Quorum auctorem quidam nostrae aetatis eruditissimi Graeci colligunt fuisse Apollinarem,"
in his *Adnotationes in Novum Testamentum* reprinted from the *Opera*, of Basel, 1540, in L. Valla,
Opera omnia, 2 vols., with an introduction by E. Garin (Turin, 1962), 1: 852, col. 2. For an
improved text of this passage see S. Camporeale, *Lorenzo Valla. Umanesimo e teologia* (Florence,
1972), 428–29. Valla did not specify "of Laodicea" when he spoke of Apollinaris, but there really
is no other Apollinaris to whom his "learned Greeks" could have plausibly been referring. See
below at note 100.

6. See his *'Collatio Novi Testamenti'. Redazione inedita*, ed. A. Perosa (Florence, 1970), 167. Perosa, xxxvii–xl, and Camporeale, *Lorenzo Valla*, 351–58, convincingly date the completion of the
Collatio to 1443.

a *locus iudicum*, i.e., the site in Athens where the city judges sat. The Dionysius of Acts was a judge, whereas the author of *The Celestial Hierarchy* was clearly a philosopher. But Acts calls Dionysius simply the Areopagite, not Epicurean, Stoic, Peripatetic, or Academic, which were the reigning philosophic sects.

2. The author does not smack of antiquity (*nec antiquitatem sapit*).

3. The eclipse at the moment of Christ's death which he claimed to have seen at Athens occurred only in Judaea; and even if it were universal, an Athenian judge would not have spoken of it in the philosophical terms used by the author.

4. None of the ancient Greek and Latin authorities know this author.

After coming to Rome, Valla substantially revised the *Collatio*.[7] At the same time, he also came into contact with the Greek and Latin scholars associated with Cardinal Bessarion. Indeed, in his *Antidotum II*, written in the spring of 1453, Valla specifically acknowledged that Bessarion had played an important role in his coming to Rome.[8] He also noted in the *Antidotum II*[9] that Bessarion had called his attention to the textual problem in John 21:22 which Valla resolved in the last version of his *Collatio*[10] exactly as Bessarion said he should.[11] It was in this final version of his collation of the New Testament, i. e., the *Adnotationes in Novum Testamentum* of the sixteenth-century editions, that Valla cited the opinion of some contemporary Greek scholar(s), that Pseudo-Dionysius was really Apolli-

7. See below for a discussion of the dating of this revision.

8. For the date of the *Antidotum II* see p. xliii of Perosa's introduction to the *Collatio* and especially Camporeale, *Lorenzo Valla*, 363–65. My text of the relevant passage is taken from Camporeale, 361, who used the autograph, Paris, BN, MS lat. 8691, f. 88v (= *Opera omnia*, 1: 339–40): "Nam cardinalis Nicaenus, vir de me optime meritus et qui ut Romam venirem auctor extitit, habet in opere meo partem; quippe illud cuius supra feci mentionem, 'si eum volo manere quid a te' [Io. 21:22], quod ego non animadverteram, ut adderem admonuit."

9. See the quotation in the previous note.

10. *Adnotationes in Novum Testamentum*, *Opera omnia*, 1: 846. col. 2; and (corrected against the unique Brussels manuscript of the treatise, Bibl. Royale 4031–33) Camporeale, *Lorenzo Valla*, 428–29, where Valla corrected the "sic volo" of the Vulgate to "si volo".

11. See L. Mohler, *Kardinal Bessarion*, 3 vols. (Paderborn, 1923–42; repr. Paderborn, 1967), 1: 70ff., and 3: 70–87 (for the Greek text of Bessarion's treatise on the passage). For the dating of Bessarion's piece see Perosa's introduction to Valla's *Collatio*, xxxiv, note 64; V. Peri, "Nicola Maniacutia: un testimone della filologia romana del XII secolo," *Aevum*, 61 (1967): 67–90, at 68ff.; and (for a view opposed to Perosa and Peri) my *Collectanea Trapezuntiana: Texts, Documents, and Bibliographies of George of Trebizond* (Binghamton, N. Y., 1984), 311, Text CIV.

naris.[12] He also added the new argument that Pope Gregory the Great
did not mean the Areopagite when he spoke of the author Dionysius.
In the *Encomium S. Thomae* delivered at Rome in 1457, just before he
died, Valla elaborated the argument of the second redaction of the *Collatio*,
and conceded that a Dionysius, *but not* the Areopagite of Acts 17:34, had,
in fact, written the Dionysian corpus.[13] He even dated this Dionysius to
the sixth century. Concomitantly, he also revealed an increased command
of Greek patristic literature, confidently listing the Greek Fathers who
knew nothing of the Dionysian corpus. Contact with Greek scholars and
access to Greek manuscripts available in Rome had proven salutary for
Valla's scholarship. Not only did he owe to Bessarion suggestions such
as that on John 21:22, but in the *Adnotationes* Valla greatly increased his
references to Greek manuscripts.[14] Bessarion and the Vatican library possessed the largest collections of Greek biblical manuscripts to be found
in the Latin West. It is difficult to believe that Valla did not take advantage of his patron's library in his search for Greek exemplars of the New
Testament.[15]

   To be sure, Bessarion himself nowhere hints that he had doubts about
Dionysius.[16] But others in Bessarion's circle did not fully share this con-

12. See note 5 above.
13. J. Vahlen, "Lorenzo Valla über Thomas von Aquino," *Vierteljahresschrift für Kultur und Literatur der Renaissance*, 1 (1886): 384–96, at 395 (repr. in Valla, *Opera omnia*, 2: 351). Although he placed him in the sixth century, Valla treated Dionysius as a respectable authority approximately coeval with Gregory the Great.
14. See Perosa in *Collatio*, xxx–xxxi, and Camporeale, *Lorenzo Valla*, 285–86.
15. Valla nowhere specifically mentions consulting Greek manuscripts in Bessarion's collection, but it is hard to suppose that he did not do so when the collection was available to him, i. e., in 1448–49 and 1455–58. At his death in 1472 Bessarion owned at least fourteen Greek manuscripts of all or part of the New Testament, ten of which are extant (Venice, Bibl. Marc., MSS Zan. gr. 5–6, 8–12, 27, 33–34). For the four lost codices see L. Labowsky, *Bessarion's Library and the Biblioteca Marciana. Six Early Inventories* (Rome, 1979), Inventory B (of 1474), nos. 504, 925, 929, and 1010. According to the inventory published by R. Devreesse, *Le fonds grec de la Bibliothèque Vaticane des origines à Paul V. ST*, 244 (Vatican City, 1965), 11–36, in the time of Pope Calixtus III (1455–58) the Vatican possessed nineteen manuscripts of all or part of the New Testament in Greek (nos. 102–114, 139–145, 155 in Devreesse's list). In comparison, even at the end of the century the Biblioteca Laurenziana only had three such manuscripts (see B. L. Ullman and P. A. Stadter, *The Public Library of Renaissance Florence* [Padua, 1972], 248, nos. 1054–1056). Valla's former teacher, Giovanni Aurispa, may have been a help here, but even his stock of Greek New Testaments was small, consisting at his death in 1459, at the most, of two codices (see A. Franceschini, *Giovanni Aurispa e la sua biblioteca: Notizie e documenti* [Padua, 1976], 80, note 80; and 99, no. 227).
16. Three times in the *In calumniatorem Platonis* (Mohler, *Kardinal Bessarion*, 2: 88.19ff., 446.7f., and 488.7ff.) Bessarion very strongly asserted that Dionysius was the pupil of St. Paul and

fidence. One such waverer seems to have been Pietro Balbi of Pisa.[17] Balbi is probably best known for his association with Nicolaus Cusanus. Balbi appears as an interlocutor in several of Cusanus' dialogues, and it was for Cusanus that Balbi translated Alcinous' (i. e., Albinus') *Disciplinarum Platonis epitome* as well as Proclus' monumental *Theologia Platonica*. Nonetheless, Bessarion probably played a larger role in Balbi's life.

Balbi entered Bessarion's *familia* earlier than anyone has hitherto supposed, and he remained closely associated with Bessarion and the members of the *Accademia Bessarionea* for the rest of his life. Fittingly, our earliest evidence connecting Balbi to Bessarion is also the earliest reference known to me describing the scholars around Bessarion as an "Academy".[18] In late 1453 or early 1454, when Bessarion was papal legate in Bologna, his young secretary, Niccolò Perotti, wrote a letter attacking Poggio Bracciolini.[19] Perotti's letter is lost, but Poggio quoted from it when he himself later wrote to Guarino Veronese.[20] One of the quoted passages runs as follows: "Quid Petrus Balbus et Athanasius [*Chalkeopoulos*], duo Achademie nostre lumina . . . ."[21] It is not improbable that Balbi had en-

---

the legendary Hierotheus, known only from Dionysius' references to him. Twice (*ibid.*, 246.21 and 488.10) Bessarion proudly noted that Dionysius was such a good Platonist that he did not hesitate to use Plato's very words in his own writings. In the *De Sacramento Eucharistiae* Bessarion frequently referred to Dionysius by titles such as "hieros", " hierotatos", "theios", and "makarios" (*ibid.*, 3, *ad indicem*). Indeed, Pseudo-Dionysius was a major source for Bessarion's argument in the treatise.

17. The literature and known facts of his life and works are summarized in A. Pratesi, "Balbi, Pietro," *DBI*, 5: 378–79; and H. D. Saffrey, "Pietro Balbi et la première traduction latine de la *Théologie platonicienne* de Proclus," in *Miscellanea codicologica F. Masai dicata MCMLXXIX*, eds. P. Cockshaw, M.-C. Garand, and P. Jodogne, 2 vols. (Ghent, 1979), 2: 425–37. New information is also to be had in P. O. Kristeller, "A Latin Translation of Gemistos Plethon's *De Fato* by Johannes Sophianos Dedicated to Nicholas of Cusa," in *Nicolò Cusano agli inizi del mondo moderno. Atti del Congresso internazionale in occasione del V centenario della morte di Nicolò Cusano, Bressanone, 6–10 settembre 1964* (Florence, 1970), 175–193, at 187–188.

18. For a discussion of the members of the "Accademia Bessarionea" as listed by Niccolò Perotti in the early 1470s see G. Mercati, *Per la cronologia della vita e degli scritti dei Niccolò Perotti arcivescovo di Siponto. ST*, 44 (Rome, 1925), 77ff.

19. The *terminus ante quem* is Poggio's letter quoting Perotti, dated 12 August (1454), in P. Bracciolini, *Epistolae*, ed. T. Tonelli, 3 vols. (Florence, 1832–61; repr. as vol. 1 in P. Bracciolini, *Opera omnia*, ed. R. Fubini, 4 vols. [Turin, 1964–69]), 3: 110; and Guarino, *Epistolario*, 3: 622. The *terminus post quem* is Perotti's letter to Battista Brenni, which started the quarrel with Poggio, dated 8 September 1453 and found in *Miscellanea di varie operette*, 8 (Venice: T. Bettinelli, 1744): 186–87, repr. in P. Bracciolini, *Opera omnia*, 4: 73–74.

20. See the previous note.

21. Whether he knew Perotti's letter or not, Donato Acciaiuoli, in a letter of 23 March 1454, also called the group of young scholars with which he was associated in Florence an "Academia"

tered Bessarion's service even before Bessarion had left Rome for Bologna in 1450.[22] In any case, after returning from Bologna, Balbi continued to serve Bessarion. The papal registers describe him as Bessarion's *cappellanus et familiaris continuus commensalis* when on 9 April 1456 he paid common services in Rome as the procurator of the abbot elect of a Basilian monastery in Calabria.[23] In 1457 Balbi acted as Bessarion's vicar at the monastery of St. Mennas in Calabria.[24] In the 1460s, even after we can document Balbi's association with Nicolaus Cusanus, Bessarion remained important for Balbi's activities in Rome, providing, for instance, the Greek exemplars of Balbi's translation of Proclus's *Theologia Platonica* for Cusanus[25] as well as the previously unknown translation of Justinian the Great's treatise *Contra Origenem* for Teodoro Lelli.[26] After Balbi became bishop of Tropea in Calabria (6 June 1463,[27] *pace* the literature on Balbi which misdates this

---

(F. Fossi, *Monumenta ad Alamanni Rinuccini vitam contexandam* . . . [Florence, 1791], 77). See A. Della Torre, *Storia dell'Accademia Platonica di Firenze* (Florence, 1902), 357ff.

22. Tradition has it that Balbi came to the papal court under the aegis of Cardinal Pietro Barbo in the 1440s during the pontificate of Eugenius IV (Pratesi, 378). If that is so, it is more likely that he joined Bessarion's household before Bessarion left Rome for Bologna. It is difficult to see why he would have been called to Bologna from Rome after Bessarion had departed.

23. M.-H. Laurent and A. Guillou, *Le "Liber visitationis" d'Athanase Chalkéopoulos (1457–1458). Contribution à l'histoire du monachisme grec en Italie méridionale*. ST, 206 (Vatican City, 1960), 239. Balbi was acting in the name of "Pauli Romani electi abbatis monasterii Ss. Helie Novi et Philareti, O. S. Bas., Militen. dioc."

24. *Ibid.*, 8.23–25, 13.5–6, 14.11–12, 17.7–9.

25. This is Munich, Bayerische Staatsbibliothek, MS Graecus 547; see Saffrey, "Pietro Balbi," 436, note 36, and in Proclus, *Théologie platonicienne*, 1, eds. H. D. Saffrey and L. G. Westerink (Paris, 1968), cxxiv.

26. See Appendix I below.

27. Reg. Vat. 493, ff. 156v–157r (new numeration), of the Archivio Segreto Vaticano, contains a copy of the letter, dated "Rome apud sanctum Petrum, anno etc. millesimo cccclxiii, octavo Idus Iunii, pontificatus nostri anno quinto," by which Pope Pius II named Balbi bishop of Tropea at the death, "extra Romanam Curiam," of Iosue (Mormile), the previous bishop. There then follow, ff. 157r–158r, copies of the five letters of the same date informing the chapter of the cathedral, the clergy of Tropea, the people of Tropea, the archbishop of Reggio Calabria, and King Ferdinand of Naples of this fact. Balbi had previously been named bishop of Nicotera (on 15 February 1461 according to local tradition [see Pratesi, 378]; on 18 January 1462 according to Eubel, 2: 203, note 1), but no mention of this earlier appointment is to be found in these letters of 1463. The election to the see of Nicotera could not in fact take effect because it was based on the false belief that the previous bishop had died (Eubel, *loc. cit.*). It is unclear exactly how soon the papal court became aware of its mistake concerning the bishopric of Nicotera. However, since Balbi seems to have still considered himself bishop of Nicotera in March 1462 (see the end of the next note), and since it is hard to believe that the papal court would have gone several years without noticing its error concerning an Italian bishopric, the date of election given by Eubel, 18 January 1462, is far more probable (Pratesi agrees).

event[28]), Bessarion used him to administer the Calabrian diocese of Gerace for Athanasius Chalkeopoulos.[29] After Bessarion's death, Balbi demonstrably maintained a close relationship with at least two Greeks of the Bessarion circle, Athanasius Chalkeopoulos and Theodore Gaza, i.e., the very same Greeks mentioned by Perotti in his letter of late 1453–early 1454.[30] Nor did he separate from his Latin friends of the *Accademia Bessarionea*. On 27 March 1479, near the end of Balbi's life,[31] another veteran of the Bessarion circle, Francesco della Rovere, now Pope Sixtus IV, granted to Balbi, his *referendarius et continuus commensalis*, the privilege of freely disposing of the benefices in the diocese of Tropea which became vacant in even-numbered months.[32] In several translations which he dedicated to Sixtus, Balbi called himself a *famulus* of the pope.[33] At Balbi's

28. Eubel, 2: 257, offers no exact date, but merely notes that Balbi paid common services for Tropea on 27 Dec. 1465. Pratesi, 379, believes that he received Tropea a few months after Nicotera, i.e., in 1461 or 1462. Saffrey, "Pietro Balbi," 429 and 435, opts for early 1462 as the date of Balbi's appointment because of the colophon of Bergamo, MS Bibl. Civica, Gamma IV 19 containing Balbi's version of Proclus' *Theologia Platonica* (Saffrey, *loc. cit.*; Kristeller, *Iter*, 1: 8): "Finis sexti et ultimi libri Procli de theologia Platonis, conversa e grego [*sic*] per me Petrum Balbum Pisanum, inclite Tropee, urbis in Calabria site, episcopum, anno domini 1462, die XXII Marcii." The colophon is no doubt correct in dating Balbi's completion of the translation, but I suspect that in its original form the colophon carried Balbi's title as bishop of Nicotera (Nicotera is also in Calabria) and that subsequently either Balbi himself or an amanuensis changed the title in the colophon to that of Tropea. The Bergamo manuscript is demonstrably not the autograph which Balbi finished on 22 March 1462 (see Saffrey). Whether the change was made in the autograph of the translation or only in an apograph such as Bergamo, MS Gamma IV 19 is irrelevant to the issue. But if my hypothesis concerning the Bergamo manuscript is correct, then Balbi must have considered himself bishop of Nicotera as late as 22 March 1462 (see note 39 below).

29. Laurent and Guillou, 213–14, where a document dated Rome, 7 May 1467 is edited, according to which Athanasius had delegated Bessarion as the administrator of his diocese and Bessarion, in turn, had delegated this responsibility to Balbi. Balbi is specifically described as *absens*.

30. In a letter of 8 September (1474?) to Alexius (Celadenus), Theodore Gaza remarked that he had come to southern Italy to live out his remaining days with his dear friends Athanasius (Chalkeopoulos) and Pietro (Balbi); see Mohler, 3: 586.13–14, and Teodoro Gaza, *Epistole*, ed. E. Pinto (Naples, 1975), 124.15–17.

31. Balbi died 9 September 1479 (Pratesi, 379).

32. That Balbi was a referendarius was not known before (he is nowhere mentioned in B. Katterbach, *Referendarii utriusque signaturae a Martino V ad Leonem XIII. ST*, 55 [Vatican City, 1931]). The document in Archivio Segreto Vaticano, Reg. Lat. 796, f. 283v, begins, "Sixtus etc. venerabili fratri Petro, episcopo Tropiensi salutem etc. . . . tibi qui referendarius et continuus commensalis noster existis quoad vixeris . . . ," and ends, "Datum Rome apud Sanctum Petrum, anno Incarnationis dominice millesimo quadragintesimo septuagesimo nono, sexto Kalendas Aprilis, anno octavo." The pope added the limitation that the privilege held as long as these benefices "dispositioni apostolice generaliter reservata non sint."

33. Both Vatican City, BAV, MS Vat. lat. 3656, containing Balbi's translation of Maximus

death, Sixtus had him buried in St. Peter's and saw to the erection of a suitable sepulchral inscription.[34] Hence, whereas we can connect Balbi to Cusanus for only a period of about four years, i.e., from ca. 1459, when Cusanus left Brixen for Rome, to 1463, when Balbi left Rome for Calabria,[35] we can trace Balbi's close association with Bessarion and the members of the Bessarion circle for most of his life.

Now, in the *De non aliud* of 1461 Cusanus makes Balbi an interlocutor and portrays him as wondering about the similarity in language and doctrine between Dionysius the Areopagite and the Neoplatonic philosopher Proclus, whom, Balbi says, he is translating at that very moment.[36] Cusanus responds that Proclus' words bear a close resemblance to those of Dio-

the Confessor's *Sermo per dialogum inter fratrem et senem*, and MS Vat. lat. 3660, containing Balbi's rendering of John Chrysostom's *Sermo de patientia et longanimitate*, have dedications to Sixtus IV; see Kristeller, *Iter*, 2: 322 and 582. From internal references both dedications would seem to date from the later 1470s.

34. The end of the sepulchral inscription states that it was installed "Sixti IV Pont. Max. iussu" (F. Ughelli, *Italia Sacra*, ed. N. Coletus, 9 (Venice, 1721): 468; and V. Forcella, *Iscrizioni delle chiese e d'altri edifici di Roma dal secolo XI fino ai giorni nostri*, 14 vols. (Rome, 1869–1884), 6: 44, no. 84).

35. There was undoubtedly a special relationship between Balbi and Cusanus. (In a preface after Cusanus' death, Balbi referred to him as *reverendus dominus meus cardinalis*; see A. M. Bandini, *Catalogus codicum latinorum Bibliothecae Mediceae Laurentianae*, 3 [Florence, 1776]: 269.) But as Kristeller, "A Latin Translation," 188, has pointed out, it is not certain that Balbi actually lived in Cusanus' household. Saffrey, "Pietro Balbi," 436, note 36, goes further and suggests that in the early 1460s Balbi was still living in Bessarion's household. However, Balbi did not accompany Bessarion on his German legation of 1460–1461 or his Venetian legation of 1463–1464. So it is dubious that he was formally part of Bessarion's household in these years. In any case, he cultivated by dedications of his patristic translations a fairly wide circle of curial personages, including Pope Pius II for Justinian's *Contra Origenem* (see the Appendix below) and John Chrysostom's *Sermo de divinis statuis* (Florence, Bibl. Laurenz., MS LXXXIX, sup. 16, f. 39r sq.; see Bandini, 3: 266ff.), Pope Paul II for Gregory of Nyssa's *De anima et resurrectione* under the title *Dialogus de immortalitate animi* (lost manuscript once at Capua; see Ughelli, *Italia Sacra*, 9: 468; and H. Brown Wicher, "Gregorius Nyssenus," *CTC*, 5: 1–250, at 65–66), Cardinal Marco Barbo for Gregory of Nyssa's *De vita B. Macrinae* (Ughelli, *loc. cit.*; Wicher, 181), Cardinal Oliviero Carafa for Gregory Nazianzenus' *Sermo de amore paupertatis* (Ughelli, *loc. cit.*), and Cardinal Francesco Piccolomini for John Chrysostom's *Sermo de eleemosyna*. A comprehensive study needs to be made of Balbi's translations and dedications. For his translations of six homelies of Gregory Nazianzenus see Sister Agnes Clare Way, "S. Gregorius Nazianzenus," *CTC*, 2: 43–192 at 138ff.

36. Nicolaus Cusanus, *Opera omnia iussu et auctoritate Academiae Literarum Heidelbergensis*, 13. *Directio speculantis seu de non aliud*, eds. L. Baur and P. Wilpert (Leipzig, 1944), 47.18ff.: "Cum enim Proculum illum Platonicum in libro de Platonis divini theologia de Graeco verterem hiis diebus in Latinum, ea ipsa quasi eodem quoque expressionis tenore ac modo repperi, quamobrem de Platonica etiam te audire theologia aliquid cupio . . . . (p. 47.27ff.) Sicut Dionysius inquit unum, quod est posterius uno simpliciter, ita et Proculus Platonem referens asserit."

nysius because Proclus copied from Plato, and Plato, in turn, had antici-pated Christian doctrine to a wondrous degree.[37] In the *De non aliud* and in other writings, Nicolaus Cusanus, like Marsilio Ficino a little while after, quite happily asserted Dionysius' Platonism.[38]

According to the *De non aliud*, Balbi accepted Cusanus' explanation of why Dionysius and Proclus sound so much alike.[39] But a text in a manuscript owned by Cusanus containing Robert Grosseteste's transla-tion of, and commentary on, Pseudo-Dionysius proves that Balbi was not fully comfortable with that explanation.

Folio 1v of MS Cus. 44 carries a lengthy note written by the scribe Petrus Ercklentz but explicitly stated to be the work of Pietro Balbi as bishop of Nicotera[40] (i.e., from January to no later than September

37. *Ibid.*, 47.29ff.

38. A good summary of Cusanus' various pronouncements concerning Pseudo-Dionysius is given by Gandillac, 375, in the article in the *DSAM* cited in note 1 above. See also Tigerstedt, *The Decline*, 22–24; and the note of R. Klibansky and J. G. Senger in their edition of Cusanus' *De venatione sapientiae* (*Opera omnia*, 12 [Hamburg, 1982], 154–55). Jacques Lefèvre d'Etaples, the later editor of Cusanus and Pseudo-Dionysius, vigorously opposed such an attitude. See Tiger-stedt, *The Decline*, 26–28, and E. F. Rice, Jr., ed., *The Prefatory Epistles of Jacques Lefèvre d'Etaples and Related Texts* (New York, 1972), 63–64, and notes 17–21 on pp. 68–69.

39. N. Cusanus, *De non aliud*, 49.14: "Video, pater, haec dubio carere." We may note here the close relationship between Balbi's status as bishop and the dates of the two dialogues of Cusa-nus in which he appears as an interlocutor. In both the *De non aliud* and the *De venatione sapientiae* of the next year, Balbi lacks an episcopal title. Klibansky and Senger, xi–xii (see note 38 above), date the *De non aliud* to the first month and a half of 1461 because they hold to the view that Balbi was named bishop of Nicotera on 15 February 1461, as local tradition has it (see note 28 above). However, Eubel's date of 18 January 1462 for Balbi's election strikes me as more plausible (see *ibid.*). Therefore, for the *De non aliud* I prefer the date of November-January 1461 put forward by Baur—Wilpert, X (see note 36 above). The probability that Balbi still thought himself bishop of Nicotera in March 1462 (see note 27 above) and the fact that he became bishop of Tropea in June 1463 do not conflict with Klibansky's and Senger's view, p. xii, that Cusanus wrote the *De venatione sapientiae* in the autumn of 1462. Such a date for the *De venatione* would indicate that Balbi became disabused of the notion that he was bishop of Nicotera in the the spring or summer of 1462. In a note of 9 December 1462 in London, BL, MS Harl. 1347, f. 296r, Giovanni Andrea Bussi referred to Balbi simply as a priest, not as a bishop; see Way, "Gregorius Nazianze-nus," 138.

40. For a description of MS Cus. 44 see J. Marx, *Verzeichnis der Handschriften-Sammlung des Hospitals zu Cues bei Bernkastel a. Mosel* (Trier, 1905), 39–40. For the identification of the transla-tion in the manuscript as that of Grosseteste see M. Grabmann, *Mittelalterliches Geistesleben*, 2 (Munich, 1936): 466, note 54 (cf. E. Vansteenberghe, *Le cardinal Nicolas de Cues (1401–1464). L'Action—La Pensée* [Paris, 1920], 414, note 1). The manuscript also contains Grosseteste's commentary; see S. H. Thomson, *The Writings of Robert Grosseteste, Bishop of Lincoln, 1235–1253* (Cambridge, 1940),55–58 and 78. Klibansky and Senger in N. Cusanus, *De venatione sapientiae*, xi, identify

1462,[41] and therefore after the date of the *De non aliud*). We may translate as follows:[42]

Lord Peter, Bishop of Nicotera, has extracted these things from certain Greek writings attached to the text of Dionysius.

It must be noted that certain external [i.e., non-Christian] philosophers, and especially Proclus, often use the speculations of Saint Dionysius and even his very words. From this we can deduce that the ancient philosophers at Athens kept Dionysius' book hidden because they had appropriated it for themselves, as he [Dionysius] relates in the present book. To refute their vainglory and temerity, so that the fathers themselves might see his divine discourses,[43] this treatise [of Dionysius] has come to light by divine dispensation. Basil the Great teaches [in his sermon] on the text "In the beginning was the Word," that they [the pagans] were wont to appropriate our works for themselves. As he says in this passage,[44] "I know many beyond the pale of the truth who, glorifying and admiring worldly wisdom, have dared to usurp in their treatises the works of others. For the devil is a thief, and he brings[45] to his servants our works in the guise of fables." These are Basil's words, while Numenius the Pythagorean most openly says: "For what is Plato except Moses speaking in Attic?" This no one can deny since Numenius is not one of ours but rather an adversary.[46] And indeed, Eusebius, the bishop of Caesarea in Palestine, attests to the very same thing, namely

the hand as that of Ercklentz (concerning whom see *ibid.*, 163–64). Kristeller, "A Latin Translation," 188 (see note 17 above), was the first to identify Balbi as the author of the note. Cf. also Tigerstedt, *The Decline*, 86, note 181.

41. For this dating see note 39 above.

42. Though cited by Marx, Klibansky-Senger, and Tigerstedt, this note of Balbi has never been published. I give the text in Appendix II.

43. Balbi has mistranslated the Greek here. "'Οφθῶσι τῶν θείων αὐτοῦ λόγων" should be placed in the previous sentence so that the passage would run: "kept it hidden so that they themselves might seem the authors of his divine discourses. In refutation of the vainglory etc." (see note 56 below).

44. At the start of the *Homelia in illud, "In principio erat verbum"* (*PG*, 31: 472 C).

45. Balbi has mistranslated as "quasi fabulas reducit" the Greek ἐκφερομυθέω, "to reveal" (see note 56 below).

46. Cf. Eusebius Pamphili, *Praeparatio evangelica*, XI, 10 *ad finem*.

that not only now but even before the coming of Christ external philosophers were accustomed to stealing our works.[47]

However, since some say that this treatise is not Dionysius' but of some later author, it is necessary also [for them] to admit that he [Dionysius] asserted some absurd and useless things, having counterfeited his works in this way as if he had been together with the apostles and had sent letters to them who were neither his contemporaries nor capable of sending letters.[48] His pretending [in Epist. 10] to prophesy to St. John in exile that he [John] would return to the region of Asia and teach as before would be the act of a man who is a deceiver and a madman seeking the glory of a prophet.[49] So too would be his saying that he was with Apollophon in the city of Helia[50] at the very time of [Christ's] saving[51] passion and at that moment observed and philosophized about the the eclipse of the sun as contrary to nature and the path of the sun at the time,[52] his having avowed his presence with the apostles at the translation of the holy corpse of the blessed Mary,[53] his having asserted the authority of his teacher Hierotheus from the words of his epitaph,[54] and his pretence to have written epistles and discourses as if to the disciples of the apostles. How much absurdity and reproof that man would deserve! And, indeed, [such condemnation] would not befit a man[55] who by morals and learning has been so greatly elevated and sublimated above all things sensible, and who had attained to the intellectual beauties and, through them, as much as it is possible, to God.

47. E. g., cf. ibid., X, 1–2. It was a general thesis of Eusebius that much Greek theological thought was correct because the Greeks borrowed from the Hebrews.

48. Either there is a scribal error here or Balbi mistranslated the Greek, translating "quirent" instead of "quiret" (ἐπέστειλε). The passage should read: "who were not his contemporaries and to whom he could not send letters" (see note 67 below).

49. One could also translate "a deceiver seeking the glory of a mad [inspired] prophet;" but the Greek reads: "τερατολόγου ἀνδρὸς καὶ προφήτου δόξαν ἐκμανῶς θηρωνένου."

50. This may be a scribal error. The town Pseudo-Dionysius speaks of is Hieropolis.

51. Perhaps salutaris should be emended to salvatoris. The Greek text in Migne has σωτηρίου (see note 67 below).

52. Pseudo-Dionysius, Epist., VII.

53. Pseudo-Dionysius, De divinis nominibus, III, ad finem.

54. Cf. ibid. Balbi's translation is unclear and does not effectively reflect the Greek (see note 67 below).

55. Balbi's Latin condenses the Greek here somewhat (ibid.).

Balbi translated the first paragraph of his note word-for-word from an anonymous Greek scholium on Pseudo-Dionysius.[56] The substance, and much of the phrasing, of this scholium can also be found in the tenth-century *Suda*[57] and in George Pachymeres' preface to his paraphrase of Pseudo-Dionysius from the thirteenth century.[58] Thus, Balbi had passed on to Cusanus a Byzantine argument for the priority of Dionysius *vis-à-vis* Proclus different from the solution proposed in the *De non aliud*. Cusanus tacitly accepted the argument of the scholium in the *De venatione sapientiae* of 1462.[59]

The opening sentences of the first paragraph ("It must be noted . . . vainglory and temerity") also can be found in a different Latin translation attributed to "quidam expositores" by Cusanus' friend, Denis the Carthusian, in his commentary on Pseudo-Dionysius in the mid–1460s.[60] Thirty-five years later, this part of the scholium, in virtually the same Latin version used by Denis, reappeared in Jacques Lefèvre d'Etaples' edition of Pseudo-Dionysius, but now attributed to Ambrogio Traversari, the Renaissance translator of the Areopagite.[61] However, even as great

56. *PG*, 4: 21 D – 24 A, entitled "Ex scholiis diligentissimi cuiusdam viri". Tigerstedt, *The Decline*, 86, n. 181, already made this identification. Klibansky and Senger on p. 155 of their edition of Cusanus' *De venatione sapientiae*, mistakenly claim that Balbi was translating George Pachymeres (see note 58 below).

57. See G. Wentzel, *Die griechische Übersetzung der* viri inlustres *des Hieronymus*. Texte und Untersuchungen zur Geschichte der altchristlichen Literatur, 12.3 (Leipzig, 1895), 40. The note is translated into English by Tigerstedt, *The Decline*, 23.

58. *PG*, 3: 116 A–B. Pachymeres and the *Suda* are virtually identical except at the end, where the *Suda* refers to Dionysius' letter to Timotheus and Pachymeres quotes from St. Basil the Great before making a transition to his paraphrase. The differences between Pachymeres and the anonymous scholiast are sufficient to prove that Balbi did not use Pachymeres. At *PG*, 4: 21 D.6–7 and D.8–10, the anonymous scholiast adds two minor phrases lacking in Pachymeres but found in Balbi (ὡς ἐν . . . βίβλῳ and καὶ κατ' οἰκονομίαν . . . καὶ ῥᾳδιουργίας καί). At the end Pachymeres introduces his paraphrase while the scholiast and Balbi quote Numenius and Eusebius.

59. *De venatione sapientiae*, eds. Klibansky and Senger, 62.15–16: "Proclus vero . . . Dionysium sequendo."

60. *Doctoris ecstatici D. Dionysii Cartusiani opera omnia* . . ., 15 (Tournai, 1902): 20, col. 2 B–C It should be said that the translation of the scholium in Denis is superior to that of Balbi in MS Cus. 44 (see the next note).

61. *Theologia vivificans . . . Dionysii celestis hierarchia* . . . (Paris: J. Higman and W. Hopyl, 1499 = *Gesamtkatalog der Wiegendrucke*, no. 8409), sign. A iii r. See Rice, *The Prefatory Epistles*, 69, note 20, who gives the full text. This text is one of three testimonia *de furtis Platonicorum*, the first two being drawn from Ficino and St. Basil. Rice, *ibid.*, 549–551, lists the editions of Pseudo-Dionysius *cum Iacobi Fabri scholiis*. When Lefèvre's edition was combined with the commentary of Denis the Carthusian, Traversari's scholium was retained. I have consulted two copies: *S. Dionysii Areopagitae . . . opera . . . omnia . . . commentariis D. Dionysii a Rickel Carthusiani elucidata* (Cologne:

an admirer of Traversari's translation of Pseudo-Dionysius as Cusanus did not have this particular version of the scholium in his copy (MS Cus. 43);[62] nor can it be found in Pope Nicholas V's and other good copies of Traversari's translation.[63] Perhaps Denis' version of the scholium comes from a medieval translator;[64] but Tigerstedt may be right in suggesting that Cusanus passed on the scholium (in this revised form) to Denis.[65] In any event, the scholium seems to have first taken on a special impor-

Io. Quentel, 1536), f. 419v (= Rice, no. CLX); and the edition of Cologne: Io. Quentel, 1556, p. 842 (= Rice, no. CLXV). Denis' version of the note differs from Lefèvre's only superficially: "Sciendum multos externorum philosophorum, maxime [et maxime Lef.] Proclum, sententiis B. [B. Lef. om.] Dionysii, imo et nudis eius vocabulis plerumque usos fuisse [immo vero ipsis quoque vocabulis nudis usos plerunque fuisse Lef.]. Unde possumus suspicari [suspicari possumus Lef.] ab his [iis Lef.] qui Athenis philosophabantur, libros sancti [beatos Lef.] Dionysii, quorum ipsemet [ipse Lef.] meminit, fuisse celatos [celatos fuisse Lef.] ut quae inde sumebant ipsi invenisse aestimarentur [invenisse ipsi putarentur Lef.]. Verum his libris inventis divina providentia id agente inanis illorum gloria atque malitia patefacte sunt [Sed divina providentia his modo libris adinventis inanis gloria illorum et malitia patefacta est Lef.]."

62. For Cusanus' admiration of Traversari's translation see L. Baur, Cusanus-Texte. III. Marginalien 1. Nicolaus Cusanus und Ps. Dionysius im Lichte der Zitate und Randbemerkungen des Cusanus. Sitzungsberichte der Heidelberger Akademie der Wissenschaften, philosophisch-historische Klasse, 1940/41, 4 (Heidelberg, 1941), 13ff.; and Kristeller, "A Latin Translation," 183–184. Professor Kristeller has also pointed out to me that Cusanus was instrumental in the diffusion of Traversari's translation in Germany; see the colophons in Giessen, Universitätsbibliothek, MSS 671 and 723 (Kristeller, Iter, 3: 540 and 541). I viewed Cusanus' copy of Traversari's translation in a microfilm from the Hill Monastic Microfilm Library. Baur, Nicolaus Cusanus und Ps. Dionysius, makes no mention of any such scholium. Furthermore, it would have been strange for Balbi to take credit for a note Cusanus already long knew from Traversari.

63. At my request Dr. Concetta Bianca checked Vatican City, BAV, MS Vat. lat. 169, belonging to Pope Nicholas V, a good friend of Traversari before becoming pope after Traversari's death (see Codices Vaticani Latini, 1, eds. M. Vattasso and P. Franchi de' Cavalieri [Rome, 1902], 131–132). I was able to consult in microfilm at the Pius XII Memorial Library, St. Louis University, BAV, MSS Chis. A V 127 and Palat. lat. 149. Dr. Arthur Field inspected for me Florence, Bibl. Laur., MS XVII, 22, as did Dr. Emil Polak, Oxford, Lincoln College, MS 49.

64. Neither the scholia translated by Anastasius the Librarian in the tenth century nor those believed translated by Robert Grosseteste in the thirteenth century have been published. Furthermore, there were in circulation Latin scholia translated from the Greek by one or more anonymous medieval scholars. See H. F. Dondaine, Le Corpus dionysien de l'Université de Paris au XIIIe siècle (Rome, 1953), 50ff., 69–71, 122ff.; E. Franceschini, "Roberto Grossatesta, vescovo di Lincoln e le sue traduzioni latini," Atti del Reale Istituto Veneto di scienze, lettere ed arti, 93.2 (1933–1934): 1–38, at 35–37; and S. H. Thomson, The Writings of Robert Grosseteste, 53–55. See also V. Rose, Verzeichnis der lateinischen Handschriften der kgl. Bibliothek zu Berlin, 1. Die Meerman-Handschriften des Sir Thomas Phillipps (Berlin, 1893), 68. None of the literature alludes to the existence of our scholium. At my request Dr. Concetta Bianca checked Vatican City, BAV, MS Vat. lat. 176, which contains the scholia translated by Anastasius. I myself could not find it in Grosseteste's commentary (MS Cus. 44).

65. Tigerstedt, The Decline, 86, note 181.

202 ~   JOHN MONFASANI

tance around 1460 with Balbi's work on Proclus for Cusanus. Certainly,
shortly thereafter Denis the Carthusian in his commentary showed considerable sensitivity to the similarities between Proclus and Pseudo-Dionysius
and frequently referred to Proclus.[66]

The second part of Balbi's note translates (but not always correctly)
part of Maximus the Confessor's preface to his commentary on Pseudo-
Dionysius.[67] Oddly enough, these lines can be read as a devastatingly sar-
castic rejection of the authenticity of Pseudo-Dionysius rather than as a
proof to the contrary. This way of reading Maximus' words may explain
a peculiarity of Grosseteste's commentary, for which Balbi's note served
as sort of an introduction in MS Cus. 44. Grosseteste incorporated Maximus' preface into his commentary, but without the passage translated by
Balbi.[68] Obviously others saw danger in this passage. For anyone with
serious doubts about the Areopagite, Balbi's note, with its recog-

66. See the large number of references listed in the indices of Denis' *Opera*, 15 and 16 (Tournai,
1902) cited in note 60 above. His chief source was Proclus' *Elements of Theology*, though he would
cite the *Liber de causis* in tandem with the *Elements* without attributing it to Proclus (in 15: 86
D, col. 2, he asserted: "auctor libri de causis, qui peripateticus fuit . . .").

67. See *PG*, 4: 21 A-C. Tigerstedt, *loc. cit.*, correctly identified the text, but wrongly cited
Wentzel, *Die griechische Übersetzung*, 40, as doubting the attribution of the prologue to Maximus
(Wentzel was talking about the anonymous scholium which follows the prologue in the *Patrologia*).

68. The preface introduces the *De celestia hierarchia*. It is not mentioned by Franceschini or Thomson
(see note 64 above), and Tigerstedt did not realize that it contains this important omission. It
is found on f. 141r–v in MS Cus. 44 (properly identified in the catalogue of Marx); see also J.
M. Mucciolus, *Catalogus codicum manuscriptorum Malatestianae Caesenatis Bibliothecae*, 2 vols. in 1
(Cesena, 1780–1784), 1: 52–53, for Cesena, Bibl. Malat., MS XII dext. 1; A. M. Bandini, *Catalogus codicum latinorum Bibliothecae Mediceae Laurentianae*, 5 vols. (Florence, 1774–1778), 4: 427, for
Florence, Bibl. Laur., MS XIII dext. 2; and H. O. Coxe, *Catalogus codicum manuscriptorum qui
in collegiis aulisque Oxoniensibus hodie adservantur*, 2 vols. (Oxford, 1852), 1.8: 48 for Oxford, Lincoln College, MS 101. The preface begins: "Nobilitatem quidem et preclarum in diviciis," and
ends "quos nunc in meas venire accidit manus." The massive omission comes after the words "maxime
autem omnium dogmatum firmissimum" (= *PG*, 4: 21 A.11), which is immediately followed
by the words, "Enarrationis quidem igitur," which is the start of the last paragraph of Maximus'
preface (= *ibid.*, 21 C.7). I do not know if Grosseteste himself or his Greek source is responsible
for the omission. In any case, Grosseteste did not know the identity of its author, as his scholium
at the start of the preface shows (I give the text from Mucciolus, 52, because the text is difficult
to read in my microfilm of MS Cus. 44): "Non inveni in exemplari Graeco nomen auctoris praescrip-
tum huic prologo. Coniicio tamen quod Dionysius archiepiscopus Alexandriae hunc prologum
scripsit. Inveni enim post finem epistolarum decem huius Dionysii Areopagitae sic scriptum Graece:
sciendum igitur alter Dionysius archiepiscopus Alexandriae, qui unus rhetorum conscripsit scholia
sancti Dionysii. Auctor autem huius prologi, ut patet in prologo, scholia super hunc librum scripsit."

nition of the real link to Proclus and its suggestion of Pseudo-Dionysius as a brazen forger, might tend to reenforce rather than to dissipate such doubts.

After Balbi's note in MS Cus. 44 there immediately follows a note in Cusanus' own hand[69] quoting the reference to Pseudo-Dionysius in the Pseudo-Athanasian *Dialogus ad Antiochum principem* and then expressing wonder at the fact that St. Athanasius cited the Areopagite's writings but Ambrose, Augustine, and Jerome did not. However, at the end of the note, Cusanus further records that John of Damascus, and, before him, Pope Gregory the Great did cite the Areopagite. Perhaps Cusanus' investigation was generated by a reading of Valla's *Collatio*.[70] But as far as I know, the Pseudo-Athanasian *Dialogus* did not exist in Latin translation.[71] So someone had to point out and translate the passage for Cusanus. Balbi is the most likely candidate. The proximity of the two notes suggests

69. "In dyalogo sancti Athanasii ad Anthiochum principem De plurimis ac necessariis questionibus dubitatis in divina scriptura, que ab omnibus Cristianis cognosci debent [PG, 28: 603; cf. Rice, *The Prefatory Epistles*, 68, n. 10]: 'Octava interrogatio: Quot ordines et quot substancie angelorum sunt? Responsio: substantia una sicud et hominum una, sed, quemadmodum magnus in theologia Dyonisius inquit, novem sunt ordines, scilicet, angeli, archangeli, principatus, potestates, virtutes, dominationes, sex alarum seraphim, et plurimum oculorum cherubim, et troni.' Considera an loquatur de Dyonisio Areopagita, sicud videtur, et tunc mirum quod Ambrosius, Augustinus, et Ieronymus ipsum Dyonisium non viderunt, qui fuerunt post Athanasium. Damascenus etiam Dyonisium allegat, qui fuit post illos tempore Eraclii. Gregorius papa ante Ioannem Damascenum Dyonisium allegat." The first part, but never the second part, of this note has been reproduced a good number of times (the only correct version is that of Klibansky-Senger): Vansteenberge, *Le cardinal Nicolas de Cues*, 26–27, note 5; Baur, *Nicolaus Cusanus und Ps. Dionysius*, 19; Tigerstedt, *The Decline*, 22–23; and Klibansky and Senger in N. Cusanus, *De venatione sapientiae*, 155.

70. We have a letter of Cusanus to Valla asking for a copy of what seems to have been the collation of the New Testament after having been shown it by the pope (Valla, *Antidotum IV* in *Opera*, 1: 340). R. Sabbadini, *Cronologia documentata della vita di Lorenzo della Valle detto il Valla*, in L. Barozzi-R. Sabbadini, *Studi sul Panormita e sul Valla* (Florence, 1891), 127 (repr. in Valla, *Opera*, 2: 433), and Perosa in Valla, *Collatio Novi Testamenti*, xlix, date the letter to 1450, while G. Mancini, *Vita di Lorenzo Valla* (Florence, 1891), 237–238, and Camporeale, *Lorenzo Valla*, 367, date it to 1453. In either case, Cusanus is speaking about the *Collatio*, which was dedicated to Pope Nicholas V in 1453, and not the *Adnotationes*. Thus it is quite possible, though not certain, that Cusanus had read the attack on Pseudo-Dionysius in the *Collatio*. However, no copy of Valla's work owned by Cusanus is known to exist today. From 1453 to 1458 Cusanus was almost continually away from Rome, and therefore was not present when Valla delivered the *Encomium S. Thomae* in 1457.

71. My search was admittedly not comprehensive, but sufficient to suggest that such a translation, if it did exist, was not easily available or generally known. I could not find a translation of this work in the literature on Cusanus' library, nor in the first two indexed volumes of Kristeller's

that Cusanus was working in conjunction with Balbi on the problem of the Areopagite. Cusanus' note in itself reflects no real doubt about Pseudo-Dionysius — or of Pseudo-Athanasius for that matter — but merely puzzlement at the silence of the fourth-century Latin Fathers when Athanasius before them and Gregory and John of Damascus after them cite the Areopagite. Clearly, after Balbi raised the issue of Pseudo-Dionysius and Proclus in 1460, Cusanus either commissioned Balbi to search for information on the problem or, at the very least, was now receptive to relevant texts which Balbi translated on his own account.

Unfortunately, except for his bland remark after Cusanus' death, that the cardinal overlooked "nichil Dyonisii, nichil Augustini, nichil Thomae" in his studies,[72] we really have no discussion of Pseudo-Dionysius in Balbi's own words. But we do have some tantalizing possibilities. As Balbi himself tells us, he searched through numerous sylloges of the Fifth Ecumenical Council under Emperor Justinian I before translating Justinian's *Contra Origenem*.[73] Thus, it is marginally possible that Balbi came across the first known attack on the authenticity of Pseudo-Dionysius, i. e., that put forward by Hypatius of Ephesus at a colloquy with "Severan" Monophysites organized by Justinian at Constantinople in 532 and reported in a letter written soon after by Innocent of Mariona.[74] Because he had access to Bessarion's library for many years, it is even more possi-

---

Iter nor in the printed catalogues of North America (De Ricci and Wilson, Bond and Faye), the Vatican, the British Library, the Biblioteca Ambrosiana (Ceruti) in Milan, the Biblioteca Medicea-Laurenziana in Florence, the Bayerische Staatsbibliothek in Munich, the Bibliothèque Nationale in Paris, and the Nationalbibliothek in Vienna. I also consulted the catalogues of early printed books for a pre-sixteenth-century translation. The first translation seems to have been that of John Reuchlin published at Hagenau in 1519, and absorbed into the *Opera* of St. Athanasius published by Jean Petit at Paris in 1520 (*De variis questionibus ad Antiochum principem*).

72. Saffrey, "Pietro Balbi," 430, lines 7–8 of the preface to Ferdinand of Naples for the translation of Proclus' *Theologia Platonica*.

73. See Appendix I below.

74. According to Innocent, Hypatius rejected Pseudo-Dionysius as a forgery on the grounds that neither Athanasius nor Cyril of Alexandria nor any other Father ever cited him. Innocent's letter is edited by E. Schwartz, *Concilium universale Constantinopolitanum sub Iustiniani habitum*, II. *Acta Conciliorum Oecumenicorum*, 4.2 (Strasbourg, 1914): 169–184. Since its first publication by C. Baronius in the sixteenth century (*Annales ecclesiasticae, ad ann.* 532), it has only been known in the Latin translation found in the conciliar collection in the tenth-century manuscript, Paris, BN, lat. 1682. For a description of this manuscript see E. Schwartz and J. Straub, *Acta Conciliorum Oecumenicorum*, IV.3.1 (Berlin, 1974): xxvii sq.; and Paris, Bibliothèque Nationale, *Catalogue général des manuscrits latins*, 2 (Paris, 1940): 122ff.

ble that Balbi read the penetrating critique of the authenticity of Pseudo-Dionysius found in Photius' *Bibliotheca*.[75] In Codex I Photius reports the four arguments against Pseudo-Dionysius which an otherwise unknown Theodorus presbyter tried to refute. These are: 1) none of the Fathers who supposedly postdate the Areopagite ever cite him; 2) Eusebius does not mention him in listing the writings of the Fathers; 3) the Areopagite relates Church customs which only developed after he supposedly lived; 4) the Areopagite cites the letter of Ignatius who lived in the time of Trajan. Photius himself never bothered to record how Theodorus refuted these arguments.[76]

In any case, Cusanus' *De non aliud* and the note in MS Cus. 44 show that Balbi worried about the authenticity of the Areopagite. But how far his doubts extended and whether or not they were fully allayed by his own researches or by Cusanus are not questions to which the evidence permits definite answers. However, Balbi does confirm that there were doubts about Pseudo-Dionysius in mid-Quattrocento Rome and, moreover, that these doubts were emanating from Greek sources quite independent of Lorenzo Valla, who did not make the link between Pseudo-Dionysius and Proclus.[77]

To corroborate this view we can call on another former member of the Bessarion circle, George of Trebizond. In his *Comparatio philosopho-*

75. For a copy of the *Bibliotheca* which Bessarion had on consignment in 1459 from the stock of Giovanni Aurispa see the letter to Nardus Palmerius in Mohler, *Kardinal Bessarion*, 3: 493. By the time of his death Bessarion owned the two most important extant manuscripts of the *Bibliotheca*. These are Venice, Bibl. Marc., MSS Zan. gr. 450 (= 652) and Zan. gr. 451 (= 537). See the concordance in Labowsky, *Bessarion's Library*, 442. Bessarion's copies may have been the only ones in Rome at the time. For a discussion of both manuscripts see E. Martini, *Textgeschichte der* Bibliothek *des Patriarchen Photios von Konstantinopel. I. Die Handschriften, Ausgaben und Übertragungen*. Abhandlungen der Königl. Sächsischen Gesellschaft der Wissenschaften, philologisch-historische Klasse, 28.6 (Leipzig, 1911): 6–19; and the introduction to R. Henry's edition of Photius, *Bibliothèque*, 1 (Paris, 1959): xxvii–xxxv. None of the inventories of the Vatican library in the fifteenth century lists a copy (Devreesse, *Le Fonds grec, ad indicem*).

76. N. G. Wilson, *Scholars of Byzantium* (London, 1983), 55, suggests that all four arguments may derive from Hypatius of Ephesus. But did Photius agree with the sceptical view? J. Stiglmahr, "Hielt Photius die sogen. Areopagitischen Schriften für echt?" *Historisches Jahrbuch der Görresgesellschaft*, 19 (1898): 91–94, said no, while I. Hausherr, "Doutes au sujet du 'Divin Denys'," *Orientalia Christiana Periodica*, 2 (1936): 484–490, said yes.

77. Much of the confusion on this point stems from A. Renaudet, *Préréforme et humanisme à Paris pendant les premières guerres d'Italie (1494–1517)*, 2nd ed. (Paris, 1953), 375–376, followed, e. g., by Aubert, 296 (see note 1 above); but Tigerstedt, *The Decline*, 89, note 221, corrects Renaudet.

rum Platonis et Aristotelis, completed in 1458 and rebutted by Bessarion as early as 1459, George responded to the charge that Dionysius copied from the *Platonici* by insisting that the opposite was true, namely, that the *Platonici* had copied from Dionysius.[78] Hence, George was not really answering the criticisms of Valla, but rather those in the Greek tradition, and he refuted them with the same tactics used by George Pachymeres. Knowledge of Proclus was not uncommon among educated Byzantines in the fifteenth century. Even such a staunch Aristotelian as George Scholarius knew Proclus well enough to label many parts of Gemistus Pletho's *Laws* as taken whole cloth from Proclus.[79] Through the 1440s Trebizond had been a member of the Bessarion circle; and in a perverse way he maintained this link even after breaking with Bessarion. He wrote his *Comparatio* of 1458 in large part to stem the Platonic "contagion" emanating from the Bessarion circle. A year later, in 1459, Trebizond finished translating for Nicolaus Cusanus Plato's *Parmenides*.[80] The question of Trebizond's inconsistency aside, the essential point is that given Trebizond's presence at the papal court, his connection with the Bessarion circle, and his association with Cusanus in the late 1450s, it is difficult to imagine Balbi not knowing about and perhaps even participating in the discussions on Dionysius against which Trebizond was reacting.

All this brings us to Balbi's long-time friend, Theodore Gaza. Gaza has a special place in this history, indeed, along with Valla, the central place. For he, and really only he, I would contend, is Lorenzo Valla's *quidam nostrae aetatis eruditissimi Graeci* who identified Pseudo-Dionysius with Apollinaris. This assertion is not new, but it has never been proven.[81]

---

78. For this dating see my *George of Trebizond. A Biography and a Study of his Rhetoric and Logic* (Leiden, 1976), 166. For George's text see his *Comparationes phylosophorum Aristotelis et Platonis* (Venice: Aldine Press, 1523) sign. G 8r. Like George Pachymeres, George singled out Proclus and Numenius as the chief culprits.

79. See Scholarius' *Letter to the Princess of the Peloponnesus*, in *Oeuvres complètes de Gennade Scholarios*, 8 vols., eds. L. Petit, X. A. Sidéridès, and M. Jugie (Paris, 1928–1936), 4: 153.23ff.; and his *Letter to the Exarch Joseph, ibid.*, 162.21ff. The last text is also to be found in Pletho, *Traité des Lois . . .*, ed. C. Alexandre, tr. A. Pellissier (Paris, 1858; repr. Amsterdam, 1966), 424 (French translation by Alexandre on p. lxxx); and *PG*, 160: 639C, from Alexandre. Cf. the opinion of Saffrey and Westerink in Proclus, *Théologie platonicienne*, 1: clviii–clix (see note 25 above): "Le XVe siècle fut vraiment, pour la *Théol. plat.*, celui d'une renaissance. L'artisan principal de cette renaissance . . . fut Georges Gémiste Pléthon."

80. Monfasani, *George of Trebizond*, 167ff.

81. Mancini, *Vita di Lorenzo Valla*, 312, says that Valla meant Gaza, and cites for evidence

Gaza settled in Rome in early 1450 after a brief visit at the end of 1449.[82] He had made the move from Ferrara under the aegis of Cardinal Bessarion and the papal intimate Giovanni Tortelli, both of whom wanted him to join the cohort of humanists translating Greek texts for Pope Nicholas V in Rome.[83] In the next five years, until Nicholas V died in March 1455, Gaza rendered into Latin Theophrastus' *De plantis*,[84] the Aristotelian *Problemata*, and Pseudo-Alexander of Aphrodisias' *Problemata*.[85] He also began his translation of Aristotle's zoological writings.[86] But Gaza did more than simply translate. He critically examined the authenticity and text of the works he translated. He was the first to recognize the apocryphal nature of the *Problemata* attributed to Alexander of Aphrodisias.[87] Again, when he turned to work on Aristotle, he rejected the received text of the Aristotelian *Problemata* as more the product of a later editor than of Aristotle himself. And because he believed that the classical editor had botched the job, he himself attempted to publish in Latin translation what amounted to a new edition of the Aristotelian *Problemata*.[88] In the case of his translation of Aristotle's *Historia animalium*, he rearranged the sequence of books. Today, against the witness of the Greek manuscripts, modern editors of the *Historia animalium* follow the order which Theodore Gaza imposed on the books in his Latin translation.[89] When faced with a garbled or lacunose text, Gaza did not hesitate to

F. Fiorentino, *Il Risorgimento filosofico nel Quattrocento* (Naples, 1885), 98; but Fiorentino makes no such identification. Mancini's assertion has been generally accepted by modern scholars, e.g., Camporeale, *Lorenzo Valla*, 429; and D. Geanakoplos, "Theodore Gaza, a Byzantine Scholar of the Palaeologan 'Renaissance' in the Italian Renaissance," *Medievalia et Humanistica*, n. s., 12 (1984): 61–81, at 70–71.

82. See the letter to Giovanni Tortelli edited by R. Sabbadini in Guarino, *Epistolario*, 3: 480–481; Sabbadini supplies a good synopsis of Gaza's life to that point in his *Carteggio di Giovanni Aurispa* (Rome, 1931), 168–170. For literature on Gaza see *Prosopographisches Lexikon der Palaiologenzeit*, 2, ed. E. Trapp with R. Walther and H.-V. Beyer (Vienna, 1977), 139; and Geanakoplos, "Theodore Gaza." The biography by Pinto in his edition of Gaza's letters (see note 30 above) is to be used with caution. I am preparing a new study of Gaza's life and works.

83. For Tortelli see the previous note; for Bessarion see the remarks of George of Trebizond in Mohler, *Kardinal Bessarion*, 3: 294.2 sq. As an example of Bessarion's affection for Gaza see his remarks at *ibid.*, 487.9 sq.

84. See C. B. Schmitt, "Theophrastus," *CTC*, 2: 239–322, at 266ff.

85. See F. E. Cranz, "Alexander Aphrodisiensis," *CTC*, 1: 77–135, at 126ff.

86. For the date of Gaza's versions under Nicholas V see my *George of Trebizond*, 150, note 79.

87. See Cranz, cited in note 85 above.

88. An analysis of this translation will be part of the study mentioned at the end of note 82 above. But see my *George of Trebizond*, 152ff.

89. Gaza transposed Bks. 7 and 9 of the *Historia animalium* as found in the manuscripts. He also suppressed Bk. 10.

substitute conjectures which are still cited today either under the false belief that Gaza had access to more correct manuscripts or simply because his readings have remained the most plausible.[90]

According to George of Trebizond, Gaza's critical daring extended beyond Aristotelian scientific texts into the realm of scripture. Writing at Rome in 1465, George exclaimed:[91]

We say, behold the impiety! I have in my hands an oration which he [Theodore Gaza] wrote against the books of Moses, which are the origin and foundation of all sacred letters.

No extant work of Gaza fits Trebizond's description, and from his brief reference it is impossible to surmise what exactly Trebizond was accusing Gaza of saying about the Pentateuch. To be sure, Trebizond was hardly an unbiased reader. But we have absolutely no reason to doubt that he had read something by Gaza on the Pentateuch.[92] Given Trebizond's reaction, it is hard to believe that Gaza's comments did not go beyond the banal observation that Moses did not write the end of Deuteronomy (34:5 sq.), where Moses's death is reported. Such an observation would not have been news at Rome. Standard Latin authorities such as the *Glossa ordinaria* (twelfth century),[93] Hugo of St. Cher (d. 1263),[94] Nicholas of Lyra (d. 1349),[95] and Gaza's own contemporary, Denis the Carthusian,[96] ac-

90. E.g., E. S. Forster (Oxford, 1927) and W. S. Hett (Cambridge, Mass., 1936–1937) in their translations of the Aristotelian *Problemata* make much use of Gaza; as did H. Aubert and F. Wimmer (Leipzig, 1860) in their edition of the *De generatione et corruptione*.

91. Monfasani, *Collectanea Trapezuntiana*, 107 (Text IX, 10): "Dicimus, vide impietatem! Est in manibus oratio quam scripsit adversus Moysi libros, qui omnium litterarum sacrarum origo sunt atque fundamentum."

92. In the case of Bessarion, we can test George's charges. George insisted that the cardinal was wrong to emend *sic* in Jn. 21:22 to *si*. George was right in so far as *sic* was not a scribal error, as Bessarion supposed, but the authentic text of the Old Latin and Jerome's revision (see my *George of Trebizond*, 92–93). George also condemned Bessarion for lapsing into doctrinal error in his attempt to explain the *zenon* of Greek eucharistic practice. In point of fact, Bessarion's explanation is difficult to square with the Latin understanding of when consecration takes place in the Eucharist (see my *Collectanea Trapezuntiana*, 169, sect. 29; and "Bessarion Latinus," *Rinascimento*, ser. 2, 21 (1981): 165–209, at 171, note 2).

93. See *PL*, 113: 506 A–B. See also G. Hoberg, *Moses und der Pentateuch* (Freiburg i. B., 1905), 72.

94. *Hugonis Cardinalis Opera omnia in universum Vetus et Novum Testamentum*, 8 vols. (Venice 1754), 1: f. 177v, col. 2.

95. Nicholas of Lyra, *Postilla in totam Bibliam* (Venice, 1488), f. 1r, col. 1, of sign. 13 (the introduction to Deuteronomy), where, for instance, Rabbi Salomon is cited to the effect that "totus iste liber scriptus fuit a Moyse excepto ultimo capitulo quod scripsit Iosue post mortem Moysi." There is also an extended discussion on whether Moses even wrote Deuteronomy.

96. Denis the Carthusian, *Opera omnia* (see note 60 above), 2 (Montreuil, 1897): 688.

knowledged the non-Mosaic authorship of these lines. Furthermore, George spoke of Gaza attacking *the books* of Moses, and not merely the last lines of Deuteronomy. Fifty years later Andreas Carlstadt denied that Moses actually wrote the Pentateuch.[97] One wonders how far in that direction Gaza himself went when he "wrote against the books of Moses."

With Gaza's general critical attitude in mind, we should now turn to a passage in Gaza's preface to his translation of Pseudo-Alexander of Aphrodisias' *Problemata*. Probably in late 1454 Gaza addressed Pope Nicholas V as follows:[98]

> Most holy father, would you take it for the moment amiss if I were to discover that the inscription of this book is false, or do you want merely the books of the *Celestial Hierarchy* to be of that most learned man, Dionysius the Athenian, lest religion suffer any loss? As for other works, however, you do not care whether or not they belong to whom they are ascribed as long as some profit can still be derived from them. I think that you prefer the latter course, and I am not afraid to seem to reject what men have for so long believed.

In this involuted, but clever opening, Gaza made it clear that he himself considered the writings attributed to the Areopagite forgeries, but in deference to the pope's feelings on the matter would not assert it. In the preface to his translation of Pseudo-Alexander Gaza had gratuitously brought up the question of Pseudo-Dionysius. He had acknowledged the pope's wishes in the matter. But, pointedly, he himself avoided endorsing the authenticity of the *Celestial Hierarchy* or any other part of the Dionysian corpus. The passage also indicates that Nicholas V knew well the opinion of Gaza and others in Rome concerning the authenticity of Dionysius.[99]

97. See K. A. Credner, *Zur Geschichte des Kanons* (Halle, 1847), 364ff.; H. Barge, *Andreas Bodenstein von Karlstadt*, 2 vols. (Leipzig, 1905), 1: 193ff. In his *De canonicis scripturis libellus* of 1520 Carlstadt asserted that Moses was responsible for the content but not the actual writing of the Pentateuch. This aspect of Carlstadt is ignored by R. J. Sider, *Andreas Bodenstein von Karlstadt: The Development of His Thought, 1517–1525* (Leiden, 1974).

98. F. E. Cranz, "The Prefaces to the Greek Editions and Latin Translations of Alexander of Aphrodisias," *Proceedings of the American Philosophical Society*, 102 (1958): 510–546, at 541: "Num aegre interim feras, pater sanctissime, si ego falsam deprehendam libri descriptionem, an libros tantum illos de hierarchia autoris esse Dionysii Atheniensis, viri doctissimi, velis ne quid religionis derogetur, cetera autem sint necne, quorum volumina esse inscribuntur, parum referre censeas modo fructus ex his aliquis capiatur? Equidem ita censere te arbitror, nec vereor ne quod hactenus per tam longum tempus crediderint homines a me reprobari videatur."

99. That Nicholas V had Valla's *Collatio Novi Testamenti* in his hands is certain from a letter

What these lines in Gaza's preface do not make clear is Gaza's judgment on the date and identity of Pseudo-Dionysius. Obviously, if Gaza
did believe that Pseudo-Dionysius was Apollinaris of Laodicea, it is no
wonder that he kept that opinion from the pope. Such an identification
was equivalent to saying that nearly a thousand years of pious Christian
study and commentary were based on an heretical author.[100]

But did Gaza make this identification? Well, the idea was hardly original to the fifteenth century. Since the seventh century it could be found
in the standard Greek commentary on Pseudo-Dionysius by Maximus the
Confessor.[101] To be sure, Maximus himself rejected the possible authorship of Apollinaris out of hand. But any reader of Maximus who doubted
the attribution to Dionysius the Areopagite might find the suggestion
of Apollinaris attractive. The followers of Apollinaris were notorious for
their practice of circulating Apollinaris' writings under the name of respected
orthodox figures in order to gain acceptance of their ideas.[102] The fact
that Proclus flourished about fifty years after Apollinaris (d. 385–395) posed
no major problem since both Proclus and those who believed in the authenticity of Dionysius claimed that Proclus drew upon a Platonic tradition
much older than Proclus himself. So one could assume that Apollinaris
simply anticipated Proclus in his borrowing from this Platonic tradition.
Indeed, the first time we know of Dionysius being cited, i.e., by the Seve-
rans at the colloquy in Constantinople in 532, Hypatius of Ephesus actu-

of Cusanus (see note 48 above) and from Valla's dedication, but this does not mean that he read
it through.

100. On Apollinaris see R. Aigrain, "Apollinaire Le Jeune," *DHGE*, 3 (Paris, 1924): 962–982;
H. Lietzmann, *Apollinaris von Laodicea und seine Schule. Texte und Untersuchungen*, 1 (Tübingen,
1904; repr. Hildesheim, 1970); E. Mühlenberg, *Apollinaris von Laodicea* (Göttingen, 1969); C.
E. Raven, *Apollinarianism* (Cambridge, 1924); and B. Altaner–A. Stuiber, *Patrologie*, 9th ed.
(Freiburg, 1978), 313–315.

101. *PG*, 4: 175 C, at the lemma καὶ μακαριωτάτην (*Beatissimamque*) in *Hier. eccl.* VII.

102. The prime text on this score is the *Adversus fraudes Apollinaristarum* (*PG*, 86: 1948–1976)
attributed to the sixth-century theologian Leontius Byzantinus, which attempts to prove that the
Apollinarians had foisted Apollinaris' *logoi* on the unsuspecting by substituting in the titles of
these works the names of Gregory Thaumaturgus, Athanasius, and Pope Julius I. For the Apol-
linarian fragments found in Leontius and a modern corroboration of Leontius' thesis see Lietzmann, *Apollinaris von Laodicea*, 103ff. Concerning the attribution of the *Adversus fraudes
Apollinaristarum*, J. H. I. Watt, "The Authenticity of Writings Ascribed to Leontius of Byzantium: A New Approach by Means of Statistics," *Studia Patristica*, 7 (Berlin, 1966): 321–336, especially 333, rejects attempts to deny the attribution to Leontius. For more literature on the *Adv.
fraudes Apoll.* see Altaner–Stuiber, *Patrologie*, 510. See also W. Speyer, *Die literarische Fälschung
im heidnischer und christlicher Altertum: Ein Versuch ihrer Deutung* (Munich, 1971), 271 ff.; and Mühlenberg, *Apollinaris von Laodicea*, 97 ff.

ally suggested that Apollinaris was the source of the Dionysian and the other false patristic testimonia adduced by the Monophysites.[103] Well into the eighteenth century the attribution to Apollinaris was still seriously debated by scholars.[104] In any case, Anastasius the Librarian omitted the key sentence in this particular scholium when translating Maximus' scholia in the ninth century.[105] Grosseteste included the sentence when translating the same scholium in the thirteenth century, but the brief reference seems not to have attracted any attention.[106] So it was only in the Greek East that a certain amount of doubt about Dionysius continued after Maximus.[107] Not by chance, in the Middle Ages Pseudo-Dionysius exercised a far greater influence amongst the Latins than he ever did amongst Byzantines.[108] Gaza, I believe, should be placed within the narrow but nevertheless real Byzantine tradition of scepticism concerning Pseudo-Dionysius.

103. *Acta Conc. Oecum.*, IV.2 (see note 74 above): 172.30–31: "Vos non suspicamur [*of fraud*], sed antiquos haereticos Apollinaristas." See also H.-C. Puech, *Libératus de Carthage et la date de l'apparition des écrits dionysiens*, in Ecole pratique des hautes études, section des sciences religieuses, *Annuaire*, an. 1930–1931, 1–39.

104. See the treatise of Bernardus de Rubeis, O. P. (d. 1775), *Dissertatio adversus Michaelem Lequienum aliosque*, in *PG*, 4: 1025ff., where he refutes (col. 1029ff.) the English scholar William Cave, who had identified Pseudo-Dionysius with Apollinaris in his *Scriptorum ecclesiasticorum historia litteraria* of 1688.

105. In Vatican City, BAV, MS Vat. lat. 176, f. 182v (seen in a print from microfilm) the scholium runs: "Arbitror enim innuere [*ex* innmare (?) *cod. corr.*] Papiam Ierapoliten. Hic enim in quarto libro Domenicarum narrationum refectiones dixit per escas in resurrectione futuras. Secundum quod dogma eadem credidit Appolinarius. Hyreneus quorum [*sic*] Ludiniensis [*sc.* Lugdunensis] in quinto sermone de heresibus hoc idem dicit et inducit testem super hiis que dicit predictum Papiam." For the presence of Maximus' scholia to the *Ecclesiastical Hierarchy* in the "Parisian" corpus of Dionysius see Dondaine (see note 64 above), 17, line 2 up. In his preface Anastasius made the point that the Greek scholia derive from John Scythopolios as well as Maximus, and in this contention he has been supported by modern scholarship; see H. U. von Balthasar, "Das Problem der Dionysius-Scholien," in his *Kosmische Liturgie. Das Weltbild Maximus des Bekenners*, 2nd ed. (Einsiedeln, 1961), 644–675.

106. I used MS Cus. 44, f. 309v, col. 2, bottom margin (= K), and Vatican City, BAV, MS Chis. A IV 129, Part 1, f. 197v, col. 2 (= V)(seen in microfilm at the Pius XII Memorial Library, St. Louis University). One needs the Greek (see note 101 above) to understand completely Grosseteste's painfully literal translation: "Ex Greco: Hoc ait enigmatizans, existimo, Papiam Hierapoleos [Herapoleos K; Ierapoleos V], eius que secundum Asiam, tunc existentem episcopum et coevum divino evangeliste Ioanne. Iste enim [est V] Papias in quarto libro dominicarum [χυριαχῶν; divinarum V] ipsius enarrationum per cibos dicens in resurrectione [reserructione V] voluptates. In quod dogma post hoc credidit Apollinarius. Qualiter igitur Apollinarii hoc sancti Dyonisii conscriptiones secundum quorundam deliramenta interimentes Apollinarium?"

107. Hausherr, "Doutes au sujet du 'Divin Denys'" (see note 76 above).

108. See the summation of the evidence for the East by P. Sherwood, J. Leroy, A. Wenger, and A. Rayez in "Denys Le Pseudo-Aréopagite," *DSAM*, 3: 286–318; and more briefly in "Denys Le Pseudo-Aréopagite," *DHGE* 14: 286–90.

As for the suggestion concerning Apollinaris, we have the testimony of Valla that at least one Greek in his time ventured it, and, given the Byzantine tradition, it is not conceivable that any other Apollinaris was meant than Apollinaris of Laodicea, the Younger.[109] But if Gaza did not propose Apollinaris, then who? No other Greek in contemporary Rome even remotely expressed in writing any doubts about Pseudo-Dionysius or demonstrated the critical daring of Gaza. John Argyropoulos seems to me the only other plausible candidate, but in the absence of evidence that he took a stand on the issue or that he had any dealings with Valla,[110] Gaza remains the only real choice.

It is no accident that as soon as Gaza arrived in Rome he recognized a kindred spirit in Lorenzo Valla. In a letter written in November 1449, almost as soon as he came to Rome from Ferrara, Gaza already called Valla *meae deliciae*.[111] Valla, in turn, when he defended himself against Poggio in 1453, listed Gaza as one of his masters in Greek along with Giovanni Aurispa, Rinuccio Aretino, and an otherwise unknown Calojannis.[112] But Aurispa and Rinuccio had taught Valla Greek in his youth. Gaza's influence began when he settled in Rome in 1450 at a time when Valla

109. In his note to Acts 17:34 (see note 5 above), Erasmus raised the issue of which Apollinaris was meant, and pointed out that in the *De viris inlustribus* Jerome named two authors, one the bishop of Hierapolis and the other bishop of Laodicea, with the name Apollinaris. Erasmus himself denied that the heretic Apollinaris was responsible for the Dionysian corpus ("Neque enim opinor haec Apollinari haeretico tribuenda"). The heretic Apollinaris of Laodicea ("the Younger") needs to be distinguished from his father ("the Elder") of the same name. For the various Christian authors named Apollinaris see *DHGE*, 3: 958ff.

110. Argyropoulos also seems not to have shown a special interest in textual history. If he had any significant contact with Valla, it would have been in the period 1454–1457 when he travelled about after the fall of Constantinople. After the standard biography, G. Cammelli, *Giovanni Argiropulo* (Florence, 1941), see for more recent literature E. Bigi, "Argiropulo, Giovanni," *DBI*, 4 (Rome, 1962): 129–131; J. E. Seigel, "The Teaching of Argyropoulos and the Rhetoric of the First Humanists," in *Action and Conviction in Early Modern Europe: Essays in Memory of E. H. Harbison*, eds. T. K. Rabb and J. E. Seigel (Princeton, 1969), 237–260; E. Garin, *La cultura filosofica del Rinascimento italiano* (Florence, 1961), 102–108, 111–121, and 346–350; and A. Field, *The Beginning of the Philosophical Renaissance in Florence, 1454–1469*, diss., Univ. of Michigan, Ann Arbor, 1980, 347–350, and *passim*; and idem, "John Argyropoulos and the 'Secret Teachings' of Plato," in this volume.

111. In the letter to Tortelli cited in note 65 above: "cupio enim non modo cum reliquis amicis et cum Laurentio Vallensi, meis deliciis, esse in urbe . . .'

112. Valla, *Opera*, 1: 339; Camporeale, *Lorenzo Valla*, 352, from Paris, BN, MS lat. 8691: ". . . et ego in Graeciam nunquam navigavi, necdum tantis praeceptoribus meis dignus sum Aurispa atque Rinucio, nedum Calojanne atque Theodoro." Cf. L. Valla, *Antidotum Primum. La prima apologia contro Poggio Bracciolini. Edizione critica con introduzione e note*, ed. A. Wesseling (Assen, 1978), 95, second note to section 50.

was already a mature scholar.[113] So in listing Gaza among his teachers, Valla was paying Gaza a considerable compliment and acknowledging Gaza's influence upon him.

Valla was bold enough to publish his critique of Pseudo-Dionysius; Gaza was not. Unlike Valla, Gaza apparently felt he could not risk offending his patrons, Nicholas V and Bessarion. Yet, if the argument of this article is correct, Gaza did publish his opinion, albeit indirectly, through Valla. Furthermore, Gaza's preface to Nicholas V for Pseudo-Alexander of Aphrodisias is our best indication that the doubts raised by Valla concerning Pseudo-Dionysius disturbed the Roman Curia, so much so that by 1454 the pope had to warn Gaza on the issue. In his well-known conservative attacks on Valla's scholarship in 1452–53, the papal secretary Poggio Bracciolini never mentioned Pseudo-Dionysius. Even if Poggio had heard of Valla's doubts concerning Pseudo-Dionysius only by word of mouth, he doubtlessly would have denounced them. In the invectives against Valla, Poggio did not hesitate to attack the contents of works which he demonstrably had not read.[114] Gaza's preface of 1454 and Poggio's silence in 1453 prove that the issue of the authenticity of the Areopagite first disturbed Rome in late 1453–early 1454, i. e., when Valla dedicated the *Collatio Novi Testamenti* to Nicholas V.[115] Thereafter, with Valla's *Encomium S. Thomae* in 1457, Gaza's preface to Pseudo-Alexander, Trebizond's *Comparatio* in 1458, and the various comments and notes of Balbi and Cusanus in the early 1460s, the issue became a subject of fairly wide debate at Rome.

I suspect that after the death of Nicholas V it was Cardinal Bessarion who more than anyone else prevented doubts concerning Pseudo-Dionysius from taking root more firmly amongst Roman intellectuals. Certainly,

---

113. It is conceivable that Gaza visited Rome in 1447–1448 and met Valla then; but even so, any close association could only have begun in 1449.

114. Attacking Valla's views on the procession of the Holy Spirit, but not knowing that they were contained in Valla's *Repastinatio totius dialectice*, Poggio attributed to Valla a separate ghost work *de trinitate* (*Opera* [see note 19 above], 1: 233: "Quid liber de trinitate?"); see my review essay of G. Zippel's edition of the *Repastinatio dialectice* in *Rivista di letteratura italiana*, 2 (1984): 177–193, at 188.

115. See note 70 above. If Gaza accurately quoted Nicholas V's prohibition against casting aspersions upon the authenticity of Pseudo-Dionysius ("libros tantum illos de hierarchia autoris esse Dionysii Atheniensis"), then Nicholas V seems to have been consciously quoting the first recension of Valla's *Collatio* ("hec dico ne illorum sequamur errorem qui ab hoc Dionysio existiment opus de celesti hierarchia fuisse compositum").

given his great authority in all things Greek, if Bessarion had seconded the doubts of Valla, Gaza, and perhaps Balbi, the 1450s would have been the decisive period in the history of the Dionysian corpus. The irony is that the Bessarion circle in the 1450s, with its sure knowledge of Proclus, its direct contact with the Greek scholiast tradition on the Areopagite, its immediate access to Codex I of Photius' *Bibliotheca*, its enjoyment of the living presence of Lorenzo Valla, and its possession in Theodore Gaza of a critical mind of great stature, was in far better position to start the revolution concerning Pseudo-Dionysius than was Erasmus in the next century, who in his own criticism did not really move much beyond what he found in Valla's *Adnotationes*.

In the long term, however, the discussion on Pseudo-Dionysius in mid-Quattrocento Rome did have its effect. Erasmus publicized specifically the Roman version of Valla's attack on Dionysius containing Gaza's attribution to Apollinaris. The troublesome similarity between Proclus and Pseudo-Dionysius, which mid-Quattrocento Rome first raised as a serious issue for Latins, was thereafter brought to the attention of readers of Cusanus and Trapezuntius. Marsilio Ficino, who read Proclus in the original, as well as Denis the Carthusian and Jacques Lefèvre, who did not, could not avoid the problem. Finally, though we cannot trace all the direct and indirect ways in which it spread, the aura of suspicion attaching to Pseudo-Dionysius in the Latin West started at Rome in the 1450s. Nicholas V's order to Theodore Gaza is proof of that.

JOHN MONFASANI

APPENDIX I

1.

Chis. G IV 97 of the Biblioteca Apostolica Vaticana is a mixed parchment and paper fifteenth-century manuscript (ff. 1–10, 15–16, 25–26, 35–36, 45–46 are parchment) of 72 written leaves in one semi-humanistic round hand (see Kristeller, *Iter*, 2: 481). Ff. 1r–51v contain the *Vita S. Athanasii* in the translation of Giovanni Tortelli with a preface to Pope Eugenius IV. Ff. 52r–72r contain two anepigraphic texts: a preface (f. 52r–v) followed by a treatise (f. 53r sq.). At the top of both ff. 52r and 53r space was left for titles which were never written. However, at the very bottom edge of f. 52 the binder failed to cut completely away the note which was meant to serve as the model for the rubricator when he wrote in the title at the top of the page. One can still read the last half of this partially excised note. It runs: ". . . Petri Balbi Tropiensis episcopi prefatio." The preface itself is manifestly addressed to a pope. As the preface also makes clear, the text that follows on f. 53r is Balbi's translation of Emperor Justinian I's *Contra Origenem*.

We can date Balbi's preface with certainty to 1462–64, and with fair probability to June–July 1463. Since Teodoro Lelli[1] is called at its start the "ecclesie Feltrentium [*sic*] presul," the preface cannot be earlier than 15 February 1462, the date Lelli was elected bishop of Feltre,[2] nor later than 7 September 1464 when Lelli was transferred from Feltre to the see of Treviso.[3] Balbi tells us in the preface that Lelli himself had gone to Bessarion to ask for the Greek exem-

---

1. Concerning Lelli, doctor of both laws, papal ambassador, polemicist, and adviser, whose brilliant career at Rome was cut short by an early death, see L. Alpago-Novello, "Teodoro de' Lelli: vescovo di Feltre (1462–64) e di Treviso (1464–66)," *Archivio Veneto*, ser. 4, 19 (1936): 238–261; J. B. Sägmüller, *Zur Geschichte des Kardinalates. Ein Traktat des Bischofs von Feltre und Treviso Teodoro de' Lelli über das Verhältnis von Primat und Kardinalat*. Römische Quartalschrift für christl. Alterthumskunde und für Kirchengeschichte, Suppl. 2 (Rome, 1893). Alpago-Novello discusses one collection of Lelli's speeches, but others exist, e.g., Vatican City, BAV, MS Ottob. lat. 233 (see Kristeller, *Iter*, 2: 413), as do other manuscripts of his writings. Lelli is responsible for an edition of St. Jerome's letters and opuscula found in MSS Vat. lat. 343 and 344 of the BAV which are reproduced in the two earliest printed editions (Rome, Pannartz and Sweynheym, 1468; and Rome, Sixtus Riessinger, ca. 1468) as well as in the deluxe manuscripts, Paris, BN, lat. 1890 and 1891 (I thank Eugene F. Rice, Jr., for advice on this aspect of Lelli's work). Lelli would reward further study.

2. Eubel, 2: 153.

3. *Ibid.*, 249.

plar. Lelli immediately (*ulla sine mora*) passed the codex on to Balbi, and when Balbi discovered in it Justinian's *Contra Origenem*, he set to translating it as best he could while preoccupied with other business. Hence, very quickly after Lelli received the manuscript from Bessarion, Balbi translated the *Contra Origenem* and, it would seem, also wrote the preface to the pope. If this reading of the preface is correct and if Balbi's title of bishop of Tropea in the note at the bottom of f. 52r of Chis. G IV 97 truly reflects Balbi's status at the time of the translation, then the only possible date for the preface and the translation is June–July 1463. Bessarion left for his Venetian legation in the first half of July 1463 and did not return to Rome until late August 1464,[4] when he almost immediately entered the papal conclave which elected Paul II on 31 August. A week later Lelli was made bishop of Treviso. There would have been virtually no time for Lelli to solicit the Greek exemplar and for Balbi to make the translation between Bessarion's return to Rome and Lelli's transfer to Treviso — not to enter into the question of Bessarion's library being probably still in storage and therefore inaccessible.[5] Indeed, to suppose otherwise means believing that Balbi's preface is addressed not to Pius II, but to Paul II within days of his election, a very dubious proposition given the matter-of-fact tone of the preface and its implication that Balbi had long experienced the pope's benign rule ("pontificum prudentissime"). Hence, the most reasonable *terminus ante quem* for Balbi's translation and preface is July 1463, before or not long after Bessarion left for Venice. Since Balbi was named bishop of Tropea on 6 June 1463, we arrive at June 1463 as the *terminus post quem*. And if this is so, the pope addressed in the preface is Pius II, who had named Balbi to the see of Nicotera and then of Tropea.

The preface does not tell us why Balbi dedicated the translation to the pope instead of to Lelli. Perhaps Balbi had already dedicated to Lelli the translation of the other conciliar texts which he mentions in the preface, and did not feel obligated to do so again. Perhaps the research was part of a project Pius II had assigned Lelli. In any case, Balbi certainly was beholden to Pius for making him a bishop, and Lelli himself was a favorite of the pope. We may also note that in 1462–1463 Cusanus wrote Lelli a number of times.[6] So Lelli and Balbi had much in common in terms of friends and patrons, quite apart from shared scholarly interests.

4. Mohler, *Kardinal Bessarion*, 1: 317; and L. Labowsky, "Bessarione," *DBI*, 9: 686–697, at 692.
5. This is exactly what Bessarion did during his French legation of 1472 (see L. Labowsky, *Bessarion's Library*, 36ff.).
6. Cusanus' full correspondence has not yet been edited; but E. Meuthen, *Die letzten Jahre des Nikolaus von Kues: Biographische Untersuchungen nach neuen Quellen* (Cologne, 1958), cites from Kues-Bernkastel, St.-Nikolaus-Hospital, MS Cus. 221, letters of 23 July 1462 (Meuthen, 111, 283 note 1, 284 note 3), 25 September 1462 (Meuthen, 287 note 5), 10 January 1463 (Meuthen, 289 note 4), and 13 March 1463 (*ibid.*).

According to the modern critical edition, the full title of the work Balbi translated is "Statement [*logos*] of our most pious Emperor, Justinian, dispatched [*katapemphtheis*] to Mena, the most saintly and blessed Archbishop and Patriarch of the felicitous City against the impious Origen and his lawless dogmas".[7] The text forms part of the controversy concerning the Origenists in the reign of Justinian, and was published by the emperor in 543.[8] As the preface informs us, Balbi used a manuscript of Cardinal Bessarion. But Schwartz lists no Marciana manuscript in the introduction to his edition nor could I find any manuscript containing this text in A. M. Zanetti - A. Bongiovanni, *Graeca divi Marci Bibliotheca codicum manu scriptorum per titulos digesta* (Venice, 1740). Labowsky, *Bessarion's Library*, reports no manuscript of this text now extant outside the Fondo Antico of the Marciana, but the earliest inventories list a lost sylloge of the Fifth Ecumenical Council (Labowsky, p. 165, no. A 196, p. 199, no. B 142 , and p. 457, no. B 142), where Balbi might have found Justinian's treatise.

2.

I give below Pietro Balbi's preface to Pope Pius II for the translation of Emperor Justinian I's *Contra Origenem* in Vatican City, BAV, MS Chis. G IV 97, f. 52r-v, followed by the *incipit* and *desinit* of the translation, ff. 53r and 72r. I have modernized the punctuation, but otherwise left the text as it is found in the manuscript.

[No rubric]

(T)heodorus, ecclesie Feltrentium [*sic*] presul, beatissime patrum, iuris consultorum eruditissimus, cum sepe mecum de sanctorum patrum institutis conferret, de hac nostra etate conquestus est quanta sit librorum iactura quantaque solertium hominum paucitas in ea presertim parte que ad nostram intemeratam fidem religionemque pertinet. Referebat denique mihi se quam diutissime pro viribus diligentiam adhibuisse ut que reperirentur priscorum patrum in conciliis gesta in unum colligeret, reperisseque aliqua

---

7. E. Schwartz, *Acta Conciliorum Oecumenicorum*. 3. *Collectio Sabbaitica* (Berlin, 1940), 189–214; upon which is based M. Amelotti and L. Migliardi Zingale, trs., *Scritti teologici ed ecclesiastici di Giustiniano* (Milano, 1977), 67–119.

8. For this date see E. Schwartz, *I. Vigiliusbriefe. II. Zur Kirchenpolitik Iustinians*. Sitzungsberichte der Bayerischen Akademie der Wissenschaften, philosophisch-historische Abteilung, an. 1940, Heft 2, p. 52. F. Diekamp, *Die origenistischen Streitigkeiten im sechsten Jahrhundert und das fünfte allgemeine Konzil* (Münster, 1899), 45–46, prefers 423 as the year of publication as do J. Hefele and H. Leclercq, *Histoire des conciles*, 2.2 (Paris, 1908): 1187.

de ceteris orbis terrarum conciliis, de quinto vero nihil aut parum. Petiit igitur a me vir solertissimus an aliquid de hoc forte apud Grecos codices vidissem. Qua equidem percontatione motus perquisivi diligenter. Reperi quedam pauca que sua dumtaxat persuasus amicitia Latina feci. Quibus transferendis inveni de quadam imperatoris Iustiniani epistola mentionem, que quidem origo causaque fuerit huius quinti concilii celebrandi. Theodorus igitur suo pristino affectus desiderio, festinus ad reverendissimum dominum Nicenum se contulit. Unde Grecum codicem acceptum ad me ulla sine mora detulit. Sed quid plura? Inter cetera que de hoc sacro quinto concilio in eodem sunt codice prefatam reperi epistolam ad patriarcham Constantinopolitanum Menam, non mutilatam aut concisam sed totam atque integram. Feci eam denique Latinam ut potui, ceteris in negotiis implicatus.

In qua, pontificum prudentissime, id precipue advertas, velim, quanta fuerit solertia quantaque diligentia apud priscos erga immaculatam puramque fidem nostram tuendam atque servandam. Videbis hic insana, nugacia, impiaque Origenis suorumque sequacium dogmata et per sacras primum litteras et per maiorum nostrorum deinde auctoritates a veris omnino Christicolis reiecta atque reprobata. Lege ergo feliciter hanc epistolam, immo potius volumen non parvum. Vale, pontifex maxime, quam diutissime.

[*Translation*]

(S)emper nobis cure fuit et est ut et Christianorum rectam immaculatam fidem et sanctissime dei catholice apostoliceque ecclesie statum per omnia ulla sine turbatione tueamur atque servemus . . . [*des.*] Anathema sit et Origeni et Adamatio, qui hec exposuit cum suis nephandis maledictisque dogmatibus, et cuique persone eiusmodi hec sentienti vel qui faveret vel aliquo prorsus modo, quocumque tempore magnifacere ac defendere auderet in Christo Iesu domino nostro, cui gloria in secula seculorum. Amen.

A P P E N D I X   II

This text is taken from the microfilm of Kues-Bernkastel, St.-Nikolaus-Hospital, MS Cus. 44, provided to me by the Hill Monastic Manuscript Library. For bibliography on the manuscript see note 40 above. The text is found on f. 1v, cols. I–II of the manuscript. For its Greek sources see notes 56 and 67 of the article; for literary and historical information see notes 43–55 of the article.

Dominus Petrus episcopus Nycotarensis ex quibusdam Grecis scripturis textui Dyonisii applicatis hec extraxit.

Notandum quod quidam externorum philosophorum et presertim Proclus sepe speculationibus beati Dionysii utuntur ac ipsis tum aridis dictionibus. Ex quo coniectura sumi potest quod prisci apud Athenas philosophorum, cum eius opus sibi vendicassent, quemadmodum in presenti commemorat libro, occultarunt. Ut patres ipsi divinos eius sermones videant,[1] divina dispensatione hic tractatus apparuit ad illorum inanem gloriam temeritatemque redarguendam. Quodque eis consuetum fuerat nostra sibi vendicare Magnus docet Basilius supra illud dictum, "In principio erat verbum", eodem in loco ita dicens hec, "complures novi eciam extra iacionem veritatis qui, cum mundanam sapientiam magnifacerent atque admirarentur, in suis tractatibus aliena occupare ausi sunt. Fur enim dyabolus est ac nostra ad suos ministros quasi fabulas reducit." Et hic quidem sic, hec eciam Numenio Pythagorico apertissime dicente, "Quid enim Plato est nisi Moyses Attice loquens?", quod nemo negare potest cum noster non sit sed pocius adversarius. Eusebius autem, Cesarie Palestinorum presul, idem ipsum testatur, quod non modo in presenciarum verum etiam ante Christi adventum externi philosophi nostra furari consueverunt.

At cum quidam hunc tractatum sancti esse Dionysii negent sed cuiusdam posteriorum, necesse est et (?)[2] fateri hunc absurda quedam et supervacanea posuisse: sua eiusmodi mentitus ac si una cum apostolis fuisset misissetque epistolas illis qui neque contemporanei sibi fuerint neque mittere epistolas quirent. Quod autem propheciam fingat ad apostolum Iohannem, in exilio cum esset, quo rursus rediret ad Asye regionem consuetaque doceret, id hominis prestigiatoris foret ac furiosi prophete gloriam venantis; quod eciam dicat se una cum Apollophone in tempore ipso salutaris passionis apud Heliam fuisse civitatem ac simul speculari et philosophari de solis defectu tamquam non secundum naturam neque de more ut tunc fuit; dixisse quoque eum offuisse una cum apostolis in translatione sancti cadaveris beate Marie; protulisse eciam sui preceptoris Hierothei auctoritatem ex verbis epithaphii; finxisse autem et epistolas et sermones tamquam ad discipulos apostolorum scripsisse eum. Quante inconvenientie ille homo atque reprehensionis dignus foret! Ac ne viro quidem convenire⟨t⟩ qui tantopere et moribus et sciencia sit elevatus sublimatusque super sensibilia omnia quique intellectuales pulchritudines attigisset atque per eas, ut fieri potest, deum.

---

1. Balbi is guilty of a mistranslation here. See note 43 of the article.

2. *et*: the ink is too faint for the word to be read in microfilm. The Greek is καί. See note 47 of the article.

AN INCONSOLABLE
FATHER
and his human-
ist consolers

JACOPO
ANTONIO
MARCELLO
VENETIAN NOBLEMAN
PATRON and MAN
of letters

B Y THE EARLY MONTHS OF 1439, Brescia had already long suffered the hor-rors of siege warfare. Having gallantly rallied the citizens to a heroic defense against Milanese forces, the humanist Francesco Barbaro, then the city's Venetian governor, called desperately for help. Responding to his call, according to panegyrists, the *provveditore* Jacopo Antonio Marcello (no mercenary, but a Venetian nobleman elected by the Senate to super-vise their hired generals) accomplished a feat "greater than human strength and scarcely credible to posterity": with men, machines, and teams of oxen he hoisted the Venetian river fleet (perhaps eighty ships—"grossissima," said one chronicler) over Alpine foothills and launched them in the Lago di Garda. Like Xerxes, King of the Persians, who had built a bridge of boats across the Hellespont in order to invade Greece, wrote Guarino Veronese years afterward, Marcello had bridged the mountains blocking the one gateway to imperilled Brescia.[1]

1. The characterization of Marcello's achievement from Guarino's letter to Marcello of Ferrara, 1458, *Epistolario*, 2:629–634, at 632: ". . . humanis viribus maius et vix posteritati credibile. . . ." The comparison to Xerxes follows. The figure of eighty ships and comment on size from the *Cronaca* of Cristoforo da Soldo, ed. G. Brizzolara, in L. A. Muratori, *Rerum italicarum scriptores*

This victory was one of many in which Marcello participated between the campaign at Casalmaggiore in 1438 and the siege of Trieste in 1463. A key military leader at a time of *terraferma* expansion, Marcello was not only a soldier but also a statesman, diplomat, author, patron of arts and letters, and the father of a little boy who died in his ninth year and, dying, broke his aged father's heart. This essay will present Marcello and his son and the episode of death, mourning, and consolation which bore fruit in a collection of humanist works of interest to students of Renaissance society and ideas.[2]

Born 17 January 1399 (or 1398) to a Venetian noble family of great antiquity and apparently vast wealth, Marcello belonged to that narrow inner circle of his city's ruling class that actually determined and executed policy.[3] His membership in that powerful elite is signalled by the offices he held: *provveditore*, or military supervisor (repeatedly); provincial gover-

---

(new ed.), 21.3 (Bologna, 1938), at 30. This incident, a famous one in Venetian history, is not usually attributed to Marcello or to any other single figure, although other works written for the nobleman do make that attribution: see below, note 50. Marcello's special role is exaggerated by the humanists who direct laudatory works to him. This deed was, in fact, recommended by experts, commanded by the Senate, and executed by Venetian forces under the command of Gattamelata, who was accompanied by the *provveditore* Marcello, an active participant in this and other episodes of the 1438–40 campaign: see R. Fabbri, "Le *Consolationes de obitu Valerii Marcelli* ed il Filelfo," *Miscellanea di studi in onore di Vittore Branca* [*Biblioteca dell' "Archivum Romanicum,"* ser. 1, vols. 178–180], 3 vols. in 4 (Florence, 1983), 3.1:227–250, at 248–249, and sources there cited. For Barbaro's role at Brescia, see esp. P. Gothein, *Francesco Barbaro (1390–1454): Frühhumanismus und Staatskunst in Venedig* (Berlin, 1932), chap. 7. Research for this essay was supported by a grant from the National Endowment for the Humanities, to which agency I am most grateful.

2. For Marcello, see esp. Fabbri, "Le *Consolationes;*" H. Martin, "Sur un portrait de Jacques-Antoine Marcelle, Sénateur vénitien (1453)," *Mémoires de la société nationale des antiquaires de France*, 59 [= ser. 6, vol. 9] (1898):229–267; and M. Meiss, *Andrea Mantegna as Illuminator: An Episode in Renaissance Art, Humanism and Diplomacy* (New York, 1957); also, G. Benadduci, *A Jacopo Antonio Marcello patrizio veneto parte di orazione consolatoria ed elegia di Francesco Filelfo e lettera di Giovanni Mario Filelfo* (Tolentino, 1894); E. A. Cicogna, *Della famiglia Marcello patrizia veneta narrazione* (Venice, 1841), 18–19; M. L. King, *Venetian Humanism in an Age of Patrician Dominance* (Princeton, 1986), Part II, Marcello profile; J. Monfasani, *George of Trebizond: A Biography and a Study of his Rhetoric and Logic* (Leiden, 1976), 174–176 and 413, addendum to p. 175, and studies therein cited; the same author's *Collectanea Trapezuntiana: Texts, Documents and Bibliographies of George of Trebizond* (Binghamton, N.Y., 1984), 235–236. The humanist works inspired by this event collected in MS 201 (U.1.5.) of the Hunterian Museum Library of the University of Glasgow (henceforth G) and discussed below were first called to my attention by Professor P. O. Kristeller. For that manuscript, see below at notes 32 and 33. This essay is a preliminary sketch of matters I shall deal with in a separate monograph.

3. For the date of birth, see Fabbri, "Le *Consolationes*," 246. The uncertainty is due to the seeming conflict between archival and literary evidence. For Venice's narrow ruling elite at this period, see King, *Venetian Humanism*, Part II, Preface.

nor (*capitano, podestà, luogotenente* of Friuli); ambassador; senator; *savio di terraferma* ("sage" of mainland affairs); ducal counsellor (several times); member and head of the prying Council of Ten; ducal elector.[4] Clearly an insider, his career was still unusual in one regard: Marcello specialized in military assignments. Most Venetian leaders appeared more frequently than he in the councils at home, or abroad in roles of governor or ambassador. They served in military roles briefly as *provveditori* or for longer terms as *capitani da mar;* the latter were invariably Venetian noblemen of high caste and could spend many years at sea. But Marcello fought on land. He not only advised the mercenary soldiers who led Venetian forces, but actually led armies into the field. He may have hankered for mainland life away from Venice's damp alleys and silent canals. Indeed, he had married into a noble Paduan family and sojourned often and unauthorizedly (to the Senate's despair) in nearby Monselice in his splendid suburban villa.[5]

As ambassador to Count Francesco Sforza (the mercenary captain, later Duke of Milan) and *provveditore* with Gattamelata, Michele Attendolo da Cotignola, and other Venetian *condottieri,* Marcello fought in the wars Venice waged with Milan throughout the second quarter of the century. From 1438 to 1440, he accompanied Venetian troops at Casalmaggiore and entered Brescia and Verona following the heroic transport of ships

4. For these offices, see the documents cited in King, *Venetian Humanism*, Part II, Marcello profile, which extends the record provided by Fabbri, "Le *Consolationes*," 246–247.
5. See M. Mallett, "Venice and its Condottieri, 1404–54," in *Renaissance Venice*, ed. J. R. Hale (Totowa, N.J. and London, 1973), 121–145, at 135–137 and notes, for the significant role of the Venetian *provveditori*, civilian administrators of the standing *terraferma* army that the city created in the course of the fifteenth century; note 91 names several of these (including Marcello) whose careers were mainly military. For the relationship of Venice's tradition of patrician naval leadership to its development of a standing army, see Mallett, "Preparations for War in Florence and Venice in the Second Half of the Fifteenth Century," in *Florence and Venice: Comparisons and Relations*, 1:*Quattrocento* (Florence, 1979), 149–164, at 161. For Marcello's three marriages see Fabbri, "Le *Consolationes*," 246. Lucia da Leone, Valerio's mother, and her family are duly praised by Pietro Perleone in his *Laudatio in Valerium eius filium puerum eximium*, one of the consolatory texts in G (pp. 189–248), at pp. 194–196. (The Perleone work—perhaps the original of that in G—is also in West Berlin's Staatsbibliothek Preussischer Kulturbesitz, cod. Lat. qu. 557, ff. 3r–108v; see Kristeller, *Iter*, 3:490.) Senate documents frequently note Marcello's presence at Monselice: for instance, on 15 October 1449, the Senate ordered the rectors of Padua to tell Marcello in Monselice to return to the field immediately (where he had been previously as ambassador to Sforza) so that they might have news of Lombardy: Archivio di Stato di Venezia (henceforth ASV), Senato-Terra, R. 2, f. 120v. From Monselice, Marcello wrote the letter to René of 1 March 1457 (printed by Martin, "Un portrait," 264–266). For the Marcello villa, see G. Pavanello in *Enciclopedia italiana*, "Monselice."

described. Sent immediately to Ravenna, a Venetian dependency, he held that city as instructed by the Senate with 2000 soldiers borrowed from the general Colleoni. In the field again in 1442 and 1444, Marcello served almost continually, ranging over Lombardy, as a military adviser from 1446 through 1454. He was knighted following a victory outside Cremona in 1446. With Sforza, the Frenchman René (Duke of Anjou, later Count of Provence, until 1442 also King of Naples) and his Italian minister Giovanni Cossa, he entered Milan in 1449. Then he held for Venice the Lombard city of Crema, a western outpost recently conquered, until the early months of 1452. But by the end of that year, tables had turned. Milan, ruled by Marcello's former colleague Sforza, had allied with Florence and won the pledged support of France and of the royal cousin King René, Marcello's once and future friend. Cornered, Venice allied with Naples. In 1453, Marcello was sent again to the field, with Pasquale Malipiero (from 1457 Doge of Venice) as colleague. Early in 1454, the French retreated, and Marcello and Malipiero went home. Shocked by Constantinople's fall the previous year, wearied by decades of tug-of-war in Lombardy, coaxed by the Pope, the Italian states made peace. The treaty signed at Lodi in April, 1454, established a new pattern of wary balance of power which lasted, not long enough, but a while.

After the settlement at Lodi, Marcello served in Venice on the Council of Ten (1458–59), as ducal counsellor (1459–60 and 1462), and ducal elector (of Cristoforo Marcello, 1462).[6] Late in 1462, he was sent to Udine in Friuli, Venice's northeastern frontier of strategic importance equal to Lombardy's. There in October, he politely requested funds for the repair of the governor's palace. Less than a year later, he was ordered to join Venice's other generals outside the walls of Trieste, defended by an Austrian army. Still in arms outside Trieste on 13 November 1463, Marcello is not heard from again.[7]

6. See King, *Venetian Humanism*, Part II, Marcello profile, for these offices.
7. The Senate granted Marcello funds in Udine (12 October 1462): ASV, Senato-Terra, R. 5, f. 20r [19r; more recent numeration in brackets here and henceforth]. He was ordered to join Count Carlo Fortebracci da Montone in the field (24 September 1463): f. 51r [50r]. He was still in the field on 24 October: f. 57r [56r]. And presumably also on 13 November 1463, for it is from there (though the author himself was in Udine) that Giorgio Bevilacqua da Lazise dates the *Excusatio adversus consolatores in obitu Valerii filii* written in Marcello's name (Verona, Bibl. Civica, cod. 1472 [henceforth V], ff. 7r–173r, at f. 173r; undated and fragmentary at the beginning [see below, note 33] in G, pp. 309/310–426). For Marcello's role at Trieste in the fall of 1463, see also D. Malipiero, *Annali veneti dall'anno 1457 al 1500*, ed. F. Longo and A. Sagredo,

That date is the last event known to me not only of Marcello's military career, but also of a career of literary activity which followed the soldier into the field.[8] For Marcello turned to literary pursuits while on campaign as much as when working in Venice or resting at Monselice: to relish translations from the Greek of works on theology or geography, and to draft Latin letters to another connoisseur who, like him, often carried a sword. René d'Anjou, ousted from the kingdom of Naples and Sicily in 1442, retired to France and began collecting things: books, art, and courtiers. In 1448, he founded one of the late medieval knightly orders—that of the Crescent. The following year, he added to its rolls Sforza and Marcello, his allies in the Lombard struggle. Sforza had told René that Marcello supported (did the Senate know?) the latter's Neapolitan ambitions (for the Frenchman lusted to return to the south). Marcello had sent René's Queen, Isabelle of Lorraine, a set of playing cards (painted by an Italian illuminator) which had once belonged to the Visconti. René made Marcello head of his navy—an honorific title. Marcello had to conjure up some new courtesy: something, he thought, appropriate to his new status as seventeenth Knight of the Order of the Crescent. He had not been able to attend the ceremony of his induction held in Avignon; but he would acknowledge the great honor in the Italian mode, with a manuscript, a dedication, some verse, a portrait, and a puzzle.[9]

In the book Marcello sent, the life of St. Maurice (patron of René's knightly order) is sandwiched between the Venetian's dedicatory letter (to Giovanni Cossa, then Senator) and a concluding epigram. These items

Archivio storico italiano, 7 (1843–44):208; M. A. Sabellico, *Historia rerum venetiarum ab urbe condita*, in A. Zeno ed., *Istorici delle cose veneziane*, 1 (Venice, 1718):724. Marcello died between the autumn of 1464 and July, 1465: see Fabbri, "Le *Consolationes*," 246.

8. It is the date of Bevilacqua's *Excusatio* (see the preceding note), the last literary work known to me associated with Marcello.

9. These items in Paris, Bibliothèque de l'Arsenal, cod. 940; Marcello's letter to Cossa and verses to René published from that manuscript by Martin, "Un portrait," 258–260 and 261–264 respectively. For the circumstances of Marcello's association with the Order of the Crescent and the preparation of the St. Maurice manuscript, see Meiss, *Andrea Mantegna*, chap. 1, which adequately incorporates Martin's inferences and corrects some dates. The date of Marcello's appointment as René's naval captain, however, on the basis of the nobleman's epitaph (published in Monfasani, *Collectanea Trapezuntiana*, 235–36, and in Fabbri, "Le *Consolationes*," 248 and elsewhere as there cited) can be assigned to 1449 (the date of the entry to Milan), not 1442 (Meiss, p. 2). For René, see esp. A. Lecoy de la Marche, *Le roi René: sa vie, son administration, ses travaux artistiques et littéraires*, 2 vols. (Paris, 1875; repr. Geneva, 1969). René's wife Isabelle's native Lorraine was at this time part of the Empire; but René himself was, of course, impeccably French.

were illustrated with masterly paintings, probably by Andrea Mantegna, of the Congress of the Order of the Crescent, of its patron saint, of Marcello, of an ideogram that the latter had designed, accompanied by an inscription in a resistant code known to the author and his addressee. A resplendent gift—but more than a gift. For this manuscript book was no mere courtly token. The prefatory and concluding material was for contemporaries and for us more important than the pious *vita* they enclosed. In the sum, as Millard Meiss has brilliantly shown, they amount to a last-chance diplomatic plea of Marcello's to his French friends not to abandon their Venetian alliance. The book and its veiled message were dispatched from the field on 1 June 1453, just as René and Cossa were setting out for Italy to join Sforza and Milan against Venice. Marcello's subtle gift arrived too late. Despite his former comrade's plea, on 10 October René declared war on the Serenissima.[10]

A declaration of war, one would think, might rupture a friendship. However, both before the 1453 crisis and afterwards, Marcello corresponded warmly with René, and confected a series of literary presents to send over the Alps. Marcello probably sent the first such gift on 5 April 1452 as he was about to embark on a mission abroad for his *patria*. He offered René at this time a miniature *De sacerdotio Christi* translated (badly) by his fellow-nobleman Lauro Quirini from the Greek text attributed to Suidas.[11] Perhaps the following winter, Marcello sent his friend another version of the same work translated by an unnamed "learned friend" who had deplored the Quirini translation. The dedicatory letter to the later version comments on the sickness of René's Queen Isabelle of Lorraine. Marcello would soon lament her death on 28 February 1453 in a separate

10. The manuscript's contents are given by Meiss, *Andrea Mantegna*, at 79–80. It is Meiss' great contribution to have identified the unknown artist, considered a masterly one even by other scholars who suggest other candidates (notably Giovanni Bellini). For a discussion of this controversy, see the sources cited by Fabbri, "Le *Consolationes*," 229–230, note 8.

11. For the Quirini translation, cf. G. Mercati, *Ultimi contributi alla storia degli umanisti*, 2 vols. (Vatican City, 1939), 1:70–85. Marcello's introductory letter is given at 81–82. Mercati assigns the letter to 1452 (the month and day are given in the manuscript) on the basis of Marcello's reference to a new duty about to be assumed. He believes this is the mission as *provveditore* with Pasquale Malipiero which in fact occurred in 1453. In April, 1452, Marcello was still in Crema, but was shortly to be replaced: cf. ASV, Senato-Terra, R. 3, f. 23r [25r]. The date, therefore, remains uncertain. For Lauro Quirini, see esp. V. Branca, ed., *Lauro Quirini umanista: studi e testi a cura di Konrad Krautter, P. O. Kristeller, Agostino Pertusi, Giorgio Ravegnani, Helmut Roob e Carlo Seno* (Florence, 1977); also King, *Venetian Humanism*, Part II, Quirini profile.

consolatory letter. But a mere letter he deemed insufficient. He ordered a new manuscript gift to be prepared, a translation (by the same fastidious but anonymous scholar who had corrected Quirini) of a homily by Chrysostom on the subject of mourning, an apt work for the learned and desolate Frenchman.[12]

After the 1453 confrontation described above, Marcello's relations with René continued and perhaps strengthened. For that royal personage was still the chosen and indeed the only recipient of these recondite literary treats. During the years from 1455 to 1459, René's friend conceived and supervised a project of considerable historical significance: the Latin translation of Strabo's *Geography*. Guarino Veronese had begun the task for Pope Nicholas V, and had completed the first seventeen books (the *Europa*) by the spring of 1455 when that pontiff and patron unkindly died — Guarino's reward of 1000 *scudi* probably uncollected. Guarino hoped for Medici patronage. But the Medici were unwilling to pay Nicholas' outstanding obligation and assume responsibility for the remainder of the translation. Marcello did. By 13 July 1458, Guarino had finished.[13] During the next fourteen months were accomplished the tasks still required to prepare a suitable work for René's growing library. A scribe copied the text itself and the introductory letters composed by Guarino (to Pope Nicholas and Marcello) and his patron (to René). And once again Marcello hired Mantegna, the probable illustrator of the St. Maurice manuscript, to paint rare portraits of Guarino offering the work to Marcello and of Marcello, in turn, offering it to his friend. On 13 September 1459, in Venice, the work was signed in Marcello's name and sent to France, where it is still.[14]

---

12. For the letter accompanying the second translation from ps.-Suidas, see Mercati, *Ultimi contributi*, 1:73–74, 77; for that on the death of Queen Isabelle, 1:77 and note 2, 82, 84; for that accompanying the Chrysostom translation, 1:77, and 82–83, with the text at 84–85.

13. For Guarino's *Strabo*, see A. Diller, *The Textual Tradition of Strabo's Geography* (Amsterdam, 1975), 126–129; Diller and P. O. Kristeller, "Strabo," in *CTC*, 2:225–233, at 225–226; Meiss, *Andrea Mantegna*, chap. 2; R. Sabbadini, "La traduzione guariniana di Strabone," *Il libro e la stampa*, 3 (1909):5–16; Sabbadini, notes to Guarino's *Epistolario*, 3:483–487. That Guarino sought Medici assistance derives from Vespasiano da Bisticci, quoted at length (and corrected) by Sabbadini in Guarino's *Epistolario*, 3:483–484.

14. The three letters appear in several of the manuscript versions of this work. Guarino's to Pope Nicholas and Marcello are published in the humanist's *Epistolario*, 2:627–634; Marcello's to René in Sabbadini, "Traduzione guariniana," 13–15. Sabbadini speculates that this last letter was actually written by Guarino, but I see no conclusive evidence for that contention. The presentation manuscript is described in Meiss, *Andrea Mantegna*, 81. He identifies it as MS 4 of the Biblio-

René's interest in geography was known to Marcello before 1459. A map and another geographical work had preceded the Strabo as a gift to the learned prince. Ludovico Martelli, the Frenchman's agent for such matters, had asked Marcello where he might locate a *mappamondo* for his master. Marcello obtained one from the Paduan bibliophile Onofrio Strozzi (son of Palla, the Florentine exile). To that item he added a manuscript of Ptolemy's *Cosmography* prefaced, as was by now his habit, with a dedicatory letter (dated 1 March 1457) to René. Like the Strabo and St. Maurice manuscripts, the book is still found in France to where Marcello sent it more than four centuries ago. It, too, may have been adorned by Mantegna's extraordinary hand.[15]

From 1452 (perhaps earlier), then, until 1459, Marcello forwarded to René works written by ancient authors and translated by contemporary scholars. His own literary contribution consisted mainly of the series of letters which accompanied those works.[16] When a sad opportunity later arose for the construction of another presentation volume, Marcello wished to preface it not simply with a letter, but a lengthy and original work of his own. The nature of those tragic circumstances and the means by which Marcello won his wish are the story we have now to tell.

On 24 April 1452, while Marcello was *provveditore* in Crema, his third wife (the Paduan noblewoman Lucia da Leone) gave birth to the last of his several children: a boy, Valerio.[17] Three months later, Marcello re-

theque Rochegude in Albi; it can now be located as MS 77 in the Bibliothèque Municipale on rue Rochegude of that city.

15. For this incident, see Meiss, *Andrea Mantegna*, 31 and 88, note 4. For the dedicatory letter, see above, note 5.

16. Marcello also sent other works to René: see Meiss, *Andrea Mantegna*, 32 and 89, note 7. Marcello also had other connections with the world of learning. Humanists addressed works to him other than the consolations discussed here: Giovanni Michele Alberto da Carrara, who wrote a verse eulogy of Marcello's military exploits entitled the *De bello Jacobi Antonii Marcelli in Italia gesto*, in G. B. Contarini, ed., *Anecdota veneta* (Venice, 1757), 309–328; G. M. Filelfo (see Benadduci, *A Jacopo Antonio Marcelli*, xx–xxi, 25–26); Janus Pannonius (see Fabbri, "Le *Consolationes*," 228–229; Monfasani, *George of Trebizond*, 175, note 198 and addendum at 413); George of Trebizond (see Monfasani, *George of Trebizond*, 175–176, note 201; the dedications are published by Monfasani in *Collectanea Trapezuntiana*, 248–251); Raffaele Zovenzoni, with whom he also had contact in Istria in 1463, and who sought out the Marcello house in Venice; see B. Ziliotto, *Raffaele Zovenzoni: la vita, i carmi* (Trieste, 1950), 21ff., 47.

17. Francesco Filelfo gives the date of 24 April (*De obitu Valerii filii consolatio*, in G, pp. 38–126, at p. 67; for this work, see below, note 22), but assigns the birth to 1453, the year of his own son's; for he says that his son Olimpio and Valerio Marcello were born the same month and year (pp. 39, 55, 67). But 1453 does not square with the consolatory texts which place Marcello in Crema at his son's birth, and back in Venice three months later. These data point to 1452. Born

turned, still vigorous but by now middle-aged, and viewed for the first
time his infant son. The child turned away from his nurse's breast, contemporaries report, to gaze upon his father's face. A special bond was
forged between the boy and the general. The child was graced (those reports
tell us, although we may assume exaggeration) with exceptional beauty,
intelligence, and agility. He developed, under his father's and a tutor's
guidance, rare sensitivity, refinement of manners, and precocious
knowledge. Skilled in Latin and Greek, he was broadly curious, but particularly inquisitive about his father's military exploits and the history of
his family and city. Thoroughly instructed in these matters, he yearned
to imitate his father, who doted upon this prodigious child, already perfect in every regard, and budding with promise of future greatness.

Valerio died before his ninth birthday. A slight illness, hardly noticed
by the household, grew into a fatal disease. The child lingered, wasted,
visited by the skilled doctors his father procured and who could do nothing for him. Coolly aware of his condition and his destiny, Valerio comfor-
ted his father, preparing him for inevitable loss, and participated in the
last pious acts religion required with otherworldly fervor. But Marcello,
unwilling to relinquish his son, anxious before the death, mourned desperately afterwards. A common event, the death of a child, in this case stirred
exceptional grief. The normal term of mourning passed, and Marcello was
still distraught. His peculiar state was noted. His friends may have noised
it about. Perhaps Marcello himself invited attention to his grief. The set
of learned men in and around Venice lifted their pens, and so did some
not so learned. Soon the series of letters ordinarily sent to comfort a mourner
had blossomed into a literary contest of considerable dimensions.

Valerio had died on New Year's Day in 1461.[18] Early in April, the immigrant humanist George of Trebizond, then in Venice, wrote his father
a consolatory letter (no hasty note but a substantial work, like the others

in 1452, moreover, Valerio would have been not quite nine at his death on 1 January 1461—the
death date also given by Filelfo, who writes on Christmas day, 1461, that the following Kalends
of January, Marcello will have grieved one year (p. 121). George of Trebizond, writing much
closer to the event than Filelfo, gives this date for Valerio's death as well: see Monfasani, *Collectanea Trapezuntiana*, 235, 243. The consolers (except Filelfo) agree that Valerio died in his ninth
year. In all, I would accept Filelfo's dates for month and day, but would place Valerio's birth
in 1452. Valerio was Marcello's youngest son at the time of the death (see the statement in G,
at p. 304, by Anonymous B; regarding that person, see below, notes 26 and 47). In 1463, perhaps,
another son, also named Valerio, was born; see Fabbri, "Le *Consolationes*," 231. For the narrative
of Valerio's life, based on the Glasgow texts, see below, note 48.

18. See the previous note.

to be described).[19] Probably at about the same time, another immigrant and humanist wrote a similar letter: the ducal secretary Niccolò Sagundino.[20] These works were followed in August by another of comparable scale by perhaps the most remarkable woman humanist of the century, Isotta Nogarola.[21] Francesco Filelfo dated his extensive *De obitu Valerii filii consolatio* from Milan on Christmas day of the same year, when Jacopo Antonio's grief had almost reached its first anniversary. Filelfo also wrote a Greek (later translated) and a Latin elegy (in the name of his patron Francesco Sforza, Marcello's former comrade-in-arms); these are undated.[22] Also undated are consolatory *opuscula* by Giovanni Mario Filelfo, Battista Guarini, Montorio Mascarello, Janus Pannonius, Pietro Perleone, and Gregorio Tifernate.[23]

19. George's letter published by Monfasani, *Collectanea Trapezuntiana*, 235–248, which edition is cited here; also in G, pp. 25–38, and the other manuscripts reported by Monfasani.

20. The *De obitu Valerii filii consolatio*, cited here in G, pp. 1–25. Also in Vatican City, BAV, MS Ottob. lat. 1732, fols. 1r–13r, and Ferrara, Bibl. Comunale Ariostea, cod. II, 135, ff. 92r–105v. In that same Ferrara codex (henceforth F) there also appear the consolatory letters of George of Trebizond (ff. 85r–91v), Pietro Perleone (106r–109r), Battista Guarini (109v–114v), and Isotta Nogarola (115–119). I have preferred the Italian form Sagundino to Secundinus because of that Greek immigrant's blending into the Venetian environment for the three decades before his death.

21. *Ad Jacobum Antonium Marcellum eius dulcissimi filii Valerii filii in obitu consolatoria* in G, pp. 133–141, but cited here in E. Abel's edition of Nogarola's *Opera quae supersunt omnia*, 2 vols. (Vienna, 1886), 2:161–178 (dated 9 August 1461).

22. The lengthy prose *Consolatio*, cited above, note 17. The autograph is Vatican City, BAV, MS Vat. lat. 1790, ff. 3r–154v. Other manuscripts exist. The work appears in many editions of Filelfo's works, but has received no critical edition. The Greek elegy (edited by Fabbri in "Le Consolationes," 243–245) is in G, pp. 127–129, and in many other manuscripts (including Vat. lat. 1790, ff. 155r–158r). A translation of the Greek elegy by Ludovico Carbone is in G, pp. 129–133, immediately following the original. The Carbone translation is also found in many manuscripts. Carbone also was the author of a Latin elegy for Marcello, not to be confused with his translation from Filelfo's Greek; see below, note 27. In addition to Carbone's translation of Filelfo's elegy, Ludovico Grifo also translated the work, in a version far less widely diffused than Carbone's. Venice, Bibl. Marciana, lat. XIV, 246 (4683), gives Carbone's translation on ff. 139r–141r and Grifo's on ff. 142r–144r. Filelfo's Latin elegy in Sforza's name (not to be confused with Carbone's or Grifo's translation of his Greek elegy) is published by Benadduci, *A Jacopo Antonio Marcello,* 17–23. For these works by Filelfo, see Fabbri, "Le Consolationes," 233ff.; for suggested dating, 237–238. For the Greek elegy, see also D. Robin, "Unknown Greek Poems of Francesco Filelfo," *RQ,* 37 (1984):173–206, at 198 and note 73.

23. For G. M. Filelfo's *Consolatio marcellina,* see Benadduci, *A Jacopo Antonio Marcello,* xx; neither that author nor I have located the work. Guarini's work is in G, pp. 179–188, cited here, and in manuscripts in Ferrara and Rome (see Kristeller, *Iter,* 1:58 and 2:360 respectively). I have seen the former: F, ff. 109v–114v. Mascarello's dedicatory letter (pp. 161–162), dialogue (pp. 162–174), and separate letter (pp. 174–179) are in G (the first dated Kal. Febr., without year). For Pannonius' verses, see Fabbri, "Le Consolationes," 232. Perleone's brief letter (Venice, Bibl. Marciana, Lat. XIV, 266 (4502), ff. 218r–221v; F, ff. 106r–109r; and other manuscripts listed

At some distance from the 1461 works by George, Sagundino, Nogarola and Filelfo were composed others which suggest Marcello's sustained interest in the literary commemorialization of his son. The Venetian citizen and learned cleric Michele Orsini, commenting on Filelfo' long *consolatio,* wrote in 1462 (26 August) an elaborate letter disputing the historical sections of that work and celebrating both Venice and the still-heartbroken Marcello.[24] In 1463, the soldier Carlo Fortebracci da Montone wrote a consolatory letter,[25] and two anonymous authors two others in July and October of that year.[26] Ludovico Carbone, a regular composer of such celebratory works at the court of Borso d'Este of Ferrara, composed an elegy probably also in 1463.[27] On 1 November 1463, while Marcello was besieging Trieste, Pietro Perleone (Riminese by birth, Venetian by adoption) wrote Marcello from Udine a long *Laudatio in Valerium eius filium puerum eximium,* revealing his close relationship with the child and the family.[28] Two days later, the Veronese Giorgio Bevilacqua da Lazise (then in Udine, an intimate of Marcello's circle) wrote to Marcello a letter introducing the last and most interesting work (dated 13 November) of this consolatory series: the *Excusatio adversus consolatores in obitu Valerii filii,* ghosted by Bevilacqua for his noble patron.[29] Marcello wished to compose a work defending his grief for a beloved son. But he had not the leisure or learning to do so himself.

in Kristeller, *Iter,* 2:9 and 454), is distinct from the *Laudatio* in G (cited above, note 5). Gregorio Tifernate's consolatory *oratio* is found in manuscripts in Trent and Vicenza; see Kristeller, *Iter,* 2:189 and 302 respectively. I have seen the Vicenza manuscript: Bibl. Comunale Bertoliana, cod. 7.1.31 (formerly 6.7.31), ff. 126v–131r, with an epigram to Valerio on f. 131r-v.

24. Orsini's *De summa venetorum origine,* cited here in the autograph cod. H.122 inf. of the Bibl. Ambrosiana in Milan (henceforth M), where it appears with the given date. It also appears in G, pp. 269–294. E. A. Cicogna reported that the work had been printed, but neither he nor I have found the edition (*Delle iscrizioni veneziane,* 6 vols. [Venice, 1824–53], 5:525). Vatican City, BAV, MS Vat. lat. 5280 (see Kristeller, *Iter,* 2:332; Fabbri, "Le *Consolationes,*" 232) contains a much larger work by Orsini dealing with the same historiographical issues as the *De origine.*

25. G, pp. 141–160.

26. G, pp. 249–268 and 295–308 respectively.

27. I have seen the work in Venice, Bibl. Marciana, Lat. XIV, 246 (4683), ff. 126r–138r; see also Fabbri, "Le *Consolationes,*" 235, note 28. It was written at the request of Borso d'Este (f. 126r), and refers to several of the Glasgow consolations and also others not otherwise known to me by Ferrarese authors (f. 137v).

28. Cited above, note 5.

29. Bevilacqua's *Excusatio* is cited above, note 7; the letter is in V, ff. 4r–6r. V may have been the manuscript sent by the author to Marcello and is cited here. G does not include the prefatory letter and is also otherwise incomplete; see below note 62.

Bevilacqua's tactful letter describes his anger for Marcello's sake. His consolers had charged that the aging soldier's grief ill-suited his dignity and reputation for courage. But Marcello's grief was justified, wrote Bevilacqua, his vicar in Udine during the Trieste siege and witness to the mourner's plight during recent months. "I cannot bear your being accused of pusillanimity," he wrote; Marcello, even grief-stricken, was fully worthy of his ancestors.[30] To defend Marcello, therefore, and silence his well-intentioned accusers, Bevilacqua had written the *Excusatio* (as Marcello had directed) as though that nobleman was the author, and addressed it to—whom else?—René: "So I have written the letter, as I persuaded you should be done, as though you yourself had composed it in your free evenings, and have addressed it from you to the divine King René.... Now I give it to you."[31]

Marcello, then, was not, as the text written in his name implies, the author of the *Excusatio*. But he seems to have approved of it even in advance of composition. Distanced somewhat by late 1463 from the tragic event which had saddened him, he saw the opportunity to construct from the works addressed to him a clever (and enormous) literary dialogue between consolers and consoled, meat for René's library. He welcomed the defense of his unstanched grief by his humanist aide, and made it, the evidence suggests, the collection's capstone work.

Bevilacqua's *Excusatio* is extant today—without the revealing letter—as the final work in a collection of consolations to Marcello on the death of Valerio that was intended for René, exquisitely prepared, left unfinished, and never sent. Apostolo Zeno saw it in the eighteenth century in the Marcello palazzo. In 1767, Jacopo Morelli spied it in an old bookstore in Venice. Nine years later, it formed part of the library of Caesar de Missy which was sold at auction by the London dealers Baker and Leigh. In the catalogue of the 18 March 1776 sale, the book is described as elegantly written and decorated. It sold for £5.5.0 to Dr. William Hunter, who also purchased many other items in the collection. Hunter's library

30. V, f. 4 bis r: "Aequo animo te pusilanimitatis crimine lacessi non patior. . . ." Bevilacqua also identifies himself as Marcello's vicar. He states that Marcello is "perdignus" of the family tradition at f. 5v.

31. V, f. 6r: "Sic epistolam scripsi quam abs te lucubratam fuisse, et a te divo Renato regi destinandam suasi. . . . Eam igitur nunc ad te do."

subsequently passed to the collection which bears his name in the University of Glasgow. There the Marcello consolations are still found.[32]

Damaged in places, it is still a beautiful manuscript clearly designed as a presentation volume comparable to the St. Maurice and Strabo manuscripts already introduced. The first page of each component work is laid out to allow for prominent initials; smaller ones head subdivisions of works in three cases. Most of these initials were exquisitely ornamented and colored. In three cases, they were not. The first page of these works lacks a heading (and in one case a text) as well as adornment, leaving authors and titles in question. The first page of the whole collection contains in the left margin a portrait of a boy (Valerio?) facing the image, in the left margin, of St. Mark, Venice's patron saint. At the foot of the page is painted a shield with a rampant lion superimposed on a neutral island landscape. The arms are neither Marcello's nor René's. The reference could be to Venice's own ferocious lion. But the connection of the manuscript with both these figures seems clear from the evidence of the works there contained: fourteen consolations for Marcello, in the last of which the Venetian (through Bevilacqua) addresses King René and asks him to judge between the merits of the father's grief and the consolers' remedies.[33]

32. Morelli notes having seen a collection of consolatory works to Marcello in his edition of the anonymous (Marcantonio Michiel's) *Notizie d'opere di disegno nella prima metà del secolo XVI*, 2nd ed. (Bologna, [1889]), 170ff. In the first edition (Bassano, 1800) of Morelli's work, however, which I have not seen but which is cited by Cicogna (*Iscrizioni*, 5:671), and quoted by Abel (preface to Nogarola's *Opera*, cxliv–cxlv, note 82), he comments at greater length. The codex "di grande pregio" had previously been seen by Zeno, Morelli notes, in the library of Federico Marcello (see also Zeno's own *Dissertazioni vossiane*, 2 vols. [Venice, 1753], 1: 297) and by himself in 1767. He further notes, as other works in consolation of Marcello, Carbone's elegy, Pannonius' verse, the Grifo translation of Filelfo's Greek elegy, and an epigram of Gregorio Tifernate. The De Missy sale was recorded as Lot 1664 of the Sotheby *Catalogue of Sales* (which absorbed the Baker and Leigh records), published in microfilm by Xerox University Microfilms, Ann Arbor, Michigan, 1972, Part I, reel 6; the film is available in Columbia University's Avery Library. The Marcello consolations appear as item no. 1662 (p. 54). I am most grateful to Dr. Sandra Sider for this information about the manuscript's voyage to Scotland. See also Fabbri, "Le *Consolationes*," 231, note 11. The manuscript is described in *A Catalogue of the Manuscripts in the Library of the Hunterian Museum in the University of Glasgow*, ed. J. Young and P. H. Aitken (Glasgow, 1908), 142–143. That description can be corrected at points, as I do in these pages. The assumption that the manuscript is at all related to Doge Niccolò Marcello appears to be without basis. I have worked from microfilm and photographs and from the detailed answers to my questions kindly provided by Mr. P. K. Escreet, Keeper of Special Collections of the University of Glasgow Library.

33. Headings and initials are lacking at pp. 249 and 295 (the opening pages of the two anonymous works); heading, initials, and text on p. 309 (the first page of Bevilacqua's letter, the author

The Glasgow codex contains fourteen of the consolatory works named earlier (by twelve authors) — almost all of the known works written in honor of the child Valerio. They include, in this order, the letters of Sagundino and George of Trebizond; the *Consolatio* and Greek elegy (with a translation by Ludovico Carbone) of Francesco Filelfo; Nogarola's letter and Fortebracci's *Consolatio*; a *Dialogus* with prefatory letter and an additional consolatory letter by Montorio Mascarello; Battista Guarini's letter and Perleone's *Laudatio;* the two anonymous letters (henceforth Anon. A and B), but between them Orsini's long letter to Filelfo; Bevilacqua's *Excusatio.* The order is roughly chronological. The *Excusatio* is probably the latest of these works and perhaps of all the consolatory literature associated with this episode.[34]

Who were the authors of the component works of the Glasgow codex, and what were their relations to Marcello? The noted humanist Francesco Filelfo does not require introduction. His *Consolatio* for Marcello is a rich, even a brilliant work, said by Filelfo's biographer to be among his best. Certainly Marcello was delighted; he may in fact have commissioned Filelfo to compose this seemingly spontaneous work. He rewarded Filelfo with a lavishly expensive gift.[35] Father of Giovanni Mario Filelfo, Francesco may have first become acquainted with the Venetian during his difficult offspring's brief career in Venice (in 1460) as the first teacher of that city's public school of rhetoric. Mario had had prior contact with René d'Anjou — as *juge du palais* at the Frenchman's court around 1450 — and was himself to write a consolation to Marcello (not in the Glasgow co-

of which I identified from the independent V). For Marcello's arms see V. Spreti *et al., Enciclopedia storico-nobiliare italiana*, 5 vols. (Bologna, 1928–35), 4:351. René's own description of his is in Lecoy de la Marche, *Le roi René*, 2.3:161, note 1. Marcello's appeal (as phrased by Bevilacqua) to René is made at several points (see below, note 60). One instance: he explains that he has collected "in hoc volumine" the works of his consolers — among them "propinqui" and "familiares," who had tried to console him "non modo epistolis, sed libellis singulari doctrina et mira orationis facultate compositis." Reading them, René will understand his grief. Now he appoints René "inter me et eiusmodi repraehensores censorem arbitrumque." V, f. 8r–v (= G, pp. 310–311).

34. It is the latest dated work, and precedes Marcello's death by perhaps as little as a year; see above, note 7.

35. For the work and the gift, see C. de' Rosmini, *Vita di Francesco Filelfo da Tolentino*, 3 vols. (Milan, 1808), 2:123–127; Benadduci, *A Jacopo Antonio Marcello*, xix–xx. Robin, who retells the incident (in "Unknown Greek Poems," 203 and note 14) points out (p. 176) Filelfo's frequent seeking of commissions, necessary for his livelihood. Filelfo's response of 27 June 1461 to a letter of Marcello's suggests that the nobleman had requested a service, perhaps the composition of a *consolatio*; the date is right: "Ego propediem quod cupis effectum dabo" (Filelfo, *Epistolarum familiarum libri xxxii* [Venice, 1502], f. 116 bis r).

dex).[36] During his unhappy sojourn in Venice, the younger Filelfo entered into fierce competition with George of Trebizond and Pietro Perleone, foreigners like himself resident in the city, for the position of public historiographer. Both his competitors, like both Filelfos, were later to console Marcello for the loss of Valerio.[37] Both knew Marcello even before that unhappy death—as did, apparently, many of the commoners of Venice's *ordo litteratorum*, ever in search of wealthy men who liked a little learning. Perleone, indeed, a teacher in Venice's public school of San Marco, had been Valerio's teacher (and Francesco Filelfo's pupil, whose friend he remained).[38] Intricate links, therefore, connect these four consolers of the saddened nobleman and seekers of his favor.

Related to this group but more remotely are Sagundino and Orsini, the former a Greek long resident in Venice, the latter a Venetian citizen. Sagundino belonged to the circle of government secretaries who occupied a sociological niche in Venice similar to that of the teachers. Like them, he actively sought the patronage of wealthy noblemen; he would have revelled in Marcello's, if he did not in fact win it. Sagundino's close friendship with Perleone is witnessed by the lengthy consolation the latter wrote for the Greek-born secretary after a tragic shipwreck.[39] Orsini was a cleric,

36. For the younger Filelfo, see G. Favre, *Vie de Jean-Marius Philelphe*, in *Mélanges d'histoire littéraire par Guillaume Favre*, 1 (Geneva, 1856):2–221, and L. Agostinelli and G. Benadduci, *Biografia e bibliografia di Giovan Mario Filelfo* (Tolentino, 1899). For his role in the school of rhetoric, see esp. as keys to a large literature the recent studies of J. B. Ross, "Venetian Schools and Teachers, Fourteenth to Early Sixteenth Century," *RQ*, 39 (1976), 521–566, esp. chronological tables; and M. Pastore Stocchi, "Scuola e cultura umanistica fra due secoli," in *Storia della cultura veneta*, 3.1 (Vicenza, 1980):93–121. See also Fabbri, "Le *Consolationes*, 234–235, note 26.

37. For the competition for this position, not in fact then created, see F. Gilbert, "Biondo, Sabellico, and the Beginnings of Venetian Official Historiography," in J. G. Rowe and W. H. Stockdale, eds., *Florilegium Historiale: Essays Presented to Wallace K. Ferguson* (Toronto 1971), 275–293; also A. Pertusi, "Gli inizi della storiografia umanistica del Quattrocento," in Pertusi, ed., *La storiografia veneziana fino al secolo XVI* (Florence, 1970), 269–332, and F. Gaeta, "Storiografia, coscienza nazionale e politica culturale nella Venezia del Rinascimento," in *Storia della cultura veneta*, 3.1:1–91 and studies there cited. For George, see Monfasani's *George of Trebizond* and *Collectanea Trapezuntiana;* for Perleone, see King, *Venetian Humanism*, Part II, Perleone profile.

38. That Perleone had been Valerio's tutor is evident from his own words: *Laudatio*, G, pp. 241ff. He corresponds frequently with his former teacher Filelfo: see the latter's *Epist. fam.*, passim. Two consolers of the Glasgow manuscript refer to Marcello's patronage of learned men: Anonymous B speaks of "our order's" enormous love for that nobleman (p. 295); Orsini calls Marcello the "father" of the "academy" of *litterati* (M, f. 15v). See also above, note 16.

39. For Sagundino, see P. D. Mastrodimitris, Νικόλαος Σεχουνδινός *(1402–1464)*. Βίος καὶ ἔργον (Athens, 1970); also King, *Venetian Humanism*, Part II, Sagundino profile, and the studies there cited. Perleone's *Epistola [consolatoria] ad Nicolaum Sagundinum* is in G. M. Lazzaroni, ed., *Miscellanea di varie operette*, 2 (Venice, 1740):43–98.

for many years the abbot of San Antonio da Vienna in Venice, where Marcello and his family had taken refuge during an invasion of plague at some time during Valerio's brief lifetime; further association with the family is suggested by his words. And Orsini was related by marriage to Pasquale Malipiero, once Marcello's colleague in the field, and at the time of Valerio's death, Doge of Venice.[40]

In Verona, Marcello had met the Nogarola family (when Isotta, probably, was still small — can this meeting be assigned to 1439, when Marcello was present at the reconquest of Verona?).[41] Perhaps at the same time he met Bevilacqua, who was in these years an admirer of both prodigious Nogarola sisters.[42] Nogarola and Bevilacqua both belonged to the city's noble clans, collaborators in Venetian domination. Also Veronese by birth was Battista Guarini, whose father Guarino Veronese translated Strabo for Marcello and inaugurated a tradition of praise for that personage. Battista had recently acquired his father's post in Ferrara on the elder scholar's death on 4 December 1460, shortly before the death of Valerio Marcello.[43] Not from Verona but nearby Vicenza came Montorio Mascarello. His relations otherwise with Marcello are not now known to me.[44] Fortebracci, a soldier and son of the notorious *condottiere* Braccio da Montone, had fought with Marcello during the wars with Milan and participated in

40. For Orsini, see King, *Venetian Humanism*, Part II, Orsini profile. That author describes the Marcello's family sanctuary at San Antonio in his *De summa venetorum origine*, M, ff. 19v–20r.

41. Nogarola refers to Marcello as "father" and remembers his "great benefits" to her family and city, which might logically have been granted following the city's liberation; cf. her consolatory letter, ed. Abel, 163–164, 174–175.

42. For Bevilacqua and his relations with the Nogarolas, see Abel, preface to Nogarola's *Opera*, xvii–xxi (and letters cited), cviii–cix; also Sabbadini, in Guarino, *Epistolario*, 3:139–141, 216–217, 226. Bevilacqua was a student of Guarino's in Verona in the late 1420's. Anonymous B reports that Bevilacqua had been much praised by the former's teacher, Giovanni Pietro (d'Avenza) da Lucca. Bevilacqua also addressed other works to Venetian patricians: the *De bello gallico* to Marco Donato, in many manuscript versions (see Kristeller, *Iter*, 1:84; 2:294, 332, 579); an oration for Andrea Donato, podestà of Verona (Vatican City, BAV, MS Vat. lat. 5108, ff. 80v–85v); commentaries on Cicero to Ludovico Foscarini (cf. the latter's *Epistolae*, Vienna, Österreichische Nationalbibliothek, cod. Lat. 441, f. 331r–v). Lorenzo Zane addressed to Bevilacqua his *De difficilimae doctrinae palma capescenda*, published by G. degli Agostini, *Notizie istorico-critiche intorno la vita e le opere degli scrittori viniziani*, 2 vols. (Venice, 1752–1754) 1:198–204.

43. Cf. Sabbadini, *Vita di Guarino Veronese*, 168. For Battista, see W. H. Woodward on the *De ordine docendi et studendi*, in *Vittorino da Feltre and Other Humanist Educators* (Cambridge, 1897; repr. New York, 1963), 159–160. E. Garin publishes that work by Battista and letters exchanged between him and his father in *Il pensiero pedagogico dell'umanesimo* (Florence, 1958), 434–471 and 422–433 respectively.

44. For orations and a letter by Mascarello, see Kristeller, *Iter*, 1:333, and 2:250, 312, 566.

the Trieste campaign of 1463 led by Marcello and his colleague Vitale Lando.[45] Anonymous A is probably a brother of Marcello's.[46] Anonymous B is perhaps a Paduan student, the acquaintance of some members of the circle of Udinese litterati whom Marcello knew in 1462–63.[47]

The group of consolers, it seems, contains sub-groups of related figures. Most had some knowledge of Marcello prior to Valerio's death. They are not, after all, so disparate. Nor do the works they wrote to comfort the bereaved nobleman, however various in size and miscellaneous in genre, differ greatly in content or theme.

The consolations as a group deal with four main issues: the boy Valerio, the father Jacopo Antonio and his Marcello ancestors, the city of Venice, and the means of consolation. Bevilacqua's *Excusatio* presents a fifth: the legitimacy of grief and consequent rejection of consolatory arguments. Each of these matters requires close attention it cannot receive here. The remaining pages of this essay will merely describe their contours.

Valerio. The authors of the Glasgow consolations are familiar with the general outline of Valerio's brief life.[48] Several dwell on the special poignancy of lost promise: for Valerio was an extraordinary child, who would surely have brought glory on the family, and that hope was now frustrated. This theme is prominent in the works of George of Trebizond, Perleone, Anonymous A, Orsini and Bevilacqua. Anonymous A, a relation,

---

45. For Fortebracci, in Venetian service from the 1440's until his death in 1479, see Mallett, "Preparations for War," 150, 153. For his presence at the siege of Trieste, see the document cited above, note 7. See also Kristeller, *Iter*, 2:50, 63, 438.

46. Describing Valerio's feeling that he would prefer his own to his father's death, Anonymous A tells Marcello that he had felt the same way about their father's death, which event he then recalls: G, p. 256.

47. Anonymous B's letter is written from Padua (G, p. 308). The author identifies himself with the circle of the learned (the *ordo litteratorum*; p. 295); he is much younger than the others who had written to console Marcello (p. 296); he will be bold enough to offer metaphysical and theological arguments. This sounds like a university student. He names the learned men with Marcello in Friuli: "Leonardo, prince of Thomists," the "doctor Hieremias," Guarnerius Martheniensis (d'Artegna?), and Giorgio da Lazise (= Bevilacqua). He had studied with Giovanni Pietro (d'Avenza) da Lucca.

48. The principal discussions of Valerio and his life upon which the following discussion draws (all references here and henceforth to G unless otherwise noted, and listed in the order of their appearance there): Sagundino (pp. 3–7); George of Trebizond (ed. Monfasani, 236–239); Filelfo (41–50); Fortebracci (144–147); Mascarello (176–178); Guarini (181–182); Perleone (211–248); Anonymous A (253–259, 261); Orsini (M, ff. 18v–20v); Anonymous B (300, 304, 306); Bevilacqua (V, ff. 34v–41v, 52v–69r, 95v–99r, 156v–158r). Filelfo, Perleone, and Bevilacqua most fully discuss Valerio. Anonymous A and Orsini add important and personal details.

not surprisingly stresses the glory lost to the Marcello family, in whose bosom God chose to place the finest of children. Perleone and Bevilacqua supply examples of ancient gods and heroes who showed special youthful promise—notably Hercules. George of Trebizond makes this issue a primary one of his brief work. Why do some die prematurely, he asks? Above all, those possessing unusual virtues. They achieve much; consequently, they die young. To this brilliant company Valerio belonged.

Predictably, Marcello's consolers praise Valerio's physical beauty (Perleone, Bevilacqua), his natural and precocious piety (Filelfo, Fortebracci, Mascarello, Perleone, Anonymous A, Bevilacqua), his intelligence (Filelfo, Perleone, Anonymous A, Orsini, Bevilacqua), his skill at games (Perleone, Anonymous A, Bevilacqua). Valerio's studies, a matter of interest to these humanists, are commented upon by several: Sagundino, Guarini, Perleone, Anonymous A, Orsini, and Bevilacqua. Of these, all but Sagundino and Bevilacqua explicitly mention Valerio's competence in both Greek and Latin, and all but Sagundino and Guarini the particular role played by Marcello himself in furthering his son's education. Bevilacqua and Perleone treat us to disquisitions on the importance of early learning, good teachers, and high motivation; the latter praises Valerio's dutiful reverence for his tutor (himself).[49]

Valerio adored his father, several of the consolers attest (Fortebracci, Mascarello, Perleone—at length, Orsini, Anonymous A, and Bevilacqua). He thirsted to hear of Marcello's deeds, and yearned for a similar glory. The latter four report touching deathbed conversations between father and son. All the consolers just named, with Sagundino, George of Trebizond, and Filelfo, describe the wasting disease and pious death. With the exceptions of Trebizond, Guarini, and Orsini, all describe Valerio's present beatitude, won by his innocence, assured by his youth. Filelfo, who had himself lost a son within weeks of Marcello, is particularly eloquent on this theme.

Certain incidents of Valerio's life are noted by several authors and in similar ways: that he was born when his father was governor of Crema; that he greeted his father with enthusiasm when at age three months he saw Marcello for the first time; that he preferred his father's to his

49. Note esp. Guarini's comments on Valerio's skill in both languages (G, pp. 181–182), and Perleone's discussion of the importance of early learning and good teachers (226–229) and description of the boy's relationship to his tutor (242–243). Both of these authors were professional teachers.

nurse's company; that having viewed a monument to the naval hero Vettore Pisani, Valerio yearned to achieve glorious deeds; that he once boldly questioned visiting senators; that he preferred, he said, to die rather than see his father die, and would, if he survived, prefer to dress in somber garments rather than see his father, in execution of a vow, so dressed; that semi-conscious on his sickbed he remembered perfectly the attending doctor, whom he had seen once before in his short life at the family villa in Monselice.

In all, these descriptions of Valerio's life are peculiarly similar. Allowing for variations in length of work and direction of argument, our authors follow the same script. This commonalty cannot be the result of direct observation of the same phenomena by twelve authors. Observation does not usually result in such unanimity. Moreover, we can be sure that only three of Marcello's consolers personally knew Valerio: the boy's tutor, Perleone; his uncle (perhaps), Anonymous A; the abbot Orsini, who reports an actual encounter with him. Sagundino and George of Trebizond, who resided in Venice prior to the death, may have known him, and Bevilacqua, possibly, if he belonged to Marcello's retinue before 1461. But as they mention no such acquaintance, it is unlikely that they knew him well, if at all. How can the common matter in the recitation of events about Valerio be explained? Did the consolers read each other's consolations? Did Marcello keep them near him and make them available to humanist friends for that purpose? Did he or one of his learned aides circulate a biographical sketch upon which most of the consolers relied? These questions remain for further exploration.

Marcello and his forebears. Given such unanimity on a series of events so private as the life of a young child, it is not surprising to find similarities in reports of Marcello's deeds and ancestry, which were alive in public record and memory. All the consolers in the Glasgow manuscript except Sagundino describe Marcello and his military career: the battle at Casalmaggiore, the heroic transport of Venetian ships to the Lago di Garda, the liberation of Brescia and Verona, the comraderie with Sforza, the entry to Milan. Some mention the defense of Ravenna. Filelfo deals with (tactfully) the battle between Sforza and Venice in Marcello's last Lombard campaign (1453–54). Perleone notes an extraordinary incident: when the Venetian troops could not be paid, Marcello paid their stipends himself from his own purse. Fortebracci notes another: when Venetian forces stormed Milan, Marcello took no booty. With some exceptions, then, the account of Marcello's wartime exploits follows, like the accounts of Valerio's life, the same script. In this case, possible scripts are available: Giovanni Michele Alberto da Carrara and Guarino Veronese had previously described these deeds quite outside the context of the consolatory literature of 1461–63, as had contemporary chroniclers.[50]

Common to eight of the Glasgow consolers is the discussion of Marcello's Roman ancestry. The Marcellos were one of the Venetian clans— like the Giustiniani (Justinianus), the Corner (Cornelius), the Miani (Aemilianus), among others—which had from the Middle Ages viewed itself as descending from noble Roman origins. Guarino Veronese had recited this tradition in his 1459 letter to Marcello. The theme is touched on again by Sagundino, Filelfo, Mascarello, Guarini, Perleone and Anonymous A. It is elaborated at great length by Orsini and Bevilacqua, who draw elaborate analogies between the careers of key Roman Marcelluses and their own contemporary Jacopo Antonio.[51] Five of the authors who remark on Marcello's Roman ancestry (all except Sagundino, Mascarello and Guarini) also describe the family's illustrious career since its migration to the Venetian lagoons. Orsini reviews Jacopo Antonio's greatest Venetian ancestors; Bevilacqua praises his grandfather Pietro, murdered in Crete. In describing the glories of Marcello's family, Filelfo takes the opportunity to praise the Venetian Senate and the whole patrician class.[52]

Venice and her myth. To console Marcello for the loss of Valerio, the

50. Descriptions of Marcello's military career: George of Trebizond (ed. Monfasani, 240–242); Filelfo (109–119; this is the section pub. by Benadduci, *A Jacopo Antonio Marcello*, 1–15); Nogarola (ed. Abel, 173–175); Fortebracci (148–151); Mascarello (166–172); Guarini (186–188); Perleone (197–210); Anonymous A (267); Orsini (M, ff. 15v–18r); Anonymous B (304–305); Bevilacqua (V, ff. 128r–137r). Perleone recalls Marcello's opening his own purse at p. 209; since the payment of soldiers was an urgent necessity and local funds were often appropriated, the incident is not implausible, particularly if Marcello were later repaid. Fortebracci's comment at p. 151; note also Orsini, M, f. 17v. Carrara's work cited above, note 16; Guarino's 1458 letter cited at note 1. For the chroniclers, see Fabbri, "Le *Consolationes*," 248–249.

51. Guarino in the letter cited note 1, at p. 630. The Glasgow consolers as follows: Sagundino (G, p. 14); Filelfo (108–109); Mascarello (178); Guarini (186); Perleone (193); Anonymous A (251, 266); Orsini (M, ff. 15v–18r, *passim*, and 23v); Bevilacqua (V, ff. 12r–19v, 23r–v, 80r–81r). For the medieval historiographical tradition, see esp. the studies of G. Fasoli ("I fondamenti della storiografia veneziana," 11–44), G. Cracco ("Il pensiero storico di fronte ai problemi del comune veneziano," 45–74), and A. Carile ("Aspetti della cronachista veneziana nei secoli XIII e XIV," 75–126) in Pertusi, ed., *Storiografia veneziana*.

52. Orsini (M, f. 24r–v); Bevilacqua (V, ff. 20r–21r); Filelfo (Benadduci ed., p. 3).

authors of the Glasgow codex not only reminded him of his own greatness and that of his family, but that of his city as well. The city's splendor, power, and antiquity thereby become prominent themes in the works
they wrote. While they drew on contemporary accounts of Marcello's
military career, as has been seen, his claim to Roman ancestry they derived not only from these but from legends long preserved in medieval
chronicles. Those chronicles again and the new humanist histories which
follow in their mold are the source of the descriptions given of Venice
and her origins. The view of Venice and of Venetian history there offered
is so far from realistic that it is called the "myth" of Venice.[53]

All the Glasgow authors praise Venice. Filelfo, Perleone, and Anonymous B do so emphatically. But for the two remaining authors—Orsini
and Bevilacqua—the history of Venice and the myth of her uniqueness
are central themes developed at length.[54] Bevilacqua surveys the main
events of Venice's early history: the flight to the lagoons of the Venetian
people during the chaotic years of Roman decay; the creation of her first
doge; her struggle against Pippin and Charlemagne and the refounding
of the city at the Rialto; the translation of the legitimizing body of Saint
Mark; the Peace of Venice of 1178 between Emperor Frederick Barbaros-
sa and the beleaguered Pope, who in gratitude regaled the Doge with
symbols of unassailable and priestly authority. Orsini's focus is more specific.
Orsini's work, it will be remembered, is not strictly a *consolatio*, although
it contains material related to Valerio's death and Marcello's grief; its whole
purpose is to clarify amicably Francesco Filelfo's report of the origin of
the Venetian people. Not the Gauls but the Trojans were the immediate
ancestors of the Veneti, Orsini argues at great length, evaluating the contradictory accounts of Strabo and Livy. Descended from the Trojans, a
free people who had fled Asia in order to preserve their immemorial liberty,
the Venetians had never been subject to any power, and the city's own
liberty, preexisting Rome's, was indisputably ancient and would last eternally. For Orsini, as for many Venetian chroniclers and historians, the

53. For the myth of Venice, see the many studies cited in King, *Venetian Humanism*, chap.
2, note 231. For the medieval chronicle tradition, see the studies of Fasoli, Cracco and Carile
cited in note 51.

54. Filelfo (G, pp. 107–109), Perleone (193–194), Anonymous B (304); Orsini (M, esp. ff. 2v–15v,
21r–28r); Bevilacqua (V, ff. 69r–95v). The matter is only of peripheral concern for the remaining
Glasgow authors.

origin of Venice in a pure tradition of freedom was an argument for the irreproachability of her present state and ambitions.

Having established that Venice was founded in freedom, Orsini (and with him Bevilacqua) celebrates Venice's long record of liberty since her founding, the justice of her domination of other cities, the antiquity of her nobility, unblemished by any admixture of lesser stock, her guardianship of the sea, the abundance of her wealth founded in busy commerce, the advantages of her site, the beauty of her buildings, her impregnability, her piety, her uniqueness in every regard. These are the strains of the Venetian *mito* so much studied by modern scholars and so prevalent in the contemporary literature.

The means of consolation. The stated goal of the authors of the Glasgow codex, however, with the exception of Orsini, is not to praise Valerio, Marcello, or Venice, but to comfort the stubbornly inconsolable father. Their works are largely devoted to recipes for consolation.

Most of the authors acknowledge the pain of Marcello's loss. They describe his great grief, in which they share. Bevilacqua does so at great length, since it is the main task of his work (to be examined in greater detail below) to describe and justify Marcello's sorrow. Perleone and Anonymous A express feelings of personal loss; the former Valerio's tutor, the latter perhaps his uncle, they had developed deep affection for the child. Filelfo companionably describes his grief at the death of his own son Olimpio: both children born the same year to fathers of the same age, they died the same year, leaving fathers who themselves stared at death. Others of the consolers had recently suffered the deaths of close relatives whom they name as they sympathize with Marcello: Sagundino had lost several children and his pregnant wife in a shipwreck in 1460; Nogarola, unmarried and childless, had recently lost her mother; as a child Fortebracci had lost his father — and it is the advice he received from wise priests then that he repeats to Marcello now. Battista Guarini, though he does not refer to the death, had lost his famous father soon before Valerio died. Marcello's comforters, therefore, do not rebuke him harshly: it is natural to mourn loved ones, especially children.[55]

---

55. Bevilacqua describes Marcello's great grief repeatedly throughout the work; important passages at V, ff. 7v–13r, 42r–52r, 97v–115r, 158r–162v, 171v–173r. The others noted: Perleone (G, pp. 235, 242, 248); Anonymous A (250–251); Filelfo (39); Sagundino (2–4, 7, 13); Nogarola

But enough is enough, they say. What is common to the human condition all human beings must accept. Death comes to all; it must be greeted without fear. To defy the certainty of death is to waver in faith, for God must be revered in adversity as well as prosperity. The faithful Christian suffers patiently, and permits God to recall one of his angels to himself. Children above all are vulnerable, and are most certainly beloved of God: they must be relinquished peaceably. Marcello should consider the evils of human existence that Valerio escaped by dying, and the vices to which he might have fallen prey, besmirching his soul, had he lived longer. Marcello had other children, a wife, a family, the hope of resurrection and of reunion with his son in heaven. He had borne bravely the death of his father Francesco, deeply beloved, his mother Magdalucia, his brother Pietro (the learned bishop), other brothers, sisters, sons, a daughter: why had the death of this one child defeated him? Marcello had always been known for his prudence and moderation—two classic virtues—and must not now degenerate from the standard of his previous behavior. A reasonable term of mourning passed, it was time to resume his normal life, especially since he was a Venetian, a nobleman, a Marcello, and a soldier.[56]

It was necessary for Marcello, more than for other fathers, to be brave. How could a hero of noble soul permit himself the indignity of prolonged and prostrate grief? He had stood firm against Piccinino, Visconti, and Sforza, and demonstrated courage and resourcefulness in the field. He was a ruler of his city, born for the good of the republic, an ornament to his great city. The consciousness of such splendor should banish grief. The brilliance of his reputation makes his present condition the more shameful. Consider the examples of great men (and a few women) who had bravely borne the death of children and other adversities, Marcello's consolers exhorted him. Among the Greeks, there were Pericles and Xenophon;

(ed. Abel, 164); Fortebracci (143, 147). Also for the legitimacy of grief: Nogarola (ed. Abel, p. 168); Guarini (179); Anonymous B (297). For the death of Guarino Veronese, see above, note 42.

56. Arguments for the acceptance of inevitable death: esp Sagundino (G, pp. 9–13, 19–22, 24); Filelfo (50–55, 57–61, 69–79); Nogarola (ed. Abel, 170–171, 176–178); Fortebracci (152–155); Anonymous A (251–253, 262–263). For the need to relinquish children esp.: Filelfo (119); Fortebracci (153); Guarini (182, 185); Perleone (248); Anonymous B (301, 305). The consolation of family and hope for reunion with Valerio: Filelfo (122–124). Previous losses: Perleone (190–192). George of Trebizond also mentions the death of a daughter, Taddea, soon after Valerio's (ed. Monfasani, 243)—no literary memorial for her! The need for moderation voiced everywhere but esp.: George of Trebizond (ed. Monfasani, 239–240, 242–245); Filelfo (119–121).

among the Romans, Aemilius Paulus, Marcus Claudius Marcellus (a presumed ancestor), the orator Cicero, the Spartan women, and Cornelia;
from Scripture, the suffering Job and the dolorous Virgin Mary; from
Venice in the present age the doges Francesco Foscari and Pasquale
Malipiero.[57]

The arguments just reviewed are commonplaces of the genre of consolation.[58] They are encountered in all the authors of the Glasgow codex
(even Orsini), although some certainly dwell more than others on one
matter or another, and the brief works develop only one issue fully, or
none at all. Sagundino, George of Trebizond, and Nogarola, for instance,
particularly emphasize the moral argument: the need to accept death and
accept adversity with strength of soul. Fortebracci and Anonymous A exhort Marcello to strengthen his faith. Perleone is intimate, naming family
members and appealing to personal motives. Reminders of Marcello's
courage as demonstrated in military feats are prominent in the works of
George of Trebizond, Filelfo, Fortebracci, Mascarello, Guarini, and Bevilacqua. Arguments for immortality are the most conspicuous themes of the
works of Filelfo and Anonymous B. The latter's work is minor. But in
Filelfo's work, the discussion of immortality amounts to a small treatise
(about one-third of the whole) of considerable interest.[59]

Death would indeed be an evil, Filelfo pointed out, if the soul were
not immortal. But its immortality can be proved in three ways. First,
souls have been observed to exist outside of bodies, as they were repeatedly by the ancient Greeks, by the saints Augustine and Jerome. Secondly,
as the Presocratics, Plato, and Aristotle have shown, the soul is wholly
immaterial and thus utterly independent of the body. While the latter,
then, is admittedly subject to death, the immaterial soul is not. Thirdly,

57. Argument that a military hero and civic leader should not grieve: Sagundino (G, pp. 14,
24–25); George of Trebizond (ed. Monfasani, 240ff.); Filelfo (87, 104); Nogarola (ed. Abel, G,
pp. 170, 172); Fortebracci (148–151); Guarini (182, 186ff.); Perleone (189); Anonymous B (304).
Examples of those who had vanquished grief: Sagundino (pp. 15–18); Filelfo (121–122); Nogaro-
lo (ed. Abel, 166–168); Fortebracci (148, 154–155); Mascarello (163); Guarini (183); Anonymous
A (251); Anonymous B (305–307); Bevilacqua (V, ff. 103v–104r, 109v–112r, 158v–160v).

58. For which see P. O. Kristeller, "Francesco Bandini and his Consolatory Dialogue upon
the Death of Simone Gondi," in his *Studies*, 411–435; the dissertation of G. W. McClure, Jr.,
*The Renaissance Vision of Solace and Tranquility: Consolation and Therapeutic Wisdom in Italian Hu-
manist Thought*, 2 vols. (University of Michigan, 1981); idem, "The Humanist Art of Mourning," to appear in *RQ* (1986). McClure's works provide guidance to a large literature on the
consolatory genre. For the convention of the literary collection of works as a memorial for the
dead, see Kristeller, "Bandini," 419–420, and the additions of Fabbri, "Le *Consolationes*," 232–233.

59. That discussion in his *Consolatio*, G, pp. 80–107, summarized below.

if the soul were not immortal, God would not be just—an evident impossibility. The evil are not always punished in this life: an injustice. The just God must therefore render justice in an afterlife. Due punishment for sin must necessarily be visited upon immortal souls. All souls, then, are immortal.

Consolation refused. Filelfo's *Consolatio* is unique in its systematic development of one of the series of consolatory arguments found in the Glasgow texts. Bevilacqua's *Excusatio*, an apology for prolonged mourning, is unique in another way. It contains all the consolatory arguments reviewed with a larger framework: that of Marcello's dialogue with René d'Anjou. The work begins and ends with exhortations to that "divine king and most serene prince," and the narrator (Marcello speaks, but Bevilacqua is author) returns to the dialogue mode several times in between. The narrator simply refuses to be consoled. He seeks solace by turning to his time-tested friend, describing his implacable grief and the many learned men and women—the most eloquent of the age—who had written to comfort him. Their consolations he includes with the present work so that René may act as judge—"arbiter"—between the bereft father and those who have, in consoling him, accused him of weakness.[60]

The accusation of weakness, the central theoretical issue of the *Excusatio*, is discussed and rebutted at several points; such discussions are interlaced with descriptions of Valerio and his death, of Marcello's great deeds, of the history of Venice. To his consolers' charge, the narrator responds that human nature compels us to mourn. He offers repeatedly examples of ancients, pagan and Christian, who suffered grief at the loss of loved ones (especially children). Christ's tears for Lazarus, the Virgin Mary's for Christ, St. Augustine's for his saintly mother (retold at length), are particularly compelling demonstrations of the legitimacy of the narrator's own sorrow.[61] But he is patient, obedient to the will of God, and absolutely rejects suicide as a remedy for his intolerable pain.[62] Besides these reflective and anecdotal responses to the accusation of weakness, the narrator presents a disputation, complete with alternations of arguments *pro*

---

60. The narrator appeals to René at V, ff. 7r–10r, 69v, 99r–v, 171v–173r.

61. Examples are offered throughout; series begin at V, ff. 113r, 140v, 145r, 150r and 153r. The examples of Christ, Mary, and Augustine respectively at ff. 113r, 148v–149r, and 150r–153r.

62. V, ff. 44r, 99r for his obedience to the divine will, which is the cause of his rejection of suicide, discussed on ff. 163v–171r. The suicide section is omitted from G.

and *contra*, on the question of whether virtue can coexist with grief.[63]The Stoic and Peripatetic views of human emotions are distinguished. The Stoics recommend a state of passionlessness, and argue that the virtuous man must overcome his emotions—including grief—if he is to remain virtuous. The Peripatetics concede the human being's innate emotionality: a father can mourn his son, and remain good. A father would be cruel to view without weeping the burial of his son, the narrator concludes. He must be permitted tears.[64]

But Marcello does not say these things. They were penned by another hand. Do they represent the true feelings of Valerio's father? Or did Marcello, coolly, find in the death of his son an opportunity for another literary game? For that matter, were the other consolations reviewed here, by Marcello's order splendidly transcribed and bound in the Glasgow manuscript volume, spontaneous expressions of sympathy? Were their authors charged by Marcello (or his agents) to write? Or did they smell the possibility of a reward (Filelfo, remember, was richly rewarded) if they wrote cleverly to console, but really to flatter, a wealthy dilettante?

Valerio died, and Marcello grieved, I suspect, genuinely. And a group of learned men, aware of the incident, were struck by the image of a powerful man devastated by sorrow. They drew on available traditions—the stories of Valerio and Marcello, the history of Venice, the genre of consolation—and wrote appropriate works. They may well have hoped thereby to win fees or advancement. And Marcello, near the end of his life, still saddened, enjoyed a last literary game, with himself at its center, played with his old friend. He produced his last book, and sent it over the Alps to the bibliophile and soldier whom he had long admired. And I too now, in a volume offered to a great scholar, tender with respect and admiration a small work.

MARGARET L. KING

---

63. V, ff. 115r–128r summarized below.
64. These concluding statements at V, ff. 158v, 160v.

A LITTLE KNOWN RENAISSANCE MANUAL OF CONSOLATION NICOLAUS MODRUSSIENSE'S
DE CONSOLATIONE
1465—1466

AS RHETORICIANS AND MORALISTS, Renaissance humanists were deeply interested in the theory and practice of providing consolation for life's sorrows. In their works appear many practical attempts to offer solace for such problems as bereavement, fear of death, illness, despair, and misfortune. Beginning with Petrarch's *De remediis utriusque fortunae* in the fourteenth century, there likewise emerged a keen interest in the theory of therapeutic *ratio* and *oratio*.[1] Though it has yet to be fully studied, this

A version of this paper was presented at the Eighteenth International Congress on Medieval Studies in Kalamazoo, Michigan, in 1983. I would like to thank Professors Charles Trinkaus and Paul Oskar Kristeller for their careful reading of the dissertation from which much of this study is drawn.

1. On Renaissance consolatory literature see A. Auer, *Johannes von Dambach und die Trostbuecher von 11. bis zum 16. Jahrhundert*. Beitraege zur Geschichte der Philosophie und Theologie des Mittelalters, 27:1–2 (Muenster, 1928); B. Langston, *Tudor Books of Consolation* (Ph.D diss., University of North Carolina, 1940); P. O. Kristeller, "Francesco Bandini and His Consolatory Dialogue Upon the Death of Simone Gondi," in his *Studies*, 411–435; F. N. M. Diekstra, "Introduction," to his *A Dialogue Between Reason and Adversity: A Late Middle English Version of Petrarch's* De remediis (Assen, 1968), 15–65; and the article by Margaret King in this volume. For studies on Giannozzo Manetti's *Dialogus consolatorius*, see J. Banker, "Mourning a Son: Childhood and Paternal Love in the *Consolatoria* of Giannozzo Manetti," *History of Childhood Quarterly: The Journal of Psychohistory*, 3 (1976): 351–362; A. de Petris, "Il *Dialogus Consolatorius* di G. Manetti e le sue fonti," *Giornale storico della letteratura italiana*, 154 (1977): 76–106; idem, "Giannozzo Manetti and his *Consolatoria*," *Bibliothèque d'humanisme et renaissance*, 45 (1979): 493–521; and my "The Art of Mourning: Autobiographical Writings on the Loss of a Son in Italian Humanist Thought (1400–1461)," *RQ*, 39 (1986): 440–475.

theoretical concern with consolatory philosophy and rhetoric reveals much
of the humanists' wider vision of the merging of wisdom and eloquence.
It is therefore worthwhile to examine this theoretical literature of consolation for what it can teach us about the character of Renaissance humanism and its contributions to the larger moral, religious, and psychological
traditions of Western thought.

   The genres of practical consolatory literature include the *epistola consolatoria*, the *oratio consolatoria* or *consolatio* (longer and more ambitious than
the *epistola*), the *oratio funebris*, and the consolatory dialogue; more purely
theoretical problems of consolation are treated in the remedial or consolatory manual, which seeks to transcend particular tragedies and misfortunes and address itself to the general problems of solace and tranquillity.[2]

2. The literature on the consolatory tradition is considerable. On ancient consolation, see among
others K. Buresch, *Consolationum a Graecis Romanisque scriptarum historia critica*. Leipziger Studien
zur classischen Philologie, 9:1 (Leipzig, 1886); Sister Mary Evaristus (Moran), *The Consolations
of Death in Ancient Greek Literature* (Washington, D.C., 1917); Sister Mary Fern, *The Latin Consolation as a Literary Type* (St. Louis, 1941). On patristic consolation, see C. Favez, *La consolation
latine chrétienne* (Paris, 1937); R. C. Gregg, *Consolation Philosophy: Greek and Christian Paideia in
Basil and the Two Gregories*. Patristic Monograph Series, 3 (Cambridge, Mass., 1975); Sister Mary
Beyenka, *Consolation in Saint Augustine* (Washington, D.C., 1950). On medieval consolation see
P. von Moos, *Consolatio: Studien zur mittellateinischen Trostliteratur ueber den Tod und zum Problem
der christlichen Trauer*. Muenstersche Mittelalter-Schriften, 3:1–4 (Munich, 1971–72). For a bibliography of sources for the consolatory tradition see von Moos, 4:19–39; for a comprehensive
list of secondary works, see *ibid.*, 40–68.
   The Trecento and Quattrocento concern with consolation has important antecedents in the tradition of the *ars dictaminis*. Some of these rhetorical manuals contain examples of consolatory letters and some discussion of consolation. See Kristeller, "Francesco Bandini," 418; Banker, 352
and 360–361; von Moos, 1:401–414. On Boncompagno, see note 23 below. On the dictaminal
tradition as a whole, see J. J. Murphy, *Rhetoric in the Middle Ages. A History of Rhetorical Theory
from St. Augustine to the Renaissance* (Berkeley, 1974).
   The humanists produced countless examples of the consolatory letter. For those of Petrarch
see his *Familiares* II, 1; IV, 12; VII, 13; XIII, 1; XIV, 3, in *Le Familiari*, ed. V. Rossi and U.
Bosco (Florence, 1933–42); his *Seniles* VIII, 5; X, 4 and 5; XI, 10 and 14; XIII, 1, 9, and 10,
in *Lettere senili*, tr. G. Fracassetti (Florence, 1869–70). Salutati's consolatory epistles may be found
in his *Epistolario*, 1:161–164; 2:68–76, 245–250, 439–456; 3:331–335, 363–368, 435–436. On his
own losses see 3:392–403, 408–422, 456–479. A consolatory letter by Leonardo Bruni to Nicola
di Vieri de' Medici is found in Leonardi Bruni *Epistolarum libri VIII*, ed. L. Mehus (Florence,
1741), 2:53–57 [= *Ep.* VI, 8]. For the consolatory letters of George of Trebizond, see *Collectanea
Trapezuntiana*, ed. J. Monfasani (Binghamton, N.Y., 1984), Texts LXIII and LXVIII. The consolatory letters of Marsilio Ficino are found in his *Opera omnia* (Basel, 1576), 1:617, 654, 660,
and 884; see also P.O. Kristeller, *Supplementum*, 2:162–167, 173–175.
   For examples of humanist funeral orations, see the orations on the death of Leonardo Bruni
by Poggio Bracciolini and Manetti printed in Bruni, *Epistolarum libri VIII*, 1:89–126; Alamanno
Rinuccini's oration on the death of Matteo Palmieri is in Rinuccini, *Lettere ed orazioni*, ed. V.
Giustiniani (Florence, 1953), 78–85; an oration of George of Trebizond's is found in the *Collectanea*, ed. Monfasani, Text CXXXII.

The most famous Renaissance manual of remedies was Petrarch's massive *De remediis utriusque fortunae* (1354?–1366), a dialogue in which Petrarch formulates remedies for the vicissitudes both of prosperity and adversity. He depicts the attempts of "Reason" (*Ratio*) to exhort his interlocutors to a state of equanimity: in Book I by pricking the vanities of "Hope" (*Spes*) and "Joy" (*Gaudium*), in Book II by stilling the laments of "Fear" (*Metus*) and "Grief" (*Dolor*). The treatise forms a handbook of rhetorical cures, providing the *medicamenta verborum* that might pacify the multifarious range of human passions. The *De remediis* seems to have been quite popular, for it appeared in more than twenty printed editions between 1474 and 1760, numerous manuscript copies, as well as adaptations and vernacular translations.[3]

Examples of the longer *consolatio* are Carlo Marsuppini's *Consolatoria oratio* (or *epistola*) of 1433 to Lorenzo and Cosimo de' Medici on the death of their mother, in P.G. Ricci, "Una consolatoria inedita del Marsuppini," *La Rinascita*, 3 (1940): 363–433; see also Francesco Filelfo's *Oratio consolatoria ad Iacobum Antonium Marcellum* of 1461 (ed. in *Orationes cum quibusdam aliis eiusdem operibus* [Basel, before 1498], sign. E2r–K1v), discussed by Margaret King in an article in this volume and by me in "The Art of Mourning."

For some examples of the consolatory dialogue, see Giovanni Conversino da Ravenna's *De consolatione de obitu filii* of 1401 (Oxford, MS Balliol 288, ff. 54vb–71va; Giannozzo Manetti's *Dialogus consolatorius* of 1438 on the death of his son (Florence, BN, MS Magl. Cl. XXI, 18, ff. 1–45 [see *Iter* 1:120]), an edition of which by A. de Petris has now been published in Edizioni di Storia e Letteratura, Rome; Bartolomeo Scala's *Dialogus de consolatione* of 1463 (Florence, Bibl. Laur., MS LIV 10, ff. 104–122v), edition by A. M. Brown in preparation; Platina's self-consolatory dialogue *De falso et vero bono dialogi* (Paris, 1630), which deals with his imprisonment by Pope Paul II in 1468–69; Aurelio Brandolini's *Dialogus de humanae vitae conditione et toleranda corporis aegritudine* (Paris, 1562). The latter two dialogues are discussed in C. Trinkaus, *In Our Image and Likeness: Humanity and Divinity in Italian Renaissance Thought* (London and Chicago, 1970), 1:294–321.

In addition to Nicolaus Modrussiensis' *De consolatione*, consolatory manuals were composed by Petrarch (*De remediis*) and Johannes von Dambach (*Consolatio theologiae*). Though more concerned with traditional pastoral concerns (e.g., those of conscience) and more directed to a monastic audience than Petrarch's manual, the latter work, completed in 1366, is still considerably humanistic, rhetorical and consolatory in character. The text was printed by Amerbach (Basel, 1492) and has been studied by Auer, *Johannes von Dambach*. Matteo Bosso's dialogue *De tolerandis adversis*, in his *Contenta*, (Strasbourg, 1509), sign. Q1–U1, may also be considered an example of this genre. In the sixteenth century, Girolamo Cardano wrote a *De consolatione* and later a massive handbook similar to Petrarch's *De remediis* entitled *De utilitate ex adversis capienda*. These works are edited in Cardano's *Opera omnia* (Lyons, 1663), 1:588–636; 2:1–282.

It should be emphasized that this is only a partial listing of sources for the consolatory tradition; in particular vast amounts of manuscript materials remain to be collected and studied. For some additional sources see my *The Renaissance Vision of Solace and Tranquillity: Consolation and Therapeutic Wisdom in Italian Humanist Thought* (Ph.D diss, Univ. of Michigan, 1981). A useful study of humanist literature on adversity and happiness (a literature which can often be classified as consolatory) is C. Trinkaus, *Adversity's Noblemen: The Italian Humanists on Happiness* (New York, 1940).

3. Petrarch's treatise as yet has no modern edition. See the edition in his *Opera omnia* (Basel,

About a century after Petrarch completed his handbook, there appeared another work intended to serve as a therapeutic manual: the *De consolatione* of Nicolaus Modrussiensis. Though little-known and never published, this work deserves to be brought to light because it is a revealing example of the Renaissance interest and innovation in consolation and because it is a useful summary of the classical and Christian consolatory traditions. It differs from Petrarch's *De remediis* in significant ways. First, whereas Petrarch's manual dealt with both "positive" and "negative" emotional states, Nicolaus' treatise is concerned only with grief and despair. Second, whereas Petrarch's manual is meant to be read for private benefit, Nicolaus' is intended to be used as a guide for those administering solace—in addition, presumably, to its alternative function as a book for private reading and comfort. In its aim to be a complete handbook, it offers a thorough framework for the theory and method of consolation. Petrarch's treatise, though containing some general, prefatory remarks on the nature, purpose, and techniques of therapeutic wisdom, chiefly aims to be a compendium of remedies. And though there are scattered general discussions of consolation in some other high medieval and Renaissance writings,[4] Nicolaus' work is unique, to my knowledge, in its attempt to construct, in an autonomous work, a systematic treatment of both the *topoi* and the administering of consolation. My purpose in this article is to examine the *De consolatione*'s genre, sources, and themes in order to place the work within its proper historical context in Renaissance thought and in the Western consolatory tradition in general. I hope to use the treatise to

1554), 1–256. On the dating of the *De remediis* see the remarks of P. G. Ricci in Francesco Petrarca, *Prose*, ed. G. Martellotti, P. G. Ricci, E. Carrara, E. Bianchi. La letteratura italiana, storia e testi, 7 (Milan and Naples, 1955), 1169–1170, and E. H. Wilkins, *Petrarch's Eight Years in Milan* (Cambridge, Mass., 1959), 65–72. For discussions of the work see K. Heitmann, *Fortuna und Virtus: Eine Studie zu Petrarcas Lebensweisheit*. Studi italiani, 1 (Cologne and Graz, 1958); the "Introduction" to Diekstra's *A Dialogue*; Trinkaus, *The Poet as Philosopher: Petrarch and the Formation of Renaissance Consciousness* (New Haven, 1979), 120–128. On manuscripts, editions, and translations of the treatise, see N. Mann, "The Manuscripts of Petrarch's *De remediis*: A Checklist," *IMU*, 14 (1971): 57–90; W. Fiske, "Francis Petrarch's Treatise *De remediis utriusque fortunae*, Texts and Versions," *Bibliographical Notices*, 3 (Florence, 1888); Heitmann, 12–14. B. Kohl suggests that the *De remediis* was the most popular philosophical work to come out of the Italian Renaissance. See his "Introduction" to the facsimile edition (Delmar, N.Y., 1980, x–xi) of Thomas Twyne's translation of the *De remediis*, the *Physicke Against Fortune* (1579).

4. For instance, such discussions can be found in Boncompagno's *Rhetorica antiqua* I, 25; see note 2 above. There was a similar epistolatory exchange between Salutati and Francesco Zabarella concerning consolation. See Salutati's *Epistolario* 3:408–422, 456–479; 4:347–361. See also Manetti's *Dialogus consolatorius* (note 2, above).

make some generalizations about the intellectual, cultural, psychological, and religious implications of the Renaissance treatment of the problem of consolation. I shall also make some suggestions concerning the character of Renaissance humanism, pastoral care, and the larger "history of the cure of souls".[5]

Nicolaus Modrussiensis (or Nicolaus Machienensis, Nicolaus Cattarus) was born in the Venetian territory of Dalmatia in the first quarter of the fifteenth century. He studied under the theologian and philosopher Paolo della Pergola in Venice. Becoming a cleric, he held ecclesiastical offices in Dalmatia (e.g., at Modrussa and Corbavia) and in Italy (e.g., at Viterbo, Ascoli, Todi, and Spoleto). He was vice-legate to Cardinal Raffaele Riario in 1478–79; in the conflict between Sixtus IV and the Florentines in 1479 he wrote an apologia for Sixtus entitled *Defensio ecclesiasticae libertatis*. He died in Rome and was buried in S. Maria del Popolo.[6] Several volumes of his library passed to the collection of Sixtus IV. Thus, though not born in Italy, he was educated in Venice and had close ties to the Italian clergy and the Papal court. His works include a *De mortalium felicitate* which he dedicated to Pius II; the *De consolatione* (1465–66) dedicated to Marco Barbo, then bishop of Vicenza; a *De bellis Gothorum* (ca. 1473); an *Oratio in funere Petri* composed (as was a similar work of Niccolò Perotti) in Rome after the death in 1474 of Cardinal Pietro Riario; the *Defensio ecclesiasticae libertatis* (1479), which he dedicated to Raffaele Riario; a *De humilitate*; and a *De titulis et auctoribus Psalmorum* (ca. 1479). Of these works, the only one to be printed was the funeral oration for Riario.[7]

5. See J. T. McNeill, *A History of the Cure of Souls* (New York, 1953). McNeill's study considers classical, Judeo-Christian, and Eastern thought in the common context of the cure of souls, providing a valuable conceptual framework that can, among other things, suggest new ways to compare and contrast classical philosophy and Christian thought.

6. For these and other details of Nicolaus' life, see C. Frati, "Evasio Leone e le sue ricerche intorno a Niccolò vescovo Modrussiense," *La Bibliofilia*, 18 (1916): 1–35 and 81–98; G. Mercati, "Note varie sopra Niccolò Modrussiense," *La Bibliofilia*, 26 (1924–25): 165–179, 253–265, 289–299, 359–372 (= Mercati, *Opere minori*, ST 79 [Vatican City, 1937], 4:205–267); citations will be from this latter edition. See also the bibliography in Mercati's *Per la cronologia della vita e degli scritti di Niccolò Perotti* . . . , ST 44 (Vatican City, 1925). Nicolaus was sent by Pope Pius II on a mission to the King of Bosnia and Sixtus IV sent him as his emissary to Lorenzo de' Medici and the Florentine government in order to request the release of Raffaele Riario, who had been imprisoned following the Pazzi conspiracy. See Mercati, "Note varie," 205–242.

7. On Nicolaus' works, see Mercati, "Note varie," 205–242. Other than a single letter, the *Oratio in funere Petri* was the only work of his published before this century, when some other of his letters have been printed in addition to the translations with dedications of Isocrates' *Ad*

Nicolaus' interests, as revealed by his works and by the books he owned, embraced both scholasticism and humanism. Aristotelian commentaries by Alexander of Hales, Duns Scotus, Albert of Saxony, and Gaetano da Thiene, now preserved in the Biblioteca Angelica in Rome, have been plausibly traced to his library.[8] His *De mortalium felicitate* cites a number of scholastic thinkers.[9] But included in the books that passed to the library of Sixtus IV in 1480 are not only several works of Aristotle, but also a variety of more literary texts, such as philosophical and rhetorical works of Cicero (including the *Tusculan Disputations*), Quintilian's *Institutes*, Macrobius' commentary on the *Somnium Scipionis*, and Calcidius' commentary on his translation of the *Timaeus*; works of Augustine, Jerome, and Lactantius are found as well. A document of the Vatican Library from 1448 identifies him as the scribe of a commentary on the epigrams of Prosper and of Aesop's fables.[10] He is probably the translator of two orations of Isocrates, the *Ad Demonicum* and the *Ad Nicoclem*. Certainly the *De consolatione*, with its frequent citations of the ancient moralists and poets, shows Nicolaus to have been well-acquainted with the authors who formed the backbone of the *studia humanitatis*.

The *De consolatione* was written in 1465–66 when Nicolaus was in Viterbo.[11] In the early nineteenth century, the Carmelite scholar Evasio Leone planned an edition, but the project was never completed.[12] A full assessment of the work's diffusion must await a complete census of the manuscripts in which it is preserved, but the first two volumes of Kristeller's *Iter Italicum* show that there were at least two copies.[13] There is also one

Nicoclem and *Ad Demonicum* which have been plausibly attributed to him, most recently by L. Gualdo Rosa, in *La fede nella "paideia": Aspetti della fortuna europea di Isocrate nei secoli XV e XVI.* Studi storici dell'Istituto storico italiano per il Medio Evo, 140–142 (Rome, 1984), 43–47. See also Frati, Mercati, and F. Lepori, "La scuola di Rialto dalla fondazione alla metà del Cinquecento," in *Storia della cultura Veneta*, 3:2 (Vicenza, 1980), 559–570.

8. See Frati, "Evasio Leone," 84–85.

9. See Mercati, "Note varie," 220–221; Lepori, 559–570. Though citing scholastic sources, Nicolaus' treatise *De mortalium felicitate* places him to some extent in the moral tradition of humanist treatises on happiness, exemplified by the treatises of Francesco Zabarella, Bartolommeo Facio, Maffeo Vegio, and Filippo Beroaldo. See Trinkaus, *Adversity's Noblemen, passim.* I have been able to study only the prologue of this dialogue, edited by Mercati, "Note varie," 246–247.

10. See *ibid.*, 209–211.

11. Frati, "Evasio Leone," 28, dates the treatise from the colophon in BAV, MS Vat. lat. 5139, f. 123v: "In arce Viterbensi secundo Pauli editum scriptumque vestro nomine, R[everendissime] P[ater] et domine."

12. See Mercati, "Note varie," 222–223.

13. MS Vat. lat. 5139 (*Iter* 2:331) and MS Vat. lat. 8764 (*Iter* 2:345). Casale Monferrato,

contemporary reference to the work made by Nicolaus' Perugian friend, the poet and humanist Francesco Maturanzio. In 1474 Maturanzio wrote Nicolaus saying that, after having heard of a recent family death, he wished that he had had Nicolaus's *De consolatione* at hand so that his grief might have been in some measure diminished.[14]

The genre of the *De consolatione* is that of the handbook: in it, Nicolaus intends to deal comprehensively with the art of giving solace by treating its theory, method, and the major *loci communes*. It is therefore a kind of *summa* for the *officium consolandi*. In his prefatory comments, Nicolaus presents his purpose in the work and alludes to the consolatory traditions to which his treatise is related:

> I have therefore attempted in this work to explain the method of consolation not according to the precise standards of philosophy— for we are not now disputing about Nature or about those finer and subtler points which are to be discussed away from the crowd, in retreat with the wise—but in a broader and cruder fashion that is capable of treating even rather high matters before the people. It is indeed our purpose to pass on precepts by which, as in the case of other disturbances [i.e., sin], so in the case of [adversities warranting] consolation, when the circumstances require it we may influence the mind of a hearer, succor those who are afflicted, and alleviate their distress as completely as possible. And I do not think I have undertaken this labor in vain, even though there exist many distin-

---

Seminario Vescovile, MS I a 8, s. XIX is a copy prepared by Evasio Leone for his planned edition of the text (*Iter* 1:40). In this article I shall cite the text from MS Vat. lat. 8764 (hereinafter cited as 'V'), a manuscript written by the scribe Stephanus Sabinus which contains emendations in what I believe to be the hand of Nicolaus. Certainly the emendations have the character of author's variants, as is clear from the various passages quoted below.

14. Mercati, "Note varie," 223, cites this letter: "Una menzione, non so se l'unica contemporanea, se ne fa nella lettera 19 luglio 1474 del Maturanzio da Vicenza. In essa egli dopo aver espresso l'immenso dolore che provò in Venezia all' udire da un concittadino in Perugia la morte della vecchia madre, aggiunge: 'Quod si *Consolationem* tuam in manibus haberem, quae ita graviter et sapienter a te est scripta ut Crantorem vel Ciceronem legere se existiment quicunque in manus sumpserint, aliqua fortasse ex parte intestinus hic minueretur dolor'(Vat. lat. 5890, f. 85v)." To my knowledge there is no evidence whether or not Nicolaus' treatise influenced other later consolatory works of the Quattrocento such as those of Platina or Brandolini. Platina wrote his *De falso et vero bono dialogi* in the late 1460s or early 1470s before Nicolaus' manuscripts had passed to the Papal library (of which he was the librarian from 1475 to his death). Many of Nicolaus' manuscripts came into the Vatican library in 1480 after his death; the *De consolatione* passed into the library later with Marco Barbo's (d. 1491) collections (see Mercati, "Note varie," 205–211).

guished works written by very knowledgable men about this method, such as all the books *On [the] Consolation [of Philosophy]* by the famous Boethius, the well-known *On Consolation* as well as the book called *On the Remedies for Misfortunes*, both by Seneca, and the shining gem of Isidore's *Synonyms*. If, indeed, the work of Cicero that he composed about this method had survived, we and all others might have been freed of this labor. There are extant, however, the greater part of his valuable consolatory epistles, and not a few similar letters exist of Cyprian, Jerome, Basil the Great, and many other deeply learned men both Greek and Latin. For many Greeks — Plato, Cleanthes, Crato, Diogenes, Epicurus, Dicaearchus, Posidonius, Carneades, Chrysippus, and Crantor whom Cicero followed — wrote on this subject.[15]

Embracing treatises, dialogues, and letters, this list is a good survey of sources in the Western tradition of consolation. Except for Plato's dialogues (the *Phaedo, Crito, Apology*, and the ps.-Platonic *Axiochus*), all the works of pagan Greeks he names are lost or survive only in fragments.[16] The most famous of these was Crantor's Περὶ πένθους, which was written to console Hippocles on the loss of his children. This work, which apparently synthesized much of the Greek literature of consolation, deeply influenced Cicero's now fragmentary *Consolatio seu de luctu minuendo* — a self-consolatory work that Cicero wrote following the death of his daughter

15. V, ff. 1v–2v: "Conatus sum igitur hoc in opere consolandi rationem explicare non quidem secundum exactam philosophiae legem — nunc enim non de rerum natura disputamus aut de illis tenuioribus [et *canc.*] magis[que *add. redactor*] minutis rebus de quibus a turba secrete cum sapientibus disserendum — sed secundum pinguiorem crassioremque rationem quae etiam in populo non ignava [aut ociosa *canc.*] possit versari. Est enim propositum nostrum praecepta tradere quibus, ut caeteris perturbationibus, ita et consolatione, quando res postulabit, auditoris animum afficere possimus ac laborantibus succurrere eorumque aegritudinem quam comodissime levare. Nec mihi vanum hunc laborem assumpsisse puto, tametsi multa a peritissimis viris egregia monumenta extent in hanc rationem [*add. supra.*; rem *canc.*] conscripta, ut sunt pene⟨s⟩ omnes illi et praeclari quidem Boetii *De consolatione* libri, et Senece, tam ille *De consolatione* codex insignis quam alter quem *De remediis fortuitorum* appellavit, Isidorique *Sinonimorum* clarissima gemmula; Ciceronis vero, si extaret opus quod de hac ipsa ratione conscripsit, forsan et nos et omnes alios hoc labore emisset [et nobis et omnibus aliis hunc laborem adimisset(?) *canc.*]. Extant tamen pleraeque eius consolatoriae dignae epistolae. Quales etiam sunt nonnullae Cypriani, Hieronymi, Basilii Magni, aliorumque complurium doctissimorum virorum tam latinorum quam graecorum. Scripserunt enim hac ipsa de re et graecorum complures: Plato, Cleantes, Crato, Diogenes, Epicurus, Dicaearchus, Possidonius, Carneades, Crysippus, et Crantor quem Cicero [illo in opere quod meminimus *canc.*] secutus est."

16. This series of Greek writers is omitted in MS Vat. lat. 5139. It resembles the list made by Jerome in *Ep. 60* (PL 22:592). See also the discussion of Greek figures in *Tusculans* I and III.

Tullia. Had this work survived, Nicolaus argues, it might have relieved him of his present task.[17] The Senecan *De consolatione codex* could refer to any or all of Seneca's three treatises, *De consolatione ad Marciam, Ad Polybium*, or *Ad Helviam*.[18] Nicolaus also cites ps.-Seneca's dialogue *De remediis fortuitorum*, Petrarch's model for his own *De remediis*. Rightly, Nicolaus gives pride of place to Boethius' *De consolatione philosophiae*, the single most important extant model in the humanist consolatory tradition. This famous dialogue addresses the specific problems of the imprisoned Boethius' misfortune and despair, before proceeding to more general discussions of happiness, the highest good, divine providence, and free will.[19] The final treatise Nicolaus cites is Isidore of Seville's *Synonyma*. Subtitled *De lamentatione animae peccatricis*, this work is a dialogue between a *deflens homo* and an *admonens ratio*. The "lamenting man" bewails various misfortunes: misery, unhappiness, exile, poverty, adversities, insults. The dialogue is a near-perfect blending of classical and Christian perspectives on the human condition. In dealing with the problem of adversity, Isidore presents classical remedies (such as "non hoc tibi soli" and "praemeditatio futurorum malorum"), but he also develops various Christian themes (such as man's state of sin, divine retribution, and redemptive suffering). And although the dialogue deals with misery, much of it deals as well with the general problems of sin, temptation, and spiritual health. Finally, in addition to these treatises and dialogues, Nicolaus also cites the genre of the consolatory letter as practised by classical and patristic authors.[20]

Though these classical and Christian sources offer various consolatory genres and *topoi*, none serves as a theoretical manual for the entire office of consolation. And this is what Nicolaus' treatise attempts to do. His nearest model for such a manual is the third book of Cicero's *Tusculan Disputations*, which discusses the malady of *aegritudo* and the method of consoling, and which, apparently, drew to some extent on Cicero's earlier

---

17. A forgery of Cicero's treatise was made in the next century and published in Venice in 1583. See E.T. Sage, *The pseudo-Ciceronian Consolation* (Chicago, 1910).

18. The *Ad Marciam*, the longest of these treatises, dealt with the loss of a son; the *Ad Polybium*, with the death of a brother. Seneca wrote the *Ad Helviam* for his mother to console her on his exile.

19. On Boethius, see P. Courcelle, *La Consolation de philosophie dans la tradition littéraire: Antécédents et postérité de Boèce* (Paris, 1967); H. R. Patch, *The Tradition of Boethius* (New York, 1935).

20. For editions, see *PL* 83:825–868. On the dialogue, see Auer, 245; Diekstra, 41.

Consolatio. Nicolaus in fact relies heavily on the *Tusculans*, despite his failure to mention it in his prefatory review of the consolatory tradition.

Having discussed the literary and philosophical traditions, Nicolaus continues his preface with a further discussion of his purposes in writing the work:

> Now all these authors [those ancient and patristic writers cited above] performed the office of consolation, and worthily and wisely to be sure. How then could others too have carried out the same service? There were a very few persons [i.e., the scholastic theologians] who were willing to teach, and, because of the wonderful sharpness of their intellects, perhaps did so abundantly enough, but [their teaching] in my judgment is too condensed and limited to meet the needs of those whose understandings have not yet had a great deal of philosophical training. I am certain that this had nothing to do with their ignorance of [the nature of] sin—for what indeed did those divine intellects not understand? Whatever light the divine providence of the All Highest has granted us shines on us through them. It is rather a question of a certain negligence, carelessness, contempt for the very easiness of the subject. Nor ought it to be a matter of shame to offer milk to the infants for whom Christ did not blush to die, particularly so since the Lord himself will ask all men, not only the philosophers, not merely those who are held to be wise, to visit and console him if he should be in prison or tribulation. Hence one may see with what necessity mortals are compelled to undertake the office of consolation, [an office] of which the Lord threatened to make himself so severe a taskmaster. Wherefore, desiring at once to benefit everyone and to show all the way to achieving what is required of them by divine and human law alike, we have laid out in order the precepts of consolation with the aid of that Helper Who alone is the best consoler of all miseries.[21]

21. V, ff. 2v–3r: "Verum hi omnes officio consolandi perfuncti sunt et quidem dignissime sapientissimeque. Caeterum quo pacto idem munus et alii [as- *canc.*] sequi possent? Pauci admodum praecipere voluerunt et hi quidem [*add. supra;* nimirum *canc.*] pro admirabili ingenii eorum acumine fortasse satis copiose, sed pro illorum desiderio [aut exigentia *canc.*] qui nondum in philosophia [aliisque liberalibus disciplinis *canc.*] admodum exercitatos habent sensus, meo iudicio et pressius et parcius. Neque id eos peccati ignoratione admisisse certo scio. Quid enim divina illa ingenia ignorarunt? a quibus nobis altissime ita ferente providentia, quicquid luminis est, illuxit. Quin

As these prefatory sections indicate, classical and Christian influences inform not only Nicolaus' view of the genres and sources of consolation, but also his notion of the consolatory office: it is an *officium* fulfilled by philosophers; it is also a duty that should be met by all Christians. Appropriately, Nicolaus' goal is to provide a practical, general guide that might serve a broad range of persons, not merely scholars. He wants to provide a useful manual that can help foster a broader, more effective practice of this philosophical and spiritual duty.

A final comment on the genre of the *De consolatione* needs to be made. As I have shown, Nicolaus could look to several classical and Christian sources for examples of consolatory discussions, but for a model of a consolatory manual, he could only have turned to the third book of Cicero's *Tusculan Disputations* or to more recent humanist writings such as Petrarch's *De remediis*. There were, however, two other literary traditions available to him, which, though they did not provide models of consolatory manuals as such, nevertheless contained works wherein questions of consolation were treated in handbook form.

First, he might have made use of a number of manuals stemming from the thirteenth-century tradition of the *ars dictaminis*, some of which include treatments of the rhetoric of consolation.[22] Several manuals, for instance, contain models for the *epistola consolatoria*. Boncompagno da Signa's *Rhetorica antiqua* contains a chapter *De consolationibus* (I, 25) in which are presented not only various types of model letters but also general comments on the nature of consolation, the proper time of administering solace, the advantages of moderate weeping, examples of those who have borne loss temperately, and other topics; furthermore, in the following chapter (I, 26) entitled *De ritu funeralis* there is a survey of funerary rites.[23]

potius negligentia aut incuria quadam et ipsius rei prae facilitate contemptu. . . . Nec pudori esse debet infantibus lac praebere pro quibus Christus mori ⟨non⟩ erubuit, praecipue cum sit ipse dominus non solos philosophos aut eos dumtaxat qui habiti sunt sapientiores, verum omnes omnino homines interrogaturus si se in carceribus et in tribulatione positum visitaverint aut consolati fuerint. Unde videre licet quanta necessitate mortales cogantur consolandi munus [sedulo *canc.*] obire, cuius se dominus tam severum exactorem comminatur [*add. supra;* promittit futurum *canc.*]. Itaque et nos universis prodesse cupientes eisque viam ostendere ad id consequendum quod divino pariter ac humano iure ab his exquiritur [et desideratur *canc.*], praecepta consolandi ex ordine digessimus, illius ope adiuti qui solus est cunctorum miserorum optimus consolator."

22. See note 2 above.

23. There are such chapters as *Quid sit consolatio, Litterae generales super consolationibus defunctorum, Litterae consolationis ad patrem et matrem pro morte filii, Quod non est tristibus in acerbitate doloris*

Though offering a considerably less theoretical, less comprehensive, and less humanistic treatment of consolation than that found in Nicolaus' work, these rhetorical manuals may have served as models for his own highly rhetorical treatise.[24]

The second tradition upon which Nicolaus may have drawn is the tradition of the confessor's manual.[25] Given his scholastic background and his training and vocation as a cleric, it is reasonable to assume that Nicolaus was familiar with the literature concerning the office of the confessional. This literature, which begins to flower in the thirteenth century with the appearance of massive *summae* for confessors and other handbooks of pastoral care,[26] is the central "therapeutic" legacy of the medieval cure of souls. Patristic writers, to be sure, had developed some of the genres

consolationis remedium exhibendum, Quod multi sancti viri flevisse super morte carorum leguntur et modum habuisse in fletu, Quod per immoderatam effusionem lacrimarum incipiant oculi caligare, Quod duplex afflictus proveniat illis qui lacrimari non possunt, Qui sint qui non indigent consolatione. Besides bereavement, some other misfortunes, such as blindness and mutilation, are also treated. For a list of the thirty sections of the *De consolationibus,* see von Moos, 2:224–225. On the following chapter, I, 26, see M. Barasche, *Gestures of Despair in Medieval and Early Renaissance Art* (New York, 1976), 88.

This tradition of the letter-writing manual will continue in the Renaissance among certain humanists. Aurelio Brandolini composed a *De ratione scribendi,* which contained chapters *De moerore, sive aegritudine sedanda; De consolatione paupertatis; De consolatione amissorum bonorum et patriae; De consolatione mortis; De consolatione caecitatis et totius corporis imbecillitatis.* I thank Fr. John W. O'Malley, S.J., for this reference. See his comments on the *De ratione scribendi* in his *Praise and Blame in Renaissance Rome: Rhetoric, Doctrine, and Reform in the Sacred Orators of the Papal Court, ca. 1450–1521* (Durham, North Carolina, 1979), 44f. O'Malley suggests 1485 as a *terminus ad quem* for the treatise. The *De ratione scribendi* was printed in Cologne in 1573 as part of an anthology of Renaissance epistolography, which includes also letters of Erasmus and Vives among others. A *Declamatio de morte* appears in some editions of Erasmus' *De conscribendis epistolis,* which was intended as a model for the Christian humanist consoler. See J.-C. Margolin, in *Erasmi Opera Omnia,* 2:1 (Amsterdam, 1971), 197, 441–445. When we find such humanists as these writing in the tradition of the *ars dictaminis* we are reminded of the continuity and overlap between the dictaminal and humanist traditions, a point stressed by Kristeller and Seigel, among others. See Kristeller, *Renaissance Thought and Its Sources* (New York, 1979), 228–259; Jerrold E. Seigel, *Rhetoric and Philosophy in Renaissance Humanism: The Union of Eloquence and Wisdom, Petrarch to Valla* (Princeton, 1968), 173–225. It is therefore important that we consider the possible influence of the dictaminal tradition on Nicolaus' treatise. A collection of studies with a bibliography on Renaissance rhetoric has recently been edited by J. J. Murphy, *Renaissance Eloquence: Studies in the Theory and Practice of Renaissance Rhetoric* (Berkeley, 1983).

24. The rhetorical nature of Nicolaus' manual is suggested by a number of characteristics: it is composed almost entirely of *loci,* it draws to a large extent on the tradition of the *epistola consolatoria* for its principles, and it provides commonplaces for the funeral oration.

25. See C. Trinkaus' suggestion in *The Poet as Philosopher,* 125, that Petrarch's *De remediis* can be seen as a type of lay *summa confessorum.*

26. For a study of the confessor's *summa* and the pastoral handbook, see T.N. Tentler, *Sin and Confession on the Eve of the Reformation* (Princeton, 1977).

of consolation, largely as a result of classical influences, but in the medieval period consolation is absorbed within the confessional tradition and subordinated to the need for salvation: sorrow comes to be associated more with contrition than with misfortune.[27] Thus a title such as that given to Johannes Nider's (d. 1438) manual for confessors, *Consolatorium timoratae conscientiae*, reveals how the notion of consolation becomes attached to the "spiritual" problem of sin and guilt rather than to the "worldly" problem of suffering and grief. Nonetheless, the confessor's *summa* could be one source for a number of therapeutic techniques that could be used effectively by the consoler — techniques dealing with the overall therapeutic scheme, and possibly some of the specific details, required for psychological healing. Though Nicolaus' treatise is clearly more a rhetorician's *summa* than a confessor's, it still betrays some of the latter's "clinical" approaches. In sum, Nicolaus' treatise represents a blend of the humanist, dictaminal, and pastoral traditions; it is this hybrid quality that gives the work its special historical interest.

Though the consolation for death is Nicolaus' primary focus, he is also concerned with the general theory of solace, and in one section mentions the related themes of poverty, power, and fame. In defining grief and in prescribing solace, Nicolaus draws from Greek dramatists (such as Menander and Euripides), Roman poets (Vergil, Ovid, Horace, Terence, Juvenal), philosophers (Plato, Cicero, Seneca), and religious writers (Jerome, Augustine, Isidore, Gregory the Great).[28] He describes well his encyclopedic range of sources when he characterizes his method in one section of his treatise as a "philosophorum theologorum satyrorum historicorumque lectio" from which he draws "ex aliis rationes, ex aliis exempla."[29] Nicolaus builds much of his manual from consolatory letters: he uses such

---

27. See W.A. Clebsch and C. Jaekle, *Pastoral Care in Historical Perspective: An Essay with Exhibits* (New York, 1964), 1–82.

28. Nicolaus may well have been acquainted with some of these sources in the original, since there is evidence to suggest that he knew Greek. See Gualdo Rosa, *La fede*, 45, note 9. It seems likely that his access to Greek sources was in some degree limited, however, for he fails to cite such well-known writings as Plutarch's *Consolatio ad uxorem* and other moral works, as well as ps.-Plutarch's *Consolatio ad Apollonium*. The latter work influenced Carlo Marsuppini's *Oratio consolatoria* of 1433 and was translated by Alamanno Rinuccini in 1463 for Cosimo de' Medici upon the death of his son. See P. G. Ricci, "Una consolatoria inedita," 372 and *passim*; Kristeller, "Bandini," 421; for Rinuccini's preface to his translation of the treatise, see Rinuccini, *Lettere ed orazioni*, 59–63.

29. V, f. 54v.

letters as Cicero's consolations to Titius (*Familiares* V, 16) and to Brutus
(*Ad Brut.* I, 9); Servius Sulpicius' famous letter to Cicero on the death
of Tullia (*Fam.* IV, 5); Cicero's letters in which he laments Tullia's loss
(*Fam.* IV, 6 and V, 13); Seneca's letter to Lucilius on the death of Flaccus
(*Ad Luc.* 63); Jerome's *consolatoriae* to Heliodorus (*Ep.* 60), Pammachius
(*Ep.* 66), Theodore (*Ep.* 75), Oceanus (*Ep.* 77); and the (perhaps pseudonymous) letter to Tyrasius.[30] Besides these letters on bereavement,
Nicolaus also draws on other types of consolatory letters, such as Cicero's
consolation to Ligarius concerning his political difficulties (*Fam.* VI, 13),
a *consolatoria* for illness by Seneca, Jerome's (or ps.-Jerome's) letters *Ad
virginem in exilium missam* and *Ad Oceanum de ferendis opprobriis hortatoria*.[31]

In the tradition of Cicero, Nicolaus couches his treatise in a clinical
framework. In his prefatory statement he says,

> ... when we professed the art of curing souls I decided that it was
> required of us — as it is of physicians of bodies — to hand down cer-
> tain general methods of healing, but to leave the particular [methods]
> and those which can occur to [any] diligent person, to the prudence
> of the doctor.[32]

Soon afterwards, he defines the tripartite scope of his healing manual:

> It is expedient for the ideal consoler to know three things: first, how
> depressed are those who stand in need of consolation; then, from
> which persons in particular they are desiring it [i.e., what is the con-
> dition of the persons in need of consolation]; thirdly, in what way
> the duty of consolation should be taken up and what matters should
> be pursued.[33]

30. No. 40 in the collection of letters doubtfully attributed to Jerome in *PL* 30.
31. No.s 4 and 41 in *PL* 30. This list is not meant to be exhaustive; the treatise may well
draw on works by these and other authors.
32. V, f. 3v: "Qua in re [*add. supra*; nobis ergo *canc.*], quando curandorum animorum artem
professi sumus, nobis [*add. supra*] veluti corporum medicis faciendum statui generales quasdam
ac praecipuas medendi rationes tradere, particulares vero et quae sedulo accidere possunt, prudentiae medici relinquere, presertim cum ipsa ex traditis principiis per se facile [*add. supra*; assequi
canc.] percipi poterunt."
33. V, f. 3v: "Consolatori optimo tria cognoscere expedit: primum qualiter affecti sint qui consolatione indigent, deinde a quibus personis illam precipue expetunt, tertio loco [*add. supra*; vero
canc.] qua ratione consolandi officium sit suscipiendum et quibus exequendum rebus." On ff. 3v–4r,
Nicolaus presents his definition of consolation: "Proinde primum quid ipsa sit consolatio videa-
mus: est igitur consolatio (quatenus ad propositum negotium spectat) amicis dictis vel factis moerentis
animi refocillatio quaedam."

Nicolaus then proceeds with what is truly a *summa* for consolers. Unlike a *summa* for confessors, however, the intended audience is general rather than clerical. Every aspect of consolation is treated. Drawing on the *Tusculans*, Book III, he begins with a detailed portrait of the nature and dangers of grief and *aegritudo*.[34] One such chapter, the *Quae nocumenta afferat aegritudo*, reveals how he combines Christian morality, medical science and his literary study to gain psychological insight. Nicolaus opens with the scriptural citation that "tristitia viri nocet cordi" (Prov. 25:20), and then discusses how the grieving mind can afflict the body with, among other things, the melancholy humor. Citing Ovid's description (*Ex Ponto* I) of his own sadness which caused a loss of appetite and sleep, he lists the medical cures of sleep, wine, and hot baths, arguing that Augustine availed himself of these remedies in his time of grief over his mother's death (*Confessions*, Book IX).[35]

Nicolaus next turns to the problems of who best can receive solace and who best can administer it. In his chapter *Qui facilius et qui minus facile consolationem admittunt*, he betrays the eye of the medieval casuist in his careful delineation of those who are receptive to solace and those who are not. "For everyone is not equally afflicted by this grief; there is variation with respect to age, condition, the times, and the evils suffered. Some indeed are quickly relieved, others more slowly, others never."[36] Most receptive to solace are youths and women; not receptive are those who are old, those who depend too much on earthly goods, and those who are irreligious.[37] For these difficult cases, Nicolaus presents separate

34. Nicolaus draws on the panorama of consolatory theory (of such figures as Cleanthes, Epicurus, and Chrysippus) presented in *Tusculans* III in his chapter *Quomodo et quibus rationibus sit consolandum*. Here also, like Cicero, he presents the body-soul analogy concerning healing (V, f. 22r–v): "Quamobrem huius aegritudinis curatori perinde atque prudenti medico faciendum est qui non bene cognitum morbum vario farmaco vel cataplasmate tentat diversisque medelis experitur, nec eorum quae conducere putat intentatum quicquam relinquit. Nititurque precipue scitus medicus morbum tollere funditus, aut si nequit, dolorem sedare laborat aut saltem minuere, et, si neque id datur comprimere, eum curat ne in amplius manas sana membra valeat vitiare. Divertere quoque minus noxiis itineribus conatur. His rationibus omnis medicorum ars procedit, quarum et medico animae nulla prorsus omittenda est."

35. See V, ff. 4v–5r.

36. V, f. 9r: "Neque enim omnes aequaliter hac aegritudine afficiuntur, sed pro varietate aetatum personarum temporum ac malorum, et alii quidem levantur celerius, alii tardius, alii vero numquam. Eorum autem animi precipue refocillantur miseriaque levantur qui sunt ad laetitiam voluptatemque proniores. Quales imprimis sunt iuvenes . . ."

37. For instance, concerning the irreligious and the pious, Nicolaus suggests (V, f. 11r): "Viri quoque irreligiosi et qui de providentia iustitiaque dei non recte sentiunt et truces nimium ac melan-

chapters of antidotes, entitled *Antidotum senum et pusillanimorum, Antidotum illorum qui rebus terrenis nimium sunt dediti, Antidotum irreligiosorum*.[38]

In his discussion of those most suited to administer solace (in the chapter *Qui homines consolandis aliis sint idonei*) Nicolaus begins by citing from Servius Sulpicius the notion that consolation is to be given by one's *propinqui* and *familiares*.[39] He then makes an interesting and subtle psychological point concerning children's natural potential to be the most effective consolers:

> Therefore friends, parents, children, or persons connected by some other necessity are best able to console, and among these the consolation of children is the most valuable, especially adolescents or little ones, if it ever chance that some of them should express themselves rather appropriately, or weep with their parent: the former is a great source of delight to parents; the latter, after it is enjoyed, constrains the parents through paternal piety to restrain themselves, lest they should cause pain or suffering to their children whom they dearly love. For this same reason the consolation of a wife or beloved friend avails greatly.[40]

Of course he also cites the efficacy of the consolation given by the wise

colici solatium accipere nesciunt, quoniam illi quidem iniuste se afflictos putant . . . At vero homines pii et deum metuentes, quoniam ea quibus premuntur [incommodis *canc.*] omnipotentis iudicio destinata recte arbitrantur, ut Job, Thobias et alii sanctorum, plerique aequo animo ferunt et consolationem lubentes amplectantur."

38. This section on the varying receptivity of people to solace and on the cure of difficult cases seems to reflect the influence of the confessional. This is hard to establish with certainty, however, since ancient rhetorical theory also addressed itself to the problem of "circumstance." It is often difficult to separate completely the rhetorical and confessional traditions, as ancient theories of "circumstance" had some impact on the notion of the "circumstances" of sin in the confessional. See D.W. Robertson, "A Note on the Classical Origin of 'Circumstance' in the Medieval Confessional," *Studies in Philology*, 43 (1946): 6–14; Tentler, 116–118.

39. V, f. 20r: "Quod optime intelligens, Servius Sulpitius scribit ad Ciceronem oportere eos per quos consolationis munus obeundum sit propinquos esse ac familiares." See Sulpitius' letter to Cicero in *Fam.* IV, 5.

40. V, f. 20r–v: "Valent ergo ad consolandum amici, parentes, filii, aut alia quavis necessitudine coniuncti, inter quos consolatio filiorum est precipua, et presertim adulescentium vel parvulorum, si quando contigit ut quipiam aptius proferant aut genitori collacriment, quorum altero parentes maxime delectantur, altero post delectationem ob pietatem paternam stringuntur, seseque cohibent ne filiis quos tenere diligunt dolorem iniciant aut eos cruciari cernant. Eadem hac ratione et uxoris amicaeque nimium dilectae consolatio egregie valet."

and pious whose words carry the meaningful weight of authority.[41] And as a highly rhetorical and philosophical treatise, the *De consolatione* is directed chiefly to the therapeutic techniques of the learned friend, the epistolary consoler, and the funeral orator.

In his treatment of the craft of consoling, Nicolaus truly creates a science. Presenting solace at the proper time; carefully approaching those in deep grief; assuring the bereaved first of one's friendship with him or her; using caution, skill, and humility in consoling the wise:[42] all these concerns are given systematic analysis. Time and again, Nicolaus' method is based on the use of ancient and patristic sources to illustrate or to construct various therapeutic methods, as in the case of the section *Quomodo aggrediendi sunt graviores aegritudines*, where he uses selections from Seneca's consolatory epistle to Lucilius (*Ad. Luc.* 63) to present the subtle technique of effectively approaching those who are in very serious grief. In formulating his principles Nicolaus shows considerable breadth in his sources. For instance, in his chapter *De tempore consolandi* he draws, among other sources, on theories of timely solace and psychological medicine in Cicero (*Tusculans* III, xxxi, 76) and in Ovid (*De remediis amoris*, 119-134), and he cites the case of Job whose consolers made no attempt to console his vehement grief for an entire week (Job 2:13).[43]

After these sections on the nature of the grief-stricken, consolers, and the administering of solace, the treatise turns to its principal subject: consolatory *topoi*, remedies, and techniques. Nicolaus presents eleven sets of *loci* which as a whole attempt to embrace almost every conceivable philosophical, emotional, and theological argument or technique of consolation. He collects all of the many traditional commonplaces such as the arguments concerning the inevitability and universality of death, the shortness and misery of life, the varieties of fortune, the benefits of death.[44] The mixture of classical and Christian sources reveals Nicolaus

41. V, f. 20v.
42. For instance, in consoling prudent men (V, f. 12v): "In consolandis gravioribus ac prudentioribus viris ut et nostri pudoris et eorum auctoritatis curemus [curamus *ms.*] rationem habere, et non illis nos praeceptores aut doctores exhibeamus, ne nostrum consilium sapientiae eorum preferre videamur, verum quicquid vel dicere vel facere voluerimus verecundius agere ac ipsorum dignitatem in omnibus conservare. Ita fiet ut et impudentiae notam pulchre effugiamus et apud eos non minus oratione quam benivolentia valeamus."
43. See V, ff. 24r–25r.
44. See Appendix, below.

as a true Christian humanist. The chapter *De bono mortis*, for instance, draws on Plato in addition to citing biblical figures and Christian martyrs. The *Locus a contrario et de incommodis vitae* contains a long citation from Augustine's lament on the human condition in the *De civitate Dei* (XXII, 22) — the same vision of human misery used by Petrarch in his *De otio religioso*[45] —; it also cites the ancient philosopher Hegesias' lost lamentation of earthly life. Sometimes the *De consolatione* presents commonplaces that are more fully Christian in nature. For instance, in the second set of *loci* there is a *Locus ab iusto* which draws principally on biblical examples and religious arguments to propose that one should see one's misfortunes as just. Nicolaus quotes an extensive passage from Isidore's *Synonyma* (I, 32–37) that deals with the divine plan and justice in the realm of human adversity. Such sections reveal how Nicolaus draws upon particular Christian assumptions about the purpose of human adversity. That is, notions of divine retribution, tribulations of the just, and redemptive suffering all reveal a new perspective concerning the divine purpose and value of suffering, a perspective not found in classical thought. It is just such notions as these — along with the Christian emphasis on Christ's Passion, on the martyrs' suffering, on other-worldly beatitude — which help to account for the absence in Christian thought of a continuous and fully developed tradition of consolation comparable to that of Greco-Roman antiquity.[46]

Many of Nicolaus' consolatory *topoi* seem to reflect the Stoic belief that evil does not consist in circumstances themselves, but in one's attitude toward them. Thus in the first set of commonplaces he presents arguments dealing with the inevitable evils of life and the benefits of death. It is in this set of *topoi* and within this same conceptual framework that Nicolaus briefly expands his perspectives from death to other problems of poverty, power, and the desire for fame.[47] In some of his chapters he

---

45. See *Opere latine di Francesco Petrarca*, 2 vols., ed. A. Bufano (Turin, 1975), 1:685.

46. It seems fair to say that consolatory genres and perspectives were generally less prominent in Christian than in classical thought. In the post-classical era, consolatory writings appear more commonly in the patristic, Renaissance, and early modern periods (generally, I believe, as a result of humanistic influences) and less commonly in the medieval period. There are only a few consolatory writings of a religious character from the medieval period (e.g., Lawrence of Durham's *Consolatio de morte amici*, Vincent of Beauvais' *Tractatus consolatorius ad Ludovicum IX regem de obitu filii*, Meister Eckhart's *Buch der goettlichen Troestung* — see von Moos).

47. As he had done for death in the *Locus a contrario et de incommodis vitae*, Nicolaus presents

also recommends the Cyrenaic practice of *praemeditatio*: the practice of fore-seeing all possible adversities in human life.[48]

One set of *loci* deals exclusively with the funeral oration, thus suggest-ing that one function of the manual was to provide help with more pub-lic forms of solace. The *De sex locis funebribus* presents the rhetorical *topoi* appropriate for funerals, such as the *Loci ab operibus suis, a genere mortis, a causa mortis*, and others. Presumably these are the commonplaces Nicolaus himself used later in his *Oratio in funere Petri*.

In other sets of commonplaces Nicolaus touches on an encyclopedic range of consolatory techniques and remedies. One set deals with the various moral or rhetorical methods for moving someone to equanimity: the con-soler can appeal to the grieving person's sense of shame concerning his grief or his fear of its repercussions; he can exhort the aggrieved to vir-tue;[49] he can use the power of *exempla*. One section of the treatise deals with *aegritudinis diversio* by which ". . . animum a moerore ad aliam curam studiumve aut cogitationem voluptuosam evocamus vel traducimus."[50] It includes chapters on various social, psychological, and behavioral reme-dies such as the compassion of friends, lamentation, study, a pleasant deed or saying, the consideration of the good features of one's life, the hope of future good. In those chapters dealing with *voluptuosa* thought or ac-tivity, we can see Nicolaus' use of the Epicurean approach to consola-tion.[51] Most interesting in this final section of the treatise is the *Locus a lamentatione*, where Nicolaus presents a lengthy argument concerning the therapeutic power of lamentation and emotional expression.[52] Among other things, he cites the notion of cathartic weeping and writing found in Ovid's thought and example. He quotes, for instance, Ovid's lines:

consolation for the concerns of poverty, weakness, and obscurity *a contrario* by discounting the life of wealth, power, and fame.

48. V, ff. 99v–102r. Cf. *Tusculans*, III.

49. In the *Locus a virtute* Nicolaus makes an interesting use of *Tusculans*, Book II, by adapting one of Cicero's arguments concerning physical *dolor* to the problem of mental grief. For other *loci* in this set see the Appendix.

50. V, f. 109r. This section of the treatise is entitled the *Quinta ratio consolandi* and is the final *ratio*.

51. Cf. *Tusculans*, Book III.

52. The inclusion of lamentation in this section may be due only to the fact that Nicolaus sees this section as a collection of general psychological remedies, a surmise which may explain as well his inclusion of a section on compassion, for example. But he may have associated lamentation with Epicurean psychology. Certainly, he develops the theme of the "voluptuous" aspects of ex-pressing sorrow.

Fleque meos casus: et quaedam flere voluptas;
Expletur lacrimis egeriturque dolor.[53]
(*Tristia* IV, iii, 37–38)
("Weep for my mischances: and weeping is a kind of pleasure;
grief is filled up and overflows through tears".)

and observes that "he [Ovid] himself put into practice this advice and wept
over his calamities in poetry." Besides presenting this poetic notion of
voluptas dolendi, he goes on to give an almost clinical explanation of the
phenomenon of lamentation. He suggests that *maeror* has a two-fold seat:
one in the body (in the form of the melancholic humor) and another in
the mind.[54] He says that some thinkers theorize that the physical melancholy is purged by weeping. Then, more importantly, he presents a theory as to why the mental *maeror* is also cured by weeping. I believe that
Nicolaus considered this discussion noteworthy, because it is one of the
sections of V that has special markings in the margins; perhaps he considered his argument somewhat unique.[55] He enumerates three reasons why
weeping is therapeutic: it entails the bitter-sweet recollection of past goods;
it releases and dissipates a painful emotion which, pent up, tears at the
mind; it encourages people to indulge in their own most suitable type
of behavior (such as solitude, asceticism, doleful writings). Thus Nicolaus
fully systematizes the notion of therapeutic lamentation.[56]

53. V, f. 111v, which reads *Flere* for the correct reading *Fleque* preserved in Vat. lat. 5139, f. 99r.
54. V, f. 112r: ". . . cum maeror duplicem habeat sedem, unam in corpore et in animo alteram,
in corpore melancoliae humorem, qui ut phisici docent precipuus in cerebro est, in animo vero
fantasiam aut opinionem malorum quibus se oppressum cernit."
55. Not only is this section bracketed but also the marginal notations, which appear to be in
Nicolaus' hand, identify the three arguments by number.
56. V, ff. 112r–113r: "(Dicit) lamentationibus et querelis opinionem malorum opido extenuari:
cuius multiplex causa est, sed precipua quoniam in lamentatione pergit homo enumerando praeterita
bona, quorum sicut possessio fuit iocunda, ita et recordatio. Quo fit ut omnis lamentatio veluti
et ira admixtam habeat cum dolore voluptatem. Hinc venit ut homo, si vel solus apud se ipsum
queratur, levetur miseria, sed multo melius si apud alium fuerit lamentatus, illa de causa quam
superius assignavimus. Levant quoque questus dolorem et ista ratione, quia animus dum continet
intra se mali spetiem, totus circa illam occupatur et eam [*add. supra*; illam *canc.*] intuendo diutius,
vehementius affligitur et cruciatur. Cum vero plorat aut querelas fundit, animus ad exteriora ex-
panditur et ab illa urente cura quodammodo se non parva ex parte avertit. Et rursum lamentationibus mitigatur aegritudo, quoniam omnis lamentatio cum voluptate est ex eo, quod homo
malis honeratus lachrimando et querendo putat convenientia sibi obire munera. Omni vero eo
quod quis⟨que⟩ sibi conveniens ducit oblectari necesse est [unumquemque *canc.*]. Unde aliquos
maerentes delectant solitudines, ut apud Homerum Bellorophontem, apud Virgilium vero Latini
uxorem; alii se sponte cruciatibus vel doloribus deputant, ut ille Terentianus Demea; alii nec [nul-

This chapter must be read in the context of earlier dictaminal and humanistic discussions of the same theme. Boncompagno treated the topic in his *Rhetorica antiqua* I, 25 (*De consolationibus*). He has sections on the legitimacy of tears and on the problems of weeping too much or not at all. There are some fairly detailed physiological and psychological observations in these sections. For instance, he warns that excessive weeping can impair the vision by blocking the optic nerve, and he argues that it is foolish "to weep excessively because through immoderate grief many are made odious to God, until sensation is lost and human bodies are dessicated".[57] But he also warns of the danger to those who are unable to weep, suggesting that "when tears are kept inside, the soul is burdened with an indescribable weight and its actions are confused, whence in either case man is accustomed to be easily undone".[58] Later, in Petrarch, one finds a profound exploration into the realm of despair and grief. The initial psychological context for Petrarch's interest in sorrow is his lovesickness, as seen in his *Rime* in such expressions as "Pascomi di dolore" (*Rime*, CXXXIV, 12).[59] But it also extended into other areas of experience. In his letters dealing with bereavement he admits having enjoyed the pleasures of grief. In *Seniles* III, 1, writing to Boccaccio with a lament for the deaths of two friends, he says, "I in truth feed upon my evils with a certain savage pleasure, and what had been sighs are now victuals; and there was realized in me that saying of David that 'tears were my bread by day and by night' [Ps. 61] or that saying of Ovid, 'care, mental anguish, and tears were nourishment' " [*Metamorphoses*, X, 75].[60] In mourning, as in lovesickness, Petrarch followed a regimen of cathartic weeping and writing. The symptoms of a *voluptas dolendi* are also found

lis *canc.*] voluptatibus nec ullis ornamentis uti volunt, quoniam illa in tantis malis putant sibi minime convenire . . ." And later (f. 113v): "Ovidius quoque ait, 'Flebilis ut noster status est, ita flebile carmen / Materiae scripto conveniente suae' [*Tristia* V, i, 5–6]".

57. For the Latin text, see von Moos, 3:217.

58. *Ibid.*

59. See A. Bobbio, "Seneca e la formazione spirituale e culturale del Petrarca," *La Bibliofilia*, 43 (1941): 246–247; *Opere latine di Francesco Petrarca*, ed. A. Bufano, 1:142, no. 69 and 196, no. 51. For other scholarship on Petrarch's notion of *voluptas dolendi*, see R. Kuhn, *The Demon of Noontide: Ennui in Western Literature* (Princeton, 1974), 71–75; F. Rico, *Vida u obra de Petrarca*, (Padua, 1974), 1:203–204. On the topic of *flendi voluptas*, see von Moos, 3:55–57.

60. Petrarch, *Opera omnia* (Basel, 1554), 847: ". . . ego vero malis meis pascor, voluptate quadam effera, et qui fuerunt gemitus cibi sunt, impletumque est in me seu Davidicum illud, 'Fuerunt mihi lachrymae meae panes die ac nocte,' sive illud Ovidianum, 'Cura dolorque animi, lachrymaeque alimenta fuere.' "

in Petrarch's descriptions of the malady of *accidia-aegritudo* in the *Secretum*, Book II, and in his discussion of *miseria-tristitia* in the *De remediis* (II, 93). After Petrarch, various other humanists discuss the ineluctability of emotion in a time of bereavement. In letters of 1400–1401 to Francesco Zabarella discussing the loss of two sons, the Florentine chancellor Coluccio Salutati presents an attack on dispassionate Stoicism in which he proclaims the legitimacy of grief. In the fall of 1401 the humanist Giovanni Conversino da Ravenna wrote a self-consolatory dialogue on the loss of a son (*De consolatione in obitu filii*) in which he defends the naturalness of emotion and asserts the salutary benefits of weeping. And in 1438 Giannozzo Manetti's *Dialogus consolatorius* on the death of his son considerably expands Salutati's attack on Stoic *apatheia*, arguing at length for the legitimacy of emotion.[61] It is difficult to know which, if any, of these writings Nicolaus knew. But whatever influences may have been involved, Nicolaus' *Locus a lamentatione* reveals another instance of the substantive interest in the psychology of sorrow that can be found in dictaminal and humanist writings. In his effort to systematize the laws of lamentation, Nicolaus displays an interesting range in his sources and arguments: he unites literary sensibilities of *voluptas dolendi*, medical notions of melancholy, psychological observations concerning the emotional and behavioral benefits of expressing sorrow.[62] It is perhaps one of the most important specific instances of Nicolaus' contribution to moral thought and psychological theory.

---

61. For Salutati's letters and Conversini's and Manetti's dialogues, see note 2 above. See also my "Art of Mourning."

62. In discussing the "pleasant" features of sorrow, Nicolaus thus seems to provide a fairly well-developed explanation of the Epicurean conception of sorrow, drawing upon such notions of *voluptuosa* sorrow as those discussed in Seneca and Petrarch (see Bobbio, 246–7). At the same time he discusses the humoral concept of melancholy. Though Petrarch drew together notions of sweet sorrow, *aegritudo*, and Christian *accidia*, he avoided the concept of melancholy; in doing so, he is perhaps following Cicero, who in the *Tusculans* for the most part discounts the humoral notion of melancholy as a basis for psychological theory. In scholastic writings the humors (including melancholy) were sometimes cited in the discussion of sins such as *accidia*. See S. Wenzel, *The Sin of Sloth: Acedia in Medieval Thought and Literature* (Chapel Hill, 1967), 59, 173–174, 186, 191–194. Boncompagno also treats melancholy in his *Rhetorica antiqua*, I, 25. As some scholars argue, melancholy becomes more popular as a sensibility beginning with late medieval poetry and it spreads into general parlance and psychological discussion. In the Elizabethan period there is a dramatic interest in the malady, the culmination of that interest being Robert Burton's *Anatomy of Melancholy* (1621). See R. Klibansky, E. Panofsky, and F. Saxl, *Saturn and Melancholy: Studies in the History of Natural Philosophy, Religion, and Art* (New York, 1964). Nicolaus' interest in weeping should be placed within the general context of the developing interest in emotion, grief, and melancholy which appears in Renaissance and early modern thought.

Finally, it is important to discuss briefly Nicolaus' final set of consola-tory *topoi*: those that are aimed at the "most wise and religious men." The first is the thoroughly Christian *Dominicae passionis devota recordatio* in which Nicolaus presents a meditation on the life and passion of Christ. Against His suffering, all human tribulation is as nothing; a pious medi-tation on the passion ". . . so lightens our mind from all its distresses that in the place of sadness it brings a marvelous sweetness and restores and strengthens the whole mind."[63] Though it is not identified as a source, some of this chapter seems to be drawn from the letter *Ad Oceanum de ferendis opprobriis hortatoria* attributed to Jerome. The second *topos*, the *Lo-cus a recordatione mortis*, draws on classical and Christian notions of the meditation on death, and includes a lengthy citation from Isidore's *Syn-onyma* (I, 47–50). Like the *loci a iusto, a voluntate divina* and *ab utili*, these last commonplaces articulate the particular Christian contribution to the problem of consolation. It is interesting that this set of *loci* for wise and pious men is preceded by a rather cynical group of topics, dealing with revenge and similar matters, which Nicolaus suggests is generally unsuit-ed for wise and religious people.[64] He thus ministers counsel to two ex-tremes. Like a good rhetorician, Nicolaus addresses his manual to a whole spectrum of people—to the pusillanimous, impious, worldly, and venge-ful; to the wise and pious; and to the array of people who fall in between.

Neither as humanist nor religious thinker can Nicolaus be said to be a major figure in Renaissance thought. There is no evidence that his *De consolatione* or any of his other writings had any significant impact. Yet his consolation manual is an historically noteworthy and revealing work not only because it exemplifies the Renaissance interest in consolation, but also because it represents an imaginative contribution to the general history of the cure of souls. In the first place, it summarizes the Renais-sance treatment of the problem of consolation. Earlier humanists had emu-lated other consolatory and remedial genres: the consolatory letter, the

63. V, f. 130r: "Harum atque similium rerum pia reputatio, credite mihi, ita animum nostrum omnibus levat angoribus ut loco tristitiae mirificam inducat suavitatem totumque recreet ac con-firmet."
64. This set is entitled *De tribus locis qui a persona accipiuntur inimici.* See the Appendix for sub-headings.

oration, the dialogue, the remedy book. Works such as Johannes von Dambach's *Consolatio theologiae* or Petrarch's *De remediis* provided comprehensive collections of consolatory topics. But Nicolaus' treatise attempts to
systematize fully the office of consolation by offering advice on general
therapeutic problems, by gathering myriad rhetorical *topoi*, and by recom-
mending various psychological remedies. Expanding and modernizing
Cicero's *Tusculans*, Nicolaus provides a guide-book to help others better
fulfill the moral and spiritual *officium consolandi*. As a comprehensive manual,
Nicolaus' discussion surpasses what can be found extant from ancient and
patristic writers or from Nicolaus' more recent dictaminal and humanist
predecessors. Culling precepts from ancient and patristic authors, he reifies
or expands a number of consolatory issues: he deals with the nature of
despair, the varying temperaments of the grief-stricken, the varying capacities of consolers; he presents theories about curing particular cases;
he codifies the therapeutic benefits of time, compassion, and (here with
a certain originality) of lamentation; he cites the techniques of friendly
chiding, of exhortation to virtue, of the use of *exempla*; he offers *solacia*
and remedies that range from the mundane (pleasant distractions) to the
sublime (the consideration of divine providence and the sufferings of Christ).
His sources include consolatory letters, more general consolatory and psychological literature, and an array of other literary, philosophical, and religious writings. Joining classical and Christian sources and perspectives,
the *De consolatione* is the complete guide for the Quattrocento humanist
and Christian.

   Nicolaus' treatise fills an important gap in the history of moral, rhetorical and spiritual care. Though there were many ancient consolatory writings, only Book III of the *Tusculan Disputations* survived to provide the
basis for a manual of consolation. Likewise, in patristic thought, though
there were numerous instances of consolatory letters, dialogues, and orations, there was no systematic manual to which the consoler could turn.
The literature of pastoral care did not offer a comprehensive manual for
consoling. In examining Ambrose's *De officiis ministrorum*, Chrysostom's
De sacerdotio, Gregory the Great's *Regula pastoralis* or Isidore of Seville's
De ecclesiasticis officiis, one does not find a fully developed and detailed program of the consolatory office, but only some general notions of the obligation to comfort the afflicted and grieving.[65] Gregory's *Regula pastoralis*

---

65. For instance, Chrysostom's *De sacerdotio* cites the pastor's responsibility "to visit the sick,

comes closest to providing a manual of "therapeutic rhetoric": the entire third book consists of admonitions and exhortations for a variety of moral and circumstantial conditions; still, the emphasis is moral and corrective rather than consolatory. The manuals of *ars dictaminis* provide some guidelines for consolatory rhetoric, and, in the case of Boncompagno's *Rhetorica antiqua*, one can find some general treatment of the problem of grief and consolation. But these dictaminal manuals lack the theoretical scope, the range of therapeutic considerations, the sense of the autonomy of the consolatory genre, and the humanistic content found in Nicolaus' manual. In sum, by composing a comprehensive manual Nicolaus can be said to have filled a void found in ancient, patristic, and medieval literature.

We do not know which, if any, other major Renaissance consolatory writings Nicolaus knew—works such as Dambach's *Consolatio theologiae*, Petrarch's *De remediis*, Manetti's *Dialogus consolatorius*, Filelfo's *Oratio consolatoria ad Marcellum*, Matteo Bosso's *De tolerandis adversis*. What is clear, however, is that in studying and emulating the consolatory models of ancient and patristic writers, he shares a concern found in numerous Renaissance humanists. This Trecento and Quattrocento humanist interest in consolation will continue into the sixteenth century and the early modern period, both in Italy and across the Alps.[66] It is plausible to argue that the Renaissance humanists' exploration into the territory of consolation serves an important function in the history of the pastoral cure of souls. The relative paucity of medieval pastoral works dealing with consolation is remedied by the spate of Renaissance and early modern writings, both lay and clerical. It is interesting that, particularly by the early modern period, pastoral writings reveal a greater sense of balance between the two faces of human despair than that which was found in medieval thought: *homo lugens* gradually achieves a greater prominence alongside his coun-

---

console the grieving, exhort the sluggish, aid the afflicted" (Greek text in *PG*, 48:685). For an analysis of the place of Gregory's *Regula pastoralis* in the medieval rhetorical tradition of preaching, see J. J. Murphy, *Rhetoric in the Middle Ages*, 292–297.

66. To name but a few works: in sixteenth-century Italy one can cite Girolamo Cardano's *De consolatione* and *De utilitate ex adversis capienda* (see note 2, above); Antonio Ricci's *Consolatione della morte* (Ferrara, 1564). Across the Alps, consolatory writings appear from the hands of three prominent figures: Erasmus' *Declamatio de morte* (note 23, above); Luther's *Tessaradecas consolatoria pro laborantibus et onerantis*, and Thomas More's *A Dialoge of Comfort Agaynst Trybulacion*. There is a wealth of consolatory writings and translations in the sixteenth and seventeenth centuries which cannot be listed here; see B. Langston, *Tudor Books of Consolation* (Ph.D diss., University of North Carolina, 1940) which lists about seventy works on consolation published between 1478 and 1600.

terpart *homo peccans*. In the fourteenth century this could be seen in Dambach's *Consolatio theologiae*, which dealt substantively with adversity in addition to treating the problems of conscience.[67] In seventeenth–century pastoral manuals this new sense of balance is striking. For instance, the Anglican divine Joseph Hall composed a treatise entitled *Heaven Upon Earth, or, Of True Peace and Tranquillitie of Minde* (1606). Using the Stoic conception of tranquillity, Hall discussed the problems of conscience and sin as well as those of misfortune, at one point making reference to Petrarch's *De remediis*.[68] John Downame's *Consolations for the Afflicted, or the Third Part of the Christian Warfare* (1613), provided a highly humanistic treatment of pain and affliction.[69] The pastor Martin Day published a *Meditations of Consolation* (in his larger work, *Monument of Mortality*, published in 1630) which dealt with "worldly" problems (such as hardship, loss of honor, death of friends, sickness, aging) and then treated "divine" problems such as bad conscience and fear of judgment.[70] In some cases such manuals drew on classical solace; in some cases they criticized it, hoping to replace "pagan" solutions with spiritual remedies; in some cases they did both. In a word, sometimes harvesting classical consolation and sometimes competing with it, early modern pastoral care was inspired by humanist thought to become more responsive to the problems of grief and sorrow.[71]

67. See Auer, *passim*; Tentler, 114, 159.

68. Joseph Hall, *Heaven Upon Earth* and *Characters of Vertues and Vices*, ed. R. Kirk (Rutgers, 1948), 104.

69. Downame quotes extensively from Seneca's moral letters as well as from his *Consolatio ad Marciam* and *De providentia*; he also cites Plutarch's *De tranquillitate animi*, ps.-Plutarch's *Consolatio ad Apollonium*, and various patristic sources, such as the treatises on patience by Cyprian, Chrysostom, and Tertullian.

70. It is worth pointing out that in his *On Comfortable Considerations for the Sicke* (1621), also later included in the 1630 *Monument of Mortality*, Day expressed an awareness of the need for reviving the role of mutual consolation. Referring to the earlier Christian era of Tertullian and Eusebius he says, "So fervent, at those dayes, was the love towards God and their neighbors (which is now waxen cold) in the mindes of Christians, and that true Christian charitie, whose propertie is (as Saint *Paul* saith) to rejoyce with them that rejoyce, to weepe with them that weepe." (*On Comfortable Considerations for the Sicke*, p. 2, in *Monument of Mortality* [London, 1630]).

71. Hall, Day, and Downame all turn to classical thought. But notwithstanding Day's and Downame's use of classical sources, they also sometimes criticize them as erroneous or incomplete. Other works which reveal a sense of competition with classical consolation include William Gilbert's *Architectonice consolationis or the Art of Building Comfort* (1640), which challenges the Stoic *consolatio* for bereavement; in France, Charles Drelincourt's *Les consolations de l'âme fidèle contre les frayeurs de la mort* (1651) attempts to replace inadequate Stoic consolations for dying with Christian remedies. The sense of competition can also be seen in works other than pastoral handbooks: the first chapter of More's *Dialoge of Comfort* is entitled *That the comfortes devised by the old paynim*

Finally, though these areas cannot be explored here with the attention they deserve, there are some larger cultural and social questions that can be asked of Renaissance consolation. The writing, translating, printing, and reading of consolation books commands a prominent place in the Renaissance and early modern periods. As a result, one might expect changes in certain private and social forms of consolation. First, the rise of literacy, the development of printing, and the spread of consolatory literature would inevitably generate a rise in private readings. Such readings, along with public consolatory oratory and, possibly, private consolatory conversation, could signify a shift in the therapeutic medium employed in European psychological and spiritual thought and practice: a shift from a predominately sacramental medium to a more rhetorical one. That is, the medieval paradigm of prayer, priestly administration, and liturgy is being complemented, or even partially replaced, by texts, by readings—by a "logotherapy," the salvific persuasion of classical and divine words.[72] Ritual yields to rhetoric. Both lay and pastoral writers attempt to make available a body of such consolatory readings. A second matter that needs further study concerns the office of consoling. Does a work such as Nicolaus' De consolatione in any way reflect the development of a new social sensibility, a greater awareness that the duty to console friends and loved ones is an important responsibility? The classical moral tradition articulated the duty of the friend and rhetor to provide solace. So, too, Christian thought called for compassion towards others, and, in Paul's words, for the charitable duty to "rejoice with those that rejoice, and to weep with those that weep" (Romans 12:15).[73] Perhaps both clergy and laity alike seek to revitalize this social office. In examining the lay forms of consolation, a number of problems could be usefully pursued. For instance, it could be instructive to consider the medieval, Renaissance, and early modern literature of consolation in the larger historical context of developments in theories of friendship, in letter-writing,

philosophers were insufficient and the cause wherefore (edited by L. L. Martz and F. Manley as volume 12 of The Complete Works of Thomas More, [New Haven, 1976]). Nicolaus' treatise, on the other hand, shows no sense of alienation from the classical tradition of consolation; it is an ideal fusion of secular and religious solace.

72. On logotherapy, see P. Laín Entralgo, The Therapy of the Word in Classical Antiquity, trs. L. Rather and J. Sharp (New Haven, 1970); also M. O'Rourke Boyle, "Erasmus' Prescription for Henry VIII: Logotherapy," RQ, 31 (1978): 161–172.

73. See note 70 above.

in the social function of rhetoric, in funerary custom and oratory, in the provenance and lay function of the *ars moriendi* manuals.[74]

As a worthy rhetorical charge and as a valuable, practical type of therapeutic wisdom, consolation is an important part of the humanist revival of eloquence and moral philosophy. Though little-known, Nicolaus' *De consolatione* sheds light on the nature of that revival. It represents the long-needed attempt to systematize, once and for all, the moral, rhetorical, and spiritual office of consoling. In terms of its structure, sources, and themes, the treatise deserves more attention as a revealing document in the history of Renaissance humanism, in the history of *mentalité* and psychological sensibility, in the general history of consolation and the cure of souls.

GEORGE W. McCLURE

---

74. The connection between consolatory letter-writing and the theory of friendship needs to be more fully developed, beginning with twelfth-century writers such as Bernard of Clairvaux, Aelred of Rielvaux, and Peter of Blois, and continuing into the early modern period. It would be interesting to consider the role played by manuals of the *ars moriendi* in the area of lay consolation. As J. T. McNeill argues, the profusion of these manuals is some indication of the laicization of psychological and spiritual care. Such manuals were generally intended to be used by lay people when clergy were unavailable to guide the dying person. It is true that this lay aspect of the tradition was due to a lack of pastors in times of epidemic, but the result may have been a greater lay interest in the role of offering comfort and guidance. On the *ars moriendi*, see J. T. McNeill, *History of the Cure of Souls*, 157–162; Sr. M. C. O'Connor, *The Art of Dying Well* (New York, 1942) and, more recently, N. L. Beaty, *The Craft of Dying: A Study in the Literary Tradition of the Ars Moriendi* (New Haven, 1970).

APPENDIX

The following appendix lists the section and chapter headings of Nicolaus Modrus-siensis' *De consolatione* as they appear in V. MS Vat. lat. 5139 presents only minor variations which have not been recorded. The "ae" diphthong is inconsistently indicated in V; here, as in the footnotes above I have transcribed the text exactly as it appears in the MS.

NICOLAI EPISCOPI MODRVSIENSIS AD DOMINVM MARCVM VICEN-TINVM PRAESVLEM LIBER DE CONSOLATIONE FOELICITER INCIPIT.

⟨LIBER PRIMVS⟩
—Qualiter affecti sunt qui consolatione egent
—Que nocumenta afferat egritudo
—Quibus incommodis aegritudo afficiat animum
—Qui facilius et qui minus facile consolationem admittunt
—Quae propria sunt antidota harum aegritudinum singularium
  —Antidotum senum et pusillanimorum
  —Antidotum illorum qui rebus terrenis nimium sunt dediti
  —Antidotum irreligiosorum
—Qui homines consolandis aliis sint idonei

SECVNDVS LIBER
—Quomodo et quibus rationibus sit consolandum
—De tempore consolandi
—Quomodo aggrediende sunt graviores egritudines
—Egritudo quibus medicaminibus funditus tollitur
  —Primus locus a munere naturae
  —Secundus locus ab universitate
  —Tertius locus a damno
    —De miseria vitae humanae
  —Quartus locus a nocumento
  —Quintus locus ab utili vel commodo
    —De bono mortis
  —Sextus locus a iudicio sapientum

—Septimus locus a contrario et de incommodis vitae
 —Quam mors sit bona
 —Contra avaritiam et de paupertate
 —Contra tyrannidem
 —Contra cupidos laudis
 —Rationes quibus vera bona a falsis discernuntur

LIBER TERTIVS
DE SECVNDA CONSOLANDI RATIONE
—Primus locus a iusto
—Secundus locus a voluntate divina
—Tertius a voluntate maiorum
—Quartus a varietate et lege fortunae
—Quintus locus a conditione humana
—Sextus locus a societate
—Septimus locus a necessitate
—Octavus locus a diligentia
—Nonus locus ab honesto
—Decimus locus ab utili

DE TERTIA CONSOLANDI RATIONE
—Primus locus a tempore debito
—Secundus locus a brevitate temporis
—Tertius locus ab inevitabilitate
—Quartus locus a comparatione alterius mali gravioris
—Quintus locus a non impuni
—Sextus locus a commemoratione peiorum
—De sex locis funebribus
 —Primus locus a re morientis
 —Secundus locus ab operibus defuncti
 —Tertius locus a genere mortis
 —Quartus locus a causa mortis
 —Quintus locus a ratione funeris
 —Sextus locus a loco mortis
—De multis aliis locis ex quibus mali opinio minuitur
 —Quomodo ex collatione boni mali opinio minuitur
 —Secundus locus a discrimine

LIBER QVARTVS
DE QVARTA CONSOLANDI RATIONE
—Primus locus a pudore
—Secundus locus ab exemplo
—Tertius locus a virtute
—Quartus locus a metu
—Quintus locus a ratione inimici

QVINTVS RATIO CONSOLANDI
—Primus locus a compassione
—Secundus locus a lamentatione
—Tertius locus a laudatione
—De propriis locis huius quintae rationis, quorum primus est a studio
    —Secundus locus a faceto dicto et facto
    —Tertius locus a spe futuri boni
    —Quartus locus a munere
    —Quintus locus ab eventu
—De tribus locis qui a persona accipiuntur inimici, quorum primus a vindicta est
    —Secundus locus a criminatione adversarii
    —Tertius locus a frustratione
—De tribus locis sapientum, quorum primus est a recordatione dominicae passionis
    —Secundus locus a cogitatione finis humani
    —Tertius locus a recordatione mortis

PSEUDO–DIONYSIUS THE AREOPAGITE AND THREE RENAISSANCE NEOPLATONISTS
CUSANUS FICINO & PICO
ON MIND AND COSMOS

I N A LECTURE FIRST PUBLISHED in 1955, Paul Oskar Kristeller emphasized
the particular importance of three fifteenth-century thinkers — Nicolaus
Cusanus, Marsilio Ficino, and Giovanni Pico della Mirandola — for the history of Renaissance Platonism.[1] Each of these figures continues to receive
considerable scholarly attention, and Ficino and Pico frequently have been
treated in relationship to one another. But Cusanus' place within the general
context of fifteenth-century thought still remains to be established in many
important respects. And there has been no comprehensive comparison of
the systems of Cusanus, Ficino, and Pico since Ernst Cassirer's brilliant
but now outdated *Individuum und Kosmos in der Philosophie der Renaissance*,
published in 1927.[2]

There are probably many reasons why Cassirer's attempt to link Cusanus,
Ficino, and Pico in a unified vision of Renaissance man and cosmos has
not borne fruit, but three appear to be especially important. First, the
Individuum und Kosmos was itself the product of a Neo-Kantian mode of
historical discourse which has largely fallen out of use in the decades since

1. P. O. Kristeller, *The Classics and Renaissance Thought* (Cambridge, Mass., 1955), Chapter 3.
2. E. Cassirer, *Individuum und Kosmos in der Philosophie der Renaissance, Studien der Bibliothek Warburg*,
10 (Leipzig, Berlin, 1927), English tr. by M. Domandi, *The Individual and the Cosmos in Renaissance Philosophy* (London, 1963).

Cassirer published his famous essay. Second, students of Cusanus since Cassirer's day have generally paid very little attention to the development of research on Italian Renaissance thought, and to research on Ficino and Pico in particular. The converse is generally true of the scholars who study Ficino, Pico and Italian Renaissance religious and intellectual history; with the exceptions of Garin and Saitta they have taken little notice of Cusanus save in an allusory way.[3] Third, although all three figures continue to be considered fundamentally "Platonist" in certain essential aspects of their thought, the precise nature of these Platonisms has become somewhat blurred because of recent scholarly emphasis upon the Aristotelian and Thomistic elements in Cusanus' positions, and Hermetic and Cabalistic elements in those of Pico and Ficino.[4]

If one turns away from this apparent historiographical impasse back to Cusanus, Ficino, and Pico themselves in search of a way to reconsider their Neoplatonisms in relationship to one another, a certain common feature of their thought emerges. Cusanus, Ficino, and Pico are the three great Renaissance students and interpreters of pseudo-Dionysius the Areopagite, though all three are of course subject to other important influences which they bring to bear in their reading of the Areopagite. It is thus not surprising that their readings and adaptions of the pseudo-Dionysius are not uniform. The differences among the three readings provide interesting indexes to the nature of the Neoplatonisms of Cusanus, Pico, and Ficino, and signal important distinctions among these Neoplatonisms.

The cosmos of the pseudo-Dionysius is intelligential and spiritual; in

3. See E. Garin, "Cusano e i platonici italiani del Quattrocento," in *Nicolò Cusano. Relazioni presentate al Convegno Interuniversitario di Bressanone* (Florence, 1961), 75–100; G. Saitta, *Nicolò Cusano e l'umanesimo italiano* (Bologna, 1957). In my *Nicolaus Cusanus: A Fifteenth-Century Vision of Man* (Leiden, 1982), I suggested some of the ways in which Cusanus' thought could be linked to various aspects of Italian humanism. See also P. O. Kristeller, "A Latin Translation of Gemistos Plethon's *De fato* by Johannes Sophianos Dedicated to Nicholas of Cusa," in *Nicolò Cusano agli inizi del mondo moderno. Atti del Congresso internazionale in occasione del V centenario della morte di Nicolò Cusano* (Florence, 1970), 175–193.

4. Important studies of Cusanus which emphasize Aristotelian and Thomistic elements in his thought include R. Haubst's *Die Christologie des Nikolaus von Kues* (Freiburg, 1956); J. Hopkins, *Nicholas of Cusa on Learned Ignorance* (Minneapolis, 1980); idem, *Nicholas of Cusa's Debate with John Wenck* (Minneapolis, 1980). At the font of the many recent studies of Hermeticism and Cabalism in Pico and Ficino are two works: D. P. Walker, *Spiritual and Demonic Magic from Ficino to Campanella* (London, 1958) and F. Yates, *Giordano Bruno and The Hermetic Tradition* (London and Chicago, 1964).

this sense it can be distinguished from a physical, elementally stratified cosmos such as the Aristotelian one that was so influential in the Latin West from Antiquity to the Scientific Revolution, and beyond. The structure of the pseudo-Dionysius' cosmos is at once monadic and triadic, its order is hierarchical and its dynamism is circular; all being and knowledge unfold from God and seek to return to Him. The pseudo-Dionysius' surviving works, four treatises and ten letters, are all concerned in one way or another with the manner in which the soul ascends to God through the powers and operations of sensible and intelligible symbols, that is, the manner in which it theologizes.[5]

According to the pseudo-Dionysius, there are two fundamental kinds of discourse about divinity; affirmative theology (*kataphatike*) and negative theology (*apophatike*). Affirmative and negative theology are tightly interwoven in the larger tradition of speculation concerning the divine as well as in Dionysius' own system, as he points out in his Ninth Letter, addressed to the bishop Titus:

> . . . the theological tradition is double, being on the one hand a tradition which is not expressed in words and which is mystical and, on the other hand, a tradition which makes manifest and is better known. One is symbolic and aims at initiation, the other is philosophical and demonstrative. What is not said is woven together with what is said. One persuades and makes known the truth of what is said, the other fulfills and situates souls in God through a mystical guidance which is not learned by teaching.[6]

For Dionysius, affirmative or cataphatic theology is an initiation into the hierarchies of the theophany of created being initially through the rites and ceremonies described in *The Ecclesiastical Hierarchy*. These rites and ceremonies constitute a kind of "Christian theurgy."

The *praxis* of the pseudo-Dionysius' theurgy (probably derived from various Alexandrine, Cappadocian, and Neoplatonic sources, the latter pos-

---

5. My discussion of the Dionysian cosmos is based on the following sources: R. Rocques, "Denys L'Areopagite (Le Pseudo-)," *DSAM*, 3, cols. 264–286; I. P. Sheldon-Williams, "The pseudo-Dionysius," in *The Cambridge History of Later Greek and Early Medieval Philosophy*, ed. A. H. Armstrong (Cambridge, 1970), 457–472; R. Rocques, *L'Univers dionysien: structure hiérarchique du monde selon Le pseudo-Denys* (Paris, 1954).

6. Letter 9.1. For the Greek text, see *PG*, 3: col. 1105d. The English translation is from J. D. Jones, *Pseudo-Dionysius Areopagite: The Divine Names and Mystical Theology* (Milwaukee, 1980), 15.

sibly including the works of Proclus) has been succinctly characterized
by I. P. Sheldon-Williams as follows:

> Theurgy, like all praxis, was the utilization of sensible objects,
> but concerned itself not with their matter but with the inherent power
> which they were supposed to derive from the *sympatheia* which binds
> the whole universe together, the sensibles to the intelligibles and
> the intelligibles to the gods, and the control of which was therefore
> an automatic means of invoking divine and demonic assistance for
> practical ends.[7]

According to this "Christian theurgy," the soul ascends from the legal
hierarchy, from the most rudimentary theophanies of rites and ceremonies received through the senses, to the purer symbolic theophanies of
the ecclesiastical hierarchy. Reception of these symbols initiates the aspiring soul into the celestial hierarchy of the intelligible world, populated
by angels and other sorts of pure intelligences. Guided by these beings
the soul passes to *gnosis* — union with the supreme causal agent which completes its process of deification. But this God to whom the initiate ascends
through various theurgic practices is not the Godhead itself. That transcendent One is approached only through negative or apophatic theology.

Apophatic theology leads to darkness (*gnophos*), the revelation of what
God is not rather than what he is. In this sense it transcends positive theology though it is not a refutation of it. Negative theology begins at the
very point where affirmative or cataphatic theology reaches its summit.
Rather than operating through rites of initiation, theurgic practices, and
analogical symbolism, as does affirmative theology, negative theology operates through discordances, through dissimilar similitudes, as Dionysius
explains in this passage from *The Celestial Hierarchy*:

> . . .the method of Divine revelation is twofold; one, indeed as is natur-
> al, proceeding through likenesses that are similar, and of a sacred
> character, but the other, through dissimilar forms, fashioning them
> into entire unlikenesses and incongruity . . . its praises are supermun-
> danely sung, by the Oracles themselves, through dissimilar revela-
> tions when they affirm that it is invisible, and infinite, and
> incomprehensible; and when there is signified, not what is, but what

7. Sheldon-Williams, 458.

is not. For this, as I think, is more appropriate to It, since, as the secret and sacerdotal tradition taught, we rightly describe its non-relationship to things created, but we do not know its superessential, and inconceivable, and unutterable indefinability. If then, the negations respecting things Divine are true, but the affirmations are inharmonious, the revelation as regards things invisible, through dissimilar representations, is more appropriate to the hiddenness of things unutterable.[8]

Apophatic theology, the principal subject of the pseudo-Dionysius' *Divine Names*, is still an intelligible operation which proceeds beyond the *gnosis* of cataphatic theology in that it empties all affirmations regarding divinity of any meaning. *Apophatike* leads the soul to a final stage wherein it experiences *agnôsia*, the revelation that God is unknowable, and *henôsis*, in which it takes leave of the celestial hierarchy and of itself and becomes lost in God.

With the notable exception of Scotus Eriugena, there was little direct or extensive acquaintance with the pseudo-Dionysius' theology in the earlier medieval period. Though there had been two translations of the pseudo-Dionysian *corpus* into Latin in the ninth century, it was not until the twelfth century that interest in him became more widespread, principally among Victorine and Cistercian thinkers. In the course of the thirteenth and fourteenth centuries, the works of the "mystical doctor," as the pseudo-Dionysius came to be known, influenced important scholastics such as Robert Grosseteste, Albertus Magnus, and Thomas Aquinas and mystics such as Meister Eckhart and Jean de Ruysbroeck. In the fifteenth century a revived and more historically informed interest in the pseudo-Dionysius emerged, inaugurated by Ambrogio Traversari's new translation of the pseudo-Dionysian *corpus* in 1436.[9] This revival of interest in the works of the pseudo-Dionysius must be seen as part of a larger Renaissance of Plato and Neoplatonism. And it is within the context of this larger Renaissance that Cusanus, Ficino, and Pico constructed their various readings of the pseudo-Dionysius.

8. *De coelesti hierarchia*, 2.2–3; *PG*, 3: cols. 140b–141a. The English translation is from J. Parker, *The Works of Dionysius the Areopagite* (London, 1897), 7–8.
9. On the influence of the pseudo-Dionysius in the Latin West from the sixth century to Nicholas of Cusa, see P. Godet, "Denys L'Areopagite (Le Pseudo-)," *DTC*, 4, cols. 318–375; for a list of translations of the pseudo-Dionysian *corpus* during that period, see col. 263. On Traversari's translations of the pseudo-Dionysius see C. L. Stinger, *Humanism and the Church Fathers: Ambrogio Traversari (1386–1439) and Christian Antiquity in the Renaissance* (Albany, 1977), 158–162.

Nicolaus Cusanus (1401–64) shared with his friend Lorenzo Valla some serious doubts as to whether the pseudo-Dionysius was indeed a contemporary of St. Paul, the man mentioned in Acts 17:16–34.[10] But his uncertainty as to when the pseudo-Dionysius actually lived did not diminish Cusanus' life-long interest in the writings of the Areopagite. The influence of the pseudo-Dionysius can be discerned in a series of Cusanus' most seminal works, beginning with the De docta ignorantia of 1440 and culminating with such late works of the 1460s as the De non-aliud (1462) and the De ludo globi (1463–64). Though certain elements of Cusanus' conception of the cosmos and his "science of God" owe much to the writings of the pseudo-Dionysius, he consistently modified and transmutated these writings in working out his own positions.[11]

For example, in the De docta ignorantia, Cusanus stated that, in some mysterious way, "visibles are in truth images of the invisibles," and that all things "have some kind of relationship to one another, however occult and incomprehensible to us."[12] But when he addressed himself to the question of further describing the structure of the universe in places such as the well-known chapters 11–13 of Book II of the De docta ignorantia he appears to have conceived of it in physical and mathematical, rather than intelligential and spiritual terms, and to have relied upon sources other

10. In a note to Kues, Hospitalbibliothek, MS 44, fol. 1r, Cusanus observed that it was "astonishing" (mirum) that neither Ambrose, Jerome nor Augustine mentioned the pseudo-Dionysius. See E. Vansteenberghe, Le Cardinal Nicholas de Cues (1401–1464): L'action-la pensée (Paris, 1920), 26, note 5. In the Apologia doctae ignorantiae of 1449, he called Maximus the Confessor the "first Greek commentator" on the pseudo-Dionysian corpus and quoted a passage from him (without, however, mentioning him by name). See Nicolaus de Cusa, Opera omnia, 2, ed. R. Klibansky (Leipzig, 1932): 20–21, lines 6–8. Several lines later, Cusanus does mention Maximus by name (line 22), placing him first in a list of commentators on the pseudo-Dionysius. The edition of the Apologia doctae ignorantiae cited above is hereafter referred to as Apologia. In his Adnotationes ad Novum Testamentum, Valla also observed that no Greek or Latin Father prior to Gregory the Great mentioned the pseudo-Dionysius. See S. I. Camporeale, Lorenzo Valla: Umanesimo e Teologia (Florence, 1972), 270, 428–30 which includes the Latin text of Valla's remarks concerning the identity of the Areopagite.

11. Cusanus does not explicitly mention the Traversari translation until the Apologia doctae ignorantiae. See Apologia, p. 10, line 16, where he refers to the De divinibus nominibus "in novissima Ambrosii Camaldulensis translatione." But Ludwig Baur convincingly argues that Cusanus was utilizing the Traversari translation (completed by 1436) when he wrote the De docta ignorantia in 1440. See his "Nicolaus Cusanus und Ps. Dionysius im Lichte der Zitate und Randbemerkungen des Cusanus. Cusanus-Texte III," Sitzungsberichte der Heidelberger Akademie der Wissenschaften, Philosophisch-historische Klasse, 1 (1941–42): 3–113.

12. Nicolaus Cusanus, Opera omnia, 1 (Leipzig, 1932), 1.11, p. 22 (this edition of the De docta ignorantia is hereafter cited as DDI).

than the works of the pseudo-Dionysius in making his arguments regarding cosmic infinity and relativity.[13]

On the other hand, in Chapter 13 of the first part of the *De coniecturis*—the companion piece to the *De docta ignorantia*—he presents a "figure of the universe" which seems to represent the monadic-triadic structure of the pseudo-Dionysian cosmos. Although Cusanus does not specifically associate this cosmogram with the pseudo-Dionysius in Chapter 13 of the *De coniecturis*, he appears to refer to it in the retrospective late work *De ludo globi*, wherein he explains the Dionysian cosmos in considerable detail to his young interlocutor, Albertus, saying that:

> The divisions of the heavens can also be sought to some extent, for certain saints have understood there to be a visible heaven and an intelligible heaven and an intellectual heaven and three divisions in each heaven so that a ninefold of heavens is completed inside a tenth where the seat of God is, above the cherubim.[14]

The cosmogram of the *De coniecturis* has a curious *fortuna* which remains to be thoroughly worked out and explained, as does the nature of the Dionysian influence that it transmits. For example, Cusanus' cosmogram of the *De coniecturis* appears in a French translation of Pico della Mirandola's *Heptaplus* by Nicolas LeFèvre de la Boderie, published in Paris in 1579. It is intended to illustrate the three worlds imagined by Antiquity and set forth by the pseudo-Dionysius in the ecclesiastical and celestial hierarchies, the exposition of which is the subject of the *Heptaplus*.[15]

13. Cassirer read these chapters of the *De docta ignorantia* as key evidences of Cusanus' "modernity," of his shattering of the hierarchical, stratified, static and finite cosmos of the scholastics (see *The Individual and the Cosmos*, 24–28). But recently Edward Grant has suggested that Cusanus' statements in Book II of the *De docta ignorantia* were based upon his reading of the pseudo-Hermetic *Book of the XXIV Philosophers* and that his reading closely parallels that of at least one scholastic, Thomas Bradwardine. See Grant's *Much Ado About Nothing: Theories of Space and Vacuum from the Middle Ages to the Scientific Revolution* (Cambridge, 1981), 138–141.

14. Nikolaus von Kues, *Philosophisch-Theologische Schriften*, ed. L. Gabriel (Vienna, 1967), 3:302–318; the passage translated in the text is on p. 318: "Possunt et caelorum discretiones aliqualiter venari. Nam caelum visibile et caelum intelligibile et caelum intellectuale quidam sancti esse comprehenderunt et in quolibet trinam distinctionem, ut novenarius caelorum in denario, ubi est sedes Dei super cherubim, perficiatur."

15. Francesco Giorgio, *L'Harmonie du monde*, et al., tr. Guy Le Fèvre de la Boderie (Paris, 1579), f. e6v. I have traced the lineage of this figure from Cusanus' *De coniecturis*, through this sixteenth-century translation of Pico's *Heptaplus* to Robert Fludd's *Cosmi maioris scilicet et minoris metaphysica* (1617) and Athanasius Kircher's *Musurgia universali* (1650) in an unpublished paper titled "Cusanus and the Renaissance Cosmos."

While Cusanus believed that in some manner the universe was a *sympatheia* in which mind and cosmos were linked through number, he also took as fundamental to his epistemology, from the *De docta ignorantia* on, the premise that on the level of rational discourse, "there is no proportion of the finite to the infinite."[16] In Chapter 3 of the *De docta ignorantia*, Cusanus described the disjunction that he believed prevailed between the knower and the thing known in these words:

> . . . the essence of things [*quidditas rerum*], which is the truth of beings and which has been sought by all philosophers and has been discovered by none of them, is unattainable in its purity; and the more profoundly we become learned in this ignorance, the closer we approach the truth.[17]

In order to speculate more truly concerning the divine, it is necessary

> . . . to raise the intellect above the meaning of words, rather than to insist upon the properties of words which cannot be properly adapted to such great intellectual mysteries. It is also necessary to use elementary examples in a transcendent way, relinquishing sensible things, so that the reader may ascend to simple intellectuality.[18]

In the *Apologia doctae ignorantiae*, Cusanus draws this distinction more sharply, contrasting the "contentions" that arise from verbal wars with the "freedom and silence" of mystical theology, and advising his adversary Johannes Wenck that in order that

> . . . he might be transferred from blindness to light, he must read with his intellect the Mystical Theology of which I have already spoken, and Maximus the monk, Hugh of St. Victor, Robert of Lincoln [Robert Grosseteste], John the Scot, the abbot of Vercelli [Thomas Gallus], and the rest of the more modern commentators

---

16. *DDI*, 1.3, pp. 8–9; see also *DDI* 1.1 for an important discussion of number.

17. *DDI*, 1.3, p. 9: "Quidditas ergo rerum, quae est entium veritas, in sua puritate inattingibilis est et per omnes philosophos investigata, sed per neminem, uti est, reperta: et quanto in hac ignorantia profundius docti fuerimus, tanto magis ipsam accedimus veritatem."

18. *DDI*, 1.2, p. 8: ". . . potius supra verborum vim intellectum effere quam proprietatibus vocabulorum insistere, quae tantis intellectualibus mysteriis proprie adaptari non possunt. Exemplaribus etiam manuductionibus necesse est transcendentur uti, linquendo sensibilia, ut ad intellectualitatem simplicem expedite lector ascendat. . . ."

of this book, and he will undoubtedly discover that until now he had been blind.[19]

Cusanus goes on to argue that the proper application of the symbolizing powers of the intellect (as distinct from the discursive powers of reason, based on the "properties of words") will lead to a revelation not of what God is, but rather what He is *not*:

> Truly all the likenesses that the holy men, even the most divine Dionysius, hypothesize, are wholly disproportionate and useless rather than useful to all those lacking in learned ignorance—that is, the knowledge of this, that they [the likenesses] are wholly disproportionate.[20]

Cusanus' early adaptation of the pseudo-Dionysian *apophatike* remained central to his "science of God," his theologizing.

In the *De non-aliud* of 1462, Cusanus portrayed himself as a student of the pseudo-Dionysius engaged in conversation with three friends studying Aristotle, Plato's *Parmenides* and Proclus' commentary on it, and Proclus' *Theology of Plato*. In the ensuing conversation on the subject of the divine nature (the "not-other"), Cusanus reiterates the position first set forth in the *De docta ignorantia* and the *Apologia doctae ignorantiae* over twenty years earlier:

> Dionysius, the greatest of the theologians, assumes the following: that it is impossible for a human being to ascend to an understanding of spiritual matters except by the guidance of perceptible forms, so that, for example, he regards visible beauty as an image of invisible beauty. Hence, Dionysius maintains that perceptible things are likenesses or images of intelligible things. However, he asserts that God, as the Beginning, precedes all intelligible things; and he purports to know that God is not among any of the things which can be either known or conceived. Hence, he believes that the only thing

---

19. *Apologia*, 20–21: "Sed si se gratiam assequi sperat, ut de caecitate ad lumen transferatur, legat cum intellectu Mysticam theologiam iam dictam, Maximum monachum, Hugonem de Sancto Victore, Robertum Lincolniensem, Iohannem Scotigenam, abbatem Vercellensem et ceteros moderniores commentatores illius libelli; et indubie se hactenus caecum fuisse reperiet."

20. *Apologia*, 24: "Sunt enim omnes similitudines, quas sancti ponunt, etiam divinissimus Dionysius, penitus improportionales et omnibus non habentibus doctam ignorantiam —huius scilicet scientiam, quod sunt penitus improportionales,— potius inutiles quam utiles."

which can be known about God (whom he affirms to be the being of all things) is that He precedes all understanding.[21]

And Cusanus follows this statement with a long series of quotations from the *Celestial Hierarchy*, the *Ecclesiastical Hierarchy*, the *Divine Names*, and the letters, wherein the pseudo-Dionysius discusses the nature of his negative theology.[22]

In his early works, particularly the *De docta ignorantia*, Cusanus also discusses the nature and purposes of *kataphatike* or affirmative theology. In Chapter 26 of the first book of the *De docta ignorantia*, Cusanus argues that the modes of worship—the *cultura*—of any religion are necessarily based on affirmative theology, on the positive assertions that it makes regarding its god.[23] But he concludes that all affirmative theology finally derives from and leads to negative theology. He pays relatively little attention to affirmative theology except in his discussions of the role that it plays in the "cult" of a religion.

Cusanus' adaptation of the pseudo-Dionysius' apophatic theology informed his conception of language. According to Cusanus, language is the product of usage and convention and it operates primarily within the realm of the reason. When it is applied to theology, language operates within the realm of affirmative theology wherein various attributes are given to God, but within the realm of negative theology it is "vision" arising out of learned ignorance that is the key:

> . . . learned ignorance raises a person to vision as does a high tower. "When placed there, he sees that which a person who roams through

21. The English translation is from J. Hopkins, *Nicholas of Cusa on God as Not-Other: A Translation and an Appraisal of De li non-aliud* (Minneapolis, 1979), 83. For the Latin text, see Nicolaus de Cusa, *Opera omnia*, 13: 1. *Directio speculantis seu de non aliud*, ed. L. Baur and P. Wilpert (Leipzig, 1944), 29–30: "Dionysius, theologorum maximus, impossibile esse praesupponit ad spiritualium intelligentiam praeterquam sensibilium formarum ductu hominem ascendere, ut visibilem scilicet pulchritudinem invisibilis decoris imaginem putet; hinc sensibilia intelligibilium similitudines seu imagines dicit, Deum autem principium asserit intelligibilia omnia praecedere, quem scire se dicit nihil omnium esse, quae sciri possunt aut concipi. Ideo hoc solum de ipso credit posse sciri, quem esse inquit omnium esse, quod scilicet omnem intellectum antecedit." This text is hereafter referred to as *De non-aliud*.

22. *Ibid.*, 83–99; *De non-aliud*, 29–38.

23. *DDI*, 1.26, p. 54: "Quoniam autem cultura Dei, qui adorandus est in spiritu et veritate, necessario se fundat in positivis Deum affirmantibus, hinc omnis religio in sua cultura necessario per theologiam affirmativam ascendit, Deum ut unum ac trinum, ut sapientissimum, piissimum, lucem inaccessibilem, vitam, veritatem, et ita de reliquis adorando. . . ."

a field is tracking by moving variously about; and he perceives the
extent to which the seeker approaches and recedes from that which
he seeks. Learned ignorance, standing upon the high region of the
intellect, judges discursive reasoning in this way."[24]

Not surprisingly, Cusanus shows no interest in the incantatory power
of words such as figured in the theurgic *praxis* of the pseudo-Dionysian
legal and ecclesiastical hierarchies.

Cusanus does link up the objects that man makes and uses with his
theology and anthropology but he does not exhibit any interest in talismans or in magical practices. For him, the objects that man creates are
manifestations of his creativity, his god-like nature, his capacity to play
cosmic games. But the objects that man makes "have no exemplar in nature" as he emphasizes in the *Idiota de mente*:

> Outside of the exemplar in our mind, the spoon has no other ex-
> emplar. Although the sculptor or painter takes exemplars from things
> that he wishes to represent, I however do not. I bring forth spoons
> and bowls from wood and jars from mud. Indeed, in doing this I
> imitate the form of no natural thing.[25]

Spoons and jars are the products and fusions, the perpetuations of the human world of culture; they do not provide man with access to or controls
over natural and celestial forces. And it is the invention and perpetuation
of this human world which provides man with a refuge against the vagaries of fortune and the temptation to attribute the events that befall him
to planetary forces over which he can have no control.

Cusanus's reception and transmutation of the pseudo-Dionysian *corpus*
differs from the readings of Giovanni Pico della Mirandola and Marsilio
Ficino in a number of significant ways. In the *Heptaplus*, Pico discussed
four worlds, the angelic, the celestial, the sublunary or elemental, and

---

24. *Apologia*, 16: ". . . doctam ignorantiam sic aliquem ad visum elevare quasi alta turris. 'Videt
enim ibi constitutus id, quod discursu vario vestigialiter quaeritur per in agro vagantem; et quantum quaerens accedit et elongatur a quaesito, ipse intuetur. Docta enim ignorantia de alta regione
intellectus existens sic iudicat de ratio-cinativo discursu'."

25. Nicholaus de Cusa, *Opera omnia*, 5, ed. L. Baur (Leipzig, 1937): 51: "Coclear extra mentis
nostrae ideam aliud non habet exemplar. Nam etsi statuarius aut pictor trahat exemplaria a rebus,
quas figurare satagit, non tamen ego, qui ex lignis coclearia et scutellas et ollas ex luto educo.
Non enim in hoc imitor figuram cuiuscumque rei naturalis."

the world of man. For his exposition of the angelic and celestial worlds, he relied heavily, though certainly not exclusively, upon the works of the pseudo-Dionysius. In the Proem to the second book of the *Heptaplus*, his exposition of the heavenly world, Pico refers to the pseudo-Dionysius as the "glory of our theology" (along with Thomas Aquinas) and in the Proem to the third book, his exposition of the angelic world, he says that he treads in the footsteps of the Areopagite.[26]

In a general description of the three worlds given in the Second Proem, Pico manifests his debt to the pseudo-Dionysius:

> In the first world, God, the primal unity, presides over the nine orders of angels as if over many spheres and, without moving, moves all toward himself. In the middle world, that is, the celestial, the empyrean heaven likewise presides like the commander of an army over nine heavenly spheres, each of which revolves with an unceasing motion; yet in imitation of God, it is itself unmoving. There are also in the elemental world, after the prime matter which is its foundation, nine spheres of corruptible forms.[27]

In addition to accepting the monadic-triadic structure of the pseudo-Dionysian cosmos, Pico also accepts the pseudo-Dionysian idea of the cosmos as an emanative *sympatheia*. Again in the Second Proem, Pico says,

> It should above all be observed, a fact on which our purpose almost wholly depends, that these three worlds are one world, not only because they are all related by one beginning and to the same end, or because regulated by appropriate numbers they are bound together both by a certain harmonious kinship of nature and by a regular ser-

26. G. Pico della Mirandola, *Heptaplus*, tr. D. Carmichael (New York, 1965), 95, 107. For the Latin text of the *Heptaplus*, see Joannes Picus Mirandulanus, *Opera omnia* (Basel, 1572 [rpt. Turin, 1971]), 1:1–62. For Pico's remarks regarding the pseudo-Dionysius in the Proem to the second book of the *Heptaplus*, see *Opera omnia*, 1:16; in the Proem to the third book, 1:23. This edition is hereafter referred to as Pico, *Opera*.

27. Carmichael tr., 78. For the Latin, see Pico, *Opera*, 1:7: "In primo mundo Deus unitas prima, novem angelorum ordinibus quasi sphaeris totidem praeest immobilisque ipse omnes movet ad se. In mundo medio, id est, coelesti coelum empyreum, novem itidem sphaeris coelestibus quasi dux exercitui praeest, quae cum singulae motu incessabili volvantur, illud tamen Deum imaginas immotum est. Sunt et in mundo elementari post materiam primam ipsius fundamentum, novem sphaerae formarum corruptibilium."

ies of ranks, but because whatever is in any of the worlds is at the same time contained in each, and there is no one of them in which is not to be found whatever is in each of the others.[28]

Pico's belief that the universe is a monadic-triadic *sympatheia* leads him to conceive of language and symbolic thought in a way that is distinct from that of Cusanus. According to Pico, words and images are part of a theophanic cosmic code:

> The early Fathers could not properly represent some things by the images of others unless trained, as I have said, in the hidden alliances and affinities of all nature. Otherwise there would be no reason why they should have represented this thing by this image, and another by another, rather than each by its opposite. But versed in all things and inspired by that Spirit which not only knows all these things but made them, they aptly symbolized the natures of one world by those which they knew corresponded to them in the other worlds. Therefore those who wish to interpret their figures of speech and allegorical meanings correctly need the same knowledge. . . .[29]

For Pico, therefore, words had a "natural" as distinct from a "conventional" signification, and by extension, affirmative theology and its goal of *gnosis* assumed for him a centrality in the "science of God" which it did not have for Cusanus. Moreover, it was Pico's conviction that there was a cosmic code to be cracked that was the basis of his attraction to "natural" magic.

28. Carmichael, tr., 77. For the Latin, see Pico, *Opera*, 1:6: ". . . magnopere observandum unde et nostra fere tota pendet intentio esse hos tres mundos mundum unum, non solum propterea quod ab uno principio et ad eundem finem omnes referant, aut quoniam debitis numeris temperati et harmonica quadam naturae cognatione atque ordinaria graduum serie colligent. Sed quoniam quicquid in omnibis simul est mundis, id et in singulis continetur, neque est aliquis unus est eis, in quo non omnia sint quae sunt in singulis. . . ."

29. Carmichael, tr., 79; Pico, *Opera*, 1:7: "Nec potuerunt antiqui patres aliis alia figuris decenter representare nisi occultas, ut ita dixerim, totius naturae et amicitias et affinitates edocti. Alioquin nulla esset ratio cur hoc potius hac imagine aliud alia quam contra repraesentassent. Sed gnari omnium rerum et acti spiritu illo qui haec omnia non solum novit, sed fecit naturas unius mundi, per ea quae illis in reliquis mundis noverant respondere aptissime figurabant. Quare eadem opus cognitione (nisi idem adsit et spiritus) his qui illorum figuras et allegoricos sensus interpretari recte voluerint." See E. H. Gombrich, "*Icones Symbolicae*: Philosophies of Symbolism and Their Bearing on Art," in *Symbolic Images: Studies in the Art of the Renaissance* (London, 1972), 123–195, for a brief but very illuminating discussion of the nature of Pico's symbolic thought.

In the famous *Oration* prefacing the nine hundred *conclusiones* which he proposed to debate publicly in Rome, Pico discussed "natural" magic in some detail, always carefully distinguishing it from demonic magic. Of "natural" magic, Pico says:

> Having carefully investigated the harmony of the universe, which the Greeks very expressively call συμπάθειαν, and having looked closely into the knowledge that natures have of each other, this second magic, applying to each thing its innate charms, which are called by magicians ἴυγγες, as if it were itself the maker, discloses in public the wonders lying in the recesses of the world, in the bosom of nature, in the storerooms and secrets of God. And as the farmer marries elm to vine so the magician marries earth to heaven, that is, lower things to the qualities and virtues of higher things.[30]

Pico devoted twenty-six *conclusiones* to the subject of "natural" magic. The nineteenth through twenty-fourth *conclusiones* reveal that for Pico, it is particular words and calls which have magical power in that they derive ultimately from the voice of God. In the twentieth conclusion he succinctly expressed this belief, saying that "whatever magical power a word has, it has to the extent that it is fashioned by the voice of God." (*Quelibet vox virtutem habet in Magia, inquantum Dei voce formatur.*)[31]

It was Pico's belief in the magical power of words that led him into the arcane world of Cabalism, in which transpositions, anagrams, and invocations deriving from the ten names of God that composed the Sephiroth and the twenty-two letters of the Hebrew alphabet would lead to a comprehension of the secrets of God and the cosmos. At the conclusion of the *Heptaplus*, Pico claimed that all *gnosis* lay concealed in the Pentateuch, and that this "Mosaic profundity" could be made accessible through the Cabalistic art. Taking the first four verses of Genesis as his example, Pico began by explaining what he proposed to do:

---

30. G. Pico della Mirandola, *On the Dignity of Man*, tr. C. G. Wallis (New York, 1965), 28. For the Latin text, see Pico, *Opera*, 1:328: "Haec universi consensum, quem significantius Graeci συμπάθειαν dicunt, introrsum perscrutatius rimata, et mutuam naturarum cognitionem habens perspectam, nativas adhibens unicuique rei et suas illecebras, quae magorum ἴυγγες nominantur, in mundi recessibus, in naturae gremio, in promptuariis arcanisque Dei latitantia miracula, quasi ipsa sit artifex, promit in publicam et sicut agricola ulmos vitibus, ita Magus terram coelo, id est, inferiora superiorum dotibus virtutibusque maritat."

31. For the texts of the nineteenth through twenty-fourth *conclusiones* see Pico, *Opera*, 1:105.

This whole passage is composed of 103 letters, which, arranged, as they are, make up the words which we read, displaying nothing but the common and trivial. But this arrangement of letters, this text, composes the shell of a secret kernel of hidden mysteries. If we open up the words and take the same letters separately and, according to the rules which the Hebrews hand down, join them together properly into the sayings that can be made up of them, they say that there will appear to us, if we are fit for hidden wisdom, many wise and wonderful doctrines. If this is done with the whole law, there will finally be brought to light by the proper placing and connecting of its elements all learning and the secrets of all the liberal disciplines.[32]

Pico went on to show how through the rearrangement of the letters of the first four verses of Genesis, the following passage would emerge: "the father, in the Son and through the Son, the beginning and end or rest, created the head, the fire, and the foundation of the great man with a good pact."[33] And for Pico this decoding represented the "holy pact" of creation in which the "little world" that is man is bound together with the "great man" that is the world in a microcosmic-macrocosmic symbiosis.

Ficino did not share the doubts held by Cusanus and Valla regarding the pseudo-Dionysius' identity; he apparently believed that he was indeed the contemporary of Paul mentioned in Acts. Ficino translated and commented upon the pseudo-Dionysius' *Divine Names* and indications of his reading of the Areopagite are evident throughout his writings. Ficino's admiration of the pseudo-Dionysius was of a high order; at the beginning of his commentary on the Areopagite's *De mystica theologia*, Ficino called him the "summit" of the Platonic disciplines and of Christian theology.

32. Carmichael tr., 170–171; Pico, *Opera*, 1:59–60: "Est tota illa scriptura tribus et centum elementis cognomentata, quae eo modo disposita, quo ibi sunt dictiones constituunt quae legimus, nihil nisi commune et triviale prae se ferentes. Corticem, scilicet, constat hic literarum ordo, hoc textum medullae interius abditae latentium mysteriorum, at vocabulis resolutis, elementa eadem divulsa si capiamus, et iuxta regulas quas ipsi tradunt, quae de eis conflari dictiones possunt, rite coagmentemus, futurum dicunt, ut elucescent nobis, si simus capaces occlusae sapientiae, mira de rebus multis secretissima dogmata, et si in tota hoc fiat lege, tum demum ex elementorum hac, quae rite statuatur, et positione et nexu, erui in lucem omnem doctrinam secretaque omnium liberalium disciplinarum. . . ."

33. Carmichael tr., 172; Pico, *Opera*, 1:61: "Pater in filio, et per filium principium et finem, sive quietem creavit, caput, ignem et fundamentum magni hominis, foedere bono. . . ." For Pico's explication of this passage, see 1:61–62.

"Searching for divine light, he investigated not so much through the intelligence as through the ardent disposition of his will, and he searched through discourse [oratio.]"[34]

It seems clear from a reference in the sixteenth book of the *Theologia platonica*, and particularly from the fourteenth chapter of the *De christiana religione*, that Ficino incorporated the nine orders of angels of the pseudo-Dionysian celestial hierarchy into the spheres of his own hierarchically ordered cosmos, itself a hybrid of the Aristotelian and Ptolemaic systems:

> Above the four elements which are moved according to substance and quality are the seven heavens of the planets. They are not moved by substance but in a certain manner by a kind of quality or, as it were, disposition. Since the movement of these planets is erratic, an eighth heaven, whose motion is more regular, is set over them. But this heaven has two motions, namely one from the East to West and another in the opposite direction. It has two qualities also, namely brilliance and splendor. For that reason, the crystalline sphere whose one motion is from the East [to the West] and has a single quality, brilliance, is ascendant over it. But since position is superior to motion and since what gives light is superior to light, therefore one ascends to the Empyrean which is entirely stable and shining throughout. The Empyrean is rightly related to the stability and light of the Trinity, and the nine other heavens to the nine orders of angels. Indeed, they are disposed in a manner consistent with Dionysius the Areopagite; three hierarchies of divine spirits, each of which contains three orders.[35]

34. Marsilio Ficino, *Opera omnia* (Basel, 1576), 2:1013: "Dionysius Areopagita Platonicae disciplinae culmen, et Christianae Theologiae columen, quaerens divinum lumen, non tam intelligentia perscrutatur, quam ardente voluntatis affectu, et oratione petit."

35. *Ibid.*, 1:19: "Super quatuor elementa, quae secundum substantiam et qualitatem mutabilia sunt, coeli septem sunt Planetarum, qui non substantia, sed quodammodo qualitate quadam, vel dispositione quasi mutantur. Quoniam vero horum motus quasi erraticus est, coelum illis octavum superponitur, cuius magis ordinatus est motus, sed coelum illud duos habet motus, ab Oriente scilicet ad Occidentem, atque econverso. Duas quoque saltem qualitates, candorem scilicet et splendorem, idcirco ab illo ad crystallinum ascenditur, cuius motus est simplex ab Oriente, qualitas quoque simplex, id est candor, sed quoniam motu superior status est, et candore superius lumen, ideo ab hoc ascenditur ad empireum omnino stabile, totumque lucens. Empireum stabilitati lucique trinitatis recte accommodatur, novem reliqui, novem ordinibus angelorum. Sunt enim quemadmodum Dionysio Areopagitae placet, hierarchiae tres spirituum divinorum, quarum quaelibet tres continet ordines."

And in related sections of the *Theologia platonica* and the *De raptu Pauli* Ficino describes three heavens which are reminiscent of the pseudo-Dionysius' ecclesiastical, celestial, and angelic hierarchies. Certainly Ficino's conception of the cosmos was informed by other mitigating Neoplatonic and scholastic sources and influences, but in the main it is intelligential and spiritual in the pseudo-Dionysian vein.[36]

The cosmos of Ficino's *Theologica platonica* and *De christiana religione* provides an interesting contrast to that of Cusanus' *De docta ignorantia*. Whereas Ficino's cosmos is a finite, closed system of hierarchically ordered spheres in which everything has its place ("totam entis ipsius latitudinem"),[37] Cusanus' cosmos is neither centered nor circumscribed according to the prevailing Aristotelian-Ptolemaic cosmology:

> Therefore the earth, which cannot be the center [of the universe], cannot be lacking in all motion . . . just as the earth is not the center of the universe, so the sphere of the fixed stars is not its circumference, although in actually comparing the earth to the heavens, the earth itself seems to be closer to the center and the heavens to the circumference. Therefore the earth is not the center of the eighth or any other sphere, nor does the appearance of the signs of the zodiac above the horizon lead to the conclusion that the earth is in the center of the eighth sphere.[38]

Every part of Cusanus' universe is in motion and so all position is relative. The *locus* of a being is not a factor in determining the particular nature of that being.

Ficino's conception of the universe as a hierarchically ordered *sympatheia* underlies his conception of knowledge as *adaequatio* — the correspondence between the knowing mind and the object of its knowledge. In Book 11, Chapter 1, of the *Theologia platonica*, Ficino explains the concept of *adaequatio* in this way:

---

36. The relevant passage from the *Theologia platonica* is in *Opera omnia*, 1:369; the *De raptu Pauli*, 1:697–706.

37. *Ibid.*, 1:238 (*Theologia platonica*, Book 10, Chapter 9).

38. *DDI*, 2.11. pp. 100–101: "Terra igitur, quae centrum esse nequit, motu omni carere non potest. . . . Sicut igitur terra non est centrum mundi, ita nec sphaera fixarum stellarum eius circumferentia, quamvis etiam, comparando terram ad caelum, ipsa terra videatur centro propinquior et caelum circumferentiae. Non est igitur centrum terra neque octavae aut alterius sphaerae, neque apparentia super horizontem sex signorum terram concludit in centro esse octavae sphaerae."

As long as the intellect is only potentially prepared to know, it is not yet united with the object potentially to be known; but when it is actually knowing, it is united with it . . . since the form of that object is inherent in the mind. . . . Thus the knowing mind and the thing known becomes one, since the form of that thing, as such, molds the mind.[39]

It is beyond the scope of this paper to trace the origins of Ficino's concept of *adaequatio*, but it is worth mentioning that his epistemology is based upon the identification of the knower with the known. In that respect it emulates many of the ancient Neoplatonic theories of knowledge which he was in the process of rediscovering and assimilating into his own system. And Ficino's epistemology may be distinguished from that of Cusanus which is always conditioned by the premise that "there is no proportion of the finite to the infinite."[40]

Ficino's conception of words and discourse is consistent with his theory of knowledge. In an important discussion of signification in Book 10, Chapter 7 of the *Theologia platonica*, Ficino argues that signification is to words what the soul is to the body:

The soul, through the instrument of the tongue, hits the air; the air, having been hit, resounds, and in resounding, takes on signification. . . . But is it by the tongue that the soul gives a word its signification? Not at all. The tongue is a body . . . it does not by itself give any signification. . . . Signification is an incorporeal, not a sensible, thing.[41]

Though a word is spoken and heard only in a moment, its signification remains in the minds of the speaker and the auditor:

39. Ficino, *Opera omnia*, 1:239: "Intellectus siquidem quamdiu potentia est intellecturus, nondum cum re potentia intelligenda coniungitur, sed quando actu intelligens est cum re actu iam intellecta. Coniungitur autem cum ea (ut volunt Peripatetici) quoniam rei illius forma inhaeret menti. Quorum vero una forma est, ipsa sunt unum: Unum ergo sit ex mente intelligente, ac re intellecta, quandoquidem rei huius forma, ut talis est, format mentem." The English version is from Paul Oskar Kristeller's *The Philosophy of Marsilio Ficino*, tr. V. Conant (Gloucester, Mass., 1964), 50.

40. See my *Nicolaus Cusanus*, especially 25–32; Chapters II and VII.

41. Ficino, *Opera omnia*, 1:234: "Anima rursus per linguam tanquam instrumentum frangit aërem, fractus aër sonat, sonando significat. . . . Sed nunquid anima significationem dat voci per linguam? Mimine. Lingua enim corpus est . . . neque significationem dat per se ullam. . . . Significatio vero res est incorporalis et insensibilis."

... this signification remains in the intelligence of the auditor although the syllables have disappeared, as it had existed in the intelligence of him who spoke before he spoke. Consequently the signification produced without intermediary by the soul of him who speaks is incorporeal.[42]

The meaning of this incorporeal signification derives ultimately from divine discourse itself:

The human soul therefore will be immortal and introduced by God into our body, like the signification introduced into the air by God. If one pays attention to this signification, it is the thought of God who speaks that one comprehends.[43]

The signification represented by human discourse is therefore innate and incorporeal, created in man by God when He made him in his image and likeness. If man properly understands the significations of words, he can hear God talking.

It was this conception of the relation between speech and signification that led to Ficino's deep interest in the magical powers of words and to his study of texts such as Proclus' *De sacrificiis et magia*, Iamblichus' *De mysteriis*, and the *Asclepius* — texts whose historical roots and theurgic practices lay close to those of the pseudo-Dionysius. And his linking of human and divine discourse was a key part of his creation of a Christian cosmos that was at the same time a pseudo-Dionysian hierarchical *sympatheia*. Within this cosmic *sympatheia*, Ficino searched for God, he theologized, in a number of different ways, including through his much-discussed astrological music and talismanic magic.[44]

Even so brief an essay as this into Cusanus', Pico's, and Ficino's views of mind and cosmos reveals some noteworthy differences in their uses of the pseudo-Dionysius' two modes of theologizing. In his *De docta ignorantia* and *Apologia doctae ignorantiae* Cusanus followed the pseudo-Dionysius'

42. *Ibid.*, 1:235: "Quae quidem significatio in audientis intellectu perpetua saepe remanet syllabis pereuntibus, sicut in loquentis mente fuerat antequam loqueretur. Significatio igitur ab anima loquente sine medio producta incorporalis est."

43. *Ibid.*: "Erit igitur hominis anima et immortalis, et huic corpori tanquam significatio aëri ab loquente Deo inserta. Quam significationem si quis animadverterit, Dei loquentis intelligit mentem."

44. See Walker, *Spiritual and Demonic Magic*, Chapter 1, Part 2 and Chapter 2, Parts 1 and 2 for a basic treatment of Ficino's interest in astrological music and talismanic magic.

apophatic or negative mode of theologizing. Believing that knowledge of created things is inaccessible to man through rational discourse and that knowledge of divine things is inaccessible through affirmative theology, he went beyond the one-dimensional pseudo-Dionysian concept of *agnô-sia* to the two-dimensional concept of "learned ignorance." Though there are places in his writings, notably the *De coniecturis* and the *De ludo globi*, where he introduces the monadic-triadic system of the pseudo-Dionysius into his discussions of the structure of the cosmos, he in the main conceives of the cosmos as an infinite sphere within which everything is in motion and precise hierarchical position seems lacking. On the other hand, both Pico and Ficino appear to have adopted, in their various ways, the intelligential cosmos of the pseudo-Dionysius and to have incorporated his celestial and angelic hierarchies into their own systems. More importantly, both also believed that the universe was a *sympatheia* and that knowledge of it was accessible to man through various means. Put another way, Pico and Ficino believed that there was a theophanic code of the universe to be cracked; they, like the Chaldeans and Neoplatonists of antiquity, were looking for *gnosis* and the operative power associated with it. In the *Heptaplus*, Pico searched for *gnosis* above all through the Cabalistic art, Ficino sought for it in words, songs, and the sympathetic powers of the stars and elements. There is much more to be said about the ways in which these three Renaissance Neoplatonists, Cusanus, Pico, and Ficino, transmitted and transformed the pseudo-Dionysius' cataphatic and apophatic theologies, the two ancient "sciences of God."

PAULINE MOFFITT WATTS

JOHN ARGYROPOULOS
and the 'SECRET TEACHINGS' of
PLATO

IN SEPTEMBER 1463, about a year after Cosimo de' Medici and Marsilio Ficino had founded their Platonic Academy, the humanist Donato Acciaiuoli described for a Castilian friend of Vespasiano da Bisticci recent intellectual changes in Florence. "Never before," he wrote, "have the humanities so flourished in this city," and many young Florentines are "so well versed in the Aristotelian and Platonic teachings that they seem to have been brought up in the Academy." To whom did Acciaiuoli credit

The present study is intended principally to reexamine some commonly held hypotheses concerning the teaching of John Argyropoulos in Florence. It touches only peripherally on Argyropoulos' place in the Latin and Greek scholastic traditions, and such a study, which I am not qualified to make, would no doubt clarify and perhaps emend some of the conclusions that follow. For the intellectual and cultural background of Argyropoulos' students, the controversies surrounding his first public appointment in Florence, and the use made of his lectures on Aristotle in the commentaries of his student Donato Acciaiuoli, see my forthcoming book, *The Origins of the Platonic Academy of Florence* (Princeton Univ. Press). The section on the public appointment has been published separately as "The *Studium Florentinum* Controversy, 1455," *History of Universities*, 3 (1983): 31–59.

In the following references to manuscripts, the abbreviations "Magl.," "Naz.," and "Ricc." are for the Fondo Magliabechiano of the Biblioteca Nazionale Centrale, Florence, the main collection of the same, and the main collection of the Biblioteca Riccardiana, Florence. All dates, unless specifically noted, are in the modern style.

Research for this study was supported by the American Academy in Rome, the American Council of Learned Societies, the Fulbright Commission, and the Harvard University Center for Italian Renaissance Studies, Villa I Tatti (through the Hanna Kiel Fellowship Fund and the Robert Lehman Foundation).

this revival? Not the Medici, nor even Ficino, but the Byzantine immigrant to Florence, John Argyropoulos.

> With great elegance, in the manner of the ancients, he has taught and is teaching moral and natural philosophy. Many books of Aristotle he has translated into Latin, and he has diligently opened up Plato's beliefs, and those secrets of his and the hidden teaching as well, to the great wonder of those who hear him lecture.[1]

Ficino himself did not dismiss the role of the Byzantines. From Byzantium, he wrote in 1464, the "spirit of Plato" had flown to Italy. But for Ficino the "spirit" had flown with the Greek text of Plato, and it had landed in his Academy.[2] Indeed, very soon after Acciaiuoli's description of the philosophical renaissance, quoted above, Ficino would emphasize his own role in the revival of Plato.[3] To learn the "basic tenets of philosophy" (*prima philosophiae sacra*), Ficino wrote in 1464, Cosimo de' Medici commissioned translations of Aristotle from John Argyropoulos. Then, to learn the "inner secrets of wisdom itself" (*intima sapientiae ipsius arcana*), Cosimo turned to some Hermetic writings and Platonic dialogues. In these works, which I translated, Ficino wrote, are revealed "all precepts of life, all principles of nature, all holy and divine mysteries."[4]

1. Letter to Alfonso de Palencia, 24 September 1463, written for Vespasiano da Bisticci, ed. in F. Fossi, *Monumenta ad Alamanni Rinuccini vitam contexendam* (Florence, 1791), 61–62: "Primum litterarum studia numquam magis in hac urbe viguerunt, multique hic adolescentes, multique iuvenes reperiuntur eruditi litteris graecis atque latinis, plerique etiam ita Aristotelicis Platonicisque disciplinis instructi, ut in Academia educati videantur. Venit enim in hanc urbem Argyropylus Bizantius. . . . [P]hilosophiam tum de vita et moribus, tum etiam de natura, summa cum elegantia antiquorum more et docet, et docuit. Plures Aristotelis libros latinos fecit, Platonis opiniones atque arcana illa et reconditam disciplinam diligenter aperuit non sine magna audientium admiratione." See A. Mondó, "Una lletra d'Alfons de Palència a Vespasià da Bisticci," in *Studi di bibliografia e di storia in onore di Tammaro de Marinis* (Verona, 1964), 3:271–281.

2. M. F., *Prooemium* to trans. of ten dialogues of Plato, to Cosimo de' Medici, in Kristeller, *Supplementum*, 2:104: ". . . e Bizantia Florentiam spiritus eius ipsis in licteris vivens Attica voce resonus ad Cosmum Medicem advolavit."

3. For Ficino's conception of the historical importance of his Academy, see P. O. Kristeller, *Il pensiero filosofico di Marsilio Ficino* (Florence, 1953), 11–20. For Ficino and Byzantium, see the general remarks of Kristeller, "Byzantine and Western Platonism in the Fifteenth Century," now in his *Renaissance Thought and Its Sources* (New York, 1979), 161–162.

4. *Prooemium* to trans. of Xenocrates, *De morte* (i.e. *Axiochus*), in *Opera omnia* (Basel, 1576; repr. Turin, 1959), 2:1965: "[Cosmus, ut] in primis philosophiae sacris initiaretur, nonnullos Aristotelis libros converti ab Ioanne Argyropylo viro doctissimo voluit, eosque diligentissime legit. Deinde ne intima sapientiae ipsius arcana sibi deessent, divi Platonis libros decem et unum Mercurii e Graeca lingua in Latinam a nobis transferri iussit, quibus omnia vitae praecepta, omnia

While there have been some important and detailed studies of the Neo-platonism of Marsilio Ficino, little effort has been made to investigate the Platonism of John Argyropoulos. At the same time many scholars, led by Eugenio Garin, have stressed the central role of Argyropoulos in the revival of Platonic studies in Florence.[5] According to Garin, the Byzantine not only wove Platonic doctrines into his public lectures on Aristotle but also directly explained, privately to his students, his preferred Platonic texts. University rules alone kept his public activity confined to Aristotle.[6] Taking up the passage from Acciaiuoli's letter quoted above, Garin has maintained that Argyropoulos taught a "secret and hidden doctrine" of Plato and hence embraced the hypothesis of a secret, Hermetic teaching passed on by Plato and his followers.[7] The common distinction between Argyropoulos' Aristotelianism and Ficino's Platonism, according to Garin, is due to Marsilio Ficino's cunning attempt to elevate his own role and that of his Medici patrons in the new Platonic studies.[8] Garin's conclusions are now widely accepted. Not unusual is the recent summary by George Holmes: the evidence that John Argyropoulos "filled his pupils with enthusiasm for Plato" is "not abundant but it is decisive."[9]

To his future students, Argyropoulos appeared to have stepped into Florence from antiquity itself. He spoke of the ancient philosophers as if he knew them first hand, and his strong accent sounding through a full beard represented an otherworldly and ancient lore.[10] Donato Acciai-

naturae principia, omnia divinarum rerum mysteria sancta panduntur." Cf. Kristeller, *Supplementum*, 1:cxxxvi–cxxxvii.

5. See especially Garin's "Donato Acciaiuoli cittadino fiorentino" (1954), in his *Medioevo e Rinascimento* (Bari, 1973), 199–267, an expanded form of an earlier article appearing in *Rinascimento* in 1950; "Platonici bizantini e platonici italiani: 1. Nuove indagini sul Pletone," in his *Studi sul Platonismo medievale* (Florence, 1958), 153–190; *La cultura filosofica del Rinascimento italiano* (Florence, 1961), 102–108; "La rinascita del Plotino" (1975), in his *Rinascite e rivoluzioni: Movimenti culturali dal XIV al XVIII secolo* (Bari, 1976), 89–129. For other works see *Bibliografia degli scritti di Eugenio Garin, 1929–1979* (Rome, 1979).

6. Garin, "Donato Acciaiuoli cittadino," 226–227; idem, "La rinascita del Plotino," 98–100.

7. Garin, "Donato Acciaiuoli cittadino," 226–229, 233. The expressions Garin uses, *arcanam illam et reconditam disciplinam* (p. 226) and "l'arcana e riposta disclipina" (p. 233), are inaccurate. The original is *arcana illa et reconditam disciplinam* (see above at note 1). For this study the distinction is important, for I shall argue that Argyropoulos was never interested in explaining any "secret teaching" of Plato.

8. Garin, "Donato Acciaiuoli cittadino," 265; idem, "La rinascita del Plotino," 96–97.

9. G. Holmes, *The Florentine Enlightenment, 1400–50* (London, 1969), 263.

10. In 1477, when Argyropoulos returned to Florence from Rome, Niccolò Michelozzi mentioned that he still had his accent but no longer his beard, and he "didn't look Greek anymore" (cited by G. Cammelli, *Giovanni Argiropulo* [Florence, 1941], 159, and now edited in part by A.

uoli's description of him in 1454 is telling: "He seemed to me not only erudite (as I had heard before I met him) but also wise and venerable, as if he had come from Greece of old."[11] Physically the impression required little from the Florentine imagination. Since the period when the Eastern Church sent to Florence her philosophers and theologians for the great ecumenical council in the late 1430s, no Florentine painter of the Adoration could neglect to include the portrait of a bearded Byzantine sage as one of the Magi.[12] Constantinople's fall to the Turks in 1453 left Florence with one of her exiles, one of these wise men from the East.

For those humanists in Florence who were accustomed to the study of Latin eloquence alone, the culture of Argyropoulos, like that of the other Byzantines, offered great enrichment.[13] He was born in Constantinople about 1410. After early training in Greek rhetoric and philosophy, he may have joined (the evidence is confusing) other Byzantine intellectuals at the Council of Florence in the late 1430s. From 1441 to 1444 he was in Padua, at the house of the Florentine exile Palla Strozzi. There he taught privately Greek rhetoric and philosophy to some Paduan nobles and polished his own Latin through conversation and instruction at the University of Padua. He may have lectured on Greek literature and language at the University, in the arts faculty; his studies were in the arts,

Verde, 'Giovanni Argiropolo e Lorenzo Buonincontri professori nello Studio Fiorentino," *Rinascimento*, ser. 2, 14 [1974]:280). Describing the lay and clerical Greeks at the Council of Florence, 1439, Vespasiano da Bisticci noted that they were dressed in the same "serious and dignified manner" which had been in use among the Greeks for "fifteen hundred years or more" (*Le vite*, ed. A. Greco, 2 vols. [Florence, 1970, 1976], 1:18–19).

11. Letter to Iacopo Ammannati, 5 August 1454, ed. G. Zippel, "Per la biografia dell'Argiropulo" (1896), now in his *Storia e cultura del Rinascimento* (Padua, 1979), 181: "Vir . . . mihi visus non solum eruditus, ut fama audieram, sed etiam sapiens, gravis et vetere illa Grecia dignus."

12. Ghirlandaio included a portrait of Argyropoulos as a Magus in his *Adoration of the Magi* (Florence, Uffizi) of 1487. The two bearded figures in Benozzo Gozzoli's *Voyage of the Magi* (Florence, Palazzo Medici-Riccardi), completed in 1459, merit closer attention. For the Renaissance representation of the Magus see R. Hatfield, *Botticelli's Uffizi "Adoration": A Study in Pictorial Content* (Princeton, 1976), *passim* (and p. 90, note 78, for Ghirlandaio's Argyropoulos), and idem, "The Compagnia de' Magi," *JWCI*, 33 (1970):107–161. For contemporary portraits of Argyropoulos, mostly miniatures, see the plates in Cammelli, *Argiropulo*, and in S. P. Lampros (or Lambros), ed., *Argyropouleia* (Athens, 1910).

13. The following survey of Argyropoulos' early career is based on Zippel, "Per la biografia"; A. Della Torre, *Storia dell'Accademia platonica di Firenze* (Florence, 1902; repr. Turin, 1968), 366–367, 380–384, 387–399, and *passim*; Cammelli, *Argiropulo*; E. Bigi, "G. A.," *DBI*, 4 (1962):129–131; and J. Monfasani, *George of Trebizond* (Leiden, 1976), 375–378 (for the problem of the date of A.'s birth). For Argyropoulos' public appointment in Florence, see my "*Studium Florentinum* Controversy, 1455," 31–59, and for additional bibliography, 50, note 19.

including Latin, that is scholastic, philosophy. By 1448 he was back in Constantinople in a prestigious position teaching at the Museum of the Xenon. When Constantinople fell to the Turks he fled, made his way to Venice, then to Padua, and spent part of the summer of 1454 in Florence, where he became acquainted with a group of young Florentine aristocrats and intellectuals led by Donato Acciaiuoli and Alamanno Rinuccini.

Not long after his short stay in Florence in the summer of 1454, Argyropoulos probably returned to Greece, to the court of Thomas Palaeologus, who held an area in the Peloponnesus not yet conquered by the Turks. By August, 1455, future students and Medici patrons in Florence won for him what was probably a lucrative position at the University, where he was expected to teach philosophy as well as, it seems, some Greek grammar and literature. He did not accept the appointment at that time. By early 1456 Thomas Palaeologus sent Argyropoulos as an ambassador to the new pope, Calixtus III. Calixtus in turn sent him first to Milan, then to France, Germany, and England. Finally, in early 1457, Argyropoulos returned to Florence and began teaching Aristotelian philosophy. He stayed in Florence some fifteen years, took up teaching in Rome in the early 1470s, returned briefly to Florence toward the end of the decade, and then went back to Rome, where he died in 1487.

In Florence, Argyropoulos was a teacher. He did little else professionally, except prepare a great number of Latin translations, mostly of Aristotle, which he presented to patrons.[14] The argument that Argyropoulos introduced Platonism to Florence is based principally on the testimony of his students and on evidence drawn from his lectures. Of these lectures several of the more formal prefatory orations or preliminary lectures (the *praefationes* or *praelectiones*) have modern editions.[15] There are also unedited

---

14. See Cammelli, *Argiropulo*, 183–184, for a list. See also C. Frati, "Le traduzioni Aristoteliche di G. Argiropulo e un'antica legatura Medicea," *La Bibliofilia*, 19 (1917):1–25.

15. From Ricc. 120, K. Müllner has edited six pieces from John Argyropoulos' introductory lectures: *Reden und Briefe italienischer Humanisten* (1899; repr. Munich, 1970), 3–56. The manuscript has been considered a possible autograph, but the hand is in fact that of Donato Acciaiuoli (see Plate I). Although the titles and style of the six pieces in Ricc. 120 would seem to indicate six separate lectures, some of the separate pieces in the manuscript are actually made up of several introductory lectures, and the "secunda lectio" for the course on the *De anima* (edited on pp. 48–53; Ricc. 120, ff. 31r–34r) should be loosely considered "a following lecture," probably the third for that academic year, 1460–1461. Some of the divisions can be clarified by comparing Donato Acciaiuoli's notebooks for the regular lectures themselves (MSS Naz. II I 103; Naz. II I 104; Magl. V 42). These contain some but not all of the introductory lectures from Ricc. 120, as well

lectures, only sporadically utilized by modern scholars, which are in manuscript notebooks diligently copied by Donato Acciaiuoli (see Plates I and II).[16] (Acciaiuoli had the "fastest hand" in Florence, a *mano velocissima*, according to Vespasiano da Bisticci, which could "take down in writing everything that Argyropoulos said in voice."[17]) Three of these notebooks are extant, and they include some fifteen hundred pages of text covering lectures delivered before 1462, the pivotal year when the Platonic Academy was founded and when Ficino began his direct and systematic study of the Platonic corpus.[18] Hence there are abundant sources, for the most part unedited, which should permit careful analysis of Argyropoulos' role in the revival of Platonism in Florence.

To be sure, affixing or removing the tag "Platonist" to a Renaissance philosopher can be risky. For Argyropoulos' "Platonism" one could look at his status within the Byzantine tradition, in relation to its earlier history from Psellus to Pletho. Platonism so permeated Byzantine philosophical culture that few Byzantines, even ardent Aristotelians, can escape being called Platonists in some sense of the word, even if they would not have so described themselves. Moreover, in the Plato-Aristotle controversy of the Quattrocento, Argyropoulos sided with the "harmonizers" by prais-

---

as other introductory material. Cf. for instance Ricc. 120, f. 31r (Plate I) and Magl. V 42, f. 8r (Plate II). For these notebooks, see notes 16, 30, below. In the notebooks the separate lectures are more clearly distinguished (labeled "1a," "2a," etc., or separated by vertical lines, pen changes, or such tags as "pridie dicebamus"). It should be noted that since Ricc. 120 is an Acciaiuoli autograph, the dates assigned in the Acciaiuoli notebooks, long recognized as autographs, no longer serve as corroborating evidence for the dates of Ricc. 120. The dates for the latter may in fact indicate when Acciaiuoli copied the pieces, after stylistic improvements. But I think they are roughly accurate. The dates from early November (or early February), seem late for the academic year, which in Florence usually began on October 18 (or January 18, for a delayed term). Indeed I have argued elsewhere that the dates Acciaiuoli assigned his autograph letters should never be trusted, and that they are often some two to three weeks later than they should be ("The *Studium Florentinum* Controversy, 1455," 51, note 32). While I find few errors in Müllner's editions, Ricc. 120 should probably be reedited with a fresh reading of the manuscript and with the material from Acciaiuoli's notebooks added and compared. For one problem with the edition, see V. Brown, "Giovanni Argiropulo on the Agent Intellect: An Edition of Ms. Magliabecchi V 42 (ff. 224–228v)," in J. R. O'Donnell, ed., *Essays in Honour of Anton Charles Pegis* (Toronto, 1974), 161, note 4; see also note 30, below.

16. See note 15, above. Although Acciaiuoli's notebooks have been called "lecture notes," they should properly be called "lecture drafts" or *reportata*. In these the student prepares the drafts from notes, usually attempting to reproduce faithfully the lectures and sometimes in consultation with the lecturer himself. Any close reading of the corrections and style of Acciaiuoli's notebooks reveals that they cannot possibly contain actual lecture notes.

17. Vespasiano da Bisticci, *Vite*, 2:25.

18. See note 15, above. For Ficino's early Platonic studies, see Kristeller, *Studies*, 196–198, and his "Marsilio Ficino as a Beginning Student of Plato," *Scriptorium*, 20 (1966):41–54. For the be-

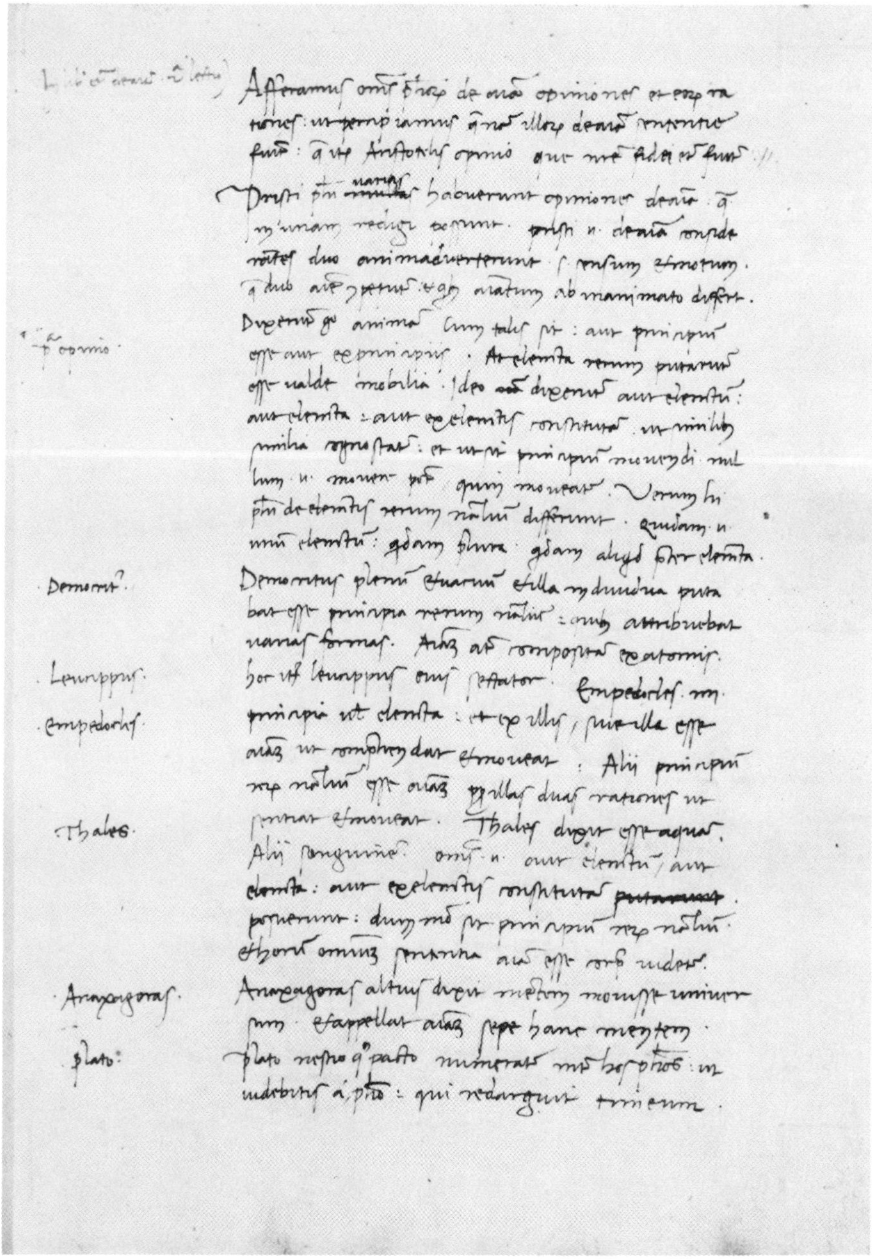

Plate I. Firenze, Bibl. Riccardiana, MS 120, f. 31r: John Argyropoulos, the beginning of a lecture on Aristotle's *De anima*, 1460. The scribe is identified as Donato Acciaiuoli.

Plate II. Firenze, BN, MS Magl. V 42, f. 8r: Donato Acciaiuoli's draft of Argyropoulos' lectures on the *De anima*, 1460–1461.

ing Bessarion's defense of Plato against George of Trebizond's rigid Aristotelianism.[19] For this too one might term Argyropoulos a "Platonist." What concerns us in this study is different, defined by the question we raised at the beginning of this essay: Is there evidence that the Platonic teaching of Argyropoulos heralded that approach toward Plato taken by Marsilio Ficino and hence that it ushered in the Neoplatonic movement itself? Did Argyropoulos, that is, attempt to convince his Florentine students that certain Platonic doctrines, express teachings and hidden ones as well, were consonant with their proper "human condition," essential to their self-understanding, and beneficial or even necessary to their desire to attain happiness?

What, we may ask, did Donato Acciaiuoli mean when he wrote that Argyropoulos opened up the "secrets" and the "hidden teaching" of Plato? The expressions appear in a letter composed on behalf of a Florentine book dealer, Vespasiano da Bisticci, and addressed to a foreign customer, where exaggerated statements of Florentine cultural and intellectual accomplishments should abound. Secret and hidden teaching could mean the sort of *prisca theologia* of Marsilio Ficino. According to Ficino, secret teachings of natural and divine wisdom had been passed down by a succession of ancient sages from the Egyptian Hermes Trismegistus to Orpheus and others, and thence to the divine Plato and his followers. Some of these could be found in ancient writings (the *Orphic Hymns*, the *Pimander* and other texts attributed to Hermes Trismegistus, the *Chaldaic Oracles*); others required an enlightened interpretation of Platonic dialogues and letters. They were "secret" because they had been cunningly kept from the masses of men, because they were "hidden" in express teachings of philosophers and poets, or because they were "removed" from one's ordinary way of looking at the world.[20] Acciaiuoli's description of Argyropoulos' role in the new studies, in September 1463, falls just a few weeks before Tommaso Benci published his Italian translation of Ficino's Latin rendering, published the previous April, of the *Pimander* of Hermes Trismegistus. The Hermetic texts were very popular, and in underscor-

---

ginning of the Academy, see also S. Gentile, S. Niccoli, and P. Viti, eds., *Marsilio Ficino e il ritorno di Platone: Mostra di manoscritti, stampe e documenti (17 maggio–16 giugno 1984)* (Florence, 1984), 175–176, no. 140.

19. Argyropoulos, letter to Bessarion, in L. Mohler, *Kardinal Bessarion*, 3 vols. (1923–42; repr. Aalen, 1967), 3:601–602.

20. See especially D. P. Walker, *The Ancient Theology: Studies in Christian Platonism from the Fifteenth to the Eighteenth Century* (London, 1972), 1–21 and *passim*.

ing the importance of ancient secret lore Acciaiuoli could have simply been reflecting current fashion.[21] We shall argue, however, that in ascribing to Argyropoulos the idea that Plato had a "hidden teaching," Acciaiuoli was using expressions that had a particular meaning of their own.

To contemporaries Argyropoulos' wisdom was neither inscrutable nor esoteric: the common tag applied to it was that it was "systematic." One of Argyropoulos' students, Alamanno Rinuccini, described in 1489 the Byzantine's early lectures. After travelling through France, Germany, and England (1456), Argyropoulos returned to Florence and

> began to teach philosophy, in no backward or piecemeal way, but (a thing which is a great aid to learning) in the order in which it was written out by Aristotle. Taking his beginning from dialectics, he went thence through his teachings on natural science and went forward in his teaching up to metaphysics, explicating Aristotle's twelve books on it over a two-year period.[22]

Indeed an important, and, for the Florentines, unconventional part of Argyropoulos' teaching was his consideration of Aristotle's philosophy as a unified whole. Leonardo Bruni and the humanists of the early Quattrocento had asserted the Stagirite's eloquence and had studied his moral philosophy; they had avoided Aristotle's speculative philosophy or treated it eclectically.[23] In the universities teachers in the arts and medicine lectured on standard texts of Aristotelian logic and dialectics, as well as on those other works of Aristotle which served as a groundwork for the professions. But Argyropoulos saw how the several parts of the Aristotelian corpus fitted together: to study philosophy, he argued, one had to begin with logic and dialectics; then one studied, in order, ethics, natural philosophy, mathematics, and finally metaphysics. When Argyropoulos spoke of education in more general terms, he added grammar and rhetoric

21. For the Benci translation, see Kristeller, "Marsilio Ficino as a Man of Letters and the Glosses Attributed to Him in the Caetani Codex of Dante," *RQ*, 36 (1983):22.

22. Rinuccini, *Lettere ed orazioni*, ed. V. R. Giustiniani (Florence, 1953), 189: "Qui peragrata Gallia, Germania et Britannia, regressus Florentiae constitit, et philosophiam non praepostere aut interrupte, sed, quod maxime ad discendum confert, quo ordine ab Aristotele perscripta est docere coepit, a dialectica principium sumens atque inde per mediam naturalem disciplinam ad metaphisicam usque docendo profectus, de qua duodecim Aristotelis libros biennio explanavit."

23. For an especially useful synopsis of Aristotle in the early Renaissance, see E. Garin, "Le traduzioni umanistiche di Aristotele nel secolo XV," *Atti e memorie dell'Accademia fiorentina di scienze morali "La Colombaria,"* ser. 2, 2 (1947–1950 [1951]):55–104.

to the beginning of the list—but these were two basic and preliminary disciplines, not part of philosophy.[24]

This scheme of sciences was Platonistic, and seems to have originated in late antiquity with the Greek Neoplatonic commentators on Aristotle. The theory then was that one proceeded up through hierarchies from things humanly perceived to the divine essences themselves.[25] In Byzantine philosophical culture the scheme was commonplace. Even the scourge of Renaissance Platonism, George of Trebizond, followed the same ascending order of logic, natural philosophy, mathematics, and metaphysics.[26]

Each step forward in the *cursus* of sciences required a grasp of the earlier sciences. In one of his first public lectures in Florence, in early 1457, Argyropoulos pointed out the necessity of preliminary instruction in logic:

After the art of grammar and oratory, if we wish to proceed to philosophy, we must first look to the art of arguing and reasoning, which is customarily called logic. Without logic—and this is as clear as noonday—nothing can be perfectly perceived and known in the active or speculative life. Afterward we should proceed at once to moral philosophy.[27]

The transition from moral to natural philosophy Argyropoulos described in an introductory lecture on the *Physics* (1458). After dialectics, our entrance to philosophy, ethics serves as our preparation for more advanced study:

For when the soul is well disposed and purged of vice, and all moral

24. For Argyropoulos' order of philosophy, see below, notes 27–30.

25. B. Tatakis, *La philosophie byzantine*, suppl. no. 2 to É. Brehier, *Histoire de la philosophie* (Paris, 1949), 179, 191, 196–197; J. A. Weisheipl, "Classification of the Sciences in Medieval Thought," *Medieval Studies*, 27 (1965):58–62.

26. George of Trebizond, *Comparationes phylosophorum Aristotelis et Platonis* (Venice, 1523; repr. Frankfurt a. M., 1965), lib. I, cap. 3 ff. His list of the sciences in his *divisio operis* at the end of I, 2, however, reads *rationalis* (including the *copia dicendi*), *naturalis*, *metaphysica*, and *mathematica*, with *moralis* separated out. But in discussing these in the following chapters, he reversed mathematics and metaphysics; the earlier order would seem to be due, therefore, to a mental lapse or an editorial or scribal error.

27. *Praefatio in libris Ethicorum quinque primis* (4 February 1457), in Müllner, ed., *Reden und Briefe*, 16 (cf. Ricc. 120, f. 8v): "Nam post grammaticam oratoriamque artem, si ad philosophiam pergere voluerimus, post argumentandi ratiocinandique artem, quae logica appellari solet, sine qua medius fidius nihil perfecte nec in activa nec in speculativa vita sciri atque percipi poterit, percipienda est statim philosophia moralis. . ."

disturbances have been stilled, one may proceed to this natural philosophy.

Then, he argued, one must not proceed "at once" to divine philosophy (metaphysics), for while through natural philosophy we know that the "essence of the soul" and "certain separated substances" exist, we are not able to perceive these things perfectly without mathematics.[28] Studies of mathematics, as Plato said, serve as "steps" which lead to metaphysics.[29]

This order of sciences indeed provided Argyropoulos with his actual program of studies. The chronological evidence we have for his lectures, from the notebooks of Donato Acciaiuoli, from extant *praefationes* and *praelectiones*, and from the testimony of his students, demonstrates conclusively that Argyropoulos did in fact adhere to his order of sciences. That is, after private lectures in logic (always labeled "first" in contemporary testimony, though it seems that they must have been given at the same time as the early lectures on ethics), Argyropoulos taught moral philosophy (the *Nicomachean Ethics*, 1457–58, and soon thereafter, on feast days, the *Politics*) and then went through natural philosophy (*Physics*, 1458–60; *De anima*, probably 1460–61; and *Meteorologica*, beginning in 1462).[30] After 1462 he may have taken up more natural philosophy. There

28. Naz. II I 103, f. 8v (from the *accessus*, here explaining the position of natural philosophy within the *ordo scientiarum*): "Ordo . . . talis esse videtur. Incipiendum a dialetica, que via modus et aditus est ad pergendum ad archana philosophie. Deinde pergendum ad istam [*sic*: *sc.* naturalem philosophiam] per moralem philosophiam, ut dispositus animus et purgatus, sedatis perturbationibus omnibus, accedat ad istam naturalem philosophiam. Ex naturali vero non statim accedendum ad divinam, sed ad mathematicam et per eam ad divinam. Atque ille Plato divinus non modo doctrina sed re ipsa ostendit per hanc proficiscendum ad divinam. Nam per naturalem philosophiam anime essentiam cognoscimus et quasdam substantias separatas esse. Non tamen possumus perfecte percipere illa sine mathematicis."

29. *Praefatio . . . in sexto libro Ethicorum* (i.e., introductory lecture to the second series of lectures on the *Ethics*, 1 February 1458), in Müllner, ed., *Reden und Briefe*, 20 (cf. Ricc. 120, f. 12v): "[S]unt . . . res mathematicae mediae inter naturales et supernaturales, ne ab extremo ad extremum sine medio fiat transitio, unde Plato scalas appellare haec solebat, quibus ab inmersis in materia ad purissimas substantias ac separatas ab omni materia posset accedi [animus noster]." In the autumn of that same year, in an introductory lecture to Aristotle's *Physics* (Naz. II I 103, f. 2v), Argyropoulos made the same argument but may have given Plotinus as the source: ". . . post philosophiam naturalem in ordine perdiscende sunt mathematice, quas Plotinus ille summus philosophus appellavit scalas." This image of the "steps" toward metaphysics appears in Plato, *Rep.* 6, 511b, and Plotinus, *Enn.*, 6.7.36. Two lectures later Argyropoulos would again speak of the intermediary sciences and mention Plato alone (see note 28, above).

30. For the dates, see the introductory lectures edited by Müllner, *Reden und Briefe*, 3–56, from Ricc. 120. Acciaiuoli's draft of the *Ethics* course, Naz. II I 104, is undated at the beginning, but the date "1456" (s.f.) appears at the top of f. 29r, at the beginning of Book 2, an indication that

were no texts of Aristotle for mathematics, and it is unlikely that Argyropoulos used other, standard texts; rather, he probably wove into his regular lectures on Aristotle a careful explanation of the function of mathematics.[31] Argyropoulos concluded the series with two years of lectures on Aristotle's *Metaphysics*.[32]

The order of sciences not only determined Argyropoulos' sequence of

the second book was probably begun before 25 March 1457. For the course on the *Politics* we have testimony only: a letter of Pierfilippo Pandolfini to Xanthus Viriatus, Magl. VI, 166, ff. 111r–112v, and Vespasiano, *Vite*, 2:13, 26 (who mentions other courses as well). Acciaiuoli's lecture draft of the *Physics* course, Naz. II I 103, is dated at the beginning 3 November 1458 (f. 1r) and at the end 2 August 1460 (f. 260v). The manuscript is complete for *Physics* 1–3, covered by Argyropoulos in 1458–1459 (cf. the *Praefatio*'s title edited by Müllner), but does not include most of the rest of the *Physics* (i.e. 4–8), except part of Book 8. Acciaiuoli probably missed the lectures at the beginning of the academic year 1459–1460; he may have been at the Council of Mantua (see Pandolfini's letter, autumn, 1459, quoted below at note 59, and A. C. de la Mare, *Vespasiano da Bisticci, Historian and Bookseller* [Ph.D. thesis, University of London, 1965], 2:325–326).

Acciaiuoli's notes from the course on the *De anima* (Magl. V 42) are dated, at the beginning, 5 November 1460 (f. 1r). Cf. also Rinuccini's letter on these lectures cited at note 35, below. For the *Meteorologica* we have an introductory lecture only, edited by Müllner, 53–56, as "In libro Mechanicorum" (Ricc. 120, f. 35r: "In libro Methaurorum"), dated 1462. In an early article Garin pointed out the correct subject of the course ("Le traduzioni umanistiche," 85–86n.). Somewhat more problematic are the courses in logic and dialectics. Bartolomeo Fonzio recorded a few glosses from Argyropoulos' lectures on the *Posterior Analytics*, and some of his other remarks as well, in one of his notebooks, Ricc. 152, ff. 185r–197r (originally foliated 174–186). The undated section is entitled (f. 185r): "Sub Ioanne Argyropylo collecta non solum ad librum posteriorum necessaria, sed etiam quaecunque ab eo dicta preter expositionem." For this MS, see Kristeller, *Iter* 1:88; S. Caroti and S. Zamponi, *Lo scrittoio di Bartolomeo Fonzio umanista fiorentino* (Milan, 1974), 41–45, no. 2. In his biographies of Donato and Piero Acciaiuoli, Vespasiano da Bisticci implies sometimes that lectures on logic were prior to, sometimes that they were concurrent with, the early lectures on the *Ethics*, and indicates that they were given privately in the morning (*Vite*, 2:11–12, 25). Both Landino's description of Acciaiuoli's early studies under Argyropoulos, and Politian's description of Lorenzo de' Medici's, list studies in dialectics "first" (Landino, funeral oration on Acciaiuoli, ed. in M. Lentzen, *Reden Cristoforo Landinos* [Munich, 1974], 72–73, and Politian, *Miscellaneorum prima centuria*, in *Opera omnia* [Basel, 1553; repr. Turin, 1971], 1:224). What is important for this study is that Argyropoulos did indeed adhere to his system, and the notion that he abandoned or distorted it to create a "civic" Aristotle, or to pander to his civic-humanist friends, cannot be supported by the available evidence (cf. Garin, "Donato Acciaiuoli cittadino," 202–203, 240–241, 245). See also Garin's "Platonici bizantini e platonici italiani," where he reviews favorably F. Masai's *Pléthon et le Platonisme de Mistra* (Paris, 1956). Masai sees Argyropoulos as the Italian exponent of Pletho's paganism, in an attempt to use a form of Platonism as the ideological foundation of political renewal and reform. For the latter thesis, see the cogent remarks of J. Monfasani, *George of Trebizond*, 160, note 124.

31. In a letter on education to his son, Alamanno Rinuccini adhered strictly to Argyropoulos' order of studies and recommended for mathematics the *Sphaera* of Johannes de Sacrobosco, the *Planetarum theorica* of Gherardus de Sabbioneta, and Euclid (*Lettere ed orazioni*, 100 and note).

32. See the quotation from Rinuccini, note 22, above; cf. Vespasiano da Bisticci, *Vite*, 2:13, 26.

courses but also helped shape his method of lecturing. One advanced to the higher science after mastering the lower one. Hence in his lectures on ethics Argyropoulos relied heavily on Aristotle's logic. And so, too, natural philosophy depended on ethics. Here, however, we cannot expect the relation to be strikingly evident in the lectures themselves. Ethics shaped not future lectures but future students. Ethics was to produce students cured of vice and rid of moral disturbances, good and hard-working, and eager to master the higher branches of philosophy.[33] But for the Florentines the transition from moral to natural philosophy presented special problems. For those who were seeking a general, humanistic education, natural philosophy was a new science.[34] Midway through Argyropoulos' lectures on the *De anima* (1460–61), Alamanno Rinuccini would write that, from Book II of Aristotle's work, the students could only relate to the fifth chapter, *De gustibus* (i.e. on eating and drinking).[35] Much later he would describe the typical Argyropoulos student as Ennius described Neoptolemus: as one, that is, who was willing to learn philosophy only part way.[36] Indeed from his first lectures in Florence John Argyropoulos himself described all philosophical learning as difficult, and learning in speculative philosophy as especially difficult. He underscored the problem by repeatedly identifying the principles of philosophy as *arcana*. After logic and dialectics, he said in 1458, we must move on to the *arcana* of philosophy, beginning with ethics.[37]

This was indeed John Argyropoulos' characteristic definition of *arcana*: secret teachings were those difficult to grasp.[38] These *arcana* embraced not just the speculative wisdom hidden in the writings of the *prisci philosophi* or the *prisci poetae*, but the teachings of all philosophy, including the relatively easy subject of Aristotle's *Ethics*.

Argyropoulos described some of the difficulties in an early lecture on

33. See above at note 28.
34. See Rinuccini's letter on education to his son, 1474, where he says that, to get a good education, it is *now* considered necessary to pass beyond rhetoric to philosophy (*Lettere ed orazioni*, 97).
35. *Lettere ed orazioni*, 55–56.
36. Letter to Roberto Salviati, 1489, in *Lettere ed orazioni*, 187–190 (ref. at 189–190).
37. See note 28, above.
38. In a preface to a translation of some of Aristotle's logic, for instance, Argyropoulos argued that all should avidly move on from studies of rhetoric to the "archana philosophiae sententiasque persubtiles Aristotelis": ed. J. Seigel in his "The Teaching of Argyropulos and the Rhetoric of the First Humanists," in *Action and Conviction in Early Modern Europe: Essays in Memory of E. H. Harbison*, eds. T. K. Rabb and J. E. Seigel (Princeton, 1969), 258.

Aristotle's *Physics*, in November, 1458, when he attempted to outline the philosopher's method (the *modus procedendi*, one of the several categories surveyed in a scholastic *accessus*):

> The method of proceeding seems to be now divisive, from which he defines, now demonstrative, partly from causes, partly from effects. He also seems to proceed by way of definition. Thus he uses these three methods. Now and then he also uses the resolutive (for there are four methods), that he might discover the cause from the effects.[39]

Although these four dialectical methods were common divisions of the Greek commentators, Argyropoulos' description (if Acciaiuoli's draft of the lectures is here faithful) is almost stammering.[40] And well it should be, as we may note as the passage continues:

> Nevertheless in this [i.e. his method] as in his other things [relating to this work], he is most difficult [to follow], and not only in the old Latin translations, but also in Greek. For at one moment he seems too laconic, at another too prolix—out of this variety the difficulty arises. . . . And this not without reason, but so that the sciences might lie hidden and with difficulty be mastered, and so that men, stirred by the clarity [or excellence] of the subject matter, would despise the labor necessary so long as they obtained such excellent [benefits] and hence emerged [from the discipline] more perfect.

Argyropoulos then turned to the problem of the origins of scientific thinking.

> One should also realize, lastly, that the sciences had a beginning, not only in our opinion but also in that of the pagans, who nevertheless held that the sciences have continuously sprung up: because at one time things were lost through a flood (one which did not cover the whole world), and at another time things were recovered. There-

---

39. Naz. II I 103, f. 9v: "Modus procedendi videtur esse nunc divisivus, ex quo diffinit, nunc demostrativus [sic], partim a causis, partim ab effectibus. Diffinitivus etiam videtur. Itaque istis tribus utitur modis. Utitur etiam interdum resolutivo (quattuor enim sunt) ut inveniat causam ab effectu."

40. For the four methods, see N. W. Gilbert, *Renaissance Concepts of Method* (New York, 1960), 24, 104–105.

fore they admit that the sciences were invented in some part of the world, as in Greece after the flood of Deucalion, but that in the world there were always sciences. They say that the Egyptians did not have the flood of Deucalion and thus the Greeks were helped by them.

Argyropoulos went on to explain that early science was necessarily unsystematic.

Therefore the sciences seemed to be crude in the beginning. For there were many philosophers who taught science obscurely and in verse — nevertheless many things were worthy and outstanding. Afterwards came Pythagoras, who seems to have extended philosophy. Later came Plato, who avoided verse and provided most fully a teaching — although he preserved some old practices by designating the principles of things in the mathematical way. Then Aristotle treated the principles of things as natural, and he did not seem to speak about the parts of the world, but as if the world had never been, not presuming any existence but only quiddity. Nevertheless he maintained the obscurity.[41]

Thus in the systematization of natural philosophy even Aristotle retained

41. Naz. II I 103, ff. 9v–10r: "Tamen in hoc ut in suis aliis est difficillimus, et non modo latine secundum traductiones antiquas sed etiam grece. Nam nunc astringit sese nimium, nunc dilatat, ex qua varietate nascitur difficultas. Lycophron poeta unum, Avicena alterum sequi videtur scribendi modum. Atque hoc non sine causa, sed ut in abdito sint scientie et cum difficultate habeantur atque rei claritate commoti homines laborem comptenant [sic], dummodo tam preclara adispiscantur atque ob hoc evadant perfectiores. Considerandum etiam illud postremo quod scientie incepere, non modo nostra sed etiam gentilium opinione, qui tamen dixerunt perpetuo fuisse obortas, quia nunc amissa per diluvium, non secundum totum mundum, nunc etiam recuperata. Concedant igitur inventas scientias in aliqua parte mundi, ut in Grecia post Deucalionis diluvium, sed in mundo semper fuisse scientias. Egiptios dicunt non habuisse Deucalionis diluvium et ideo Greci habuerunt adiumentum ab illis. Itaque crude videbantur in illo principio esse scientie. Fuerunt enim multi philosophi qui obscure et carminibus tradiderunt scientiam, tamen multa digna ac preclara. Postea venit Pythagoras qui amplificasse philosophiam videtur. Postea Plato, qui omissis carminibus amplissime dedit doctrinam, etsi reservavit antiqua nonnulla apellando principia rerum modo mathematico. Aristoteles postea adeo loquutus est de principiis rerum ut naturalia sunt, nec videtur loqui de partibus mundi sed ac si mundus numquam fuisset, non accipiendo existentiam ullam sed quidditatem. Tamen obscuritatem retinuit." The previous year, in an early lecture on the *Ethics*, Argyropoulos also referred to the flood in explaining Aristotle's distinction between moral and intellectual virtues in *Eth. Nic.* 2.1 (1103a 1–3). Moral virtues require doctrine, intellectual virtues invention, which in turn requires experience and time. Although pagans believe in the eternity of the world, they also, like Christians, believe in this process of discovery, since they think they have suffered losses through floods and continental and oceanic dislocations. (MS Naz. II I 104, f. 29r.) For a later discussion of the question, see the lectures on the *De anima*, Magl. V 42, f. 231v.

some of the confusion of the earlier philosophers: the poetic obscurities of a former age, which the Stagirite cleared up in several disciplines, yet have remained in natural science.

Aristotle could be systematic only because he stood at the end of a great philosophical tradition, one that was unified and that should be studied in its unity.[42] After the simple preservation and transmission of many Greek texts, the doctrine of a unified philosophical tradition must rank as the most strikingly evident Byzantine contribution to Renaissance Platonism. Marsilio Ficino seized on the hypothesis at once.[43] But Argyropoulos placed Aristotle at the pinnacle of this tradition. As for the pre-Socratic poetic philosophers, theirs was no "oracular wisdom" or secret teachings that the good philosopher should want to recover and pass on; rather, the *prisci philosophi* were crude and unscientific. If their teachings were "hidden away," it was because they were obscure. For Argyropoulos, the text itself of Aristotle required him to explore pre-Peripatetic philosophical traditions—directly or indirectly Aristotle referred often to earlier traditions, and Argyropoulos was either clever enough to identify the indirect references or diligent enough to look them up in available commentaries. We shall focus here on his attitude toward Platonic and pre-Socratic (or pseudo pre-Socratic) "secrets."

In the lectures, we find that the "unity" of ancient philosophy was not something that Argyropoulos accepted passively; rather, he critically and carefully identified three stages of ancient wisdom: the pre-Socratic or poetic, the Platonic, and the Aristotelian. He analyzed each in terms of what it contributed to the development of the specific sciences, ethics, natural philosophy, mathematics, and metaphysics. Argyropoulos included the earliest philosophers, from Zoroaster to Anaxagoras, within the "unified tradition," but he ignored them in his lectures except where Aristotle himself spoke of an earlier tradition. When he took up these pre-Socratics, as in the quotation above, Argyropoulos mentioned their "obscurity" and their philosophizing "in verse." An excellent summary of Argyropoulos's opinion of the first centuries of philosophy appears in an early lecture on Aristotle's

---

42. *Too* unified, one might say, for in an *accessus* Argyropoulos has Aristotle studying "sub praeceptore Socrate primo, deinde Platone" (*Praefatio in libris Ethicorum quinque primis*, in Müllner, ed., *Reden und Briefe*, 15; cf. Ricc. 120, f. 8r). Noted by E. B. Fryde, *Humanism and Humanist Historiography* (London, 1983), 63.

43. *Opera*, 2:1537. Cf. A. Keller, "Two Byzantine Scholars and Their Reception in Italy," *WCI*, 20 (1957):363–366, and P. O. Kristeller, "Byzantine and Western Platonism," 161–162.

De anima (1460). In the passage, which we shall quote at length, Argyropoulos passed by the earliest philosophers and poets in favor of the three figures who created the classical philosophical tradition, Socrates, Plato, and Aristotle:

> There were three outstanding geniuses. I omit Zoroaster and many others up through Anaxagoras who taught philosophy obscurely and in verse. There were, then, three: Socrates, Plato, and Aristotle. Socrates drove men to the sciences through discourses on moral philosophy: thus he is called a moral philosopher although he was a speculative philosopher of the first rank. He saw that the men of his time were devoted to forensic eloquence; he called them away from this and urged them on to the study of wisdom and self-perfection. For man is born imperfect, but he has the power to perfect himself and then also to perfect others. In this way, therefore, Socrates drove on the rest. After him was the divine Plato, most perfect in every discipline, supreme in poetry and the most eloquent of all, a moral, natural, mathematical, and especially a speculative thinker, as we may understand from his writings: he, however, followed Socrates' practice of not putting the sciences in order. After him came Aristotle, who studied under Plato for twenty-one years and gave the supreme order to the sciences.[44]

Argyropoulos never gratuitously wove Platonic teachings into his lectures on Aristotle. To be sure, he did follow standard academic practice in his introductory lectures or *praelectiones* and outline a variety of ancient teachings. In a prefatory section on the definition of philosophy he reproduced the Pythagorean definition ("amor sapientiae"), the Platonic ("cog-

---

44. Magl. V 42, f. 2v: "Fuerint enim tria preclara ingenia. Omitto Zorostrem [*sic*] et multos alios usque ad Anaxagoram, qui obscure et carminibus tradiderunt philosophiam. Fuerunt igitur tres, scilicet Socrates, Plato, Aristoteles. Socrates disserendo per moralem philosophiam compellebat homines ad scientias et ideo apellatus est moralis, quamquam speculativus summus fuerit. Videbat ea tempestate homines deditos eloquentie forensi, a qua avocabat et compellebat deinde ad studium sapientie et perfectiones suas. Homo enim nascitur imperfectus sed aptus per potentias ut perficiatur, ut etiam deinde perficiat alios. Socrates igitur hoc pacto compellebat reliquos. Post hunc fuit Plato divinus, qui, perfectissimus in omni facultate—in poesi summus, eloquentissimus omnium, moralis, naturalis, mathematicus, et maxime speculativus, ut ex scriptis eius intelligi licet—non tamen tradidit ordinem scientie, sequutus Socratis morem. Post hunc Aristoteles qui XXI annos audivit Platonem et dedit ordinem scientiarum summum. . ."

nitio eorum quae sunt," or "similitudo qua deo similis homo quoad possit fieri potest," or "excogitatio mortis"), and the Aristotelian ("artium
ars scientiarumque scientia").[45] But these highly schematic, formal list-
ings implied no endorsement of any one position — and a scholar's recent
attempt to isolate the Platonic definitions as Argyropoulos' favorite has
not been backed by supporting evidence.[46]

It cannot be denied, on the other hand, that Argyropoulos took up
the Platonic teachings with a great deal of care and empathy. Argyropoulos' overall opinion of Aristotle's critique of Plato followed well-worn paths:
(1) Aristotle is really criticizing not Plato but common opinions attributed to Plato, opinions taken up by some of Plato's followers; (2) Aristotle's arguments against Plato are artificial, disputatious, and sophistic,
designed solely to impress his audience with the distinctiveness of his own
doctrine. (Argyropoulos avoided, however, the heavy-handed moralistic
judgments common to humanist exegesis, that the Stagirite was a *discipu-
lus ingratus*.) Where Aristotle criticizes Plato's theory of Ideas (e.g., in
passages in the *Nicomachean Ethics* and the *De anima*), Argyropoulos examined the respective positions at some length.[47] According to Vespasiano
da Bisticci, Argyropoulos indeed fancied himself something of an authority
on the Platonic Ideas.[48]

In one of his first lectures in Florence, Argyropoulos outlined the Platonic theory as follows. Plato posited one god as the king above the heavens,
in whose intelligence are the species of all inferior things. This god holds
these species "causatively," not "essentially." Through self-understanding
this god creates a second god, who has in his mind the formal reasons
of all species, which are in him "essentially." This second god, through
self-understanding, produces the other species, the third god of the universe
and then a fourth god of all other things, and then both things that are
"male" and things that are "female." These "males" and "females" are
to be understood as the "form" and the "matter" of created things, and
each of these has its corresponding Idea. "Universal" can be considered

45. *Praefatio in libris Ethicorum quinque primis*, in Müllner, ed., *Reden und Briefe*, 5 (cf. Ricc.
120, f. 2r).

46. E. Garin, "La rinascita del Plotino," 99.

47. A long passage from the lectures on the *Ethics* is paraphrased below. Cf. the lectures on
the *De anima*, Magl. V 42, esp. ff. 25r–27v, 46r–48r.

48. Vespasiano, *Vite*, 1:346–347.

in any one of three ways, according as it is *before, in,* or *after* a concrete referent. The first universal—the formal reason itself, the definition of each species, and the Ideas—is in the divine mind; the second universal is the common *ratio* of the universal itself which is in individual and particular things, as the "humanity" in this or that human; the third universal is deduced from individual things as the species or the genus derived from the species, and this third rests in our intellect. In his *Ethics* Aristotle opposed Plato's theory of Ideas, Argyropoulos argued, with this syllogism: (a) of those things in which there is an earlier and a later there is not one Idea; (b) in things morally good there is an earlier and later; (c) *ergo,* there can not be an Idea of the morally good. The "good," Argyropoulos stated, can be considered in two ways, either as "goodness itself," or as the subject in which goodness rests. Aristotle's reasoning is valid against this second form only. Hence his arguments as a whole do not oppose Plato and are sophistic.[49]

49. Paraphrased from the lectures on the *Ethics,* Naz. II I 104, f. 15r-v: "*His igitur omissis.* Hac in parte Philosophus impugnare intendit opinionem Platonis, qui posuit summum bonum esse Ideam. Eius opinionem latissime exposuit Argyropolus hoc modo. Dicebat Plato summum esse supercelestem et regem omnium deum, in cuius intelligentia essent omnes speties rerum inferiorum, sed causative tantum non autem essentialiter. Hic intelligendo seipsum ab eterno generat alium deum secundum, qui secundus deus habet in mente sua omnia, idest rationes formales omnium spetierum, que sunt in eo essentialiter et sunt de substantia ipsius et ibi habet spetiem, primo totius mundi deinde speties omnium aliarum rerum. Itaque illas intuens, idest seipsum intelligens, producit omnes alias speties omnium rerum inferiorum et creatarum. [*In margin without signe de renvoi:* In primo illo dicuntur rationes, in secundo exemplaria. Rationes dicuntur, inquam, in primo causative, veluti de sole dicuntur, qui causative generat ranam, equum et alia animalia.] Producit quoque tertios et quartos deos et deinceps non modo mares sed etiam feminas. Quod ita intelligendum est quod cum ad omnia que creantur duo concurrant, materia scilicet et forma, et unicuique istorum conrespondeant sue idee, ille que ordinantur ad formas possunt apellari masculino nomine, que ad materias feminino. Dicimus autem materias, quoniam secundum diversas formas diversificantur etiam materie. Alia enim est materia hominis, alia equi et sic de singulis. Intelligendum tamen de materia propinqua natura remotaque—etiam prima dicitur—una est materia omnium. *De universali.* Notandum quod triplex est universale, unum ante rem, aliud in re, tertium post rem. Primum universale est ipsa ratio formalis et diffinitio cuiuscumque spetiei et idea que est in mente divina. Secundum est ratio conmunis ipsius universalis que est in singulis particularibus, ut 'humanitas' in hoc et illo homine. Tertium quod deducitur ab ipsis singularibus, utputa ipsa speties predicamentalis vel genus quod abstrahitur ab ipsis spetiebus et est in nostro intellectu. *Huius opinionis.* Contra Platonem hoc modo. Eorum in quibus est prius et posterius non est una idea. Sed in bonis est prius et posterius. Ergo etc. Minor probatur a Philosopho inductive, quod cum bonum dicatur in omnibus predicamentis, prius tamen de uno quam de altero dicitur, ut de subiecta prius quam de accidentibus. Sed hec ratio non arguit contra mentem Platonis et est sophistica. Sciendum igitur quod bifariam potest considerari bonum, aut ⟨ut⟩ importat bonitatem dumtaxat aut ut importat etiam subiectum in quo est. Et hoc secundo modo considerando

Argyropoulos' Plato is here, to be sure, Neoplatonic. This view of the Platonic cosmos was well known in Byzantine circles. George of Trebizond took it up in his attack on Plato, and Cardinal Bessarion described it at some length in Book Three of his answer to George, *In calumniatorem Platonis*.[50] In another introductory lecture on Aristotle, in 1458, Argyropoulos would once again take up the Platonistic *schema* of the second, third, and fourth gods; but this time he concluded the survey with a Peripatetic response:

> But the Peripatetics and Aristotle himself, the prince of the Peripatetics, posit one god, highest, immortal, perpetual, and most perfect, who holds eternally all innate perfection; according to the opinion of some he deduces our souls, by which our bodies are informed, from the potency of matter; [and he says] there is, however, a single intellect, perpetual, and immortal, by the power of which all rational souls understand and act according to reason. Therefore the souls have no innate virtue or knowledge, nor any innate happiness and perfection, but they are like a blank slate and are able to acquire happiness for themselves with their operations.

Argyropoulos then concluded:

> Compelled by this belief, by which he considered us appropriately to gain happiness through our human operations, the philosopher wanted to expose the way by which one could proceed to this happiness, and this he did by teaching us this doctrine [*sc.* of natural philosophy] with the greatest systematization and the greatest diligence.[51]

---

valet ratio Aristotelis. Primo autem modo minime, quia secundum eam rationem non dicitur esse in aliquo predicamento. Etiam de tali bono intellexit Plato et sic non valet contra illum huiusmodi ratio."

50. George of Trebizond, *Comparationes*, lib. II, cap. 1; Bessarion, *In calumniatorem Platonis*, in Mohler, ed., *Kardinal Bessarion*, 2:223–225 (III.2), 239–243 (III.6), 279–281 (III.13).

51. *Praefatio . . . in sexto libro Ethicorum*, in Müllner, ed., *Reden und Briefe*, 24 (cf. Ricc. 120, f. 14v): "At Peripatetici atque ipse Aristoteles, Peripateticorum princeps, unum deum ponit summum, inmortalem, perpetuum, perfectissimum, qui omnem perfectionem habet ab aeterno innatam, animas vero, quibus nostra corpora informantur, secundum nonnullorum opinionem deduci de potentia materiae; esse tamen intellectum unicum, perpetuum et inmortalem, cuius vi omnes rationales animae intelligerent atque secundum rationem operarentur. Itaque non innatam habere

Here as elsewhere Argyropoulos' exposition has led him to what he knows and likes best, the systematic study of Aristotle. Even where his explanations of Plato's teaching are lengthy, sympathetic, and detailed, and even where, as apparently here, he thinks that Aristotle erroneously believed in the unity of the intellect, Argyropoulos still returned to his Aristotelian philosophy, the best route to true human wisdom and perfection.

Plato's major contribution, emphasized Argyropoulos, was to be the first to present a "clear," unfettered teaching of certain philosophical principles. Earlier philosophers taught "obscurely" or "in verse." Taking up certain Pythagorean and corpuscular theories, Argyropoulos explained to his students why the teachings appear so curious: philosophy at that time was thoroughly confused (*vehementer indigesta*).[52] Early teachings on the soul reflect this confusion, and certain doctrines, especially where the soul is defined purely by physical characteristics, should be accepted as metaphors.[53]

The earliest philosophers may indeed have been "obscure" but they were by no means "subtle." Their thinking was necessarily limited, in that dialectical reasoning had not yet been invented. In his lectures on the *Nicomachean Ethics*, Argyropoulos took up Aristotle's distinction between two kinds of universal term, one predicable of the agent and the other of the object (7.3; 1147a). Aristotle, Argyropoulos stated, always takes the middle ground with such distinctions. Plato, he continued, "was the first to have discovered these ways of making distinctions." Later Aristotle made wide use of these methods of distinguishing, so that "all those

virtutem ullam aut scientiam, non felicitatem aut perfectionem, sed esse tamquam tabulam abrasam ac suis operationibus posse sibi felicitatem in vita acquirere. Hac opinione compulsus Philosophus, qua arbitrabatur humanis operationibus oportere felicitatem nostram acquiri, iter patefacere voluit quo ad illam posset accedi, cum hanc doctrinam nobis summo ordine summaque diligentia tradidit." The doctrine of the single intellect derives from Averroës, whose approach toward Aristotle Argyropoulos would have studied in Padua in the early 1440s. Here it seems that Argyropoulos is not actually embracing the doctrine but does see it as useful for understanding Aristotle. The doctrine, condemned by theologians and opposed vehemently by Ficino, was never especially popular in Florence, and in 1460 Argyropoulos attacked it in his lectures on the soul: see Brown, "Giovanni Argiropulo," 163.

52. Lectures on the *De anima*, Magl. V 42, f. 43r.

53. *Ibid.*, ff. 44r, 55r, 199r. Argyropoulos began describing such doctrines as metaphorical in his lectures on the *De anima* (1460–1461) and this terminology may be due to the influence of his Florentine contemporaries. One quotation (f. 55r) reads: "Sed hec [*sc.* opinio de anima] Platonis est vehementer subtilis accipiendo eam non ut verba sonant sed ut significatur per verba methaphorica." And later (f. 199r): Aristotle spoke "confusedly" about the *phantasia*, following the *prisci philosophi* who called it *imaginatio*. We shall discuss it "proprie et non methaphorice."

'ironies' of the sophists, whom he always hated intensely, could be removed."[54] Later, in lectures on the *De anima*, Argyropoulos repeated the
theme with the question of whether there could be color without sight.
One must distinguish, he said, between "color itself" and "color" in any
particular circumstance. "Before Plato," Argyropoulos explained, "these distinctions were not made, and people spoke in a simple manner." Later
Aristotle "in a wonderful fashion amplified on these methods."[55]

The lectures of Argyropoulos as recorded by Donato Acciaiuoli repeat
the aforementioned themes time and again, whenever the Byzantine is
compelled by the text of Aristotle to take up Platonic theories. Nothing
in the lectures reveals the "Platonic enthusiasm" scholars have suggested
they contain. To be sure, other evidence for Argyropoulos' Platonism has
been adduced. Eugenio Garin has argued at length that Argyropoulos had
already studied a codex of Plotinus before Marsilio Ficino had acquired
the skills to do the same. No one has yet demonstrated how such study,
if it indeed did take place, affected any lectures in the classroom.[56] Acciaiuoli's notebooks give no solid evidence that Argyropoulos was promoting
Plotinus before his students.[57] Garin also has argued that once in a lecture
on the soul Argyropoulos, opposing Aristotle, insisted on the autonomy
of the mind in respect to the sensible phantasm. "Sed dominus Ioannes exponit quod . . . intelligit quando vult, et non indiget presentia phantasmatis" — so reads Acciaiuoli's draft of the lectures, cited by Garin. But an
examination of the manuscript reveals that Argyropoulos is not opposing
Aristotle at all. He is here (at *De anima* 430a 14f.) simply explaining the
textbook doctrine of the agent intellect, which, unlike the possible intellect which uses phantasms, uses intelligible species as objects of thought.[58]

54. Naz. II I 104, f. 110r.
55. Magl. V 42, f. 192v.
56. "La rinascita del Plotino," 91 ff.
57. See note 29, above. This is the only instance I have seen, in some fifteen hundred pages
of Acciaiuoli's notes, of any reference to Plotinus.
58. E. Garin, "La rinascita del Plotino," 99: ". . . l'Argiropulo contra Aristotele insisteva sull'
autonomia della mente rispetto al fantasma: 'sed dominus Joannes— sottolineava nei suoi appunti
l'Acciaiuoli—exponit quod . . . intelligit quando vult, et non indiget presentia phantasmatis.'"
(Garin cites Magl. V 42, f. 225r. I shall be citing Brown's edition of ff. 224r–228v in her "Giovanni
Argiropulo," 166 and note.)
In Greek the passage being glossed concludes as follows (*De anima* 3, 430a 14f., ed. W. D.
Ross [Oxford, 1961]): καὶ ἔστιν ὁ μὲν τοιοῦτος νοῦς τῷ πάντα γίνεσθαι, ὁ δὲ τῷ πάντα ποιεῖν,
ὡς ἕξις τις, οἷον τὸ φῶς· In his translation of the *De anima*, Argyropoulos handled the conclusion
in this way: "Atque quidam est intellectus talis ut omnia fiat; quidam talis ut omnia agat atque

There remains one important and well known piece of evidence for Argyropoulos' Platonism. It appears in a letter of one of his students, where we learn that the Byzantine at least once taught Plato privately.

In the autumn of 1459 Pierfilippo Pandolfini sent to Donato Acciaiuoli a description of John Argyropoulos' teaching of Plato. The oft-quoted letter indeed seems to demonstrate the Byzantine's enthusiasm for Plato and could suggest, as Garin has argued, that only academic constraints kept his public lectures tied to the texts of Aristotle. The relevant section from the letter follows:

The afternoon of the last day of September, a Sunday, Vespasiano and I went to John and found him reading Plato. Several of our group were with him. He put his book aside and spoke with us for a while. After many words were bandied about we at last brought him to a discourse which would have pleased you immensely — on Plato, namely, whom he praised with enthusiasm and of whom he related some things incredible and truly unheard-of. "With many words (he said) I shall show you how great was the prudence and wisdom of Plato, whom all, even if they do not know his teaching, admire greatly." At once he began: "I shall explain to you this man's dialogue entitled *Meno*. You ought to be satisfied with this one, for how great is its doctrine, eloquence, prudence, and wisdom you will surely observe if you wish to hear." Then he explained it, with such order, such elegance, such richness and variety of expression, that

efficiat, qui quidem habitus est quidam et perinde ac lumen" (ed. V. Brown, 164). The part Garin has Acciaiuoli emphasizing (*sottolineando*) is in the margin. Argyropoulos' original gloss in the text follows (ed. Brown, 166): "Nota quod intellectus agens est philosophi sententia *ut habitus* quidam, et per hoc vult philosophus intellectum agentem esse actu et intelligere semper. Nam antequam generetur habitus in intellectu, sine presentia specierum non potest percipere; at non est in potestate sua tunc intelligere cum vult. At cum acquisivit habitum, potest speculari cum vult, id est non indiget presentia rei."

In her edition of this passage, V. Brown included two marginal additions that Acciaiuoli added to this gloss. The first reads as follows: "Expositores accipiunt ut habitus, id est ut quedam perfectio." Brown identifies the source as Aegidius Romanus' commentary on the *De anima*. The second marginal addition appears just below it: "Sed dominus Ioannes exponit quod est ut habitus, quasi intelligit quando vult et non indiget presentia phantasmatis aut alicuius exterioris, ut intellectus possibilis qui non eo pacto est ut habitus quidam" (*ed. cit.*, 166). See Magl. V 42, f. 225r, for the relative location of the two glosses. Acciaiuoli's marginal gloss, therefore, merely explains Argyropoulos' own commentary. Acciaiuoli has distinguished Argyropoulos' gloss from that of the *expositores*, who interpreted the agent intellect simply as *quaedam perfectio*. The gloss in no way opposes Aristotle. Nor is it Neoplatonic.

as much as we marveled at Plato himself, whose many divine teachings we heard, we marveled no less at the eloquence of John.[59]

What does the letter reveal? We have no transcription of the described "lecture" and any conclusions as to its content must remain speculative. We shall venture a few anyway. In the first place, the lecture was on the *Meno*, and this dialogue was one of the poorest Argyropoulos could have chosen had he wanted to outline for his students something close to Ficino's "Platonic theology."[60] The *Meno* begins with the distinction between the thing-in-itself (i.e. virtue in itself) and the particular thing (any virtue); to illustrate this sort of distinction, Plato has Socrates ask whether "white" is "color" or "a color" (74c). Here we do not have to stretch our imaginations far to imagine how Argyropoulos would describe what he saw as a marvelous Platonic invention in the field of logic and dialectics. The dialogue deals also with the theory of recollection, whether certain ideas are held innately or acquired by our efforts; it includes the famous episode where Socrates educes certain mathematical principles from an uneducated boy. This, too, is a theme ideally suited as a backdrop to Argyropoulos' conception of Aristotelian science. Even if Pierfilippo Pandolfini maintained that what Argyropoulos taught were *inaudita*, we can yet surmise that on that Sunday afternoon Argyropoulos' students heard some rather familiar themes, developed, to be sure, with a "richness" and

---

59. The letter is undated, one of several from Pierfilippo Pandolfini in a fragmentary section, ff. 104r–115v, of Magl. VI 166, containing letters from August 1459 to August 1460. The last day of September 1459 was a Sunday, and the date therefore seems secure. The section reads as follows (f. 108r–v; cf. E. Garin, *La cultura filosofica*, 119): "Pridie Kalendas Octobris, qui fuit dies dominicus, post meridiem ego et Vespasianus dominum Joannem adivimus eumque Platonem legentem invenimus. Erant et cum illo nostrorum quidam. Hic posito libro aliquantulum confabulatus est, multisque verbis ultro citroque habitis in eum tandem sermonem provenimus qui tibi profecto non iniocundus fuisset: in Platonis [*sic*], dico, quem cum vehementer laudasset eiusque nonnulla incredibilia prorsus atque inaudita retulisset, 'multis,' inquit, 'vobis [verbis *Garin corr.*] ostendam quanta prudentia ac sapientia Plato, quem omnes vel eius disciplinae ignari non mediocriter admirantur, fuit.' Statimque exorsus: 'Eius viri,' inquit, 'vobis dialogum, qui *Menon* inscrib < it > ur, declarabo. Hoc enim uno Platonis contenti esse debebitis, in quo quanta doctrina, quanta eloquentia, quanta denique et prudentia et sapientia insit, profecto si audire volueritis prospicietis.' Eumque denique tanto ordine, tanta elegantia, tanta dicendi ubertate et copia explicavit, ut non magis Platonem ipsum, cum [cuius *Garin corr.*] multa divina audiebamus, quam huius viri eloquentiam admiraremur."

60. To be sure, this conclusion is somewhat impressionistic, and could be tested through a complete index of Ficino's works. Those indices now available (Kristeller, *Il pensiero filosofico*, as well as some recent editions of Ficino) show very few direct citations of the *Meno*.

"elegance" (as the letter reads) unsuited to a class lecture. Indeed the letter states that the students marveled at Argyropoulos' "eloquence" and "order." Did the Byzantine leave his students thirsty for more Platonic wisdom, doctrines of the soul and of love, the secret teachings and wonderful metaphors contained in the *Phaedo*, *Philebus*, or the *Symposium*? Possibly, but only because they were not getting such doctrines from their Florentine *maestro*. As Argyropoulos said before he began talking about the *Meno*: "You ought to be satisfied with this one." Indeed, within a year Pierfilippo Pandolfini would once again refer to Argyropoulos' teaching: I have heard so many divine things, he wrote, that "now for the first time I have begun to admire Aristotle as the prince of philosophers."[61]

Argyropoulos' accomplishments in Florence were many. He showed how Aristotelian philosophy was a unified whole, whereas Florentines had before been accustomed to study the Peripatetic discipline (as Rinuccini later implied) "in a backward or piecemeal way."[62] He introduced the Florentines to the "hidden teaching" of ancient poets and philosophers: Plato had been the first to outline expressly many of the doctrines and methods that became part of the Aristotelian system; and the early poetic philosophers with their obscure figments had given the system its first form. He was fascinated by this Aristotelian system and knew that it had a history, that the sciences had a "beginning." Hence he praised the pre-Socratics, Socrates, and Plato. And his students could, and many did, move freely between his lectures and those of Marsilio Ficino. Yet Argyropoulos could never praise Plato at Aristotle's expense, and his only serious endeavor in Florence was an explanation of the Aristotelian system. So devoted was he to the "true Aristotle" that in his first lectures in Florence, on the *Nicomachean Ethics*, he inserted a running critique of Leonardo Bruni's translation of the text—Filelfo warned him at once that he was treading on hallowed and sensitive ground.[63] Even more boldly (accord-

61. Letter to Xanthus Viriatus, Magl. VI 166, f. 112r: "In quorum [*sc.* librorum philosophiae naturalis] declaratione tot et tanta audiuntur divina ut nunc primo Aristotelem philosophorum principem admirari incipiam."

62. See note 22, above.

63. If Acciaiuoli's notebook is at all faithful, from his first lectures on the *Nicomachean Ethics* Argyropoulos often quoted the Greek and then gave his students a translation "correcting" that of Leonardo Bruni (Naz. II I 104). Filelfo's warning—this is the only negative thing I am hearing about you from Florence—appears in a letter of November 1457 (ed. É. Legrand, *Cent-dix lettres grecques de François Filelfe* [Paris, 1892], 93).

ing to testimony of Politian) Argyropoulos claimed that Cicero did not know his Aristotle![64] These "indiscretions" underscore his diligence. By the sixteenth century, classical scholars would credit Argyropoulos, not Leonardo Bruni, with having broken with the medieval tradition of translating Aristotle.[65] In his own time, with his skillful, careful explanation of Aristotle, based on the original sources, he remained at the forefront of Florentine intellectual life.

As we noted earlier, in the mid-1460s Marsilio Ficino claimed that, through Cosimo's efforts, he had translated the works of Plato while Argyropoulos had made available Aristotle. Our conclusion here is that Ficino has described rather well Argyropoulos' influence: The Byzantine recreated for the Florentines the system that Aristotle had built. While Ficino had from the beginning an independent, theoretical, dialectical relationship with the Platonic corpus, so that he was continuously adding to what he had accomplished previously, Argyropoulos described his project from the beginning—a reconstruction of the Aristotelian system— and he set about to fill in the details. Perhaps it was fitting that in 1471, lured by Sixtus IV, he left Florence for Rome: by now he had surely completed both the lecture series and the translations of Aristotle.

The nature of Argyropoulos' teaching, as outlined above, may explain why there is such a curious silence between him and Marsilio Ficino. Ficino's reference to Argyropoulos, cited earlier, is the only one he gave; Argyropoulos never seems to have mentioned Ficino. (There is complete silence between Ficino and Argyropoulos' most loyal student, Alamanno Rinuccini. Between Ficino and Argyropoulos' most enthusiastic student, Donato Acciaiuoli, nothing is heard until the 1470s, when Ficino urged Donato to play the patron to an impoverished son of Carlo Marsuppini.[66]) How-

---

64. E. Garin, "Ἐνδελέχεια e ἐντελέχεια nelle discussioni umanistiche," *Atene e Roma*, ser. 3, 5 (1937):177–187; J. Kraye, "Cicero, Stoicism, and Textual Criticism: Politian on κατόρθωμα," *Rinascimento*, ser. 2, 23 (1983):83–87. Politian's testimony may be true, although Argyropoulos' critique of Cicero does not appear where one might expect it, in Acciaiuoli's redaction, that is, of the lectures on the *De anima* (Magl. V 42).

65. C. B. Schmitt, *Aristotle and the Renaissance* (Cambridge, Mass., and London, 1983), 69–72.

66. Ficino, *Opera*, 1:655. In describing this silence I have followed Kristeller, "L'état présent des études sur Marsile Ficin," in *Platon et Aristote à la Renaissance* (Paris, 1976), 68, who raises this as a question yet to be answered. There are other possibilities besides the one I am offering in the conclusion to this essay. First, there was a great deal of nastiness in the controversy between Argyropoulos' students, led by Donato Acciaiuoli and Alamanno Rinuccini, and the supporters of Cristoforo Landino, who presumably included Poggio Bracciolini and Marsilio Ficino, over the status of the humanist chairs at the University of Florence in the mid-1450s. While I

ever highly Argyropoulos may have regarded Ficino's translations or his
other attempts to *reproduce* Greek antiquity, it seems likely that, with his
particular view of the progress of the disciplines, he could only have considered the Ficinian "Platonic theology" as philosophically retrogressive.
Aristotelian science had developed through three steps, from the *prisci
philosophi* to Plato to Aristotle, and Ficino was demonstrating far too much
enthusiasm for the first two—for the early, secret wisdom and the poetic
obscurities—for his philosophy to be palatable to an Argyropoulos. The
sciences, as they had naturally developed, Ficino was throwing into confusion.[67] From the other side, Ficino, as it seems according to the style
of his philosophical discourse, would have likely considered Argyropoulos a skilled expounder of Aristotle, a learned translator, but limited in
scope and imagination. We would have to agree with Ficino, if indeed
that was his opinion, save for the tag "limited," which ill suits the leading Peripatetic of early Renaissance Florence.

ARTHUR FIELD

have argued that John Argyropoulos was not at the center of the controversy, this has not definitely
been proven, and it remains true that several of those who became his students engaged in polem-
ics with the supporters of Landino ("The *Studium Florentinum* Controversy, 1455"). R. Cardini
has argued that in 1458 Argyropoulos and Landino were throwing barbs at one another in their
inaugural orations at the Florentine University (*La critica del Landino*, 71 ff.). Secondly, Argyropoulos
evidently viewed Latin philosophers generally as second-rate thinkers (as in the reference to Cicero,
noted above; see also note 67, below). Latins took the Greeks as vain and too apt to conceal their
intellectual borrowings. The latter opinion is particularly evident in Poggio Bracciolini and Cristoforo
Landino (especially in the latter's early lectures on Virgil, in Rome, Biblioteca Casanatense, MS
1368, and in Florence, Biblioteca Laurenziana, MS 52, 32), but it also appears, in its own way,
in Ficino's endorsement of the pre-Greek *prisca theologia*. Thirdly, as I mentioned earlier, Argyropoulos
attacked Bruni's translation of Aristotle. This of course was an attack on a Florentine Chancellor,
could only have infuriated Ficino's friend Poggio Bracciolini, and may also have provoked a "patriotic"
reaction from Ficino himself. Fourthly, Argyropoulos appears at times to have been sympathetic
to Averroistic doctrines, which Ficino condemned strongly (see the end of note 51, above). Fifth-
ly, Ficino and many of his circle were not, particularly in the earlier period, the social equals
of the better-born disciples of John Argyropoulos.

67. Whom did Argyropoulos consider to be the best interpreter of Plato? According to Vespasiano da Bisticci, Argyropoulos thought that "among the Latins" (!) none could approach Narcis-
sus Verdunus! (*Vite*, 1:346–347). *Addendum*: The identification of the hand of MS Ricc. 120 in
note 15 as that of Donato Acciaiuoli was earlier made by S. Caroti in "La rinascita della scienza,"
in *La corte il mare i mercatanti ...*, catalogue of the exhibit "Firenze e la Toscana dei Medici nell'Europa
dell Cinquecento" (Florence, 1980), 132.

SCALA, PLATINA and LORENZO

de' MEDICI in 1474

THE THREE LETTERS of the humanist and chancellor of Florence, Bartolomeo Scala, transcribed below form part of a collection of autograph letters in the Archivio Borromeo in Isola Bella.[1] The letters consist of four folios, Fondo Autografi S 6, folios 1–4, the first being an original state letter from the Florentine Signoria to Francesco Gualterotti, Florentine ambassador in Milan, dated 20 February 1497, subscribed with Scala's name as chancellor, but not autograph. The remaining folios consist of autograph drafts of letters, possibly coming from the collection now in Modena, Biblioteca Estense, MS Campori Appendice 235 (Gamma P 2, 5), to be described fully in my forthcoming edition of Scala's writings. Folios 2–3

---

1. In June 1984 I received from Professor Kristeller what he called "a surprise . . . which you may consider a rather mixed blessing": six autograph and very illegible drafts of letters by Bartolomeo Scala. Since they have to be added to my forthcoming edition of Scala's writings, they were indeed a mixed blessing, but following the adage *beneficia plura recipit qui scit reddere*, I am delighted to be able to return to Paul, in *omaggio* and gratitude for all the help and encouragement he has given me for more than twenty-five years, part of his *beneficium* in the form of these transcriptions — without however asking for more! I would not have been able to do so in the required time but for the kindness of Signor Pier Giacomo Pisoni, who gave me generous help with xeroxes and with his own transcription. I would like to thank him and Count Vitaliano Borromeo for permission to publish; also Jill Kraye at the Warburg Institute and Professor Nicolai Rubinstein for their help. All the autograph draft letters will be included in my edition of Scala's *Political and Humanistic Writings* to be published by the Scuola Normale Superiore di Pisa, Nuova Collezione di Testi umanistici inediti o rari.

contain four letters probably drafted in late April–May 1474, one to Bartolomeo Sacchi, called Platina, one to Sacramoro Sacramori, formerly Milanese ambassador in Florence, now in Rome, and two to Lorenzo de' Medici. The draft to Sacramoro (f. 2r–v, not edited here) "jokingly" chides him for being less kind to Scala than was the Neapolitan ambassador, Marino Tomacelli, before "more seriously" going on to discuss the divided opinions in Florence about a new peace treaty.[2] Folio 4 contains draft letters to the Bishop of Aleria, Ardicino della Porta, and to Pope Innocent VIII relating to the benefice Scala was hoping to obtain in July 1487.[3]

The letters I edit here are of great interest for the light they throw on the literary scene in Florence in 1474. This was the period dominated by Cristoforo Landino's teaching in the university and by Marsilio Ficino's neoplatonic discussions at Careggi, which together stimulated new interests and new attitudes to moral problems and philology: which is better, the active or the contemplative life, does happiness lie in acts of will or reason, what is the relation between language and philosophy? These are all topics discussed in writings like Ficino's letter *On Happiness* and his *Oratio ad Deum theologica*, which influenced Lorenzo de' Medici's poem the *Altercazione* of 1474; the dialogue *De optimo cive* which Platina sent to Lorenzo in April 1474; and Landino's *Disputationes Camaldulenses* written probably towards the end of the previous year, which Cardini describes as a *svolta* or turning point in Florence. After it, he says, a book like Pliny's *Natural History*, which Landino was translating into Italian at this time, served as a source for the discovery of philosophical truths rather than historical fact, the first step in a Platonising ascent from the visible to the invisible.[4]

All these writings are referred to directly or indirectly by Scala, who like Landino was strongly influenced by the revival of Platonic thought. His letter to Platina and his first letter to Lorenzo de' Medici were written in response to Platina's dialogue to Lorenzo, *De optimo cive*, thanks

2. On the changing diplomatic relationships in Italy in 1474 that preceded the eventual signing of a new treaty between Florence, Venice and Milan on 2 November, see Lorenzo de' Medici, *Lettere* (Florence, 1977), 2:477–84 (Excursus I) and 485–90 (Excursus II).

3. They are probably the two letters Scala refers to in a letter to Giovanni Lanfredini dated 2 July 1497: "Con questa vi mando mie lettere al Papa et a Monsignore Arelia;" see Alison Brown, *Bartolomeo Scala, 1430–1497, Chancellor of Florence: the Humanist as Bureaucrat* (Princeton, 1979), 108–9.

4. See R. Cardini, *La critica del Landino* (Florence, 1973), 113–232, esp. 152–61; on the date of the *Disputationes*, 152, note 37. On the other writings, see notes 5 and 7 below.

to which we are able to date his letters with some certainty to late April–May 1474.[5] In this dialogue Cosimo de' Medici plays the part of Socrates in propounding to his grandson Lorenzo Platonic doctrines about the state, showing the growing influence of Platonism on the way the Medici's role in the city was perceived.[6] Its political relevance was not lost on Scala, who writes both to Platina and to Lorenzo to commend it. To Platina he welcomes the use of Cosimo as model of "the best citizen" who now seems to live again in Lorenzo, "called by everyone another Cosimo returned to the city." To Lorenzo he emphasises the moral seriousness of the dialogue, "in which you hang upon the lips of your grandfather, drinking wisdom from him as a baby drinks from the breast of his mother."

Scala's second letter to Lorenzo is longer and more interesting. He begins by apologizing for being so long in replying, not due to negligence but to the fact that, "captivated by the sweetness and adornment of your oration, captivated by the gravity and opinions of your writing," he had to read it over and over again before he felt satisfied. The whole letter, he goes on, is highly polished and worthy of a serious and wise man, especially the part discussing virtues and their opposites which was written less in an oratorical manner than in the learned manner of the philosophers. What does he refer to? Presumably the *Altercazione*, despite describing it as a letter rather than a poem. Certainly the "oration" would describe its sixth chapter, which was modelled on Ficino's *Oratio ad Deum theologica*; and the subject matter and treatment corresponds to the rest of the poem, part of which Gentile Becchi described on 15 March 1474 as "Lorenzo's three chapters *de summo bono*."[7] Unless Lorenzo wrote a

---

5. Platina's *De optimo cive* is edited by F. Battaglia (Bologna, 1944). On its date, see N. Rubinstein, "Il *De optimo cive* del Platina," in *Atti del Convegno su Bartolomeo Sacchi, detto il Platina* (forthcoming), quoting from the *Protocolli del carteggio di Lorenzo il Magnifico per gli anni 1473–4, 1477–92*, ed. M. Del Piazzo (Florence, 1956), 512, that Lorenzo wrote to thank Platina on 23 April 1474; on 4 May Donato Acciaiuoli also wrote to Platina about his dialogue (Rubinstein, *ibid.*).

6. On the political relevance of the dialogue, see my article in *The Journal of Modern History*, 58 (1986): 383–413, "Platonism in Fifteenth Century Florence and Its Contribution to Early Modern Political Thinking"; cf. Rubinstein, above.

7. See M. Martelli, *Studi laurenziani* (Florence, 1965), 13–15. On the "guazzabuglio dell'*Altercazione*," and its relationship to Ficino's writings, *ibid.*, 1–35; Kristeller, *Studies*, 213–19; A. Rochon, *La jeunesse de Laurent de Médicis (1449–1478)* (Paris, 1963), 475–543; and Lorenzo de' Medici, *Lettere*, ed. R. Fubini (Florence, 1977), 1:496–98, 510–11, 517–18. The *Altercazione* is edited by A. Simioni, in Lorenzo de' Medici, *Opere*, vol. 2 (Bari, 1937), and by G. Cavalli, in idem, *Tutte le opere*, vol. 3 (Milan, 1958). Ficino's *Oratio* and his letter *De felicitate* are in his *Opera* (Basle,

prose version or a separate letter to Scala on similar material, we must suppose that Scala was writing to praise the *Altercazione*, or at least that part of it in which Lorenzo discusses his own and Ficino's idea of the highest good within a strictly philosophical framework.[8]

"Enough of this. Other matters press." And so Scala goes on to discuss a new topic, the controversy he was involved in through claiming primacy for letters over arms at the end of his last letter to Lorenzo: no one before himself had dared to adjudicate between them; some put pleasure first, or riches, or disparaging all such things, laugh at human labours and prefer a life of solitude; but nothing equals a life dedicated to the administration of a republic. Despite being criticised for this opinion, he continues, he is as yet unmoved. Letters seem to him to be much more immortal than those superior beings which some defend. For although everything at length dies and disappears, we continue to speak, and what survives longest we honour with the name of immortality, which properly belongs to divine things. Nor does he mean by "letters" simply the alphabet, about whose origin there is much controversy (here quoting from Pliny's topical *Natural History* on possible inventors of the alphabet), but rather the whole discipline of the liberal arts and the knowledge of human and divine things, that is, wisdom itself, "a lettered man" meaning someone who devotes himself to these studies.

In his own inimitable and pithy way Scala encapsulates the humanist programme in a few words. Not as original as he claims, of course, since he was hardly the first to defend the supremacy of letters over arms, nor the importance of a life of public service. Nor was his interpretation of humanism new, since Landino had been lecturing on its philosophical basis since at least 1458. Nevertheless, in terms of his own development, the ideas Scala expresses here about language and philosophy are entirely consistent with the Platonising attitude to speech and names he had been developing since the early 1450s, when he and Landino were students of Carlo Marsuppini. From what is probably his earliest writing in 1453 to his poem "La Nencia", which was written c. 1474, possibly at the time

1576, repr. Turin, 1962), 1:662–65 [692–95]; cf. P. O. Kristeller, *Supplementum*, 1:40–46. On the influence of Landino's *Disputationes Camaldulenses* (ed. P. Lohe [Florence, 1980]), see J. B. Wadsworth in *Modern Philology*, 50 (1952): 23–31, and Martelli, 23–26.

8. On 15 April 1474 Ficino also wrote to Lorenzo to praise the *Altercazione*, *Opera*, 1: 655–56 [685–86], cf. Fubini, above, 518; on "la parte più strettamente filosofica," Martelli, *Studi*, esp. 34–35.

of his letter to Lorenzo, he stresses the importance of names which must be invented with great care and may well, in the case of the gods, represent cosmic Ideas or principles of reason, if only we interpret them rightly.[9] Although his apologue "On Letters" does not survive, his reference to it in a late letter to Poliziano shows how little his attitude had changed during his life: "When I said you held a Triumph over Letters I didn't mean you were the enemy of Letters . . . but rather that they are placed in an exalted and difficult place. . . . Nor did the Goths or any of those barbarians hold triumphs over Letters, it seems to me, since they neither knew them, nor had ever heard their name, let alone approached them with arms and fought them. . . ."[10]

Scala always liked to respond to Lorenzo's creative bursts with writings of his own.[11] On this occasion his reply throws interesting light not only on Lorenzo's *Altercazione* but on the ideas of the circle in which he moved.

ALISON BROWN

9. See Brown, *Scala*, 258, 259–62; on Landino, *ibid.*, 264. On the date of "La Nencia," Rochon, *La jeunesse*, 357–99; although always associated with Lorenzo's "Nencia da Barberino", Scala's poem also reflects the influence of the *Altercazione* in the contrast it draws between the country dweller, Gedon, or 'little farm', and Politus, the city-dweller, Pan being described in similar terms. ("Pan, quale ogni pastore onora e venera, / il cui nome in Arcadia si celebra / che impera a quel che si corrompe o genera," *Alterc.* IV, 4–6; "Ipse etiam deus Arcadiae, quem numina ruris / cuncta colunt, latis qui possidet omnia campis / . . . / non unquam est nostros contemni passus honores," "La Nencia", lines 22–3, 25, cited by Rochon, 378, who suggests he may represent Lorenzo in Scala's poem). Spring 1474 is not ruled out as a possible date for the competition of "La Nencia", which Scala suggests could be read by Lorenzo and Sigismondo della Stufa if the "peremnes pluviae" kept them at home, Lorenzo also referring to the "nimie pluvie" which encouraged him to return home from Pisa in a letter to Ficino of [18-19 March 1474]; see Rochon, 376; Lorenzo de' Medici, *Lettere*, 1:514 (lett. 159).
10. A. Poliziano, *Opera omnia* (Lyons, 1533), 146–47, Scala to Poliziano [1494].
11. Brown, *Scala*, 272–3; Martelli, *Studi laurenziani*, 55.

TEXTS

In transcribing the letters I have followed the criteria to be adopted in my forth-coming edition of Scala's writings. I have normalised the spelling by restoring the diphthong *ae* except in the prefix *pre-*, and I have introduced my own punctuation and paragraphs. All corrections given in the apparatus are by Scala unless otherwise noted.

I. Bartolomeo Scala to Bartolomeo Sacchi, [April–May 1474][a]. Autograph draft. Archivio Borromeo. Fondo Autografi, S 6 (B. Scala), f. 2r.

Bartholomeus Scala Bartholomeo Platynae.

Inciderunt litterae ad me tuae in infidelem tabellarium. Aliquot enim occultae dies vix tandem et resignatae quidem prodierunt. Utrumque molestum fuit, sed mora molestior. Verum ita res habet:
5 sunt epistolis quoque sui casus. Eas legi avidissime, non minus Dia-logi quoque tui[b] legendi studiosus. Percommode autem ad civem principem civitatis quid optimo conveniat civi scribis; neque ad prin-cipem solum sed ad doctissimum virum, Musarum cultorem, bo-narum omnium artium sectatorem et ducem. Videorne tribuere nimis
10 multa huic aetati? Sed, mihi crede, Platyna, laudari pro meritis satis illa virtus non potest.

Probo etiam tuum consilium qui Cosmum[c] disputantem de civis optimi officio feceris optimum civem lumenque et decus totius civi-lis sapientiae. Recognoscet sese Laurentius in dictis avi. Fama enim
15 percrebuit et mihi ita videtur avitos mores, gravitatem, sapientiam, ita referre Laurentium nepotem, ut iam redditum urbi nostrae al-terum Cosmum omnes fateantur; atque ita alterum ut nihil praeter aetatem habeat alterum: animum esse eundem, idem ingenium, mentem eandem quae Cosmo fuerit.
20 Certo scio apud talem virum minime opus erit alicuius patroci-

---

3 enim: *s.s. corr. ex* postquam   vix: *s.s. add.*   et: *corr. ex* ac   quidem prodier-unt: *s.s. corr. ex* sunt redditae; et *s.s. del.*   4 'S' *ante* Verum *del.*   6 studiosus: *s.s. corr. ex* Avidus   7 scripsisti *post* civitatis *del.*   9 -ne: *s.s. corr. ex* fortasse lego (?) plura   10 utinam *post* Sed *del.*   12 Probo: *s.s. corr. ex* laudo   15 avitos *ex* autem *corr.*   virtutem *post* avitos *del.*   16 nostrae: *ex* nostrum (?) *corr.*   18 animum: *ex* animus *corr.*   esse eundem: *s.s. corr. ex* idem   19 mentem: *corr. ex* mens

nio, ut scripta tua cara acceptaque habeat et collocet inter delitias.
Ipsum enim existimo satis doctrina elegantiaque tua scriptis esse
tuis patrocinatum. Tamen, si evenerit, viri boni faciam officium,
nec meritae laudi tuae deero, magis adeo ut in tua consulam meae
25 quam quod tu nostra aut alicuius egeas. Vera enim gloria ex aliena
vocula non pendet. Ipsa per se substat satis neque indiga opis extra-
neae ultro et propagatur et regnat. Adde quod Medices ipse eo est
iudicio, ut nihil habeat opus adventitio aliquo testimonio ut de
litteris recte diiudicet. Tamen geram tibi morem et quidem multo
30 melius cum legero. Quod equidem dabo operam ut scribam ad te
postea omnibus de rebus cumulatius. Vale.

a. For the date, see the introduction above.
b. *De optimo cive*, dedicated to Lorenzo de'Medici; see above.
c. Cosimo de' Medici, one of the interlocutors in the dialogue.

II. Scala to Lorenzo de' Medici, [April–May 1474?]. Autograph draft.
MS cit., ff. 2v–3r.

Laurentio Medici.
Postea quam legi Platynae libros duos quos ad te nuper inscripsit
et disputantem et praecipientem Cosmum de cive optimo[a] fecit, te
autem pendentem ab ore avi eiusque sapientiam haurientem tan-
5 quam a[b] matris ubere infantem, mutavi sententiam, qua non recte inscriptos ad te qui et disputasses putarem. Veritus sum enim
ne levior haberi res posset minusque vi esset auctoritatis si quid ad

---

21 Te enim satis existimo patrocinatum. Tamen si videro viri boni atque amici
faciam officium. Semper enim amavi te ex quo cognovi *ante* ut *del.*   22 Ipsum:
s.s. corr. ex te   25 me *post* tu *del.*   aliq- *ante* alicuius *del.*   egeas: *s.s. corr. ex* in-
digeas   ex: *s.s. add.*   26 pendet: *s.s. corr. ex* indiget   27 ultro: *s.s. add.*   Laurentius *ante* Medices *del.*   28 est *post* iudicio *del.*   testimonio: *ex* testimoniae *corr.*
29 recte: *s.s. add.*   30 ut *correxi*: et MS *ut vid.*

2 duos: *s.s. add.*   3 Cosmum: *s.s. add.*   fecit: *s.s. corr. ex* cognovi   4 eiusque:
-que *s.s. add.*   5 ab *bis auctor, alt. postea del.*   6 inscriptos: *corr. ex* inscriptam
putarem *scripsi*: putaram MS   enim: *s.s. add.*

gratiam factum dictumve esse in philosophia videatur. Quae quidem
ut casta, ut gravis, ut omnis fuci, omnis assentationis et vanitatis
10   expers, maiestatem fert prae se quandam atque ad colendum amplectandumque sese homines impellit, ita si praeter dignitatem vilioribus inservire sit coacta ministeriis et, ut aequo animo ferrent,
copiosam est pollicita mercedem, quaeso te, quid contra istam virtutem detractio ⟨non⟩ potest ⟨efficere⟩? Laudant plerique te atque
15   admirantur. Si quid obloquuntur pauci, mihi crede, negligendi sunt,
orandumque ut meliorem mentem det Deus. Et quamquam, ut tu
multo nosti quam ego melius, gloria nostra nihil est nisi in Domino gloriemur, tamen illustras tu quidem communem patriam nostram, quod ego non possum non multi facere nec continere me
20   quin efferar. Tu autem recte feceris si caeteris posthabitis non tibi
solum, sed quotquot audire te volent, struxeris in caelum viam. Vale.

a. See Introduction and Scala's letter to Platina above.

III. Scala to Lorenzo de' Medici, [April–May 1474?]. Autograph draft.
MS cit., f. 3r–v.

Bartholomeus Scala Laurentio Medici.
Quod sum ad rescribendum tardior, velim negligentiam non accuses meam. Captus enim suavitate atque ornatu tuae orationis,
captus gravitate atque sententiis tuarum litterarum, minime una
5   lectione contentus sum. Nisi enim expleta etiam atque etiam lecti-

---

8 potius quam ad rem *post* gratiam *del.* (quam ad rem *s.s.*)   dictumve esse: *s.s.*
add.   9 assentationis . . . vanitatis: *corr. ex* assentatione . . . vanitate   10–11 colendum amplectandumque: *corr. ex* colendam amplectandamque   11 Induerit (?) vili-
bus (?) *del. ante* vilioribus   12 aequo . . . ferrent: *s.s. corr. ex* sustinerent   13 Barth:
post copiosam *supra lineam primam folii sequentis, quasi pro salutatione novae epistolae,
postea autem del.*   pollicita *correxi:* pollicitus *ut vid.* MS   contra: *s.s. add.*   istam:
corr. ex ista (?)   14 ad *ante* atque *del.*   19–20 nec . . . efferar: *s.s. corr. ex* habere
autem immortali dei gratias quod

2 Quod: *s.s. corr. ex* Si   quam tu *ante* tardior *del.*   3 meam: *s.s. add.*   atque
. . . tuae: *s.s. add.*   4 tuarum litterarum: *s.s. add.*   5 enim: *s.s. add.*

tando animi voluptate, nullae vires sunt adscribendum ingenii.
Nam mihi quidem ita modo evenit, ut his qui in suavissimum aliquem atque insolitum cibum avidissimi inciderunt. Ingurgiter plus-
culum, nec nisi plenus e manibus, ut cutem hirudinis. Omnis tua
10 epistola ornatissima est gravique et sapienti viro digna. Ille in ea
praeclarissimus est locus quo de virtutibus earumque contrariis
non oratorio magis quam philosophorum doctissimo more dispu-
tas. In universa autem vereor ne amori et benivolentiae erga me
tuae nimium tribueris. Quamvis enim scio longissime es ab omni
15 vanitate et turpi assentatiuncula, quamvis summum iudicium est
tuum, summa auctoritas, tamen non possum quin pleraque in me
a te dicta non desiderem. Sed haec quidem ut vis. Aliud modo instat.
    Civimus pugnam de litteris. Eas negant quidam tenere primum
dignitatis locum qui nostram ad te superiorem epistolam legerunt,
20 in cuius calce nos principatum litteris tradidimus. Diu fuisse de
dignitate armorum certamen cum litteris; neminem adhuc praeter
me modo inter haec diiudicere ausum. Praesto futuros qui voluptatem anteferant, qui divitiis multa plus tribuant, qui etiam spretis
his omnibus rideant labores humanos et solitudine atque otio magis
25 delectentur—administrationi denique reipublicae, quae quidem studia atque operam nostram patriae civibusque impertit, nihil omnino aequiperandum esse—alios item alia studia prelaturos pro varietate ingeniorum; me prepropere nimis dixisse pro litteris sententiam.
Haec atque huiusmodi complura inveniuntur quae contra dicant

---

6 animi: *s.s. add.*   adscribendum: *s.s. add.*   7 Nam: *s.s. add.*   modo: *s.s. add.*
8 atque: *s.s. add.*   avidissimi *s.s. corr. ex* incider fame lic- (?)   9 nec: *s.s. corr. ex*
Ac   e manibus: *s.s. add.*   hirudinis *emendavi:* hirudines *MS*   10 Ille: *corr. ex*
Illud   11 quo: *corr. ex* quem   13 Illud *del. ante* In   autem: *s.s. add.*   14 tuae:
s.s. add.   15 est: *s.s. add.*   16 a te de me (de me *s.s.*) dicta non desiderem *ante*
in *del.*   18 principatum *del. ante* primum   20 principatum: *s.s. corr. ex* primus
tradidimus: *s.s. corr. ex* notavimus; concessimus assigne *ante del.*   in ambiguo fuisse
post Diu *del.*   21 armorum: *emendavi ex* armis   22 ausum *post* modo *del.*
24 omnia humana *ante* labores *del.*   magis: *s.s. add.*   25 Denique agendo *ante*
administrationi *del.*; administrationi *corr. ex* -tionem   quibus *ante* quae *del.*   facit
ante, ut *post* quidem *del.*   26 aequari nihil posse *del. ante* nihil   27 prelaturos:
pre- *s.s. corr. ex* ante-   28 dixisse: *s.s. corr. ex* tulisse

30   qui litteris his nostris primas invident, me tamen loco nondum
      movent.
          Et litterae quidem mihi inter res omnes mortalium solae videri
      solent multo, quam illa superiora quae defendunt nonnulli, magis
      immortales. Etsi enim occidunt cuncta nostra tandem et diu nihil
35   extat, tamen solemus ita loqui et quae diuturniora sunt immortali-
      tatis quae sua est rerum divinarum nomine honestare. Litteras au-
      tem non elementa modo earumque figuras intelligi volo—quan-
      quam formarum quoque talium inventores excellenti quadam gloria
      celebrentur, cuiusque prima sit, nobilissimae inter se gentes enixissime
40   contendant. Aegyptii, qui et Isim colunt quod prima quemadmodum
      res signis variis notarentur apud se ostenderit, Phoenices, Iudei,
      Graeci, omnes id sibi decus adscribere nituntur. Et Graeci quidem
      Cadmum, Iudei Mosem, Phoenicos Mercurium admirantur. Assiri-
      os etiam in partem venire disceptationis huius Plinius[a] auctor est.
45   Nec publice modo petitur ista palma, sed privati etiam quidam
      confidentissime prodeunt in medium seque suo fraudari honore non
      patiuntur: Cecrops Atheniensis, Linus Thebanus et troianis tempori-
      bus Palamedes Argivus; Aristoteles Epicarmum mavult. Talis de
      inventione litterarum pugna est.
50   —At ego, inquam, non de his solum litteris intelligi velim, sed
      de his potius quibus omnium bonarum artium disciplina humanarum
      divinarumque rerum notitia, quae est proprie sapientia, continetur;
      quae nos, iam usitatissimo vocabulo appellamus "litteras," et qui
      huiusmodi se studiis dediderunt atque excoluerunt animum doctri-
55   nis bonis, "litteratos." Ad has sum ego te hortatus, et praeclarissi-
      mam esse rem atque haberi testatus sum. Quae quidem sententia nescio
      utrum plus assertorum an rationum habeat. Sed longior iam

---

    30 dic *del. post* qui   nondum: -dum *s.s. corr. ex* modo   32 quidem: *s.s. add*
mortalium: corr. ex mortalem   33 immortales *del. ante* multo, quae *del. post*
34 alia (?) *del. post* nostra   37 eas tantum *del. post* non   et *del. post* quanquam
42 Syri *post* Graeci *s.s. add., postea del.*   id: *s.s. corr. ex* enim (?)   decus: *s.s. add.*
43 Cadmum: *corr. ex* Cadmus   44 etiam : *s.s. add.*   45 quidam: *s.s. add.*   46 suo:
corr. ex sue   honore: *s.s. corr. ex* gloria   51 div- *del. post* disciplina   52 est proprie:
s.s. add.   est *del. post* sapientia   continetur: *corr. ex* continentur   55 bonis: *s.s.*
add.   56 esse: *s.s. add.*

sum. Itaque in aliud ea tempus differemus, nostra in praesentia opinione contenti, et Musas modo nostras Bellonae, Veneri, Mer-
60   curio et Plutoni anteferemus. Quod si vel paulum repugnaverimus, video statim fore ut te litterarum principe et defensore ne mutire quidem contra quisquam audeat. Vale.

a. Pliny, *Nat. Hist.* VII, 56, 192.

58–9 nostra . . . opinione: *s.s. corr. ex* Nunc (Atque *s.s. del.*) opinione nostra
59 erimus *del. post* contenti   modo: *s.s. add.*

NOTE sullo 'SCRITTOIO' di
MARSILIO FICINO

IN UN PRECEDENTE lavoro dedicato allo studio del codice Magliabechiano VIII 1441 della Biblioteca Nazionale di Firenze, archetipo dei libri V e VI delle *Epistolae* di Marsilio Ficino, mi ero riservato di tornare in altra sede su di un problema di natura paleografica scaturito dall'esame di questo manoscritto. Mi limitavo ad affermare che avrebbero concorso alla trascrizione del Magliabechiano quattro mani: quella del Ficino — che oltre a scrivere per intero alcune lettere, avrebbe corretto estesamente tutto il manoscritto — e quelle di tre suoi collaboratori, il primo dei quali ne avrebbe copiati più di tre quarti, degli altri due, il secondo poche carte, il terzo appena una singola lettera. Se della scrittura di quest'ultimo dichiaravo di non conoscere altri esempi, e di quella del secondo avevo potuto indicare soltanto due lettere originali, scritte a nome del Ficino, per quanto concerneva il primo, oltre ad attribuire alla sua mano alcuni codici ed epistole, avevo proposto l'identificazione con un amanuense notoriamente legato al Ficino, Luca Fabiani.[1]

1. V. S. Gentile, "Un codice Magliabechiano delle Epistole di Marsilio Ficino," *Interpres*, 3 (1980): 86–89 e note. Per quanto concerne il secondo copista va fatta tuttavia una correzione. Non a lui — come ho proposto (*ibid.*, 88, nota 29) — ma al Fabiani si deve attribuire la lettera originale d'accompagnamento conservata nell'incunabolo Magliabechiano B 5 18 della Biblioteca Nazionale di Firenze, contenente il *De christiana religione* del Ficino; cfr. idem, in *Marsilio Ficino e il ritorno di Platone. Mostra di manoscritti stampe e documenti*, Catalogo a cura di S. Gentile, S. Niccoli, P. Viti, premessa di E. Garin (Firenze, 1984), 86 sg., no. 67. Sul cod. Magliabechiano v. anche *ibid.*, 99–101, no. 75.

Rilevavo anche come questa partizione non s'accordasse con le affermazioni di quanti, in precedenza, avevano toccato l'argomento 'mani' relativamente a questo manoscritto. Arnaldo Della Torre ne aveva distinte due sole, quella del Ficino e quella di un suo amanuense non meglio identificato,[2] e due ne aveva riconosciute pure Paul Oskar Kristeller—per parte sua avanzando cautamente la proposta di attribuire la seconda a Sebastiano Salvini, cugino del filosofo[3]—, respingendo la tesi nel frattempo sostenuta da Martin Sicherl,[4] il quale aveva dichiarato autografo l'intero manoscritto, conformemente alla sua teoria che attribuisce al Ficino due diversi tipi di scrittura: la ben nota e caratteristica minuta corsiva (*Gelehrtenschrift*) e una *Rheinschrift*, nella fattispecie, un'umanistica corsiva 'quasi calligrafica'.

Tornare sull'argomento non pare inopportuno: se la differenza di vedute tra il Della Torre, il Kristeller e chi scrive, si riduce sostanzialmente a un'ulteriore distinzione di mani e a un diverso nome per il copista principale, l'accettazione della tesi del Sicherl verrebbe a mutare radicalmente quanto si è sinora pensato, dal punto di vista della paternità grafica, non solo del Magliabechiano, ma di molti altri manoscritti d'ambiente ficiniano, che da copie esemplate ad opera di un amanuense, sia pure stretto 'familiare' del filosofo, assurgerebbero al rango di autografi. Il tornarvi sopra diviene tanto più necessario se prendiamo atto che la tesi sostenuta dal Sicherl—ribadita in un secondo saggio espressamente intitolato "Die Humanistenkursive Marsilio Ficinos",[5] in cui risponde ad alcune osservazioni pertinenti del Kristeller, e da lui data poi per scontata in una terza recente pubblicazione dedicata all'esame del Supplément grec 212 della Bibliothèque Nationale di Parigi[6]—sembra costituire oggi l'ultima e definitiva parola sulla dibattuta questione.

I risultati di un'indagine condotta su buona parte del materiale manoscritto per un qualche verso legato all'ambiente ficiniano, credo confortino

2. V. A. Della Torre, *Storia dell'Accademia platonica di Firenze* (Firenze, 1902; rist. anast. Torino 1968), 92.

3. V. P. O. Kristeller, "Some Original Letters and Autograph Manuscripts of Marsilio Ficino," in *Studi di bibliografia e storia in onore di Tammaro de Marinis* (Verona, 1964), 3:18 e nota 3, 26.

4. V. M. Sicherl, "Neuendeckte Handschriften von Marsilio Ficino und Johannes Reuchlin," *Scriptorium*, 16 (1962): 55.

5. Idem, "Die Humanistenkursive Marsilio Ficinos," in *Studia codicologica*, hrsg. K. Treu (Berlin, 1977), 443–450.

6. Idem., "Druckmanuskripte der Platoniker-uebersetzungen Marsilio Ficinos," *Italia Medioevale e Umanistica*, 20 (1977): 323–339.

l'ipotesi alternativa a cui si è sin qui soltanto accenato, di attribuire la vessata *Rheinschrift* non al Ficino, ma al suo fido amanuense Luca Fabiani. Inoltre, dato che comunque è all'interno dell'officina del filosofo che va ricercata questa 'mano'—ed è questo l'unico punto su cui vi sia unanime consenso—, non parrà inutile gettarvi uno sguardo e fare alcune considerazioni preliminari che servano sia al nostro immediato proposito, sia a delineare un primo, seppur sommario, quadro di questo ambiente grafico, che possa servire da orientamento per ulteriori ricerche.

* * *

Comincerei con qualche osservazione sulla mano tradizionale del Ficino, vale a dire su quella minuta corsiva che gli viene concordemente riconosciuta. E' una scrittura, se vogliamo, 'da dotto', ricca di caratteri distintivi, che le conferiscono un aspetto difficilmente confondibile. Vi si ravvisa, accanto ad un limitato uso di legature, una spiccata tendenza a mantenere le singole lettere ben distinte, accompagnata e messa in risalto da un tratto di penna generalmente assai marcato. Questa tendenza non viene meno neppure negli esempi più veloci della sua scrittura, dove la rapidità è favorita da un ricorso puntuale alle risorse del sistema abbreviativo tardo-medievale, piuttosto che ad un aumento della corsività del tracciato, che si limita, in genere, al raddoppiamento delle aste, specie di quella della 'd', per consentire la legatura a destra. Quanto poi alla forma delle singole lettere, le più caratteristiche sono state messe bene in rilievo dal Kristeller;[7] mi limiterò pertanto ad attirare l'attenzione sulla singolare e direi significativa mescolanza di elementi 'moderni'—cioè della tradizione corsiva tardo-medievale—e 'antichi', o, se si preferisce, 'umanistici', che contraddistingue la minuta corsiva del Ficino, e che sembrerebbe rappresentare il riflesso, sul piano grafico, della sua complessa formazione culturale: noteremo, ad esempio, accanto alla 'a' corsiva chiusa una 'a' dalla spalla alta, la 'r' rotonda che s'accompagna alla 'r' diritta, la 's' tonda che si alterna in fine di parola con la variante diritta, e così via.

Queste caratteristiche—unite a quelle indicate dal Kristeller—restano costanti lungo quasi tutto l'arco della produzione grafica del filosofo. Si può dire che già nel Riccardiano 135, che risale agli anni 1455–56, ed è

---

7. V. Kristeller, "Some Original Letters," 10.

interamente di mano del Ficino,[8] la sua minuta corsiva risulta, per così dire, formata. Converrà sottolineare, invece, come di fronte ad altre scritture 'di dotti' dell'epoca—si pensi al Pico[9]—, la minuta ficiniana solo raramente, in qualche appunto o frettolosa nota marginale, presenta difficoltà di lettura. Al contrario, quando vergata con cura, appare persino in grado di gareggiare per chiarezza con gli esempi più calligrafici e rigorosamente 'umanistici' dei suoi amanuensi. Il Ficino del resto se ne servì non soltanto per copiare l'intero Vaticano lat. 7705—nel quale, a mio parere, va riconosciuta la copia di dedica del *Commentarium in Convivium*, che il filosofo scrisse di suo pugno per Giovanni di Niccolò Cavalcanti [10]—, ma anche per correggere il testo e arricchire di *notabilia* i margini di alcuni codici di dedica contenenti opere sue,[11] per collaborare alla trascrizione di altri manoscritti, che pure non erano destinati al suo uso personale,[12] nonché per vergare gli originali di alcune sue lettere.[13]

Non bisogna poi dimenticare che della minuta corsiva ficiniana esistono esempi particolarmente posati ed eleganti, come la lettera di dedica a Bernardo del Nero che figura sotto il frontespizio di un esemplare dell'*editio princeps* delle sue *Epistolae*, oggi a Durham[14] [tav. I]; oppure le cc. 195r–

8. Su questo MS v. Gentile, in *Marsilio Ficino . . . Mostra*, 14 sg., no. 12 e tavv. III–IV.

9. Sulla scrittura del Conte della Mirandola abbiamo un significativo giudizio dello stesso Ficino in una lettera a Germain de Ganay edita da Kristeller, *Supplementum*, 2:92: "Moliebatur (*scil. Pico*) quotidie tria: concordiam Aristotelis cum Platone, enarrationes in eloquia sacra, confutationes astrologorum, omnia quidem tam facunde quam subtiliter disputata, sed quam stilo luculenta, tam novis obscurisque characteribus adumbrata, ut vix ab eo legi possent. Itaque necdum absoluta ab eodem vel recognita sunt nec ab aliis nisi forte vaticinentur exscribi possunt."

10. Cfr. S. Gentile, "Per la storia del testo del *Commentarium in Convivium* di Marsilio Ficino," *Rinascimento*, ser. 2, 21 (1981): 26 sg.

11. E' questo il caso di sette manoscritti del *Commentarium in Convivium*; v. *ibid.*, 20, nota 1.

12. Sono di mano del Ficino le cc. 190r–193v, 195r–211v del già citato Parigino Supplément grec 212, il MS utilizzato da Aldo per stampare nel 1497 l'edizione principe delle traduzioni ficiniane di Giamblico e di altri neoplatonici, nonché del *De voluptate*; cfr. Sicherl, "Druckmanuskripte," 326 sg. e tav. VII, 1; Kristeller, *Iter*, 3:214 sg. Sull'edizione aldina [Hain 9358; IGI 5096], v. Gentile, in *Marsilio Ficino . . . Mostra*, 131 sg., no. 101. Di mano del Ficino è anche la c. 124r–v (e parte di c. 134r) del cod. II IX 2 della Biblioteca Nazionale di Firenze, appartenuto a Pietro del Nero e contenente il primo libro dell'epistolario ficiniano (v. *ibid.*, 89 sg., no. 69 II e tav. XXI).

13. Le lettere originali autografe del Ficino sono elencate dal Kristeller, "Some Original Letters," 11, 16 sg. Ad esse va aggiunta la lettera a Michele Mercati del primo aprile 1466 esposta alla mostra del Ficino alla Biblioteca Laurenziana; v. Gentile, in *Marsilio Ficino . . . Mostra*, 48, no. 36 e tav. XII.

14. Cfr. Kristeller, "Some Original Letters," 16 sg., 23, 33; A. I. Doyle, E. Rainey e D. B. Wilson, *Manuscript to Print: Tradition and Innovation in the Renaissance Book* (Durham, 1975), 15, no. 17 (con tav.).

Tav. I. Durham, University Library, MS SR 2 C 22.

204v del summenzionato Supplément grec 212,[15] che sono veramente un bell'esempio del grado di ricercatezza che la sua minuta corsiva può raggiungere.

La dignità 'libraria' conferita dal Ficino alla sua scrittura usuale nei casi appena citati, già di per sé fa dubitare dell'esistenza di una *Rheinschrift* diversa da questa minuta corsiva. Del resto, se prendiamo in considerazione le testimonianze dei contemporanei sulla mano del Ficino—espresse da Ber-

15. Cfr. supra, 340, nota 6, e 342, nota 12.

nardo Bembo nei margini del Canoniciano class. Lat. 156 della Bodleian Library di Oxford,[16] e da Pietro del Nero nel cod. II IX 2 della Biblioteca Nazionale di Firenze[17] — e le sue personali attestazioni di autografia — ad esempio nella dedicatoria del Vaticano lat. 7705,[18] nella sottoscrizione alle Pandette Laurenziane[19] e nella lettera a Bernardo del Nero che abbiamo prima ricordato[20] — si vedrà che queste riguardano solo e soltanto la sua scrittura 'usuale'.

* * *

Ad un altro aspetto del panorama grafico fiorentino dell'epoca, diverso da quello rappresentato dalla minuta corsiva ficiniana, si ricollegano le scritture dei suoi amanuensi, che impiegano un'umanistica corsiva sobria ed elegante, generalmente caratterizzata da un certa inclinazione verso destra del tracciato.

Questo sia detto in generale, ma occorrerà far subito delle precisazioni. Innanzi tutto con 'i suoi amanuensi' ho inteso indicare un determinato gruppetto di collaboratori del Ficino, che rispondono ai nomi — già noti agli studiosi, seppure in misura diversa — di Sebastiano Salvini, Rutilio, Ficino Ficini e, ovviamente, Luca Fabiani. Essi hanno in comune, oltre al tipo di scrittura — si noterà subito che dal punto di vista grafico costituiscono un insieme singolarmente compatto e uniforme, segno sintomatico della loro appartenenza ad un medesimo ambiente culturale —, la prerogativa di essere vissuti, anche se probabilmente in momenti e per periodi diversi (e con qualche dubbio per Rutilio), in casa del filosofo. Ed è questa una condizione necessaria, come s'è già accennato, per considerarli possibili candidati alla paternità della discussa *Rheinschrift*; perché, in alcuni codici, essa s'accompagna con promiscuità tale alla minuta corsiva ficiniana da non potersi che attribuire ad un collaboratore molto stretto, se non ad un vero e proprio segretario personale del filosofo.

E' tuttavia opportuno ricordare, per non correre il rischio di falsare il

16. Cfr. M. Ficino, *Commentaire sur le Banquet de Platon*, a cura di R. Marcel, (Paris 1956; rist. anast. 1978), 40, 43; Kristeller, "Some Original Letters," 10, 29 e tav. VII.
17. V. Gentile, in *Marsilio Ficino . . . Mostra*, 89 sg., no. 69 II e tav. XXI.
18. V. idem, "Per la storia," 26 sg.
19. V. Kristeller, "Some Original Letters," 10, 24 e tav. I; cfr. P. Viti in *Marsilio Ficino . . . Mostra*, 184 sg., no. 54.
20. V. supra, nota 14; in calce alla lettera il Ficino ha aggiunto *manu propria*.

quadro, che questi quattro copisti non furono i soli a trascrivere codici ficiniani.

Si ricordi, ad esempio, come in una lettera a Taddeo Ugoleto, bibliotecario di Mattia Corvino, il Ficino scriva di aver dato a copiare la sua traduzione *ad sensum* del *De mysteriis* di Giamblico ad un *Antonius librarius*, di cui appare convincente l'identificazione proposta con il ben noto amanuense fiorentino Antonio Sinibaldi.[21]

Se comunque la trascrizione del *De mysteriis* era stata commissionata al Sinibaldi dall'Ugoleto stesso, troviamo mani diverse da quelle dei quattro copisti summenzionati in più d'un codice contenente scritti del Ficino con correzioni autografe, e quindi verosimilmente a lui molto vicini: è il caso di alcuni manoscritti del *Commentarium in Convivium*, copiati in umanistica corsiva—salvo uno in *antiqua*—da scrivani diversi a cui per ora non saprei dare un nome.[22]

Del resto, anche per quel che concerne i codici di lusso, preziosamente decorati, per lo più destinati alla biblioteca dei Medici, se ve ne sono alcuni di mano del Salvini e del Fabiani, altri sembrerebbero da attribuirsi a copisti 'esterni' all'officina del filosofo.

Ad alcuni di costoro è possibile attribuire con ragionevole certezza più d'un codice. Così, ad esempio, ad uno stesso amanuense si devono il Vaticano lat. 1789 [tav. II]—che è la copia di dedica a Giuliano de'Medici

---

21. V. M. Ficino, *Opera quae hactenus extitere et quae in lucem nunc primum prodiere omnia* (Basileae, 1576; rist. anast. Torino, 1962²), 1:903; cfr. J. Huszti, "Tendenze platonizzanti alla corte di Mattia Corvino," *Giornale critico della filosofia italiana*, 11 (1930): 233; Kristeller, *Supplementum*, 1:clxxi; idem, *Studies*, 126; idem, "A New Work on the Origin and Development of Humanistic Script," *Manuscripta*, 5 (1961): 40; K. Csapodi-Gardony, "Les scripteurs de la bibliothèque du roi Matthias," *Scriptorium*, 17 (1963): 29 sg. Il Kristeller, *Supplementum*, 1: clxx sg., cita come esempio di trascrizioni di opere del Ficino effettuate da copisti (*librarii*) esterni alla sua officina, due lettere del filosofo a Martino Uranio (v. Ficino, *Opera*, 901, 921)—ove tuttavia l'espressione *librarii nostri*, nella seconda delle due lettere, probabilmente indica proprio 'gli' scrivani del Ficino—e un'altra lettera, a Carlo Ristori, relativa alla copia del *pius noster Plato* ad opera di un *impius Germanus* (v. *ibid.*, 856). Su Antonio Sinibaldi v. G. Cencetti, *Lineamenti di storia della scrittura latina* (Bologna, 1954), 279–281; T. De Marinis, *La biblioteca napoletana dei re d'Aragona* (Milano, 1957), 1:52–55; 2:312 sg.; B. L. Ullman, *The Origin and Development of Humanistic Script* (Roma, 1960), 118–123; J. Wardrop, *The Script of Humanism. Some Aspects of Humanistic Script 1460–1560* (Oxford, 1963), 9 e nota 3; J. J. G. Alexander e A. C. de la Mare, *The Italian Manuscripts in the Library of Major J. R. Abbey* (London, 1969), XXVI, nota 3; E. Casamassima, "Literulae latinae," in S. Caroti e S. Zamponi, *Lo scrittoio di Bartolomeo Fonzio umanista fiorentino* (Milano, 1974), XXIV sg., XXXII, nota 46.

22. Cfr. Gentile, "Per la storia," 20, nota 1. Il codice in *antiqua* è lo Strozzi 98 (v. *ibid.*, 7; cfr. idem, in *Marsilio Ficino ... Mostra*, 60 sg., no. 46).

Tav. II. Città del Vaticano, Biblioteca Apostolica Vaticana, MS Vaticano lat. 1789, c.7r.

del primo libro delle *Epistolae* — e il Laurenziano XXI 9, testimone molto importante, e fino a poco tempo fa unico manoscritto, del *De christiana religione*:[23] l'uno e l'altro sono copiati in una corsiva umanistica molto posata, tra le cui caratteristiche si possono indicare le aste delle 's' e delle 'f' che non discendono al di sotto del rigo — mentre è la 'r' (diritta) che talora allunga il tratto verticale in basso — e la presenza sporadica, accanto alla 'd' diritta, della 'd' di forma onciale.

A un secondo copista si attribuiranno tre manoscritti Laurenziani (i primi due, segnati LXXXII 6–7, contengono la traduzione ficiniana dei *Dialogi* platonici;[24] il terzo, segnato LXXXII 15, raccoglie una silloge di neo-platonici, sempre nella versione del Ficino [25]), il cod. 143 della Biblioteca Durazzo di Genova, nel quale troviamo altre traduzioni ficiniane (Alci-noo, Speusippo, Pitagora),[26] il cod. lat. 2613 della Bibliothèque Natio-nale di Parigi [tav. III] — unico manoscritto comprendente le traduzioni del Ficino del *De mystica theologia* e del *De divinis nominibus* dello pseudo-Dionigi[27] — e le pp. 229–402 del cod. R VI E f 11 della Naròdni a Univer-sitni Knihova di Praga, ove figurano nuovamente le traduzioni di Alci-noo, Speusippo e Pitagora, seguite dall'*Argumentum* e dal commento del Ficino al *Fedro* platonico.[28]

La scrittura impiegata in questi codici è una bastarda all'antica, in cui si nota, tra l'altro, la presenza di alcuni degli arcaismi grafici che il Wardrop ha chiamato "the stock-in-trade of northern scribes", quali la 'c' capitale che racchiude al suo interno la lettera seguente, la 'a' onciale di grande modulo e la 'q' capitale d'origine epigrafica, e, in genere, l'inserzione di lettere maiuscole in luogo delle corrispondenti minuscole.[29]

23. Cfr. idem, in *Marsilio Ficino ... Mostra*, 84 sg., no. 65 e tav. XIX.

24. V. *ibid.*, 113–116, no. 89 I–II, e la tav. tra p. 98 e p. 99.

25. V. *ibid.*, 128 sg., no. 99 e la tav. tra p. 130 e p. 131.

26. V. D. Puncuh, *I manoscritti della raccolta Durazzo* (Genova, 1979), 212–214, no. 143 e tav. 91.

27. V. Kristeller, *Supplementum*, 1:xxxvii; idem, *Iter*, 3:216; Gentile, in *Marsilio Ficino ... Mo-stra*, 157, no. 121.

28. V. Sicherl, "Druckmanuskripte," 336 sg.; M. J. B. Allen, *Marsilio Ficino and the Phaedran Charioteer* (Berkeley-Los Angeles-London, 1981), 65–70, 131, 253–255, e la tav. tra p. 70 e p. 71; Kristeller, *Iter*, 3:165.

29. V. Wardrop, *The Script*, 16. Forse converrà spiegare perché abbiamo definito 'una corsiva umanistica molto posata' la scrittura del copista che ha trascritto il Vaticano lat. 1789 e il Lauren-ziano XXI 9 e 'bastarda all'antica' la scrittura di questo secondo amanuense. Nel primo caso siamo davanti a una scrittura che pur essendo impiegata e tracciata come una 'libraria', ritiene tuttavia l'andamento corsivo che è evidentemente alla sua base; nel secondo caso, invece, abbiamo l'inserzio-ne di elementi 'corsivo-cancelereschi' su una base 'libraria' (*antiqua*). A rigore anche la prima

Inter virtutem naturalem atque cognitricem hoc interest potissimum, quod naturalis virtutis actio fertur foras ac desinit in
subiectum. Cognitricis vero virtutis actio permanet penes ipsam, qua
propter haec quidem circulare non nihil habet: quod enim in orbe
movetur versatur circa se ipsum, redit quod semper unde discessit. Illa
vero rectam videtur lineam imitari ab altero usque puncto in alterum
desinentem. Corpori quidem sola competit eiusmodi actio motusque
consimilis. Intellectui vero convenit actio circularis: cum et cogitatio quaelibet in se videlicet quodammodo permanens circulare non nihil habeat, et imaginatio quidem magis quam sensus, ratio quoque
magis quam imaginatio, intellectus denique tanquam cognitio summa circularis est summopere. Hinc fit ut anima inter intellectum cor-
pusque media mediam habeat actionem motumque similiter tum orbis
tum recti participem. Una siquidem intellectus ipsius actio est intellec-
tio ex se exordiens et orbiculariter remeans in se ipsam. Quatenus
vero se sua quae intelligit, eatenus intelligit, efficit, movet, regit alia.
Hic igitur recta quaedam linea tendens in alia orbem intimum commuta-
tur, videlicet unde profecta. Haec igitur actio circa alia intimam
non distrahit actionem. Anima vero et animadversione sui facit
circulum et vegetatione corporis negotiisque circa corpus rectam lineam imitatur. Sed quoniam haec non dependet ab illa, nimirum anima sic agendo distracta videtur, et apud eam operatio altera vicissim impedit alteram. Verum si ad mentem quidem circuitus
attinet, ad animam vero motio quaedam mixta, ad corpus denique
recta, unde nam caelestis revolutio provenit. Non a corporea quidem

Tav. III. Paris, Bibliothèque Nationale,
MS lat. 2613, c.70v.

Parimenti ad una stessa mano sono dovuti due manoscritti ficiniani destinati a Bernardo Bembo, del *De raptu Pauli*, attualmente alla Bibliotheek
der Rijksuniversiteit di Leida con la segnatura BPL 160a,[30] e delle *Quinque claves platonicae sapientiae* — cod. B F 44 (già B 13) della Cornell University Library [tav. IV][31] —, che sono copiati in un'umanistica corsiva
rotondeggiante, affine agli esempi più posati di Pietro Cennini e di Bartolomeo Fonzio.[32]

* * *

Per tornare agli amanuensi 'del Ficino', il più noto di essi è certamente
Sebastiano Salvini, grazie al bel saggio che gli ha dedicato Paul Oskar
Kristeller.[33]

Divenuto ben presto orfano dei genitori, il Salvini venne allevato dal
Ficino — che gli era cugino per parte di madre — e da Antonio degli Agli.
Non fu soltanto un semplice copista; discepolo del suo illustre *amitinus*,
coltivò in modo speciale gli studi teologici, tanto da divenire, agli inizi
degli anni ottanta, *sacrae paginae professor*. Di suo ci sono giunti alcuni
opuscoli — d'argomento prevalentemente teologico —, una rilevante silloge
di epistole, dei sermoni, una parafrasi dei *Salmi* e una versione in volgare —
che seguiva una precedente sua rielaborazione del testo latino — dell'*Epistola
di Rabbi Samuel*.

Non fu dunque amanuense di professione; anzi, come vediamo da alcune sue sottoscrizioni — al Guelferbitano 3011 [= 12 Aug. 4to][34] e al

---

potrebbe essere definita 'bastarda all'antica', ma bisogna tenere presente che la sua origine è affatto
diversa.

30. Su questo MS v. Kristeller, *Supplementum*, 1:xxxi; idem, *Studies*, 159; M. Ficino, *Théologie
Platonicienne de l'immortalité des âmes*, a cura di R. Marcel, 3 (Paris, 1970), 256.

31. V. Kristeller, *Studies*, 166 sg.; Ficino, *Théologie*, 3:255 sg. Su questi due manoscritti del
Bembo v. anche P. O. Kristeller, "Marsilio Ficino e Venezia," in *Miscellanea di studi in onore di
Vittore Branca, 3: Umanesimo e Rinascimento a Firenze e a Venezia* (Firenze, 1983), 479 e note 27–29.

32. Cfr. Casamassima, "Literulae," XXIV.

33. P. O. Kristeller, "Sebastiano Salvini, a Florentine Humanist and Theologian, and a Member of Marsilio Ficino's Platonic Academy," in *Didascaliae, Studies in Honor of Anselm M. Albareda*,
ed. S. Prete (New York, 1961), 207–243. V. anche M.E. Cosenza, *Biographical and Bibliographical
Dictionary of the Italian Humanists and the World of Classical Scholarship in Italy, 1300–1800* (Boston,
1962), 4:3164 sg.

34. V. Kristeller, "Sebastiano Salvini," 243 sg.; idem, *Iter*, 3:733; *Bibliotheca Corviniana*, a cura
di C. Csapodi e K. Csapodi-Gardony (Gyoma-Budapest, 1969), 77, no. 175, tav. CXXXVIII.

Prima clauis Platonicę sapientię Marsi
lij Ficinj Florentini. Elementa mouetur
mobiliter celestes sperę mouentur stabi
liter. Animę stant mobiliter. Angeli stat
stabiliter. Deus est ipse status & unitas.

VIDEMVS elementa a
terra usq; ad cęlum moue
ri mobiliter: mobiliter inq;
quoniam a rectissima motionis norma
non nunq; uel ob impedimentum uel ob
aliam quandam causam quodammodo
dimoueri uidentur. Cęlestia uo corpora
mouentur quidem: sed stabiliter. Nam
in ipsorum naturali motu continue per
seuerant. Proinde status motu longe per
fectior iudicatur. Motus enim statu ne
cessario indiget: sed non contra. Quá cô
rem si motus motu nobis ab inferiorib;
ad superiora nunc ascendentibus pfectior
gradatim occurrit: multo magis status
ipse statu gradatim pfectior debet occurre.

Prima clauis.

Tav. IV. Ithaca (New York), Cornell University Library, MS F 44, c.1r.

Riccardiano 797[35] — egli teneva a sottolineare le ragioni non venali della sua attività di *scriptor*, dichiarando, ad esempio, nel Riccardiano 797:

> Transcripsit manu propria preclarum hoc opus Sebastianus Salvinus, amitinus eiusdem Marsilii Ficini, philosophi insignis, theologie professor et artium, amicitia ad transcribendum ductus.[36]

Non sono pochi, comunque, i manoscritti che ci sono pervenuti vergati di sua mano. Oltre ai già citati Riccardiano e Guelferbitano, ne abbiamo altri tre con la sua sottoscrizione: due contengono opere del Ficino — e sono i Laurenziani XXI 8[37] e LI 11[38] — ; il terzo, invece — il cod. II IV 31 della Biblioteca Nazionale di Firenze — , gli *Aphorismi medicinae* di Mosè Maimonide, che il Salvini esemplò per Giorgio Ciprio, un medico non estraneo al circolo ficiniano.[39]

Ma non soltanto i codici sottoscritti sono di sua mano. Il Kristeller ha infatti indicato quattro manoscritti che ritiene possano essere interamente di mano del Salvini: i Magliabechiani XXXIV 15 e XXXIV 72, il Riccardiano 1454 e il Vaticano lat. 5140, contenenti suoi opuscoli e lettere.[40] Ha poi suggerito di attribuirgli alcune carte inserite nella copia dell'incunabolo dell'*Epistola di Rabbi Samuel* appartenente alla Jewish Theological Society of America di New York, e delle annotazioni che compaiono in un altro esemplare della medesima edizione, posseduto dalla Biblioteca Nazionale di Firenze;[41] sempre in questa biblioteca ha riconosciuto interventi di mano del Salvini nel cod. Conventi soppressi A 2 737, nel quale figurano le *Hystoriae* di Antonio degli Agli.[42] E ancora al Kristeller dobbiamo la segnalazione di due lettere autografe del Salvini, la prima conservata all'Archivio di Stato di Firenze, datata 1477 e diretta a Lorenzo d'Medici,[43]

---

35. V. Kristeller, "Sebastiano Salvini," 241 e tav. I; Gentile, in *Marsilio Ficino . . . Mostra*, 120 sg., no. 94.

36. La sottoscrizione figura nel MS a c. 255v, in calce al quarto libro dell'epistolario; v. *ibid.*

37. V. Kristeller, "Sebastiano Salvini," 216 sg., 239 e tav. IV; Gentile, in *Marsilio Ficino . . . Mostra*, 70–72, no. 55 e tav. XVI.

38. V. Kristeller, "Sebastiano Salvini," 239; idem, "Some Original Letters," tav. V; Gentile, in *Marsilio Ficino . . . Mostra*, 91, no. 69 IV.

39. V. Kristeller, "Sebastiano Salvini," 214, 240.

40. V. *ibid.*, 240–242 e tav. II (dal Vaticano lat. 5140); sul MS Vaticano v. anche Gentile, "Un codice Magliabechiano," 116, nota 102.

41. V. Kristeller, "Sebastiano Salvini," 238 sg. e tav. III (dall'esemplare di New York).

42. V. *ibid.*, 217 e nota 69.

43. ASF, Mediceo avanti il principato (d'ora in avanti = MAP), XXII 408; v. *ibid.*, 239.

Tav. V. Firenze, Biblioteca Medicea Laurenziana,
MS LXXX 12, c.2r.

la seconda nel fondo Ginori Conti della Biblioteca Nazionale di Firenze,
indirizzata a Piero Soderini in data del 26 luglio 1503.[44]

Per quel che concerne poi i manoscritti di opere del Ficino, il Kristeller
attribuisce al Salvini la trascrizione della sezione cartacea del Laurenziano
LXXXIII 18—comprendente una silloge di diciassette epistole, in prevalenza
del Ficino[45]—, limitandosi per il resto a ricordare, senza pronunziarsi,
quanto proposto dal Della Torre, il quale aveva riconosciuto la mano del
Salvini in due manoscritti del primo libro dell'epistolario ficiniano—il cod.
II IX 2 della Biblioteca Nazionale di Firenze, da noi già ricordato, e il
Laurenziano Strozzi 101—e nel Laurenziano XC sup. 43, in cui si trovano
riuniti i primi otto libri della raccolta epistolare.[46] Vi è infine un'ultimo
manoscritto, il Laurenziano LXXXIII 12 [tav. V], la cui sezione mem-

44. Ginori Conti, XXIX 108; la lettera è datata "VI K⟨a⟩l⟨enda⟩s Julii 1503 Flor⟨rentiae⟩".
V. Kristeller, "Some Original Letters," 9, nota 4, che dà però come segnatura MS 64; cfr. infra,
353, nota 50.
45. Cfr. Kristeller, "Sebastiano Salvini," 239 sg.; Gentile, "Un codice Magliabechiano," 116
sg., nota 103; idem, in *Marsilio Ficino . . . Mostra*, 105, no. 80.
46. V. Kristeller, "Sebastiano Salvini," 217.

branacea, contenente l'*Argumentum in platonicam theologiam*, viene attribuita al Salvini da un altro studioso del Ficino, Raymond Marcel.[47]

Queste attribuzioni paiono fondate. Sarà sufficiente eliminare quella del Della Torre concernente il Laurenziano XC sup. 43 — su cui torneremo in seguito a proposito di Luca Fabiani[48] — e correggere le affermazioni di quello studioso relative ai due manoscritti del primo libro dell'epistolario.[49] Per il resto, le aggiunte che si potrebbero fare al già lungo elenco sono minime. Ci limiteremo a segnalare l'esistenza di un terza lettera autografa del Salvini [tav. VI], conservata anch'essa nel fondo Ginori Conti della Biblioteca Nazionale di Firenze, senza data, diretta a Niccolò Michelozzi.[50]

Anche ad un esame superficiale delle lettere e dei codici sopra elencati, ci si rende conto che la realizzazione più 'classica' e frequente della scrittura del Salvini è quella che compare — per citare i manoscritti più noti — nel Laurenziano LI 11, nel Riccardiano 797 e nel Guelferbitano 3011 [= 12 Aug. 4to], dove fa bella mostra di sé un'umanistica corsiva dal tracciato molto regolare, leggermente inclinato verso destra. Per quel che riguarda la forma delle lettere, rari appaiono, anche quando si saranno oramai diffusi in ambiente fiorentino, gli arcaismi grafici d'influenza settentrionale; una peculiarità che si può dire costante della mano del Salvini, consiste piuttosto nella posizione assunta dalla legatura 'et', in cui l'originario primo tratto della 'e' si mantiene sempre al di sotto del rigo.

A questa corsiva il Salvini sembrerebbe essere rimasto fedele lungo tutta la sua sia pure occasionale attività di amanuense: la vediamo impiegata nel primo dei suoi codici sottoscritti — il Laurenziano LI 11, finito di trascrivere il 21 febbraio 1476 (stile fiorentino)[51] — e la ritroviamo sostanzialmente identica nell'ultimo documento datato che gli possiamo attribuire, la lettera a Piero Soderini del fondo Ginori Conti, con la quale scendiamo al 26 luglio 1503.

---

47. V. Ficino, *Théologie*, 3:255; cfr. Gentile, in *Marsilio Ficino . . . Mostra*, 92, no. 70.

48. V. infra, 374–379.

49. Sul Laurenziano Strozzi 101 e il cod. II IX 2 della Biblioteca Nazionale di Firenze, v. Gentile, in *Marsilio Ficino . . . Mostra*, 89–91, no. 69 II–III.

50. E' segnata Ginori Conti XXIX 64; cfr. supra, nota 44. Evidentemente il Kristeller, "Some Original Letters," 9, nota 4, ha confuso tra loro le due lettere del Salvini conservate in questo fondo manoscritto.

51. C. 122r: "Transcripsit hunc librum Bastianus Salvinus presbyter VIIII K⟨a⟩l⟨endas⟩ Mar⟨tias⟩ MCCCCLXXVI", da intendersi secondo lo stile fiorentino (cfr. idem, "Sebastiano Salvini," 239).

Salue. Saluinus tuus nequit esse saluus, nisi salute[m] tua[m] secum aliquis tueatur. Tue-
bitur aut[em], nisi priuatus fueris ijs que conducunt ad ipsam salut[em] felicius co[n]sequen-
da. Dato g[itur] op[er]am mi suauissime Nicolae, si lubet, ut quemadmodum ana a Magnanimo
Laurentio Medici ip[s]e donatus, ita doner ab[s] q[ue] vir undi[que] liberalis ne[que] apud anim[um] ip[s]a-
.i. apud diuum Laurentium hospitio uidear prohiberi .2. Vale[t] & da op[er]am ut intelligam
bas meas litteras apud R[ ] pondus habuisse .2.

Tuus Sebastianus Saluinus .2.

In una diversa realizzazione, una 'bastarda all'antica' chiaramente d'apparato, che sembrerebbe isolata nella produzione grafica del Salvini, si presenta invece la sua mano nel Laurenziano XXI 8, sottoscritto e datato 11 febbraio 1490 (stile fiorentino). Questo codice, riccamente miniato da Attavante, è l'esemplare di dedica a Lorenzo de'Medici di alcuni opuscoli e traduzioni giovanili del Ficino e del suo commento al *Filebo* platonico.[52] Qui la scrittura del Salvini, che nella sua forma da noi definita 'classica' raggiunge risultati di grande eleganza in preziosi codicetti di piccolo formato, appare estremamente posata, nell'evidente sforzo di adeguarsi all'alto grado di ricercatezza del codice, in modo da soddisfare il gusto dell'epoca e dell'ambiente.

* * *

Di una documentazione assai ridotta possiamo disporre per quel Rutilio che viene annoverato tra i copisti del Ficino in virtù del solo codice sicuramente da lui sottoscritto, il Vaticano lat. 2929.[53] E' questo l'esemplare del *Commentarium in Convivium* inviato a Giovanni Antonio Campano unitamente a una lettera—che vi si legge in calce, sempre di mano dell'amanuense—in cui il Ficino pregava il Campano di presentare al cardinale Francesco Piccolomini una seconda copia della medesima opera,[54] l'odierno Vaticano Chigiano E IV 122.[55]

Nel codice destinato al Campano, Rutilio si è sottoscritto due volte, la prima a c. 161r, alla fine del *Commentarium in Convivium* [tav. VII]: "ἀντώνηὰν [sic] Dum vivit ista vivo Rutilius servus ex voto", e poi, a c. 162v, dopo la lettera d'accompagnamento: "Rutilius Marsilii servus ex voto et Divae ἀντὼνῄε [sic] servulus". Proprio da questa seconda sottoscrizione si è dedotto che Rutilio potesse essere uno scrivano del Ficino, mentre il riferimento a una Antonia è stato accostato a due luoghi del testamento del filosofo in cui è menzionata una *domina Antonia sua servens*, alla quale

---

52. V. supra, 351 nota 37.

53. Sul MS v. Kristeller, *Supplementum*, 1:xl; idem, "Some Original Letters," 31; idem, *Iter*, 2:357; Ficino, *Commentaire*, 42.

54. V. Kristeller, *Supplementum*, 1:89; Ficino, *Commentaire*, 266.

55. Sul MS v. Kristeller, *Supplementum*, 1:xlv; idem, "Some Original Letters," 32; idem, *Iter*, 2:479, 604; Ficino, *Commentaire*, 41 sg.

egli lasciò una certa somma di denaro da destinarsi a *subsidium dotium* delle figlie.[56]

Ma al nostro Rutilio viene ricollegata anche un'altra sottoscrizione, che compare in alcuni manoscritti contenenti la traduzione volgare del *Pimander*, opera del confilosofo ficiniano Tommaso Benci. Anche questo è un colophon singolare, e mette conto riportarlo, secondo la lezione del Laurenziano XXVII 9:

> Finito illibro di Merchurio Trismegisto di grecho in latino translato per Marsilio Ficino fiorentino daprile 1463 Et facto vulgare da Ru.Sil. ad 10 di settembre 1463.[57]

Ha infatti dato luogo ad un'interpretazione non troppo convincente da parte del Della Torre,[58] che ha suggerito di "sottintendere un *scritto* a quel complemento d'agente *da Ru.Sil.*, il quale verrebbe ad essere così semplicemente il copista", al fine di evitare contraddizioni col proemio — indirizzato a Francesco di Nerone — in cui il Benci si attribuisce esplicitamente la paternità della traduzione; soluzione questa — d'intendere *Ru.Sil.* come il copista — che è stata poi accettata dal Kristeller, il quale a sua volta ha proposto l'identificazione — per l'affinità dei nomi — di *Ru.Sil.* col Rutilio copista del Vaticano lat. 2929.[59]

L'interpretazione del Della Torre lascia tuttavia dei punti oscuri. Si noterà innanzi tutto che il colophon con *Ru.Sil.* compare, con leggere varianti, in diversi manoscritti del volgarizzamento del *Pimander*, e segnatamente in cinque dei complessivi sedici testimoni che ci hanno tramandato questa versione.[60] Se si trattasse quindi soltanto della sottoscrizione del copista, resterebbe pur sempre da determinare a quale dei cinque codici che la presentano vada riferita: un confronto tra la scrittura che compare nel Laurenziano XXVII 9 e quella del Vaticano lat. 2929 non consente d'attribuire entrambi questi codici a Rutilio, come proposto dal Kristeller, trattandosi chiaramente di mani diverse. Ma questo sarebbe ancora il meno: una difficoltà più grave viene dalla forma in cui questo colophon figura in un

---

56. V. Kristeller, *Supplementum*, 2:194 sg., 332. Il testamento del Ficino e stato edito anche da R. Marcel, *Marsile Ficin (1433–1499)*, (Paris, 1958), 740–746.

57. Tale sottoscrizione figura a c. 70r del MS Laurenziano, sul quale v. Niccoli, in *Marsilio Ficino ... Mostra*, 41–43, no. 30, tav. XI.

58. V. Della Torre, *Storia*, 558, nota 1.

59. V. Kristeller, *Supplementum*, 1:cxxxi, clxviii; cfr. Marcel, *Marsile Ficin*, 258, nota 1.

60. Cfr. Niccoli, in *Marsilio Ficino ... Mostra*, 42, no. 30.

altro manoscritto del *Pimander* volgare segnalato dal Kristeller, il cod. A
IX 28 [= Gaslini 47] della Biblioteca Universitaria di Genova, un ricco
miscellaneo appartenuto proprio alla famiglia del traduttore, i Benci. Così
è riportato l'explicit del *Pimandro* da Giuliano Tanturli, a cui dobbiamo
un dettagliata descrizione del manoscritto:

> . . . da quali sono chomprese tutte lechose. Finito illibro di Merchurio
> trismegisto digrecho inlatino tranlatato da Marsilio Ficino fiorenti-
> no daprile 1463 et facto vulghare da Tommaso Benci disettembre
> 1463. Laus deo,[61]

dove *Tommaso Benci* occupa esattamente il posto che ha *Ru.Sil.* negli altri
codici. E se ciò porta ad escludere definitivamente l'interpretazione data
dal Della Torre del colophon del Laurenziano XXVII 9, lascia però senza
risposta la questione dell'origine di *Ru.Sil.*, dal momento che una corruzione da *Tommaso Benci*—eventualmente avvenuta nell'archetipo dei
manoscritti recanti questo colophon—non pare certo probabile da un punto
di vista paleografico.

Le spiegazioni che vengono in mente sono diverse: si può pensare a una
corruzione più grave, e postulare, ad esempio (per un salto da uguale a
uguale), la caduta nella sottoscrizione di *Tommaso Benci et scritto da* prima
di *Ru.Sil.*, che allora potrebbe veramente indicare il nome del copista; oppure pensare a una sostituzione voluta di *Ru.Sil.* in luogo di Tommaso
Benci, che potrebbe essere stata opera sia di un copista (Rutilio?), sia dello stesso Benci, forse desideroso in un primo momento di non comparire
come autore del volgarizzamento; *Ru.Sil.* sarebbe allora da intendersi come
uno pseudonimo del Benci.

Si deve riconoscere che queste spiegazioni[62] sono assai poco convincenti,
e ci si dovrà accontentare, per ora, d'avere attirato l'attenzione su questo
strano caso e tornare al Vaticano lat. 2929 e alla mano di Rutilio.

Questi scrive in un'umanistica corsiva affine a quella del Salvini, ma dal
tracciato meno regolare, quasi ondeggiante, talora inclinato verso destra,
talaltra diritto.

Sulla base della sottoscrizione e della scrittura del Vaticano lat. 2929
sono stati attribuiti a Rutilio altri codici. Dell'improbabilità di una sua

---

61. V. G. Tanturli, "I Benci copisti. Vicende della cultura fiorentina volgare tra Antonio Pucci
e il Ficino," *Studi di filologia italiana*, 36 (1978): 288 sg.
62. L'una e l'altra sono riportate da Niccoli, in *Marsilio Ficino . . . Mostra*, 42, no. 30.

identificazione con l'amanuense che ha copiato il Laurenziano XXVII 9—per altro in *antiqua*—s'è detto. Ma Raymond Marcel, editore del *Commentarium in Convivium*, ha riconosciuto la mano del nostro copista anche nel Vindobonense lat. 2472 e nel già citato Chigiano E IV 22, entrambi contenenti il testo del *Commentarium*. Se il codice di Vienna risulta scritto da mano diversa,[63] per quel che concerne il Chigiano non si può che essere d'accordo; evidentemente il Ficino fece copiare a Rutilio entrambi gli esemplari del *Commentarium* inviati al Campano, anche quello destinato al cardinale Piccolomini.

C'e poi un terzo manoscritto del *Commentarium* da attribuirsi con ogni probabilità a Rutilio sul fondamento del confronto della scrittura: il cod. 1 della Biblioteca Serlupi, contenente anche, d'altra mano, vari opuscoli giovanili del Ficino.[64]

* * *

Personaggio più conosciuto di Rutilio è Ficino Ficini, nipote del filosofo.[65] Figlio di Cherubino, sembra sia vissuto accanto all'illustre zio negli anni che ne precedettero la morte, facendosi evidentemente benvolere, a giudicare almeno dal testamento del Ficino, che gli lasciò in eredità, "in recompensationem servitiorum eidem testatori prestitorum", non solo "omnes libros et quaternos", ma addirittura la villa di Careggi.[66] Sappiamo inoltre che fu tra i discepoli di Francesco Cattani da Diacceto[67] e che venne giustiziato nel 1530 per via delle sue manifeste simpatie filo-medicee.[68]

La mano di Ficino Ficini è stata proposta all'attenzione degli studiosi dal Kristeller, che per primo pubblicò la riproduzione di una sua lettera a Francesco Gaddi, allora appartenente alla Collezione De Marinis, datata 16 settembre 1497 *ex agro Charegio*.[69] Si conosceva poi una sua nota di

---

63. V. Ficino, *Commentaire*, 41. La mano che ha trascritto il cod. di Vienna (sul quale v. anche Kristeller, *Supplementum*, 1:1 sg.; idem, "Some Original Letters," 32; idem, *Iter*, 3:62) è piuttosto molto simile a quella che ha vergato i manoscritti ficiniani di Leida e della Cornell University (per i quali v. supra, note 30–31).

64. V. Gentile, in *Marsilio Ficino . . . Mostra*, 64 sg., no. 49.

65. Su Ficino Ficini, v. Della Torre, *Storia*, 103, nota 1, 833; Kristeller, *Supplementum*, 2:334.

66. V. *ibid.*, 196.

67. V. idem, *Studies*, 322, nota 189.

68. V. idem, *Supplementum*, 2:334; Cosenza, *Biographical Dictionary*, 2:1394.

69. V. Kristeller, "Some Original Letters," 13 e tav. IV; *Nuovi documenti per la storia del Rinascimento*, raccolti e pubblicati da T. De Marinis e A. Perosa (Firenze, 1970), 7 e nota 6, 42, e tav. XIV.

possesso, su di un codice appartenuto al Ficino, il Riccardiano 76, che evidentemente faceva parte dei manoscritti compresi nel lascito della biblioteca al nipote.[70]

E' un'umanistica corsiva molto simile ad una delle realizzazioni in cui si presenta—come avremo modo di vedere—la presunta *Rheinschrift* ficiniana, anche se è possibile distinguerla da essa per alcune sue peculiarità quali la 'r' che non lega con la lettera seguente, terminando con uno svolazzo, la 's' tonda, che in principio di parola si alterna con la variante diritta, la 'e' in due tempi con l'occhiello superiore alto, una legatura 'et' piuttosto particolare.

Proprio fondandosi sul confronto con la lettera a Francesco Gaddi, il Sicherl ha potuto attribuire a Ficino Ficini la sezione (cc. 1r–35v) del Parigino lat. 2614 contenente la traduzione e il commento del Ficino al *De mystica theologia* dello pseudo-Dionigi,[71] e le cc. 186r–189v del già citato Parigino Supplément grec 212, corrispondenti al *Prohemium Marsilii Ficini ... in Alcinoi et Speusippi et Pythagorae opuscula ab eo e graeca lingua in latinam traducta*.[72] Di queste attribuzioni del Sicherl soltanto la seconda è valida, mentre la prima risulta errata, trattandosi della stessa mano che egli ha generalmente considerato come la *Rheinschrift* del Ficino, e che personalmente ritengo invece appartenere a Luca Fabiani.[73]

Riconosciamo invece la sua mano chiaramente in una lettera originale del Ficino ad Aldo Manuzio [tav. VIII], oggi inserita in un codice miscellaneo della Biblioteca Vaticana, il Reginense lat. 2023, alla c. 173r-v,[74] in cui si parla, tra l'altro, proprio di quella edizione aldina di cui il Parigino Supplément grec, come ha dimostrato il Sicherl, ci ha conservato parte del manoscritto usato per la stampa.[75] Troviamo infine annotazioni di mano di Ficino Ficini nel Riccardiano 426—il manoscritto del *Nuovo Testamento* appartenuto allo zio[76]—, nel Magliabechiano XX 58, *codex*

70. Cfr. Kristeller, *Supplementum*, 2:334; Gentile, in *Marsilio Ficino ... Mostra*, 55–57, no. 43.

71. V. Sicherl, "Die Humanistenkursive," 443 sg.; precedentemente il Sicherl, "Neuendeckte Handschriften," 56, aveva attribuito la trascrizione di questo MS al Ficino, in *Rheinschrift*. Sul MS, v. Kristeller, *Iter*, 3:216.

72. V. Sicherl, "Druckmanuskripte," 325; cfr. idem, "Neuendeckte Handschriften," 55; idem, "Die Humanistenkursive," 443.

73. Cfr. Gentile, in *Marsilio Ficino ... Mostra*, 157, no. 121.

74. Cfr. *ibid.*, 131, no. 101. Il testo di questa lettera, che reca la data del primo luglio 1497, è stato edito dal Kristeller, *Supplementum*, 2:95 sg. (cfr. *ibid.*, 1:xliv; idem, *Iter*, 2:412).

75. V. Sicherl, "Druckmanuskripte."

76. V. Gentile, in *Marsilio Ficino ... Mostra*, 79 sg., no. 61.

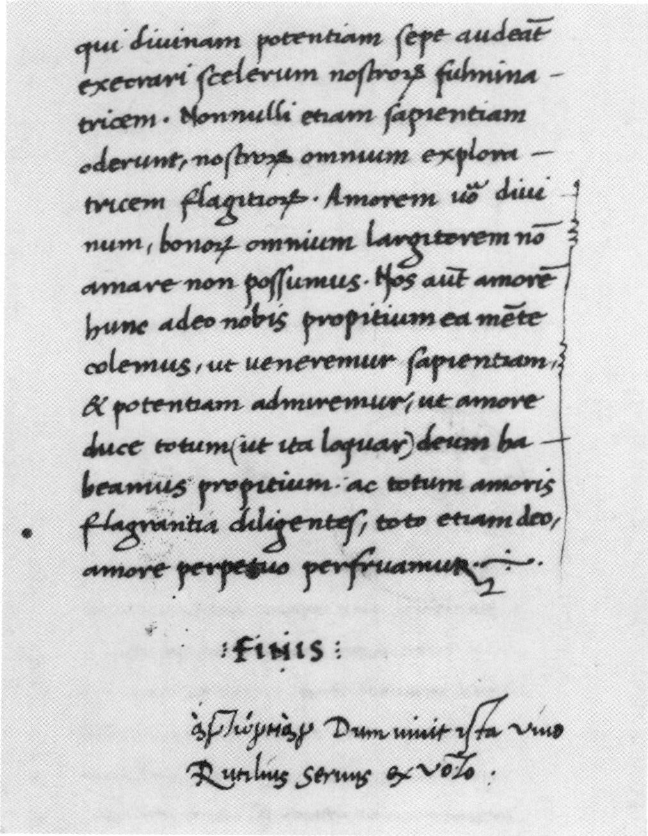

Tav. VII. Città del Vaticano, Biblioteca Apostolica Vaticana, MS Vaticano lat. 2929, c.161r.

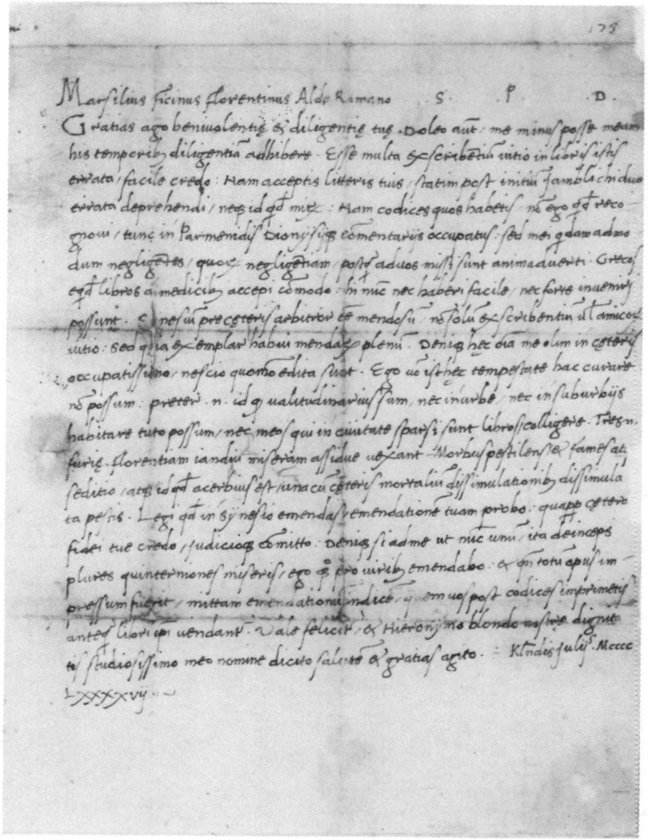

Tav. VIII. Città del Vaticano, Biblioteca Apostolica Vaticana, MS Reginense lat. 2023, c.173r.

unicus della *Disputatio contra iudicium astrologorum* — sul quale avremo occasione di tornare più avanti[77] —, e in due edizioni principi di opere ficiniane: la prima, del *De sole et lumine* — che fu stampato a Firenze il 31 gennaio 1492 (stile fiorentino) per i tipi di Antonio Miscomini —, è oggi alla Biblioteca Laurenziana;[78] la seconda, dei *Commentaria in Platonem* — usciti, sempre a Firenze, il 2 dicembre 1496, dalla stamperia di Lorenzo d'Alopa —, si trova invece alla Biblioteca Consorziale della Città d'Arezzo.[79]

* * *

E passiamo finalmente a parlare di quel Luca Fabiani che abbiamo tante volte menzionato.[80]

La prima traccia della sua esistenza ci viene da una lettera del Ficino intitolata *Discendi et loquendi ratio*, diretta appunto "Lucae Fabiano scribae suo" e databile grosso modo agli inizi del 1477.[81] Della sua vita anteriormente a questa data sappiamo soltanto che era originario di un famiglia contadina di Montegonzi nel piviere di Cavriglia.[82]

Su come Luca sia giunto in casa del Ficino da Montegonzi, non c'informa certo la lettera del filosofo, di carattere esortativo e moraleggiante, rivelatrice piuttosto, nel tono paterno usato dal Ficino con il suo scrivano, di un certa familiarità tra i due. Al più si potrà considerare, in via del tutto ipotetica, l'eventualità che un legame, un qualche punto di contatto, venisse loro per il tramite della madre del Ficino, Alessandra di Nan-

---

77. V. infra, 381, 388–394.

78. V. Gentile, *Marsilio Ficino ... Mostra*, 154 sg., no. 119, tav. XXXV/a–b.

79. V. *ibid.*, 155 sg., no. 120. Correzioni di mano di Ficino Ficini figurano anche nell'esemplare dell'edizione principe dell'*Epistolae* ficiniane di Durham (sul quale v. supra, 342 e nota 14).

80. Sul Fabiani, oltre agli studi che si citeranno via via, v. Della Torre, *Storia*, 102, nota 2; Kristeller, *Supplementum*, 2:333; Cosenza, *Biographical Dictionary*, 3:2017 sg.; K. Csapodi-Gardony, "Les scripteurs," 42.

81. V. Ficino, *Opera*, 742.

82. Nei registri del Catasto relativi al popolo di San Piero a Montegonzi nel piviere di Cavriglia (Quartiere di Santa Croce), è possibile rintracciare le portate del nonno di ser Luca, Agnolo di Nanni di Piero. V. ASF, Catasto 1043: estimo del 1459, c. 566r; Catasto 947: estimo del 1460, cc. 568r–569v; Catasto 1113: estimo del 1487, cc. 674r–676v. In quest'ultima portata Angelo risulta avere 103 anni (ma 67 nel 1459 e 78 nel 1460), Fabiano, padre di Luca, 53 (37 nel 1459, 40 nel 1460), e fanno la loro comparsa "M⟨adonn⟩a Serafina, dona di Fabiano", di anni 50, "Nicholo di Fabiano d'Agnolo" di anni 16 e "Tonio di Fabiano" di anni 8; gli ultimi due sono evidentemente fratelli di Luca, che tuttavia non è menzionato in questa portata, con ogni probabilità perché già si trovava a Firenze, presso il Ficino (cfr. infra, note 98 e 147). Forse del bisnonno di ser Luca è una portata del 13 agosto 1427 (Catasto 115, c. 22r) di un Nanni di Agnolo.

noccio, nativa della vicina Montevarchi,[83] località in cui già il nonno del nostro amanuense possedeva un appezzamento di terreno.[84]

Ma se non è possibile indicare l'occasione dell'incontro tra il Ficino e il Fabiani, la presenza dell'amanuense nella casa del filosofo viene confermata da una seconda lettera di quest'ultimo — che segue la precedente di circa un anno —, diretta a ser Bastiano Foresi, in cui figura un poscritto che mette conto riportare:

> Ipse Lucas Marsilii scriba, qui hanc epistolam transcripsi, me tibi commendo atque oro, si modo tanto munere dignus tibi videor, ut tantum me ames quantum ab ipso Marsilio amari te video. Patronus, Foresi, meus te tantum amat quantum ipse amas amari. Vale.[85]

Qui il Fabiani, oltre a prodursi senza timori reverenziali in battute di gusto tipicamente ficiniano, ci appare impegnato a svolgere una mansione che diremmo consona più ad un segretario che ad un amanuense in senso stretto, quella cioè di trascrivere le lettere del suo *patronus*, verosimilmente dalla minuta nella trasmissiva. Ed è un fatto, questo, che non solo legittima — come ha visto il Kristeller[86] — l'esistenza di lettere del Ficino originali e non autografe, ma ci permetterà anche, più avanti, di fare alcune considerazioni di un certo interesse.

Per il resto, se si escludono le allusioni a un *puer noster* e a uno *scriba noster*, forse da riferirsi al Fabiani, che troviamo in altre due epistole del Ficino non lontane cronologicamente da quelle ora menzionate,[87] lo scrivano sembra scomparire per un lungo periodo dall'orizzonte del filosofo.

Farà infatti la sua ricomparsa soltanto dopo una decina d'anni, nel Laurenziano LXXXII 11 — che assieme all'LXXXII 10 forma la copia di dedica del Plotino tradotto e commentato dal Ficino, donato da Filippo Valori a Lorenzo de'Medici. Vi leggiamo infatti, nell'ultima carta (c. 407r): "Ego Lucas Marsilii Ficini amanuensis exscripsi hoc opus et finem imposui in agro Caregio die XII novembris 1490" [tav. IX].[88]

---

83. Cfr. Marcel, *Marsile Ficin*, 123, 735, no. 5; Ficino, *Opera*, 615 (lettera a Matteo Corsini).

84. ASF, Catasto 1043, c. 566r (a lapis): "Un pezo ditera posta nella corte di Montevarchi . . .". Non risulta confermata da documenti la parentela col Ficino attribuita al Fabiani dal Cosenza, *Biographical Dictionary*, 3:2018: "Son of Fabianus who married a daughter of Agnolo di Giusto Ficino".

85. V. Ficino, *Opera*, 788.

86. V. Kristeller, "Some Original Letters," 9 e nota 6.

87. V. Ficino, *Opera*, 730 (a Giovanni Cavalcanti), 781 (cfr. infra, 394 e nota 161).

88. Cfr. Kristeller, *Supplementum*, 1:xii; Gentile, in *Marsilio Ficino . . . Mostra*, 150, no. 115 II.

Ego Lucas Marsilij ficini amanuensis exscripsi hoc opus et
finem imposui In agro Caregio die xij. Nouembris. 1490 :–

Marsilius ficinus Magnanimo Petro Medici . s.
Cum idibus Nouembribus in Agro Caregio una cum Magnani
mo Laurentio Medice deambularem multaq̃ Platonis my
steria ultro citroq̃ interpretaremur decidi forte interloquen
dum e sapientia in fortunam cepiq̃ hanc acrius incusare q̃
Platoni lucem affectanti seculis iam multis obstiterit Tum ille
noli inquit Marsili Platone nostrum infortunatū dicere : nisi for
san me fore putes infortunatū Sermonem quidem tunc nostrum
his dictis absoluimus Sed nunquid mortis causa deinde scitē
Laurentium licet infortunatū existimare : simulq̃ Platonis
fortunā funditus corruisse. Absit ut animum illum minus
felicem putem quem e corporis compedibus euolantem nouo
quodam applausu letus ether exceperit: grandiore stella in
Laurentiana morte cadente : mirisq̃ flammis ex alto per Ca
regnanos agros triduo corruscantibus. Sed biduo ante obitū
Jupiter rubente dextera sacras iaculatus arces terruit
vrbem mox orbam tanto patre futura: Terruit hostes gra
ue nequid forsan aduersus inuictum domum Medicam mo
lirentur. Itaq̃ nec Laurentius heros nec heroicus Petrus
Laurentij filius ob ea que nuper cōtigerunt minus posthac
felix est iudicandus : nec propterea Plato noster infortunatus.
Cuius caput hactenus salutari prorsus umbra Lauri fouebat.
Nunc pedes iam firmissima petra nituntur. Plotinus demū
manibus nūc tuis apprehensus seniorem interea Platonē pijs
humeris substinebit : teq̃ duce producet in lucem. xv. Maij 1492 .

Al Plotino seguirono, nel giro di poco più di un anno, altri due codici copiati e sottoscritti dal Fabiani, vale a dire il Laurenziano Strozzi 97—comprendente la parafrasi del *De mysteriis* di Giamblico, con la dedica al cardinale Giovanni de'Medici, seguita da altre traduzioni e opuscoli del Ficino[89]—, e il Laurenziano LXXXIII 11, in cui troviamo riuniti e dedicati a Lorenzo de'Medici l'*Argumentum in platonicam theologiam* e altri trattatelli facenti parte del secondo libro dell'epistolario ficiniano.[90]

In questi due ultimi manoscritti il Fabiani si è sottoscritto in forma leggermente diversa e cioè, nel Laurenziano Strozzi 97 (c. 205v): "Lucas Fabiani de Ficinis notarius florentinus veloci calamo exaravit XXX iulii MCCCCLXXXXI Florentiae", e, nel Laurenziano LXXXIII 11 (c. 98v): "Lucas Fabiani [*corretto da* Fabianus] de Ficinis notarius florentinus veloci calamo exaravit VII septembris MCCCCLXXXXI Florentiae".

La differenza tra queste sottoscrizioni e quella del Laurenziano LXXXII 11 consiste nella trasformazione di "Lucas Marsilii Ficini amanuensis" in "Lucas Fabiani de Ficinis notarius florentinus."

Il *de Ficinis* sembra ufficializzare, per così dire, la familiarità che abbiamo detto trasparire dalle lettere sopra citate, e sarà forse da leggersi nel senso di una vera e propria adozione dello scrivano da parte del filosofo. E' del resto normale, in documenti più tardi, trovare il Fabiani indicato come Luca Ficini: si può ricordare al proposito un distico di Alessandro Braccesi— da ascriversi con ogni probabilità al 1503—,

> Est tibi caesaries ingens corpusque pusillum
> Sic ut sit maior corpore caesaries,

indirizzato appunto "ad Lucam Ficinium."[91]

La lettera a Piero de'Medici che figura di seguito alla sottoscrizione (v. tav. IX) è anch'essa di mano del Fabiani, che ve l'aggiunse in un secondo tempo.

89. V. Kristeller, *Supplementum*, 1:xv; Gentile, in *Marsilio Ficino . . . Mostra*, 126–128, no. 98.

90. V. Kristeller, *Supplementum*, 1:xiii; Gentile, in *Marsilio Ficino . . . Mostra*, 96 sg., no. 73. Per quanto diremo cade l'ipotesi fatta dal Marcel (v. Ficin, *Théologie*, 3:254 sg.) di correggere la data di sottoscrizione di questo MS, 1491, in 1481 (cfr. Gentile, in *Marsilio Ficino . . . Mostra*, 96 sg., no. 73).

91. V. A. Braccius, *Carmina*, ed. A. Perosa (Florentiae, 1944), 145. Da un confronto col Laurenziano XCI sup. 41, c. 52v, risulta che l'epigramma è indirizzato "ad Lucam Ficinium" non "ad Lucam Ficinum", lezione quest'ultima che è anche in A.M. Bandinius, *Catalogus codicum latinorum Bibliothecae Mediceae Laurentianae*, 3 (Florentiae, 1776), 793; la lezione corretta dà invece il Della Torre, *Storia*, 102, nota 2.

Quanto poi al *notarius florentinus*, il fatto che non si conoscano documenti in cui il Fabiani venga fregiato di questo titolo anteriori alla data di sottoscrizione, induce a credere che la sua omissione nel Laurenziano LXXXII 11 non sia casuale. L'amanuense del Ficino compare infatti per la prima volta in veste di notaio in un atto rogato il 17 settembre 1491 ("in palatio residentie illustrissime Dominationis florentine") da ser Giuliano di Giovanni della Valle, "presentibus ser Andrea Romuli Laurentii et ser Luca Fabbiani Angeli de monte Ghontio, ambobus notariis florentinis, testibus".[92] Non il suo nome, ma la sua mano è poi presente in una missiva del 22 novembre 1491 a firma degli Otto di Pratica,[93] anteriore di solo pochi mesi a una postilla, sottoscritta e datata 18 aprile 1492 [tav. X] — aggiunta in calce ad un registro di lettere dell'ambasciatore fiorentino a Roma, Piero Alamanni — in cui ser Luca si dichiara coadiutore di Bartolomeo Scala, che era allora primo Cancelliere.[94]

92. ASF, Notarile antecosimiano G 533 (libri del notaio Giuliano di Giovanni della Valle contenenti atti degli anni 1488–1497), c. 5r (del secondo libro); va notato che nell'atto "Fabbiani Angeli" è aggiunto con inchiostro diverso in uno spazio lasciato bianco. Nello stesso libro, alle cc. 48v–49r, è conservato anche l'atto d'emancipazione di ser Luca, ad opera del padre Fabiano, avvenuta il 3 marzo 1492 (stile fiorentino); cfr. ASF, Consigli della Repubblica, Emancipazioni 12, c. 150v.

93. ASF, Signori, Otto di Pratica, Dieci di Balìa, Missive originali 4, c. 76r–v. Per il vero la mano di ser Luca compare in documenti della Cancelleria anche di data anteriore al 1491. Ad esempio in ASF, Signori, Carteggi, Minutari 13, c. 1r–v, ove troviamo una lettera diretta a Innocenzo VIII e datata 19 ottobre 1484, che il Fabiani evidentemente copiò in un secondo tempo, come suggerisce del resto il fatto che già la terza lettera di quel registro (la seconda non ha data) è del 5 maggio 1493. E in ASF, Signori, Carteggi, Minutari 16, c. 1r–v, figura una "Copia litterarum transmissarum per Henricum regem Angliae et Franc⟨orum⟩ ac etiam dominum Hiberniae Dominis Prioribus Libertatis et Vexill⟨ifer⟩o Iustitiae populi florentini", copiata e sottoscritta dal Fabiani — "Copiata ac rescripta per me Lucam Fabiani Angeli notarium publicum florentinum ad fidem me s⟨ub⟩s⟨scrip⟩s⟨i⟩" — in data verosimilmente posteriore a quella dell'epistola stessa, vale a dire al 19 febbraio 1490, da intendersi secondo lo stile dell'Incarnazione, in uso in Inghilterra. Ciò pare confermato dal fatto che essa precede altre due epistole, sempre di mano di ser Luca, datate rispettivamente 13 luglio 1491 e 7 gennaio 1491 (stile fiorentino).

94. ASF, Signori, Otto di Pratica, Dieci di Balìa, Legazioni e Commissarie 19, c. 145v: "Ser Antonius Petri de Colle cum florentino legato D⟨omino⟩ Petro Alamanno apud summum Pont⟨ificem⟩ Innocentium p⟨a⟩p⟨am⟩ octavum hac presenti die XVIII Aprilis MCCCCLXXXXII presens volumen epistolarum ex florentina lege mihi Luce Ficino magnifici cancell⟨arii⟩ Bartholomei Scalae coadiutori (coadiutori *nell'interlinea*) consignavit. Ego Lucas Fab⟨iani⟩ not⟨arius⟩ florentinus in rei testimonium manu propria scripsi et s⟨ub⟩s⟨cri⟩ps⟨i⟩"; cfr. A. Brown, *Bartolomeo Scala, 1430–1497, Chancellor of Florence. The Humanist as Bureaucrat* (Princeton, 1979), 189, nota 66; *Il notaio nella civiltà fiorentina, secoli XIII–XVI, Mostra nella Biblioteca Medicea Laurenziana* (Firenze, 1984), 94 sg., no. 93. Nei *Ricordi di Paolo Vettori al cardinale de' Medici sopra le cose di Firenze*, editi da R. von Albertini in appendice al suo *Firenze dalla repubblica al principato. Storia e coscienza politica*, trad. C. Cristofolini (Torino, 1970), è ricordato a p. 358 un ser Lorenzo (*sic*) Ficini tra i coadiutori "a tempo di Lorenzo" della "Cancelleria degli Otto della Pratica e Dieci".

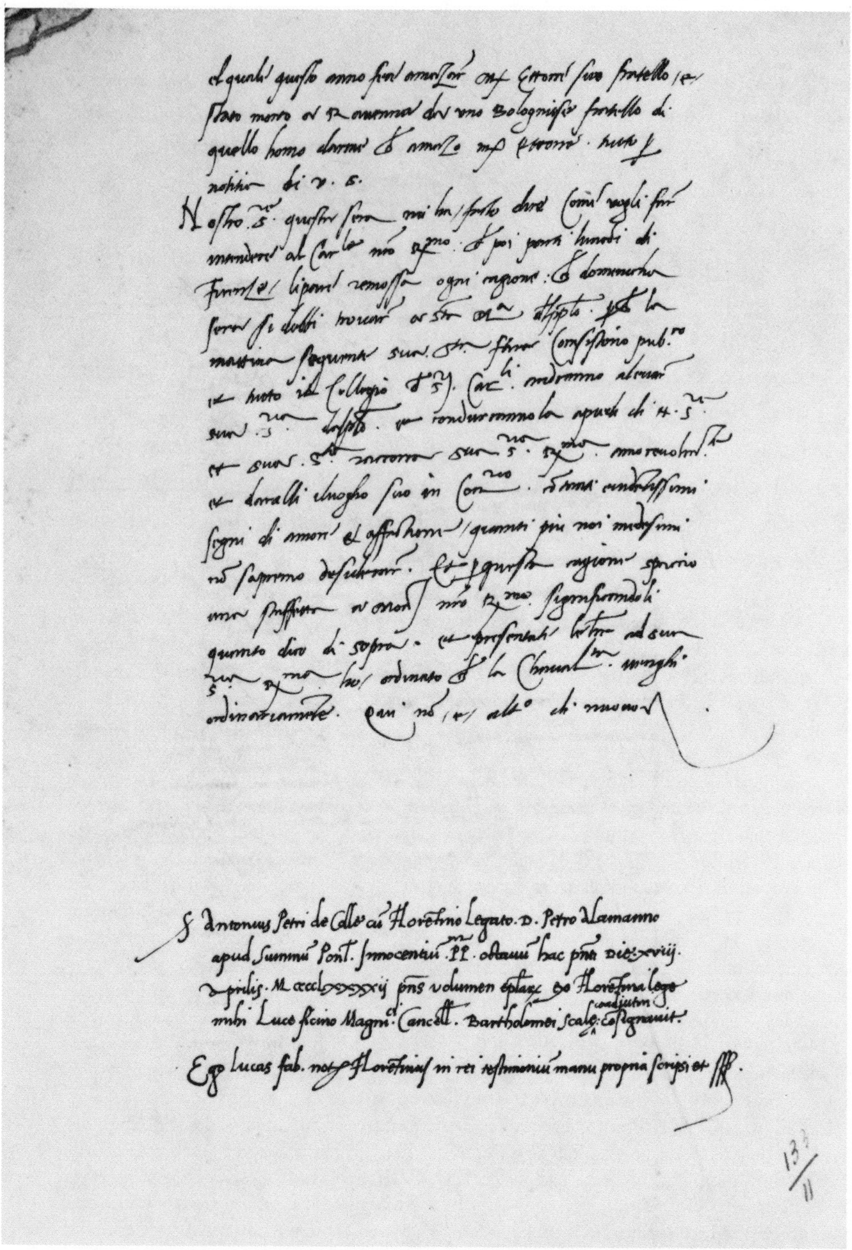

Tav. X. Firenze, Archivio di Stato, Otto di Pratica, Dieci di Balìa,
Legazioni e Commissarie 19, c.145v.

Il fatto che ser Luca si dichiari coadiutore dello Scala induce a pensare che egli sia succeduto in questa carica a ser Filippo d'Andrea Redditi. Il Redditi infatti, deputato dallo Scala a suo coadiutore nel 1488 per un primo triennio,[95] e confermato dalla Signoria assieme a tutti i cancellieri e i coadiutori per un secondo triennio il 23 novembre 1490,[96] venne cacciato dalla Cancelleria e interdetto agli uffici del notariato con deliberazione presa dai Signori il 15 aprile 1491.[97]

A ciò s'aggiunga che, stando alla dichiarazione da lui fatta per il pagamento della Decima repubblicana nel 1498, il Fabiani entrò 'ufficialmente' in Firenze e "venne a graveza" per la prima volta proprio nel 1491.[98]

Probabilmente il Fabiani fece quindi il suo ingresso in Cancelleria in sostituzione del Redditi alla fine del 1491, iniziando così una lunga carriera cancelleresca che si protrasse per circa 26 anni.[99] Da un registro degli

95. V. D. Marzi, *La cancelleria della Repubblica fiorentina* (Rocca San Casciano, 1910), 611; cfr. ASF, Signori e Collegi, Deliberazioni fatte in forza di speciale autorità 36 (c. 138r–v della numerazione a lapis), 37 (c. 70v).

96. V. ASF, Signori e Collegi, Bastardelli di sbozzi 11, c. 31v.

97. V. ASF, Signori e Collegi, Deliberazioni, Duplicati 26, c. 13r–v (numerazione a lapis). Dalla provvisione del 1488 concernente la Cancelleria (v. supra, nota 95), apprendiamo che allo Scala venne lasciata la libertà di scegliersi il coadiutore, purché questi avesse 25 anni e fosse immatricolato nell'Arte dei Giudici e dei Notai. Dobbiamo pertanto ritenere che il Fabiani, quando subentrò al Redditi, rispondesse a questi requisiti.

98. V. ASF, Decima repubblicana 32, c. 435r (scritta di mano di ser Luca): "Q⟨uartiere⟩ S⟨an⟩to G⟨iovan⟩ni G⟨onfalo⟩ne Chiavi. Ser Lucha figliuolo emanceppato di Fabiano d'Agnolo (*segue spazio bianco*) da Monte Gonzi popolo di san Piero Maggiore venne a graveza in Firenze nel 1491. Hebbe lagraveza nel Q⟨uartie⟩re di S⟨anta⟩ M⟨aria⟩ No⟨vella⟩ G⟨onfalo⟩ne L⟨eo⟩ne B⟨ian⟩co"; di mano coeva in margine si legge: "Entro in Firenze nel 91 no. 439 1/2" Nella dichiarazione il Fabiani scrisse poi le sue "substanze", che consistevano in un appezzamento di terreno nella "corte" di Montevarchi, tre appezzamenti in quella di Montegonzi, parte di una casa nel "castello" di Montegonzi, metà di un altro appezzamento di terreno nella "corte" di Montevarchi. Tranne quest'ultimo, che acquistò successivamente, egli ricevette gli altri beni in dono dal padre in occasione della sua emancipazione ("Hebbe tucti esopradecti beni da d⟨ec⟩to Fabiano suo padre in premio della emanceppatione nientedimeno riservatosi lusufructo depsi durante la sua vita"; per l'emancipazione di ser Luca, v. supra, nota 92. Il padre inoltre si occupava di tutti i terreni del figlio ("Lavora et fa lavorare esopradecti beni Fabiano d'Agnolo d⟨ec⟩to"). Ser Luca, invece, come abbiamo già osservato, continuò a vivere a Firenze, presso il Ficino; ne è riprova il fatto che il gonfalone (Leone Bianco) nel quale il copista fece la sua prima dichiarazione nel 1491 è lo stesso in cui l'aveva fatta il Ficino nel 1480, così come quella del 1498 è stata fatta da entrambi nel gonfalone Chiavi (per il Ficino, v. Viti, in *Marsilio Ficino . . . Mostra*, 193 sg., no. 167).

99. Si segnala che ad un prima recognizione, estesa, ma tuttavia non esaustiva, la mano di ser Luca compare nei seguenti registri dell'ASF: Signori, Carteggi, Minutari 13, 14, 16; Signori, Otto di Pratica, Dieci di Balìa, Missive originali 4; Signori, Otto di Pratica, Dieci di Balìa, Legazioni e Commissarie 19; Signori, Carteggi, Missive I Cancelleria 50, 51; Signori, Otto di Pratica, Dieci di Balìa 66; Signori, Otto di Pratica, Deliberazioni e Partiti, Condotte e Stanziamenti 5, 11; Dieci di Balìa, Deliberazioni, Condotte, Stanziamenti 37, 51, 53, 56, 59. Troviamo invece il suo nome

Otto di Pratica apprendiamo infatti che egli fu messo a riposo con un vitalizio, in ricompensa del suo fedele operato, pari alla metà dello stipendio da lui sino ad allora percepito, il 2 gennaio 1517.[100]

Questa lunga milizia cancelleresca non valse tuttavia ad allontanarlo dal Ficino. Del resto basterà dare un'occhiata al testamento di quest'ultimo per accorgersi non soltanto della riconoscenza che egli portava a ser Luca — destinatario con Ficino Ficini dei lasciti più cospicui —, ma anche del fatto che essi continuarono a vivere sotto lo stesso tetto.[101] Luca, comunque, non smise di copiare codici per l'oramai anziano filosofo, come avremo modo di vedere più avanti.

Non è qui il caso di seguire il Fabiani nella sua carriera cancelleresca successiva alla morte del Ficino, avvenuta nel 1499. Si ricorderà soltanto che egli fu della segreteria dei Dieci ai tempi del Machiavelli, e che il suo nome compare più volte nelle lettere di Biagio Buonaccorsi — suo 'familiare', avendo sposato una nipote del Ficino — e di Agostino Vespucci, dirette al Segretario fiorentino.[102] Non credo tuttavia fuori luogo riportare parte

e le retribuzioni da lui percepite in ASF, Dieci di Balìa, Deliberazioni, Condotte, Stanziamenti 34-36, 41-43, 45-46, 49-61; e poi — dopo la sostituzione, avvenuta il 10 giugno 1514, della magistratura dei Dieci con quella degli Otto di Pratica — in ASF, Otto di Pratica, Deliberazioni e Partiti, Condotte e Stanziamenti 6, 11. La mano del Fabiani figura anche, come segnalatomi dal dott. Paolo Viti, in un registro di atti di ser Alessandro Braccesi (v. ASF, Notarile antecosimiano B 2318, c. 459r), ove egli scrisse la notifica della concessione di una "tregua" da parte dei Dieci di Balìa in data 3 agosto 1495. Qualche dato sull'attività cancelleresca di ser Luca in Marzi, *La cancelleria*, 268, 295, nota 4, 327 e nota 8 (quest'ultimo riferimento a ser Luca risulta però inesatto); O. Tommasini, *La vita e gli scritti di Niccolò Machiavelli* (Torino-Roma-Firenze, 1883), 1:556, 667, nota 1; *Il notaio*, 94 sg., no. 93, 95 sg., no. 95, 143, no. 148.

100. ASF, Otto di Pratica, Deliberazioni e Partiti, Condotte e Stanziamenti 6, c. 57v: "Die secunda Ianuarii MDXVI more florentino . . . Dicta die. Prefati Domini etc. deliberaverunt et deliberando voluerunt quod pro remuneratione et ser Lucae de Ficinis solvantur sibi in futurum durante eius vita librae tredecim s⟨olidi⟩ decem p⟨iccio⟩li singulo quoque mense, hoc est dimidium salarii quod sibi solutum fuit usque ad suprascriptam diem commissione eorum magistratus, hac tamen conditione, quod sit liber ab omni onere et obligatione Cancelleriae eorum magistratus, ut recognoscerent longam servitutem in eorum Cancelleria". Se quanto osservato sulla probabile data d'ingresso del Fabiani in Cancelleria ha il conforto dei documenti, qualche dubbio per quanto concerne il momento della sua immatricolazione ci viene da uno squittinio — della cui esistenza mi ha informato il dott. Paolo Viti — per l'elezione dei consoli dell'Arte dei Giudici e dei Notai, dove, tra i non veduti, figura anche, al numero 249, "ser Luca di Fabiano da Montegonzi" (v. ASF, Tratte 60, c. 376r della numerazione a lapis). Il fatto che l'elenco dei veduti (nonché la filigrana) corrisponda, con qualche minima differenza, a quello che figura in ASF, Tratte 62, cc. 385r–391r, che conserva lo squittinio per l'elezione del camerlengo della medesima arte, datato "Die 19 martii 1488" (stile fiorentino), porterebbe a supporre la contemporaneità dei due squittini, e, di conseguenza, l'immatricolazione di ser Luca intorno al 1489 (cfr. *Il notaio*, 143, no. 148).

101. V. Kristeller, *Supplementum*, 2:194 sg., 200; cfr. anche supra, nota 98.

102. V. N. Machiavelli, *Tutte le opere*, a cura di M. Martelli (Firenze, 1971), 1024 (lett. 18),

di una di queste lettere—scritta il 20 ottobre del 1501 dal Vespucci al Machiavelli, allora in Francia—in cui del Fabiani si tesse un elogio che tocca, tra le altre cose, proprio la sua scrittura:

> Lucas noster, qui tantopere satagit Cancellerie et domus, quam sibi a fundamentis erexit, obque ista duo erumnossus, se tibi commendat. Positus enim inter sacrum et saxum crudciatur [sic] misere: solvere fisco quod debet nequit, et nisi prius solvat seque a Speculo liberet, fieri non potest (ut suis virtutibus merebatur optabatque) in Alphani loco scriba ordinari; que res nequaquam fieret ei difficilis, ni spes nominandi in consilio, ab eo in cuius manu facultas est, sibi deesset; commendat se tamen omnipotenti Domino et cunctis amicis. Scis etenim ipse quantopere fide et taciturnitate valeat, quantumve in scribendo velociter et concinne literarum caracteres exprimat; cui quin reditus tuus suffragetur, cum bonis faveas, veri quidem simile non est.[103]

1029 (lett. 25), 1030 (lett. 26), 1052 (lett. 64), 1092 (lett. 131), 1094 (lett. 135). Gli accenni contenuti in queste lettere a un "Luca", a un "ser Luca", oppure a un "Lucas noster", sempre da riferirsi, a giudicare dal contesto, a un membro della Cancelleria, sono stati intesi come riguardanti Luca degli Albizzi—tranne il "ser Luca" della lett. 25—negli indici dell'ed. machiavelliana cit. e di quella precedente, curata da F. Gaeta (N. Machiavelli, *Lettere* [Milano, 1961]). Già il Marzi, *La cancelleria*, 300, aveva identificato col Fabiani il "Lucas . . . noster" della lett. 18, oltreché il ser Luca della lett. 25. Vediamo comunque che nella monumentale edizione curata dal Bertelli tali accenni vengono correttamente riferiti a ser Luca, col quale tuttavia viene anche identificato un omonimo ser Luca—omesso negli indici delle due edd. precedenti—, maestro di Guido Machiavelli (v. N. Machiavelli, *Opere*, a cura di S. Bertelli, 11: *Appendice. Indici* [Verona, 1982], 194), che lo nomina in una lettera al padre del 17 aprile 1527 (=lett. 322 dell' ed. Martelli), data in cui il Fabiani, come vedremo, era già morto da qualche anno. Nella recentissima edizione di F. Gaeta (N. Machiavelli, *Opere*, 3: *Lettere* [Torino, 1984]) si segue l'ed. Bertelli, tranne che in due casi: il Fabiani non è più identificato con il maestro di Guido Machiavelli, ma in compenso lo si scambia nuovamente—nella lettera del Buonaccorsi al Machiavelli del 20 settembre 1501 (=lett. 26 dell'ed. Martelli)—con Luca degli Albizzi. Per i rapporti del Fabiani col Buonaccorsi, v. il diario di quest'ultimo, edito da D. Fachard, *Biagio Buonaccorsi. Sa vie. Son temps. Son oeuvre* (Bologna, 1976), 14, 175, 182, 198, 205, ove è più volte menzionato "ser Luca di Fabiano da Montegonzi decto de' Ficini". Da scartare l'interpretazione data a questo "decto de' Ficini" da M. Martelli, "La *Historia florentinorum* di Bartolomeo Scala," *Interpres*, 4 (1981-82): 16, nota 22, che vorrebbe intenderlo come corrispondente a un "sopraddetto, sopra ricordato" a differenza del Fachard, che giustamente traduce "dit", cioè "detto, soprannominato".

    103. V. Machiavelli, *Tutte le opere*, 1024 (lett. 18; ho leggermente modificato l'interpunzione). Ricordiamo anche che ser Luca fu testimone—assieme ad Antonio Vespucci, Bartolomeo Dei, Piero Buonaccorsi, Filippo Lippi da Pratovecchio, Giovanni Biagi da Poppi, Bartolomeo Ruffini—del primo testamento del Machiavelli, rogato il 22 novembre 1511 da ser Francesco Ottaviani d'Arezzo (v. Tommasini, *La vita*, 1:556).

E concluderei questi appunti sul Fabiani, rilevando come egli morì il 16 dicembre del 1520,[104] non senza ricordare tuttavia il nome di un suo figlio, notaio anch'egli, che proprio nel nome, *Marsilius de Ficinis*, ci dà forse la miglior prova della devozione di ser Luca per il filosofo.[105]

Possiamo adesso passare all'esame di alcuni manoscritti copiati dal Fabiani, tenendo presente due dati emersi da quanto si è osservato sulla sua vita: innanzitutto la possibilità di attingere esempi 'sicuri' della sua scrittura ad una nuova fonte, vale a dire ai registri della Cancelleria, da aggiungersi ai codici sottoscritti; e poi la constatazione dell'esistenza di un legame per lo meno ventennale, di grande familiarità, tra lui e il Ficino; ed era questa, si rammenterà, la condizione che abbiamo detto necessaria per un'eventuale attribuzione della discussa *Rheinschrift*.

Per quel che concerne il primo punto, bisogna considerare, infatti, che i codici sottoscritti dal Fabiani appartengono tutti, per la splendida veste esteriore, e, in particolare, per la ricchezza delle miniature, alla categoria dei manoscritti di gran pregio, coll'implicazione ovvia e conseguente dell'impiego da parte dell'amanuense della sua mano 'migliore'. Pertanto quella che è generalmente indicata come 'la' scrittura di ser Luca, in realtà rappresenta solo un aspetto della produzione di questo amanuense, corrispondente a quella realizzazione d'apparato che nel Salvini abbiamo visto rappresentata da un solo manoscritto—per altro copiato agli inizi del 1492, vale a dire nella stessa epoca di quelli sottoscritti dal Fabiani—il Laurenziano XXI 8.[106]

Ma se per il Salvini questo resterà un caso isolato, del Fabiani si possono segnalare, al di fuori di quelli sottoscritti, altri codici, del medesimo grado di fattura, anche se non tutti altrettanto sontuosamente decorati, la cui attribuzione appare sicura: ad esempio il Guelferbitano 2994 [= 10 Aug. 4to] della Herzog-August Bibliothek di Wolfenbuettel,[107] fatto copiare probabilmente attorno al 1490 da Filippo Valori per Mattia Cor-

---

104. V. ASF, Morti, Serie della "Grascia" 6, c. 390r: "MDXX Dicembre . . . Ser Lucha Fecini riposto in san P⟨ier⟩o Magiore mori adi 16 Dicembre".

105. Il primo registro dei protocolli del figlio di ser Luca ha l'intestazione: "1533. Hic est liber protocollorum mei ser Marsilii olim ser Luce de Ficinis notarii florentini . . ."; in quella che apre il secondo registro dei suoi atti egli si dice "notarius publicus florentinus imperialique auctoritate iudex ordinarius notariusque publicus"; v. ASF, Notarile antecosimiano F 274. Ci è pervenuto anche un atto notarile rogato da ser Luca stesso, esterno alla Cancelleria, datato 2 settembre 1516, in ASF, Notarile antecosimiano, busta II 23 (cfr. Kristeller, *Supplementum*, 2:333).

106. V. supra, 351, 355 e nota 37.

107. V. Kristeller, *Supplementum*, 1:lii; idem, *Iter*, 3:733; *Bibliotheca Corviniana*, 77, no. 174, tavv. CXXXVI–CXXXVII.

vino, contenente la traduzione e il commento del Ficino alla *Interpretatio Prisciani Lydi in Theophrastum de intellectu et phantasia*, che del resto è già stato attribuito al Fabiani—con un altro 'corviniano'—da Edith Hoffman e da Emanuele Casamassima;[108] e poi il cod. HB XV 65 della Wuerttembergische Landesbibliothek di Stoccarda [tav. XI]—da ritenersi copiato tra l'aprile e il settembre del 1492—comprendente il *De comparatione solis ad Deum* del Ficino, preceduto da una dedicatoria a Eberardo conte del Wuerttemberg;[109] e infine il Laurenziano Acquisti e Doni 665, esemplare di dedica a Piero de'Medici del *De sole* e di altri opuscoli ficiniani, la cui trascrizione venne completata con ogni probabilità il primo marzo del 1492.[110] La stessa realizzazione, ma in un codice di minori pretese—cartaceo, non miniato, con appena i titoli in rosso—, si ritrova anche nel MS Riccardiano 147—in cui figura nuovamente l'*Interpretatio Prisciani Lydi in Theophrastum*, con la dedica a Filippo Valori (datata 25 marzo 1489)[111]—che il Sicherl attribuisce al Ficino in *Rheinschrift*.[112]

Questi che abbiamo appena ricordato sono gli esempi più posati della scrittura del Fabiani. Ma vi è poi un discreto gruppo di codici in cui la mano di ser Luca compare sia in tracciati più rapidi che in realizzazioni diverse, per le quali conviene ricorrere, come punto fermo da cui muovere per un utile confronto, non ai codici sottoscritti ma ai registri della Cancelleria.

E' questo il caso di due manoscritti contenenti il commento *In Epistolas Pauli*, composto dal Ficino dopo il 1496.[113] Sono il cod. VII A 8 della Biblioteca Nazionale di Napoli [tav. XII] [114] e il Conventi soppressi G 4 489 della Nazionale di Firenze.[115] In essi la testeggiatura delle aste delle lettere, nonché l'accentuazione di alcuni vezzi 'calligrafico-cancellereschi'—

108. V. E. Casamassima, "Note e osservazioni su alcuni copisti dei codici Corviniani," *Ungheria d'oggi*, 5 (1965): 80–82; cfr. Gentile, in *Marsilio Ficino . . . Mostra*, 125, no. 97.

109. V. Kristeller, *Supplementum*, 1:xlviii; idem, *Iter*, 3:712; Gentile, in *Marsilio Ficino . . . Mostra*, 153, no. 118. Il Marcel, *Marsile Ficin*, 525 e nota 2, attribuisce questo codice alla mano del Ficino.

110. Su questo MS, che prima d'essere acquistato dalla Laurenziana appartenne alla Dyson Perrins Library di Malvern, v. Kristeller, *Supplementum*, 1:xxxiii; Gentile, in *Marsilio Ficino . . . Mostra*, 153 sg., no. 118 e la tav. tra p. 162 e p. 163.

111. V. Kristeller, *Supplementum*, 1:xviii; Gentile, in *Marsilio Ficino . . . Mostra*, 125 sg., no. 97 e tav. XXX.

112. V. Sicherl, "Neuendeckte Handschriften," 57; idem, "Die Humanistenkursive," 449 sg.

113. V. Kristeller, *Supplementum*, 1:lxxxi sg.; Gentile, in *Marsilio Ficino . . . Mostra*, 158, no. 122.

114. V. Kristeller, *Supplementum*, 1:xxxvi; idem, *Iter*, 1:422; Gentile, in *Marsilio Ficino . . . Mostra*, 158 sg., no. 122.

115. V. Kristeller, *Supplementum*, 1:xxvi; idem, *Iter*, 1:159; Gentile, in *Marsilio Ficino . . . Mostra*, 158 sg., no. 122 e tav. XXXVI.

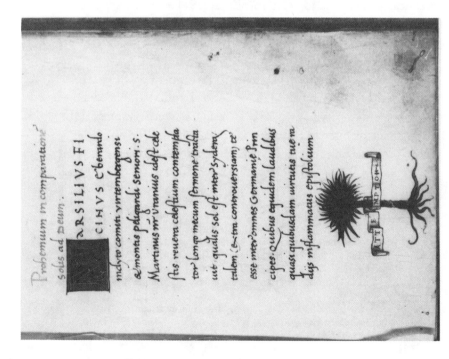

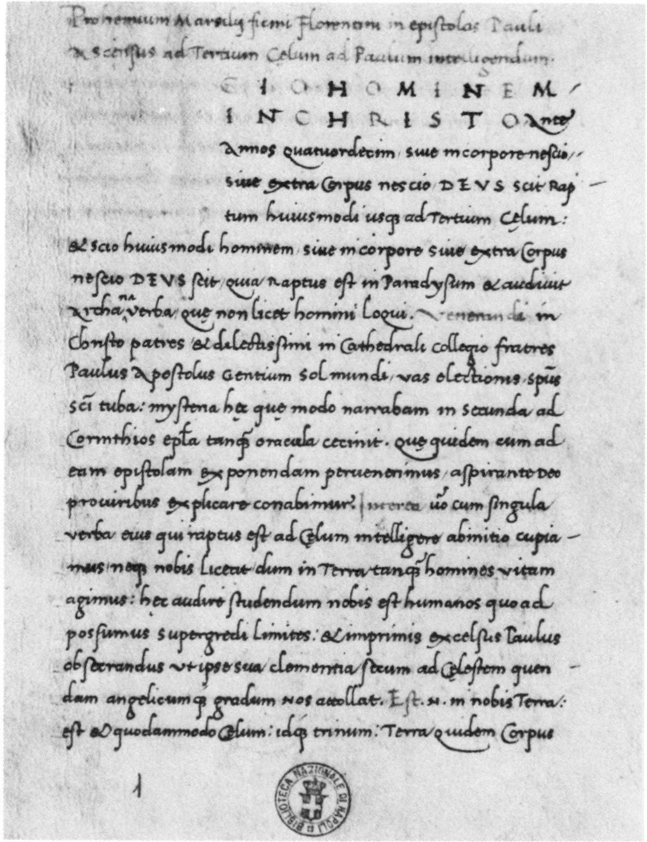

Tav. XII. Napoli, Biblioteca Nazionale, MS VII A 8, c.1r.

Tav. XI. Stuttgart, Württembergische Landesbibliothek, MS HB XV 65, c.7r.

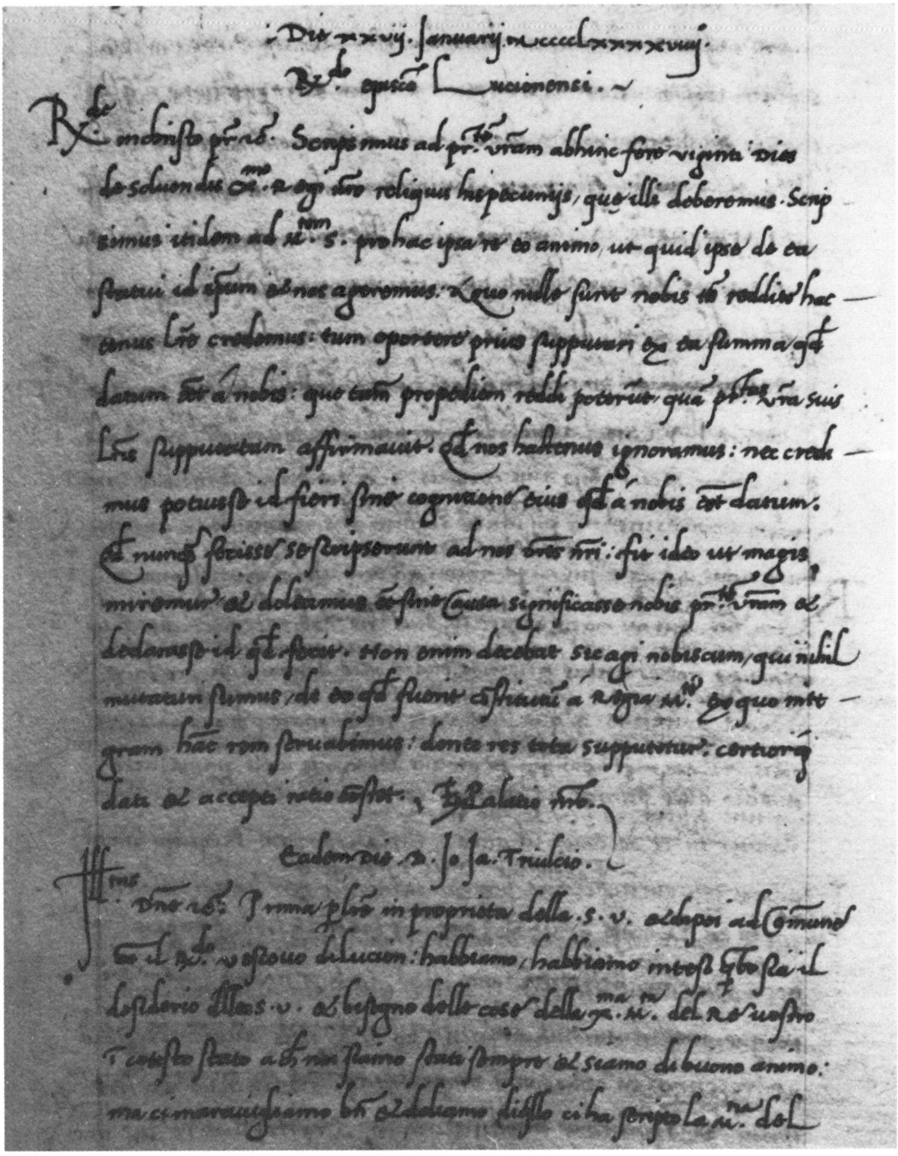

Tav. XIII. Firenze, Archivio di Stato, Signori, Carteggi, Missive I Cancelleria 51, c.177r.

Die . vij . Januarij 1491
Joannes stephanus Mediolanensium principis orator venit
Die . vij . Ingressusque auditorium summi magistratus
eoque salute nomine sui principis salutato: multisque
quibus [illegible] illius erga rem. pu. [illegible] dictis
demonstravit se a suo Principe missum ut Dno angelo
succederet etc. Responsumque illi est a Nicholao donato
primo iustitie signifero et benivole et amice etc. atque eadem
die muneribus publicis donatus est.

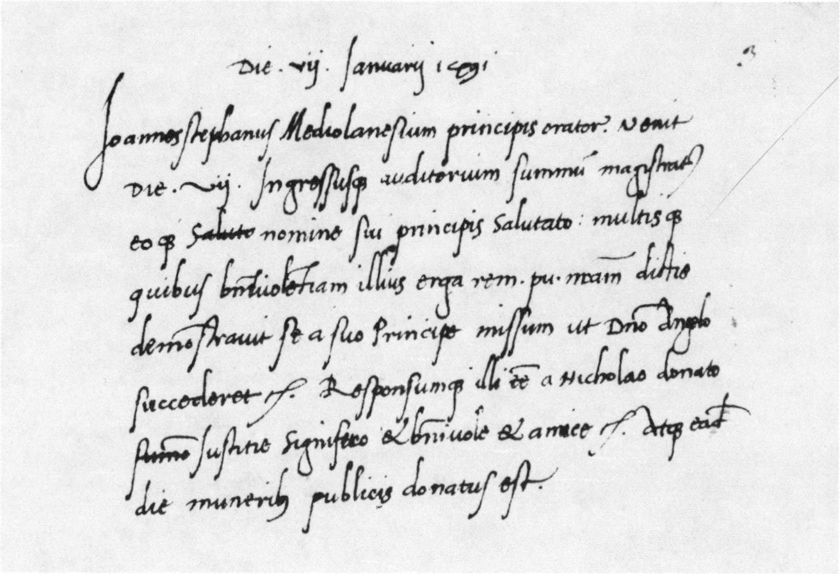

Tav. XIV. Firenze, Archivio di Stato, Signori, Carteggi, Minutari 16, c.3r.

pur non intaccando, ovviamente, la sostanziale identità di mano con i codici sottoscritti—danno luogo ad una realizzazione diversa, che ritroviamo in forme molto simili nella scrittura impiegata da ser Luca per gli usi della Cancelleria negli ultimi anni del secolo [tav. XIII].[116]

Così pure per il Laurenziano XC sup. 43,[117] che fu verosimilmente ultimato il 18 ottobre 1490, il termine di paragone più prossimo ci viene dalla Cancelleria, questa volta con documenti che appartengono ai primi anni della carriera del Fabiani in quegli uffici [tav. XIV], risalenti cioè agli inizi del 1492.[118]

In base a questo confronto tuttavia, l'attribuzione a ser Luca del Laurenziano—che raccoglie, come abbiamo avuto modo di osservare, i primi otto libri dell'epistolario ficiniano—risulta ovvia solo per quel che con-

116. La tavola che qui si presenta è tratta da ASF, Signori, Carteggi, Missive I Cancelleria 51, c. 177r (numerazione a lapis), in cui figura una lettera al vescovo di Luchon datata 27 gennaio 1499 (stile fiorentino) scritta da ser Luca, tra altre due lettere, sempre di sua mano.

117. V. Della Torre, *Storia*, 85 e nota 1, 841–843; Kristeller, *Supplementum*, 1:xiv; Gentile, in *Marsilio Ficino ... Mostra*, 141 sg., no. 109 e tav. XXXII.

118. La tavola proviene da ASF, Signori, Carteggi, Minutari 16, c. 3r, ed è il breve resoconto della presentazione davanti alla Signoria del nuovo ambasciatore milanese in data 7 gennaio 1491 (stile fiorentino), di mano di ser Luca.

cerne le ultime carte (cc. 378r–384v) [tav. XV], mentre non si può fran-
camente dire la stessa cosa per le prime 346, che presentano, dal punto
di vista della scrittura, un aspetto alquanto diverso [tav. XVI]. C'è poi
una sezione di circa trenta carte (cc. 346v–378r), in cui la scrittura del
copista si presenta in una realizzazione intermedia tra le due appena distinte [tav. XVII].

Queste considerazioni ci permettono di avanzare l'ipotesi che nel codice
non si debbano riconoscere più mani, bensì diverse realizzazioni di una
stessa mano. E in effetti la scrittura della prima parte del codice si distingue da quella della seconda per delle particolarità che non precludono affatto l'attribuzione ad un solo copista – quali il modulo più piccolo, il minor
divario tra corpo e asta delle lettere, la mancata recezione di quegli influssi
che si son detti d'origine settentrionale – e tuttavia la rendono più com-
patta, uniforme, con risultati molto vicini a quella che abbiamo definito
l'umanistica corsiva 'classica' del Salvini, con la quale del resto è stata anche
confusa, come s'è accennato in precedenza, dal Della Torre.[119]

Una volta accettata questa ipotesi – che si tratti di un solo copista,
ragionevolmente identificabile col Fabiani sul fondamento del confronto
tra la scrittura che compare nelle ultime carte del Laurenziano e i suoi
esempi 'cancellereschi' – resta da vedere se queste differenze siano dovute
a un'interruzione nella copiatura del manoscritto – se si debba cioè am-
mettere che sia trascorso del tempo tra una realizzazione e l'altra – o se,
invece, vadano attribuite a una libera scelta del copista, capace di scrivere
con uguale scioltezza in una maniera come nell'altra, nel medesimo periodo di tempo.

Dirò subito che la prima ipotesi sembra la più probabile. Tra i manoscritti
d'ambiente ficiniano dovuti a questa mano possiamo infatti distinguere
due gruppi: i codici che appartengono al primo si possono datare, per ragioni
prevalentemente di contenuto, attorno agli anni 1481–1486 e sono scritti
nella stessa realizzazione della prima parte del Laurenziano (che d'ora in
avanti indicheremo con "Fabiani B"); quelli che appartengono al secondo
sono da assegnarsi invece, per la stessa ragione, ad epoca più tarda
(1487–1492 circa), e sono copiati invece nella realizzazione dell'ultima parte
del Laurenziano (che d'ora in poi designeremo con "Fabiani C").

Del resto anche l'esame codicologico del MS Laurenziano ci fornisce

119. V. supra, 352 e nota 46.

...ſſimus ficimus Florentinus B...mo in ... pri et Dno
Marco Veneto Car.li divi Marci suppliciter se commedat
Vides ne q(uod) sit callidus Calderinus n(oste)r? ego cogitavit hic tan-
diu facillimum tutissimumq(ue) viaticum. Quo salvus semper
et Florentiam petat et repetat Romam. Salutationib(us)
enim se semper fulcit/armat(que) tuis. Quibus et ipse salvus
eat per tela per ignes: et salvum reddat amicum. Salvum
tibi quoq(ue) renuntiet: Salutationes vero tue sunt: sive abs te eat
sive ad te redeant. hunc equidem quem modo Callidum apel-
labam, apello prudentem. Ceteri namq(ue) sortis eiusdem ho(m)i(n)es
plurimum dormitant ad fores insipientum. Sed noster
interim isthic ad fores vigilat sapientis. ut hauriat salutem a domino. Quam et impertit amicis. immo etiam ut
inveniat vitam. Sperat n(im). ibi dumtaxat se victurum
ubi potissimum vivitur intellectu. Siquidem et legit et memi-
minit/intellectum da mihi et vivam. Vivo igitur felix
ante alios venerande patrone noster: tuosq(ue) clientes h(abe)as
commendatos. ... 27 aug f 80

Finis octavi epistolarum libri.
Die xviiij. Octobris MccccLxxx.

~ Florentie ·

humanis operibus nos uoti compotes pro uiribus efficit. neq? ab errat
unq? neq? fallitur. Alioquin sapientia reuera non ēet. Cum uo causa
consequendi finis sapia sit necessarium ē eam ad felicitatem totum ua-
lere. Preterea ij dumtaxat quibus bona plurima assunt beati dicūt.
Hi tam non prius beati sunt q? bona ipsis presentia prosint. neq? profuit
unq? nisi illis utantur. Sola .n. siue usu possessio nihil momenti ad felicitatem habet. uerum tam nec usus ? sufficit. Pot .n. quis male uti ego
quo contingit ut ledatur potius q? adiuuetur. ut igitur possessioni usu
addimus: sic ? usui rectitudine addere decet. ? e utamur solum, uerum ? recte utamur. ut aut singulis recte utamur sola nobis sapi
entia prestat. quodquid licet martibus intueri. inquibus illi dum
taxat qui artis periti sunt tam materia q? instrumentis recte utunt.
Eadem quoq? ratione ut diuitiis, sanitate, forma, robore, ac ceteris
que bona uocamur. utamur recte sapia efficit. Qua pp in omi possessio
ne, usu, opatione. causa prospere beneq? agendi scientia est. Nam qui
sine mente ? possidet multa ? utitur, tanto leditur magis q? possidet
plura, pluribus ue abutitur. sane qui insipiens, quo minus agit,
minus errat. Minus errans minus ? male agit. Minus aut male
agens, minus est miser. Agit certe minus si paup sit q? si diues. Si
debilis q? si robustus. Timidus q? audax. Piger q? uigil. Tardus q? ue
lox. hebes q? sagax. Itaq? nulla eorum que insuperioribus bona nu-
cupabantur ipse bona sunt. Nam si illis inscitia prest, tanto de-
teriora sunt, q? eorum contraria. qto uberius improbo duci ani-
micula scelerum possit suppeditare. Sin aut prudentia sapietiaq?

Tav. XVI. Firenze, Biblioteca Medicea Laurenziana, MS XC sup. 43, c.2r.

nutriendos & tanqᵐedico fouendos confirmandosq̃ comendo.

vale & carissime compater & optime medice atq̃ lege feliciter.

De materia silentij purgatio qn amicos literis non respondem.

ARSILIVS FICINVS Philippo ca
lori Sal. Accepimus iampridem epistolam tuam

mᵉ ᷅alor non mihi solum. sed etiam petro Hero Philippoq̃
Carduccio. ac denicq̃ academicis cunctis comunem. Et mihil
mirum sit nullum adhuc nostrum epistole respondisse. dum
alij alios quotidie responsurus arbitrarentur. Accedit adhᵉc
q̃ dialecticus quidam ex academia cum audiret reprᵉhᵉdi
nos q̃ valoris nostri optam, valoris plenam quodammodo ⸗
peruficere tam longo silentio uideremur in hunc ferme ⸗
modum argumentari cepit. Facile ostendi potest amica nᵒ̃
tam nos q̃ philippum ipsum diuturni huius silentij causam
extitisse. Quaeq̃ ipsum potius q̃ nostrum quemqua ᵉᵉ repre
hendendum. Sano si philippus ᷅alor est amicus noster ⸗
certe ualor est noster. Rursus si ipse valor est noster: utiq̃
ipse est noster ualor. Ao si ille est noster ᷅alor. consequens
est ut illo absente mihil ipᵐ penitus ualeamus. Ergo ᷅alor re
deat subito uox nostra redibit. Ingenium nobis illo dat. illo
rapit. Cum iᵒ̃ hec ille dialecticus conclusisset. alij omnes letis
simo statim applausu consensere. Vnus dumtaxat in argu
mentando paulo curiosior. non amorem quidem erga te co
munem simul & singularem improbare. sed ipsam argumētaⁿⁱˢ.

un elemento a favore di questa ipotesi. Si noterà infatti che in questo codice la prima e l'ultima carta del quinterno iniziale sono scritte in quella realizzazione intermedia tra "Fabiani B" e "Fabiani C", che abbiamo individuato alle cc. 346v–378r. Il fatto che a c. 10 figuri come filigrana un' 'aquila', che è la stessa che ritroviamo da c. 351 in poi (le altre carte hanno invece per filigrana una 'forbice'),[120] indica come il bifolio esterno del primo fascicolo vada ritenuto un'aggiunta successiva. Ciò pare confermare da un lato l'effettiva posteriorità di "Fabiani C" rispetto a "Fabiani B", dall'altro il fatto che tutto il codice sia opera dello stesso copista, il quale avrà sostituito in un secondo tempo le cc. 1 e 10, verosimilmente — se supponiamo che il codice non fosse stato ancora rilegato — perché la prima carta s'era deteriorata.

Tra i manoscritti ficiniani più tardi copiati in "Fabiani C" un posto di rilievo occupa il Monacense lat. 10781 della Staatsbibliothek di Monaco — contenente i libri IX–XI delle *Epistolae* del Ficino, seguiti da alcune lettere di Bartolomeo Scala [121] — che sembrerebbe ricollegarsi al Laurenziano XC sup. 43 più strettamente di quanto l'attuale lontananza dei due codici non lasci immaginare. Perché i due manoscritti s'integrano a vicenda non soltanto in ragione del contenuto — comprendono infatti, l'uno i libri I–VIII, l'altro i libri IX–XI dell'epistolario ficiniano — , ma anche sotto il profilo paleografico, visto che il codice di Monaco è copiato in "Fabiani C", come le ultime carte del Laurenziano. Ne risulta una continuità che non viene smentita da altri elementi, di natura codicologica, comuni ai due manoscritti, almeno per quanto si può giudicare, per il Monacense, da riproduzioni fotografiche.[122]

Tra gli altri manoscritti copiati in "Fabiani C" ricordiamo poi il Guelferbitano 2924 [= 2 Aug. 4to] della Herzog-August Bibliothek di Wolfenbuettel — contenente il *Liber de vaticinio somniorum* di Sinesio, nella traduzione del Ficino, insieme ai libri III–IV delle *Epistolae* — che è stato attribuito al Fabiani da Edith Hoffman e Emanuele Casamassima.[123] Questo manoscritto ha in comune con l'altro 'corviniano' segnalato in

120. L' 'aquila' è simile a Briquet 85 e 86 (v. C. M. Briquet, *Les Filigranes. Dictionnaire historique des marques du papier dès leur apparition vers 1282 jusqu'en 1600* [Genève, 1907], 1:24), la 'forbice' a Briquet 3766 e 3767 (v. *ibid.*, 239).
121. V. Kristeller, *Supplementum*, 1:xxxv sg.; idem, *Iter*, 3:619.
122. Cfr. Gentile, in *Marsilio Ficino . . . Mostra*, 141 sg., no. 109.
123. V. Kristeller, *Supplementum*, 1:lii; idem, *Iter*, 3:733; Casamassima, "Note e osservazioni," 31 sg.; *Bibliotheca Corviniana*, 77, no. 173 e tavv. CXXXIV–CXXXV.

precedenza, la sontuosità e il tipo di decorazione, mentre se ne distacca per la scrittura, che risponde piuttosto a questa realizzazione. Sempre in "Fabiani C" è stato copiato, a mio avviso, anche il Vaticano lat. 5953, un voluminoso codice utilizzato dallo Allen per la sua edizione del *Commentarium in Philebum* e appartenuto a Pier Leoni da Spoleto, in cui sono raccolti commenti, traduzioni e opuscoli del Ficino.[124] Così pure nel miscellaneo Parigino lat. 2614 — le cui prime 35 carte contengono il *De mystica theologia* dello pseudo-Dionigi nella versione e col commento del Ficino, preceduto dalla dedica a Giovanni de'Medici — troviamo un mano che, come s'è anticipato, non è quella di Ficino Ficini, bensì nuovamente "Fabiani C".[125] Ed infine è stato attribuito recentemente a ser Luca anche il Laurenziano LXVIII 26 — comprendente non opere del Ficino, ma il testo mutilo dell'*Historia florentinorum* di Bartolomeo Scala, di cui ser Luca, come si ricorderà, fu coadiutore in Cancelleria — copiato sempre nella stessa realizzazione.[126]

Vi è poi un certo numero di manoscritti, in cui il Sicherl ha riconosciuto — accanto alla minuta corsiva del Ficino — la famosa *Rheinschrift*, e che sarei incline ad attribuire invece a ser Luca, sempre in "Fabiani C".

Alludo alle cc. 212r–221v del già citato Parigino Supplément grec 212, in cui figurano le traduzioni ficiniane del *De occasionibus* e di parte del *De abstinentia* di Porfirio, che il Fabiani avrebbe trascritto alternandosi nella copiatura con un altro amanuense.[127] Così pure gli assegnerei le cc. 144r–172r del cod. F 20 della Biblioteca Vallicelliana di Roma — dove ritroviamo le traduzioni di Porfirio seguite da quella (parziale) del *De daemonibus* di Psello, tutte con estese correzioni di mano del Ficino, e da un passo, sempre sui demoni, "ex tomistis" — e molte delle numerose annotazioni che figurano nei margini dei testi greci, in ispecie del *De mysteriis* di Giamblico — che occupa le cc. 1r–136v —, destinate poi a confluire nella

124. V. Kristeller, *Supplementum*, 1:xli sg.; idem, *Iter*, 2:378; J. Ruysschaert, "Nouvelles recherches au sujet de la bibliothèque de Pier Leoni, médecin de Laurent le Magnifique," *Académie royale de Belgique. Bulletin de la classe des lettres et des sciences morales et politiques*, ser. 5, 46 (1960): 55 sg. e tav. II, a; M. J. B. Allen, ed. and tr., *Marsilio Ficino: The "Philebus" Commentary* (Berkeley-Los Angeles-London, 1975), 536 sg., nota 205 e tav. [II]; Gentile, in *Marsilio Ficino . . . Mostra*, 33, no. 24.

125. V. Kristeller, *Supplementum*, 1:xxxvii; idem, *Iter*, 3:216; Gentile, in *Marsilio Ficino . . . Mostra*, 157, no. 121. Sull'attribuzione a Ficino Ficini v. supra, 359 e nota 71.

126. V. A. Brown, *Bartolomeo Scala*, 189, nota 66, 297, nota 3; cfr. Martelli, "La *Historia florentinorum*," 16 e nota 22.

127. Cfr. supra, 359 e nota 72.

traduzione *ad sensum* di quest'opera che il Ficino dedicò nel 1489 al cardinale Giovanni de'Medici.[128] Sono inoltre da aggiungere le cc. 130r–148r del Riccardiano 76, comprendenti la traduzione del *De somniis* di Sinesio;[129] le annotazioni che figurano nei margini di un famoso codice di Plotino, il Parigino greco 1816, contrassegnate da Paul Henry con la sigla "F5";[130] e, infine, alcune carte del Magliabechiano XX 58, il manoscritto della *Disputatio contra iudicium astrologorum*, su cui ci soffermeremo piu avanti.[131] Accanto a questi manoscritti va poi collocata una lettera originale del Ficino a Francesco Gaddi, datata 11 ottobre 1488,[132] che, assieme ad altre due non menzionate dal Sicherl—la prima diretta a Bernardo Dovizi, del 25 ottobre 1490 [tav. XVIII],[133] la seconda a Lorenzo de'Medici, del primo dicembre di quello stesso anno[134]—e a parte della minuta di un'altra lettera, che nella sua forma definitiva risulta diretta a Braccio Martelli,[135] vanno assegnate a ser Luca in "Fabiani C".

Risultano ugualmente scritte in "Fabiani C" le correzioni e aggiunte, marginali e interlineari, che troviamo nel Laurenziano LXXIII 39, unico esemplare manoscritto dei tre libri del *De vita*, probabilmente di poco posteriore all'edizione principe di quest'opera, che il solito Filippo Valori aveva

---

128. V. M. Sicherl, *Die Handschriften, Ausgaben, und Uebersetzungen von Iamblichos "De mysteriis"* (Berlin, 1957), 22–37; idem, "Neuendeckte Handscriften," 50, 54, 60, no. 20; idem, "Die Humanistenkursive," 448 e tav. 3 a–b (la tav. 3a tuttavia non presenta annotazioni di mano del Fabiani); Kristeller, "Some Original Letters," 31; idem, *Iter*, 2:132 sg.

129. V. Sicherl, *Die Handschriften*, 25 sg., 36; idem, "Neuendeckte Handscriften," 55, 60, no. 16; idem, "Die Humanistenkursive," 449; Kristeller, "Some Original Letters," 27; Gentile, in *Marsilio Ficino ... Mostra*, 55–57, no. 43.

130. V. P. Henry, *Etudes Plotiniennes, 2: Les manuscrits des Ennéades* (Bruxelles-Paris, 1948), 45–62; Sicherl, "Neuendeckte Handscriften," 61, no. 24; idem, "Die Humanistenkursive," 443, 445–449; Kristeller, "Some Original Letters," 30; Gentile, in *Marsilio Ficino ... Mostra*, 31 sg., no. 23.

131. V. infra, 389–394.

132. Su questa lettera, facente parte sino a pochi anni or sono della Collezione De Marinis, v. Kristeller, "Some Original Letters," 12 sg., 28 e tav. III; *Nuovi documenti*, 7 e nota 5, 39 e tav. 11; Sicherl, "Die Humanistenkursive," 449.

133. ASF, MAP XLI 551; v. Kristeller, *Supplementum*, 1:xxviii; idem, "Some Original Letters," 24; *Autografi dell'Archivio Mediceo avanti il Principato*, a cura di A.M. Fortuna e C. Lunghetti (Firenze, 1977), 126 (la lettera è erroneamente attribuita dai curatori alla mano di Ficino Ficini); Gentile, in *Marsilio Ficino ... Mostra*, 142, no. 110 I.

134. ASF, Carte Strozziane I 137; v. Kristeller, *Supplementum*, 1:xxviii; idem, "Some Original Letters," 24; Gentile, *Marsilio Ficino ... Mostra*, 142 sg., no. 110 II.

135. Si tratta di un foglietto attualmente incollato per un margine sul verso della seconda guardia anteriore di un esemplare dell' "editio princeps" dell' *Expositio libri Ethicorum Aristotelis* di Donato Acciaiuoli (GKW 140; IGI 14), conservato alla Biblioteca Nazionale di Firenze e segnato Incun. Magliabechiano C 1 10. La prima delle due mani che vi figurano sul recto è riconoscibile per quella di Luca Fabiani; cfr. Kristeller, *Iter*, 2:512; Gentile, in *Marsilio Ficino ... Mostra*, 143 sg., no. 111.

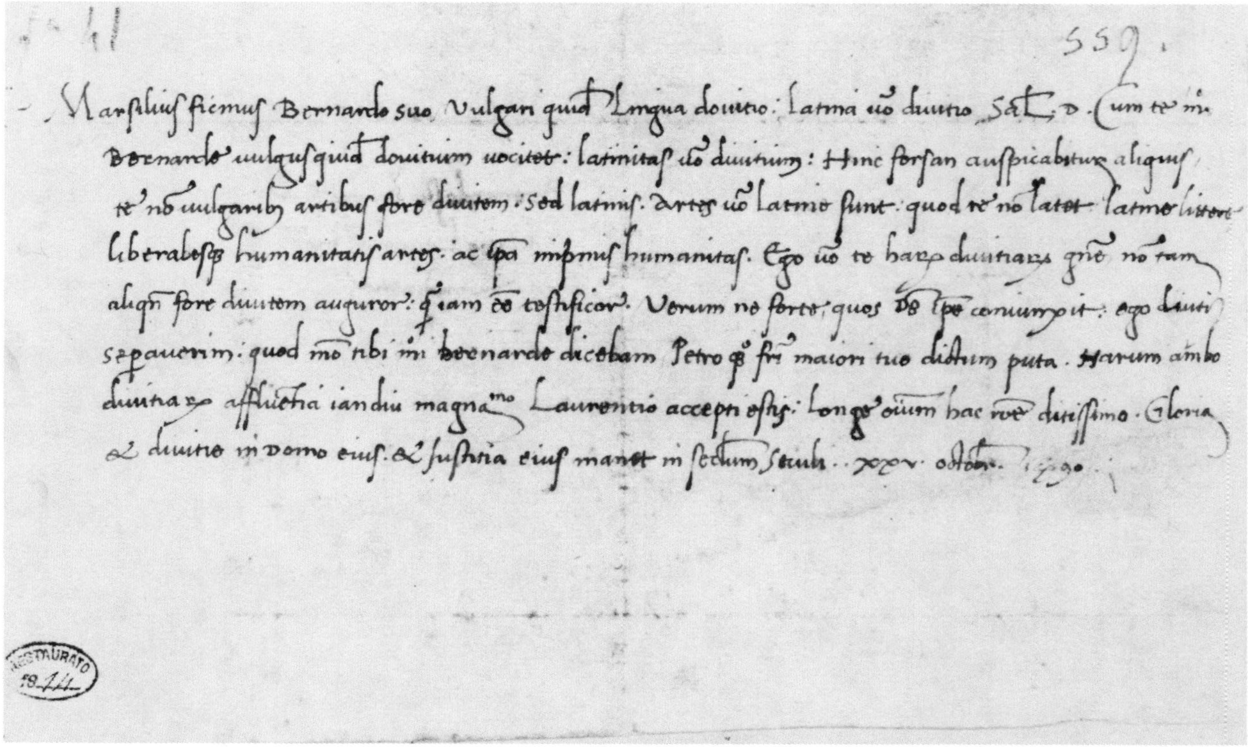

550

Marsilius Ficinus Bernardo suo Vulgari quid Longius quid Latina uia diuina S.P.D. (cum te...)

Tav. XVIII. Firenze, Archivio di Stato, Mediceo avanti il principato, XLI 551.

fatto copiare in *antiqua*, e decorare da Attavante, per poi dedicarlo a Lorenzo de'Medici.[136] Una lunga aggiunta marginale in "Fabiani C" figura anche nel cod. Ashburnham 917, contenente il *De cura valitudinis eorum qui incumbunt studio litterarum*.[137]

Dopo aver enumerato i manoscritti copiati in "Fabiani C", passerei ad esaminare quelli in cui incontriamo la realizzazione che compare nella prima parte del Laurenziano XC sup. 43 e che abbiamo indicato con "Fabiani B".

Il solo codice di mia conoscenza interamente esemplato in questa realizzazione è il Conventi soppressi E 1,2562 della Biblioteca Nazionale di Firenze. E' un codice molto importante, l'unico ad averci trasmesso la versione ficiniana di Plotino disgiunta dal commento, che il Fabiani probabilmente terminò di copiare per Giovanni Pico della Mirandola—della cui mano figurano nei margini del codice alcune postille—non molto dopo il 16 gennaio 1486, giorno in cui il Ficino, come sappiamo, ultimò questa traduzione.[138]

Vi sono poi codici latini e greci, copiati da altri amanuensi, con note di ser Luca in "Fabiani B". Come il Laurenziano XXI 21—che raccoglie traduzioni e opuscoli giovanili del Ficino—in cui i titoli dei capitoli della traduzione dell'*Alcinoi platonici liber de doctrina Platonis* appaiono aggiunti in un secondo tempo dalla sua mano,[139] e il Riccardiano 797—uno dei codici copiati e sottoscritti dal Salvini—, dove in margine ad un'importante lettera appartenente al VII libro dell'epistolario ficiniano il Fabiani ha posto due aggiunte che non figurano nelle edizioni a stampa.[140] Così pure a c. 117v di un altro codice da noi già incontrato, il Riccardiano 76,[141] troviamo una lunga annotazione di mano del Fabiani, pubblicata

---

136. V. Kristeller, *Supplementum*, 1:x sg.; Gentile, in *Marsilio Ficino . . . Mostra*, 133–136, no. 103 e tav. XXXI. In "Fabiani C" sono inoltre alcune correzioni al testo e l'aggiunta in inchiostro rosso dei titoli dei capitoli del *De daemonibus* di Psello nel Vaticano Ottob. lat. 1531 (cfr. Kristeller, *Supplementum*, 1:xliv; idem, *Iter*, 2:431; Gentile, in *Marsilio Ficino . . . Mostra*, 130, no. 100 I). Correzioni in "Fabiani C" figurano anche nel Guelferbitano 2706 [= 73 Aug. 2°], comprendente i primi otto libri delle *Epistolae* del Ficino (cfr. Kristeller, *Supplementum*, 1:li sg.; *Bibliotheca Corviniana*, 76, no. 170).
137. V. Kristeller, *Supplementum*, 1: xvi sg.; idem, *Iter*, 1:91; Gentile, in *Marsilio Ficino . . . Mostra*, 132 sg., no. 102.
138. V. Kristeller, *Supplementum*, 1:xxvi; idem, *Iter*, 1:158; Gentile, in *Marsilio Ficino . . . Mostra*, 146 sg., no. 114 e tav. XXXIII.
139. V. Kristeller, *Supplementum*, 1:ix; Gentile, in *Marsilio Ficino . . . Mostra*, 44 sg., no. 32.
140. Cfr. Gentile, in *Marsilio Ficino . . . Mostra*, 120 sg., no. 94.
141. V. supra, 359 e nota 70.

da Eugenio Garin assieme alle altre note marginali—in massima parte di mano del Ficino—che accompagnano il testo della famosa orazione di Giuliano al Sole.[142] Inoltre, sempre in margine a un testo greco—il commento di Olimpiodoro e Damascio al *Fedone* e al *Filebo* platonici—, s'incontrano nel Riccardiano 37 annotazioni, pubblicate dal Westerink, sia di mano dell'amanuense che del Ficino, alcune delle quali utilizzate poi nella *Theologia platonica*, e pertanto da ritenere anteriori alla pubblicazione di quest'opera, avvenuta in Firenze il 7 novembre 1482.[143]

Veniamo così al codice da cui avevamo preso le mosse, vale a dire al Magliabechiano VIII 1441.

Anche in questo manoscritto figurano realizzazioni diverse di una stessa mano, che è quella del copista principale, di cui s'è suggerita l'identificazione con Luca Fabiani. Vi possiamo infatti distinguere una prima realizzazione, più 'nervosa' e generalmente più rapida—che indicheremo con "Fabiani A"—e una seconda realizzazione dal tracciato più posato e regolare, che è la stessa da noi già individuata in altri codici e indicata con "Fabiani B".

Al fine di sincerarsi di questa identità di mano si raffrontino, per quel che concerne "Fabiani B", la c. 227r del Laurenziano XC sup. 43 [tav. XIX], copiata in questa realizzazione, e la c. 2r del Magliabechiano [tav. XX], le quali offrono la possibilità di un agevole confronto presentando entrambe l'inizio del quinto libro delle *Epistolae*. Quanto a "Fabiani A"—l'altra realizzazione presente nel Magliabechiano, generalmente più rapida e 'nervosa'—si deve notare che essa si distingue da "Fabiani B" non soltanto per la maggior rapidità del tracciato, come potrebbe forse sembrare a prima vista. La prova più evidente di ciò è fornita da un codicetto membranaceo di pregevole e accurata fattura, il Riccardiano 2684 [tav. XXI]—"Facto in Firenze adi XXVIII digiungno 1478"—contenente i *Sermoni morali* del Ficino,[144] al quale si possono aggiungere alcune carte copiate in bella sia nel Magliabechiano VIII 1441 che nel Magliabechiano XX 58 (sul quale ci soffermeremo fra breve), e numerose lettere originali del filosofo, una delle quali con correzioni autografe, anch'esse trascritte con gran cura in

---

142. V. E. Garin, *Studi sul platonismo medievale* (Firenze, 1958), 190–214.

143. V. L. G. Westerink, "Ficino's Marginal Notes on Olympiodorus in Riccardi Greek MS 37," *Traditio*, 24 (1968): 352–378; cfr. Sicherl, "Neuendeckte Handschriften," 60, no. 12; idem, "Die Humanistenkursive," 444, nota 4, 447–449 e tav. 4a; Gentile, in *Marsilio Ficino . . . Mostra*, 110 sg., no. 86 e tav. XXVII/b.

144. V. Kristeller, *Supplementum*, 1:xx sg.; idem, *Iter*, 1:221; 2:517; Gentile, "Un codice Magliabechiano," 94, nota 44; idem, in *Marsilio Ficino . . . Mostra*, 101 sg., no. 76 e tav. XXVI.

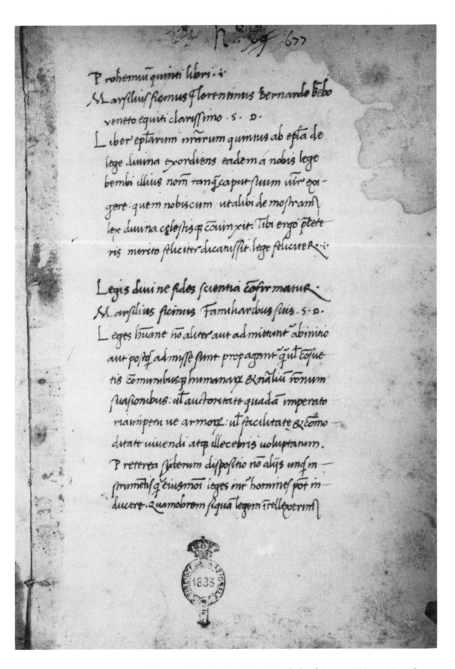

Tav. XIX. Firenze, Biblioteca Nazionale, MS Magliabechiano VIII 1441, c.2r.

Prohemium quinti libri·

MARSILIVS FICINV
FLORENTINVS BER

nardo bembo veneto equiti clarissimo · s· d·

Liber eptarum nrarum quintus ab epta de lege
diuina exordiens eadem a nobis lege bembi illius nomen tanq̃ caput
suum uidetur exigere. quem nobiscum ut alibi demonstrauimus lex di
uina celestisq̃ coniumpit. Tibi ergo preceptoris merito feliciter dicatuf
sit: Lege feliciter ·i·

Leges diuine fides scientia confirmatur ·i·

Marsilius Ficinus Familiaribus suis · s· d· Leges
humane non aliter aut admittuntur ab initio aut postq̃ ad misse sūt
propagantur q̃ ut consuetis comunibusq̃ humanars̄ & naturalium
rationum suasionibus· ut auctoritate quadam imperatoria impetu uel
armos̄ ut facilitate & commoditate uiuendi atq̃ illecebris uoluptatū·
Preterea siderum dispositio nō alijs unq̃ īstrumētis q̃ eius mōi leges inter
homines pōt inducere· quamobrem siquam legem intellexerimus apd
homines sane mentis & ortam aliq̃ & latissime propagatam / dum ·
probabiles illi multorum argumentationes aduersarent̄: cum arma
potentum contra illam ubiq̃ seuirent· Dum palam omnis humane
uoluptatis usus spesq̃ ab ea prorsus auferretur: Legem eius mōi / neq̃
humanā ēē neq̃ a celesti stuto pendere / sed diuinā omino & a supcelesti
quadam potentia proficisci necessario concludemus· Quod aūt necessa
ria probatione concludit̄ Id procul dubio certa scientia c̄oprehenditur·

Tav. XX. Firenze, Biblioteca Medicea Laurenziana, MS XC sup. 43, c.227r.

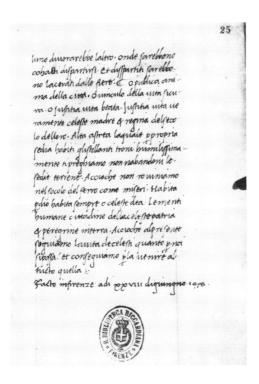

Tav. XXI. Firenze, Biblioteca Riccardiana, MS 2684, c.25r.

questa realizzazione, entrate poi a far parte dei libri IV e V delle *Epistolae*.[145]

Riterrei piuttosto che si debba considerare "Fabiani A" anteriore a "Fabiani B",[146] e che essa vada collocata negli anni 1476–1481, datazione che

145. Cfr. idem, "Un codice Magliabechiano," 87 sg. e nota 25, 95 sg. e nota 51, 105 sg. e nota 76. Aggiungiamo che è copiata in "Fabiani A" anche una singola lettera a c. 149r del MS Laurenziano Strozzi 101, contenente il primo libro dell'epistolario ficiniano; v. idem, in *Marsilio Ficino ... Mostra*, 90 sg., no. 69 III.

146. Alla posteriorità di "Fabiani B" rispetto a "Fabiani A" non osta il fatto che le cc. 2r–4v del Magliabechiano VIII 1441, le sole nel MS vergate in "Fabiani B", precedano carte in "Fabiani

ci viene suggerita da molteplici elementi: dal colophon del Riccardiano 2684, dall'esistenza di lettere originali in questa realizzazione appartenenti ai libri IV e V dell'epistolario ficiniano, dallo stesso Magliabechiano VIII 1441, archetipo dei libri V e VI, nonché, come vedremo, dal Magliabechiano XX 58. Vi sono inoltre alcuni esemplari dell'edizione principe del *De christiana religione* del Ficino — che fu stampata a Firenze nel 1476 — recanti correzioni, aggiunte, lettere d'accompagnamento, scritte nella stessa realizzazione.[147]

Sempre a proposito del Magliabechiano VIII 1441 va poi rilevato che una singola epistola, che non compare nei testimoni derivanti da questo codice archetipo, e che perciò stesso è da ritenersi più recente del resto del manoscritto, è copiata in "Fabiani C". Il tracciato piuttosto incerto con cui è stata copiata questa epistola, può far pensare a una delle prime sperimentazioni dell'amanuense in questa realizzazione.[148]

Dobbiamo infine notare che l'esistenza di lettere originali del Ficino, in ispecie appartenenti ai libri quarto e quinto delle *Epistolae*, vergate da una mano che sembrerebbe potersi identificare con quella del Fabiani, è importante anche per un'altra ragione, e cioè per il significato particolare che viene ad assumere, alla luce di questa constatazione, il poscritto più sopra riportato di "Lucas Marsilii scriba" in calce ad una lettera del Ficino a Bastiano Foresi.[149]

Se si considera infatti che sia il Magliabechiano — e all'interno di questo la lettera al Foresi, che appartiene al quinto libro della raccolta —, sia le lettere originali, sono ascrivibili allo stesso ben determinato torno di tempo, vale a dire agli anni 1476-1481, ai quali ci riportano le prime testimonianze su Luca Fabiani *Marsilii scriba*, e si associa poi a questa considerazione quanto ci viene rivelato dal poscritto, e in particolare da

A". Le cc. 2r–4v con ogni probabilità furono infatti copiate e inserite nel MS solo in un secondo tempo.

147. V. idem, in *Marsilio Ficino . . . Mostra*, 85–87, note 66–67. Si segnala che anche la dichiarazione che il Ficino presentò al Catasto nel 1480 per il Quartiere di Santa Maria Novella, Gonfalone Leone Bianco — v. ASF, Catasto 1014/2, c. 344r (numerazione a lapis) — è scritta in "Fabiani A". In questa dichiarazione — per massima parte illeggibile a causa dei danni provocati dall' alluvione del 1557 (cfr. Viti, in *Marsilio Ficino . . . Mostra*, 193, no. 167) — con molta difficoltà alla voce "Incharichi" si legge, sotto "M⟨esser⟩ Marsilio deta danni 47 [?]", "un garzone che mi governa", frase che forse si può riferire al Fabiani stesso.

148. Tale lettera figura nel MS Magliabechiano a c. 39r; cfr. Gentile, "Un codice Magliabechiano," 86, nota 16, 92, nota 39.

149. V. supra, 362.

quel "qui hanc epistolam transcripsi"—e cioè che l'amanuense aveva l'incarico di copiare le lettere del Ficino—, diviene oltremodo probabile, anche per questa ragione di natura extra-grafica, che il Fabiani e lo scrivano che ha trascritto le lettere originali siano la stessa persona. Tanto più che la medesima mano proprio in quell'epoca era impegnata in un'opera strettamente connessa con la copiatura delle trasmissive, vale a dire la registrazione delle stesse nel copialettere, che poi sarebbe divenuto l'archetipo della tradizione canonica dei libri V e VI delle *Epistolae* e che oggi riconosciamo nel Magliabechiano VIII 1441.[150]

* * *

Accanto all'archetipo dei libri V e VI dell'epistolario ficiniano non si può non ricordare un altro codice ficiniano proveniente dal medesimo fondo manoscritto, il Magliabechiano XX 58.[151] Questo codice è noto per essere l'unico testimone ad averci trasmesso il testo della incompiuta *Disputatio contra iudicium astrologorum*, sia pure in una forma—come si constaterà facilmente dall'edizione del Kristeller—piuttosto confusa.[152]

Così come è giunto sino a noi, esso presenta infatti—analogamente al Magliabechiano VIII 1441—un aspetto non uniforme, con alcune carte trascritte in pulito, altre che ebbero evidente funzione di mala copia,[153] e altre ancora su cui il filosofo annotò materiale ancora allo stato grezzo di appunti, probabilmente in vista di una stesura definitiva, che, a giudicare almeno dallo stato del manoscritto, non vi fu mai.

Per quel che concerne le mani, se si escludono gli interventi dell'autore—che oltre ad aver scritto parte del testo, lo rivide poi in più luoghi—e di un altro amanuense, che si limitò a trascrivere le ultime due carte, il rimanente è di mano del copista che abbiamo identificato con Luca Fa-

---

150. Cfr. Gentile, "Un codice Magliabechiano," 87 sg., nota 25. Per il rapporto archetipo-trasmissiva, v. anche idem, in *Marsilio Ficino . . . Mostra*, 100, no. 75, e in particolare le tavv. XXIV (tratta dal MS Magliabechiano) e XXV (proveniente dal cod. II 162 della Biblioteca Comunale Ariostea di Ferrara, contenente lettere originali del Ficino scritte in "Fabiani A").

151. V. Kristeller, *Supplementum*, 1:xxiii sg.; idem, "Some Original Letters," 18 e nota 3, 26; idem, *Iter*, 1:138; Sicherl, "Neuendeckte Handschriften," 55; idem, "Die Humanistenkursive," 447 sg.; Gentile, in *Marsilio Ficino . . . Mostra*, 97–99, no. 74 e tavv. XXII–XXIII.

152. V. Kristeller, *Supplementum*, 1:cxxxix–cxli; 2:11–76.

153. Significativo al proposito il caso del proemio, di cui troviamo alle cc. 1r–3v la copia in pulito, di mano del Fabiani, e, alla c. 30r–v, la minuta, di mano del Ficino; cfr. Gentile, in *Marsilio Ficino . . . Mostra*, 98, no. 74, e tavv. XXII–XXIII.

biani, ed è vergato per lo più in "Fabiani A" [tav. XXII], ma in parte anche in "Fabiani C" [tav. XXIII], vale a dire in quella realizzazione che figura nelle ultime carte del Laurenziano XC sup. 43.[154]

Le carte trascritte in "Fabiani C"—cc. 11r–14r (in parte di mano del Ficino) e 51v–54v—si distinguono dal resto del codice sia ad un esame di carattere codicologico, in particolare della fascicolazione e delle filigrane,[155] come pure sotto il profilo del contenuto. Difatti, se è cosa nota che nella *Disputatio* si incontrano passi estrapolati dalla *Theologia platonica*, assieme ad altri, che invece, redatti originariamente nel Magliabechiano, passarono successivamente nel commento a Plotino,[156] si osserverà che mentre gli uni risultano vergati dal copista in "Fabiani A", gli altri lo sono in "Fabiani C".

Si noterà inoltre che la c. 10v in origine non doveva essere seguita dalle attuali cc. 11–15 (contenenti il primo passo parallelo del commento a Plotino, in "Fabiani C"), ma dal fascicolo successivo (cc. 16–29), che è trascritto nella stessa realizzazione del primo, e cioè in "Fabiani A". Tra l'altro i due fascicoli si ricollegavano in maniera esplicita anche per quanto concerne il testo, prima che questo venisse corretto in funzione dell'inserzione del fascicolo intermedio.[157]

---

154. Così andrà suddiviso il codice, per quanto concerne la paternità grafica, tra il Ficino e il suo amanuense: cc. 1r–10v (sino a "persuasionem inducit") "Fabiani A"; c. 11r–v (sino a "impeditur extrinsecus") "Fabiani C"; c. 11v ("Ac sepe— remota videtur") Ficino; cc. 11v–12v (sino a "necessario sequitur") "Fabiani C"; cc. 12v–13r (sino a "debere") Ficino; c. 13r–v (sino a "ferme numerum") "Fabiani C"; cc. 13v–14r Ficino; cc. 14v–15v bianche; cc. 16r–29v "Fabiani A"; cc. 30r–31r (sino a "servus exiret") Ficino; c. 31r–v "Fabiani A"; c. 32r ("Sunt—presentes") Ficino; cc. 32r–50v "Fabiani A"; c. 51r (sino a "Porphyriusque detestantur") Ficino; cc. 51r–54v "Fabiani C"; c. 55r–v bianca; cc. 56r–57r Ficino; c. 57v bianca; cc. 58r–64r (sino a "removere non potest") "Fabiani A"; cc. 64r–65v (sino a "contemnere ceperit") Ficino; a c. 66r s'alternano Ficino e "Fabiani A"; cc. 66r–67v ("Hieremias— egrediendi moram") "Fabiani A"; cc. 67v–68r (da "Quod celi") Ficino. Ad una terza mano si devono le cc. 68v–69r.

155. Per quel concerne la fascicolazione abbiamo un quinterno (cc. 1–10) con l'aggiunta di una carta singola (c. 11), un duerno (cc. 12–15), un setterno (cc. 16–29), un senione (cc. 30–41), un quinterno (cc. 42–51), un duerno (cc. 52–55), un quinterno (cc. 56–65), un duerno (cc. 66–69). Quanto alle filigrane vi troviamo un 'cane', simile a Briquet 3645 (v. Briquet, *Les Filigranes*, 1:234), alle cc. 1–10, 16–29, 30–41 (tranne le cc. 33 e 36), 66–69; poi un 'giglio' (alle cc. 12–14), un 'grifone' (alle cc. 33 e 36), un' 'aquila' (alle cc. 42–51) e un 'cappello di cardinale' (alle cc. 52–55) non identificabili con nessuno dei tipi elencati dal Briquet.

156. Cfr. Kristeller, *Supplementum*, 1:cxxxix sg.; Gentile, in *Marsilio Ficino*, 98, no. 74.

157. C. 10v termina con una citazione dagli *Oracula* attribuiti a Zoroastro (v. tav. XXI; la cit. greca è di mano del Ficino): "Si animos pulsat (*scil.* deus), quia illi hac et illac, sursum deorsumque libere volubiles sunt, pulsat et libere, ita ut alliciat, non trahat, non cogat, sed persuadeat. Quod Zoroaster ita testatur: πατὴρ οὐ φόβον ἐνθρώσκει πειθὼ δ'ἐπιχέει, id est, Pater non incutit metum sed persuasionem inducit" (cfr. *Oracles Chaldaïques, avec un choix de commentaires anciens,*

Plato m̄ in libro de re p. decimo q̄
p̄ virtuta putat humana arbitrij libe̅
tatem non tolli p̄uīna prouidentiā
sed seruari. Nec̄ id quiat in uirtā
q̄ nra sicut inp̄stia de z̄ futura scrip̄
ti sunt rerū euentuf, ita q̄ euentuū
causę mediq̄ agendi. Et sicut opa n̄ra
nota sunt deo ita & n̄ra uoluntas qū
nrorum ē operum causa & modus
libere agendi. Q̄ uare diuina p̄uisio
si reddit necessaria n̄ra opa, reddit
necessarium similiter agendi modū.
Hoc ē n̄ra indies libertate. Q̄ in deus
n̄iarum oim̄ temptator cuiq̄ rei co̅
seruat, nō sub trahit n̄r̄am quā dederat.
S.u dum regit cunctas singula pro sin
gulorum regit nā. Ad scendentibus
elementis ad adscensum conducit,
descendentibus ad descendendum. Si
regit animalium motū qa ille nā
natura sua progressiuus est confert
ad gradiendū. Si cælos ducit, qa ob ro
tunditate, nā uolubiles sunt, confert
ad circuitus ambitū. Si animos pul
sat, qa illi, sursū deorsū q̄ libere
uolubiles sunt, pulsat q̄ libere: ita ut
alliciat, nō trahat, nō cogat, sed
p̄suadeat. Q̄uod Zoroastre ita testātur
πάντη δὲ φόβον ἐκβάλλοντα, ἤγουν ὁ Ζωροάστρης ἔφη·
ł Pater non incutit metum, ſʒ p̄suasio-
ne inducit ::—

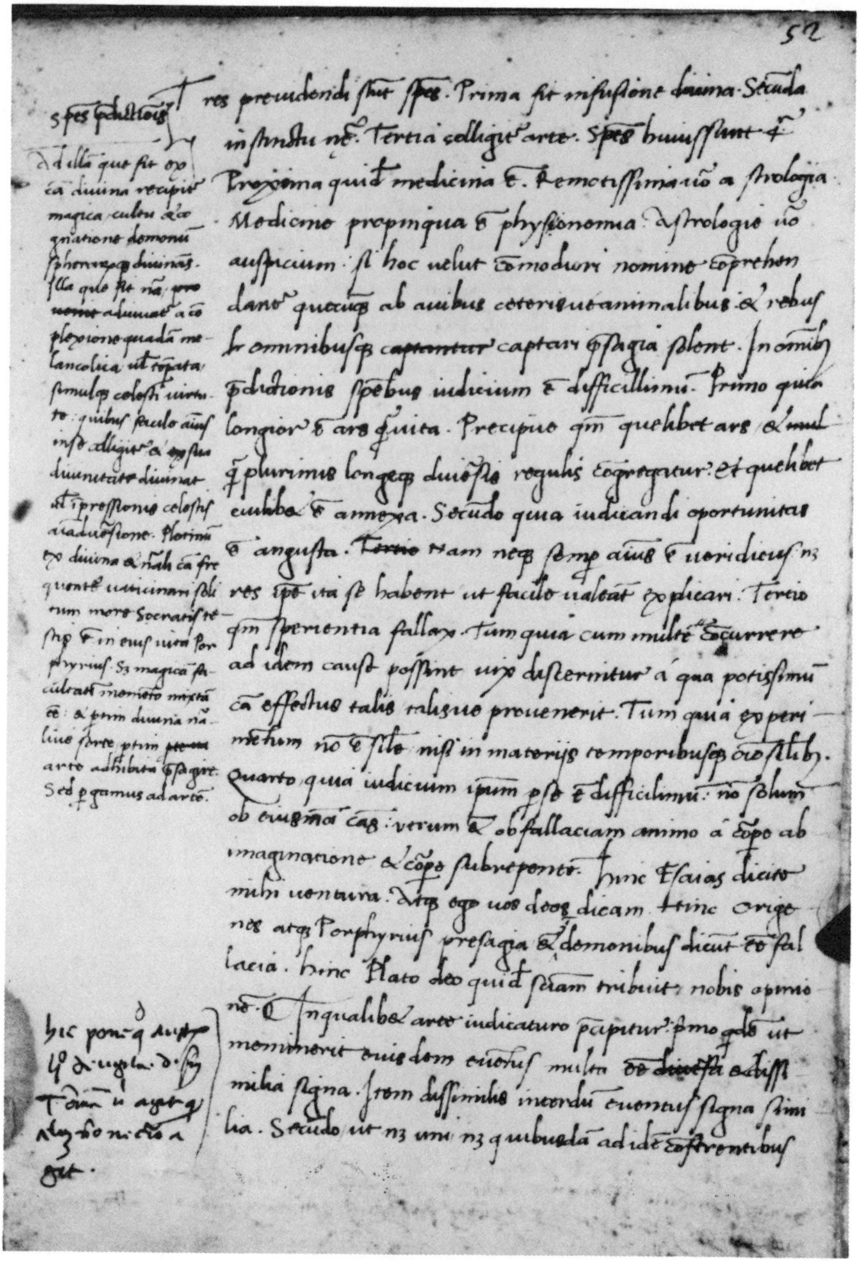

Tav. XXIII. Firenze, Biblioteca Nazionale, MS Magliabechiano XX 58, c.52r.

Ci sono insomma indizi sufficienti a suggerire la possibilità che le carte vergate in "Fabiani A" appartengano ad un'ipotetica prima stesura della *Disputatio*, mentre quelle che risultano copiate in "Fabiani C" siano invece aggiunte posteriori—avvenute non prima della seconda metà degli anni ottanta—, legate alla parte preesistente in maniera per altro approssimativa.[158]

D'altro canto siamo indotti a supporre che possa esservi stato un certo divario cronologico nella stesura delle diverse parti del Magliabechiano XX 58 anche dall'evidente contraddizione tra le testimonianze circa una datazione della *Disputatio* al 1477,[159] e quanto leggiamo a c. 65v del manoscritto a proposito della longevità di Paolo del Pozzo Toscanelli, del quale si dice che, a dispetto di previsioni astrologiche avverse, avrebbe raggiunto la veneranda età di ottantacinque anni, un'asserzione che il Ficino non può aver fatto anteriormente al 1482, anno in cui il Toscanelli, nato nel 1397, morì, "sanus prorsus corpore sanaque mente", appunto ottantacinquenne.[160]

Va poi rilevato che tra le testimonianze attestanti il 1477 come data di composizione della *Disputatio*, ce n'è una che per noi è di particolare interesse. Mi riferisco alle poche righe di presentazione che il Ficino ac-

---

a cura di E. Des Places [Paris, 1971], 69, fr. 14). A c. 16r il testo originale leggeva: "Igitur ne putet forte aliquis divinam providentiam singulis vim inferre, meminisse oportet voluntatem Dei malle universi bonum quam apparens alicuius particule commodum . . .", poi corretto dal Ficino in: "Igitur nemo putet divinam providentiam vel ex se ipsa vel per celum singula necessaria reddere, sed meminerit quisque voluntatem Dei malle universi bonum quam propriam alicuius particule qualitatem" (cfr. Kristeller, *Supplementum*, 2:21). Inoltre il richiamo in fine di fascicolo, a c. 10v, "Ipsum", è su rasura, scritto su un precedente "Igitur." Queste correzioni s'erano rese necessarie dopo l'inserzione alle cc. 11r–14r (le cc. 14v–15v sono bianche) del passo che leggiamo in Ficino, *Opera*, 1679 (da "Ipsum bonum")—1681 (sino a "debeat proficisci"); cfr. Kristeller, *Supplementum*, 2:16–19.

158. Cfr. Gentile, in *Marsilio Ficino . . . Mostra*, 98, no. 74.

159. Il 14 giugno il Ficino scriveva a Bernardo Bembo (v. Ficino, *Opera*, 771): "Ut autem te nunc de praesentibus studiis nostris faciam certiorem, compono librum de providentia Dei atque humani arbitrii libertate, in quo illa astrologorum iudicia, quae providentiae libertatique detrahunt, pro ingenii facultate redarguo". Del 28 giugno dello stesso anno è un'altra lettera (v. *ibid.*, 776; cfr. Kristeller, *Supplementum*, 1:31), a Francesco Marescalchi, in cui il Ficino accenna alla composizione di quest'opera: "Quartum [*scil.* quaeris] quid componam. Compono librum de providentia Dei et humani arbitrii libertate, in quo agitur contra astrorum necessitatem fatumque astrologorum". Di poco posteriore a queste due lettere parrebbe quella a Francesco Ippoliti che si cita nel testo. Sulla datazione della *Disputatio* al 1477, cfr. Kristeller, *Supplementum*, 1:cxxxix–cxli; E. Garin, *Lo zodiaco della vita. La polemica sull' astrologia dal Trecento al Cinquecento* (Bari, 1976), 70.

160. Cfr. Kristeller, *Supplementum*, 2:66: "Quinque enim et octuaginta annos implevit [*scil.* Paulus Orticinus] sano prorsus corpore sanaque mente". Da notare che "Quinque–octuaginta" è correzione del Ficino da un precedente "Quatuor enim iam et octuaginta".

compagnò al *prooemium* della *Disputatio* nell'occasione del suo invio a Francesco Ippoliti, conte di Gazoldo:

> Librum scripsi contra vana astrologorum iudicia. Mitto ad te proemium. Reliquum mittam cum primum scriba noster exscripserit.[161]

Se uniamo alla probabilità che lo *scriba noster* e il Fabiani siano la stessa persona — si ricordi la lettera indirizzata proprio allora dal Ficino "Lucae Fabiano scribae suo", e il poscritto, di poco più tardi, della lettera al Foresi ("Ipse Lucas Marsilii scriba . . .") — il fatto che le parti trascritte in ordine nel manoscritto della *Disputatio* sono opera di quel copista che crediamo di poter identificare con ser Luca, avremo, in questo concorso di indizi, un ulteriore elemento a favore della nostra attribuzione.

* * *

Con queste considerazioni sul Magliabechiano XX 58 terminano le note sui rapporti tra il Ficino e il Fabiani. A proposito della scrittura di quest'ultimo vorrei soltanto aggiungere che l'avergli attribuito 'mani' a prima vista dissimili — si pensi, come casi estremi, agli esempi più tardi della Cancelleria da un lato e al Riccardiano 2684 dall'altro —, che abbiamo poi potuto accostare tra loro con l'aiuto di gradazioni intermedie, grazie soprattutto al Laurenziano XC sup. 43, trova conforto nel caso analogo offerto da un amanuense contemporaneo del Fabiani, il ben noto Antonio Sinibaldi.[162]

Si prendano ad esempio due manoscritti firmati dal Sinibaldi: il Riccardiano 1449 [tav. XXIV], comprendente l'epistola consolatoria di Giovanni Nesi a Braccio Martelli datata 9 settembre 1476,[163] e il Magliabechiano XXX 239 [tav. XXV], nel quale l'amanuense fiorentino copiò per Neri Capponi la *Monarchia* dantesca.[164]

---

161. V. Ficino, *Opera*, 781.
162. Per il Sinibaldi v. supra, nota 21.
163. V. *I manoscritti della R. Biblioteca Riccardiana di Firenze, 1:Manoscritti italiani*, a cura di S. Morpurgo (Roma, 1900), 477; De Marinis, *La biblioteca*, 1:54 (con tav. del MS); Ullman, *The Origin*, 121.
164. V. Kristeller, "A New Work on the Origin and Development of Humanistic Script," *Manuscripta*, 5 (1961): 38; idem, *Iter*, 1:127. A c. 87r del MS si legge: "Antonius Sinibaldus florentinus fideliter transcripsit ad instantiam Neri de Capponis negociatore clarissimo [*sic*]".

IOHANNES NESIVS ADOLESCÉS
BRACCIO MARTELLO VIRO CLARMO.
VM CENANTIBVS HO
bis nuntiatum esset de obitu
patris tui preclarissimi viri
equitisq; insignis: sane omnes eque
ac nostrum erat grauiter molesteq;
tulimus. hancq; calamitatem com
munem existimauimus cum nro
iudicio: tum uel maxime opinione
atq; sententia charissimi patrie:
quem cum intuerer uideremq; eum
prenimio merore ingemiscere con
queri condolere Lamentari deplorie
tanti uiri interitum animo uehe
menter angebar: tum eo dolore
quem patris tui morte susceperam
tum eo quo pater mirum imodum
premebatur; quem cum aliqtulum

Tav. XXIV. Firenze, Biblioteca Riccardiana, MS 1449, c.1r.

humani gēnris erit hic prīcipuū p̄ quod oīa
que̅ inferius probanda sunt erunt mani
festa sufficienter. Esse aūt fine̅ huiꝰ ciui
litatis et illius & nō ē̄ vniū omniū
fine̅ arbitrari stultū ē.

Vnc aūt uidendum ē qd sit finis to
tius humane̅ ciuilitatis quo viso
prīusquam dimidiū laboris erit trāsactū
iuxta phylosophum ad Nichomacū et ad
euidentiam eiꝰ quod querit aduertendū
ē q̄ queadmodum ē finis aliqs ad que̅ n̄a
producit pollicem et aliꝰ abhoc ad que̅
manū totam & rirsus aliꝰ ab utroq ad
que̅ singulare horum alius ad que̅ ordi
nant domestica comunitate aliꝰ ad que̅
uicinia et aliꝰ ad que̅ ciuitate et ali
ad que̅ regnum et deniq, optimus adque̅
vniuersaliter genus humanū deus eterꝰ
arte sua que̅ n̄a sua ē inesse p̄ducit

Tav. XXV. Firenze, Biblioteca Nazionale, MS Magliabechiano XXX 239, c.3r.

Nel primo caso abbiamo a che fare con un codicetto di piccolo formato scritto in un'umanistica corsiva affine a quella impiegata dal Fabiani nel Riccardiano 2684 (= "Fabiani A"), nonché a quella che abbiamo definito la mano 'classica' del Salvini; nel secondo caso una scrittura di modulo più grande, affine agli esempi di ser Luca provenienti dalla Cancelleria, caratterizzata da un netto accentuarsi di quei vezzi 'settentrionali' che contraddistinguono la scrittura di ser Luca 'cancelliere'. Se per il codice della *Monarchia* non è possibile stabilire una data precisa—anche se è certamente della fine del '400, inizi del '500—, colpisce, ed è assai significativa, la vicinanza cronologica fra i due Riccardiani: quello che attribuiamo a ser Luca, che "fu facto in Firenze adi XXVIII digiungno 1478", e la lettera al Martelli che è datata, come si è visto, 9 settembre 1476.[165]

SEBASTIANO GENTILE

---

165. Non ho potuto tenere conto di un recente saggio, uscito mentre il presente lavoro era in corso di stampa, di A. C. de la Mare, "New Research on Humanistic Scribes in Florence," in *Miniatura fiorentina del Rinascimento, 1440–1525. Un primo censimento*, a cura di A. Garzelli (Firenze, 1985), 1:395–600, che tratta anche l'ambiente scrittorio ficiniano.

MARSILIO FICINO's INTERPRETATION
OF PLATO's TIMAEUS
AND ITS MYTH OF THE DEMIURGE

ONE OF THE MOST STRIKING formulations of the Renaissance ideal of man and a witness to its complex originality, as well as to its deep indebtedness to both classical and medieval traditions, appears in Ficino's huge *Theologia Platonica*, which was finished by 1474 but not published until 1482. In book III, chapter 2, he argues:

> Under God everything in creation is each some one entity in itself, but soul is simultaneously all things. In herself she possesses the images of things divine from which she depends, and the reasons and models of lower things which in a way she also produces. As the middle of all, she possesses the power of all; and, if this is so, she passes into all. As the true connecting link of all in the world, she does not abandon others when she goes forth into some one individual thing; but, while she preserves all, she goes forth into individuals. Justly we are entitled to call her, therefore, the center of nature, the universal mean, the chain or succession of the world, the face of all, the knot and bond of the universe.[1]

---

1. Ed. and tr. R. Marcel, *Marsile Ficin: Théologie Platonicienne de l'immortalité des âmes*, 3 vols. (Paris, 1964–1970), 1: 141–142: "Reliqua enim sub Deo unum quiddam in se singula sunt, haec omnia simul. Imagines in se possidet divinorum, a quibus ipsa dependet, inferiorum rationes et

This paean to the ontological status of soul as an entity unique in creation in its power to become all things and in its function as the universal copula is, though this has not been generally recognized, both an elaboration of, and a subtle transformation of, an earlier passage on love that Ficino composed for his long and influential commentary on Plato's *Symposium* in 1468–69, known in its original Latin version as the *De amore*. In the third chapter of the third speech where Cavalcanti is expatiating on the contribution of Eryximachus, Ficino writes:

> Thus, since they are the works of one artificer and members of the same machine and are mutually alike in their being and living, all the world's parts are bound together with a mutual love. We are justly entitled to call love, therefore, the perpetual knot and bond of the world, the motionless prop and stay of its parts, and the solid foundation of the whole machine.[2]

Here love is the focus of attention: it is love that is "the knot and bond of the world" and thus the principle of cosmic harmony and unity. In the later *Theologia Platonica* Ficino turns away from love to focus on soul and deliberately transfers his description of love's powers to soul, making it, not love, the universal bond. More interestingly still, he replaces the static metaphors in his earlier description — 'immobile prop and stay" and "solid foundation' — with more dynamic images that stem from the notion that soul passes through and into all. In other words, whereas the passage in the *De amore* concerns itself with love as the power instilled by the divine artificer into the world machine in order to maintain its harmony and unity and is not directly concerned with man, or even with

exemplaria, quae quodammodo et ipsa producit. Et cum media omnium sit, vires possidet omnium. [Quod] si ita est, transit in omnia. Et quia ipsa vera est universorum connexio, dum in alia migrat, non deserit alia, sed migrat in singula, ac semper cuncta conservat, ut merito dici possit centrum naturae, universorum medium, mundi series, vultus omnium nodusque et copula mundi." All translations from Ficino are my own.

2. Ed. and tr. R. Marcel, *Marsile Ficin: Commentaire sur le Banquet de Platon* (Paris, 1956), 165: "Quamobrem omnes mundi partes quia unius artificis opera sunt eiusdem machine membra inter se in essendo et vivendo similia, mutua quadam caritate sibi invicem vinciuntur, ut merito dici possit amor nodus perpetuus et copula mundi partiumque eius immobile substentaculum ac firmum totius machine fundamentum." For the most recent accounts of the complex textual situation and the status of Marcel's archetype, see J. A. Devereux, "The Textual History of Ficino's *De amore*," *RQ*, 28 (1975): 173–182, and S. Gentile, "Per la storia del testo del 'Commentarium in Convivium' di Marsilio Ficino," *Rinascimento*, ser. 2, 21 (1981): 3–27.

human love at all, the passage in the third book of the *Theologia Platonica* is anthropocentric. Not only has soul supplanted love by virtue of acquiring its powers, soul has become the ontological and epistemological mirror of the universe, since it possesses within images of the divine Ideas (*formulae idearum*) and at the same time reasons and models (*formae* in the restricted sense) of all lower things which "in a way" she produces. Whereas formerly love had been envisaged as the knot and bond holding the created world together, so it is now soul that is the universal knot and bond; and, furthermore, she produces the lower world herself, since she possesses the reasons and models of all that is in it, even as she continues to contemplate the higher realm of the intelligibles. Indeed, the two realms meet in her as "nature's centre" and "the universal mean." While it is true that Ficino is speaking of soul in general and not just of the human soul or even of the highest souls (those of the planetary spheres and their demonic attendants), we can legitimately assume—since the gravamen of the *Theologia Platonica* in its entirety is to argue for the immortality of man's soul—that Ficino's paean to soul is also a paean to man's potentialities and to his unique status in the eyes of the Creator in whose image he was made. For the implied analogy is ultimately with God Himself as the *artifex, opifex* or *faber*, the maker of the world. Just as God is the artificer of the whole, so man's soul is the artificer of lower things precisely because the *formulae* or *imagines* of the divine Ideas she possesses within become, when oriented towards the lower world, the *rationes* and *exemplaria* of each thing in that world.

It is my contention here that neither these passages in particular, nor Ficino's views at large, can be fully understood without an appreciation of his interpretation of the Demiurge myth in Plato's *Timaeus*, a myth that was central to his view of man's creative powers and to his sense of Plato's adumbration of Christian truths concerning both God the Creator and His creation of the world in time. The absence of any recognition of Ficino's indebtedness to the myth for his signal views on man has hitherto prevented us from unravelling the sources of the age's dawning recognition that man was not an artisan solely but a creator, who, having been once created, must continue himself to create in God's image and likeness.

***

Ficino almost certainly began his studies of Plato's actual dialogues with the *Timaeus*, since it was one of the dialogues available to him in Latin translation and since it had been the subject of several Latin commentaries, beginning with Calcidius' in the fourth century AD and culminating with that of William of Conches in the twelfth. By 1484 Ficino had published his own Latin translation of all Plato's dialogues, and, to accompany the *Timaeus* translation, a lengthy introduction or commentary.[3] This he revised and amplified in 1492 and republished in 1496 in a volume of six Plato commentaries.[4] Interestingly, in his youthful enthusiasm for Plato and before he had mastered Greek, he had prior to 1457 already composed

---

3. *Platonis opera omnia* (Florence, 148[4]). It is located after Ficino's *Republic* translation and prior to his *Timaeus* translation (which is in turn succeeded by his *Critias* translation). For the complex bibliographical situation, see P. O. Kristeller, "The First Printed Edition of Plato's Works and the Date of its Publication (1484)," in *Science and History: Studies in Honor of Edward Rosen, Studia Copernicana XVI*, ed. E. Hilfstein, P. Czartoryski, and F. D. Grande (Wroclaw, 1978), 25–35. In an earlier study, *Supplementum*, 1: cxxi, Kristeller dates the commentary as from "not much before the year 1484" and notes on pp. xi–xii, xxxiv, cxxi, and cliv–clv that the 1484 text can also be found in two manuscripts, the Laurenziana's MS 82, 7, and Modena, Biblioteca Estense, MS Estensis lat. 469, again flanked by the *Republic* and *Timaeus* translations. The commentary is broken down into chapters with headings (but these are not numbered). It and the *Symposium* commentary are the only two commentaries, as distinct from introductions or epitomes, to appear in this great Plato edition.

The second edition of the *Platonis opera omnia* was published in Venice in 1491 and incorporated the corrigenda affixed to the 1484 edition; apart from a few variants, mainly orthographic and accidental, it is identical with the 1484 text as amended by the corrigenda. The *Timaeus* commentary (entitled a *Compendium*) appears on ff. 241r–252r (sigs. G-H4).

4. *Commentaria in Platonem* (Florence, 1496), ff. 59–93. The chapters are now numbered with headings and five passages missing in the 1484/91 version have been added; added too are *distinctiones et summae capitum* (as is the case with other commentaries in the 1496 edition). Ficino had commenced this final version by Nov. 7, 1492, and probably finished it by the close of the year; still further minor additions must have been inserted just prior to publication — perhaps when the *summae* were included — for *summa* 24 has an account of two exorcisms that were conducted as late as Oct. 1493 and Dec. 1494. See Kristeller, *Supplementum*, 1: cxxi.

This final 1496 version was then reprinted in the second edition of Ficino's *Opera omnia*, published in Basel in 1576 (rept. Turin, 1959, 1983), at 2: 1438–1485. As identified by Kristeller, *Supplementum*, 1: 78–79, the five additional passages appear on pp. 1450–51, 1453, 1461, 1461v–1463, and 1463r-v. While those on pp. 1453 and 1461 consist of only a few lines, that on pp. 1463r-v constitutes most of chapter XLI, that on pp. 1450–1451 the whole of chapter XXVII, and that on pp. 1461v–1463 the greater part of chapter XXXVII and the whole of chapters XXXVIII, XXXVIIII and XL.

There are, however, some discrepancies, hitherto unnoted, between the presentations in the 1496 and 1576 editions. First, the 1496 presentation has none of the diagrams found in the 1576 edition. Second, the 1496 presentation transposes what appear in the 1576 volume as chapters 26 and 27 (i.e. chapter 27 appears as chapter 26 and vice versa). Third, the 1496 volume misnumbers chapter 35 and has two chapters 34 instead; this mistake is never corrected and thus its chapters 40 and 42 are the 1576 edition's chapters 41 and 4[3] (see note 46 below). Finally, the 1496

a *Timaeus* commentary which is now lost. Upon reading this Cosimo and Landino had urged Ficino to dedicate himself to acquiring the learning needed to work with the Greek texts themselves (*Opera*, 929.2).[5] The dialogue seems to have thus engaged him throughout his long career as a scholar, philosopher and Christian apologist; and he emerged as an authority on this as on so many other Platonic and Platonist texts. Indeed, since he was the only scholar to publish a full commentary on the *Timaeus* in the fifteenth century, as André Chastel has reminded us,[6] his interpretation became, both because of its intrinsic excellence and because of the absence of challenging alternatives, the definitive Renaissance interpretation and subsequently the one that held the stage until superseded by the accounts of the nineteenth and twentieth centuries and notably, for English readers, by those of A. E. Taylor and F. M. Cornford. Determining Ficino's views is thus of some considerable interest; for it will

volume has a different and expanded version of what appears in the 1576 edition as chapter 4[5]: the first half—up to "Galeni mentem cum Platonica mente coniunxit"—appears as its chapter 44 (because of the misnumbering of chapter 35 and no subsequent correction), while the last half— beginning "Post haec autem perfectam hominis"—appears as its chapter 46 (f. 80r). In between, appearing as its chapter 45, is a passage which is printed quite separately in the 1576 edition on pp. 1484–1485 and entitled *De exspiratione et respiratione secundum Platonem atque Galenum* (this title the 1496 volume presents as its chapter 45 heading). Given the anomalous position of the Galen passage in the 1576 edition, the 1496 presentation undoubtedly reflects Ficino's intentions. Thus we should be alert to the discrepancies not only between the 1484/91 and 1496/1576 versions, but also between the 1496 and 1576 presentations of what is basically the same version if we disregard the corrigenda for the 1484/91 Plato translation which Ficino affixed to the 1496 *summae*.

For some reason the first edition of Ficino's *Opera omnia* published in Basel in 1561 and the third edition published in Paris in 1641 omit the five additional passages, the third edition being a reprinting of the first and not of the second edition (see Kristeller, *Supplementum*, 1: lxxiii); and a similar situation pertains with regard to passages also omitted in the *Parmenides* commentary.

As is customary, all general references to Ficino's works will be to the second edition of the *Opera omnia*.

5. Kristeller hypothesizes that this early version was quite different from the commentary as we now have it in its two versions. He identifies it rather with another lost work which Ficino refers to either as the *Libri quatuor institutionum ad Platonicam disciplinam* or as the *Declarationes Platonicae disciplinae*, and which he had dedicated to Cristoforo Landino (*Supplementum*, 1: cxx–cxxi, clxiii–clxiv). It was probably heavily indebted to Calcidius and was almost certainly his first Plato commentary.

6. *Marsile Ficin et l'art* (Geneva and Lille, 1954), 99; see also A. Chastel, *Arte e umanesimo a Firenze al tempo di Lorenzo il Magnifico*, tr. R. Federici (Turin, 1964), 221, and F. A. Yates, *The French Academies of the Sixteenth Century* (London, 1947), 87–88. In a forthcoming entry in the *Catalogus translationum et commentariorum*, however, James Hankins will treat of a number of unpublished sets of glosses on the *Timaeus* (only some of which have been previously identified) from the late 11th through the 15th centuries by such varied figures as Bernard of Chartres, Wenceslaus Boragk, Guillaume Fichet, Pico della Mirandola, and Pier Leoni, the physician of Lorenzo the Magnificent.

enable us to see how a remarkable age came to terms with a remarkable text, one from the Greek past that had been the object nonetheless of sustained meditation and enquiry throughout later antiquity by Aristotelians as well as Platonists, and again in the first flowering of medieval philosophy. It had therefore entered fully into the intellectual life of the West in a way that no other Plato text (and the *Parmenides* is no exception) could possibly have done, given the inaccessibility of the Plato canon to the Latin world for nigh on a millennium prior to the translations of Ficino and those of his older and younger humanist contemporaries.[7]

As the solitary commentator of the Quattrocento, Ficino must have felt that he had a new and special contribution to make. But between him and the light of the *Timaeus* itself stretched the long shadows not only of ancient commentary, as was the case with certain other dialogues he deemed crucial for an understanding of Plato, but also of the medieval commentary Calcidius had inspired. But Calcidius' translation only goes up as far as 53c and Calcidius' commentary skips over the opening sections of the dialogue and concentrates on the matter following 31c; it too ends at 53c. The commentary is obviously incomplete for Calcidius lists 27 sections (*tractatus*) in his introduction while only 16 remain; these are divided between two books, the first dealing with 31c–39c, the second with 39c–53c. Calcidius deals at length with the theory of proportions and with the implications for astronomy; in the process he borrows extensively from an earlier commentary by the Peripatetic Adrastus of Aphrodisias.[8] He also deals with the notion that each element has three

7. For the humanist versions, see especially E. Garin, "Ricerche sulle traduzioni di Platone nella prima metà del sec. XV," in *Medioevo e Rinascimento: studi in onore di Bruno Nardi* (Florence, 1955), 1: 339–374; also J. Hankins, *Latin Translations of Plato in the Renaissance* (Ph.D. diss., Columbia University, 1984), app. A and B. None of the humanists, incidentally, seems to have embarked on a translation of the *Timaeus*.

For the story of the *Parmenides*, see R. Klibansky, "Plato's Parmenides in the Middle Ages and the Renaissance," in *Medieval and Renaissance Studies*, ed. R. Hunt and R. Klibansky, 1 (London, 1943), 281–330; this has been reissued with another influential essay under the title of that essay as *The Continuity of the Platonic Tradition during the Middle Ages* (Munich, 1981). For the partial Latin version available to the Middle Ages, see *Corpus Platonicum Medii Aevi: Plato Latinus III: Parmenides usque ad finem primae hypothesis necnon Procli Commentarium in Parmenidem pars ultima adhuc inedita interprete Guillelmo de Moerbeka*, ed. R. Klibansky and C. Labowsky (London, 1953), 5–21. For the Moerbeke translation of Proclus' *Parmenides* commentary we now have the important edition by C. Steel, *Proclus: Commentaire sur le Parménide de Platon, traduction de Guillaume de Moerbeke*, 2 vols. (Louvain and Leiden, 1982 and 1985).

8. Extracts from Adrastus are preserved in a treatise by the early second-century Middle Platonist,

qualities and sets up an ingenious scheme of consequent analogies where he seems to be indebted to Numenius directly or indirectly. He then turns to the complicated issue of the world's eternity and to the various possible meanings of "created" (*genêtos*) and eventually rejects the idea that the world was created in time. Other issues he pursues are providence and fate, the nature and number of the demons, and the theory that matter is potentially both corporeal and incorporeal, a theory also expounded by other Middle Platonists such as Albinus and Apuleius. Ficino was familiar with the *Timaeus* epitomes of both these men, as he was with the summary account by Diogenes Laertius,[9] and with the notable essay by Plutarch, the *De animae procreatione in Timaeo*,[10] all four authors testifying to the centrality of the *Timaeus* in the Middle Platonic tradition and to its status as the Platonic dialogue *par excellence*.

I wish to stress "other Middle Platonists" because I am persuaded by the force of John Dillon's objections to the view put forward by Calcidius' great modern editor, J. H. Waszink,[11] that Calcidius was influenced by the *Timaeus* Commentary of Plotinus' distinguished disciple, Porphyry

Theon of Smyrna, entitled *Expositio rerum mathematicarum ad legendum Platonem utilium* (ed. E. Hiller, Leipzig, 1878). Theon acknowledges his debts to Adrastus among others, and quotes verbatim from him. Ficino's own translation of this treatise survives in two manuscripts; see Kristeller, *Supplementum*, 1: cxlvi–cxlvii.

9. Albinus, known to Ficino and his contemporaries as Alcinous, wrote a careful summary of the *Timaeus* (or of an earlier epitome of it) in chapters 7 to 26 of his handbook to Platonism entitled *Didaskalikos*, a handbook Ficino translated in full, *Opera omnia*, 2: 1946–1962; see Kristeller, *Supplementum*, 1: cxxxv–cxxxvi, 104.

The first four chapters of Apuleius' *De Platone et eius dogmate* treat of Plato's life, but the rest of his first book is based on the *Timaeus'* physics (from the first principles to specific maladies). In the Greekless days of his nonage Ficino must perforce have turned to Apuleius as to Calcidius.

In his *Lives of the Philosophers* 3.67ff. Diogenes Laertius presents us with a systematic exposition of Plato's thought which is based on the *Timaeus*.

10. *Moralia* 1012a–1030c with a summary from 1030d to 1032f. It argues that Plato believed in temporal creation but also that he was espousing dualist views; see note 32 below. Plutarch also discussed passages from the *Timaeus* in other works such as "Platonic Questions" (*Moralia* 999c–1011f), "Fate" (*ibid.* 568b–574f), and "The Face in the Moon" (*ibid.* 920a–945e), all of which were familiar to Ficino.

11. *Calcidius: In Timaeum* (London and Leiden, 1962; 2nd. ed. 1975); this is volume 4 in the series *Corpus Platonicum Medii Aevi* (see note 7 above). Waszink's long introduction (in Latin) gives a full account of Calcidius' views and sources, pp. xvii–cvi. See also his *Studien zum Timaioskommentar des Calcidius*, 1 (Leiden, 1964); J. C. M. van Winden, *Calcidius on Matter: His Doctrine and Sources* (Leiden, 1959); J. den Boeft, *Calcidius on Fate: His Doctrine and Sources* (Leiden, 1970); idem, *Calcidius on Demons: Commentarius Chapters 127–136* (Leiden, 1977). These four studies are volumes 12, 9, 18, and 33 respectively of the series *Philosophia antiqua*.

(c. 232–305 AD).[12] Dillon observes, "to the unprejudiced eye there is nothing in Calcidius that requires us to postulate his acquaintance with any distinctively Neoplatonic doctrine, and much to suggest that he knew nothing of Porphyry's *Commentary*."[13] Instead, he proffers other sources "from which Calcidius departs very little" except to add "explanatory comments and elaborations," among them Adrastus and a follower of Numenius (perhaps even Numenius himself), plus Middle Platonists generally. "Nowhere," Dillon concludes, "does Calcidius show any knowledge of that technique of allegorical interpretation which is such a feature of Neoplatonic commentary" (p. 403); and we should bear in mind that Waszink does accept the profound indebtedness of Porphyry to Numenius and therefore, by extension of his own argument, of Calcidius to Numenius. Calcidius may not be a mindless compiler but he is a compiler nonetheless of Middle Platonic doctrines: "there is at any rate nothing that connects him with the Neoplatonist movement" (p. 408). This is even true of the metaphysical scheme he deploys with its hierarchy of three principles: the Good (not the Plotinian One), Mind (*Nous*), and a second Mind (identified with the World Soul but not with the Plotinian hypostasis Soul).

Ficino was unacquainted, of course, with our notion of "Middle Platonism" and supposed, following Augustine and Proclus, a direct line of intellectual succession from Plato and his immediate successors down through the sceptical tradition of Carneades and Arcesilaus to Plutarch, Albinus, Apuleius and Numenius and thence on to Plotinus, Iamblichus and the later Neoplatonists. Ficino certainly regarded Calcidius as a member of this Platonic succession. In a letter to Martinus Uranius (alias Martin Prenninger) of June 1489 he deals explicitly with the succession and lists Calcidius' *Timaeus* commentary as one of the "Platonic books" to be found "among the Latins," along with the translations of the Areopagite, many things in Augustine, Boethius' *Consolatio*, Apuleius' treatise on demons, Macrobius' exposition of the *Somnium Scipionis*, Avicebron's *Fons vitae*, Alfarabi's *De causis*, much in Henry of Ghent, Avicenna, and Scotus,

---

12. The extant fragments have been edited by A. R. Sodano, *Porphyrii in Platonis Timaeum commentariorum fragmenta* (Naples, 1964).

13. *The Middle Platonists 80 B.C. to A.D. 220* (Ithaca, New York, 1977), 401–408 at 403. Waszink's argument, he claims, requires Calcidius to have picked and chosen "very selectively" from Porphyry. Certainly Calcidius never mentions any of the Neoplatonists by name.

and in the work of Ficino's own contemporaries, Bessarion and Cusanus.[14] But in his own *Timaeus* commentary Ficino barely refers to Calcidius: once to say that he had written at length on proportion and harmony, and then to note that he had also written on the problems of sight.[15] This is not conclusive evidence in itself of his having dismissed Calcidius, since paucity of explicit references to an ancient authority, or to a medieval one of unimpeachable authority such as Aquinas, often goes along with real and occasionally extensive indebtedness, as is the case frequently with regard to Proclus. Nevertheless, it is unlikely that the older Ficino would have regarded Calcidius as seriously as the younger Ficino,[16] once he had gained access to the original Plato text and to the canon at large, and access too to the *De mundo*, the treatise by Timaeus Locrus thought to be Plato's immediate source.[17] One main reason for Ficino's

14. *Opera omnia*, 1: 899; other references to "Platonicus noster Chalcidius" occur on 489 and 852 where he is cited as an authority on the stars and their role in influencing disasters and supernatural events. The letter has been edited and discussed by Klibansky, *Continuity*, 42–47; and discussed by P. O. Kristeller, *The Philosophy of Marsilio Ficino* (New York, 1943; repr. Gloucester, Mass., 1964), 26–27, and by R. Marcel, *Marsile Ficin (1433–1499)* (Paris, 1958), 606–607.

15. *Opera omnia*, 2: 1446 and 1463; cf. 1663.

16. A manuscript in the Ambrosiana in Milan (Ambrosianus S. 14 sup., ff. 5–98v) contains the Calcidius commentary and has abundant marginal notes; it also contains Bruni's translation of the *Gorgias*, Apuleius' *De deo Socratis*, and Cicero's *Topics*. The arms it bears are those of Ficino—a sword between two stars—and a note at f. 172r testifies that he had copied out the whole manuscript himself during the months of February and March 1454 (Florentine style) while he was still twenty. See Klibansky, *Continuity*, 30; Kristeller, *Supplementum*, 1: liv; idem, *Iter Italicum* 1 (London and Leiden, 1963), 342; idem, "Some Original Letters and Autograph Manuscripts of Marsilio Ficino," in *Studi di bibliografia e di storia in onore di Tammaro de Marinis* (Verona, 1964), 3: 19, 29; and Waszink, cviii.

Insofar as Ficino went beyond his youthful understanding of Plato, he went, *pari passu*, beyond Calcidius; even so he continued to refer to him on mathematical and astronomical matters and never wholly neglected, let alone formally rejected, him.

17. Timaeus Locrus' cosmological treatise *Peri psychas kosmô kai physios*, known more generally as *De mundo*, is now considered to be merely a summary of Plato's *Timaeus* dating from the first century AD, or at the earliest from the second or third centuries BC. Composed in a literary (i.e. pseudo) Doric, the putative language of the Pythagoreans in Italy and Sicily, it is probably a pious forgery by a Pythagorean revivalist. However, the Neoplatonists regarded it as the genuine work of Timaeus, the speaker in Plato's dialogue, and therefore as Plato's source. Ficino and his contemporaries were under the same illusion: in an early letter to Cavalcanti he writes, "Our Plato in the *Timaeus*, following and supporting the Pythagorean Timaeus, tells us that God created the world" and that Timaeus was his "master" (*Opera omnia*, 1: 629–30). Even so, he concentrates on Plato's text and mentions the *De mundo* only in passing (e.g. 2: 1466.1; cf. 1594.1). Obviously he regarded the *Timaeus* (perhaps in part because of its length) as the more authoritative. For the dating and style of the *De mundo* and a detailed commentary, see M. Baltes, *Timaios*

decision to embark on a full-scale *Timaeus* commentary therefore must have been to remedy the deficiencies of Calcidius' partial work: not so much to negate or refute it as to explore metaphysical dimensions that Calcidius had either not touched on or touched on but briefly.

Whatever his intrinsic merits or demerits as a Platonist, Calcidius had served as the inspiration of several medieval commentators and notably for a group in the twelfth century conveniently referred to as the School of Chartres, a group especially interested in cosmological issues. The master of these *Timaeus* commentators was William of Conches whose "glosses" Ficino apparently knew; for he mentions William in an early work, the *De voluptate* of 1457, in the company, significantly, of Apuleius, Ptolemy and Calcidius, "noble Platonists" all, who had argued for the intellectual nature of pleasure in Plato and for his agreement in this regard with Aristotle. All four commentators are Latin—Ficino had not yet learned Greek—and are cited for their having interpreted "the opinion that Plato had propounded in the *Timaeus* in the obscurest terms."[18] It is hardly a memorable reference to William, and Ficino never afterwards referred to him,[19] not even in the Uranius letter, where he is careful to list the succession of Latin Platonists, including the Scholastics and his own contemporaries.[20] But it does at least testify to his knowledge of William and therefore presumably of the contributions of the Chartrean school which

---

Lokros: Uber die Natur des Kosmos und der Seele, Philosophia antiqua, 21 (Leiden, 1972). For a critical edition of the text, and, among other matters, a full description of the many Renaissance manuscripts, see W. Marg, *Timaeus Locrus: De natura mundi et animae*, Philosophia antiqua, 24 (Leiden, 1972). Ficino certainly knew the text in the Laurenziana's manuscript 59, 1 since he had used it in 1462 for his Plato translations. Among other manuscripts in the Laurenziana with the *De mundo* are 28,29 and 85,9 and Conv. soppr. 103 and 108 (Marg, 8–9, 11, 12, 32 and 43).

18. *Opera omnia*, 1: 997ff.: "Nam Apuleius, Calcidius, Contius, Ptolemeus Platonici nobiles eo, quem breviter referam, modo Platonis sententiam obscurissimis in Timaeo verbis positam interpretantur." The "Contius" here was first identified as William of Conches by Klibansky, *Continuity*, 36 and 43 (where at note 5 he argues that "Contius" should be corrected to "Concius"). See also Kristeller, *Studies*, 40; and S. Gentile, "In margine all'epistola 'De Divino furore' di Marsilio Ficino," *Rinascimento*, ser. 2, 23 (1983): 43–47.

19. Indeed, Marcel argues that Ficino only knew of William through John of Salisbury (*Marsile Ficin*, 645); but see Gentile's objection ("In margine," 45, note 4).

Writing in 1506, Corsi, Ficino's biographer, makes no mention of William in listing the Latin Platonists who served as Ficino's authorities (*Vita Marsilii Ficini*, IV).

20. Klibansky, *Continuity*, 43, suggests that this omission may be accounted for "by considering Marsiglio's philosophical development which had led him away from the medieval commentators on the Timaeus to Greek Neoplatonic exegesis;" but this is surely a blanket consideration affecting all the Latin commentators on Plato whom Ficino encountered in his youth.

climaxed in William; and the date suggests that the glosses would have been one of Ficino's primary sources for the first version of his *Timaeus* commentary written prior to 1457 but no longer extant.[21]

* * *

Why did the *Timaeus* engage the attention of Ficino's medieval predecessors? For all intents and purposes the only Plato text available to the Latin West (thanks to Calcidius' partial Latin translation and to some fragments that had been translated by Cicero),[22] it was the object of enquiry on the part of scholars interested in the history of natural science and cosmology, and prepared to follow in the footsteps of the more liberal-minded Church Fathers and to look to the contributions of pagan antiquity, and pre-eminently, following Augustine, of Plato. But it was also an inherently challenging text that begged comparison with Genesis; and the similarities inevitably raised the question of influence. Had Plato gained access to the Mosaic mysteries during an Egyptian sojourn? Or had these same mysteries been transmitted already to the Greek sages long before and been inherited by Plato as he sat at the feet of Pythagoreans? Or had Plato arrived at a cosmology reminiscent of Moses' by way of his natural reason alone? Or had he, too, been granted divine revelation, if not as sublime as that granted to Moses, then at least sufficient to prepare the gentiles for the reception later of Christian truths? The question of influence was more than academic: it bore directly on the hotly-debated issues

21. S. Gentile, S. Niccoli, and P. Viti, *Marsilio Ficino e il ritorno di Platone: manoscritti, stampe e documenti* (Florence, 1984), 8–9. This catalogue for the Ficino exhibition, held in the Laurenziana from May 17th to June 16th 1984 to commemorate the five hundredth anniversary of the publication of the great Plato edition of 1484, is an important work of codicological and bibliographical scholarship.

See also Gentile, "In margine," 43–47, who argues for William's glosses as a "probable source" for Ficino's vernacular treatise of 1457, the *Di Dio et anima* (ed. Kristeller, *Supplementum*, 2: 128–158); he even suggests that Ficino may have known other works by William. But all evidence is wanting thus far, and in the case of the passage he cites from the *Di Dio et anima* Ficino might well have turned, I believe, to John of Salisbury's *Policraticus* 7. 5, rather than to William's glosses, recently edited, incidentally, by É. Jeauneau as *Guillaume de Conches: Glosae super Platonem* (Paris, 1965); see note 28 below.

22. For Cicero's translation, only fragments of which have survived, see F. Pini, ed., *M. T. Ciceronis Timaeus* (Milan, 1965), and R. Giomini, "Osservazioni sul testo del Timeo ciceroniano," *Rivista di cultura classica e medioevale*, 11 (1969): 251–254. In Burnet's edition (1902) of the *Timaeus*—the edition I shall refer to throughout—the fragments correspond to 27d6–37c1, 38c4–43b4, and 46a–47b2.

of the salvation of the virtuous pagan, the gift of a "natural religion" to those who were not God's chosen people, and concomitantly, the value of pagan learning as an object of Christian study, and more especially the learning of Plato.

Apart from the ongoing fascination with the dialogue's science and mathematics, a fascination reinforced by the orientation of Calcidius' commentary (though, we should recall, it only extends from 31c to 53c), the focus of the medieval commentators' interest in the *Timaeus* was the nature and function of Plato's great myth of the Demiurge. At 28a Plato had Timaeus himself argue that

> all that becomes must needs become by the agency of some cause; for without a cause nothing can come to be. Now whenever the maker of anything looks to that which is always unchanging and uses a model of that description in fashioning the form and quality of his work, all that he thus accomplishes must be good. If he looks to something that has come to be and uses a generated model, it will not be good.[23]

He continues at 28c:

> The maker and father of this universe it is a hard task to find, and having found him it would be impossible to declare him to all mankind. Be that as it may, we must go back to this question about the world: After which of the two models did its builder frame it — after that which is always in the same unchanging state, or after that which has come to be?... Everyone, then, must see that he looked to the eternal; for the world is the best of things that have become, and he is the best of causes.

The creator was entirely free from jealousy and desired that all things should resemble him as much as lay within their power (29e). Thus the world came into being as a living creature truly endowed by the providence of God with soul and intelligence (30bc).

Timaeus proceeds to speak of the World Soul and of the various har-

---

23. I am quoting from the translation by F. M. Cornford, *Plato's Cosmology: The "Timaeus" of Plato translated with a running commentary* (London, 1937).

monic relationships underlying the structural principles that govern its body. Eventually he depicts the Demiurge addressing his own offspring, the "younger gods," and commanding them to take over the task of completing man and the lower world. He will himself sow the divine seed of the soul, but leave it to them to "weave" it with the mortal elements. Accordingly, he mingles the soul ingredients with the elements in his mighty cup (completing the mix of metaphors!) and assigns the resulting individual soul-drops each to one of the stars, there being an equal number of stars and soul-drops. Then the Demiurge declares the laws of destiny to each soul in its new star chariot,[24] before taking some of them and sowing them in the earth, while taking others and sowing them in the moon or in the other "instruments of time," meaning presumably the planets (41c–42d). The "younger gods" are left to fashion mortal bodies for the souls; this apparently means bodies for the lunar souls and the other planetary souls as well as for terrestrial souls, though the syntax is ambiguous enough for an interpreter to argue that only the terrestrial souls will be provided with mortal bodies, whereas those committed to a thorough-going demonology can argue otherwise. Having pronounced these ordinances, the Demiurge "continued to abide by the wont of his own nature" while his children "took heed to their father's ordinance and set about obeying it" (42e).

Several pages later Timaeus returns to the dominant theme of creation. At 47eff. he declares that

> the generation of this universe was a mixed result of the combination of Necessity and Reason (*Nous*). Reason overruled Necessity by persuading her to guide the greatest part of the things that become towards what is best; in that way and on that principle this universe was fashioned in the beginning by the victory of reasonable persuasion over Necessity.

Timaeus does not establish specific connections or equations between his earlier references to the Demiurge as father, maker and artificer and this

---

24. This reference to a chariot, and the references at 44de and 69c, were associated with similar references in the *Phaedrus* 247b and passim, in the *Phaedo* 113d, and in the *Laws* 10, 898e–899e, and continually cited by the Neoplatonists as evidence that Plato believed in the "astral" body, vehicle or envelope; see E. R. Dodds, *Proclus: The Elements of Theology*, 2nd. ed. (Oxford, 1963), appendix.

later reference to *Nous*, nor between the earlier references to the "cup" or the "laws of destiny" and this later reference to "Necessity," though it was precisely these connections or equations that were to fascinate later commentators among the Neoplatonists and in the school of Chartres.

While this complex myth clearly invited comparison with the Mosaic account of the world's creation,[25] it presented the Chartreans with a number of points difficult to reconcile with Genesis. The debate, and notably William of Conches' contribution, has been carefully examined by Tullio Gregory,[26] and I wish to draw attention only to some very general points as they bear on our understanding of Ficino's relationship to the medieval *Timaeus* tradition, always keeping in mind the fact that he refers to "Contius" just once in his writings and at a very early date, several years before he became immersed in the study of Greek and thoroughly conversant with the problems of Plato exegesis. The possibility exists indeed that he may have been just as indebted at the outset of his preoccupation with Plato to the important comments on the *Timaeus* in Aristotle's *De caelo* and *De generatione et corruptione*,[27] or even to the *Policraticus* of John of Salisbury, William's contemporary.[28]

First, Plato depicts the Demiurge as looking up at the eternal pattern,

25. There are of course two accounts in Genesis of man's creation: 1. 26–27 and 2. 7 (and for Eve 2. 21–22).

26. *Anima Mundi: La filosofia di Guglielmo di Conches e la scuola di Chartres* (Florence, 1955). Other important studies include: J. M. Parent, *La doctrine de la création dans l'École de Chartres* (Paris-Ottawa, 1938); T. Gregory, *Platonismo medievale: studi e ricerche* (Rome, 1958), chap. 4 ("Il Timeo e i problemi del platonismo medievale"); M.-D. Chenu, *La théologie au douzième siècle* (Paris 1957), 118–128 ("Le platonisme du *Timée* et de Boèce"); E. Garin, *Studi sul platonismo medievale* (Florence, 1958), chap. 1 ("Di alcuni aspetti del platonismo medievale, in particolare nel XII secolo"); É. Jeauneau, *Lectio philosophorum: recherches sur l'École de Chartres* (Amsterdam, 1973), esp Part II, chap. 2; and L. Bianchi, *L'errore di Aristotele: la polemica contro l'eternità del mondo nel XII. secolo* (Florence, 1984). The introduction to Jeauneau's actual edition of William's *Glosae* is mainly concerned with textual and other descriptive matters, but see pp. 26–31.

27. See G. S. Claghorn, *Aristotle's Criticism of Plato's Timaeus* (The Hague, 1954). Aristotle's scientific and literalist approach was transmitted the length of antiquity as far as Simplicius' commentary on the *De caelo*, and constituted a familiar alternative to the Neoplatonists' allegorical approach.

For a survey of the *fortuna* of the *Timaeus* in antiquity, see M. Baltes, *Die Weltentstehung des platonischen Timaios nach den antiken Interpreten*, Philosophia antiqua, 30 and 35 (Leiden, 1976–78) 2 vols.; vol. 2 is devoted to Proclus. For Plotinus' views in particular, see J.-M. Charrue, *Plotin Lecteur de Platon* (Paris, 1978), 117–155.

28. The *Policraticus* 7. 5 contains a section on the *Timaeus* and on its parallels with Genesis. Ficino seems to have mistaken the title for the author, whom he refers to as Policrates, e.g. *Opera omnia*, 1: 44, 72, 763, and 780. For the confusion, see Kristeller, *Studies*, 40, note 36.

the Ideas, in order to employ them as his models for all that he creates, though Timaeus seems to be concerned here only with the creation of souls and not with the material world. In other words, Plato depicts the Ideas as logically, and therefore — given the nature of the myth — as ontologically, prior to and thus superior to the Creator-Demiurge. Thus the Demiurge exists between the sublime Ideas and the souls for whom the Ideas serve as patterns or models. If we recall that Timaeus asserts at 47eff. that "mind" (nous) and "necessity" share the work of creation, necessity being responsible under mind for the "greater part," then we are forced into the position of having to suppose that Nous looked up at the sublime Ideas which far transcended him as he transcended the World Soul and his own sons, the younger gods, and all inferior souls. This is the consequence of Plato's objective idealism. We should note, if only in passing, that the Ideas in question are not those of such virtues as Fortitude or Temperance as they appear in the Republic and Phaedrus, but are the Ideas of kinds of being, the species of souls or Soul. But Plato nowhere else discusses such an Idea of souls or Soul and the conception is fraught with difficulties. Hypothetically, since the Ideas are above Mind, the Demiurge, we could entertain the notion that there was an Idea of Mind and that the Demiurge may look up at an Idea of himself; but these are speculative reaches we need not pursue here. Commentators since antiquity had reinterpreted Plato's myth to mean that the Demiurge looked within rather than above at the Ideas as they dwelt in his own mind; and Proclus was accused of having betrayed Plato in this matter by subordinating the Ideas to Mind.[29] Once we accept the image of a mind looking within to its own ideas, it seems almost inevitable that we submit the thoughts to the thinker. By an easy transition a Christian can then equate the thinker with God and the act of creation as His turning within to model the world after His own thoughts and to make it out of them. Plato's subordinate Demiurge becomes a symbol of God in his omniscience and omnipotence, the supreme Maker of Genesis.

This brings us to the second difficulty facing William and his contemporary Timaeus commentators. Plato's term dêmiourgos does not mean

29. See E. Zeller and R. Mondolfo, La filosofia dei Greci nel suo sviluppo storico, Part 3, vol. 6, ed. Giuseppe Martano (Florence, 1961), 155n. On the exceedingly complicated problem of determining Plotinus' views as to whether the demiurge should be equated with Mind or Soul or both, see Charrue, 123–127, 133–139.

"creator" but a skilled artisan, a worker in the quotidian sense of a cobbler who crafts comfortable shoes, or a cook who bakes an aromatic cake; the contrast is with the *idiôtês*, someone with no professional expertise or skill.[30] Though the term has a remote, even a grandiose, ring to our ears, it was in everyday usage in ancient Greece and had none of the mythological dimensions it has since acquired precisely because of Plato's decision to use it in this dialogue. His Demiurge is an artisan who gazes up at the Ideas in order to make his World Soul and other souls as a potter in the five towns would shape and decorate a Spode tureen. Had the *Timaeus'* speaker been the pithy Socrates and not the Pythagorean from Locri, these mundane overtones might have survived. Even so, Plato himself also refers to the Demiurge as God, or the god (*ho theos*) — to distinguish him from the lesser gods, his sons (30a, b, d, 31b, 32b, 34a, 55c, 56c, 69b, 73b), and as "father" and "begetter" (28c, 37c, 41a). And thus Plato's artificer was taken to signify the supreme source of all being, and his humble cosmic craftsman became the Hebrews' architect of the worlds.[31] In turn the act of creation became an act of God's will, an act, moreover, that occurred in time, or, more accurately, began time. Ancient Platonist commentators, with a few exceptions that included the influential Plutarch of Chaeronea, had interpreted Plato to be portraying the world as eternal, like his pupil Aristotle.[32] The primary task for any

---

30. Liddell and Scott also note that *dêmiourgos* could also signify a magistrate in many Greek states. In antiquity the Platonic *dêmiourgos* itself was variously interpreted; see A.-J. Festugière, *La révélation d'Hermès Trismégiste*, 4 vols. (Paris, 1945–1954), 4: 275–292.

31. See especially J. Moreau, " 'Opifex, id est Creator': remarques sur le platonisme de Chartres," *Archives für Geschichte der Philosophie*, 56 (1974): 33–49. This is precisely the situation also in the *Corpus Hermeticum*, especially in the first treatise, where the *Timaeus* is obviously the source of much of the imagery and argumentation; see Festugière, *Révélation*, 2: 92–152. The impact of the *Corpus Hermeticum* on Ficino's conception of the *Timaeus* is yet to be explored, but was limited, I believe, to his earlier years as a scholar and superseded by the authority of Proclus.

Note that it became customary for the later Neoplatonists to distinguish between "the creator" and "the father" (*poiêtên kai patera*) of 28c3; see, for example, Proclus, *In Timaeum* I. 303.27ff. (ed. Diehl, 3 vols. [Leipzig, 1903–1906]).

32. Ficino praises Plutarch, Atticus, and Severus for contending that the world's creation took place in, or with, time in chapter 13 of his *Timaeus* commentary (*Opera omnia*, 2: 1443.3; cf. 1594.1). He could take ironical pleasure in the fact that Aristotle, in his *De caelo* 280a28–32, 283a2ff. and in his *Physics* 251b17, had claimed that Plato believed in the world's temporal generation, though he had censured him for it. Later Platonists on the other hand (with a few exceptions) had themselves censured Aristotle for misunderstanding Plato's position. Ficino's major source here was Proclus' *Timaeus* commentary I. 275.3–339.2 (ed. Diehl) where Plutarch's views are discussed at 1. 276.30ff., 286.20–289.6, the views of Atticus at 1.276.30ff., 283.30–285.7, 286.20–289.6, and the views of Severus at 1. 289.6–290.3. The three thinkers are aligned at 3. 212.8–9. For Aristotle's influential views on the *Timaeus*, see Claghorn's study cited above.

Christian commentator on the *Timaeus* was to demonstrate the opposite, and he could exploit the ambiguities in Plato's formulation of the myth; for it appears to depict a moment when the Demiurge gazed up at the eternal realities before he took the clay of spiritual matter to mould it to their various forms. Nevertheless, the conception of a supreme Creator exercising the supreme act of His unconditioned Will brings with it from the Hebrew tradition the parallel conception of a linear time that is quite foreign to the cyclical conceptions familiar to Plato and his contemporaries and championed by Aristotle.

A third difficulty for the Chartreans was Plato's declaration that the created world is "like" the Demiurge and endowed therefore with intelligence (*nous*) and also, "since intelligence cannot be present in anything devoid of soul," with soul (29e–30c); for the world came into being as "a living creature truly endowed with both soul and intelligence." To view the whole of creation as "a living creature" is to postulate a World Soul (and possibly a World Spirit) that transcends all individual souls as the body of the material cosmos transcends any one body within it. Obviously Plato did not mean simply a soul for the earth alone (though elsewhere, Ficino maintains, he entertained this intriguing hypothesis),[33] but a soul for the whole cosmos. This cosmic soul would necessarily include all individual souls — the higher souls of the celestial spheres, the demon souls in the trains of the planetary gods, the souls of mortal men, and even the irrational souls of brutes. At the same time, he was just as obviously referring to an individual, single soul and not to the genre soul or to a hypostasis Soul, soul in the abstract; and this individual soul, even more patently so than the Demiurge, was below the Ideas, a created, not a self-creating, entity. Accommodating such a universal soul-being into the conceptual system of Christianity was no easy matter. Some accepted it at face value and tried to adjust their metaphysical schemes accordingly; others identified it with the concept of Nature; others went so far as to see it as an adumbration of the concept of the Holy Ghost; and at one point in his career William of Conches actually argued for its identification with the third person of the Trinity as did apparently his contemporary Abelard.[34] Still others rejected it altogether as an error of animism

---

33. See my *The Platonism of Marsilio Ficino* (Los Angeles, 1984), 140–141.

34. William seems to have entertained this identification in his glosses on Boethius and in the first, but not the final, version of his glosses on the *Timaeus*. See Gregory, *Anima Mundi*, 17, 37, 133–151; also Garin, *Platonismo medievale*, 82–84.

or pantheism. Most seem to have accorded it a kind of half-belief, since it was conducive to an appreciation of the spirituality of nature if not of matter itself and helped to explain miraculous, magical and supernatural events and phenomena that would otherwise have defied explanation. Interest in the World Soul attained its medieval apogee with William's speculations in his *glosae* on the *Timaeus*.[35] Thereafter, awareness of the difficulties attending the concept increased and it was not to enjoy a thorough revival until Ficino's own speculative work in the second half of the fifteenth century, work which in turn influenced a host of magi, alchemists, astrologers, Paracelsian doctors, mystical mathematicians, theosophists, and occultists throughout the later Renaissance, including, significantly, cosmologists and chemists now recognized among the fathers of modern science.[36]

Finally, of the major difficulties, there was the problem posed by the *Timaeus'* statement that the Demiurge put his sons, "the younger gods," in charge of completing the material creation, including the task of supplying bodies for the souls inferior to themselves, those sown in the planets and the moon as well as those sown on earth. To Christians the myth implied that the angels had a vital role in the act of creation; and it was difficult to align it with the Genesis account of God Himself creating Adam from the dust of the earth and Eve from Adam's rib, where no younger god or angel is present to assist Him. Indeed the angels are no less contingent on His Will than the lower creatures, and traditionally played no role in the creation. On the other hand, Christians had always regarded them as the instruments of God's providence once creation had occurred; and Plato's myth could be adjusted to signify the guardian, not the creative, roles of the Demiurge's sons. This was an inevitable consequence of identifying the Demiurge with God and the sublime Ideas with His thoughts.

Thus the Christian commentators of the twelfth century were able to accommodate the major discrepancies between the *Timaeus* and Genesis ac-

35. Gregory, *Anima Mundi*, chap. 3 passim; also Chenu, 118–128.

36. There is no comprehensive study of Renaissance conceptions of the World Soul, but see: D. P. Walker, *Spiritual and Demonic Magic: From Ficino to Campanella* (London, 1958; repr. Notre Dame, 1975), chaps. 1 and 2; F. A. Yates, *Giordano Bruno and the Hermetic Tradition* (London and Chicago, 1964), chap. 4 and passim; E. Garin, *Lo zodiaco della vita: La polemica sull'astrologia dal Trecento al Cinquecento* (Rome and Bari, 1976); and A. G. Debus, *The Chemical Philosophy: Paracelsian Science and Medicine in the Sixteenth and Seventeenth Centuries* (New York, 1977).

counts to their own satisfaction and in accordance with suggestions in the various Church Fathers and in Calcidius himself.[37] Such an accommodation was predicated on identifying Plato's Demiurge with the Creator God, even though this identification was bitterly opposed in some quarters as Gregory has observed.[38] Anyone with Ficino's acumen and learning would certainly have been aware of the many difficulties as well as the advantages of effecting a complete reconciliation between the two authoritative texts on the beginning of things, the one a divinely inspired revelation, the other the poetic vision of a philosopher drawing upon Pythagorean and Egyptian wisdom. Whatever his debts to Calcidius and to William of Conches' glosses, and perhaps to John of Salisbury, Plutarch and others, Ficino saw clearly that the dialogue needed further interpretation and that the figure of the Demiurge and his relationship to the universal Ideas required an analysis that was more truly Platonic than was possible to Calcidius or William. That the *Timaeus* had garnered such a harvest of Latin interest in the West, while most of the other dialogues had remained unknown or unread, was largely an accident caused by the survival of Calcidius' truncated translation and attendant commentary and of the fragments translated by Cicero. It did not mean that the dialogue had received a definitive reading or that the Latin commentators had penetrated to the heart of its labyrinthine metaphysics, however valuable their insights on particular issues raised in the sections available to them.

* * *

Did Ficino therefore reject the *interpretatio Christiana*, or, what amounts

37. Interestingly, there is some slight evidence that Calcidius may have been a Christian: he dedicated his commentary and translation to an "Ossius" whom most scholars have identified with the centenarian Bishop of Cordova (c. 256–357/8 A.D.), an influential advisor to Constantine who played a major role at the councils of Nicaea and Sardica (Waszink however challenges this identification on pp. ix–xv); and he quotes the Hebraei 7 times, the Scriptures 4 times, Moses, Symmachus, and Solomon twice each, and Origen, Philo and the "Hebraica philosophia" once each. Ficino's allusion to him as "Platonicus noster" in a sermon on the Magi and their star (*Opera omnia*, 1: 489) may imply that he thought of him as a Christian, but I doubt it since he also uses "noster" of Plato.

38. *Anima Mundi*, 115–121, and chaps. 3 and 4 *passim*; also his *Platonismo medievale*, 53–150. See also Chenu, 112ff. The controversy echoed the earlier debate among the Fathers over the same problem; see H. A. Wolfson, "Plato's Preexistent Matter in Patristic Philosophy," in *The Classical Tradition: Literary and Historical Studies in Honor of Harry Caplan*, ed. L. Wallach (Ithaca, New York, 1966), 409–420.

to the same thing, the Christian view of the nature and function of the Timaean Demiurge?

So far as I know, only one scholar has spoken directly to Ficino's attitude on this matter. In an illuminating article on the Renaissance understanding of the notion of "creating" as contrasted with merely "making," and on the vital links between Ficino and his older friend but disciple, Cristoforo Landino, Professor E. N. Tigerstedt briefly examines Ficino's views on the *Timaeus* and concludes that he rejected the Christian interpretation, though he finds this an odd and unexpected turn of events. He writes, "In the long introduction to his translation, he [Ficino] explicitly discusses the Demiurge and his work and comes to the reluctant conclusion that he is not the Christian God and his work not the biblical creation"; and a couple of paragraphs later he refers to Ficino's "repudiation" of the *interpretatio Christiana*.[39] By the "long introduction" he means the *Timaeus* commentary in its first extant version as it appeared in the Plato editions of 1484 and 1491.

Should Tigerstedt be correct, we have an anomalous situation: if Ficino rejected the belief that the *Timaeus* contained Mosaic, or at least quasi Mosaic, truths, it would be tantamount to his rejecting one of Plato's most revered and traditionally authoritative texts, a text that had mingled "theological" with "physical" matters in the "marvellous manner" Plato deployed in his other great dialogues, the *Parmenides, Philebus, Symposium, Phaedrus*, and *Republic*; for these were the works in which Ficino was assured of the presence of sublime mysteries and the secrets of highest theology, and upon which he had based his entire apologetic program to win intelligent men over to the Christian faith and to the service of Catholic orthodoxy. It would be bizarre if the *Timaeus*, which Ficino always associated with these dialogues and had singled out for extensive commentary, turned out to be the sole masterpiece where Plato had failed to adumbrate Christian truths and had been led astray by a Pythagorean master.[40] Tigerstedt duly acknowledges this potential contradiction when he suggests that it must have been "a hard thing" for Ficino publicly to accept that "the Christian and Mosaic truth is lacking" in one of the principal works of "his beloved Plato, whom he usually tries to Christianize."

39. "The Poet as Creator: Origins of a Metaphor," *Comparative Literature Studies*, 5 (1968): 455–488, at 460–461.

40. Apuleius, *De Platone et eius dogmate*, 1. 3, insists on Plato's dependence on the Pythagoreans; and the view became a Neoplatonic commonplace.

As our starting point, let us take up his observation that "the Christian and Mosaic truth is lacking"; for Tigerstedt is quoting from the opening sentence of chapter ten of Ficino's own *Timaeus* commentary. In the 1576 Basel edition of Ficino's *Opera omnia*, the edition in general use today, the sentence reads very differently however: "Thus the Christian and Mosaic truth abides (*manet*)." Tigerstedt rejects *manet* as a corruption and refers us to the sentence as it appears in the earlier, and often more authoritative, texts of the commentary in Ficino's *Platonis opera omnia* editions of 1484 and 1491. There, he claims, Ficino wrote *mancat* meaning "is lacking": *Mancat ergo christiana et mosayca veritas*.[41] First we must remind ourselves that classical Latin has no such verb as *mancare* and that Tigerstedt is almost certainly thinking of the common Italian verb meaning indeed "to lack" or "to be insufficient." Hypothetically, we might grant Ficino a very late Latin form aping the vernacular verb, but this would run counter to the generally consistent classical, or at least humanist, Latinity of Ficino's style which eschews such late forms, particularly when alternative forms of unimpeachable Latinity are ready to hand, as is the case here, where he could have used *carere*, *egere* or even *deesse*.[42] Second, to my eyes the reading in the 1484 and 1491 editions, as also in the authoritative 1496 edition of the second extant version, is not *mancat* but merely the subjunctive form *maneat*.[43] For some preliminary support for this *maneat* reading, and since it is a matter of considerable import, let us turn to two passages in the *Timaeus* commentary where Ficino juxtaposes the Platonic with the Mosaic truth and deliberates on their compatibility.

In chapter 24 he considers the Demiurge's creation of the four elements according to the formula that the elements all exist in the Demiurge by way of their Ideas, in the World Soul by way of their reasons, in Nature

41. Pp. 460 and 479, note 34. Tigerstedt is quoting from a copy of the 1491 edition in the Royal Library, Stockholm.

42. There is a Latin adjective *mancus*, meaning "lame" or "crippled," from which derives the Italian adjective *manco*, meaning "left-handed" or "ominous," and thence a noun meaning "lack" or "defect," and thence, finally, the common verb *mancare*. In his *Glossarium mediae et infimae Latinitatis*, Du Cange lists *mancare* in a minor entry as a synonym for the active verb *mutilare*, but records nothing that suggests that *mancat* in this late Latin sense could ever mean "is mutilated."

43. *Commentaria* (1496), f. 61v; *Platonis Opera* (1484), sig. et.iiir, col. 2; *Platonis Opera* (1491), f. 242v. col. 1 (sig. G2v). For the 1484 edition I have used the copy in the Huntington library in San Marino, California, and for the 1491 edition the copy in the Elmer Belt library at UCLA. Sebastiano Gentile has kindly confirmed for me that the Laurenziana's MS 82, 7, f. 170v, also has *maneat*. This is the most authoritative manuscript of Ficino's translation of the *Timaeus* as it appeared in the *Platonis Opera* of 1484.

by way of their seeds, in the heavens by way of their powers (*virtutes*), and in the subcelestial world by way of their forms. Accordingly, he argues, "all things exist in all things ... but each according to the capacity of the receiver." Thus the celestials exist in the elements "in an elementary way" while the elements exist in heaven "in a heavenly way." He concludes:

> There is agreement therefore between Moses and Plato—whom Numenius refers to as another Moses—for whereas Moses writes, "In the beginning God made heaven and earth," Plato writes, "First God made fire and earth"; for Plato means by "fire" the heavens, since from the outset he had been concerned with the centre and circumference of the world's sphere—this being his topic—and had introduced the [other] elements for their sake.[44]

In other words, Ficino is convinced that the *Timaeus* account of the creation of heaven and of earth can be brought directly into accord with the Genesis account. We should note in passing the reference to the Numenian dictum, one of numerous references to it in Ficino's oeuvre.[45] The Renaissance Platonists accepted it as valuable evidence for Plato's indebtedness, however tangentially, to the Hebrew scriptures, and for the notion that he was an Attic Moses purveying to the gentiles an essentially Mosaic wisdom.

Later in his commentary in chapter 41 Ficino considers the manner in which all souls, those of the gods, demons and men, along with the world spheres themselves and the universal species, "proceed" without intermediary causes directly from the divine intellect, the creator (*opifex*) of the world. He writes,

> You will observe that when Plato declares that God rested in His own nature (*habitu*) when He issued His commands, but that His ministers followed after Him, it is because nothing of mutability

44. *Commentaria*, f. 66v (= *Opera omnia*, 2: 1449): "Concludemus denique concordiam inter Mosem et Platonem, quem Numenius alterum cognominat Mosem. Quod enim Moses ait: In principio fecit Deus celum et terram [Genesis 1.1], Plato ait: Deus primo ignem fecit et terram [Timaeus 31b6–7], ignem intelligens precipue celum. Principio enim in sphera mundi centrum consideravit et ambitum, reliqua horum gratia interiecit." Ficino surely had in mind Augustine's almost identical argumentation in his *De civitate Dei* VIII. 11.

45. Ficino is recalling Numenius' description of Plato as "a Moses speaking Attic Greek" (*apud* Clement of Alexandria, *Stromateis* 1.22; cf. Eusebius, *Praeparatio evangelica* 9.6.411a). He refers to this witticism on numerous occasions, e.g. *Opera omnia*, 1: 29, 394, 866.3.

can exist in God even while He rules over and moves things that move, whereas in His ministers His providence comes closer to a certain changeableness. Throughout this argument you can therefore see, in a marvellous way, that Plato is confirming God's statement in Moses, "I am who am."[46]

The equation of the God of Genesis with the Timaean Demiurge is here made quite explicit and Ficino sees Plato as providing us with a "marvellous" confirmation of the Mosaic truth.

This evidence alone justifies us in assuming that for Ficino the Mosaic truth "abided" in the *Timaeus* and that he did in general align himself with the *interpretatio Christiana* of the dialogue, as we might have anticipated for a variety of reasons. His interpretation of this work was all of a piece with his interpretation of its companion dialogues and does not constitute, as Tigerstedt would have us believe, an exception, an exception that would be inexplicable given Ficino's lifetime assumptions concerning Plato, and given the fervor and consistency with which he pursued his apologetic goals.

* * *

Nevertheless, while the testimony of chapters 24 and 41 confirms the *maneat/manet* readings for the opening of chapter 10 and indicates the broad direction of Ficino's commitment to discovering Mosaic truths in the *Timaeus*, further, more fundamental questions arise directly we seek confirmation of Ficino's claim that it is not only the Mosaic truth but the Christian truth which also "abides" there. For whereas the two truths are one with regard to the mystery of the world's creation, they are somewhat different, though not from a Christian viewpoint opposed, with regard to their definitions of the Creator Himself. While one might legitimately maintain that Plato's work served to confirm the Mosaic account

---

46. *Commentaria*, f. 77r (= *Opera omnia*, 2: 1463): "Notabis insuper ubi ait Deum in suo habitu permanere dum mandat, ministros autem sequi, nihil mutabilitatis in Deo esse dum mobilia regit et movet, in ministris autem eius providentiam esse mutationi cuidam propinquiorem. Denique in his omnibus Mosaicum illud: Ego sum qui sum [Exodus 3.14], cognosces mirifice confirmatum." In the *Commentaria* the chapter is misnumbered 40; see note 4 above. For his last point Ficino was surely again indebted to Augustine's *De civitate Dei* VIII. 11, since Augustine testifies that it was Plato's adherence to the truth of this Mosaic dictum that had impressed him most and almost convinced him that Plato could not have been "unacquainted with the sacred books."

of creation, it was impossible for any knowledgeable interpreter to believe that Plato had arrived at a perfect understanding of the Christian
Creator. On this issue Ficino advanced into speculative territory in his
Timaeus commentary that had been left inadequately explored by William or his contemporaries and that was undoubtedly opened up for him
by his careful study, I believe, of the works of Proclus, and in particular
of the huge *Timaeus* commentary,[47] a work that was unknown to or at
any rate inaccessible to the school of Chartres.[48] Though extant only up
to the commentary on 44d, and in Ficino's defective manuscript up to
that on 35b,[49] it provided him with the panoply of ancient Neoplatonic
interpretation of the dialogue. He turned to it as frequently as he turned
to Proclus' monumental *Theologia Platonica* and to his great commentary
on the *Parmenides.*[50] He was in a unique position, moreover, to draw upon
these sources. Only two or three other scholars in the West possessed
the mastery of the terminology and distinctions of later Neoplatonic discourse to be able to read Proclus with confidence and comprehension;

47. There is a fine French translation by A.-J. Festugière entitled *Proclus: Commentaire sur le
Timée,* 5 vols. (Paris, 1966–1968) and based on Diehl's text. For a study of its cosmogony, see
Baltes, *Weltentstehung,* vol. 2 *passim.*

48. We do, however, have fragments of a Latin translation by the thirteenth-century Dominican William of Moerbeke which correspond in Diehl's edition, volume 2, to 207.21–212.28;
214.13–16; 219.2–11; 236.20–28; 241.28–31; 242.24–243.1; 243.29–253.16; and 253.26–257.9.
They have been edited by G. Verbeke, "Guillaume de Moerbeke, traducteur de Proclus," *Revue
philosophique de Louvain,* 51 (1953): 358–373.

49. In his "Platonismus und Textüberlieferung," in *Griechische Kodikologie und Textüberlieferung,*
ed. D. Harlfinger (Darmstadt, 1980), 556, Professor Martin Sicherl observes that Ficino's exemplar was the Riccardiana's MS gr. 24 which breaks off in the middle of the third book (ed. Diehl,
2: 169.4; cf. 1: xi). It contains scholia in Greek and Latin, but only the most important Greek
scholia were edited by Diehl in the first volume of his edition, pp. 459–474.

We are now in a position to recognize that Proclus did in fact complete his commentary; see
Festugière, *Proclus: Commentaire sur le Timée,* 1: 10–11. Calcidius' commentary goes as far as 53c3
where Ficino stopped his formal commentary too. When it came to adding the *annotationes et
summae capitum* for 53c4–92c, he was therefore on his own. This was a pressing reason surely
for embarking on his new *Timaeus* translation, if not the commentary itself; for his predecessors
in the Middle Ages had known the dialogue by less than half its total length.

50. See my "Ficino's Theory of the Five Substances and the Neoplatonists' *Parmenides,*" *Journal
of Medieval and Renaissance Studies,* 12 (1983): 19–44, especially 32–42; also F. Joukovsky, "Plotin
dans les éditions et les commentaires de Porphyre, Jamblique et Proclus à la Renaissance," *Bibliothèque d'Humanisme et Renaissance,* 42 (1980), 395–398. Ficino borrowed the title of his own *magnum opus* from Proclus' *Theologia Platonica.*

On the evidence of a letter to Uranius written in the August of 1492 (*Opera omnia* 1: 937),
it seems that Ficino only became familiar with Proclus' long commentary on the *Republic* quite
late in his studies. The manuscript he consulted has been identified as the Laurenziana's MS 80,
9 and it contains only the first twelve of Proclus' sixteen treatises.

and none besides himself possessed the scholarly dedication and energy, and had the specific occasion, to devote to a sustained study of what will always remain an excessively difficult, highly technical product of the pagan scholasticism of the fifth century.[51]

Many intricate problems of elucidation and indebtedness arise at every turn, and I wish merely to establish the Proclean connection. In order to do so, let me turn to the opening chapters of Ficino's commentary, those that lead up to the observation that the truth "abides" in the *Timaeus,* and survey the grounds of Ficino's approach.

The first chapter follows Proclus in linking the *Timaeus* to the *Parmenides.* In antiquity the two dialogues together served as the second, the climactic, part of the Neoplatonists' teaching cycle.[52] Both works, Ficino and Proclus argue, are Pythagorean in inspiration:[53] and their interlocutors are Pythagoreans, not Socrates, nor, as is the case in the *Laws* and *Letters,* Plato himself.[54] Hence for Ficino they embody a serious playfulness that is midway between the games of Socrates and the certainties that Plato himself occasionally voiced. They are concerned in other words with what Ficino viewed as probabilities, opinions that Plato did not necessarily accept in their entirety or at face value, but that went beyond the scientific knowledge of the Heracliteans, and later of the Aristotelians, and beyond the ethical and political wisdom of Socrates, insofar as they treated of the highest mysteries of theology under the veil of allegorical and figurative language.[55]

Ficino also follows Proclus in subordinating the *Timaeus,* along with all the other works of Plato, to the authority of the *Parmenides* — from

---

51. The eminent Proclus scholar, Father H. D. Saffrey, has paid tribute to Ficino's mastery of the Athenian scholastic in his "Notes platoniciennes de Marsile Ficin dans un manuscrit de Proclus, cod. Riccardianus 70," *Bibliothèque d'Humanisme et Renaissance,* 21 (1959): 161–184, at 180–181.

52. For this cycle see L. G. Westerink, *Anonymous Prolegomena to Platonic Philosophy* (Amsterdam, 1962), xxxvii–xxxviii; also B. D. Larsen, *Jamblique de Chalcis: Exégète et philosophe* (Aarhus, 1972), 333–334, and, for Iamblichus' views on the *Timaeus* and its centrality in the Plato canon (to which Proclus was apparently deeply indebted), 390–418.

53. Proclus begins his *Timaeus* commentary by turning to the Pythagoreans, assuming that Plato adopted their theory of divine causality (ed. Diehl, 1: 1.25ff; cf. 1: 15.23–18.28). Thereafter they are continually invoked, as they had been, Larsen argues, by Iamblichus.

54. See the preface to Ficino's Plato translations, reprinted in his *Opera omnia,* 1: 766.2; also Ficino's *Theologia Platonica* 17. 4 (ed. Marcel, 3: 168–169).

55. See my "Marsilio Ficino on Plato's Pythagorean Eye," *Modern Language Notes,* 97 (1982): 171–182 at 174–177.

Proclus' viewpoint Plato's supreme achievement in metaphysics and the one dialogue that could always be called upon to shed light on Plato's meanings and intentions in any other work.[56] Throughout, Ficino sub-scribes to the principle of complementarity. In the opening sentence of his initial chapter, he asserts that

> just as Plato includes in the *Parmenides*, to the extent that he can, all the classes of things divine, so he embraces in the *Timaeus* every-thing in the realm of nature; and in each dialogue he is principally a Pythagorean speaking a Pythagorean part; . . . for things divine are the principles and exemplars of things natural, and things natur-al are the effects and images of things divine.[57]

Accordingly, Ficino continues, when Plato treats in the *Parmenides* of things divine, he will in the process (*interim*) "descend" to things natural; cor-respondingly, when he treats of things natural in the *Timaeus*, frequently he "rises" to things divine. This Platonic union of "divinity" with "na-ture" is fully justified since nature is divinity's "instrument." The subject of the *Timaeus* is "universal nature herself"—defined here, again follow-ing Proclus, as a "certain seminary, a life-giving power infused through the whole world and subject to the World Soul, though ruling herself over matter and giving birth to individual things according to the same order as they are conceived by Soul."[58] From the onset Ficino warns us, however, that nature is not the sole theme. The dialogue also treats of things divine in the course of its examination of things natural, and when it does so we must align it with the *Parmenides* and the metaphysics enun-ciated therein.

This link with the *Parmenides*, which from Ficino's standpoint is ab-

---

56. For the preeminence of the *Parmenides* in Proclus' system, see H. D. Saffrey and L. G. Wester-ink, *Proclus: Théologie Platonicienne*, 4 vols. so far, 6 planned (Paris, 1968–), 1: lxxiii–lxxv; also Saffrey, "Notes platoniciennes," 168–169. On the subordinate preeminence of the *Timaeus*, see Proclus' *Timaeus* Commentary 1. 13.4–14.2 (ed. Diehl); also Larsen, 377.

57. *Commentaria*, f. 59r (= *Opera omnia*, 2: 1438): "Quemadmodum in Parmenide cuncta divino-rum genera pro viribus comprehendit, sic omnia in Timeo complectitur naturalia, et utrobique plurimum Pythagoricus est sub persona Pythagorica disputans. . . . Quoniam vero divina quidem naturalium principia et exemplaria sunt, naturalia vero divinorum effectus atque imagines."

58. *Ibid.*: "ipsa universi natura, id est seminaria quedam et vivifica virtus toti infusa mundo, anime quidem mundane subdita, materie vero presidens eodemque ordine singula pariens quo et anima ipsa concepit;" cf. the prologue to Proclus' *Timaeus* commentary (ed. Diehl, 1: 10.10–21; 1: 11.9–20).

solutely critical, was unappreciated by the Middle Ages; necessarily so, given its unfamiliarity with the full text of the *Parmenides*[59] or with the extent of Proclus' views on that dialogue's supremacy. It was now to be renewed if the *Timaeus* was to be understood correctly by Ficino's Florentine contemporaries. Of immediate interest is Ficino's importation of Proclus' elaborate metaphysical schemata, which he derived with remarkable scholarly insight and skill from the *Timaeus* and *Parmenides* commentaries, into his analysis of Plato's book on the world and on nature; an importation that renders his own *Timaeus* commentary, or at least large portions of it, markedly different in its working presuppositions from the *tractatus* of Calcidius or the *glosae* of William.[60]

The foundations for this importation are laid out in the next few chapters where Ficino seems to be following pretty closely the prologue Proclus wrote for his commentary. While chapters three to six deal with the dialogue's recapitulation of the *Republic* at 17a–19b, with the prefatory story of the Atlantids at 19b–27b, and with the nature of prayer at 27b–d,[61] chapters two, seven and eight set forth the doctrine of the three transcendent causes or principles of creation: the efficient, exemplary and final, indentified respectively with the divine power, the divine understanding and the divine will. Here Ficino is glossing the *Timaeus* 28a4–6 and is very much dependent on Proclus' analyses.[62] For Proclus interprets Plato to be referring to the efficient cause at 27d5–28c5; to the exemplary cause at 28c5–29d6; and to the final cause, that is, to the Good, at 29d7–30b6. The doctrine of the three true causes, as contrasted to the two accessory

59. A part of the dialogue, we recall, appeared in Proclus' *Parmenides* commentary, which Moerbeke had translated into Latin. See volume 3 of the *Plato Latinus* cited in note 7 above.

60. Any future edition will have to determine the extent of these various debts to Proclus as well as to comments on the *Timaeus* in Aristotle, Plutarch, Plotinus, Porphyry, Iamblichus, Macrobius, Origen, Augustine, and sundry medieval commentators including William of Conches. It will have to assess Ficino's use of the summary material in Albinus, Apuleius, and Diogenes Laertius; and his use, if any, of the *De mundo* attributed to Timaeus Locrus. It will have to look to the influence of Galen and the Galenic tradition, and to the conceivable, though unlikely, possibility that Ficino was acquainted with a *Timaeus* commentary written by the Byzantine Psellus in the eleventh century. Finally, it will have to chart the varying debts to Calcidius. In all, an ophidian labour for some infant Hercules of scholarship.

61. Proclus' prologue, again perhaps following Iamblichus, argues that the *Timaeus*' recapitulations of both the *Republic* and the Atlantis story are likewise concerned with the science of nature and the world, the dialogue's overriding theme. See 1: 29.31–30.30, 53.24–55.26 for the *Republic* resumé, and 1: 77.24–80.8 for the Atlantis story. For Proclus' commentary on the section on prayer and its influence on Ficino's sixth chapter, see, briefly, Joukovsky, 398.

62. Ed. Diehl, 1: 2.1ff.; 2.29ff.; 17.17ff.

causes of form and matter, the Neoplatonists derived in the first place
from their interpretation of Plato's *Second Letter* at 312e. But they then
read it into the *Timaeus'* reference at 68e–69a to "divine" (as contrasted
with "necessary") causes,[63] or to what Proclus refers to in his prologue
as "first," "sovereign," and "primordial" causes.[64] In his second chapter
Ficino refers to them as "external causes" (*extrinsecus principia*). All things
ultimately depend on these "external" causes more than they depend on
the two "internal" causes of form and matter. But two of the external
causes are themselves subordinate to the final cause, the Good; for, writes
Ficino in chapter eight, "the One itself and the Good is above all essence
and intellect and is the cause of both," the One and the Good being identical as Plato proves "in the *Republic* book VI, in the *Parmenides* and in
the *Sophist*."[65] Thus Plato's book of nature is necessarily a study of divine causality, a study, that is, of the Pythagoreans' three "primordial"
causes. Again Ficino is following Proclus in supposing not only that the
Timaeus has a Pythagorean speaker and is therefore the vehicle for
Pythagorean metaphysics — the Pythagoreans being the original formula-
tors of the three causes doctrine — but that Plato was articulating their
views, and not his own, throughout the dialogue.[66] Once more, we
should recall that Calcidius did not begin his commentary until 31c and
thus omitted all direct consideration of this section of the dialogue deemed
so important by the Neoplatonists for its Pythagorean matter, matter which
Ficino in turn regarded as the lifeblood of Platonism itself.

Finally in the ninth and tenth chapters Ficino outlines the metaphysical
system he saw embedded in the *Timaeus* by drawing upon Proclus' entities and distinctions. They are two particularly revealing chapters for us
since they bracket the summary sentence *maneat ergo christiana et mosayca
veritas*. In chapter nine he begins by considering the status of matter, which
from our modern viewpoint the *Timaeus* assumes has been generated already

---

63. For the actual origins of Proclus' doctrine of the three causes, see W. Theiler, *Die Vor-
bereitung des Neuplatonismus* (Berlin, 1930), 17–34.

64. Ed. Diehl, 1:1.23–24 (*archêgikôn*); 2.4 (*kuriôteron*); 3.3 (*prôtourgous*); at 3.12 he refers to
them as "true" causes. Cf. Dodds' commentary on proposition 75 in his edition of Proclus' *Elements of Theology*, 240ff., where he refers us also to Proclus' *Parmenides* commentary 1059.11ff.

65. *Commentaria*, f. 61v (= *Opera omnia*, 2: 1441): "Proinde unum ipsum atque bonum esse
super essentiam omnem et intellectum, atque esse causam utriusque in sexto Reipublice atque
in Parmenide et Sofista evidenter ostendit."

66. See Proclus' *Timaeus* commentary, 1. 2.29ff. (ed. Diehl); also Ficino's letter to Cavalcanti
cited in note 17 above.

and been subjected to the world's architect for him to fabricate the world. Such matter had long been the subject of controversy, and Ficino asks,

> Now is God, the author of the world, the same as the producer (*effector*) of matter? The school of Ammonius and Origen[67] will respond that they are indeed one and the same person. They will contend that in the *Parmenides* Plato treats of matter as something received from God, but that in the *Timaeus* he is thinking of it as something that had being, as it were, before it had well-being; for Plato supposes it to receive well-being from the same divinity who had already granted it being. On the other hand, the general school of Platonists will reply to the contrary. They will contend that the god who made matter and the god who subsequently formed it were not one and the same. Matter they will argue exists from the highest Good, but is subsequently formed by intellect and then moved by soul. Or, to be more exact, the three states, first of existing, then of being formed, and finally of being moved, all derive from the first Good; but the state of existing derives from the first alone, that of being formed from the first Good by way of intellect, and that of being moved (that is, of moving and of being formed as the result of motion) derives from the first Good by way of intellect and soul together.[68]

The predictable analogy here is with the potter, his wheel and his "comb" (*pecten*).

67. Ficino assumed that Ammonius [Saccas] was the teacher of Plotinus and the Christian Origen, and that Ammonius himself was a Christian (*Opera omnia*, 2: 1621.2 and 1663.3). Porphyry (apud Eusebius, *Historia ecclesiastica*, 6. 19. 7) affirms that Ammonius had been born and nurtured a Christian but had then been converted to philosophy. Ficino probably knew this reference at first hand; if so, he would also know that Eusebius had rejected the notion that Ammonius had renounced Christianity as perfidious Porphyrian propaganda. Here he supposes, with Eusebius, that Ammonius and Origen were in agreement over and against Plotinus and a majority of his followers.

68. *Commentaria*, f. 61v (= *Opera omnia*, 2: 1441): "Sed nunquid Deus mundi auctor idem et materie est effector? Respondebit hic Ammonii et Origenis scola eundem esse; et in Parmenide quidem tractari quemadmodum materia esse a Deo accipit, in Timeo vero qua ratione ab eodem accipit bene esse prius autem quodammodo esse quam bene esse excogitari. Respondebit aliter communis Platonicorum scola non eundem esse Deum qui materiam facit et qui format proxime; immo materiam a summo quidem bono esse, ab intellectu vero formari, ab anima postremo moveri; immo vero omnia hec a primo, sed esse a primo tantum, formari a primo per intellectum, moveri et movendo formari mobiliter a primo per intellectum simul et animam." Cf. *Opera omnia*, 1: 492–493.

The crux of Ficino's argument, which goes well beyond the suppositions in Calcidius' long final section on matter, turns on the logic that proximate to the One there must exist a realm that is superlatively united, proximate to the Good a realm that is superlatively good. Because of the complexity, opposing qualities, diverse effects, and deformity of its material body, our world is neither superlatively united nor superlatively good. Accordingly, the majority of Platonists postulate another realm emanating directly from the divine unity and goodness: this is an intelligible and intellectual realm, not a visible, and it possesses all the models for the products of the visible world. This higher realm, says Ficino, the Platonists call "the divine intellect but not the Good itself: it is the eminently good son of the Good."[69]

It is here that he inserts a significant qualification: "If we understand that this intellect or son is of one substance with what precedes it (i.e. the Good), then we shall be bringing Plato into accord more with Christian theology. However, the rest of Plato's interpreters will object."[70] Elsewhere I have examined this passage in the light of other trinitarian analyses in Ficino's works, and most pertinently that of Plato's Second Letter 312e.[71] Suffice it to say that Ficino moved circumspectly. He was willing to entertain, and indeed to promote, the notion that Plato had dimly perceived the mystery of the Trinity and that a Christian interpreter could turn to the dialogues and find material susceptible of an orthodox reading. Nonetheless, Plato had not been able to arrive at the full light of the orthodox vision of the Three-in-One and in this respect his Neoplatonic successors were correct in extracting a subordinationist metaphysical system from his works. As the second hypostasis, Mind or Intellect (*Nous*) is subordinate to the prime hypostasis, the One: as the son of the Good it has emanated from, and is therefore ontologically subsequent to, the Good, different from it in kind and therefore in substance. To regard Mind as consubstantial with the prime hypostasis is to adopt the orthodox Catholic view of the Son's relationship to the Father as determined

---

69. *Commentaria*, f. 61v (= *Opera omnia*, 2: 1442): "[Mundus alter] quem quidem divinum intellectum nominant, non ipsum bonum, sed optimum boni filium."

70. *Ibid.*: "Quem [intellectum] si unius cum primo substantie esse intelligamus, Platonem Christiane theologie magis conciliabimus, sed coeteri Platonis interpretes reclamabunt."

71. "Marsilio Ficino on Plato, the Neoplatonists and the Christian Doctrine of the Trinity," *RQ*, 37 (1984): 555–584.

and defined by the councils of Nicaea and Constantinople. This approach Ficino regarded as a justifiable adaptation of Plato, one that Plato himself, had he lived to see the coming of the Saviour, would certainly have embraced as the ultimate truth. But such an approach did not reflect Plato's own intentions as the Neoplatonists, the "general school" of his interpreters, had accurately grasped; and insofar as Plato's metaphysics was subordinationist, Ficino could see that it anticipated the theological position of Arius and his followers, who, like Plato, were to deny the consubstantiality of Son and Father. In brief, surprising as it may first appear, Ficino seems quite prepared to acknowledge the "Arian" cast of Plato's metaphysics and to accept this as a major limitation in accommodating him to Christianity. It constitutes a notable confession on the part of Plato's most enthusiastic and distinguished Renaissance apologist.

It is at this juncture that Ficino pens the sentence that Tigerstedt misread. But we must now concern ourselves with the sentence following, for it has a crucial bearing on our understanding both of Ficino's intentions in writing a *Timaeus* commentary and of the limitations of his debt to Proclus as well as more obviously to Calcidius and to the commentators who took Calcidius as their guide. It reads: "Meanwhile, and since it corresponds to the view of the majority of Plato's interpreters, let us suppose that Plato or Pythagoras opined that between the visible world and the Good itself there exists an intelligible world which is an image of the Good but is the model itself for the corporeal world."[72] If we ignore the fact that in all the editions *Manet ergo* inaugurates a new chapter (with a heading moreover that reinforces the division), then the function of the *ergo* and the significance of Ficino's choice of the subjunctive in the text for the 1484, 1491 and 1496 editions at last become apparent. His line of argument runs: "If we follow Ammonius and Origen and argue that Intellect and the Good are of one substance, the rest of Plato's interpreters will object, but we will be reconciling Plato to a greater extent with Christian theology and the Christian and Mosaic truth may therefore abide. In the meanwhile, however, let us examine the view of the majority of Plato's interpreters who argue that Intellect and the Good are different in substance."

---

72. *Commentaria*, f. 61v (= *Opera omnia*, 2: 1442.2): "Ac interim si pluribus placet interpretum forsan fuerit hec vel Platonis opinio vel Pythagore intelligibilem mundum inter visibilem atque ipsum bonum esse medium, imaginem quidem boni, exemplar vero corporei mundi."

Accordingly, in chapter 10 Ficino proceeds to outline the metaphysical scheme of the five hypostases (the One and the Good being identified though treated separately on the grounds that they are the same in essence though formally distinguished): these five are, the One, Intellect, the World Soul, Nature and the corporeal World. The scheme itself is a variation on the familiar late Neoplatonic scheme, to which it is clearly indebted, of: the One, Intellect, Soul, Bodily Forms, and Matter; and it corresponds to the scheme Ficino put forward—among others, incidentally—in his *Symposium* commentary 2.3 and 7.13, and then adopted throughout his long *Parmenides* commentary, his major treatment of the subject.[73] Matter itself, as chapters eleven to fourteen will make clear, is not for Ficino an ontological category, for two reasons. If we think of it, he says, in the Pythagorean manner, as Plato does in his *Philebus,* as "the infinite," then it is one element in the pairing "the infinite, the limit" which defines every level below the One. But if we restrict the term "matter" to mean the "prime unformed material" of things, then we can see that Plato's *Timaeus* rejects the thesis that such prime matter "is equal to the world's maker," and even rejects the thesis—though here Ficino stood on shakier ground—that such matter exists before the creation of the world, that it came before the world "in any temporal way," even though, from the standpoint of someone considering the logic of events accompanying the creation, it can be said to have preceded the creation.[74] As a corollary, Ficino defends Plato's decision to depict prime matter as "tossed prior to the world in an orderly manner" (*materiam ante mundum ordinate iactatam*) by taking him to mean that God had immediately ordered matter in order to prevent it from having any time to degenerate into complete disorder (*erraturam fuisse procul ab ordine quantum in se est nisi statim desuper ordinata fuisset*). And he deliberately avoids at this point any consideration of the poets' "chaos." In short, whether taken in the Pythagorean sense as "the infinite" or in the sense of "the prime unformed material," matter is "created" by God. In turn God creates the four realms

73. See Allen, "Ficino's Theory of the Five Substances," *passim.*
74. Cf. chapters 40 and 42 (*Commentaria,* ff. 77–8; i.e. *Opera omnia,* 2: 1463 and 1464, i.e. chapters 41 and 43). See Wolfson, "Plato's Pre-existent Matter" and also Ficino's own *Opera omnia,* 1: 492–493, where Ficino clearly distinguishes between "prime matter" (which pre-exists all form and even spatial extension) and "body" (which is such matter extended and ready to receive sundry forms).

of Intellect, Soul, Nature and Body by imposing the "limit" of His Ideas, and of their lower replicas or manifestations, on the "infinite" formlessness of that prime matter (and Ficino makes it quite plain in chapter 11 that what is to be Soul begins as "unformed" matter and only becomes Soul when formed in a particular way by God).[75]

* * *

In the light of this decision to go ahead anyway with an account of the metaphysics of the *Timaeus* as interpreted by the non-Christian majority of the Neoplatonists of antiquity, was Professor Tigerstedt perhaps correct after all in his contention that Ficino rejected the *interpretatio Christiana*, despite his slip with *maneat?*

I do not think so. To begin with, Ficino had always been wary of Proclus' scholasticism, and had objected on frequent occasions to what he considered the unnecessary multiplication of metaphysical entities and therefore of divinities in the Proclean system. In his opinion Proclus and his school had read much of Plato's text too literally and had been unable to deal satisfactorily with the allegorical and figurative dimensions of the master's thought. Proclus' account of the *Timaeus,* therefore, though useful and deserving of evaluation after the obscurity of a millennium, was not one that Ficino would be likely to adopt in its entirety or without considerable reservations. Though Ficino was always cognizant, furthermore, of the proto-Arian subordinationism of Plato's metaphysics in the opinion of the majority of interpreters, he seems not to have considered this a real obstacle or serious objection to harnessing Plato to the cause of Christian apologetics. This might even indicate on his part a tolerance for, if not a sympathy for, the Arian position itself or at least for those who entertained such a position prior to the time of the fourth-century councils which clarified the dogma of the Trinity. In this he was assuredly influenced by the subordinationist metaphysics of the great third-century Christian Platonist, Origen, whose work he deeply admired and whose reputation underwent a significant revival during the Renaissance and

75. On the original formlessness of all the hypostases below the One (and Ficino thinks of them as the primal "chaoses"), see my "Cosmogony and Love; the Role of Phaedrus in Ficino's *Symposium* Commentary," *Journal of Medieval and Renaissance Studies*, 10 (1980): 131–153 at 139–148 (an analysis of the *De amore* 1.3).

notably in Ficino's Florence;[76] even so, we must bear in mind that Ficino distinguishes Origen, and his putative teacher Ammonius, from the
rest of Plato's interpreters precisely over the issue of the Son's consubstantiality with the Father. I believe Ficino recognized and accepted the proto-
Arian metaphysics of the *Timaeus,* as of other dialogues, even as he was
assured that it contained Mosaic truths along with the truths of natural
science. While Calcidius and William might have helped him to comprehend its natural and Mosaic truths respectively, the Neoplatonists, pre-
eminently Proclus, were the only reliable guides to the intricacies of its
metaphysics;[77] often we hear him say that he would explore their views
at greater length "were I not afraid of prolixity on the one hand and of
novelty on the other."[78] Clearly, he was in search of a more "professional"
interpretation that could call upon the "wonderful insights of Iamblichus,
Syrianus and Proclus," while avoiding their errors of overliteralness and
elaboration and their postulation of too many classes of intermediate and,
from Ficino's standpoint, novel divinities. Their views had to be duly
weighed, since they alone possessed the keys to the *Timaeus'* metaphysics
and an understanding of the dialogue's special status in the Plato canon,
an understanding certainly denied to the medieval commentators and, it
would seem at least in part, to Calcidius before them.

The principal drawback to an accommodation with Christianity remained
the Demiurge, whom Proclus and the Neoplatonists had identified with
Intellect, the second hypostasis in the Plotinian ontological scheme. Here
the Mosaic account was superior in that it attributed the creation to God
alone, identified by the Christian Platonists with the One, not with Intellect, whom they identified with Angel in the abstract or with the highest
angels in particular, the seraphim.[79] But the *Timaeus* had depicted a "son"

76. See E. Wind, "The Revival of Origen," in *Studies in Art and Literature for Belle da Costa
Greene* (Princeton, 1954), 412–424; reissued in his *The Eloquence of Symbols: Studies in Humanist
Art,* ed. J. Anderson (Oxford, 1983), 42–55.

77. Tigerstedt's contention that "Plotinus was a deadly foe to any interpretation of the *Timaeus*
which made the Demiurge into a Jewish-Christian Creator" and that to him "the creation is an
eternal, timeless act . . . [and] not, as Christianity believes, a free, spontaneous act of the Divine
Will" (p. 461) is historically correct. But Ficino did not interpret Plotinus in this way, and I
question Tigerstedt's opinion that "it was doubtless Plotinus who is indicated by the 'Platonici
interpretes' who oppose the *interpretatio Christiana* of the Demiurge" (*ibid.*); rather the evidence
points, as we have seen, to Proclus, to his master Syrianus, and to their predecessor Iamblichus.

78. *Commentaria,* f. 65r (= *Opera omnia,* 2: 1447.2): "Preterea nisi vererer partim prolixitatem,
partim etiam novitatem, recenserem mira quedam Iamblici et Siriani Proclique commenta."

79. See Ficino's *Philebus* commentary 1. 26 (*Opera omnia,* 2: 1232).

as the creator even though it had identified this son with Intellect. It was the revelation of Christianity that had proclaimed the authentic Trinity and therefore the role of the second and third persons in the creation. Plato had correctly perceived that a "son" would create the world even though he had misidentified this "son"; for it was impossible for him to be able to perceive the ultimate mystery of the Son's relationship to the Father, or how the One in its threefold unity could be Father and Son, could be transcendent and yet the God of creation.

Nevertheless, Plato's creation book had come very close indeed to the ultimate Christian mystery, and would not lead us astray if we took Genesis as our guide to interpreting the true significance of its Demiurge, even though Moses himself had not openly revealed the mystery of the Trinity in Genesis. But it raises, of course, the predictable question: Why read Plato's incomplete, adumbratory, poetic account of creation with its insufficient understanding of the nature of the Creator, when one could study the detailed explications of the Mosaic mystery itself by such Christian masters as Origen, Augustine and Aquinas? The answer involves the Renaissance's myths of the ancient past. If the Greeks and other peoples had also been the recipients of divine revelation of any kind, not as sublime as that granted the Hebrews but enough to prepare them to some degree for the advent of Christianity, then their philosophies and poetic visions were assuredly the embodiment of that revelation, and could be profitably studied by learned and subtle men. This ecumenism depends not only on the view, rejected by many, that God had spoken through the pagan Sibyls, poets, prophets and philosophers; but also on the view that some men could be hooked by the pleasure of mastering the difficulties involved in understanding these pagan texts and led by way of the hermeneutical and intellectual challenges towards the contemplation of the mysteries of true religion that other, more humble men merely accepted and adored.[80] In other words, Ficino and his peers seem to have been interested, not so much in converting Moslems, Jews and Averroists, as in reviving or strengthening the wavering or sceptical faith of the subtle, the sophistical, the *ingeniosi,* men committed to the ways of reason

---

80. See Ficino's *Theologia Platonica* 14.10 (ed. Marcel, 2: 283): "Omnes tamen quodammodo Deum colunt et coluere semper, neque tamen semper fuit hominum depravata natura, neque rudes tantum homines adorant, sed etiam ingeniosi et sapientes, quod ostenderunt Persarum Magi, Aegyptii sacerdotes, prophetae Hebrei, Orphici, Pythagorici, Platonicique philosophi, ac Prisci Theologi Christianorum."

who were born to Christianity but demanded rational grounds for their belief. A large part of Ficino's success as an apologist derived from his recognition that such men needed to be encountered on their own terms and led by means of intellectual examination and enquiry to a trust in the learned folly of the Cross. And none could wish for a more demanding text than the *Timaeus* in this regard, the object of study by some of the greatest ancient and Christian intellects and one of the "most clever" of all the "marvellous" books of the "divine" Plato.

In reviving Proclus' account of the dialogue's metaphysics, however, Ficino must have felt, not that he was engineering a radical break with the medieval tradition, but that he was amplifying and modifying that tradition and bringing it into line with the tradition of authentic Platonism. Simultaneously he was surely aware of the dangers of insisting upon too full a reconciliation, not so much between the Mosaic and Platonic accounts of creation, where he found, like the medieval commentators before him, a wonderfully sustained and consistent agreement; as between the Platonic and Christian views of the Creator Himself,[81] Christian views, moreover, that had either not been fully revealed to Moses, or, if revealed, had been entrusted by him to a group of initiates who then interpreted the text of Genesis by drawing upon cabbalistic lore and its numerological methods.[82] For it was not over the creation that the *Timaeus* had erred, where the Mosaic and Platonic accounts both emphasize the beauty of the world and the harmonies it embodies (though the Platonic account is much more explicitly concerned with these and perhaps especially attractive to Ficino for that reason), but over the threefold nature of the one Creator whom it had envisaged in a proto-Arian mould.

Despite his acceptance of the basic principles and intentions of the *interpretatio Christiana,* it was an "Arian" *Timaeus,* therefore, that Ficino presented to the Quattrocento in the belief that Christians could profit from its study as the Greek counterpart to Genesis. That he made no attempt to palliate

81. Justin Martyr (c. 100–c. 165 AD) was the first Christian apologist to maintain this second, more revolutionary agreement in the sincere belief that the Greek thinkers had had access to the works of Moses (*First Apology* 44.8; 59.1). He argues that in His Goodness "God created all things in the beginning out of unformed matter" and that Plato had taught the same in his *Timaeus* (*Ibid.* 10.2; 59.1ff; see Wolfson, "Plato's Preexistent Matter," 412–413). Subsequent apologists became much more hesitant.

82. See Pico's *Oratio* and the proem to the second *expositio* of his *Heptaplus* (ed. E. Garin, [Florence, 1942], 154–158 and 222).

the subordinationist nature of the dialogue's metaphysics is itself significant: obviously he did not feel it presented an insurmountable barrier or
a perilous temptation to those who sought to comprehend its secrets. But
his infusion of a resuscitated Neoplatonism into the study of the *Timaeus'*
myth, and his insistence that the work be read in the light of other Platonic masterworks such as the *Parmenides,* must needs have compelled a
contemporary reader towards an understanding of the dialogue that was
considerably removed from, though not necessarily incompatible with,
the old Christian interpretation. We must assume that Ficino believed
that those he guided in this new way would arrive at an interpretation
that was still Christian, but more informed and more profound and therefore ultimately more truly Platonic. If the judicious entertainment of "Arian" positions for a while could serve these higher ends, then so much
the better for the *ingeniosus,* and for the establishment for an intellectual
Christian of the authority of Plato as a guide to the rational understanding of the world's making and even in part of the world's maker.[83]

* * *

Ficino's *Timaeus* commentary, its genesis and its tributary traditions,
as well as the general topic of Neoplatonic metaphysics as Ficino understood it, require much more research before we can begin to assess his
ultimate contribution to the fortune of the *Timaeus* in the Renaissance.
But this introductory survey has already indicated something of Ficino's
independence and even originality. As with the *Parmenides* and *Phaedrus,*
we can see him charting his own course while eager to draw upon the
diverse, and sometimes diverging, traditions available to him; for his
Timaeus is cast in the image of the Florentine Renaissance and its preoc-
cupations, not of Proclus' dying Athens, or William's mystical Chartres.
    By way of a single but illuminating illustration, let me return to the
theme of man's creativity, where, I believe, an understanding of Ficino's
commentary can prove invaluable, given both his profound and enduring
impact on the culture and philosophy of his epoch, and the centrality of
the *Timaeus* in the formation and maturation of his own Platonism; and

---

83. We should recall that the traditional Neoplatonic subtitle for the dialogue was *De mundo,*
or, and this was Ficino's favourite variation, *De generatione mundi.* For the history of the *skopos*
in antiquity, see Larsen, 391–394.

given too his contemporaries' recognition of the dialogue's affinities with Genesis and their familiarity with the Demiurge myth.

In the article already referred to, Professor Tigerstedt suggests that perhaps we should return to the *Timaeus* as a source for the idea of poetic creativity in Landino, since "for centuries, the divine craftsman, the Demiurge, of this dialogue has been interpreted as the Christian God, creating the world after his Ideas, as a work of order and beauty, a work of art—if not as a poet, then certainly as an artisan or artist" (p. 460). "But," he continues, "if we hesitate to ascribe to the *Timaeus* any deeper influence on Landino's idea of poetic creativity, it is because of Ficino's interpretation,... [since] Ficino's repudiation of the *interpretatio Christiana* makes it improbable that Landino should have been inspired by the dialogue" (pp. 460–461). We are now in a position, however, of being able to entertain this suggestion seriously, given our clearer understanding of Ficino's relationship to his medieval predecessors, the authors of the "old" Christian view, and given our recognition that he did indeed accept the validity of the *Timaeus'* creation myth as a vehicle of Mosaic truth. Since it is widely accepted that Landino, though Ficino's senior, was his ardent disciple in most philosophical and Platonic matters, we can legitimately suppose that the Demiurge, as interpreted by Marsilio, was probably a primary source for Landino's notion of poetic creativity, as Tigerstedt had momentarily surmised. At least the hypothesis is worth exploring now that the undergirding of his main objection has been removed.

Furthermore, there is a fascinating consequence. Once we acknowledge the inherent subordinationism, the "Arianism" of Plato's metaphysics here as elsewhere, then the creation described by the *Timaeus* is the work of the second Plotinian hypostasis, the Intellect, the work of a creator, as we have seen, in the Arian mould. However unsatisfactory this might be from the standpoint of the orthodox dogma of the Trinity, it has ramifications nevertheless that can be quite satisfactorily accommodated to such views. In verses at the very heart of his account of creation Moses had declared that man was made in God's image and likeness.[84] While the

---

84. Genesis 1. 26–27: "Et ait: Faciamus hominem ad imaginem et similitudinem nostram. . . . Et creavit Deus hominem ad imaginem suam: ad imaginem Dei creavit illum: masculum et feminam creavit eos." See C. Trinkaus, *In Our Image and Likeness: Humanity and Divinity in Italian Humanist Thought*, 2 vols. (London and Chicago, 1970), 461–504 (on Ficino), 712–721 (on Landino), and *passim*.

Arians' rejection of the consubstantiality of the three persons in the God-head had been pronounced heretical, such subordinationism was perfectly acceptable when applied to man made in God's image. Indeed, "Arian" man, compounded of the *unitas, mens* and *anima* in a hierarchical series, was much more acceptable as a model, at least for post-lapsarian man, than the mystical unitive notion that he mirrored in some way God's con-substantiality. The subordinationist model comes into its own, in other words, when we turn aside from a consideration of the Creator to a con-sideration of the creature made in his similitude. More specifically, the Demiurge as Intellect comes into its own as the model for the human intelligence (*mens*) as the creator of its own intelligible reality. Whereas the Mosaic Creator creates *ex nihilo*, Plato's Demiurge creates *ex ideis*. Though made in God's image, man cannot fashion from nothing. Rather, like the Platonic Demiurge, he must fashion from ideas: not from fanta-sies and notions peculiar to himself and the vagaries of that inferior faculty, the imagination; but from *formulae idearum*, from the models of the eter-nal Ideas in God which God has planted in man's mind, and to which man can turn in order to fashion the reasons and forms of lower things.[85]

The Demiurge is Plato's authoritative image for a mind thinking or contemplating ideas and then employing them as models to fashion a lower world; is an image, that is, for paradigmatic man who must fashion *ex ideis*. At this point we should recall the memorable passage from the *The-ologia Platonica* 3.2 cited at the outset, and especially the lines: "soul is simultaneously all things. In herself she possesses the images of things divine from which she depends, and the reasons and models of lower things which in a way she also produces." Less quotable perhaps than the lines immediately succeeding them, they are in several respects just as reveal-ing; for they depict soul as another, though lesser, Demiurge, one, ironi-cally, that corresponds more closely to the Demiurge of Plato's original intention (since he is subordinate to objective ideas which he gazes up at in order to create) than to the Christianized Demiurge that Ficino in-herited from the medieval commentators (who gazes within to his own ineffable and subjective ideas).

To conclude. Ficino accepted the Timaean Demiurge as an analogue for the Creator God of Genesis and in that critical regard was happy to

---

85. For the complicated theory of the *formulae idearum*, see Kristeller, *Philosophy*, 236ff.

acknowledge his debt to the *interpretatio Christiana.* At the same time, the original Plato myth, as intepreted by the ancient Neoplatonists who identified the Demiurge with Intellect, also had its impact on Ficino's notions of creativity: not so much of divine creativity, where Christian presuppositions continued to govern him, as of human creativity. For the Neoplatonic view of the Demiurge sees the creator as a mind working with ideas, even, given Plato's insistence that the Demiurge gazes up at them, with pre-existent, and therefore superior, ideas. It is radically opposed to the notion of a God creating out of nothing from within. Applied to God Himself such a view led inevitably to heretical "Arian" notions of a creator God who is subordinate to a higher God, or even to the Manichaean blasphemy that the act of creation was somehow determined, the inexorable outcome of emanation rather than the wholly willed and so contingent act of an omnipotent and loving Father. But applied to man, it provided Ficino and his admirers, among them Landino, with a model for soul's ability to fashion and sustain its twin worlds of mind and matter and to bind them together as the universal copula. While Ficino exercised care and circumspection in arguing for the Timaean Demiurge as a model for God, he could use it unreservedly as a model for man. But even then he remained in one respect under the sway of Christian metaphysics; for he credited Plato with espousing the theory of the world's creation in time, and not, as the majority of Neoplatonists would have it, in eternity. The combination of the Neoplatonic interpretation of the Demiurge's relationship to the pre-eminent Ideas, and to the eternal world he fashions, with the Hebraeo-Christian belief in time and change as the condition of contingent reality, intelligible as well as sensible, thus accounts for the second and more familiar dimension of Ficino's paean to man: his emphasis on soul as a perpetually moving, time-immersed essence that passes into and through all things. In sum, Ficino's debt to the great myth of the *Timaeus* is exceedingly complicated even as it constitutes a primary source for his own visionary account of perfected and perfecting man, of the human demiurge as the "face" of the universe, as the "chain" or "succession" of the created world.

Assuredly, the most eloquent testimony to Ficino's revival of the Demiurge myth is the fresco that Raphael painted just a few years later in the Stanza della Segnatura in the Vatican, where a red-robed, aged Plato holds the *Timaeus* — or at least an Italian version of it — under his left arm. It is not because of the work's scientific concerns with nature and the physical universe that Raphael included it there as the representative book of Platonic wisdom, as Plato *par excellence*. While the younger, blue-robed Aristotle clasps his *Nicomachean Ethics* in one hand and gestures with the other to the world beneath him, Plato, like Moses, like the Demiurge himself, points upwards with his right forefinger towards the arch that frames both the philosophers against a clouded but azure heaven, the realm of the hidden Ideas, of the eternal patterns of all things in created nature and of all things created by man. But these include the luminous fresco itself, which is thus testifying to its own intellectual inception and to the intelligible source of its harmonious beauty and authority.

MICHAEL J. B. ALLEN

IAMBLICHUS, SYNESIUS AND THE CHALDAEAN ORA-CLES IN MARSILIO FICINO'S DE VITA LIBRI TRES: HERMETIC MAGIC OR NEOPLATO-NIC MAGIC?

AFTER DAME FRANCES YATES PUBLISHED her *Giordano Bruno and the Hermetic Tradition* in 1964, the word "Hermetic" and its cognates became terms to conjure with. Following Yates's lead, other scholars have treated "Hermetic" as if it were roughly synonymous with "magical," and they have often tried to understand the meaning of these two words for Renaissance culture by referring to the thought of Marsilio Ficino, especially his *De vita coelitus comparanda*. This treatise on astrological medicine, hereinafter called *De vita III*, is the third part of *De vita libri tres*, completed in 1489 and widely read thereafter as the most important statement of a philosophical theory of magic in the early modern period.[1] While I agree that Ficino's philosophy became the basis of European thinking about magic in the post-medieval centuries, I have argued elsewhere that Ficino's contributions to the theory of magic should not be called "Hermetic." The Hermetic λόγοι that Ficino translated from Greek, and

---

1. F. Yates, *Giordano Bruno and the Hermetic Tradition* (London, 1964), 44–82; idem, "The Hermetic Tradition in Renaissance Science," in C. S. Singleton, ed., *Art, Science and History in the Renaissance* (Baltimore, 1968), 255–74. For Yates's influence in this regard on other writers, see my "Natural Magic, Hermetism and Occultism in Early Modern Science," forthcoming in *Reappraisals of the Scientific Revolution*, ed. R. Westman and D. Lindberg. See also *Marsilii Ficini . . . opera et quae hactenus extitere* (1576; repr. Turin, 1959), 1: 529–572, hereafter cited as Ficino, *DVCC*. Other references to Ficino's works will be to this same edition as Ficino, *Opera*.

the Latin *Asclepius* that he cited say little of theoretical interest about magic. Hence Ficino looked to other sources from antiquity and the Middle Ages for the metaphysical and cosmological ingredients of his magic, ingredients lacking in the *Hermetica*. In three previous papers I have tried to show how Ficino found the principles of his magic not in the *Corpus Hermeticum* but in Plotinus, Proclus, Thomas Aquinas and other thinkers of comparable stature.[2] Here, I shall extend this line of argument to three texts of later Neoplatonism—the *De insomniis* of Synesius, the *De mysteriis* of Iamblichus, and the *Oracula Chaldaica*.

Synesius, Iamblichus and the Chaldaeans all appear in the twenty-sixth and concluding chapter of *De vita III*, where Ficino picks up threads of his commentary on Plotinus which had originally inspired his iatromathematical treatise and which formed the substance of its first chapter. Because Ficino cites Plotinus regularly in *De vita III* and because he wrote a long commentary on the *Enneads*, the reader can consult the commentary to illuminate Ficino's use of Plotinus as a theoretician of magic; the influence of Hermes Trismegistus is more difficult to determine.[3] Most of what scholars have mistaken for Ficino's commentary on the *Hermetica* (despite Professor Kristeller's identification of the material) was actually written by Lefèvre d'Etaples. Moreover, Ficino mentions Hermes in only three passages of *De vita III*, only twice by name.[4] To discover Ficino's attitude toward the meager magical content of the *Hermetica*, we must examine the context of those parts of *De vita III* in which Hermes appears. Ficino's use of various Neoplatonic philosophers in those contexts will be especially enlightening.

All three sections of *De vita III* that make use of Ficino's *Hermetica* refer

2. Copenhaver, "Hermes Tristmegistus, Proclus and the Question of a Theory of Magic in the Renaissance," read at the Folger Library Conference on Hermes Trismegistus in March, 1982, and forthcoming in the papers of that conference; idem, "Scholastic Philosophy and Renaissance Magic in the *De vita* of Marsilio Ficino," *RQ*, 37 (1984): 523–554; idem, "Renaissance Magic and Neoplatonic Philosophy: *Ennead* 4.3–5 in Ficino's *De vita coelitus comparanda*," forthcoming in *Atti del Convegno internazionale di studi sul Marsilio Ficino*, Naples, Florence, Figline Valdarno, May, 1984.

3. Ficino, *DVCC*, 570–72; on *DVCC*, the *Enneads* and Ficino's Plotinus commentary, see Copenhaver, "*Ennead* 4.3–5."

4. Ficino, *DVCC*, 548, 561, 571–2; cf. 540–41, 550 where the references are not to Ficino's Greek *Hermetica* or to the Latin *Asclepius* but to the *Liber Hermetis de XV stellis* and the *De virtutibus septem herbarum*, two of the "popular" *Hermetica* of the Middle Ages, on which see A.-J. Festugière, *La Révélation d'Hermès Trismégiste* (Paris, 1950–54), 1: 146–186, esp. 169; Kristeller, *Supplementum* 1: cxxix–cxxi; cf. Yates, *Bruno*, 28–35, and especially 40, note 1.

o the same two "god-making" passages of the *Asclepius*.[5] Ficino made no attempt in *De vita III* to ground his theory of magic in a close reading of the fourteen Hermetic λόγοι which he had translated because, as I believe, any attempt to derive such material from the eclectic and philosophically jejune *Hermetica* would have been fruitless. The three passages that use the *Asclepius* are not so much references to philosophical arguments as appeals to authority, the venerable authority of the Hermes whom Ficino thought to be a contemporary of Moses.[6] Ficino's clearest intention in the three passages is to show that the god-making magic described in the *Asclepius* is *efficacious*, i.e., that the artificial, material structure of a talisman or statue can cause it to be inhabited or animated by a spiritual being, a demon. Analysis of Ficino's reasoning and sources in these passages will also reveal an obscurer purpose: to admit that this *efficacious* magic might nonetheless be *illegitimate*, an idolatrous breach of the first and second commandments and a sin against religion.

Ficino's reader waits until the thirteenth chapter of *De vita III* for his first encounter with Hermes, a single sentence in a list of authorities — including Synesius, Iamblichus and the Chaldaeans — who claim that magicians can cause spiritual beings to enter material objects. Arguing at this point for the *efficacy* of talismanic magic, Ficino makes no clear statement about its *legitimacy*.[7] But in chapter twenty, having announced his suspicion that the evident power of talismans arises *naturally* from the matter that constitutes them rather than *artificially* from the figures that they bear, he hesitates, writing that

> the Egyptians attribute so much to statues and images fabricated with astrological and magical technique that they believe spirits of the stars are sealed inside them. But some think that these spirits of the stars . . . are demons . . . , [and] whatever they may be, . . . they think they are implanted in statues and talismans no differently than demons

---

5. *Asclep.* 23–24, 37–38; subsequent references to this work will include page and line numbers from the Budé text (Paris, 1946) of Nock and Festugière.

6. On the use of Hermes in doxographic or genealogical as opposed to theoretical contexts, see Copenhaver, "Natural Magic."

7. Ficino, *DVCC*, 548: Quales [imagines quae moverentur] et Trismegistus ait Aegyptios ex certis mundi materiis facere consuevisse et in eas opportune animas daemonum inserere solitos atque animam avi sui Mercurii; *Asclep.* 23 (326.1–2), 37 (347.13–20, 348.3–6), 38 (348.19–349.1); for other authorities listed in this passage, see *infra*, notes 13, 16, 27, 29, 33 and Copenhaver, "Proclus."

sometimes possess human bodies. . . . We believe that these things can actually be done by demons not so much because they are constrained by a particular [kind] of matter as because they enjoy being worshipped. We will discuss this elsewhere more carefully.[8]

Having once again established the *efficacy* of talismans, imputing it either to material or demonic agency, Ficino then raises the issue of *legitimacy* by comparing the animation of statues to demonic possession and by identifying an obviously evil motivation for the activity of the demons. Then Ficino abruptly suspends this religiously sensitive discussion of the Hermetic statues, which make their final appearance in the final chapter of *De vita III*.

Mercurius enters this concluding chapter as a precursor of Plotinus, the inspiration of Plotinus' belief that

the ancient priests or magicians used to capture something divine and wondrous in statues. . . . [Plotinus] along with Trismegistus supposes that, strictly speaking, divinities altogether separated from matter are not captured through material objects but cosmic [divinities] only, as I have said from the beginning and as Synesius agrees. . . . Mercurius, whom Plotinus follows, says that these are aerial demons—not celestial, much less anything higher— . . . [and] he adds songs resembling the heavens in which, he says, they take delight and thus remain longer in the statues and do good for men or else do them harm. [Mercurius] also says that when the wise men of Egypt, who were also priests, could not convince people by rational means that the gods existed. . . , they devised this magical enticement (*illicium*) by which, attracting demons into statues, they declared them to be divinities. But Iamblichus condemns the Egyptians because they not only took the demons as steps, as it were, on the path to higher gods but also frequently adored them. . . . Mercurius says that the [Egyptian] priests took from the nature of the world

8. Ficino, *DVCC*, 561: Aegyptii tantum statuis imaginibusque attribuunt arte astronomica et magica fabricatis ut spiritus stellarum in eis includi putent. Spiritus autem stellarum intelligunt alii quidem . . . demonas . . . qualescunque sint, inseri statuis et imaginibus arbitrantur, non aliter ac daemones soleant humana nonnunquam corpora occupare. . . . Quae quidem nos per daemonas fieri posse putamus non tam materia certa cohibitos quam cultu gaudentes. Sed haec alibi diligentius; *Asclep.* 24 (326.9–11), 37 (347.15–18), 38 (349.5–6); Aug. *Civ. D.* 8.24, 10.11; D. P. Walker, *Spiritual and Demonic Magic from Ficino to Campanella*, Studies of the Warburg Institute, 22 (London, 1958), 41, note 2.

a suitable power and mixed it in [with the statues]. Plotinus followed him. . . .[9]

This last point on which Ficino heard Hermetic echoes in Plotinus introduces an allusion to Plotinus' theory of seminal reasons, an important technical component in the metaphysics of Plotinus' magic and also in Ficino's.[10] Given Plotinus' importance for Ficino in *De vita III* and elsewhere, his filiation with Hermes in chapter twenty-six would seem to imply a positive evaluation of Hermetic statue-magic. When Ficino finds Hermes and Plotinus agreeing that only cosmic — as opposed to hypercosmic — *numina* enter the statues, the *Asclepius* and the *Enneads* become the basis for a theologically cautious approach to lower cosmic powers rather than high gods. On the other hand, the *numina mundana* of the *Asclepius* are demons lured by an idolatrous rite to enter statues where they can do harm to humans, and (as Augustine had warned) the Egyptians who first made the statues used a deception, a "magical enticement," to trick their people into a blasphemous belief. The demons take delight in astrological song, recalling the illicit worship condemned in chapter twenty and the demonic chants scorned by Michael Psellos in chapter thirteen.[11] If chapter thirteen was silent on the legitimacy of statue-magic and if chapter twenty seemed to condemn it, what may we conclude from the ambiguities of chapter twenty-six? Can we learn anything from the other authorities — Synesius, Iamblichus, the Chaldaeans — associated with these ambivalent references to the *Asclepius*?

---

9. Ficino, *DVCC*, 571: Plotinus . . . Mercurium imitatus ait veteres sacerdotes sive magos in statuis . . . divinum aliquid et mirandum suscipere solitos. Vult autem una cum Trismegisto per materialia haec non proprie suscipi numina penitus a materia segregata sed mundana tantum, ut ab initio dixi et Synesius approbat. . . . Mercurius ipse, quem Plotinus sequitur, inquit daemonas aerios non coelestes nedum sublimiores. . . . Adiungit cantus coelestibus similes quibus, ait, eos delectari statuisque sic adesse diutius et prodesse hominibus vel obesse. Addit sapientes quondam Aegyptios, qui et sacerdotes erant, quum non possent rationibus persuadere populo esse deos, . . . excogitasse magicum hoc ⟨illicium⟩ quo, demonas allicientes in statuas, esse numina declararent. Sed Iamblichus damnat Aegyptios quod daemonas non solum ut gradus quosdam ad superiores deos investigandos acceperint sed plurimum adoraverint. . . . Mercurius sacerdotes ait accepisse virtutem a mundi natura convenientem eamque miscuisse. Sequutus hunc Plotinus. . .; the Basel, 1576, edition has *illicitum* in the passage above; for the important emendation to *illicium* I am grateful to the editorial work of Carol Kaske and John Clarke on *DVCC*; *Asclep.* 24 (326.9–11, 14–15), 37 (347.10–15, 18–19; 348.8–10), 38 (349.3–7, 8–11); Plot. *Enn.* 4.3.11.1–2, 8–10, 134–14, 16–18, 23–24.

10. On seminal reasons in Plotinus and Ficino, see Copenhaver, "*Ennead* 4.3–5."

11. Aug. *Civ. D.* 8.24; *supra*, n. 8; for Michael Psellos, *infra*, note 27.

Ficino, who translated Synesius' treatise *On Dreams*, calls on that work in chapter twenty-six to confirm that hypercosmic gods play no part in statue-magic; the matter of statues, which are artificial forms of lower nature, attracts only *numina mundana*, cosmic divinities. Ficino had made the same point in his first chapter, where he also cited *De insomniis* to show that lower material forms, acting as baits or lures for higher entities, can attract at least some powers of Soul. "Such congruities of forms to reasons of the World-Soul," wrote Ficino, "Zoroaster called divine baits (*illices*), and Synesius also confirmed that they are magical lures (*illecebrae*)."[12] Synesius appeared again in chapter thirteen in the list of authorities on animated statues, where Ficino's purpose was to show that matter can receive demonic and divine as well as celestial gifts. Ficino took all this material on magical enticement (though not on pneumatology, another important influence from Synesius) from the first two sections of *De insomniis*. He found these preliminaries useful, no doubt, because of their evident derivation from Plotinus' exposition of natural magic in *Ennead* 4.4.30–45. "Nature is everywhere a sorceress, as Plotinus says and Synesius also, everywhere enticing particular things with particular baits." Recapitulating Plotinus' account of cosmic sympathy as the basis of natural magic, Synesius insisted that such magic can provoke divine responses. All members of the cosmos are

> parts of one living organism. . . . Even to some god, of those who dwell *within* the universe, a stone from hence and a herb is a befitting offering; for in sympathizing with these he is yielding to nature and is bewitched. . . . [But] whatsoever of the divine element is *outside* the cosmos can in no wise be moved by sorcery.[13]

---

12. Ficino, *DVCC*, pp. 531, 571: Congruitates igitur eiusmodi formarum ad rationes animae mundi Zoroaster divinas illices appellavit quas et Synesius magicas esse illecebras confirmavit; cf. Syn. *Insomn.* 132c3–4: καὶ μή ποτε αἱ μάγων ἴυγγες αὖται, which in his translation of Synesius (*Opera*, p. 1969) Ficino renders: Consideratione vero dignum est utrum huc tendant illices vel motacillae magorum; see also *infra*, note 13. The edition of *De insomniis* by N. Terzaghi in *Synesii Cyrenensis opuscula*, Scriptores graeci et latini consilio Academiae Lynceorum editi (Rome, 1944), supersedes the text in Migne, *PG*. For an English version, see A. Fitzgerald, *The Essays and Hymns of Synesius of Cyrene* (Oxford, 1930), which contains an extensive introduction and notes. See also J. Bregman, *Synesius of Cyrene, Philosopher-Bishop* (Berkeley, 1982), 145–154; C. Lacombrade, *Synésios de Cyrène, Hellène et Chrétien* (Paris, 1951), 150–169. Walker, *Magic*, 39, note 1 also mentions Synesius as an important source for Neoplatonic pneumatology, another important ingredient in Ficino's magic.

13. Ficino, *DVCC*, 549, 570: Ubique igitur natura maga est, ut inquit Plotinus atque Synesius,

To this Plotinian material Synesius added the notion of ἴυγγες or magical charms, which he would have found in various Neoplatonic commentaries on the *Oracula Chaldaica*. The ἴυγγες of the *Chaldaean Oracles*—which are both magical material objects and immaterial processions from the Father— became Ficino's *illices* and *illecebrae*, magical lures to attract divine powers. Since the original ἴυγξ was a bird, the wryneck, whose striking behavior seemed a visible sign for invisible powers capable of attracting the circling heavenly gods, Synesius used it to introduce an analogy between the act of casting a spell (θέλγειν) and the act of giving a signal (σημαίνειν). Like other Neoplatonists of his era, he wished to distinguish a base, illegitimate magic from a nobler, licit magic, and he drew his distinction on the basis of the distance between matter and mind. As a magic of signs rather than things, divination had a greater share in the divine intellect than the lower γοητεία that bound the magus downward to matter.[14] Thus, at the end of his introductory remarks, Synesius saw no danger in explaining μαντεία or divination, but in his "law-abiding treatise" he found no place for τελεταί, which Ficino translated pleonastically as *"expiationes ... solennitatesque,"* "purifications and rituals."[15]

What were the rituals to which Synesius objected? From his own ac-

videlicet certa quaedam pabulis ubique certis inescans...; Syn. *Insomn.* 132d10–13: ἑνὸς γὰρ ἦν ἄμφω ζῴου, καὶ ἔστιν αὐτοῖς τι μᾶλλον ἑτέρον πρὸς ἄλληλα· καὶ δὴ καὶ θεῷ τινι τῶν εἴσω τοῦ κόσμου λίθος ἐνθένδε καὶ βοτάνη προσήκει, οἷς ὁμοιοπαθῶν εἴκει τῇ φύσει καὶ γοητεύεται; Ficino, *Opera*, 2: 1969: Ambo enim illa et unius animalis sunt membra. . . . Atqui et alicui deo ex deorum numero mundanorum lapis hic herbave congruit, quibus quasi compatiens naturae caedit ac veluti fascinatur; Fitzgerald, *Essays and Hymns*, 329–330 (my italics); Plot. *Enn.* 4.4.40.1–12, 42.14–17, 43.12–19; Copenhaver, "Proclus."

14. Syn. *Insomn.* 131a7–9, 132c3–5, 133b14–15; A. Smith, *Porphyry's Place in the Neoplatonic Tradition: A Study in Post-Plotinian Neoplatonism* (The Hague, 1974), 90 ff., discusses the notion of higher and lower theurgies (*infra*, note 19), beginning with such earlier authorities as Rosán, Lewy and Sodano. From Ficino's translation of Syn. *Insomn.* 132c3–4 (*supra*, note 12), it is clear that he identified the physical ἴυγξ as, among other things, the *motacilla* or wagtail (cf. Plin. *HN* 37.156), although the ἴυγξ of the ancients was the wryneck, *Jynx torquilla*. Ficino also mentions the *motacilla* in *DVCC*, 533. On various aspects of the ἴυγξ, see *Orac. Chald.* frgs. 77, 206 (Des Places); Michael Psellos *Comm. in Orac. Chald.* 133a3–b4, 1149a10–b11; Psellos, *Expos. dogm. Chald.* 1149c1–1152a6; *Oratio Ioannis Pici Mirandulani*, in G. Pico della Mirandola, *De hominis dignitate, Heptaplus, De ente et uno e scritti vari*, ed. E. Garin (Florence, 1942), 152; Gossen, "Ἴυγξ," Pauly-Wissowa, *RE*, 20/2, coll. 1384–86; Hans Lewy, *Chaldaean Oracles and Theurgy: Mysticism, Magic and Platonism in the Later Roman Empire*. Publications de l'institut français d'archéologie orientale, recherches d'archéologie, de philologie et d'histoire, 12 (Cairo, 1956), 132–134, 156–157, 249–252.

15. Syn. *Insomn.* 133b15–c2: ... καὶ τελετὰς μέν, ἀλλὰ μηδὲ ὁ λόγος κινείτω, νόμῳ πολιτείας πειθόμενος· μαντικὴν δὲ ἀνεμέσητον ἀποδέξασθαι; Ficino, *Opera*, 2: 1969: Expiationes quidem solennitatesque sed nihil in praesentia sermo moveat civili tantum legi fidem adhibens; Fitzgerald, *Essays and Hymns*, 330.

count we may gather that illicit τελεταί were those magical procedures that trapped the magus in matter, unlike the higher rites of divine mantic that released him. That statue-magic (which Proclus called τελεστιχή from τελεῖν, "to consecrate") was the ritual that offended Synesius seems likely when we turn to Iamblichus' views on the subject—Iamblichus, whom Ficino cited along with Synesius as an authority on the statues.[16]

Iamblichus wrote De mysteriis, which Ficino also translated, in response to Porphyry's Letter to Anebo, a skeptical query into divination, theurgy and the role of gods and demons therein.[17] In general, Iamblichus' strategy was to make the cause for efficacious, legitimate theurgy and divination through a series of distinctions and exculpations. He ascribed any evil detected in these practices to human rather than divine agency, or to demons rather than higher divinities, or to bad demons rather than good demons. He also distinguished bad ritual, marred by human error and evil, from good rites guided by divine intention.[18] In particular, he described theurgy, including its ritual components, as a continuous process of two stages, a lower initiatory theurgy and a higher culminating theurgy. Lower theurgy, which appealed to cosmic gods, depended principally on the ritual manipulation of material σύμβολα and συνθήματα appropriate to such lower divinities; its efficacy came from the συμπάθεια that unified and vitalized the living cosmos. But the efficacy of higher theurgy addressed to hypercosmic gods originated in divine love, φιλία, that transcended cosmic sympathy. Although the higher theurgy still included ritual elements, its final stage was immaterial νόησις or intellection that led to union with the divine; the theurge reached these heights, however, from lower initial rites more dependent on material objects. These lower rites had their own sphere of efficacy, but since their power flowed from cosmic sympathy such effects were confined to the world of nature and to the lower divinities assigned to that realm. Unless they led the operator to the immaterial, noetic stages of higher theurgy, whose autonomous

16. Ficino, DVCC, 549, 571; E. R. Dodds, The Greeks and the Irrational (Berkeley, 1968), 291–95.

17. R. T. Wallis, Neoplatonism (London, 1972), 105–110, 120– 23; on Iamblichus, theurgy and De mysteriis, see also Les Mystères d'Égypte, ed. E. Des Places (Paris, 1966), 5–33; B. D. Larsen, Jamblique de Chalcis, Exégète et philosophe (Aarhus, 1972), 148–196; A. H. Armstrong, ed., The Cambridge History of Later Greek and Early Medieval Philosophy (Cambridge, 1970), 283–301; and especially, Smith, Porphyry's Place, 81–150.

18. Iamb. Myst. 82.9–15, 83.16–84.4, 91.9–92.7, 103.2–10, 114.3–115.15, 142.18–143.3, 144.1–8, 155.18–156.3, 160.15–161.2, 176.3–178.2, 219.12–18.

powers transcended the cosmos, the material rites of lower theurgy were worse than incomplete. They were dangerous.[19]

The perils in lower theurgy stemmed from human evil or human ignorance, not from any fault of the gods. If human operators were evil, if they confused the special rites required by the differing natures of hypercosmic and cosmic gods, if they made mistakes in conducting the rituals, if they forgot that the lower theurgy of sympathies was only antecedent to the higher theurgy of intellection, they might find themselves not rising to divine union but mired in the depths of otherness and vulnerable to the fierce, capricious powers governing there.[20] Even worse than failed or incomplete attempts at theurgy were other rituals that were not theurgic at all. To distinguish such practices from theurgy, Iamblichus called them φαντασμάτων θαυματουργία, the "thaumaturgy of phantasms" or "wonder-working through illusions." The genuine theurge contemplated the true essential forms (εἴδη) of the gods, but the thaumaturge only handled their false artificial images (εἴδωλα). If this trickery derived any good from power descending from on high, through the cycling heavens, down to the darkest margins of the All, such good was merely physical; it came from magical technique, not theurgic contemplation. In describing this non-theurgic magic, Iamblichus had especially in mind εἰδωλοποιία, the making of images, which he condemned at length in De mysteriis. He ended his critique of the thaumaturgy of statues with a comment that recalls Ficino's claim in De vita III to be describing images but not approving them: "One must know about the nature of this thaumaturgy but by no means use it or trust it."[21]

Iamblichus shunned statue-magic not only as a distraction from theurgy but also as an invitation to evil, perverse demons who deceived men and harmed them: "If we were to speak truthfully now about images and the evil demons who pretend to appear as gods and good demons, it is clear that a great maleficent host streams into them from that source...."[22] Ficino knew what Iamblichus feared. He cited his anxieties

19. Smith, Porphyry's Place, 90–99, 105–107, 110, 149; Iamb. Myst. 96.11–98.15, 126.17–127.3, 135.14–136.10, 139.1–4, 184.1–13, 209.4–211.18.

20. Iamb. Myst. 70.18–71.18, 72.12–17, 82.9–15, 88.5–9, 176.13–177.12, 196.13–197.11, 227.1–228.12, 229.17–230.6, 231.5– 232.9.

21. Iamb. Myst. 167.9–15, 169.1–170.2, 170.7–10, 171.5–13, 175.13–14: ὥστε εἰδέναι μὲν χρὴ καὶ ταύτην τὴν θαυματουργίαν τίνα ἔχει φύσιν, χρῆσθαι δὲ ἢ πιστεύειν αὐτῇ μηδαμῶς; Ficino, DVCC, 530; cf. Opera, 1: 573; 2: 1891; Walker, Magic, 42, note 3.

22. Iamb. Myst. 190.8–12: Εἰ γὰρ ἀληθῶς ἄρτι ἐλέγομεν περὶ τῶ εἰδώλων καὶ τῶν κακῶν

in chapter fifteen of *De vita III* while describing correspondences between types of images and varieties of demons, and again in chapter eighteen, after having set forth warnings from St. Thomas on demonic images:

> Iamblichus says that those who neglect sanctity and the highest piety, who put their trust in images alone and expect divine gifts from them, are most often deceived in this regard by evil demons who rush in under the guise of good divinities. Yet he does not deny that certain natural goods can result from images constructed according to legitimate principles of astrology.[23]

Ficino's most striking restatement of Iamblichus' view that statue-magic was demonic thaumaturgy rather than divine theurgy comes in chapter twenty-six, where

> Iamblichus condemns the Egyptians . . . because they frequently adore the demons. In fact, he prefers the Chaldaeans to the Egyptians as not possessed by demons — Chaldaeans, I maintain, who were ministers of religion, for we suspect that Chaldaean as well as Egyptian astrologers tried somehow to attract demons through celestial harmony into earthen statues.

The demon-ridden Egyptians whom Iamblichus repudiates here are, of course, the *deorum fictores* of the *Asclepius*, for the gods they made were mere εἴδωλα, mere baits for evil demons, no true gods at all.[24]

The Chaldaeans whom Iamblichus admired were, according to Ficino, "ministers of religion"; they were *not* makers of demonic astrological images. Chaldaeans or Magi or followers of Zoroaster appear frequently in *De vita III* as proponents of various astrological doctrines, most of them

δαιμόνων τῶν ὑποκρινομένων τὴν τῶν θεῶν καὶ τῶν ἀγαθῶν δαιμόνων παρουσίαν, πολὺ δήπου τι καταφαίνεται ἐντεῦθεν ἐπιρρέον τὸ κακοποιὸν φῦλον. *Ibid.* 82.9–15, 129.18–130.6, 172.15–17, 176.13–178.11, 190.4–191.11.

23. Ficino, *DVCC*, 551, 558: Iamblichus ait eos qui, religione summa sanctimoniaque posthabita, imaginibus duntaxat confisi, ab eis divina sperant munera, hac in re a malis daemonibus saepissime falli sub praetextu bonorum numinum occurrentibus. Contingere tamen ex imaginibus legitima astrologiae ratione constructis naturalia quaedam bona non negat; Iamb. *Myst.* 91.9–15, 130.3–6, 172.15–17, 176.13–177.10, 178.4–5, 190.9–191.5; Ficino, *Opera*, 2: 1881, 1886, 1891–93; Aquinas, *Summa Contra Gentiles*, III, 104–105; *De occultis operibus naturae*, 17, 20; Copenhaver, "Scholastic Philosophy."

24. Ficino, *DVCC*, 571: Sed Iamblichus damnat Aegyptios quod daemonas . . . plurimum adoraverint. Chaldaeos vero daemonibus non occupatos Aegyptiis anteponit — Chaldaeos, inquam, religionis antistites, nam astrologos tam Chaldaeorum quam Aegyptiorum quodammodo tentavisse daemonas per harmoniam coelestem in statuas fictiles trahere suspicemus; cf. Iamb. *Myst.* 167.9–176.2, 246.16–20, 247.11–248.2; Ficino, *Opera*, 2: 1890–92, 1901; *Asclep.* 38 (349.8).

unrelated to the issue of demonolatry and traceable to Macrobius, Albumasar, Peter of Abano and other sources.[25] Another set of Ficino's Chaldaean references, however, comes from the *Oracula Chaldaica*. They contain theological teachings. Zoroaster, for example, called material forms "divine baits" for powers of Soul, and a precept of his Chaldaean disciples encouraged the mix of medical and theological concerns that we find in Ficino: "Raise up a fiery mind to the work of piety, and you will save a fallen body." From Michael Psellos' *Commentary on the Chaldaean Oracles*, Ficino would have known that this "work of piety" referred to "the methods of the rituals," i.e., to theurgy, but he also knew that Iamblichus treated pious theurgy as just the antithesis of demonolatry.[26] More problematic is the following item from Ficino's list of authorities on animated statues in chapter thirteen:

> To evoke a spirit from Hecate, the Magi, . . . followers of Zoroaster, used a sort of golden ball marked with celestial characters and containing a sapphire within; as they chanted, it was whirled about on a sort of thong made from bull's hide. I gladly omit the incantations, of course, for Psellus the Platonist also disapproves and derides them.

Actually, it was in reference to the entire description of these material ἴυγγες that Psellos said "the whole thing is silly talk," but, as far as Ficino knew, this bit of nonsense—clearly a recipe for demon-worship— did not come from the *Oracles* themselves. Nothing corresponding to it occurs in the compilation of *Oracles* available in his time.[27] Moreover, Psel-

---

25. Ficino, *DVCC*, 542, 552, 556, 560, 562, 567; Macrob. *Comm.* 19.1; Yates, *Bruno*, 54, 70; M. J. B. Allen, *The Platonism of Marsilio Ficino: A Study of his* Phaedrus *Commentary, Its Sources and Genesis* (Berkeley, 1984), 118–19; C. Bezold, F. Boll and W. Gundel, *Sternglaube und Sterndeutung: Die Geschichte und das Wesen der Astrologie* (Leipzig, 1926), 21, 25, 29, 91–95.

26. Ficino, *DVCC*, 565: . . . praeceptum illud Chaldaeorum: . . . Si mentem ad pietatis opus ardentem erexeris, corpus quoque caducum servabis; *Orac. Chald.* frg. 128: . . . ἐκτείνας πύριον νοῦν ἔργον ἐπ' εὐσεβίης ῥευστὸν καὶ σῶμα σαώσεις; Psellos *Comm.* 1140b1–11: . . . ἔργα δὲ εὐσεβείας παρὰ Χαλδαίοις αἱ τῶν τελετῶν μέθοδοι; Iamb. *Myst.* 178.3–18; *supra*, note 12; cf. *DVCC*, 531, 533, 534, 562; *Orac. Chald.* frg. 150; Psellos *Comm.* 1132b1–13, c1–11.

27. Ficino, *DVCC*, 548–49: Magi quinetiam Zoroastri sectatores ad evocandum ab Hecate spiritum utebantur aurea quadam pila characteribus insignita coelestium cui et saphyrus erat insertus, et scutica quadam facta tauri corio vertebatur atque interim excantabant. Sed cantiones equidem libenter omitto. Nam et Psellus Platonicus eas improbat atque deridet; Psellos *Comm.* 1133a3–b4: Ἔστι δὲ τὸ πᾶν φλύαρον; *Oracula magica Zoroastris cum scholiis Plethonis et Pselli*, in *Sibyllina oracula* . . . *emendata ac restituta* . . . *opera et studio Servatii Gallaei* (Amsterdam, 1689), 78–91; cf. E. Des Places, ed., *Oracles Chaldaïques avec un choix de commentaires anciens* (Paris, 1971), 52–53, frgs. 77, 206, 223.

los' analysis of ἴυγγες that are mentioned in the *Oracles* known to Ficino treats them not as physical devices for working magic but as immaterial powers flowing from above, much like the "divine baits" of Zoroaster that attract soul to matter. Thus, one can discern throughout *De vita III* at least a rough distinction between Chaldaean piety and Chaldaean astrology, a division that corresponds to what Ficino saw as Iamblichus' choice of the Chaldaeans over the Egyptians.[28] The implication of this distinction—as in general of Ficino's use of Iamblichus in the "Hermetic" contexts of *De vita III*—is to devalue Hermetic statue-magic and elevate the status of Chaldaean theurgy.[29] One may call Ficino's iatromathematics "Chaldaean" or "Hermetic" with equal imprecision.

Thus far, our analysis of Iamblichus, the *Chaldaean Oracles* and Synesius in *De vita III* indicates that Hermetic statues and astrological talismans are to be avoided as demonic thaumaturgy. Even genuine but lower theurgy is a danger unless it leads to νόησις and the higher gods. For Ficino, as philosopher and Platonist, the attractions of noetic theurgy were powerful. His whole philosophical career was a pledge of fealty to what Iamblichus called the "intellectual and incorporeal law of the priestly [art that governs] ... every part of theurgy." But the laws of theurgy that Iamblichus proclaimed gave small comfort to Ficino the physician. In Iamblichus' view, only men of poor character would show much interest in the merely physical efficacy—including therapeutic efficacy—of lower theurgy which, when confined to its own material sphere, kept the operator vulnerable to demonic affliction. The ambitions of a perfected theurgy were, for Iamblichus, necessarily hypercosmic.[30] If the Platonist in Ficino was perhaps tempted to follow this sublime path in his magic, the Christian in him must have trembled to aim so high except through rituals sanctioned by the Church.

Had Plotinus been Ficino's only guide in constructing a theory of magic, his choices would have been simpler and his results—if one may speculate—clearer. Plotinus never mentioned theurgy, a Chaldaean novelty

28. *Oracula magica Zoroastris*, 80–81, 89; *Orac. Chald.* frg. 77; Psellos *Comm.* 1149a10-b11; *supra*, notes 12, 24.
29. Ficino, *DVCC*, 549, 571; for other uses of Iamblichus in *DVCC* not yet discussed, see *ibid.*, 538, 549, 562–65, 571–72; Iamb. *Myst.* 100. 3–7, 11–18, 108.10–11, 111.5-9, 114.7-9, 118.16–119.4, 134.7-9, 169.4–14, 175.15–178.2, 215.1–7, 230.4–6, 232.10–234.4, 253.5-6, 255.9–11, 258.6–11, 269.9–270.7, 271.3–12; Ficino, *Opera*, 2: 1882–87, 1891–92, 1901–02, 1904.
30. Iamb. *Myst.* 219.1–225.3, 225.3–5: ... νοερὸν καὶ ἀσώματον ἱερατικῆς θεσμὸν διαμελετῶσιπερὶ πάντα τῆς θεουργίας τὰ μέρη; *supra*, note 19.

introduced into Neoplatonism by Porphyry. Magic for Plotinus was entirely a product of sympathy in the All. Like all else, sympathy could be traced to causes transcending the cosmos, but it opened no route to those causes for the sage. Because there was no magic without sympathy, all magic for Plotinus was natural magic. Had Ficino been content to advocate nothing more than non-demonic, natural magic for medical uses, this constraint might have suited his purposes. But from such sources as Iamblichus, Psellos and the *Chaldaean Oracles*, Ficino learned of a magic that reached beyond sympathetic effects and acted as a bridge to νόησις and ἕνωσις, intellection and union.[31] Knowledge of these more ambitious practices put temptation and complication in Ficino's way. As the higher noetic theurgy, initiated in a lower magical theurgy, approached the divine Mind, it appealed strongly to the fundamental Platonist yearning for pure immaterial union in the One, yet from a Christian point of view the unorthodox rituals required to satisfy such yearnings were at best gravely suspect. Faced with these conflicts, Ficino brought his treatise on magic to an ambiguous, perplexing conclusion in its twenty-sixth chapter.

The last authority whom Ficino cites in this last chapter is Iamblichus, whom he calls upon to reinforce a point taken from Plotinus, a point that seems to contradict the Plotinian principle of a purely sympathetic, cosmic magic. Given the proper connections among ideas, forms and seminal reasons, writes Ficino,

> higher gifts may also sometimes descend, in so far as reasons in the World-Soul are joined to intellectual forms of that same Soul and through them to ideas of the divine Mind, as Iamblichus also agrees.

Actually, the integrity of Plotinus' theory of magic was secure for attentive readers who, like Ficino, knew that magic, an artificial human action, could not *cause* the descent of divine gifts. Men wise enough to recognize the gifts simply took advantage of their presence, through magic or through prayer. Magic is given in the nature of things, divinely ordained, and some men are clever enough to find it. When Plotinus briefly mentioned the divinized statues of Hermes, he used them simply to illustrate the general metaphysical principle that even material objects accessible to humans could be fit receptacles for the divine—though they

---

31. Iamb. *Myst.* 162.13–164.5, 207.7–208.6; Dodds, *Irrational*, 285; Smith, *Porphyry's Place*, 92–94, 122–127, 147; *supra*, notes 19, 28; Copenhaver, "*Ennead* 4.3–5."

became so as a consequence neither of divine intention nor of human manipulation.[32] Iamblichus broadened and transformed this principle, as Ficino noted at several points:

> Iamblichus confirms that not only celestial but even demonic and divine powers and effects can be caught in material objects which are naturally in sympathy with higher beings if they are collected and gathered in from various places at the proper time and in the correct manner.

So taken was Iamblichus with the magic of material objects duly purified and suitably assembled that he described them as working *ex opere operato*.[33] This automatic action might have been a desirable addition to a purely natural magic. But since "higher gifts may also sometimes descend," Ficino must have recognized that the continuity of lower with higher theurgy in Iamblichus opened a path to divinity that was philosophically enticing but religiously menacing.

More attention to the historicity of his sources might have resolved some of Ficino's confusions. His admiration for the *Hermetica* and his interest in their εἰδωλοποιία were, after all, results of an error in dating. In addition, it is worth recalling that the philosophy of Ficino's *Platonici* saw considerable change over a period of centuries: Plotinus began to write in A.D. 253; Porphyry, who introduced the *Oracles* to Neoplatonism, edited the *Enneads* after 298; Iamblichus wrote *De mysteriis* before 300; Synesius' treatise on dreams dates from 405-406; Proclus died in 485; Psellos studied the Neoplatonists in the eleventh century.[34] All the successors of Plotinus altered his themes and added to them, and if Ficino had been

32. Ficino, *DVCC*, 572: Fieri vero posse quandoque ut rationibus ad formas sic adhibitis sublimiora quoque dona descendant, quatenus rationes in anima mundi coniunctae sunt intellectualibus eiusdem animae formis atque per illas divinae mentis ideis. Quod et Iamblichus approbat ubi de sacrificiis agit; cf. *ibid.*, 549, 565; Iamb. *Myst.* 169.4–14, 232.5–234.4; Ficino, *Opera*, 2: 1736, 1745–48, 1891, 1898–99; Plot. *Enn.* 4.3.8.19–21, 11.1–6; 4.4.31.8–15, 24–29, 48–50, 32.1–32, 34.33–38, 35.4–8, 22–23, 36.25–27, 37.17–20, 40.1–9, 42.6–19; Smith, *Porphyry's Place*, 127–28; Copenhaver, "*Ennead* 4.3-5."

33. Ficino, *DVCC*, 549: Iamblichus in materiis quae naturaliter superis consentaneae sint et opportune riteque collectae undique conflataeque fuerint vires effectusque non solum coelestes sed etiam daemonicos et divinos suscipi posse confirmat; Iamb. *Myst.* 96.11–97.19, 232.5–234.4; Ficino, *Opera*, 2: 1882, 1898–99; *supra*, notes 13, 23, 32.

34. Walker, *The Ancient Theology: Studies in Christian Platonism from the Fifteenth to the Eighteenth Century* (London, 1972), 17–21; F. Purnell, Jr., "Francesco Patrizi and the Critics of Hermes

interested in their development as much as their ideas, he might have been more sensitive to the contradictions among them. Yet in the end, other sources of tension in Ficino's magic, especially those arising from Christianity, were more basic. Neoplatonic magic had been notorious in Latin Christianity since Augustine wrote the *City of God*, and it was to remain so despite Ficino's learned efforts to reconcile magic with philosophy and religion. Clarifying the tension between Ficino's learning and his faith helps us understand the motivation of the last sentence of *De vita III*, a confession of Christian orthodoxy: ". . . how impure was the superstition of the pagan people, but by contrast how pure the piety of the Gospel. . . ."[35]

BRIAN P. COPENHAVER

Trismegistus," *Journal of Medieval and Renaissance Studies*, 6 (1976): 155–178; Wallis, *Neoplatonism*, 39, 46–7, 138, 162; Bergman, *Synesius*, 145; Larsen, *Jamblique*, 195–96.

35. Ficino, *DVCC*, 572: Qua de re alibi nos opportunius disputabimus, ubi etiam apparebit quam impura superstitio populi gentilis extiterit, contra vero quam pura pietas Evangelica fuerit, quod magna ex parte in libro *De religione christiana* iam fecimus; *supra*, notes 8, 11; Copenhaver, "Scholastic Philosophy."

NEOPLATONIC CURRENTS AND GASPARE VISCONTI'S FRAG— MENTUM (MS TRIV 1093)

N EARLY TWENTY YEARS AGO, Paul Oskar Kristeller published an article in which he explicitly recognized the importance of currents other than Florentine Neoplatonism in the growth and spread of Renaissance thought and culture.[1] This balanced view is clearly the one to be adopted. But it remains the case, as studies since 1970 on philosophy and literature, as on the arts, have continued to indicate, and as my own work on the Italian mythological plays of the late fifteenth century has begun to reveal, that the importance of the Neoplatonic currents emanating from Florence cannot be minimized.

The diffusion of these currents, and especially of Neoplatonic love theory, was of prime importance in the development of Renaissance artistic theory and iconography, as is well known, and repercussions were felt in literature and in music, both in Italy and in the rest of Europe as the sixteenth century progressed.[2] However, it is also interesting to note the promptness of

1. "La diffusione europea del platonismo fiorentino," in *Il pensiero italiano del Rinascimento e il tempo nostro. Atti del V Convegno Internazionale del Centro di Studi Umanistici*, Montepulciano, 8–13 agosto 1968, ed. G. Tarugi (Florence, 1970), 23–41; an earlier version in English "The European Significance of Florentine Platonism," in *Medieval and Renaissance Studies*, Proceedings of the Southeastern Institute of Medieval and Renaissance Studies, Summer 1967, ed. J. M. Headley (Chapel Hill, 1968), 206–229.
2. To mention a few key works: A. Chastel, *Marsile Ficin et l'art* (Geneva, 1954; repr. 1975);

this diffusion within Italy, but outside of Florence, and among those not normally associated with the Platonic revival. I refer specifically to the poets of the Northern courts of fifteenth-century Italy.

In response to Kristeller's call in the above-mentioned article for documentation of the diffusion of these ideas, I offer the text at hand, which illustrates both early Italian diffusion of Florentine Neoplatonism, and the special interest held for poets by Ficino's *Commentarium in Convivium de amore.*

The text is a *Fragmentum* found in MS Trivulziano 1093, a *zibaldone*, or collection of writings, of the Milanese poet, statesman and courtier, Gaspare Visconti (1461–1499).[3] The manuscript, of III + 185 paper folios, can be dated to the years around 1496, a date which appears in a contemporary hand upside-down at the bottom of the verso of the unnumbered front flyleaf.[4] The composition of the bulk of the manuscript (excluding posthumous additions) can be situated with certainty only between 1493 and 1499. The former date is that of the publication of Visconti's *Rithmi*, none of whose poems appear in the present manuscript.[5] The

idem, *Art et humanisme au temps de Laurent le Magnifique* (Paris, 1961; 3rd ed. 1981); E. H. Gombrich, "Botticelli's Mythologies, A Study in the Neoplatonic Symbolism of his Circle," *JWCI*, 8 (1945): 7–60; E. Panofsky, *Studies in Iconology. Humanistic Themes in the Art of the Renaissance* (New York, 1962); idem, *Idea. A Concept in Art Theory*, tr. J. J. S. Peake (New York, 1968); E. Wind, *Pagan Mysteries in the Renaissance* (New York, 1968); A. Buck, *Der Platonismus in den Dichtungen Lorenzo de' Medicis* (Berlin, 1936); idem, *Der Einfluss des Platonismus auf die volkssprachliche Literatur im Florentiner Quattrocento* (Krefeld, 1965); J. Festugière, *La philosophie de l'amour de Marsile Ficin et son influence sur la littérature française au XVIᵉ siècle* (Paris, 1941); D. P. Walker, "Ficino's 'Spiritus' and Music," *Annales musicologiques*, 1 (1935): 131–150; idem, "The Harmony of the Spheres," in *Studies in Musical Science in the Late Renaissance* (London and Leiden, 1978), 1–13. And see J. C. Nelson, *Renaissance Theory of Love* (New York and London, 1963).

3. Descriptions of the manuscript are in G. Porro, *Catalogo dei codici manoscritti della Trivulziana* (Turin, 1884), 463–464, and Gasparo Visconti, *I canzonieri per Beatrice d'Este e per Bianca Maria Sforza*, ed. P. Bongrani (Milan, 1979), xix–xxiii. Even if the body of poetic texts published from this manuscript by Bongrani must be termed a finished collection, additions and insertions throughout the manuscript by the author (and posthumously by others), as well as the inclusion of a play, *Pasithea* (ff. 75v–100r), seem to me to require the use of the term *zibaldone*. The play and Visconti's biography are presented in C. M. Pyle, "Toward Vernacular Comedy: Gaspare Visconti's *Pasithea*," in *Il teatro italiano del rinascimento* (Milan, 1980), 349–360, and idem, *Politian's "Orfeo" and Other "Favole Mitologiche" in the Context of Late Quattrocento Italy* (Diss., Columbia University, New York, 1976). The play appears in a diplomatic edition in the latter work; it is now published in *Teatro delle corti padane*, ed. A. Tissoni Benvenuti and M. P. Mussini Sacchi (Turin, 1983).

4. This folio bears on its recto in pencil the number 264, which also appears on the label of the Biblioteca Belgioiosa inside the front cover. It continues around the inside of the spine of the book, gathering the sixteen quires, and is pierced by the stitches which join the quires to a sheepskin cover, now backed with blue-grey cardboard.

5. Porro, *Catalogo*, 463–464. The colophon of the printed volume reads in part: . . . F. TAN-

latter is the year of the poet's death. The collection of poems on ff. 2v–42r is dedicated at f. 1r to Beatrice d'Este Sforza, Duchess of Milan. Her death in January 1497 is thus the *terminus ad quem* for this portion of the manuscript, and probably for the play *Pasithea* (ff. 75v–100r) as well.[6] Visconti made use of this *canzoniere* twice, dedicating it once to Beatrice (the presentation copy is Triv. 2157 on purple parchment; cf. Porro, pp. 462–63; Bongrani, pp. xxiii–xxiv), and once, with additions from ff. 44r–134r, to Bianca Maria Sforza, wife of the Hapsburg Emperor Maximilian I (this presentation copy is Vienna, Österreichische Nationalbibliothek, MS Series nova 2621 on parchment[7]). MS Triv. 1093 is clearly the working draft for the collections. It is written by scribes, probably in Visconti's employ, and corrected by the author.[8]

Bongrani (pp. xix–xxiii) discerns seven hands in the manuscript, including that of the author (A_t), which he identifies by means of comparison with the hand of a signed letter in the Archivio di Stato, Mantua, which I have seen (Gonzaga Busta 1614: segn. E. XLIX. 2, published by Bongrani, Tavola I). The hand A_5 he treats, correctly I believe, as operating after Visconti's death to insert in blank spaces various compositions presumably found among the poet's papers. I do not see this work as that of an undiscriminating and uninterested scribe hastily completing a sorry task, as does Bongrani (p. xxxii). Rather, it appears to me a work of devotion, albeit one perhaps completed in haste. The hand of A_5 does indeed seem to be a fast-moving hand, but speed is not always to be attributed to lack of interest or intellectual nonchalance (witness the hand of Angelo Poliziano), although it can sometimes, and in the case of A_5 does, result in errors. In support of the scribe's involvement in his task is the density of the compositions gathered, and his own avowed interest in copying the text we are here considering, evident in his closing words:

CIVS GORNIGER (sic)/POETA MEDIOLANENSIS HOS RHI/THMOS MAGNIFICI AC SPLENDI/DISSIMI EQVITIS GASPARIS VI/CECOMITIS LINGVA VFRNA/CVLA (sic) COMPOSITOS . . . IN MILLE / EXEMPLA IMPRIMI IVS/SIT MEDIOLANI : AN/NO A SALVTIFERO / VIRGINIS : PARTV. / M.CCCC.LXXXXIII. / QVARTO CALEN/DAS MARTIAS. / FINIS. My transcription here, from the copy I have seen in the Biblioteca Nazionale Centrale "Vittorio Emanuele II," Rome, does not agree with that in Hain at number 16078. Bongrani's consistent reference to the book as *Rithimi* is puzzling.

6. Pyle, "Towards Vernacular Comedy," 351; idem, *Politian's "Orfeo"*, 187–190.

7. O. Mazal and F. Unterkircher, *Katalog der abendländischen Handschriften der Österreichischen Nationalbibliothek. "Series Nova,"* Teil 2.1 (Vienna, 1963), 286–287; cf. Bongrani, xxiv–xxv.

8. Bongrani, xx, xxxv–xxxix; cf. Pyle, *Politian's "Orfeo"*, 188–190.

Hactenus inventum summa cura exscripsimus (f. 132r: not *excripsim*, as in Bongrani, p. xxxii).

This text, then, probably inserted by A₅ after the poet's death on March 8, 1499, bears the title at f. 131r: *Fragmentum*, and is there said to be by Magnificus Dominus Gasparus Vicecomes. It is in Italian prose with a Northern patina, and inspection proves it to be composed of portions of the early Orations of Ficino's *De amore*, with minor additions by the *Fragmentum*'s author.[9] Ficino's Latin commentary had been composed at least by July of 1469,[10] and was printed with Ficino's translations of Plato at Florence in 1484 and Venice in 1491, both editions available during the lifetime of Gaspare Visconti, and in particular during the years of composition of MS Triv. 1093.

Comparison of our text with corresponding sentences of Ficino's own vernacular translation of his *De amore* (*Sopra lo amore*), completed by 1474 but not printed until 1544 (and then, seemingly, in response to a transla-

---

9. See the collation with Ficino's *De amore* below. I cannot begin to give a complete bibliography on this work here. I cite the basic or classic works on the subject, and those recent works to which the reader may turn for further references. The text appears in the second volume of Ficino's *Opera omnia* (Basel, 1576; repr. Turin, 1959), 2: 1320–1363; and, edited from BAV, MS Vat. lat. 7705, in M. Ficin, *Commentaire sur le Banquet de Platon*, ed. and tr. R. Marcel (Paris, 1956; repr. 1978). On this edition, see P. O. Kristeller, "Some Original Letters and Autograph Manuscripts of Marsilio Ficino," in *Studi di bibliografia e di storia in onore di Tammaro De Marinis*, 3 [Verona, 1964]: 17–18). See too, *Marsilio Ficino's Commentary on Plato's Symposium*, ed. and tr. S. R. Jayne (Columbia, Missouri, 1944); J. A. Devereux, "The Textual History of Ficino's *De amore*," *RQ*, 28 (1975): 173–182; S. Gentile, "Per la storia del testo del 'Commentarium in Convivium' di Marsilio Ficino," *Rinascimento*, ser. 2, 21 (1981): 3–27 (it should perhaps be stated once and for all that the note in MS Vat. lat. 7705 at f. Ir is in the hand of Gaetano Marini (1740–1815), according to Prof. A. Campana [personal communication], and contrary to Gentile, 15, note 1 and Marcel's introduction to Ficin, *Commentaire*, 40); indispensable now is the catalogue, *Marsilio Ficino e il ritorno di Platone. Mostra di manoscritti, stampe e documenti*, 17 maggio–16 giugno 1984, eds. S. Gentile, S. Niccoli, P. Viti (Florence, 1984), esp. 60–69.

The manuscripts of the Latin version of *De amore* are listed in Marcel's edition (pp. 39–45), in Devereux's article with additions (174–175) and now in Gentile's article (20, note 1). Compare the list of Ficino manuscripts in Kristeller, *Supplementum*, 1: v–lv and 2: 368–369. Devereux's list includes two others found by Kristeller: Morgan Library MS M. 918 (cf. P. O. Kristeller, "Marsilio Ficino as a Beginning Student of Plato," *Scriptorium*, 20 [1966]: 48, note 23) and MS Scale VII (olim XXXIII) in the Biblioteca del Vittoriale, Gardone (cf. Devereux, 179–180; Gentile, 20, note 1).

Printed editions, beginning with *Platonis opera omnia*, 2 vols., Florence, [1484] (Hain *13062); and 1 vol., Venice, 1491 (Hain *13063), which contain Ficino's *De amore* are referred to in the above-mentioned works, and cf. *Supplementum*, 1: lvii–lxxv.

10. Ficin, *Commentaire*, 45; Gentile, 9–19; *Marsilio Ficino e il ritorno di Platone*, 60–61.

tion by Ercole Barbarasa of the same year[11]), shows the Trivulziana text's borrowings to have been translated and paraphrased independently. Accepting the attribution of the text to Visconti made by the hand A$_5$, we are thus in the presence of an extract of portions of Ficino's Latin text noted down and reworked in Italian translation by Gaspare Visconti.

Most of this Italian text can be related to specific points in the first and third Orations of Ficino's *Commentary*. I give the collation by sentence (referring to Marcel's easily available edition), in lieu of a second apparatus:

Triv. 1093	Ficino, *De amore* (Marcel)
1	I.2. par. 2.1–3
2	I.2. par. 2.4
3	I.2. par. 3.1
4	I.2. par. 3.12
5	I.3. par. 1.3
6	I.3. par. 1.2,1
7, 8	I.3. par. 1.1
	(cf. par. 4)
9	(cf. I.3. par. 4)
10, 11	I.2. par. 3.2–7
12	I.2. par. 3.8–9
13	(cf. I.4. par. 2.1)
14	I.2. par. 3.10
15	I.2. par. 3.11
16	(cf. I.4 par. 1.2)
17	III.2. par. 1.1.
	(cf. III.1. par. 1.4)
18	III.2. par. 1.2–7

11. P. O. Kristeller, "Marsilio Ficino as a Man of Letters and the Glosses Attributed to Him in the Caetani Codex of Dante," *RQ*, 36 (1983): 24. The editions are: Marsilio Ficino, *Sopra lo Amore o ver' Convito di Platone* (Florence, Neri Dortelata, November, 1544); *Il comento di Marsilio Ficino sopra il Convito di Platone, & esso Convito, tradotti in lingua toscana per Hercole Barbarasa da Terni* (Rome, Francesco Priscianese Fiorentino, 1544, before April 19: cf. *Marsilio Ficino e il ritorno*, 69). Marcel prints the dedicatory letter to the Barbarasa (misspelled Barbarassa) translation at Ficin, *Commentaire*, 269. The Italian version was edited, on the basis of the Florentine edition and with a preface dated 1914, by Giuseppe Rensi (not Rienzi: Marcel, 274) in the series Cultura dell'Anima (Lanciano: Carabba Editore). On this edition have been based subsequent printings, such as those of Milan, 1973 (preface by G. Ottaviano) and a more recent printing by Atanor in Rome. A critical edition by S. Niccoli is announced as "in corso di stampa" in *Marsilio Ficino e il ritorno di Platone*, 65 (and see 65–69). I have not yet been able to locate this edition.

19	?
20	III.2. par. 1.7–8
21	III.2. par. 1.9 (with addition by Visconti) (cf. VI.3. par. 4 and VI.4. par. 1)
22–25	III.2. par. 1.10–13
26	III.2. par. 2.1
27	III.2. par. 2.2
28	III.2. par. 2.3–4
29	III.2. par. 2.5 (with addition by Visconti)
30	(Addition by Visconti)
31	III.2. par. 2.10–11
32	III.2. par. 2.12
33	III.2. par. 2.13
34	III.2. par. 3.1
35	III.2. par. 3.2 (with addition by Visconti)
36	III.2. par. 3.3
37	III.2. par. 3.4
38	III.2. par. 3.5 (with addition by Visconti)
39	III.2. par. 3.6
40	V.8. par. 4.2 (cf. III.3. par. 1.1 and par. 2.1)
41	Summary by Visconti (cf. above, 1 and 2)

The extracts are arranged to form a coherent whole, beginning and ending with the three points of love's nobility as found in its antiquity (elaborated in sentences 3–9), its greatness as perceived in its present manifestations (sentences 10–15), and its utility as seen in the consequences of its activity (sentences 16–19). The text then launches into a further discussion of the consequences of love (sentences 20–25) and its unifying function and power (sentences 26–40). Sentence 41 is a recapitulation of sentences 1 and 2.

At one or two points in the text, Visconti seems to rephrase or extend Ficino's ideas a trifle (sentences 19?, 21, 29, 30, 35, 38, 41), exhibiting the philosophical bent evident in his poetic and dramatic works. Interestingly, and perhaps worth further textual comparison, his text includes none of the mentions in Oratio III, cap. ii of the cosmic order (spheric arrangement, concentricity, and so forth).[12]

Visconti's interest in Ficino's commentary does not stop with the text here reproduced. In the dedicatory letter of his *canzoniere* for his patroness, and apparently kindred soul, Beatrice d'Este Sforza (Triv. 1093, ff. 1r–2r; Bongrani, pp. 4–7), Visconti's study of Ficino also shows itself. Here he is defending the lessons of love against the opinions of theologians, false philosophers, and those of small intelligence who say love is ignobly born. Again we find a clear and systematic treatment of the questions and, near the beginning, clear echoes of Ficino's *De amore*, in particular those parts of it found in the text from MS Triv. 1093. For example, Visconti states in his dedicatory letter that true philosophers term Love the most eminent among the eminent gods (Bongrani, p. 5; cf. *Fragmentum*, sent. 3–4). He goes on to refer to Plato's *Phaedrus* and *Alcibiades* (accepted by Ficino and included in his edition of 1484[13]). Finally, he argues against those who say Love is not noble and ancient, using the argument that the Creator kept Love (Charity) close to himself, and through Love divided the Chaos into harmonious elements (Bongrani, p. 5; cf. *Fragmentum*, sent. 6–9).

These examples serve to suggest that the reworking of Ficino's *De amore* in MS Triv. 1093 is not distant in time from the dedicatory letter to Beatrice. Bongrani dates the presentation manuscript for Beatrice (Triv. 2157)

---

12. The omissions, like the arrangement of the text, are most likely a sign of Gaspare Visconti's own interests, rather than an indication of another version of the text by Ficino; cf. Devereux, 173.

13. Cf. Kristeller, "Marsilio Ficino as a Beginning," 44–45. The Phaedrus commentary is edited and translated by M. J. B. Allen as *Marsilio Ficino and the Phaedran Charioteer* (Berkeley, Los Angeles, London, 1981); cf. idem, *The Platonism of Marsilio Ficino. A Study of his Phaedrus Commentary* (Berkeley, Los Angeles, London, 1984).

at 1495–1496 (p. xxxiv, n. 3; cf. p. xxiii, n. 2). Thus the present text, probably earlier than the letter to Beatrice in which Visconti makes his own use of the concepts found in Ficino's *De amore*, would date from about 1495.

* * *

In editing Visconti's *Fragmentum*, I have adopted modern conventions of punctuation and paragraphing. I retain the orthography and linguistic patina of Northern fifteenth-century Italy, although when necessary for comprehension I have divided words and joined them according to modern usage. Accents are also in keeping with modern usage. In one or two places, I have chosen to expand abbreviations in keeping with the dominant usage in the text (e.g. p[raese]nte in sentence 2). I have normalized capitalization, for instance of the word Chaos (e.g. sentence 5), and eliminated majuscules where they do not enhance understanding. The text is accompanied by an apparatus giving the manuscript's readings. I have numbered the sentences for the purposes of the above discussion.[14]

CYNTHIA M. PYLE

14. I wish to thank my friend and colleague Antonia Tissoni Benvenuti for reviewing this edition and making helpful comments. The staffs of the Biblioteca Trivulziana and of the Warburg Institute were, as always, most helpful.

Appendix

Gaspare Visconti's *Fragmentum*

The following text is taken from Milan, Bibl. Trivulziana, MS 1093, ff. 131r–132r. For bibliography see note 3 above. In the margin the scribe added the following *Notabilia*; sent. 4, "Plato;" sent. 6, "Hesiodus, Parmenides, Acusileus, Orpheus, Mercurius;" sent. 20 "Dio Areopagita;" sent. 37, "Empedocles;" sent. 40, "Eriximachus."

Fragmentum Magnifici Domini Gasparis Vicecomitis.

1. Se[1] nui vogliamo laudare alchuna cosa è neccessario laudarla da cose antecedente, et etiam da praesente et conseguente. 2. Le cose antecedente mostrano la nobilità, le praesente la magnitudine, le conseguente la utilità.

3. Lo amore adoncha per le cose antecedente se dice essere stato praecipuo et antiquissimo. 4. Così Phaedro disputa apresso a Platone in el quale la nobilità apertissimamente è dimonstrata, affirmando lui l'amore esser antiquissimo de tutti li dei. 5. A Platone similmente è aparso quando lui scrive el Chaos nel Thimeo, perché in quello li colloca et constituisse l'amore. 6. De questa medesma sententia esser stato Hesiodo legiamo ne la Theogonia, et in libro de la natura [di] Parmenide pithagorico et Acusileo poeta et Orpheo et Mercurio: essendo manifesto che'l chaos era avante el mondo, et essendo l'amor collocato in quello, precesse Saturno, Jove et tutti gli altri dei. 7. Per tanto Orpheo domanda l'amore essere antiquissimo et perfecto in sé medesmo, et etiam consultissimo.[2] 8. Et credo in questo seguir la sententia di Mercurio Trismegisto che sente tal cosa. 9. Et questo che è proximo al vero, imo verissimo, non è da negare perché, se l'amore de la divina virtù non havesse precesso quel Chaos, che da sua natura già molto tempo era rude, impolito, confuso et indigesto, per niuno modo havria desiderato questa forma, la qual nui vediamo, del mondo.

10. Oltra di questo, quanta sia la magnitudine de l'amore si può compraehendere per questo: se li mortali e li dei fanno li comandamenti de l'amore, et spesse volte domati et incatenati senteno li colpi de quello ne la mente et ne l'animo suo, chi è quello che dubitarà apellarlo grande? 11. Et de questa openione fu Orpheo et Hesiodo. 12. Admirabile etiam l'amore predica Phedro, et rende questa

---

1. mu (*sic*) *del.*
2. consulissimo ti *supra scr.*

causa apressa a Platone perché ciaschuno chi se vede illaqueato et irretito de la pulchritudine de alchuna cosa la suole admirare. 13. Et veramente non è altro amore se non desiderio de perfruer dela pulchritudine. 14. Et se dice etiam fare li dei (o³ vero cum alchun altro vocabulo vogli apellar gli angeli): admirando mai se satiano de contemplare la divina bellezza, et li mortali la spetia et la forma de li corpi eleganti. 15. Et tal grandeza et admirabilità de amore se monstra ne le cose presente.

16. Possiamo anchor laudar l'amor da cose consequente. 17. Per la qual cosa non mediocre utilità se monstra de quello, el quale certamente se sforza de far deffender et conservar ogni cosa. 18. Veramente a quello è per sua natura innata et ingenita (f. 131v) una certa cupidità de propagare, manifestare et generare una absoluta et consummata perfectione, quale in niuna altra cosa possiamo vedere, salvo che in Dio, il che la divina intelligentia, studiosissimamente havendo contemplato in sé dicta perfectione, la voluntà subito de epsa intelligentia desidera de edure et manifestare in luce tutte le cose. 19. Et questo è che ha in sé de generare el flagrantissimo amore.

20. Non immeritamente Dionisio nostro Areopagita dice che'l divino amore non è potuto lassar el Re de tutte le cose star senza foecundità de procreatione et germinatione, essendo etiam el transito de lo infinito de tal amore, dedito a propagatione et germinatione, transfuso dal summo auctore Idio in tutte le altre cose. 21. Per questo amore gli sancti spirti de Idio moveno i celi et ciaschuni danno li suoi doni uno a l'altro et l'altro a l'altro secondo che seguено per ordine. 22. Per questo le stelle diffondano el lume suo neli elementi. 23. Per questo el fuocho col suo calore move lo aere, lo aere l'aqua, l'aqua la terra; et vice versa [la] terra tira a sé l'aqua et questa tira lo aere, et lo aere el focho. 24. Le herbe simelmente et gli arbori per amor desiderose de propagare la sua semenza generano cose simile a sé. 25. Li animali etiam bruti et li huomeni grandissimamente son rapiti et inflammati da queste illecebre cupidità et esce de amore a procreare sobole.

26. Il che, se lo amore è certo fare ogni cosa, perché non comprobaremo⁴ tutte le cose esser conservate da quello? 27. Lo officio de epso è sempre di conservare et fare. 28. Certamente le cose simili par consistano per cose de una medesma et simel natura, et l'amore tira la cosa simile ad una cosa a sé simile. 29. Ciaschune parte de la terra per uno amore mutuo ingenito et naturale copulante se conferissano a le altre parte simile de sé; ita ché una parte aiuta l'altra, et l'altra l'altra, et mai non se disiungano per amore, et così se conserva el tutto. 30. In tal modo

3. e MS
4. tt del.

tutti gli altri elementi procedeno. 31. Platone nel libro del regno[5] dice che'l celo[6] se move per uno innato et naturale amore et l'anima del ciel è tutta insema in ciaschuni puncti del celo. 32. El celo adunque, desideroso de perfruir de la (f. 132r) sua anima, per tal causa corre aciò possa perfruire de tutta l'anima da ogni canto per tutte le sue parte. 33. Et vola celerrimamente aciò che quanto sia possibile, lui sia tutto insiema de ogni canto dove da ogni canto l'anima è tutta insieme. 34. La qual cosa, se così non se facesse, essendo abandonata in qualche parte, in tal unitate nasceria una discordia che dissolveria tal cosa. 35. Qual unità un mutuo amore de dicte parte se la fa et conserva, et per niuno modo la lassa perire. 36. La qual cosa è licito a vederla ne li humori deli nostri corpi et neli elementi del mondo. 37. Per la concordia de li quali, sì come dice Empedocle pithagoreo, el[7] mondo[8] et etiam el corpo nostro consiste; per la discordia se destrue la concordia de tal pace. 38. Et amore ce presta una certa vicissitudine, ché si uno piglia[9] de l'altro, quello li rende. 39. Per tanto Orpheo dice, "Tu, amore, rege le habene de tutte le cose." 40. Eriximaco commemora apresso a Platone esser niuna arte che lo amore non trova et governa et non sia maestro de quella.

41. Sì che l'amore, per l'antiquità, è nobilissimo; poi, per esser subiecta ogni cosa a quello, è grande et admirabile; tercio, perché da lui procede tutti li beni et è causa et fomento de ogni cosa, si como havemo demonstrato, ha inenarrabile utilità in sé.[10]

---

5. el *del.*
6. cilo *MS*
7. del *del.*; el *supra scr.*
8. per la concordia de li quali *del.*
9. dal *del.*; del *supra scr.*
10. Hactenus inventum summa cura exscripsimus *subscr.*

THE
RAFFAELE
MAFFEI
MONUMENT
IN VOLTERRA
SMALL-TOWN PATRONAGE
IN THE RENAISSANCE

THE SEPULCHRAL MONUMENT in honor of the humanist Raffaele Maffei in the church of San Lino in Volterra has received little scholarly attention. This is partly due to two deceptively clear references to the work made by Vasari which have been the bases for later accounts. In his discussion of Silvio Cosini, Vasari states that after working in Pisa in 1523 and then in Montenero, Cosini ". . . in Volterra fece la sepoltura di messer Raffaello Volaterrano, uomo dottissimo, nella quale lo ritrasse di naturale sopra una cassa di marmo con alcuni ornamenti e figure."[1] This account attributes to Cosini the central element of the monument, the reclining figure of Raffaele Maffei holding a ribbon with the Virgilian tag *Sic itur ad astra* (*Aeneid* 9, 641), and probably some surrounding decoration. In his life of Giovanni Angelo Montorsoli, Vasari writes that the sculptor ". . . porta-

See Plate 1. The research for this study was done with the support of a Summer Stipend from the National Endowment for the Humanities, 1983. The author wishes to thank Professor Sebastiano Di Blasi for assistance with the Italian texts. Professors Kathleen Weil-Garris Brandt, Sheila ffolliott, Charles Dempsey, Werner Gundersheimer, Elizabeth Cropper, and Paul Watson read the manuscript at various stages and offered useful advice. In the Italian and Latin citations all abbreviations have been expanded, capitalization and punctuation have been modernized, and "u" and "v" have been distinguished.
1. Giorgio Vasari, *Le vite de' più eccellenti pittori ed architettori,* annotated by Gaetano Milanesi 9 vols. (Florence, 1878–85), 4:482–483.

segli occasione di partire [from Perugia], se n'ando a lavorare a Volterra, nella sepoltura di M[esser] Raffaello Maffei detto il Volaterrano, nella quale, che si faceva di marmo, intaglio alcune cose che mostrarono quell'ingegno dovere fare un giorno qualche buona riuscita. La quale opera finita [he went to Florence]. . . .[2] Although no date is provided for Montorsoli's work in Volterra, the subsequent reference to his time in Florence with Michelangelo in the Medici Chapel would indicate 1524.

While Vasari identifies Cosini and Montorsoli with the monument in Volterra, he remains vague as to the distribution of the work and date of completion. This is not surprising since the history of the monument is complicated. While unpublished archival material provides more definite information concerning the genesis and construction of the monument, many questions must remain open. The unravelling of the history of the monument will shed light on problems relating to small-town artistic patronage and the chronology of Silvio Cosini and Giovanni Angelo Montorsoli, two artists whose activities remain difficult to date precisely.

I

As Vasari noted, the monument was in honor of a "uomo dottissimo." Raffaele Maffei (commonly called "il Volterrano", 1456–1522) was a significant representative of early Cinquecento Italian humanism.[3] He belonged to a Volterran family which made its fortune in the Curia Romana, where he himself served as a papal scriptor. He had broad scholarly interests, ranging from classical history and culture through modern politics. His major work was the large *Commentariorum Urbanorum libri octo et triginta* (Rome, 1506), an early example of Renaissance encyclopedism. A devoted student of Greek, Maffei translated a variety of classical and

2. *Ibid.,* 6:630

3. For Raffaele Maffei, see B. Falconcini, *Vita del buon servo di Dio Raffaello Maffei detto il Volterrano* (Rome, 1722); P. Paschini, "Una famiglia di curiali: I Maffei di Volterra," *Rivista di storia della chiesa in Italia,* 7 (1953): 337–376, at 344–356, 363–367; J. F. D'Amico, "A Humanist Response to Martin Luther: Raffaele Maffei's *Apologeticus,*" *The Sixteenth Century Journal,* 6.2 (1975): 37–56; idem, "Papal History and Curial Reform in the Renaissance: Raffaele Maffei's *Breuis Historia* of Julius II and Leo X," *Archivum Historiae Pontificiae,* 18 (1980): 75–128; idem, *Renaissance Humanism in Papal Rome: Humanists and Churchmen on the Eve of the Reformation* (Baltimore, 1983), chaps. 3, 8, 9.

patristic writers. He was deeply religious, and spent his last years in religious contemplation and composition.

Maffei's career in the Curia was limited by his decision to marry, a union which produced one surviving daughter, named Lucilla. More successful in the Curia was Raffaele's brother Mario (1463–1537), a priest and a close associate of the Medici popes.[4] Among his other positions Mario was a canon of St. Peter's, which led Julius II to make him one of the supervisors of the *fabbrica* of St. Peter's in 1507.[5] Mario was a close companion of Leo X, who appointed him bishop of Aquino in 1516, and the pope's cousin, Cardinal Giulio de'Medici. Mario was an artistic advisor to Leo and Cardinal Giulio. On one occasion Leo requested that Mario write an epitaph to be placed under windows being built for the University of Rome (the *Sapienza*).[6] Cardinal Giulio consulted Mario for the decorations of his new villa, the Villa Madama, and entrusted him with the task of supervising the completion of its construction.[7] As proof of

4. On Mario, see Falconcini, *passim;* A. Ferraioli, "Il Ruolo della corte di Leone X," *Archivio della Società Romana di Storia Patria,* 38 (1915): 261–269; L. Pescetti, "Mario Maffei (1463–1537)," *Rassegna volterrana,* 6 (1932): 65–91; Paschini, 356–363, 369–376; L. Pescetti, "Le nozze di Lucrezia Borgia in una lettera inedita di Jacopo Gherardi a Mario Maffei," *Rassegna volterrana,* 21–22 (1955): 1–6; J. Ruysschaert, "Recherches des deux bibliothèques romaines Maffei des XVe et XVIe siècles," *La Bibliofilia,* 60 (1958): 306–355; D'Amico, "Papal History and Curial Reform, 83–84; idem, *Renaissance Humanism in Papal Rome,* chaps. 3, 4; and idem, "Reformed and Unreformed Bishops in Renaissance Rome," in the forthcoming *Proceedings of the American Historical Association, 1983.*

5. See C. L. Frommel, "Die Peterskirche unter Papst Julius II. im Licht neuer Dokumente," *Römisches Jahrbuch für Kunstgeschichte,* 17 (1976): 93–95.

6. Mario discusses this in an undated, mutilated letter, in Rome, BN, Lettere autografe, A.95.64, to Paolo Riccobaldi del Bava, from Rome: "Assi a mettere un distico sotto le finestre dello studio che papa Leone vuole si fornicata lo studio. Io ne ho facti due; et perche ha donato la gabella dello studio a Romani, che con quella si puo avanzare per lo edificio et alcune altre immunita, io atutto alluddolo ho facti questi, et cosi ne fa tu et messer Raffaello qualche uno.

> Dona recognoscit Decimi iam Roma Leonis,
> Dum Phebo et Musis nobile surgit opus.

> Munera magna dedit Decimus Leo. Romule, plaude
> Cum populo: Musis nunc quoque tecta parat."

For other examples of Mario's poetry, see Vatican City, BAV, MS Ottob. Lat. 2860, ff. 110v, 119r, 184r–v. Maffei remained interested in Roman artistic activities all his life. On a trip to Rome in 1534 he noted that the new pope, Paul III, planned to have a portico built from his palace of San Marco to the church of Ss. Apostoli; see Rome, BN, Lettere autografe, A.95.45 (2), letter dated Nov. 28, 1534.

7. See R. Lefevre, "Note sulla 'vigna' del Cardinal Giulio a Monte Mario," *Studi romani,* 9 (1961): 394–403; idem, "La 'vigna' del cardinale Giulio de'Medici e il vescovo d'Aquino," *Strenna dei romanisti,*

his appreciation, Giulio translated Mario from Aquino to the diocese of Cavaillon in France in 1524.

With the money from his ecclesiastical and curial offices, Mario built a palace in Volterra and a villa at nearby Villamagna. He kept careful watch over these enterprises through correspondence with Paolo Riccobaldi del Bava who had married his niece Lucilla before 1515.[8] Since there was no surviving male child in the family, the Maffei depended on Riccobaldi for the continuity of the family name. Mario even adopted Paolo in 1525 with the proviso that he assume the Maffei name. Riccobaldi's son Giulio, born in 1523, was the ultimate inheritor of the Maffei fortune. It is through the often detailed correspondence between Mario in Rome and in Villamagna, and Riccobaldi in Volterra and in Florence, that we can follow the history of the monument for Raffaele.

The Maffei family was involved in a variety of artistic enterprises in the first decades of the sixteenth century. Raffaele endowed the Poor Clares' convent at San Lino with 8,000 scudi in 1480. This is the church where he would be buried. He also contributed to the refurbishing of the Duomo in Volterra. Raffaele had built a *sepultura* in the village of Pomerance in honor of his friend the Greek-Italian poet Michele Marullo, who in 1500 had drowned in the river Cecina near Volterra when returning to Florence after a visit to Raffaele. Maffei may have felt responsible for the poet's untimely death and erected the monument as a testimony to their friendship.[9]

The greatest of the Maffei's undertakings was their palace in Volterra.[10] The palace is mentioned regularly in the Maffei correspondence from

22 (1961): 171–177; idem, "Un prelato del '500, Mario Maffei, e la costruzione di Villa Madama," *L'Urbe*, 33 (1969): 1–11; idem, *Villa Madama* (Rome, 1975), 107–117.

8. The Maffei correspondence is divided among four depositories. The most significant collection of Mario's letters is in Rome, BN, Lettere autografe, A.95.1 to A.98.68, originally part of the Archivio Maffei in Volterra. References to these letters hereafter will be simply to shelf marks. The other major collection is the Archivio Maffei housed in the Biblioteca Comunale Guarnacciana in Volterra. Among the large number of *buste* in this Archivio, *buste* 105 and 110 relate to Mario. Also in the Volterra library is a collection of letters in *buste,* XLVII/ 2 / 1, XLVII/ 2 / 1 (1) and XLVII/ 2 / 1 (2). In the Biblioteca Apostolica Vaticana, there are two collections of copies of letters from Raffaele and Mario Maffei, MS Barb Lat. 2517, and MS Ottob. Lat. 2413. Finally, in Forlì, Bibl. Comunale, Autografi Piancastelli, *busta* 1340, there is a collection of letters of Raffaele and Mario Maffei.

9. For the *sepultura,* which no longer exists, see G. Fatini, "Spigolatura ariostesco-volterrana," *Rassegna volterrana,* 1 (1924): 106–114, at 112.

10. For the palace, which still stands, see C. Ricci, *Volterra* (Bergamo, 1905), 83–84, and plates 59 and 61. A few letters from the Bibl. Nazionale Centrale "Vittorio Emanuele" in Rome on

1513 through the early 1530's. A number of architects, sculptors and stone-masons from Volterra, Rome, and Florence carried out Mario's intentions under Riccobaldi's supervision. In some cases Mario himself seems to have had a hand in making designs for the palace. Once, when sending a design for some rooms, Mario hoped that he would not be mocked as was an unnamed cardinal who preferred to solicit designs from artists without great reputations. Since the general plans had to be communicated through letters, there were several occasions when Paolo had to suffer the brunt of Mario's displeasure with the progress of work on the palace. The palace was sufficiently complete by 1527 for an inscription praising the Maffei family to be added to the exterior.[11] The villa at Villamagna also forms a prominent theme in the Maffei correspondence. Mario lived there after his return to Volterra from Rome in the spring of 1526.[12]

In addition to these private buildings, Mario contributed to the physical well-being of the city and church of Volterra. As the commendary abbot of the Camaldolese Badia of Saints Justin and Clement in Volterra, Mario had its cloister rebuilt in the 1520's and again concerned himself with its design.[13] Similarly, as an archpriest of the Duomo of Volterra, he restored the chapel of San Gherardo, the Maffei family's patron saint. Included in Mario's plans for his chapel were sacred vessels displaying the coat of arms of Cardinal Giulio de'Medici.[14] There are even indications that Mario considered refurbishing other buildings and constructing a public library in Volterra.[15] On a smaller scale, in 1535 he commissioned a golden head of St. Mario from a Florentine *orefice* as a gift for the Duomo of Volterra.[16] Also for the Duomo, Mario obtained from Rome a silver

the palace are cited in F. Sricchia Santoro, "Daniele da Volterra," *Paragone*, n.s., 33 (1967): 3–34, at notes 5 and 7.

11. A.95.8 (3), June 9, 1521: "Delle volte delle due camere ti mando questo disegno, ma non mi dilegiare come fa el cardinale che dice non vuole disegni di dipintori di tanta riputatione; credo lo intenderai facilissimamente." For the inscription on the palace, see Pescetti, "Mario Maffei," 83.

12. A local guide book, *Il Volterrano: carte del territorio*, ed. Renato Volpini (Pisa, 1976), 30, ascribes the villa and palace to Baldassare Peruzzi without support. However, see below, note 36, where Peruzzi might also be associated with the Maffei.

13. See A. Cinci, *Storia di Volterra*, (Volterra, 1885; repr., Bologna, 1977), chap. 7, and L. Consortini, *La Badia dei Ss. Giusto e Clemente* (Lucca, 1915), 24–28. See also A.95.13 (6), Sept. 12, 1523.

14. See Pescetti, "Mario Maffei," 90–91, note 4. Maffei was involved in the construction in 1518, see A.95.5 (7). See G. Leoncini, *Illustrazioni sulla Cattedrale di Volterra* (Siena, 1869), 348.

15. See A.95.16 (1), January 5, 1524, and Volterra, XLVII/ 2 / 1 (2), March 19, 1537.

16. See A.95.47 (6), June 30, no year; Archivio Maffei *busta* 110, 1535: "Item addi 30 [di giugno?] mandai a Messer Paolo scudi dieci d'oro di sole per mano di Betto, che li rimettessi allo

reliquary for the head of San Ottaviano and a silver, jeweled crucifix to replace one by Pollaiuolo (1470) lost during the civil disorders of 1530.[17] The monument in honor of Raffaele was, therefore, but one of several artistic projects which absorbed the Maffei's time and money in the early sixteenth century.

Taken as a group, these activities show the Maffei attempting to duplicate in Volterra the artistic and architectural preferences of the High Renaissance. In so doing, Mario selected men of quality, if not of outstanding reputations, who were associated with the best artists in Rome and Florence, and who afterwards established themselves as masters. The monies accumulated through his several curial and episcopal offices and land holdings in Rome and Volterra, the knowledge of architectural principles acquired in Rome and connections to important Tuscan artistic centers, provided Mario with both the ability and background to act as an important local patron.

II

In selecting artists to work for them, the Maffei could call on the local stone workers in Volterra. But despite this ready pool, they also sought sculptors, stone-cutters, architects and masons from Rome, Florence and other Tuscan cities. The correspondence names a number of artists, some of whom can be identified. But others must remain unknown. Among these men were some with whom the Maffei developed a close relationship, treating them as friends.[18]

From the late 1510's until the mid–1530's the Maffei made constant use of a master builder named Giovanni.[19] The Maffei did not further

orefice della testa a Fiorenza, et resterà solo haver dieci altri scudi." Idem, August 9, 1535: "Andero domattina, Deo dante, a Volterra per la testa di sancto Mario. Scudi octo di sole, lire 5." There are several letters from Giovanni Battista Riccobaldi del Bava, Paolo's brother, from Florence to Paolo relating to the head; see A.98.17 (2), July 6, 1535; A.98.18, Aug. 2, 1535; A.98.19 (1), Aug. 4, 1535; A.98.19 (2), Aug. 8, 1535; A.98.19 (3), Aug. 18, 1535.

17. Volterra, XLVII/ 2 / 1 (2), March 19, 1534, Paolo to Mario, who was then in Rome, where the head of Sant'Ottaviano (presently in the Duomo) and the cross of silver are discussed. See Ricci, *Volterra,* 129, and E. Carli *Volterra nel Medioevo e nel Rinascimento* (Pisa, 1978), 79–80, and figure 144.

18. See Volterra, XLVII/ 2 / 1 (1), letter dated Rome, Nov. 10, 1535, from Mario to Paolo, who was then in Florence, where a *scarpellino* is called *mio amico.*

19. See A.95.5 (2), Jan. 1518; A.95.11 (8), March 28, 1523; A.95.5 (2), Rome, 1518; A.95.5

identify him and we may assume that he was a local resident. He recruited other workers for the palace and oversaw important parts of its contruction. Obviously Giovanni was a man with whom the Maffei felt comfortable and whose advice they trusted. In view of his long association with the Maffei, this maestro Giovanni probably contributed to all their architectural enterprises.

Several sculptors mentioned in the correspondence worked on the Duomo of Volterra in the 1520's. Among these is a Florentine architect named maestro Chimento who worked for the Maffei in various capacities from the middle of the second decade of the century.[20] Also involved in the Duomo were Giusto di Traviano di Cuiffone di San Giusto, described as a *vecchio scarpellino*, Chimento's nephew, maestro Jacopo, and Raffaele la Cioli.[21] Cioli had a not always happy relationship with the Maffei throughout the 1520's.[22] Outside of the Duomo project, the correspondence also mentions a maestro Domenico *scarpellino* who had connections with Florence and Rome, and a Pietro *scarpellino*, who, like Domenico, worked on the palace.[23] In addition to these men there are several sculptors active in Maffei projects in the 1520's and 1530's whose identity must remain for the time unknown. Among these are a Michele Gherardo *muratore*, a Raphaello *scarpellino*, who seems not to have been Cioli,[24] a *scarpellino da Montecatini*, a maestro Francesco, and a Giovanni *scarpellino* who will be discussed below.[25]

3), Rome, 1525; A.95.30 (1), from San Donnino, Feb. 12, 1527; A.95.31 (2), Feb. 28, 1524; A.95.31 (3), Aug. 4, 1527; A.95.31 (4), Aug. 13, 1527; Volterra, XLVII/ 2 / 1 (2), Aug. 21, 1527, Nov. 24, 1528; A.95.31 (1), May 28, 1528; Volterra, XLVII/ 2 / 1, June 20, 1528; also A.95.60 (2), s. a.; A.95.53 (6), s.l., s.a.

20. See M. Battistini, "Raffaello Cioli da Settignano lavorò in Volterra ai primi del '500," *Rassegna volterrana*, 1 (1924): 128–130, at 128. Also A.95.2 (1), April 15, 1515; A.95.3 (4), June 23, 1516; A.95.4 (4), April 4, 1517; A.95.13 (6), Sept. 12, 1523; A.95.3 (4), June 23, s.a.

21. Volterra, XLVII/ 2 / 1 (2), Jan. 24, 1520, and A.95.22 (1), Nov. 11, 1524. See also F. A. Lesi, "La Cattedrale di Volterra: arte e storia," *Rassegna volterrana*, 50–51 (1974): 5–70, at 61, and Battistini, "Cioli," 128.

22. See Battistini, "Cioli," and Volterra, XLVII/ 2 / 1, Jan. 24, 1520; Nov. 24, 1528; Jan. , 1528; June 7, 1532; A.95.7 (6), Oct. 5, 1520. See also Carli, *Volterra*, fig. 87.

23. See A.96.59 (1), Jan. 6, 1520; A.96.59 (2), Jan. 13, 1520; A.96.59 (4), Jan. 30, 1520; A.96.59 (6), Feb. 18, 1520; A.95.8 (1), Dec. 22, 1520, and Battistini, "Cioli," 68.

24. See A.95.4 (5), May 7, 1517; A.95.13 (6), Sept. 12, 1523; A.95.19 (1), April 2, 1524; A.95.45 (3), Dec. 3, 1534; A.95.43 (11), Sept. 20, s.a.; Archivio Maffei *busta* 110, account book for year 1534, and the record of a payment of 20 ducats to Gherardo in Volterra, XLVII/ 2 / , s.d., s.l. For Raphaello *scarpellino*, see Volterra, XLVII/ 2 / 1 (2), Jan. 7, 1528, Nov. 24, 1528 and June 7, 1532.

25. For the *scarpellino da Montecatini*, see Volterra, XLVII/ 2 / 1 (2), Nov. 24, 1528 and A.95.5

Two other artists appear regularly in the letters and the surviving account books. One is Meo *scarpellino,* who is also called Meo del Sodo *scarpellino da Volterra.*[26] His association with the Maffei must have been a close one since they trusted him with the completion of important elements of the palace, although there was some friction with him over his work and wages. We have no other information on him. More certain is the role Mario Maffei played in the career of Daniele Ricciarelli, called "da Volterra" (1509–1566).[27] As a local boy (he is referred to as "Nello" by the Maffei[28]), it was natural for Mario to take an interest in him. Daniele's most important commission for the Maffei seems to have been the sgraffitto work on the facade of the palace. It is also probable that Mario played some role in advancing Daniele's career in Rome.

This extensive contact of the Maffei with sculptors, architects, and stoneworkers forms the background to the monument in honor of Raffaele. Further, the problems they occasionally had in these other projects foreshadowed the troubles the Maffei would encounter in obtaining from the selected sculptor the finished monument. The Maffei's attempt to recruit the necessary talent to construct the *sepultura* and the difficulties they encountered makes its story illustrative of the trials facing patrons in small towns.

(2), Jan. 1518. For maestro Francesco, see A.95.2 (2), Aug. 1515. For Giovanni *scarpellino,* see below note 68.

26. See A.95.35 (1), Aug. 17, 1530; A.95.35 (2), Sept. 20, 1530; Volterra XLVII/ 2 / 1 (1), Oct. 15, 1530, where Meo is sent to Rome; A.94.13 (4), Sept. 6, 1533; A.95.21 (3), Sept. 21, 1533. Archivio Maffei *busta* 110 has an account book listing payments to Meo for work done in both Rome and Volterra. See A.95.57 (4), Aug. 3, 1535, in which there is mention of a "banco secondo el modello del Farnese." A.95.58 (1), Sept. 21, 1535; and A.96.21 (6), Sept. 27, 1535.

27. See R. S. Maffei, "Intorno ai pittori Ricciarelli e Rossetti," *Rassegna mensile di storia, letteratura ed arte per la città di Volterra e suo territorio,* 3 (1926): 27–31; M. L. Mez, "Daniele da Volterra," *Rassegna volterrana,* 7 (1933): 3–64; F. Sricchia Santoro, "Daniele da Volterra", *Paragone,* n.s., 33 (1967): 3–34, and Carli, *Volterra,* 63–69. Mario may also have helped another artist from Volterra, Giovanni Zacchi; see R. S. Maffei, *Giovanni di Zaccaria Zacchi scultore volterrano (1512–1516)* (Melfi, 1906).

28. See Archivio Maffei *busta* 110 for the account books of 1535, where Daniele is called "Nello dipintore." See also Maffei, "Intorno ai pittori," 29, for citations. Although conjectural, the Maffei might have also employed Rosso Fiorentino. In 1521 Rosso painted a "Madonna with the Child Jesus, John the Baptist, and Saint Bartholomew" for the church of Villamagna, the locality of Mario's villa. See R. S. Maffei, "Una tavola ignorata del Rosso Fiorentino," *Rassegna mensile di storia, letteratura ed arte per la città di Volterra e suo territorio,* 2 (1925): 105–107; reproduction in Carli, *Volterra,* fig. 126.

III

Raffaele Maffei died on January 22, 1522. Two weeks later, on February 3, Mario wrote to Riccobaldi discussing the funeral rites for the dead man and urging him to be restrained in external manifestations of grief. In this letter, Mario spoke approvingly of Paolo's suggestion of erecting a *sepultura* in honor of the deceased and even proposed a commemorative epitaph.[29] Mario favored Paolo's proposal because it offered an opportunity both to commemorate his brother and to fulfill a plan to erect a chapel dedicated to San Gherardo, a Franciscan from Villamagna, who was the Maffei's patron saint.[30] Immediately prior to Raffaele's death Mario discussed with Paolo the chapel and its placement in San Lino. Mario proposed as a model a chapel in Santa Maria degli Angeli in Florence which contained a picture of San Gherardo with a diadem.[31] Mario mentioned the *sepultura* again in May 1522, when he asked Riccobaldi to investigate the best means of securing the necessary marble from Lunigiana or Campiglia. Mario promised that he would have a design ready for the monument.[32] Riccobaldi must have been unable to execute Mario's orders since on October 25, 1525, Mario again wrote to Paolo to ascertain the expense

29. This letter is in A.95.9, and is reproduced with some variants in Falconcini, 213: "Quanto all'Esequie bisogna molto ben vedere quello avemo a fare, perche ne e fatte parecchie, che non si ponno equipare, a far meno forse non è bene. Dipoi sono fatte quelle del Papa di fresco [Leo X had died in Dec. 1521], et opposita juxta se posita etc. A me pare che in la Chiesa di S. Lino congreghiate una mattina quanti potete abili a dire mese, e li senza poma alcuna facciate pregare Dio per l'anima sua. Et quando a Voi non piaccia il parer mio, fate come pare a Voi; purche non entriate in frenetico di drappelloni. Quello che dici della sepultura bella molto mi pare, a farassi omnino, et sara cosa piu durabile. L'epitaphio farai come ti pare pur, poche parole v[erbi] g[ratia]

Raphaeli Mafei Graecis, Latinis litteris eruditissimo vitae sanctitate ac omni virtutum genere ornatissimo, Marius Fr[ater] ad tempus p[osuit]."

30. On San Gherardo, see D. Francioni, *Vita del Beato Gherardo da Villamagna* (Florence, 1886). In the Archivio Maffei *busta* 110, there is a letter Mario wrote to Raffaele on Jan. 4, 1522, on the proposed chapel. See also Pescetti, "Mario Maffei," 81.

31. See the letter of Jan. 4, 1522 in Pescetti, "Mario Maffei," 81, which discusses papal approval for the veneration of San Gherardo.

32. See Falconcini, 214: "Della sepoltura di M. Raffaello non credere che io mi sia dimenticato. Vedi tu di costa cominciare a investigare e domandare sopra di questo, e vedi dove sarebbe meglio far venire i marmi, o da Luni, o da Campiglia, overo abbozzati da Firenze. Io similmente di qua farò fare qualche disegno, et avvisa sopra di questo."

of obtaining the marble for the *sepultura*. At the same time Mario wrote that he had had made an appropriate design.[33]

No mention of the monument appears in the correspondence for a year. The demands placed on Mario in preparing for his departure from Rome, in continuing work at San Donnino and the palace as well as problems in obtaining the necessary marble explain this delay.[34] Despite this hiatus Mario remained committed to building the *sepultura* and considered his arrival in Volterra an opportunity to expedite the tomb and other pressing matters.[35] Even while in Rome, Mario had not completely ignored the monument and its design. He had had copies made of a tomb in Santa Maria del Popolo to use as a model for the *sepultura*. When he left Rome, he did not take these designs with him, but asked one of his functionaries in Rome, Marcello Fucci of Città di Castello, to send them to him. Fucci in a letter of October 22, 1526, wrote that he was unable to obtain the designs Mario had requested from a certain Baldassare.[36] Later Fucci obtained a design of a tomb in Santa Maria del Popolo which he sent to Mario on January 23, 1527, although it was mutilated.[37] Fucci obtained from a sculptor in Rome a full design of the *sepultura* lacking only an epitaph and intended to send it to Mario at a convenient time.[38] Mario

33. Volterra XLVII/ 2 / 1: "Vorrei che si pensare alla sepoltura di messer Raphaello, et che tu investigarsi donde e manco spesa far venir del marmo, o da Campiglia, o da Luna. Intendo che'l marmo di Campiglia e marmo gentil et buono. Quoniam [?] fusse cosi, sara buono ordinare che se piglli dili. Advisarmi quanto e da Campiglia a Volterra et quanto e da Luna, et donde lo fa venire Alberto, et sieti a mente qui non fugge tempo di giorni ne di septimane, recordatene. Io ho facto far uno disegno che credo saro aproposto. Quanto sarra i tempi, telo mandero."

34. See the letter from Mario to Paolo on the bequest by Raffaele to the nuns of San Lino, A.95.27 (5), April 14, 1526: "La sepultura ti ricordo et vedi donde hanno ha venire piu commodamente li marmi."

35. In an undated letter in Volterra XLVII/ 2 / 1, Oct. 7, Mario wrote that "Io so venuto qua per vivare[?] a S. Donnino et costi le cose et fare la sepultura di [Messer] Raffaello et el chiostro di S. Justo et ancor qualche altra opera laudabile, et in questo voglio voltar tutta la mia entrata et non in altri lavori donec ista erunt perfecta." Although no date is given, the letter probably refers to Mario's arrival in Volterra in 1526.

36. See A.97.21 (3), Oct. 22, 1526: "Non ho mai trovato Baldassare acio li potesse parlare di quelli desegni dello sepulture. Io si[?] lo trovo li faro lambasciada, et vedero anchor di mandare el desegno di quelli dal Popolo che V. S. men ha avisato." This Baldassare may have been Peruzzi who might have been associated with the Maffei villa in Villamagna. See above note 12.

37. See A.97.22 (1), Jan. 23, 1527: "Mando el desegno da una di quelle sepulture belle dal Popolo, el quale per essere cusi piegato non so si se guastare; pur lo mando per havermelo chiesto V. S. tante volte."

38. See A.97.22 (2), Feb. 23, 1527: "La sepultura di Capella tandem e fornita, cioe di mettar su ogni cosa excepto che si pense se habia a fare lepitaffio, et hassi a pulire e lustrare."

had obviously sought his inspiration for his brother's tomb in Santa Maria del Popolo which was the great center of funerary sculpture in High Renaissance Rome.[39]

Despite the dispatch of the design and his plans to have a contract drawn up for the *sepultura*, the unsettled state of Tuscany in 1527 prevented any work being accomplished.[40] In addition to the political disturbances, the Maffei architectural activities kept the *sepultura* only a design through 1528. Indeed, Mario felt that work on the tomb would be expedited if it could be done in Florence.[41] It was perhaps these problems and delays as well as the obvious expense of a marble tomb that led Riccobaldi on January 26, 1528 to propose to Mario a wooden monument in the palace that could be cheaply, and no doubt quickly, constructed. Further, Riccobaldi's letter indicates that he was having difficulties with the artist selected to do the monument.[42] As will be seen, Mario rejected Paolo's suggestion.

Seven years after the death of Raffaele, a contract was finally drawn up on January 21, 1529. A rough draft of it survives.[43] The Maffei seem

39. For Santa Maria del Popolo, see *Umanesimo e primo Rinascimento in S. Maria del Popolo*, eds. R. Cannata, A. Cavallano, and C. Strinati (Rome, 1981).

40. See A.95.30 (4), April 2, 1527: "Io lo dicto di sette porte da camere et sale di cenci fiorentini, bisogna fare unaltro pacto con qualche altra cosa che debade et poi fare un terzo cottimi della sepultura, ma tra le guerre delli homini et quello de Dio con questo arrabiato tempo io non so pensar di far cosa alcuna."

41. Volterra XLVII/ 2 / 1, July 3, 1528: "Voglio attendere alla sepultura et se si potessi praticare a Firenze gia ne haverei cavate le mani."

42. Volterra, Archivio Maffei *busta* 105, Jan. 26, 1528: "Della sepultura ho grandissimo piacere che lhabe la casa [?] et parmi nhabbi buon mercato meglio di 50 [scudi], si la conduce nel modo di quel mezzo di legno che io ucelisi [?], sara molto bella. Ho facto bene ad volere le securta, che io per me non havevo molta fede sopra di lui soli. Parmi volontaroso et piu cupido dho noia che de guadagno che e buon parte."

43. Forlì, Autografi *busta* 1340 (see above note 8); on the verso side "De Raphaellis sepultura" is written. The contract is dated "1529 die 21 Jan." "Pacti et conditioni che chiede messer Mario Maffei da mastro Johannino da Firenze scarpb⟨e⟩llinus cioe. . . che lui ha soscripto in sua mano che mastro Johannino facia una sepultura secondo el desegno di mano sua et secondo quello che ve ag⟨i⟩unto, cioe el nome di Cristo in un sole et le due figurette, una dello agnolo Raffaello senza Tobia et laltra di Sancto Gherardo frate, et in scambi delle a quile due mozi avivi in festone alta quanto puo ire et larghe sette braccia lavorata di marmo di Carrara nuovo, fine et senza vene, conducta et posta in opera in S. Lino in Volterra a ogni sua spesa tanto di marmo come di vetura, gabella et manufactura et ogni altra spesa, ordinaria o vero extraordinaria che vi intervenisse, et questo si oblighi a fare in fra termine di uno anno cominciando a . . . calande Frebraio [Marzo *crossed out*] proximo davenire, et dando decto mastro Johannino bona securta in Pisa [Volterra *crossed out*], dicto messer Mario li dara 200 scudi vz., di prestate 50 scudi et a . . . Marzo 25 altri scudi, et poi in capo di sei mesi 50 scudi, se havera comprati li marmi et lavorati secondo el tempo corso, et in capo alanno li dara altri 50 scudi similiter lavorando, et di poi li altri 50 li dara finito el lavoro tutto et messo in opera che non vi manchi niente, et volendo far questo si oblighi alla

to have considered their relative a candidate for sainthood and wanted a sumptuous monument to honor him. The contract is addressed to a sculptor named "Johannino da Firenze scarpellino" who agreed to carve from the best Carrara marble a *sepultura* according to the design of his own hand for the sum of 200 scudi d'oro to be paid in four installments with a 40 lire bonus if beautifully done. The contract specifies that the monument was to consist of two small statues, one of the Archangel Raphael without Tobias, in honor of the deceased, and the other of San Gherardo, the family patron. Further, in the decorations surrounding the statues (*festoni*), the sculptor was to supply two small life-like boy figures (*mozi*) who were to be inserted instead of eagles. There was to be added the name of Christ in the form of $\overline{\text{IC}} + \overline{\text{XC}}$ enclosed in a sun burst, a device the Maffei usually placed at the head of their writings. A fine of 50 scudi was specified if the sculptor did not complete the work within one year. With the exception of the Latin epitaph which Mario was to write,[44] the central reclining figure of Raffaele Maffei, a dog accompanying Raphael, and the two facing reliefs of the Maffei coat of arms (half-stags rampant, one with a bishop's mitre representing Mario),[45] this contract details the major elements of the present monument. The contract is witnessed by several men including Pietro Danto *orafo,* "Frate detto Albigo da Certaldo," Niccolò del Benino Casieri of the bank of Andrea da Ricasoli, Simone del Nicholaio da Poggibonsi, and another banker, Piero of Pisa.

The major problem relating to the contract is the identity of the sculptor referred to as "Johannino da Firenze." There are a number of candidates. Although the maestro Giovanni mentioned above would be a logical prospect, the letters do not connect him to the *sepultura.* Since Giovanni is not called a sculptor nor from Florence, his candidature is doubtful. In

pena di 50 scudi appl⟨i⟩carsi la meta alla mensa del vescovo di Volterra et laltra meta alli canonici non servando. Et se lui non po dar stansa in Volterra, diala a Firenze et le pene la meta a S. Maria Nova di Firenze, laltra meta a S. Pietro di Firenze." On one side of the document are the name of the witnesses and on the other the following: "40 lire piu se sara bela et bene facta a iudicio di chi intende."

44. The epitaph on the monument reads: CRISTO SERVATORI/ RAPHAELI MAFFEO GERARDI MAFF. DOCTRINA/ PIETATE AC SANCTITATE CVM QVOVIS ANTI/ QVORUM COMPARANDO VT EIVS INDICANT/ OPERA EGREGIA TESTANTVR MIRACVLA/ VIX. AN. LXX. M. XI. D. VIII. OBIIT AN. SAL./ M. D. XIII. VII. KAL. FEBR./ MARIVS MAFFEVS EPS. CAVALICEN./ FRATRI SANCTIS. P.

45. For the Maffei coat of arms, see Ruysschaert, "Recherches des deux bibliothèques...," 309–310.

a letter of June 1536, there is mention of a "Giovanni scarpeleino" who made a model of a cornice which Riccobaldi judged to be too large. Possibly this cornice was connected with the *sepultura* since there is mention of Silvio Cosini who did work on the tomb. The correspondence gives no other indication of this man's work.[46] Isolated references to a "Johanni" and a "Johannello" appear, but their dates and exact duties are uncertain.[47] Since the *scarpellino* mentioned in the contract is not a Volterran, and from other indications in the contract was more associated with Florence and Pisa than Volterra, we may assume that the Maffei sought a sculptor from outside their hometown and one whom they had not previously employed. These speculations lead to a consideration of Vasari's candidate, Montorsoli.[48]

Giovanni Angelo Montorsoli's (1507–1563) activities are rather obscure for this period so that there is no additional direct support for Montorsoli's association with the *sepultura* apart from Vasari's account. According to Vasari, Montorsoli worked in Rome, Perugia, Arezzo, and Volterra before assisting Michelangelo in the Medici Chapel, a chronology which is obviously incorrect since no work on the Maffei monument was done before 1524 when Montorsoli arrived in Florence. Vasari's possible attribution of part of the monument to Montorsoli had been questioned by some scholars since the monument in honor of Mario Maffei in the Duomo of Volterra (ca. 1537–1538) is usually ascribed to that sculptor, although with little evidence.[49] On the other hand, Vasari's statement has led some art historians to suspect the accepted date of Montorsoli's birth since Vasari's narrative would date the *sepultura* about 1523 when Montorsoli would have been only 16 years of age.[50] The result of all this is to compromise the authority of Vasari's account. The basis for any identification of Mon-

46. See A.95.58 (5), June 27, 1536, quoted in note 66.

47. A.95.53. (6), s.d., s. l., and A.95.53 (7), s.d., s.l.

48. For Montorsoli, see *Allgemeines Lexicon der Bildenden Kunstler*, ed. U. Thieme (Leipzig, 1913), 25: 99–100; A. Venturi, *Storia dell'arte italiana*, vol. 9, *La scultura del Cinquecento* (Milan, 1936), 103–153; C. Manara, *Montorsoli e la sua opera genovese* (Genoa, 1959); S. Bottari, "Angelo di Michele," in *DBI*, 3: 230–232; J. Pope-Hennessy, *Italian High Renaissance and Baroque Sculpture: Catalogue* (Phaedon, 1963), 57–58; T. Verellen, "Cosmas and Damian in the New Sacristy," *JWCI*, 42 (1979): 272–277; and S. ffolliott, *Civic Sculpture in the High Renaissance: Montorsoli's Fountains at Messina* (Ann Arbor, 1984).

49. For Mario Maffei's tomb, see Venturi, 120 and fig. 96, and Carli, *Volterra*, 90 and figs. 89 and 90. I have found no material on this tomb.

50. See Manara, 22, and Pope-Hennessy, 57.

torsoli with "Johannino da Firenze" must be established outside Vasari's account.

Montorsoli's movements after the suspension of work in the Medici Chapel in 1527 and his entry into the Servite Order on October 7, 1530, are unknown, except for Vasari's statement that he went to Poggibonsi to live with his uncle, Giovanni Norchiati, a learned chaplain of San Lorenzo in Florence.[51] If Vasari is right, Montorsoli was in the vicinity of Volterra at the appropriate time. Although born in the town of Montorsoli near Florence, he did on occasion style himself *Florentinus* so that the appellation "da Firenze" would not have been improper.[52] The contract itself leaves a space after the name "Johannino da Firenze cioe" indicating that this might not have been the name commonly given the sculptor. If the name "Johannino" is meant to distinguish him from an older man of the same name such as Montorsoli's uncle Giovanni, then the form does not exclude Montorsoli. Since the contract mentions Florence and Pisa, someone with Montorsoli's growing reputation in Tuscany would circumstantially fit the description.[53] But even if "Johannino da Firenze" can be identified with Montorsoli, there is no proof that "Johannino" actually fulfilled the contract's stipulations since his name does not appear again in the correspondence. Moreover, the style of the *sepultura* is not close to other works executed by Montorsoli. Montorsoli's connection with the monument must, for the time, remain doubtful.

IV

Two brief mentions of the *sepultura* later in 1529 indicate that work was progressing but that there were money problems and some disagreements over the form of the piece.[54] It is possible that an undated letter in which Mario states that is is necessary to come to some agreement with

51. For Norchiati, see ffolliott, *Civic Sculpture,* 2 and 196, note 23.
52. Manara, 63, note 10, cites the following: "Johannes Angelus de Monte Ursulo Florentinus."
53. Also possible are the father and uncle of Silvio Cosini, both named Giovanni. They were from areas near Florence and associated with Pisa. But, again, there is no support outside conjecture for their association with the *sepultura.*
54. Volterra XLVII/ 2 / 1, July 15, 1529: ". . . bisogna providere ancora alla sepultura. . . ." And *ibid.*: "Quello della sepultura manda a chiedere denari, non mi giovo fare pacti chiari di pagamente di tre volte la dimandi inanzi. . . .'

a sculptor refers to the work then being undertaken.[55] There is, however, no further mention of the *sepultura* until 1531. This lacuna is not surprising since the years between the contract and 1531 were difficult ones for the Maffei, Volterra, and all of Tuscany. Volterra was the scene of much political and military disorder as a result of the revolt of the Florentines against the Medici after the Sack of Rome and the papal-Spanish campaign to reestablish Medici hegemony in Tuscany in 1529–30. Volterra was especially ravaged by the military forces crossing the Tuscan hills, since she was internally divided between the supporters of the Medici and the defenders of the Florentine Republic. The Maffei were strongly pro-Medici and central actors in the crisis in Volterra. Because of their strong Medici sympathies, Paolo Riccobaldi, who was a member of the city government, had to flee with his son Giulio, and Mario had to take refuge in Bologna. The Florentine military adventurer, Francesco Ferrucci, and his troops caused great damage to the city and looted public and private holdings, including those of the Maffei.[56] The artistic treasures of Volterra especially suffered. It took the relative peace of 1531 before anything could be accomplished on the *sepultura*. However, there is no further discussion of the terms of the contract with "Johannino da Firenze." This might mean that his part of the monument had been accomplished or that the war had interrupted his work and he was no longer involved.

Even with the end of hostilities new problems interfered with the completion of the monument. The key document on the state of the *sepultura* and its sculptor after the contract is a letter from Riccobaldi to Mario dated November 11, 1531, in which Paolo discussed in detail negotiations with Silvio Cosini (1495–1549), called Silvio Pisano.[57] Since this letter is so important in the history of the monument as well as of interest in itself as an indication of relations between a patron and his employee, the relevant section is here translated:

55. A.93.53 (3), Nov. 29, s.a.: "De scultore [?] oportet ut ego et tu cum illo una sumus. Aliter nihil fieri [potest]. . . ."

56. See *Volterra e Francesco Ferrucci: scritti di M. Cavalini, L. Pescetti e G. Pilastri* (Volterra, 1930); M. Cavallini, "Sopra la guerra del 1529–1530," *Rassegna volterrana*, 5.2 (1931): 1–13, and L. Pescetti, *La storia di Volterra* (Volterra, 1963), chap. 8.

57. For Cosini, see *Allgemeines Lexikon,* 7: 503–504; P. Bacci, "Gli *angeli* di Silvio Cosini nel Duomo di Pisa (1528–1530) con documenti inediti e commenti relativi alla sua vita," *Bollettino d'arte del Ministero della Pubblica Istruzione,* 11 (1917): 111–132; C. Gamba, "Silvio Cosini," *Dedalo,* 10 (1920): 228–254; and Venturi, 487–496.

Your Lordship [i.e. Mario] is right to complain about Silvio Pisano for being faithless to you and because you did not have the satisfaction of seeing the completion of the sepulchre of your great brother and my father-in-law. And since you write that you would like to hear my opinion about what ought to be done, I certainly see little good in the situation. When your Lordship had the contract at hand, it was possible legally to compel him [Silvio] by means of his guarantor [to finish the work], but having lost it, as it seems you are hinting to me, and he not being in Florentine territory [Riccobaldi was then in Florence], I do not know how one may act either against him since he is in another's service, or against his guarantor without a contract. And when I consider well the letter of Silvio by which he clearly shows that he is resolved not to finish the said tomb if your Lordship does not give him 50 scudi d'oro more, or if you do not pay for it [a price] assessed by two masters of art, I judge that the lesser evil would be to accept one of the two alternatives rather than to enter into other useless altercations, and I would recommend paying him [the price] which would be assessed [by the two masters] rather than to give the 50 scudi, since in this way your Lordship does not show that you want to depart from justice, and in giving the 50 scudi more it will seem that your Lordship tacitly admits to not having given him a just price from the beginning, and in truth it might be so. Then I said to Messer Cornelio [del Fine, a Maffei confidant] and again, if I remember well, to you, that Silvio had become so involved that it was necessary either that he not keep to the design you showed me or that he do much work for us gratis [i.e., that he was doing more than the original design stipulated]. Since the matter has gone this way, I advise your Lordship that you write to Silvio a letter that is not too harsh but humane, exhorting him to come to give the finishing touches to the tomb and promise to satisfy him according to the assessment made by the art experts, in as much as he does not want to remain contented with what was first agreed. If you try another way, since he is working for the Doria, and your Lordship cannot produce the necessary contract, I doubt that you will ever see in these times the tomb finished by the hands of Silvio. Would that I were lying.[58]

58. Volterra, XLVII/ 2 / 1 (2), dated "Die San Martini" (Nov. 11, 1531): "Di Silvio Pisano

This letter confirms Vasari's attribution of the *sepultura,* or at least part of it, to Silvio Cosini. Although it does not specify which section of the tomb was the source of the disagreement, we do know from other sources that Silvio was working on the reclining figure of Raffaele Maffei, and that the work must have been rather advanced at that time.[59] Obviously other material and correspondence between the Maffei and Cosini have not survived. Unfortunately, there is no mention of the rest of the monument described in the 1529 contract, so we do not know if Cosini was involved in the entire structure. Whether the 50 scudi demanded by Cosini was part of the original contract which stipulated a 40 scudi bonus for work well done or a means by which he sought to extricate himself from a bothersome commission which was holding him back from bigger things cannot be determined. Certainly Cosini was in demand and knew how to exploit a favorable situation.

Before he went to work for the Maffei, Cosini had developed a lucrative career in Pisa, where his family lived, and in Montenero. The Maffei may have selected Cosini on the basis of his altar in Montenero since it is stylistically similar to the Maffei *sepultura.*[60] A major advance in Cosini's career came with his selection to work on the palace of the Doria

la S. V. ha ragione di dolersi, et per haver li mancato di fede, et perche la non ha el contento di vedere la perfectione della sepultura di tanto suo fratello et meo socero. Et inquanto ne scrive che vorria intendere el parer mio quid agendum, certamente io ce vedo poco del buono. Quanto V. S. havessi hauto impromptu le scripture, era per via di iustitia dastrignerlo suo fideiussore; ma havendole perdute, come mi pare naccenni, et lui non stando del fiorentino, non conosco come si possi agitare o contra el principale stando al servitio di chi e, o contral fideiussore senza scripture. Et considerando io molto bene la lettera di Silvio, per la quale dimosta altucto esser resoluto di non finire la detta sepultura, se V. S. non li da piu 50 [scudi] doro, o vero senon gli la pagha per quello sara stimata per duo maestri del arte, giudico chel manco male sia adceptare uno delli duo partiti, che entrare in altre altercationi inutili, et lauderei piu pagarla per quello fussi stimata, che dar li 50 [scudi], perche a questo modo V. S. mostrerra non si voler partir dal iusto, et dando li 50 [scudi] piu, parra che V. S. tacitamente confessi non haverli dato da principio prezzo conveniente, et in verita sia. Alhora dixi a messer Cornelio et ancora, se bene mi ricordo, alla S. V. che Silvio si era aviluppato, et che bisognava o che non mantenessi lopera secondo el disegno mostratomi da V. S. o vero che lui ci mertessi molte dellopere sue gratis. Conforto la S. V., poiche la cosa è ita cosi, che la scrivi una lettera a Silvio non corrucciata, ma humana exhortandolo ad venire ad dare l'ultima mano alla sepultura, et li promerti satisfarlo come sara giudicato da duo periti del arte, quanto non vogli star contento a quanto prima era convenuto. Tenendo altro modo, dubito, essendo lui a servitio del Doria, et non havendo V. S. da mostrare le scripture necessarie, che la non vedera a questi tempi per le mani di Silvio la sepultura absoluta. Quid, utinam mentire⟨m⟩."

59. See below note 61.
60. See Bacci, "Gli *angeli,*" 119, fig. 4.

in Genoa in 1531, a project on which Montorsoli was also engaged. It was this commission that led Riccobaldi to doubt that Cosini would ever finish the tomb. Certainly Cosini's defection was a bitter blow to the Maffei, more so to their pride than to their finances.

Despite Mario's annoyance, Riccobaldi was probably correct in arguing that there was little that they could have done to force Cosini to return to complete the commission once the contract was lost. Indeed, in a letter of November 30, 1531, well-known to Cosini scholars, the Volterran Camilio Incontri wrote to Mario from Pisa to confirm that Silvio was in Genoa and that he had no intention of returning to complete the *sepultura*. Incontri concluded that another sculptor should be found to finish the monument that was already half completed. Incontri proposed Stagio Stagi of Pietrasanta who was then working on the Duomo at Pisa to replace Cosini.[61] It is on the basis of Incontri's letter that Stagio Stagi (1496–1563) is usually associated with the Maffei tomb, although his contribution is not verified by any other evidence.[62] Stagio had worked with Cosini in Pisa and was a natural candidate for such a task. However, in view of Cosini's further connection with the *sepultura,* Stagio's contribution remains doubtful.

For reasons which we can only guess, Cosini returned to Volterra to work for the Maffei in July 1532. In a letter of July 20, 1532, Mario wrote

61. Letter in Falconcini, 214–215: "Reverendissimo domino. Pochi giorni sono scrissi a V. S. per la via di Firenze quanto mi accadeva circa la sepoltura della buona memoria di Messer Raffaello; e se a sorte per il lungo viaggio le lettere non fossero arrivate, di nuovo fo intendere a V. S. come Silvio si trova a Genova con animo di non tornare piu qua, secondo ho relazione, in modoche non possiamo procedere con esso. I mallevadori non so chi siano, et il notaro che ne fu rogato ancor non trovo, in modo non ci vedo altro rimedio, che allogare quest'opera ad un'altro scultore. Li marmi faremo consegnare a chi commettera Vostra Signoria, quali ho veduti, e son quasi ammezzati di lavoro, massime il volto di Messer Raffaello e quasi finito, e renderli buon'aria. Questo di ho parlato ad uno scultore si trova qua a lavorare di Duomo, chiamato Staggio da Pietra Santa, ottimo scultore, secondo ho relazione, e ne ho vedute sue opere, quale torrebbe a finire quest'opera. Quando V. S. si spiccasse da Silvio—altrimenti non vuol convenire insieme—gli ho promesso che Ella vuole allogare dell'opera ad altri, e levarla onninamente a Silvio come mancatore di fede e traditore. Sicche V. S. mi avvisera quanto vuole si facci, che tanto eseguiro, quanto Ella ne commettera. Il Sig. Giovanni dell'Antella mostra aver desiderio di far cosa grata a V. S., e raccomandasi a Ella offerendoli che tutto quello si potra fare in benefizio suo, lo fara volentieri. Io ancora a V. S. mi raccomando, quam bene valeat. Pisis, 30 Novembris 1531. Camillus Incontrius." Incontri, who acted for the Maffei on other matters, wrote a diary of Ferrucci's control of Volterra, *Infortuni occorsi alla città di Volterra nell'anno 1529 e 1530: Narrazione sincrona dei fatti del Ferrucci a Volterra notati per Camillo Incontri,* ed. M. Battistini (Volterra, 1920).

62. On Stagio, see C. Arù, "Scultori della Versilia: Lorenzo e Stagio Stagi da Pietrasanta," *L'arte,* 12 (1909): 269–287, and Venturi, 10.1, 477–486.

that Silvio had returned, and that he was to continue his work on the *sepultura*. Seemingly, in the meantime, the Maffei had not lost their ill-will toward Cosini.[63] This letter further establishes that Mario had become very sensitive about the unfinished monument. He ordered Riccobaldi to keep everyone away from it while Silvio worked. The monument and its troubles must have become a source of gossip for the Volterrans whose negative comments belittled the entire enterprise. Mario seems to have been generally pleased with Silvio's work. Surprisingly, Mario had still not written the epitaph for the monument which now Riccobaldi was to supply.[64]

V

The Maffei correspondence provides little further information about the monument. It was still incomplete in November 1532, indicating that Silvio had not hurried as Mario wished. Amazingly, Mario at that late date claimed not to have seen the piece in person, relying on Riccobaldi's descriptions of the progress and problems of the *sepultura*. Indeed, after an entire decade Mario had grown tired of the enterprise: as he put it, he was "stucco di quelli stucchi."[65] Since further notice of the tomb is lacking, it may be presumed that the piece was finished sometime in 1533. The cadaver of Raffaele Maffei, however, was not transferred to the San Lino *sepultura* until 1538.[66]

A coda to the Maffei-Cosini relationship came in 1536 when Mario was solliciting designs for a chapel he planned to build. One sculptor proposed

63. See the mutilated letter, A.95.40 (4), July 20, 1532: "E venuto Sylvio scarpellino per lavorare due cose. Vorrei che tu facessi una che li fussi cucinato, laltra che tu ordinassi che potessi lavorare in San Lino che in ogni modo visi ha da lavorare et che nissuno vedessi li lavori donec cum esse perfectum opus. So certo che non sara per la invita curiosita in tutti li volteranni, non per imparne che universamente nissuno inimicissime [?] ma per apponere . . . dimere et dir male, et se mai fu hora e riducta alla feccia. Se possit . . . mi sara caro et costori cose desidera et universamente omnis in [San] Lino. Nosti hominem; esto illi lenis con pochi blanditie et pochi pan. . . . Non poteva gia venir in tempo piu screncio [?] pur la voglia che ho . . . [fi]nirla, so per partir tutto el scripto."

64. See the mutilated letter, A.95.40 (3), dated July 15, 1532: "Mi pare molto che si aspetti Silvio. . . . Mandami quando achade quello epitaphio che tu facessi al deposito."

65. A.95.40 (6), Nov. 13, 1532: "Avisarmi come ti riesce la sepultura et siquid offendit che non puo esser di meno, io non vista in opera; et tamen so stucco di quelli stucchi."

66. See Paschini, 369.

so grand a design that Mario thought that he was being asked to do a
theater or another St. Peter's in Rome.[67] Writing at the same time, Riccobaldi commented that this sculptor, whom he called "Giovanni scarpellino", proposed a work which seem to him to be overly ambitious.
Riccobaldi was anxious that Mario decide upon the sculptor and even felt
it might be advisable to await Silvio Cosini, if he wanted to accept him.[68]
It would be intriguing to know if this sculptor was Montorsoli who was
at work on a chapel on Santissima Annunziata in Florence from 1535 to
1537.[69] Whoever he was, Mario was anxious that the sculptor chosen
not be Cosini because of the previous difficulties and consequent shame
he had experienced.[70]

Despite the difficulties surrounding the commission, the Maffei did finally see the memorial to their relative completed. The *sepultura* in High
Renaissance style became a further lasting tribute to the Maffei family,
their financial success and artistic taste. Their wealth and tenacity allowed
them to triumph in their disagreements with Cosini, even if they had
to compromise. In the disturbed political state of Tuscany between 1529
and 1531 the Maffei had trouble hiring and keeping an accomplished sculptor at work. Their ultimate success testifies to the advantage a patron
enjoyed in any conflict with most artists in the Renaissance.

JOHN F. D'AMICO

---

67. See A.95.50 (4), June 27, 1536: "Io credo che cotesto scarpellino sia pazo overo ha inteso
che io voglio far un theatro over San Pier in Roma, [et] mi lasciai gonfiare che non voleva esser
mancho di un bracchia et mezo, et, come vedo, se si facessi la cappella sana tutta cornice, io no
la voglio piu che due terzi ne ci puo star magiore, et rimandero costa el desegno quanto voglio
le boze et lasco poi el pensieri a me del lavoro. In genere manderlo prima che ti parli certo e
che non chiese piu che 20 solli del braccio de haver del pazo di un camino ce [?] tutte mie spese
mi chiese cento scudi." Possibly this chapel was the one in the Duomo where Paolo and Giulio
Maffei erected Mario's *sepultura*.

68. A.95.58 (5), July 27, 1536, Paolo to Mario: "Giovanni scarpellino m'ha dato il modello
del cornecione, che gle lo mando. Parmi una cosa molto grande. . . . Resolvisi quello vuol fare,
et advisi, che non sara forse male al defferire et aspectar Silvio, volendo abboccarsi seco."

69. For Montorsoli's activities at this time, see ffolliott, *Civic Sculpture*, pp. 2–4.

70. Same letter as above, note 67, "Di Silvio non mi curo ne mi da lanimo [?] di tenerlo per
la difficulta et sconcio [?] piu che per la spesa benche allui solo non senza [?] molta pure e disagio,
ne ancor ho da far lavoro [?] dallui addesso."

"Monumento al Ven. Raffaello Maffei" (Ed. Alinari)
P.I.N. 8723. Volterra—Chiesa di S. Lino.

LEGEND AND REALITY
THE FRIENDSHIP BETWEEN
MORE–AND–ERASMUS

THE NAMES OF THOMAS MORE AND ERASMUS of Rotterdam have been joined so closely since the sixteenth century that we hardly think of one without the other. Indeed, their friendship is so famous as to be legendary. But legends often lack in completeness what they possess in charm, and such is the case with the tale of More and Erasmus.[1]

The standard portraits of the relationship in the scholarly literature are unabashedly positive. E. E. Reynolds writes, "It is not extravagant to say that the meeting of More and Erasmus was a case of love at first sight."[2] Margaret Mann Phillips describes the relationship as "a friendship without a shadow."[3] Similarly, in the most recent account of the friendship, Roland Galibois explains,

> Il faut ici constater qu'au jour le jour, dans cette amitié, et concrète-ment parlant, c'est Erasme qui reçoit, More qui donne, qu'il s'agisse de services rendus, d'hébergement, de cadeaux généreux, de protec-

---

1. Especially positive accounts of the friendship between More and Erasmus can be found in: R. W. Chambers, *Thomas More* (London, 1935); G. Marc'hadour, *Thomas More* (Paris, 1971); M. M. Phillips, *Erasmus and the Northern Renaissance* (London, 1949); E. E. Reynolds, *Thomas More and Erasmus* (New York, 1965); and F. Seebohm, *The Oxford Reformers* (London, 1869).

2. E. E. Reynolds, *The Field is Won* (Milwaukee, 1968), 36.

3. M. M. Phillips, *Erasmus*, 101.

tion, de conseils, etc. More toutefois est bien conscient de jouir de l'estime du plus grand écrivain de son temps et d'être soutenu par lui dans la pratique du loisir culturel, que ses charges de juge ou de ministre semblent lui interdire de la plus frustrante façon.

More est toujours consulté dans les moments difficiles; c'est lui aussi qui intervient en faveur d'Érasme quand il s'agit d'obtenir pensions, subsides, conversion monétaire profitable à l'ami hollandaise, etc. C'est Érasme, par ailleurs, qui étend la réputation de More, à tous les points de vue, qui lui assure une grande place tant dans l'histoire tout court que dans l'histoire des lettres. C'est lui qui signale à Hutten, à de Brie, à Budé et à Faber, dans quelques-unes de ses lettres les plus longues et les plus travaillées, non seulement le grand talent d'écrivain, mais encore les vertus exceptionnelles de More, comme homme, comme père, éducateur, époux, citoyen, juriste, chancelier, etc.[4]

The standard account of the relationship between More and Erasmus is a chronicle of good fellowship, mutual devotion, and generous assistance.

Nonetheless, even though this is the picture of the friendship that More and Erasmus themselves give us in their writings, and even though it contains much that is true, it is seriously incomplete. We have no reason to doubt that the two were close friends, but the relationship must also be seen in terms of each man's private hopes and public aspirations. It is the aim of this essay to suggest a broader context in which the friendship can be reexamined. That is, the relationship must first be looked at in relation to each man's involvement in the intellectual movement that we now call Renaissance humanism and in what Paul Oskar Kristeller has called the "cult of friendship" in the humanists' dealings with each other.[5] And we must also ask how the two men's respective professional aspirations affected their friendship.

***

Whenever the friendship of More and Erasmus is spoken of, what comes to mind are the statements in their correspondence that suggest that each

4. R. Galibois, "Introduction," in G. Marc'hadour and R. Galibois, eds. and trs., *Erasme de Rotterdam et Thomas More: Correspondance* (Sherbrooke, 1985), xlvi.

5. P. O. Kristeller, "Thomas More as a Renaissance Humanist," *Moreana,* 65–66 (1980): 14.

enjoyed a special place in the other's heart. In the first surviving letter Erasmus begs to hear from More, writing, "Dearest Thomas, I ask you to cure, adding a bit of interest, the sick mood that I have caught from yearning too long for yourself and your letters."[6] Summarizing to his friend Robert Fisher the joys of his first visit to England, Erasmus asks, "Did Nature ever create anything kinder, sweeter, or more harmonious than the character of Thomas More?"[7] Five years later he praises More warmly to Richard Whitford, saying that More is someone "so full of eloquence that he could not fail to carry any argument, even with an enemy, and whom I regard with such affection that, even if he ordered me to join the rope-circle and dance, I should obey him without hesitation."[8] And when he learns of More's execution he writes, "I feel as if I had died with More, so closely were our two souls united."[9]

And Thomas More responds in kind. Citing Ovid, he tells Erasmus in 1516, "We are 'together, you and I, a crowd'; that is my feeling, and I think I could live happily with you in any wilderness."[10] Ten years later he refers to Erasmus as "dearest of all men."[11] In 1529 he closes a letter, "Farewell, dearest Erasmus, more than half of my soul."[12] And after giving up the Chancellorship in 1532, More writes a long letter warmly praising Erasmus' accomplishments. Among other things he says:

My dear Erasmus, we are not all Erasmuses; the gracious gift which

6. *Collected Works of Erasmus*, vol. 1: *The Correspondence of Erasmus, Letters 1 to 141*, tr. R. A. B. Mynors and D. F. S. Thomson (Toronto, 1974), Ep. 114, p. 227. "Illud extra iocum oramus, mellitissime Thoma, ut aegritudinem, quam ex nimium diuturno tui tuorumque scriptorum desyderio cepimus, usura aliqua sarcias" (*Opus Epistolarum Des. Erasmi Roterdami*, eds. P. S. and H. M. Allen, 12 vols. [1906–58], 1:266, hereafter cited as *EE*).

7. *Collected Works*, vol. 1, Ep. 118, p. 236. "Thomae Mori ingenio quid unquam finxit natura vel mollius, vel dulcius, vel felicius?" (*EE*, 1:274).

8. *Collected Works*, vol. 2: *Letters 142 to 297*, tr. R. A. B. Mynors and D. F. S. Thomson (Toronto, 1975), Ep. 191, p. 112. "Toma Moro cuius (uti scis) tanta est facundia, ut nihil non possit persuadere vel hosti; tanta autem hominem charitate complector ut etiam si saltare me restimque ductare iubeat, sim non gravatim obtemperaturus" (*EE*, 1:422).

9. Reynolds, *More and Erasmus*, 238. "In Moro mihi videor extinctus, adeo μία ψυχή iuxta Pythagoram duobus erat" *EE*, 10:221).

10. *Collected Works*, vol. 4: *Letters 446 to 593*, tr. R. A. B. Mynors and D. F. S. Thomson (Toronto, 1977), Ep. 481, p. 117. "Nos duo turba sumus apud animum meum; qui mihi videor feliciter posse tecum quavis in solitudine vivere" (*EE*, 2:372).

11. *St. Thomas More: Selected Letters*, ed. E. F. Rogers (New Haven, 1961), 165. "Vale, Erasme, mortalium omnium charissime" (*EE*, 6:442).

12. *Selected Letters*, 172; cf. Horace, *Odes*, I. iii. 8. "Vale, charissime Erasme, plusquam anime mee dimidium" (*EE*, 8:294).

God has granted to you, practically alone of all mankind, that gift all of us must wait to receive. With the exception of yourself, who would dare to promise what you produce? Though burdened by the weight of your years and constantly suffering from illnesses that would prove exhausting and overwhelming for a healthy young man, still never, all through the years of your entire life, have you failed to give an account to all the world with outstanding publications, as if neither the weight of years nor ill health could in any way diminish that record. While this one fact alone is, in the judgment of all men, like a miracle, still, amazingly, the miracle is magnified by the fact that the host of brawling critics surrounding you have in no way deterred you from publishing, though apparently they had the power to crush the heart of a Hercules.[13]

Such expressions of mutual admiration and affection have generally been accepted at face value. The result is the legend of the friendship. But as with any other legend, we should approach this one cautiously, and carefully consider how much truth the tale contains. Or perhaps a better way to put this is that we should consider what the legend omits.

As mentioned above, two factors can affect the way we read the correspondence between the two friends. The first is that both More and Erasmus were humanists. That is, they were part of the movement which has come to be called Renaissance humanism.

What need concern us most here is that moral philosophy is contained in the *studia humanitatis,* and (a point frequently forgotten) that friendship is an important theme in ancient moral philosophy.[14] Consequently,

13. *Selected Letters,* 174. "Neque enim, mi Erasme, omnes sumus Erasmi, ut quod mortalium omnium uni propemodum tibi propitius donavit Deus, id nos conveniat omnes expectare. Quis enim praeter te alius id polliceri audeat quod tu praestas? qui praeter aetatis ingravescentis incommoda, sic assiduis afflictus morbis ut fatigare atque obruere iuvenem valentem queant, quotannis tamen totius temporis tui rationem, tanquam nihil inde neque anni graves, neque adversa valetudo surriperet, aeditis libris optimis orbi toti nunquam cessas reddere. Quae res una, quum reputantibus universis miraculi vicum habeat, ad stuporem tamen usque miraculum geminat, quod nihil te deterrent a scribendo (qui vel herculeum pectus oppressuri viderentur) tot undique in te surgentes vitilitigatores tui" (*EE,* 10:32).

14. For example, Aristotle devotes two entire books of his *Nicomachean Ethics* (8 and 9) to the concept, and friendship was a central notion for the Epicureans. See, for example, L. Dugas, *L'amitié antique d'après les moeurs populaire et les théories des philosophes* (Paris, 1894); and J. C. Fraisse, *Philia: la notion d'amitié dans la philosophie antique: essai sur un problème perdu et retrouvé* (Paris, 1974).

friendship became an important theme in Renaissance humanism. For example, in connection with his theory of Platonic or divine love, Marsilio Ficino claimed that friendship was the force that joined together the members of his Florentine Academy. And Plutarch's theme of how to distinguish a true friend from a flatterer was often explored by Renaissance writers.

A major reason, then, that friendship is such a conspicuous theme in the dealings between humanists is that they are self-consciously imitating a theme and literary conventions from classical moral philosophy.[15] This is not to say that there were not genuine friendships between humanists, but that the idea of friendship was so important that the language of friendship became the established convention in exchanges between humanists. In other words, when we come upon expressions of love or friendship between humanists, we must read them with sixteenth-century, not twentieth-century, sensibilities. We must be prepared to see them perhaps only as literary or epistolary conventions and not necessarily as expressions of genuine feeling.[16]

To see the conventions of the cult of friendship, we need look only at the letters between humanists. There we find total strangers pledging love and affection for each other on the basis of their common commitment to classical study or simply because they were commended by a common acquaintance. A particularly striking example of this can be seen in Thomas More's famous letter to Martin Dorp. Dorp had written two letters (one of which was insufferably proud) against Erasmus' proposed edition of the New Testament and the *Praise of Folly*, a book that Erasmus dedicated to More. More did not know Dorp personally and we cannot imagine that Dorp's actions made More especially well disposed towards him. Nonetheless, More begins his letter:

If I were as free to visit you as I strongly desire to do, my dear

15. Kristeller writes, "The friendship between scholars is one of the characteristic features of Renaissance humanism, and as so many other things, it is an inheritance from classical philosophy and literature where friendship appears as a prominent topic of moral discussion in Plato, Aristotle, Epicurus, Cicero and others." ("Thomas More as a Renaissance Humanist," 14).

16. For example, although on the surface Erasmus' letters to Servatius suggest some emotional involvement, D. F. S. Thompson argues that the letters follow the conventions of a well-established monastic epistolary tradition "Erasmus as Poet in the Context of Northern Humanism," *De Gulden Passer*, 47 [1969]: 192 ff.).

> Dorp, . . . I would be enjoying your actual company—the sweetest
> pleasure I could have enjoyed; for Erasmus has implanted in my heart
> an extraordinary longing to see you, to get acquainted with you,
> and to love you.[17]

And he ends it in the same spirit:

> Goodbye, my dearest Dorp, and be truly convinced that no one,
> even in your native Holland, is more interested in you than is More
> among the British, sundered from all the world; and you are no less
> dear to him than you are to Erasmus. For you cannot be any dearer,
> not even to me.[18]

More's words may be laced with irony as well as exhibiting the conventions of friendship. But in any event, since More had little patience with
pride and arrogance, it is virtually impossible that his actual feelings towards
Dorp were reflected in words of such affection.

This is not to say that the humanists were insincere or hypocritical.
There was certainly some good feeling that they shared by their mutual
commitment to the study of antiquity, but it is unrealistic to believe that
all of the protestations of love and friendship meant what they would mean
if uttered by people today. The humanists came to use the conventions
of friendship in their business dealings in a way that we do not do now,
and they understood each other as doing this. There thus developed a kind
of "cult of friendship" which governed their business dealings with each
other.

The importance of all of this, of course, is that Renaissance humanism
is the intellectual tradition in which More and Erasmus operate. And since
the conventions of friendship were such a part of the humanists' ordinary
dealings with each other, More and Erasmus must have used them in the
same way. It should come as no surprise, then, when we find them writ-

---

17. *Selected Letters*, 8. "Si mihi ad te venire tam esset liberum, quam vehementer, mi Dorpi,
cupio, . . . tum quo nihil mihi iucundius potuisset accidere, teipso interea praesens praesente per-
fruerer, cuius videndi, cognoscendi, complectendique, mirum pectori meo desiderium insevit Erasmus" (*The Correspondence of Sir Thomas More*, ed. E. F. Rogers [Princeton, 1947], Ep. 15, p. 28).

18. *Selected Letters*, 64. "Vale, charissime Dorpi, vereque tibi persuade, neminem esse tui magis
vel in Hollandia tua studiosum, quam sit Morus apud toto divisos ab orbe Britannos, ut cui non
minus charus es quam ipsi es Erasmo. Nam charior esse non potes, ne mihi quidem" (*Correspondence*, Ep. 15, p. 74).

ing to casual acquaintances with the same apparent affection that they express to each other.

For example, Erasmus writes to Antonius of Luxembourg:

> Despite the fact that we have spent so few days in each other's company, my dear Antonius, still I must confess I am attracted to you by a kind of natural affection, just as iron is attracted by a magnet. Indeed the affection I entertain for you is so extraordinarily warm that it is not outdone even by my ardent love for [James] Batt himself; and him I cherish more than my very being.[19]

And the same is true with More. His letter to Martin Dorp has already been cited. And receiving a translation of Lucian dedicated to him by Conrad Goclenius, More writes in appreciation:

> [Erasmus'] frequent enthusiastic statements of your ability and learning made you dear to me before I knew you. And now really since this additional pledge, so to call it, of your affection and good will toward me in turn, although I loved you so much before that I thought I could not love you more, yet somehow or other, to that earlier love for you I feel a considerable increase has accrued.[20]

* * *

In addition to the cult of friendship in Renaissance humanism, however, we must also consider how this famous friendship was affected by each man's professional aspirations. Both men were ambitious, and there is no reason to think that they were unconcerned with advancing their careers and reputations. In fact, an important part of the bond that joined them through the years was probably the belief that each could help the other's career.

19. *Collected Works*, vol. 2, Ep. 147, pp. 21–22. "Etsi mihi tecum perpaucorum dierum consuetudo intercessit, Antoni humanissime, tamen nescio quomodo fatali quodam amore erga te ducor, mihi crede, non aliter quam a magnete ferrum trahitur, adeoque incredibili tui amore flagro, ut Battum ipsum quam te non amem effusius; quem tamen meipso etiam plus diligo" (*EE*, 1:349).

20. *Selected Letters*, 153. "Quocirca nihil me fefellit Erasmus noster, cuius illustri et crebra de tua virtute et doctrina predicatione prius mihi factus es charus quam notus. Iam vero postquam hoc accessit tanquam tuae vicissim erga me charitatis ac benevolentiae pignus, nec sane ob ullum meritum meum, etsi ante sic te dilexi, ut supra non posse mihi viderer, tamen nescio quo modo illi priori erga te amori meo, cumulum non exiguum accrevisse sentio" (*Correspondence*, Ep. 113, pp. 272–73).

Thomas More was most likely very ambitious for public success, despite his serious consideration of the monastic life. More was unusually talented in many ways, he had a knack for attracting the attention of older men in positions of power, and he was a public performer. When one puts all of these qualities together, it would be remarkable if he were not ambitious. Also, the frequency with which More talks about the great dangers of pride suggests that it was one of his main temptations. That is, More struggled against falling into the sin because of the awareness he had of his own considerable abilities and the temptations that success must have led him to — the temptation to give into the "delite and lyking of oure selfe" that More defines as the core of the sin.[21] The intensity of his preoccupation with pride was doubtless a sign of the size of his own ambition.[22]

More probably aimed at a public career early in his life. His father had set him to study law for this kind of career, but Thomas saw that in the sixteenth century there was a new avenue to Court — being known as an accomplished writer and orator. During the Renaissance the writings of antiquity were studied not only by scholars, but by men who aspired to power. A polished, classical Latin had become the tongue of government and diplomacy, and the ability to write and speak good Latin was then as much an entrée to government service as a record of political loyalty is today. If More wanted to complement his legal reputation with a literary one, his best supporter would be an important man of letters from Europe — and no one would be better than Erasmus.

Of course, for Erasmus the story would be different because his mission was to advance good learning in the hope that social and religious reform would follow. To do this he needed financial security, independence, and as much peace of mind as possible. Once he left the monastery,

21. In the *Four Last Things* More identifies pride as "an high estimation of ourselves" (*The English Works of Sir Thomas More*, ed. W. E. Campbell [London, 1931], 1: 477); in the *Treatise on the Passion* he labels it the "delite and lyking of oure selfe" (*The Yale Edition of the Complete Works of St. Thomas More*, vol. 13, ed. G. E. Haupt [New Haven, 1976], 9). In addition to material prosperity, More identifies being placed in authority over other men as a major temptation to pride. On More's understanding of pride, see my essay, "Pride and the Public Good: Thomas More's Use of Plato in *Utopia*," *Journal of the History of Philosophy*, 20 (1982): 329–54.

22. On More's public aspirations or accomplishments see: G. R. Elton, "Thomas More, Councillor (1517–1529)," in R. S. Sylvester, ed., *St. Thomas More: Action and Contemplation* (New Haven, 1972); J. A. Guy, *The Public Career of Sir Thomas More* (Brighton, Sussex, 1980), and J. Mermel, "Preparations for a Politic Life: Sir Thomas More's Entry into the King's Service," *The Journal of Medieval and Renaissance Studies*, 7 (1977): 53–66.

he was dependent on the largesse of one person or another. And as we read Erasmus' letters we can see just how large a concern money was for him. Thus some secure source of income would solve one of his main problems. It was in England that Erasmus was first appreciated for the great scholar that he was, and he probably thought that his best hopes lay there. For a number of years Erasmus seriously considered making England his adopted home, and he probably hoped that More could give him an important boost in getting the kind of financial support he needed. After all, More was a promising young man who had a talent for getting to know important men in English life.

At the same time, Erasmus was impressed with his friend's oratorical skill, and he probably saw ways that this too could help him. Erasmus was aware that in order to accomplish the work he had in mind he would need defenders as well as money. The application of humanistic learning to theology was not welcomed in all quarters, and Erasmus could not fight the entire war alone. In the first place, time spent on defending himself or his cause was time taken away from the important task at hand — restoring good learning. And then writing in his own cause would seem self-serving. A defense by a reputable third party was more strategically sound from a rhetorical point of view because it would appear more objective. Thomas More could play this part perfectly. Moreover, if Erasmus was serious about settling in England, an English defender with a public reputation would be ideal for making Erasmus' case both in England and to the learned of Europe.

* * *

If the character of the friendship between More and Erasmus was professional as well as personal, then explaining important events in the relationship by appealing only to the good feeling between the two will not give the whole story. We should see what they might look like in a different light.

Obviously, one article cannot explore all the relevant texts and speculate about the friendship in enough depth.[23] But it can at least suggest some areas that have been overlooked and merit further investigation. Accordingly, let us take a brief look at three of the most important events

---

23. In the hope of eventually providing a full account, I am currently at work on a book that reinterprets the friendship between the two humanists.

in the friendship: Erasmus' dedicating *The Praise of Folly* to More, More's
letter defending Erasmus to Martin Dorp, and Erasmus' involvement in
the publication of *Utopia*.

The traditional explanation for the dedication of *Folly* to Thomas More
is that it was done in testimony to the relationship between the two
men.[24] This comes mainly from the pen of Erasmus. The Dutch humanist
gives three different accounts of what led him to compose *Folly*, but all
of them tie More in some way to the book's inception. He writes to Ulrich von Hutten that More suggested that he write the book. He tells
Martin Dorp that he wrote it in More's home while recuperating from
a kidney ailment. And he explains in the dedicatory epistle that while crossing the Alps, Erasmus thought of More's pleasant company, their common studies, and the Greek pun on More's name and was moved to pen
an encomium of folly (Ep. 222). Since the two men did share much in
the way of outlook, interests, and sense of humor, the personal connection between Erasmus and More probably was one factor in the dedication.

However, if we look at the rest of the epistle, another reason for the
dedication presents itself quite strongly. For after the initial section of
the letter in which Erasmus tells of the book's composition and praises
More, he embarks on a section more than twice as long in which he gets
to his main point: "And so you will readily accept this little declamation
not only as a memento of your friend, but also as an object of your
patronage and defense, since it is dedicated to you and henceforth is not
mine but yours. For there will probably be no lack of quarrelsome quib-
blers who will attack it unjustly."[25] Erasmus expects the book to be attacked, he appoints More its chief defender, and he then launches into
his own defense of it. Closing the letter with a final compliment to More
and bidding him adieu, Erasmus reminds him (and the world) what is
expected of him: "But why am I saying all this to you? — you are such
an extraordinary advocate that you can make a strong defense even if the
case itself is weak. Farewell, most learned More, and defend vigorously
this your *Moria*."[26]

24. M. M. Phillips writes, "The very conception [of *Folly*] was a tribute to [the] friendship"
(*Erasmus and the Northern Renaissance*, 100).
25. "Erasmus' Prefatory Letter to Thomas More," in *The Praise of Folly*, tr. C. Miller (New
Haven, 1979), 2. "Hanc igitur declamatiunculam non solum lubens accipies ceu μνημόσυνον tui
sodalis, verum etiam tuendam suscipies, utpote tibi dicatam iamque tuam, non meam" (*EE*, 1:460).
26. "Erasmus to More," tr. Miller, 5, "Sed quid ego hec tibi, patrono tam singulari ut causas

Thus the dedication is not simply out of friendship. Erasmus needed professional assistance, and More was a logical choice for the assignment. More's oratorical abilities are about the only skills that Erasmus gives unambiguous praise to. More's reputation as a humanist was enhanced by being associated with an important group of English scholars (John Colet, William Grocyn, Thomas Linacre and William Lily). Furthermore, More was now on the rise in public life. He had a private law practice and had become an undersheriff of London in 1510, and he was doubtless attracting the attention of important men. More would make an ideal defender for *Folly* should the occasion arise.

Of course, the occasion did arise, for a work such as *Folly* could hardly escape the notice of the guardians of the status quo attacked in its pages. Those most offended were the theologians at Louvain, who believed that such satire undermined their authority, and they persuaded a young teacher of philosophy and aspiring theologian named Martin Dorp to write against Erasmus. Dorp's target was not only *Folly* but the edition of the Greek New Testament that Erasmus was working on.

Dorp wrote two letters. The first (Ep. 304) was civil and evenly divided between *Folly* and the New Testament. Dorp received a serious and courteous reply from Erasmus.[27] The second letter (Ep. 347) is a petty broadside against what Dorp takes as the encroachment of humane learning into theology. It attacks the study of Greek and overflows with pride and arrogance, which is probably the reason that Erasmus suppressed his response to it. Thomas More, however, penned a lengthy reply.

More and Erasmus met in Bruges after they had both seen the first letter, but not the second. Erasmus may have composed at least an abbreviated version of his reply. The two friends must have discussed the matter, and it is difficult to believe that Erasmus would not have told More what needed to be said—what the important issues were, which the spurious ones, what had been said, what needed to be said again, what new points needed to be made. In October More wrote to Dorp and sent Erasmus a copy.

More's letter opens with some conventional pleasantries and then chides Dorp for the pettiness of his letter. More then begins the heart of the letter—an attack on the role of dialectic in sixteenth-century theology and

etiam non optimas optime tamen tueri possis? Vale, disertissime More, et Moriam tuam gnaviter defende" (*EE*, 1:461–62).

27. Erasmus responded with an abbreviated version of Ep. 337. The original letter has not survived.

intolerance of the study of Greek and the application of humanistic methodology to theology.

Only at this point, 1347 lines into a letter of 1613 lines, does More
first mention *Folly*, and even then his defense is neither extensive nor ringing. More remarks that Erasmus' own defense of himself is sufficient and
he then resumes attacking Dorp. Faulting the young man's pride, More
accuses Dorp of thinking that theologians are too important to be satir-
ized. More seriously, he charges Dorp with slandering the bishops. And
having actually said little about *Folly*, More concludes, "All of this then,
my dear Dorp, is my view on *Folly*. . . . Although I have now left nothing untouched, certainly, as far as I know, I have omitted nothing
deliberately."[28]

In general, then, More's letter is not very concerned with *The Praise
of Folly*. He defends Erasmus' (and other humanists') approach to theology, with its attention to the importance of Greek and restoring texts;
he attacks the dialectical approach of contemporary university theologians;
and he reprimands Dorp's pride. That is, More's letter is not so much
a defense of Erasmus as More's initial foray into religious controversy.
The epistle to Dorp is not as polemical as More's subsequent religious
writings, but it takes up a basic issue which would be at the heart of
his concerns when he took up his pen against the reformers: what are
the authentic sources of divine wisdom to consult in order to find out
what we need to believe and do to be saved? Until the end, Thomas More
maintained the importance of Scripture, the writings of the Fathers, and
the traditions of the Church that were sanctioned by councils and persisted through time. More would have been deeply troubled by Martin Dorp's
ideas about the importance of scholastic commentaries, dialectical theology, the personal superiority of theologians, and the relative unimportance
of Greek and the restoration and study of the Church's earliest writings.

And how does Erasmus react to More's actions? In short, he does not.
Erasmus' sole reference to More's letter to Dorp is, "Your defense of me
I have not yet finished."[29] As far as we know, More's subsequent "What

---

28. *Selected Letters*, 62. "Istud ergo totum de Moria, mea, mi Dorpi, sententia. . . . Quanquam
iam nunc nihil intactum reliquimus, certe, quod sciam, nihil per dissimulationem pretermisimus"
(*Correspondence*, Ep. 15, pp. 72-3).

29. *Collected Works*, vol. 3, Ep. 412, p. 292. "Apologiam pro me tuam nondum totam legi"
(*EE*, 2:243).

think you of my letter to Dorp? I very much want to know" was met only by silence.[30]

The silence is surprising. It is just as puzzling as why More says so little in support of a book dedicated to him and carrying his name in the punning title. Erasmus' remark that he has not finished reading the letter is so surprising as to be doubtful. Such facts are significant, but what do they mean?

At the very least, this episode probably suggests that More and Erasmus were not of one mind about *Folly* and its defense. The exchange could suggest any or all of the following: More's own disapproval of parts of *Folly*, some unhappiness at having had the book dedicated to him, an attempt to stay out of the heart of the controversy, and Erasmus' disappointment at More's letter.[31] Perhaps we have an early sign of a major religious difference between More and Erasmus, with More being more explicitly concerned with salvation and Erasmus more directly concerned with good letters. Since More's name was prominently attached to a book that was being threatened with censure by the Louvain theologians, he could not afford to remain silent. However, he could (and did) "defend" the book in a way that distanced himself from it. Erasmus would doubtless recognize what More was doing and probably decided simply to let the matter pass in silence.

The third episode worth examining is the publication of *Utopia*. As we know from the correspondence between More and Erasmus and between Erasmus and others, Erasmus handled the publication of *Utopia*. He even included a letter in the prefatory material. This is conventionally taken to be an unambiguous sign of the friendship between the two humanists.

However, as with the two previous episodes, there is more here than is immediately apparent. In this case, it is Erasmus who distances himself from More's work. Even though he agreed to arrange for the book's publication, Erasmus must have set anonymity as one of the terms of his help. Accordingly, he and/or More concoted the fiction that Peter Giles handled

---

30. *Collected Works*, vol. 3, Ep. 424, p. 316. "De epistolio nostro ad Dorpium percupio scire quid sentias" (*EE*, 2:261).

31. Richard Marius speculates that More may not have known about the content of *Folly* and not been asked by Erasmus about the dedication. "It is just possible," he ventures, "that More was offended by *The Praise of Folly* and embarrassed at having his name so conspicuously attached to the work. The book is unlike anything More ever did himself." (*Thomas More* [New York, 1985], 95).

it. This illusion is created by More's prefatory epistle to Giles ("Therefore, provided it be done with the consent of Hythlodaeus, in the matter
of publishing which remains I shall follow my friend's advice, and yours
first and foremost" [Ep. 25]), continued in a letter presenting a copy of
Utopia to William Warham ("a friend of mine, a citizen of Antwerp [Peter
Giles], allowed his affection to outweigh his judgment, thought it worthy of publication, and without my knowledge had it printed" [Ep. 31]),
and reaffirmed in a letter to a member of the royal court ("I had it in
mind to betroth my *Utopia* to Cardinal Wolsey alone (if my friend Peter
had not, without my knowledge, as you know, ravished her of the first
flower of her maidenhood)" [Ep. 32]).[32] Erasmus further concealed his
connection to the work by instructing Giles to address his prefatory epistle to Busleyden rather than to Erasmus (Ep. 477) and by not including
a prefatory letter himself until the third edition in 1518.

But why does Erasmus distance himself from a book that he is seeing
through the press and that is written by a friend? A number of reasons
could account for this, but the most important is probably that Erasmus
had some reservations about just how good *Utopia* was.[33] This is evi-
denced by what little he says about the book when he has the opportunity to commend it. In his prefatory epistle to *Utopia* Erasmus praises More's
many abilities and then says to Froben, "For these reasons we have sent
you his *Progymnasmata* and his *Utopia* so that, if you think well, they may
go out to the world and to posterity with the recommendation of having
been printed by you. Such is the reputation of your press that, if it is
known that a book has come from the house of Froben, that is enough
to have it please the learned world."[34] Thus the letter praises the press

32. *The Yale Edition of the Complete Works of St. Thomas More*, vol. 4: *Utopia*, eds. J. H. Hexter
and E. Surtz, S.J. (New Haven, 1965), 45; "Quod reliquum est de aedendo: sequar amicorum
consilium: atque in primis tuum" (*Ibid*, 44). *Selected Letters*, 89; "Antverpiensis quidam amicus
meus [Petrus Aegidius] elapsum potius quam elaboratum, amori indulgens suo editione dignum
putavit, atque insciente me curavit excudendum" (*Correspondence*, Ep. 31, p. 87). *Selected Letters*,
89; "Ego Utopiam meam uni Cardinali Wolsaeo (si non eam ante meus Petrus, me, ut scis, insciente, multasset primum virginitatis florem) animo desponderam" (*Correspondence*, Ep. 32, p. 87).
33. At least two other possibilities suggest themselves. Having been attacked for what he said
in *Folly*, Erasmus may not have wanted his name associated with the satire in *Utopia* in order
to protect himself from further abuse. It is also conceivable that Erasmus' disappointment over
More's letter to Dorp came into play.
34. *Utopia*, 3; "Proinde misimus ad te progymnasmata illius, & Utopiam, ut si videtur tuis
excusa typis orbi posteritatique commendentur, Quando ea est tuae officinae autoritas, ut liber
vel hoc nomine placeat eruditis, si cognitum sit e Frobenianis aedibus prodisse" (*Utopia*, 2).

of Froben more than it lauds *Utopia*. And Erasmus' famous description of More to Ulrich von Hutten is similarly void of anything particularly positive about *Utopia*. Erasmus writes:

> [More] published his *Utopia* for the purpose of showing what are the things that occasion mischief in commonwealths, having the English constitution especially in view, which he so thoroughly knows and understands. He had written the second book at his leisure, and afterward, when he found it was required, added the first off-hand. Hence there is some inequality in the style.[35]

Erasmus offers an excuse for the book's style. But while this is a friendly gesture, it is not a compliment.

But if Erasmus had genuine reservations about the book, why would he help it into the world at all? Here we must consider again the professional side of the friendship between More and Erasmus and see how the two friends were advancing each other's interest. When we look at More's letters to Erasmus at this time in their relationship we see More acting as Erasmus' financial agent in England, so there is no question how More is assisting Erasmus. At the same time, More probably believed that a position at Court was finally within reach and that getting it would be easier if he could bolster his reputation as a humanist. And what would show better that he possessed both the rhetorical skills and political insight that belonged at Court than publishing a political treatise?[36] Erasmus was the logical person to turn to for his help in such a matter and the

---

35. *The Epistles of Erasmus*, ed. F. M. Nichols (1918; repr. New York, 1962) 3: 398. "Utopiam hoc consilio aedidit, ut indicaret quibus rebus fiat ut minus commode habeant respublicae; sed Britannicam potissimum effinxit, quam habet penitus perspectam cognitamque. Secundum librum prius scripserat per ocium, mox per occasionem primum adiecit ex tempore. Atque hinc nonnulla dictionis inaequalitas" (*EE*, 4:21).

36. More was especially anxious that Erasmus get testimonials for *Utopia* from government officials. In September of 1516 More wrote to Erasmus, "I am most anxious . . . that [*Utopia*] be handsomely set off with the highest of recommendations, if possible, from several people, both intellectuals and distinguished statesmen" (*Selected Letters*, 76). ("Misi ad te iam pridem Nusquamam, quam ego gestio et brevi prodire et bene ornatam etiam egregia et magnifica laude, eaque si fieri posset a pluribus non litteratis modo, sed etiam his qui sint ab administranda republica celebrati" [*EE*, 2:346].) A month later he wrote again, "I am anxious to find out if it meets with the approval of Tunstal, and Busleyden, and your Chancellor" (*Selected Letters*, 80). ("Cupio scire an Tonstallus probet, an Buslydius, an Cancellarius vester" [*EE*, 2:372].) Cuthbert Tunstal served Henry VIII; Busleyden was a member of the Great Council of Mechlin; the "Chancellor" was Jean le Sauvage, Chancellor of Burgundy and Castille.

Dutch humanist was hardly in a position to refuse. Indeed, it is probably not a coincidence that More points out in each of his letters to Erasmus that relate to *Utopia* how he is looking after Erasmus' financial welfare.[37] Nonetheless, while Erasmus agreed to help More, he evidently was willing to do only so much. He would arrange for a good European printer and for testimonials of the book, but he would keep his name from being associated with it.

* * *

So what can we conclude on the basis of all this? For a variety of reasons, the relationship between More and Erasmus is more complicated and a shade darker than its traditional picture. Their way of writing to each other is affected by the humanists' cult of friendship, so their letters probably suggest more affection than existed, especially early in the relationship. In light of the way the two of them helped each other's career, we can see that the glue holding them together was not only mutual affection, but professional advantage. And considering that both of them could have been more generous to each other (More in his defense of Erasmus to Dorp and Erasmus in publicly supporting *Utopia*), we can imagine that the friendship experienced some significant strains that are hidden beneath the epistolary conventions. The relationship was neither as one-dimensional nor untroubled as we have been led to believe by both principals and their respective biographers. However, it was more human and thus more interesting.

THOMAS I. WHITE

37. Epistles 461 (sending the manuscript to Erasmus), 467 (asking Erasmus to arrange for prefatory letters from scholars and statesmen), 468 (inquiring after these letters), 499 (reporting his reaction to Tunstal's letter and his Utopian "dream") and 502 (saying how anxious he is to receive the book) all contain detailed reports of More's efforts ranging from handling currency for Erasmus, to trying to get him a horse, to working on patronage for the Dutch scholar.

THE MYTH OF
VENICE
in the thought of Guillaume
POSTEL

Venice has been enshrined in the myth for a great part of its history. Early Christian legends described the arrival of Saint Mark in the Venetian lagoon after a violent storm and his subsequent establishment of the church at Aquileia from which the Patriarchate of Venice was established.[1]

1. See F. C. Lane, *Venice, A Maritime Republic* (Baltimore, 1973), 87–91; W. J. Bouwsma, *Venice and the Defense of Republican Liberty* (Berkeley, 1968), 52–59. See also F. Gaeta, "Alcune onsiderazione sul mito di Venezia," *Bibliothèque d'Humanisme et Renaissance. Travaux et documents*, 23 (1961); G. Fasoli, "Nascita di un mito," in *Studi storici in onore di Gioacchino Volpe* (Florence, 1958), 1: 445–479; R. Pecchioli, "Il 'mito' di Venezia e la crisi fiorentina intorno al 1500," *Studi storici*, 3 (1962). Also consult the rich bibliography in B. Pullan, *Rich and Poor in Renaissance Venice* (Cambridge, Mass., 1971). Also see the very important study of F. Gaeta, "L'Idea di Venezia," in *Storia della cultura veneta*, ed. N. Pozza. 3.3 (eds. G. Arnaldi and M. Pastore Stocchi; Vicenza, 1981): 563–641; and M. T. Muraro, "La Festa a Venezia e le sue manifestazioni rappresentive: la compagnia della calza e le momarie," *ibid.*, 315–341; R. Maschio, "Le Scuole grandi a Venezia," *ibid.*, 193–206; F. Gaeta, "Storiografia, coscienza nazionale e politica culturale nella Venezia del Rinascimento," *ibid.*, 3.1: 1–91; and V. Branca, "L'Umanesimo veneziano alla fine del Quattrocento: Ermolao Barbaro e il suo circolo," *ibid.*, 3.1: 123–175. See also the important studies of M. Gilmore, "Myth and Reality in Venetian Political Theory," in *Renaissance Venice*, ed. J. R. Hale (Totowa, N. J., 1973), 431–442; F. Gilbert, "The Venetian Constitution in Florentine Political Thought," in *Florentine Studies. Politics and Society in Renaissance Florence*, ed. N. Rubinstein (London, 1968), 466–472; the same, "Religion and Politics in the Thought of Gasparo Conarini," in T. Rabb and J. Seigel, eds., *Action and Conviction in Early Modern Europe: Essays in Memory of E. H. Harbison* (Princeton, 1969), 90–116; B. Pullan, "Service to the Venetian State: Aspects of Myth and Reality in the Early Seventeenth Century," *Studi secenteschi*, 5 (1964): 95–148; G. Benzoni, *Venezia nell'età della Contrariforma* (Milano, 1973); G. Roellenbleck, *Venezia scena*

The legends of Saint Mark enhanced the myths which proclaimed Venice's sovereign, independent birth and gave to Venice a providential origin.[2] Mulier has recently noted that the myth of Venice had an historical and a political side.[3]

According to the Venetians' version of their history, their city had been free since its origin, and Venetians had preserved their liberty in subsequent years.[4]

> As early as the eleventh century Giovanni Diacono sang the praises of this liberty in his famous chronicle. In his version, the geographical element played a decisive role. . . . Moreover, the very founding of the city in the midst of such an inhospitable body of water under pressure from attacking Huns qualified as nothing short of a miracle.[5]

The myth of Venice was also enhanced by Gasparo Contarini (1483–1542), a Venetian patrician and cardinal who wrote *De magistratibus et republica Venetorum*, which was published at Venice in 1543. In his book, as Franco Gaeta remarks, he idealized Venetian institutions and government: "Lo Stato veneziano—era la conclusione di Contarini—era stato fondato e si reggeva non sulla forza, ma sul consenso. Il *temperamentum* che lo *status nobilium* si era dato ne faceva un *unicum* nella storia."[6]

Concerning the humiliation of Venice by the League of Cambrai Contarini wrote that: ". . . ea rerum angustia perturbatus Venetus populus, adeo nihil in nobilitatem est molitus, ut lachrymantes omnes se suaque obtulerint ad reipublicae defensionem reque ipsa praestiterint."[7] Franco

dell'ultimo dialogo umanista: l'Heptaplomeres di Jean Bodin (ca. 1590). Centro Tedesco di Studi Veneziani, *Quaderni*, 29 (Venice, 1984); my "The Home of Coronaeus in Jean Bodin's *Colloquium Heptaplomeres*: An Example of a Venetian Academy," in *Acta Conventus Neo-Latini Bononiensi* (Binghamton, N.Y., 1985), 277–83; F. C. Lane, *Venice and History* (Baltimore, 1966); and E Muir, *Civic Ritual in Renaissance Venice* (Princeton, 1981). The latter work is an excellent contribution to Venetian studies and is especially significant for the scope of this study.

2. See B. Marx, *Venezia-Altera Roma? Ipotesi sull' Umanesimo veneziano*. Centro Tedesco di Stud Veneziani, *Quaderni*, 10 (Venice, 1978); and my *Guillaume Postel. Prophet of the Restitution of A Things* (The Hague, 1981), 69–92.

3. E. O. G. Haitsma Mulier, *The Myth of Venice and Dutch Republican Thought in the Seventeenth Century*, trans. G. T. Moran (Assen, 1980), 13–19.

4. *Ibid.*, 5–18. See also Gaeta, "L'Idea di Venezia," 566–571, 578–580, 600–602.

5. Mulier, *The Myth of Venice*, 13.

6. Gaeta, "L'Idea di Venezia," 639.

7. *Ibid.*

Gaeta notes that Contarini believed that salvation could come from a political process, ". . . quando la politica fosse costruzione di uno Stato giusto e di una società giusta che fossero la premessa di una salvazione individuale e collettiva."[8] Contarini believed that Venice represented the model of such a state ". . . nel quale gli uomini potessero *bene beateque vivere* perché l'ordinamento che essa si era data si rifaceva delle strutture 'naturali'."[9] Jean Bodin also placed the setting of his dialogue, entitled *Colloquium heptaplomeres de rerum sublimium arcanis abditis*, in Venice and praised Venice for the hospitality and the freedom accorded to citizens and visitors. Bodin writes:

> Whereas other cities and districts are threatened by civil wars or fear of tyrants or harsh exactions of taxes or the most annoying inquiries into one's activities, this seemed to be nearly the only city that offers immunity and freedom from all these kinds of servitude.[10]

The Doge's Palace also bears witness to the numerous myths concerning Venice. On the frieze in the Sala Grimani, Venice is depicted along with Architecture, Geography and Laws. In the same room Noah and his ark are represented and are reminders of Venice's salvation from the

8. *Ibid.*

9. *Ibid.* Contarini was not without some criticism of Venice, however; see G. Cozzi, "Authority and the Law in Renaissance Venice," in *Renaissance Venice*, 335–336; also note Cozzi's "Cultura, politica e religione nella 'publica storiografia' veneziana dell' 500," *Bollettino dell' Istituto di Storia della Società e dello Stato Veneziano*, 5–6 (1963–1964), 215–294. Also see H. Jedin, "Gasparo Contarini e il contributo veneziano alla riforma cattolica," in V. Branca, ed., *La civiltà veneziana del Rinascimento* (Florence, 1958), 104–124. For a discussion of Venetian society after the War of the League of Cambrai, see F. Gilbert, "Venice in the Crisis of the League of Cambrai," in *Renaissance Venice*, 274–290. For a concise discussion of the contributions of Contarini and Giannotti see Mulier, *The Myth of Venice*, 20–25. He notes, p. 24, that in the writings of both Contarini and Giannotti Venice's history and institutions acquired that mythic dimension which was to dominate discussions of the *Serenissima* and government in general (whether mixed or not). Even Monsignor della Casa, a member of the Venetian tribunal of Inquisitors, praises Venice as "Questa inclita città ad divino miracolo, e non ad opera humana . . ." (Venice, Bibl. del Museo Civico Correr, cod. Cic. 2/40/16, 1R, f. 37r. The manuscript was formerly part of the collection of the church of the Ara Coeli in Rome).

10. Jean Bodin, *Colloquium of the Seven about Secrets of the Sublime*, trans. (with introduction and annotations) M. L. Kuntz (Princeton, 1975), 3. It is interesting to note that Petrarch (*Letter*, tr. M. Bishop [Bloomington, 1966], 234; Muir, *Civic Ritual*, 22) described Venice in 1364 in terms which are similar to those in the *Colloquium Heptaplomeres*. Petrarch said that:

> The august city of Venice rejoices, the one home today of liberty, peace, and justice, the one refuge of honorable men, the one port to which can repair the storm-tossed, tyrant-hounded craft of men who seek the good life.

waters. In the Sala delle Quattro Porte, Tintoretto decorated the ceiling with paintings of Jupiter symbolically granting to Venice the dominion of the Adriatic, and of Juno offering to Venice the peacock and the thunderbolt. In the ceiling decoration of the Sala del Collegio, Veronese depicted Venice enthroned with Justice and Peace; in other paintings on the walls Venice is associated with mythological figures which represent the Virtues. Venetian artists often demonstrated Venice's relationship to Saint Mark. Among the best known examples are Tintoretto's paintings about the miracles of Saint Mark and the final deposition of his corpse in Venice. These paintings about Saint Mark and the stories perpetuated about him emphasized the special relationship of the Saint to the city of Venice as well as the Christianity of Venice. Frederic C. Lane notes that "the myths of Venice have enduring vitality. . . . Some myths have even been makers of reality and moulded Venice's history."[11]

From these general observations about the myth of Venice we shall now consider the myth of Venice in the thought of a specific author. Guillaume Postel (1510–1581), a French humanist in the circle of Francis I until his prophecies about the universal monarchy caused him to lose favor, also fashioned a myth about Venice which made use of the current *leggenda*.[12] It is likely that Contarini's *De magistratibus et republica Venetorum* influenced Postel in his own formulations. In 1541 Postel wrote *De republica seu magistratibus atheniensium liber*, in which he made no mention of the Venetian state. Yet by 1547 Venice had become the central focus of Postel's intellectual and spiritual life. Venice and a mysterious woman whom he venerated as the Venetian Virgin dominated his metaphysical speculations. Postel used the myth of Venice not only to justify his excessive admiration for her, but he also wove the old myths into his own new mythology of prophetic utterances about Venice and her role in restitution of all things.[13]

11. Lane, *Venice, A Maritime Republic*, 87–91.

12. For the life and thought of Postel see W. J. Bouwsma, *Concordia Mundi: The Career and Thought of Guillaume Postel* (Cambridge, Mass., 1957); and Kuntz, *Guillaume Postel*. Also see the numerous articles and books of François Secret, many of which are listed in his *Bibliographie des manuscrits de Guillaume Postel* (Geneva, 1970). Also see J.-C. Margolin, ed., *Guillaume Postel 1581–1981: Actes du colloque international d'Avranches 5–9 septembre 1981* (Paris, 1985); and M. L. Kuntz, ed., *Postello, Venezia e il suo mondo*, forthcoming, which contains the acts of an international congress held in Venice in 1982.

13. See my "Guillaume Postel and the World State: Restitution and the Universal Monarchy,"

Postel probably visited Venice for the first time in 1536, when he sailed from this port on his first visit to the Orient as a legate of Jean de la Forest, the King's representative at the court of Emperor Suleiman the Great. In 1537 Postel returned to Venice and remained there for at least a year. During his sojourn Postel developed a deep friendship with Daniel Bomberg, the famous Dutch editor of Hebrew books in Venice. The close relationship between these men flourished because of their common interests in ancient languages and in printing.[14] During his numerous visits to Venice and especially during his stay at the Ospedaletto of SS. Giovanni e Paolo from 1547 to 1549, Postel developed a profound knowledge of Venice; and as his knowledge of Venice increased, so also did his love for this city of the sea. In 1555 he wrote two books in the Venetian dialect: *Le prime nove dell'altro mondo* and *Il libro della divina ordinatione*.[15] In addition, Postel wrote an appendix to the *Chronicon* of Carion (Venice, 1556), which appeared without the name of Postel, but which can be attributed to him thanks to a manuscript from his own hand; this appendix reveals a great familiarity with Venetian life.[16] Postel writes, for example, of a violent storm which buffeted Chioggia with wind, thunder, and lightning.[17] He also describes a lightning bolt which struck the cornice of the Church of San Zaccaria and left such a precise cut that one would think that a geometer had made the measure for its removal.[18] Postel also comments upon the great beauty of San Zaccaria's cornice and notes that it was destroyed in the storm which also caused the destruction of many

History of European Ideas, 4 (1983): 299–323, 445–465; *Guglielmo Postello e la "Vergine Veneziana": Appunti storici sulla vita spirituale dell' Ospedaletto nel Cinquecento*. Centro Tedesco di Studi Veneziani, *Quaderni*, 21 (Venice, 1981); and "L'Orientalismo di Guglielmo Postello e Venezia," to be published by the Fondazione Giorgio Cini in the series *Civiltà veneziana. L' Oriente e Venezia*.

14. Kuntz, *Guillaume Postel*, 26–27.

15. Because of these books the Venetian Inquisitors decided to put Postel in the prison near Sant' Apostoli. For an excellent account of the Venetian trial of Postel see A. Stella, "Il Processo veneziano di Guglielmo Postel," *Rivista di storia della chiesa in Italia*, 22 (1968): 425–466. Also see Guillaume Postel, *Apologies et Retractions*, ed. F. Secret (Nieuwkoop, 1972), 189–216.

16. For a confirmation of Postel's authorship, see London, BL, MS Sloane 1411 (henceforth cited as B), f. 2v, where Postel writes: ". . . cuius vita est a me in multis locis subindicata magis quam descripta, videlicet, in expositione tabulae de restitutione sive de quaternariis, et in principio vangelii aeterni, et in appendice ad Chronicum Charionis anno 1553 ad signum capitis Erasmi Venetiis excusa. . . ." See also *Carionis Chronicon, Liber cui brevitate, perspicuitate . . . Appendix rerum . . .* (Venice, Valgrisius, 1556), 465–576.

17. *Carionis Chronicon*, 518.

18. *Ibid.*

boats which the Venetians call *barchele*.[19] In the same appendix Postel also speaks of the plague which attacked Venice in 1528, and he mentions the death of Marco Antonio Trevisan in 1554 and praises the great piety of the man.[20]

When Postel returned to Venice after his first sojourn in the Orient, he brought with him many ancient books and the alphabets of twelve ancient languages. He revealed that he had met at Venice priests of the Eastern Church who affirmed that the scriptures existed in their original languages at the time when the primitive Christian church was free from avarice and strife.[21] He also noted that these priests of the Eastern Church whom he met in Venice indicated that many ancient books were then in the course of publication at Venice in the *lingua Hieronymiana, seu Dalmatarum aut Illiriorum* for distribution to the East.[22]

Events which took place in Venice and episodes in the lives of noble Venetians fill the pages of Postel's books and manuscripts. Venice made such an indelible mark on Postel's consciousness that every aspect of Venetian life, great or small, held interest for him. The concept of Venice which Postel formulated, however, was much more complex and profound than mere fascination. Postel wove his idea of Venice into the fabric of his conceptions about the *restitutio omnium*, and consequently the city assumes a central role in the imminent instauration of God's Kingdom on earth in which Postel fervently believed.[23] Postel writes that Venice is the city preferred by God after Jerusalem. He describes Venice as "the most perfect magistracy" and as the "idea of the perfect principate."[24] With vivid

19. *Ibid.*

20. *Ibid.*, 518, 537–538.

21. See Postel's *Linguarum duodecim characteribus differentium alphabetum, introductio* ... (Paris, P. Vidovaeus Verlonensis, March, 1538), sig. Gv. The signature should be Hiiv.

22. *Ibid.* Postel wrote: "Hanc autem historiam potes audire ab omnibus illorum sacerdotibus, et Venetiis, et in tota Dalmatia pariter, et ab omni populo, qui mihi haec recitarunt quum de suarum literarum origine requirerem. Excuduntur permulti admodum libri harum duarum linguarum Venetiis ut illic distrahantur."

23. See my *Guillaume Postel*, 19–28, 69–72, 89–107, 112–127, 132–138, 151–155; and *Guglielmo Postello*, 3–23.

24. B, ff. 243v, 244r. See also *Il libro della divina ordinatione* (Padua, 1555), sigs. Aiii^r, B^r–Bii^v. For the role which Postel believed had been assigned to Venice see, for example, Paris, BN, MS lat. 3398 (henceforth cited as P), f. 6v: "Sic est pater in loculis sacris a toto genere humano habendus, ita tamen ut illa sacrosancta idea vel similitudo sapientiae summae, quam Plato merito, si visibilis alicubi esset, attracturam putaret universum ad sui conspectum, suae demonstrationis (post conspectas Ierosolymae et Ianiculi Venetiarumque Aquileianas sedes) basim Parisiis ponere voluerit."

imagery he identifies God's chosen city as the *sacrosancta regalitas veraque Ierusalem* and as a bride adorned for her husband who resides in the maternal seat of the final resting place of John Mark.[25] When Postel refers to Venice as *Ierusalema Ponentina*, he is designating her role in the coming of the second Messiah.[26]

Postel felt the need to justify his own profound esteem for Venice and, more importantly, the care and love of God for this city. Since God has need of nothing, as Postel affirms, reasons must be sought to explain His own incomparable Providence for Venice. Postel's concept of Venice as a utopian city appears rather paradoxical in light of the fact that he was condemned by the Venetian Inquisition in 1555.[27] Although he was judged by the Inquisition to be mad and guilty of heretical opinions, Postel dissociated his own negative opinion of the Inquisition from his deeply rooted concept of the magnanimous and millenarian destiny of Venice.

Postel lists specific reasons to justify the central role which Venice assumes in the divine design. God has favored Venice because she has maintained a stable government for more than eight centuries in contrast to other cities where cruelty, violence, and ambition follow the overthrow of princes and governments.[28] According to Postel, a stable government is an essential factor in the coming of the Kingdom of God. He equates the stability of Venetian political institutions to the practices of the ancient Kittim, praised by the prophet Jeremiah for the steadfastness of their faith and the stability of their political institutions.[29] In Postel's elaborate mythology he links the Kittim to the ancient Etruscans and by association, to Janus, whom

Venice is second only to Jerusalem in Postel's concept. The right of the Janiculum had passed to Venice because of Rome's apostasy.

25. B, f. 243r.

26. *Il libro della divina ordinatione*, sig. Ciir. For a discussion of the Ponentine Jews in the Ghetto Vecchio in Venice see C. Roth, *History of the Jews in Venice* (New York, 1975), 65–69.

27. The records of the trial are found in Venice, Archivio di Stato, Sant' Uffizio, Processi, Buste 12, 159. Professor Aldo Stella (see above note 15) has transcribed the relevant documents; see also Secret (*ibid.*).

28. "Venendo donque per certissime historie tanto Roma medesima, dove è la prima sedia del re di re per il suo ponteficato inferiore, come lo imperio romano, et come il regno di Franza, o Gallia, liquali sono li primi et piu grandi et famosi stati del mondo ponentino, havere con infinito sangue, crudelta, violentie, ambitioni et altri inconvenienti sostenuto tanta diversa damnosissima de principi, come mutationi nel governo suo, egli è di necessita che sopra del stato venetiano sia la principal cura della Providenza divina." *Il libro della divina ordinatione*, sig. Biiʳ.

29. B, f. 222v: "Ieremias ideo notavit, dicendo Insulam Chittim sive Italiae, quae, licet sit tota fere Italia peninsula, tamen proprie inter Arnum et Tyberum est, numquam suos deos mutasse. . . ."

he also calls Noah, celebrated as the second father of the Hebrews, Christians, Ishmaelites, and of all peoples and also as a king, judge, and priest of the greatest wisdom and piety.[30] In his doctrine of universal restitution Postel attaches the greatest significance to Noah by emphasizing Noah's piety and the contribution which he made to man's progress. Postel minimizes man's fall through Adam and concentrates instead upon the gift of language which God gave to Adam and upon the renaissance of civilization under Noah. It is interesting to note in passing that the same role of priest, king, and judge which Postel attributes to Noah is also the role which he assigns to the angelic Pope who will also serve as righteous king and most just judge in the universal monarchy whose establishment Postel proclaims as imminent. Postel often speaks of civilization "snatched from the waves" because of Noah, and relates Noah's salvation from the waves to the countless times God has "snatched Venice from the waves."

Although mankind was given a second chance under Noah, the sons of Abraham divided the sacred kingdom of Israel and strayed from the worship of the one true God. Consequently, according to Postel's mythology, another Jerusalem of stable institutions and pure religion must assume the function of the old Jerusalem. Venice is that city which God has chosen as the new Jerusalem. Postel writes of Venice and her role: "Venetia enim nusquam pagana sed ex Christianis primo conflata est," and "Esse vero Jerusalem translatam Venetias ob sacrorum inviolabilitatem patet."[31] Postel writes that because Noah and his descendants were snatched from the waters of the flood, they had been called *Gallim* and that *Gallia* was the name given to their nation; in like manner, Venice was founded upon the waters and had been repeatedly saved from the waters by Divine Providence.[32]

30. Postel was undoubtedly following the counterfeit histories of Annius of Viterbo. For a discussion of the significance of these spurious histories, see D. C. Allen, *Mysteriously Meant. The Rediscovery of Pagan Symbolism and Allegorical Interpretation in the Renaissance* (Baltimore, 1970), 61–62, 72–73, 111. Also see Guillaume Postel, *De Etruria regionis originibus*, ed. G. Cipriani (Rome, 1986). Throughout Postel's *Le thrésor ou recoeuil des prophéties de l'univers*, Paris, BN, MS franc. 2113, ff. 27r–124r, Annius is clearly seen as an influence. This text has been published by F. Secret, *Le Thrésor des prophéties de l'univers* . . . (La Haye, 1969). Postel's *De Etruriae regionis . . . originibus* . . . (Florence, 1551) also reflects the influence of Annius. For specific reference to the passages indicated in the text, see P, f. 5r–v, and B, f. 173r.

31. B, f. 300v and f. 196v; also *Il libro della divina ordinatione*, sig. Ciii^r.

32. B, ff. 196v–197r.

In formulating his justification for Venice's special providence Postel attributes great significance to her geographical position. He notes that all things come from water and from water derive their unity and cohesion.[33] Divine Providence was responsible for Venice's origin from the sea and has safeguarded her, so that she may fulfill her own appropriate role in human and divine history in the "restitution of all things." In this regard he notes that Venice, "civitatem maris antonomasticum esse basim restitutionis omnium."[34] Venice and Jerusalem enjoy a unique rapport because they reveal in an extraordinary way the plans God has for them in history no less than their special divine protection and preservation.[35]

In addition to his designation of Venice as the "new Jerusalem," Postel also called Venice the "new Rome." Noah, whom Postel identifies not only with Janus but also Bacchus, established his own sacred republic on the Janiculum; consequently, since Israel had fallen into apostasy, the right of God's Kingdom on earth passed to Rome, where the sacred mount of Janiculum is located.[36] Rome, after a period, also fell into the worship of idols, and her priests crucified Christ, who had taken refuge in Rome, for the second time because of their wantonness. Rome, therefore, lost the right of primogeniture which had been established by Noah on the Janiculum, and this right passed then to Venice, making her the new Jerusalem and the new Rome.[37] A little later we shall return to the significance of this double inheritance of Venice.

In his praise of Venice Postel often calls attention to *Pubblico Bene*, which he describes as the goal to which every true citizen, Venetian or otherwise, must aspire.[38] Love, exemplified by *Pubblico Bene*, reflects the true

33. Paris, BN, MS lat. 3402, f. 72v. Postel writes: "Prima in ordine est vis extractionis omnium entium creatorum de aqua illa primaria, de qua omnia sunt."

34. B, f. 24v. Note also the important statement about water and Venice in B, f. 244v, where Postel writes: "Nam aquae sunt universi vinculum. Civitas autem celeberrima solaque Virgo inter civitates aquarum est Venetiarum civitas. . . ."

35. ". . . ubi iam cum Eliae virtute et spiritu adibat Jesus priusquam visibiliter illuc veniret et veteris testamenti sacramentum agninum completurus et novi in suo corpore bina sacramenta instituturus. Et ideo Venetiis atque Aquileiae, ubi episcopatus b. Marci est positus et trium Iohannum virtus in Christo Iesu personaliter unita stat sepultaque iacet, basis victoriae mundi posita est." B, f. 245r.

36. P, f. 5v.

37. P, f. 5v, 6r. See also Paris, BN, MS lat. 3677, f. 56r; and B, ff. 199r, 431r.

38. *Il libro della divina ordinatione*, sig. Bii^{r-v}: "Conciosia donque che egli è di necessita di glorificar et lodar Iddio, per le opere particolari del la sua providenza, vedendo che maggior cura sua è stata da mille anni in qua sopra di Venetia, che di tutta la Christianita insieme, quanto a l'apparente

love which is divine. Venice demonstrates the meaning of *Pubblico Bene* by her care of the sick, the orphans, the poor, and the aged in her *scuole* and in her *luoghi pii*. Postel compares the love demonstrated by the *Pubblico Bene* to the love which God has for Venice as if it were a *Pubblico Bene Divino*.[39] In addition, the stability of Venetian institutions as a first cause of the *Pubblico Bene* is for Postel an example of that *perennitas* which is a sign of divine love for the city. Postel describes such *perennitas* as "Divinitatis verissima entitas et humanitatis in summum perfectionis per matrem conductae."[40] *Perennitas*, which is both divine and human, assures the continuity of all things. The feminine nature of *perennitas* is connected to the second person of the Trinity, Christ-Shekinah, which is the presence of God in the universe from whom, in whom, and through whom all things exist.[41]

This concept of *perennitas* is significant for Postel's designation of Venice as the new Jerusalem and the new Rome. The *perennitas* of Venice depends on the fact that Jerusalem, considered masculine by Postel, and Rome, considered feminine, are united and reborn in Venice which is the offspring of each. The divine concepts of *perennitas* and of *Pubblico Bene*, exemplified in the perfect republic of Venice, are personified and actualized in the person of a mysterious woman, exalted by Postel as the Venetian Virgin or the *mater mundi*. In Postel's social, political, and religious philosophy the Venetian Virgin becomes a living example of the virtues of Christ, and in her life and work are reflected God's care and protection of Venice.[42]

Postel immortalized this holy woman in three of his books and in countless manuscripts. From the year 1547, when he met her at the *Ospedaletto* of Saints John and Paul, until the year of his death, 1581, Postel constantly celebrated the virtues and the merits of this unusual woman whose life exercised an enormous influence on the development of his thought. Docu-

---

conservatione del publico bene, egli è di necessita di far due cose." Also note sig. Biii[r]: ". . . donde si vede chiarissimamente che di Venetia Iddio ha havuto maggior cura che di tutto quanto il mondo et massimamente di Ierusalem."

39. *Ibid.*, sig. Bii[v].

40. P, f. 3r.

41. *Ibid.*

42. See *Les tres merveilleuses victoires des femmes* (Paris, 1553); *Il libro della divina ordinatione* (Padua, 1555); and *Le prime nove del altro mondo* (Padua, 1555). Venice and the Venetian Virgin are also discussed in numerous manuscripts of Postel, several of which have already been cited.

ments in the archive of Venice reveal without doubt that Postel did not invent his own *madre divina* nor did he assign to her a pseudonym.[43] According to some documents her name was Zuana, which is Venetian dialect for Giovanna, the name given her by her parents.[44] Postel believed that her name, Giovanna, was a sign of destiny, since she crowned the work of the three Johns.[45] Postel placed the birth of Zuana about 1496 in the environs of Padua or Verona. She gave no indication of the name of her parents nor of their nationality. Postel relates that when asked about her parentage, she replied: "Nissuno sa donde io sia."[46]

Postel met this mysterious woman upon his arrival in Venice in 1547 after his separation from the Jesuits in Rome. The Venetian Virgin was about fifty years old, very small and frail, when Postel met her.[47] She had left the home of her parents at a young age to devote herself to a chaste life in the service of God. After she had spent a period of preparation in prayer and meditation among persons unknown to her and had reached an acceptable age, she was sent to Padua where she worked with the sick in a a hospital.[48] Later she went to Venice to care for the poor and the infirm. Her service in Venice appears to have begun about 1520.[49] Before obtaining a permanent location for her services Zuana had an "open kitchen" in the square near the Church of Saints John and Paul and cared for the ill in makeshift shelters.[50] Zuana's concern for the needy of Venice

43. See my *Guillaume Postel*, 69–93, 101–108; and *Guglielmo Postello*.

44. See Venice, Archivio di Stato, Ospedali e luoghi pii, busta 910 (MS not numbered). I am indebted to Dott. Giuseppe Ellero of the Istituzione di Ricovero e Educazione, Venice for providing a summary of the inventory, dated Dec. 28, 1533, which not only mentions the name of Zuana, but also lists her meager personal effects: a few handkerchiefs, table napkins and cutlery, a cloak, and a cap.

45. Paris, BN, MS lat. 3401, f. 3r.

46. *Le Prime nove del altro mondo*, sig. Br. Postel writes: "Quantunche Iddio m'habbi fatto quella gratia la quale io preferisco a tutte quelle che furon mai fatte sopra la terra a pura creatura, salvo quelle d'intorno al Salvatore d'haver havuto come padre spirituale conversatione con la creatura, la cui historia io voglio scrivere, niente dimanco mai ho potuto o far tanto che questa mi fosse aggiunta per sua maestà, ch'io sapessi overo il luogo proprio della sua nativítà, over il nome delli suoi parenti et sangue. Et quantunche io essendo gia mosso, et tutto commosso per le stupende cose ch'io in lei di continuo vedevo, spesso gli dimandassi, mai mi volse rispondere a proposito, ma solamente mi diceva: la terra et il sangue non hanno parte in cielo, cercate la generatione vera del cielo. Nissuno sa donde io sia."

47. See above notes 41 and 42; and Paris, BN, MS franc. 2115, f. 105v.

48. *Le prime nove del altro mondo*, sig. Bi^r.

49. *Ibid.* See also Paris, BN, MS franc. 2115, f. 105v.

50. *Ibid.* See also my *Guglielmo Postello*, 6–8.

developed from her conviction that on the day of Universal Judgment everyone must indicate before God if he had searched out the poor and needy to give them aid and comfort.[51] Postel commented especially upon the extraordinary work of Zuana during the dire plague which engulfed Venice in 1528 and of her success in securing food for the poor by preaching charity to the rich. It was, in fact, during the great year of suffering that the Venetian Virgin induced wealthy Venetians to build a permanent habitation for her mission adjacent to the Church of Saints John and Paul.[52]

Postel affirms that the merits of the Venetian Virgin are so extraordinary that they are the cause of the divine grace reserved for Venice. Postel repeatedly glorifies Venice as the home of the Venetian Virgin, into whose person the spirit of God descended, and in whom Christ was living. This "immutation" of the Venetian Virgin took place in 1540 in Venice at the *Ospedaletto*, which Postel called *Xenodochius* because the Venetian Virgin received strangers there.[53] The divine presence which was alive in her revealed to her the mystery of the *restitutio omnium*, which she must in turn reveal to a chosen *figlioletto* who would also become her spiritual father.[54] According to Postel's account, the Venetian Virgin told him about a divine edict revealed to her, which proclaimed God's desire that all creatures be reunited in one sheepfold and that there be a general pardon for all without exception. She also revealed to Postel that the Age of Restitution must begin with him who "lives and works in the spirit and virtue of Elias."[55] Madre Zuana stated that Postel had been chosen as the new Elias of the fourth age, that is, the Age of Restitution of all things, and had received the spirit and virtue of Elias which had been passed down to him through her. The Venetian Virgin had assumed the identity of *Eliana* or *Elianus Secundus* in whom dwelled the universal spirit of mater-

---

51. *Le Prime nove del altro mondo*, sig. Bii^r.

52. Among the noble Venetians were Domingo Loredan, Zuane Basegio, Baldisera Spinelli, Jacomo Foscarini, Lodovico de' Viscardi, Jacomo Paralion, Lorenzo Lotto, and Zuanmaria Zonta (Giunta). For the documents of the Ospedaletto see the *Libro di partte et determinationi diverse. Prencipia 1546 finno 1604, Ospedale dei derelitti*, Archivio storico di Istituzioni di Ricovero e Educazione, Venice. I am grateful to Dott. Giuseppe Ellero for use of these rare documents. See my *Guglielmo Postello*, 7, 21 n. 3.

53. B, f. 432r; Paris, BN, MS franc. 2115, f. 112v.

54. B, f. 439r–v; Paris, BN, MS franc. 2115, f. 105v.

55. B, f. 439v.

nity.[56] Postel wrote that the supreme power of truth which was imma-
nent in Elias had been bestowed upon the Venetian Virgin and her chosen
"little son."[57]

In Postel's mythology of Venice and the Venetian Virgin the virtues
which abounded in her made Venice a participant in the *Eliana virtus*, since
she had chosen Venice as her home.[58] Postel's association of the Venetian Virgin and her merits with Venice is crucial to his myth of Venice
as the new Jerusalem and the new Rome. Postel links Zuana with David,
who symbolizes, in the Cabala, the Shekinah, who is the presence of God
in the world.[59] According to Postel, Zuana is the custodian of the "Keys
of David" which without doubt represent the Psalms, "the third grade
after that of the prophets and the first grade of the Laws."[60] The Psalms
of David unite wisdom and human reason with the obscurity of revelation. They also reveal the "continued presence of Elias, through whom
the composite of 'El' and 'Jah' indicates the union of created wisdom."[61]
Since Zuana is the custodian of the keys of David which join human reason to revelation, she becomes the feminine mediatrix whose responsibility it is to proclaim the true Church of God predicated on the virtues,
which make men participants in the Church of God.[62] The renaissance
of the Church will be characterized by a universal restitution, a universal
pardon, and a universal baptism; an "Angelic Feminine Papacy" will pre-
side over the reborn Church.[63] Postel reports that the Venetian Virgin
said, in regard to the feminine papacy, that: "Io son el Signor perche esso
habita in me et per questo io son in esso il Papa Santo Reformatore del
mondo."[64] This new Angelic Papacy develops from the Venetian Virgin
because in her the presence of Christ resides. Consequently, she, as custodian of the keys of David and as the Angelic Papessa of the Reformed
Church, is called by Postel "la personele Ierusalem." The city of the Venetian Virgin becomes the new, real and true Jerusalem.[65]

56. B, f. 429r.
57. See my *Guillaume Postel*, 90.
58. Paris, BN, MS lat. 3399, f. 13v.
59. Kuntz, *Guillaume Postel*, 87–88.
60. *Le prime nove del altro mondo*, sig. Giii*.
61. Kuntz, *Guillaume Postel*, 88–89.
62. Paris, BN, MS lat. 3677, f. 3r.
63. Kuntz, *Guillaume Postel*, 81.
64. London, BL, MS Sloane 1410, f. 51v.
65. Postel writes: "Cest pour quo'y ceste ame heureuse seconde femme du superieur Abraham

Postel believed that four principles were essential for the restoration of God's Church which he refers to as the *Monarchia universalis* and the *eupolitia*. These principles, which are the substructures of the restored church, and are indeed Postel's platform of restitution, are *amor Dei, unitiva virtus, charitas in proximum*, and *virtus diffusiva sui*.[66] The Venetian Virgin possesses all these four virtues in the highest grade. These virtues also abound in the city of Venice, home of the Venetian Virgin and of John Mark, whom Postel describes as "Ille paterfamilias ... sive elevatus vir qui est in secundo loco quadripartitae sapientiae ... maxime excelleret cum matre mundi."[67] Venice was chosen through divine will to be the final resting place of John Mark and the Venetian Virgin, and to be the new Jerusalem for the restitution of all things. Consequently, Venice is the true form of that *Politia* which must be translated to all the world.[68] Venice is the perfect example of the temporal state over which Christ presides.[69] Venice represents the masculine form of the papal magistracy, thanks to John Mark, who established his own patriarchy first at Aquileia and then at Venice; on the other hand, Venice is represented also as the feminine form of the temporal state preserved by God for more than a thousand years. The stability of the Venetian state allowed the active virtues of charity to be developed. This active charity has been especially demonstrated by the Venetian Virgin who is the symbol of a universal maternity which gives life to the world.[70] Venice in its own dual aspect of a feminine, temporal magistracy and a masculine, papal patriarchy represents the union between the male and female which produces virtuous sons and daughters.[71] One notes that in Postel's mind the Angelic Papacy is also feminine because of the virtue of the Venetian Virgin in whom the Reformed Papacy resides through Christ. Of Venice's role Postel writes:

(qui apres Sarah eut a femme ceste Iehochannah, comme avant deux mille et 500 ans est revelé, ainsi quil est escript en Ghemara, au chapitre Sanct Sanctorum, our Codess haccadassim) se disoit estre la personele Ierusalem habitee par son signeur cache et environné dedens elle par excellence, pour y recoevillir, en les excusant, toutes ses brebietes. . . ." Paris, BN, MS franc. 2115, ff. 110v–111r.

66. B. f. 439v.
67. B, f. 240r.
68. B, f. 243r.
69. *Ibid.*
70. *Ibid.*
71. *Ibid.*

Sic et Venetiis, eo quod ibi perfectior magistratus totius mundi . . .
stat, vota totius generis humani impetrarunt, ut sacrosancta regalitas veraque Ierusalem, de coelo veniens in sua foeminea specie, quae
Christi (quatenus rex est) propria est videretur, et per triginta annos
aut supra exercendo summum opus et maxime regium huius mundi, quo opus est tetrapolitana charitas appareret et nomine Matris
Iochannae complendo trium Johannum opus GRATIAM DOMINI
in se completam esse demonstraret. . . .[72]

In the passage cited above Postel describes Venice as the *perfectior magistratus*, the *sancrosancta regalitas* and the *vera Ierusalem*. The virtues of the
Venetian Virgin have been responsible for these lofty designations. In her
life and work she has illustrated the meaning of *tetrapolitana charitas* to
such a degree that the grace of the Lord crowns her head. *Tetrapolitana
charitas* is defined by Postel as the care of poor adults, male and female,
and the education of young orphans of both sexes. This charity which
defines the life and the meaning of the Venetian Virgin Postel also attributed to Venice. He pays great tribute to Venice as an example of a
true "angelic papacy" in the following statement:

Et ad hoc opus rex vere pius et papa vere angelicus est in exemplum
Venetum mundo datus, cui uni functioni tanquam suae filiae naturae
habitu gratiae vestitae Deus unitrinus omnia quae in mundo sunt
comparavit. . . . Ad hoc extremum opus persona mundi quarta et summo angelicoque papatu et regno verissimo et summa gratia Domini
ornata est ut totum mundum in admirationem et imitationem trahat atque etiam intrare ad hoc convivium compellat salva libertatis
ratione.[73]

The fourth person of the world to whom Postel refers in the significant statement cited above is the Venetian Virgin, the bride of Christ,
in whom he dwells most fully. She is the personification of the divine
ecclesia, she the most true and chaste bride.[74] The city of Venice is also
a chaste bride of the Church of God because of the merits of the Venetian

72. B, f. 243v.
73. *Ibid.*
74. B, f. 431r.

Virgin and of the works of charity evident in the city.[75] In this regard
Postel writes: "Civitas autem celeberrima solaque virgo inter civitates aquarum est Venetiarum civitas."[76]

The foundation upon which a restoration of the Church resides is the
love of God demonstrated by works of charity. The active practice of charity
is so important in Postel's concept of reform that he writes: "Nam si quis
se dicit amare Deum et fratrem suum quemvis hominem non habet in
charitate perfecta dilectum, mentitur."[77] The Venetians are not guilty of
this fault, since they have established *luoghi pii* for the care of the poor
and the sick and have honored the requests of the Venetian Virgin for
a permanent hospital near the Church of Saints John and Paul. Postel also
cites Marco Antonio Trevisan as an example of a pious Venetian who merit-
ed a long life because of his aid to the poor.[78] Because Venice has shown
that she possesses the feminine virtue of charity, she has been chosen as
the location of the magistracy in the universal monarchy which Postel her-
alds in his role of *figliolo* of the Venetian Virgin, Mother of the World.[79]

In addition to all the merits of Venice which Postel exalted, another
praiseworthy aspect, which is also significant for his concept of Venice
as the most perfect magistracy, is the role of Venice as a city of art. *Perennitas*, which Postel defines as sign of God's love for Venice,[80] has been
granted by "that *numen* of salvation and is present in gold, in glass, and
in many other substances or objects, even in the art of the future."[81] The
association of *perennitas* with art could be an allusion to Venetian art, of
which Postel was undoubtedly conscious and appreciative.

It is not surprising that Postel uses art and the practice of art in his
own philosophic system, since he pursued the artistic craft in the making

75. On the charity practiced in Venice see the masterful work of Pullan, *Rich and Poor in Renaissance Venice* (above, note 1).

76. B, f. 244v.

77. *Ibid.* Note also f. 396r, where Postel writes again about charity: "Nam charitas omnia credit,
omnia sustinet, omnia suffert. Quisquis non habet hunc spiritum supportandi et excusandi omnes,
seipsum autem etiam postquam omnia fecisset maxime accusandi, praecipue in tanta opinionum
multitudine, ille sane veritatis non est capax et non est missus a Deo."

78. *Carionis Chronicon,* 537–538. See note 20 above.

79. B, f. 244v.

80. P, f. 3r.

81. *Ibid.*: "Ideo semper et aeterno testamento nomine Berith perennitas illa . . . per Iesum sive
per salutis numen concessa in auro videtur ut in vitro aliisque multis Ressis, aut rebus, est, etiam
arte futura, ab salute Deus Iudaeus, id est, artis summae et possessor et institutor."

of maps.[82] He demonstrated his acquaintance with the language of art when he wrote of the whiteness of the glaze used in the making of maiolica.[83] He also linked philosophy and art in a discussion of the potentiality of the divine nature. He used the word *tivilere*, which, according to his definition, is a word that indicates *activum passibile et agere*.[84] He also describes the "*numen* of salvation," *Deus Iudaeus*, as the founder and possessor of the most sublime art.[85] In Postel's philosophic system art and architecture are often used as analogues. One can suggest that Postel shares some ideas with those represented in the canvases of Tintoretto. In this regard, one recalls that Postel believed that the *restitutio omnium* had been announced at Venice in 1540, when the Venetian Virgin had been infused with the spirit of Christ; that this *restitutio omnium* would be proclaimed universally after he had received the miraculous "immutation" from the Venetian Virgin in Paris in 1552. Postel was convinced that the *orbis concordia* would begin in 1556. When this date proved to be in error, he corrected the date to 1566.[86] The reason for the revised date of 1566 was very likely an exorcism which took place in front of the cathedral of Laon. According to Postel, the demon fled the body of the young girl when the host was placed before the face of the demonic. Postel interpreted this so called "Miracle of Laon" as a sign of the presence of God and of His victory over Satan; in addition, he believed this to be a certain sign of the restitution of all things. In a painting by Tintoretto the year 1566 is also signaled as the year of universal concord. This painting, entitled *La Madonna dei Tesorieri*, once decorated the Magistrato dei Camerlenghi at the Rialto and later the Church of Saints John and Paul. The painting now hangs in the gallery of the Accademia. In the lower left corner of

82. See, for example, *Theatrum orbis terrarum Abrahami Orteli Antverp. geographi regii* (Antwerp, "apud Ioannem Bapt. Urintium," 1603), ff. C3 v, I r, 21r.

83. Postel writes: "Representatae autem sunt illae similium plane illorum vasorum candori quos porcellanam dicunt, aut quae nomine maiolicae majoricaeve seu faventinae suppellectilis nuncupantur." This text also has been cited by F. Secret, "Une vision au paradis," *Bibliothèque d'Humanisme et Renaissance*, 35 (1973): 101.

84. London, British Library, MS Sloane 1412, f. 184v. Postel states: "Iam nullus est qui dubitet deum esse essentiam, unitatem, veritatem, bonitatem; quare in ea re, quam maxime toti orbi dedit, demonstranda non immorabor. Videndum vero est quo modo activum, agibile seu et agere aut tivilere, ut ita compendii gratia loquar, sit in deo." In the margin of the manuscript Postel writes; "Tivilere est artis vocabulum notans activum passibile et agere."

85. P, f. 3r. See note 80 above.

86. B, f. 338r.

this painting there is a column base on which is inscribed the following: "unanimis concordiae simbolus 1566." Thus, the theme of universal concord so dear to Postel who proclaimed that its inception would begin in 1566 also appears to be a theme appropriate to the concepts of Tintoretto.[87] There is still another theme which is important to both Postel and Tintoretto and which again conceptually links Postel to Venetian painting. In numerous works Postel relates the manna which God sent to the Israelites in the desert with the eucharistic host, since, as he maintains, the significance of manna and the eucharistic host is the same: both are signs of God's love and care for His people. The identification of manna with the host is also a theme which appears in several paintings of Tintoretto. In the Church of San Giorgio Maggiore, behind the great altar, hangs one of the last works of Tintoretto, the *Raccolta della Manna*. Facing this painting is another by Tintoretto from the same period entitled *L'Ultima Cena*. Tintoretto had also used the theme of manna in one of the panels of the ceiling painting in the Scuola di San Rocco and in a canvas which hangs in the Fondazione Giorgio Cini.

The themes found in Postel's writings harmonize with the themes expressed in the religious paintings of Tintoretto. Postel's concept of the state as art is directly related to Venice, which Postel describes as the example of a temporal state which is the ideal model for all states in the world. Consequently, the seat of temporal power of the universal monarchy must be located in the most serene republic of Venice. If Postel ever viewed Venice in a less idealized conception, he never revealed this in his writings. No criticisms of Venice ever appear in the writings of Postel. Venice became a symbol of the merits of the Venetian Virgin, and in spite of the retractions which Postel was forced to make about the Venetian Virgin, he maintained his idealized view of Venice and the Venetian Virgin until his death. He praised Venice as the "magistracy most perfect" and the most worthy symbol of the temple of Solomon, erected for the praise and glory of God's name. The political structure of Venice, the piety and charity demonstrated by her citizens, the authority of the *Zohar* and of other secret commentaries which designate the *Civitas Maris* as the seat and the foundation of the *restitutio omnium* point to Venice as the most

87. For the life and work of Tintoretto see F. P. B. Osmaston, *The Art and Genius of Tintoretto*, 2 vols. (London, 1915); E. von der Bercken, *Die Gemälde des Jacopo Tintoretto* (Munich, 1942); H. Tietze, *Tintoretto* (New York, 1948). Also note the recent work of D. Rosand, *Painting in Cinquecento Venice: Titian, Veronese, Tintoretto* (New Haven, 1982).

perfect idea of the universal state.[88] More important than all of the accolades heaped upon Venice, however, is Postel's praise of the Venetian Virgin, his Mother Johanna, in whom the spirit of Christ and the Church lives and through whom Venice is unusually favored.

Postel emphasized that a *Politia* whose citizens reveal the presence of God in their lives is the true "art of all arts." He writes: "Hic est ars artis omnium artium ducatus ex gratia et ex natura compositus."[89] Postel repeatedly proclaims that Venice is the ideal of the perfect magistracy and is the "ars artium, quae est perfectissima politia regnoque perfecto et aurea modernanda, cuiusque desiderio totum genus humanum ardet."[90] According to Postel, the true artist is he who, with restored reason, collaborates with God in the foundation of the universal monarchy which is the Church of God on earth. Postel sees himself as the artist who must introduce the life of heroes among the lives of men.[91] In his own imagined role as *propheta* and *comprehensor* and *congregator mundi* Postel believed that he has fulfilled the true role of artist.[92] The spirit of Christ within man makes of him an artist because the teaching of true art comes from the supreme artist who is God. Since Postel had been taught by the Venetian Virgin in whom the spirit of Christ dwelled, he considered himself an artist. In like manner, Venetian artists such as Tintoretto fulfilled the Postellian concept of true artist.

The artists and the art of Venice and the art of the Venetian magistracy and institutions fulfilled Venice's providential role in the restitution of all things as the "most perfect magistracy" and the true art of arts; therefore, Venice is exalted by Postel as a state which is indeed a work of art. The myth of Venice formed the basis of Postel's political and religious philosophy which emphasized the unity of all things. Venice became the paradigm for all states which were to be united in the universal monarchy. The myth of Venice and the merits of the Venetian Virgin became the reality of Postel's existence, and in this mythic reality he found new life and hope.

MARION LEATHERS KUNTZ

---

88. B, f. 251r.
89. Paris, BN, MS lat. 3677, f. 51r.
90. *Ibid.*, f. 51v.
91. See P, f. 15r.
92. *Ibid.*. Paris, BN, MS lat. 3677, f. 51r.

THE HERMETIST AS HERETIC: AN UNPUBLISHED

C E N S U R E

OF FOIX DE CANDALE'S PIMANDRE

O NE OF THE MASTERPIECES of sixteenth-century French Hermeticism
was the massive commentary on the *Pimander* published in 1579 by
François de Foix, Duke of Candale and Bishop of Aire.[1] Devout Hermetist, alchemist, mathematician and savant, Foix de Candale was a powerful
and respected figure in the Bordeaux intellectual community. His earlier
edition and Latin and French translations of the *Corpus hermeticum* played
an important role in the diffusion of Hermeticism's textual sources, while
his prolix vernacular commentary established him as perhaps the most extravagant of the apologists for the Christian interpretation of the Hermetica in an era which Jean Dagens has termed the 'golden age' of religious

1. F. de Foix, *Le Pimandre de Mercure Trismegiste de la philosophie chrestienne, cognoissance du verbe
divin, & de l'excellence des oeuvres de Dieu, traduit de l'exemplaire Grec, avec collation de tres-amples commentaires* (Bordeaux, 1579). The work was dedicated to Marguerite de France, Queen of Navarre.
The French translation without commentary had appeared in a separate edition in 1574, the same
year Foix published his edition of the Greek text and Latin translation. In the present paper all
references to *Le Pimandre* are to the 1579 edition with commentary. For background on the work
see J. Dagens, "Le commentaire du Pimandre de François de Candale," in *Mélanges d'histoire littéraire offerts à Daniel Mornet* (Paris, 1951), 21–26; J. Harrie, "Duplessis-Mornay, Foix Candale and
the Hermetic Religion of the World," *RQ*, 31 (1978): 499–514; R. Marcel, "La fortune d'Hermès
Trismégiste à la Renaissance," in *L'humanisme français au début de la Renaissance*. XIVe Colloque
International de Tours (Paris, 1973), 137–153.

Hermetism.[2] Indeed Foix's enthusiasm for the elusive Egyptian philosopher-priest set him somewhat apart from the mainstream of French Hermeticism, which was characterized, as D. P. Walker has noted, by a generally more cautious attitude toward the employment of the ancient pagan theologians than was displayed by Italian contemporaries.[3] Rather than viewing Hermes Trismegistus as a contemporary of Moses, for example, as the more conservative Hermetists had, Foix de Candale argued that he was prior to Abraham and that his writings anticipated and agreed with divine Scripture, and hence ought to be employed in explicating Christian doctrine. Furthermore, his own synthesis of Christianity and Hermetic gnosticism in *Le Pimandre* led Foix to a doctrinal position which was, in the words of Jeanne Harrie, "close to formal, if unconscious, heresy" on several crucial issues.[4]

That a powerful and influential ecclesiastical figure should have produced one of the most important Hermetic tracts of the French Renaissance is surely fascinating and must have provoked considerable comment at the time, at least among those scholars with the fortitude to tackle the commentary's nearly eight hundred pages in folio. Particularly when viewed against the background of the bitter religious conflict between Catholic and Huguenot, François de Foix's idiosyncratic reading of the Hermetic significance of the Christian mysteries must have seemed a dangerous and provocative undertaking. Yet until now we have no direct evidence of any formal orthodox response to Foix's challenge.

In a brief but illuminating article published over thirty years ago Jean Dagens called attention to an unusual exchange in the correspondence of Marin Mersenne which raised some interesting questions about the *fortuna* of Foix de Candale's great commentary. In a letter to Mersenne on 16 January 1626 Robert Cornier addressed the question of the orthodoxy of Foix's work in response to a doubt raised previously by Mersenne himself:

2. J. Dagens, "Hermétisme et cabale en France de Lefèvre d'Étaples à Bossuet," *Revue de littérature comparée*, 35 (1961): 5–16 at 6. For biographical details on Foix (1502–94), see P. Tamizey de Larroque, ed., *Notes et documents inédits pour servir à la biographie de Christophe et de François de Foix-Candale, évêques d'Aire* (Bordeaux, 1877); J. Harrie, *François Foix de Candale and the Hermetic Tradition in Sixteenth Century France* (dissertation, U. of California, Riverside, 1975).

3. D. P. Walker, "The *Prisca Theologia* in France," *JWCI*, 17 (1954): 204–259, reprinted in his *The Ancient Theology* (Ithaca, N.Y., 1972), 63–131.

4. Harrie, "Duplessis-Mornay," 510. On Foix's dating of Hermes, cf. Walker, *The Ancient Theology*, 69.

J'ay tousjours creu que Mr de Candalles en son oeuvre sur Trismegiste, parloit plus tost aegyptien ou platoniquement que Chrestiennement, et aiant aultrefois mis le nez dens cet autheur, j'ay creu que ce qui s'y lisoit qui peut faire ombrage à la creance catholique, estoit plus tost un tesmoignage de la congnoissance confuse qu' avoient ces antiens philosophes de nostre theologie, que non pas un reproche contre celuy qui les à emploiés dens ce commentaire. Aussy n'ay je pas oüy parler qu' il ait jamais esté censuré; toutesfois il y a si long temps que je n'ay veu ce livre que je ne veux pas entreprendre de le deffendre. Quand je pourray l'avoir veu, je vous en diray davantage puisque vous le desirés de moy, encore que je sois peu capable d'adjouster rien à vostre jugment.[5]

As a mathematician Mersenne was quite familiar with François de Foix's work as an editor and expositor of Euclid, and was clearly also aware of his Hermetic interests as well.[6] As a devout Catholic, however, the enthusiastic religious-philosophical syncretism of the *Pimandre* commentary would have given him pause, particularly if he had heard rumors of an ecclesiastical censure of the work as Cornier implies.

Eleven days later Cornier wrote again from Rouen. The situation remained in doubt.

Je croy ce que vous me dictes pour le Sieur de Candalles, mais trouvés bon aussi, je vous prie, que j'interprete tousjours le plus benignement qu'il me sera possible les actions d'autruy jusques à ce que il ne me soit plus loisible de le faire. L'*Index* des livres prohibez en contient tant de françois qu'il me semble n'y avoir pas beaucoup d'apparence d'excuser la censure sur la langue françoise. Mais peut estre encor que je me trompe en croiant que cet autheur ne soit pas censuré. Il fauldra veoir. Je pensois en recouvrer un, mais l'on l'a presté à un homme qui este à Paris, de sorte que je suis obligé d'en attendre le retour.[7]

5. M. Mersenne, *Correspondance*, ed. P. Tannery, C. de Waard, R. Pintard, 1 (Paris, 1945), 327–328. Cf. Dagens, "Le commentaire," 24.

6. Foix published an edition of the *Elements* at Paris in 1566 which included a 'Book XVI' of his own devising dealing with regular solids. An expanded version with two additional books on solids appeared at Paris in 1578. Mersenne referred to Foix's edition of the Hermetica in his *Vérité des sciences*; cf. his *Correspondance*, 1: 327 note.

7. *Ibid.*, 1: 353.

With the explicit reference to the *Index* the question becomes more focused. Apparently Mersenne had expressed a concern that François de Foix's work had attracted the attention of the Congregation of the Index and perhaps even received a formal censure. Cornier, unaware of any such proceeding, was willing to give the good bishop the benefit of the doubt. So too, for that matter, was Dagens, who commented that Cornier's response on behalf of François de Foix showed that he "understood perfectly the spirit of the Commentary."[8] That may well be true, but it does not address Mersenne's doubts, which should at least serve to alert us to the fact that nearly a half century after its appearance Mersenne believed — perhaps vaguely recollected — that Foix de Candale's *Pimandre* had been called into question on theological grounds. Was there any basis for his suspicions? A little-known document preserved in the Biblioteca Apostolica Vaticana suggests that there was.

Vaticanus latinus 6207 is a miscellaneous manuscript of the late sixteenth century which contains numerous comments and *censurae* relating for the most part to contemporary printed books, together with some notes regarding works prohibited by the Congregation of the Index.[9] Folios 80r–82r contain a copy of a detailed Latin *censura* of François de Foix's commentary on the *Pimander* composed shortly after its appearance by Antonius Lullus, vicar-general of the diocese of Besançon. From the heading we learn that the piece was excerpted from a letter sent on 14 March 1580 to Cardinal St. Severina at Rome. This hitherto unpublished *censura* is an important source, for it provides us with concrete evidence that at least some of the potentially heretical implications of Foix's religious Hermeticism were noticed by contemporaries and formally brought to the attention of Church authorities.

The author of the censure, Antoine Lull, or Lulle, was a Spanish grammarian from Mallorca, a relative of the famous Ramon Lull. He published several works on grammar and rhetoric and corresponded with Erasmus and Ramus among others.[10] Well along in years, he was around seventy

8. Dagens, "Le commentaire," 24.

9. For a description of the contents it is still necessary to consult the handwritten *Inventarium librorum latinorum Mss. Bib. Vat.*, 7 (1643), 158–163. The titles of three other *censurae* from the MS are listed by P. O. Kristeller, *Iter*, 2: 338.

10. On Lull (c. 1510–1582) see J. F. and L. G. Michaud, eds., *Biographie universelle ancienne et moderne* (Paris, s. d.), 25 cols. 468–469; J. C. F. Hoefer, *Nouvelle biographie général*, 32 (Paris,

when he composed his indictment of the *Pimandre*, and the tone of the piece clearly reflects his impatience with the theological license of the period. Underlying the specific doctrinal criticisms he offers of Foix's positions is the general conviction that the Bishop of Aire, representing an area of Huguenot strength and closely tied by bonds of blood and affection to Henry of Navarre, was advancing views which could serve the spread of Protestantism.

The man to whom Lull confided his fears was Cardinal Giulio Antonio Santori, Archbishop of St. Severina, head of a special Congregation charged with overseeing publications in the Greek and Hebrew tongues. The head of the Congregation of the Index at the time was Cardinal Guglielmo Sirleto, Prefect of the Vatican Library, and apparently the two Congregations were somewhat complementary in function. Here is how the English biblical scholar Gregory Martin, who lived in Rome for a year and a half in the late 1570's, described their responsibilities:

> There is also a *Congregatio Indicis librorum*, where Cardinal Sirletus is President. in this are five or sixe Cardinals (namely C. Paleottus) and about twentie Doctors, Divines and Canonistes. Of this depende al like Congregations *per totum orbem*. Here are al suspected bookes examined, naughty bookes condemned, other some purged, here is made the Cataloge or table or *Index librorum prohibitorum*, which no man may read without licence of the holy Inquisition. *Magister S. Palatii* (by whose censure bookes are printed) is in this Congregation, and by it and with the authoritie therof directeth his doings.
>
> Also Cardinal S. Severinae is President in an other particular Congregation about Hebrew bookes, the Rabbines commentaries, the Talmud, the preaching to the Jewes, where he is ordinarily present and president.[11]

1863), col. 228. Among his published works are *De oratione libri septem* (Basel, [1558]) and *Progymnasmata rhetorica* (Basel, [1550–51]).

11. G. Martin, *Roma sancta (1581)*, G. B. Parks, ed., (Rome, 1969), 257–258. Martin had lived in Rome from December 1576 through June 1578 and completed his *Roma sancta* at Reims in April of 1581. On Giulio Santori as Cardinal St. Severina, cf. Eubel, 3:44; G. Hofmann, "Santori," *Enciclopedia cattolica*, 10 (1953): col. 1884; J. Mercier, "Santorio," *DTC*, 14 (1939): cols. 1104–5. Among his other accomplishments Santori served as prefect of the Congregation for the Propagation of the Faith and was co-founder with Gregory XIII of the Greek College of St. Athanasius in 1577.

In another passage Martin refers to the two as "the Congregation of such as allow or disallow of al bookes, discerning betwene the Heretical and Catholike, the corrupt and scandalous and hurtful from the contrary," and "the Congregation of Graecians and Hebricians and such have best skil of the Tongues, for the resolving of such questions as may arise therein."[12]

Clearly Antoine Lull's decision to forward his censure of François de Foix's commentary to Cardinal St. Severina was motivated by more than philological considerations. From his comments it is clear that he would class it with the 'suspected bookes' that should be examined by the Congregation of the Index. His writing to Santori was possibly motivated by the fact that the Hermetic texts were in Greek and would thus fall within the purview of the latter's Congregation, or by personal acquaintance. Lull had himself prepared an introduction to a Greek edition of Basil the Great's περὶ γραμματικῆς γυμνασίας and had perhaps had occasion to deal with the Congregation previously.[13] Be that as it may, it would appear from the opening lines of his missive that Lull himself, or at any rate someone other than Cardinal St. Severina, had initiated the investigation into Foix's book; the censor is careful to identify the author and the volume in question, not assuming his audience's familiarity with the work, and gives no indication that he is responding to a request from any church authority in offering his criticisms. After voicing his concerns about the orthodoxy of what he takes to be Foix's identification of the human mind with God's essence, Lull remarks, "I would like to hear what more learned men think." What we have then is a document intended to bring the question of the doctrinal orthodoxy of Foix's commentary to ecclesiastical authorities in a position to decide the issue.

What were the potentially dangerous teachings Lull found lurking in François de Foix's *Pimandre*? Basically there were two: the real presence of the divine essence in man and an interpretation of the sacrament of the Eucharist which came dangerously close to denying the real presence of the body of Christ in the consecrated Host. On the first point Lull argued that the Bishop of Aire had put forward the view that man was composed

---

12. Martin, 241. Unfortunately the biographical sources are vague concerning the formal title and responsibilities of Santori's Congregation.

13. Basilius Magnus, περὶ γραμματικῆς γυμνασίας βιβλίον 'Αντωνίου τοῦ Λούλλου εἰς αὐτὸ τοῦτο προμελέτησις (Basel, [1553]).

of three parts, body, soul and the Holy Spirit, identifying the latter with our mind (*mens*), which thus became an eternal rather than a temporal being, implying a dangerous mixing of the divine nature with the material realm. Although Foix had sought to buttress his position with references to Irenaeus and passages from Scripture, Lull was unconvinced. "To me," he complained, "these doctrines seem to smack of the Gnostics and Manichaeans." Though some legitimate authorities could perhaps be cited in support of the claim that the Holy Spirit was present in the souls of justified individuals, it was quite another thing to claim that a bare natural faculty of man could be identified with a person of the Trinity. "That man's mind, considered apart from its intellectual actualization (*sine intelligentia*), is the Holy Spirit and God Omnipotent none but the ancient theology (*vetus theologia*) held."[14] By implication, any attempt to import such a conception of man's nature from a Hermetic world-view into Christian theology was dangerously heretical, blurring the distinction between man and God and radically altering the character of salvation.

Lull's condemnation of Foix de Candale's interpretation of the Eucharist was likewise harsh, sharpened by his reading of the crucial passages against the background of the bitter interconfessional debates then raging in France. We know that François de Foix took a particular interest in the sacrament of the Eucharist for he made it the subject of a special treatise which he dedicated to Henry III in 1584.[15] Yet rather than taking sides on that hotly debated issue Foix seems to have sought to achieve something of a neutral position by interpreting the sacrament from an Hermetic perspective as providing a means by which the participant is united with Christ and thus purified of corporeal attachments.[16] From Lull's perspective, however, it was inevitable that any account of the Eucharist would be seen as fraught with implications for the ongoing debate over transubstantiation, and Foix's

---

14. Lull mentions Cardinal Bessarion's citation of Basil and Cyril on the real presence of the Holy Spirit in the justified, with the opposite view supported by Ambrose, Jerome and the majority of commentators. Peter Lombard, he notes, upheld a censure on this position in the *Sentences*. Although Bessarion cites Basil and Cyril in his theological writings on the Holy Spirit, I have been unable to identify any particular passage Lull may have had in mind. See, for example, Bessarion's *De spiritus sancti processione ad Alexium Lascarin Philanthropinum*, E. Candal, ed., *Concilium Florentinum. Documenta et scriptores*, ser. B, 7.2 (Rome, 1961), and his *De sacramento eucharistiae*, in L. Mohler, *Kardinal Bessarion als Theologe, Humanist und Staatsmann*, 3 (Paderborn, 1942), 1–69.

15. Paris, BN, MS français 1886 contains his "Traicte du Saint-Sacrement." Cf. Harrie, "Duplessis-Mornay," 502.

16. *Ibid.*, 509, 513.

references to Christ's bodily 'essence' or 'substance' as present in the Host raised a warning flag. Could this not be interpreted to mean that Christ's body was not really present, but only ideally or imaginarily so (*per ideam et imaginationem tantum et fidem*)? The openness of such a formulation to a Protestant interpretation would be obvious. Or if, as Foix held, the essence or substance of Christ's body could be present in the sacrament, wouldn't that commit one by implication to an exaggerated metaphysical realism whereby the ideas, substances or essences of things can exist extramentally independent of the things themselves? "Even if the Scotists posit realities of this sort," Lull commented, "I don't think they would posit them in this way in the case of the sacrament."[17]

While it was perhaps in keeping with François de Foix's personal character and family connections to avoid sectarian formulae in his discussion of the Eucharist, Lull was quick to see the implications therein for Catholic orthodoxy. In spite of Foix's obvious connections both secular and ecclesiastical he did not hesitate to voice his doubts about the Bishop of Aire to a higher authority. "The man's greatness (*amplitudo*) frightens me," he told Santori, "but I have real doubts about Aquitaine." The strength of the Calvinist threat in the southwest of France was not to be taken lightly. Seen against the background of that threat Foix de Candale's Christian Hermeticism was of serious concern.

What effect, if any, did Lull's protest to Rome produce? We have no evidence to suggest that a formal inquiry into the *Pimandre* was ever opened, and the fact that François de Foix was willing to dedicate his *Traicte du Saint-Sacrement* to Henry III as late as 1584 would seem to indicate that he was then still enthusiastic about his prospects for reconciling the theological conflict over the Eucharist by his Hermetic analysis of the sacrament. It may well be that Foix's powerful ties to the Valois, Bourbon and Hapsburg families together with his status as bishop served to protect his rather eccentric intellectual pursuits from official scrutiny. In 1587, at the age of seventy-five, he was nominated by Henry III for appointment to the College of Cardinals, but the nomination was rejected by Pope Sixtus V. Although the reasons for the Pope's refusal seem to have been largely

17. The association of Scotism with a metaphysical doctrine of exaggerated realism is of long standing. Cf. P. Minges, *Ioannis Duns Scoti doctrina philosophica et theologica*, 2nd ed., (Quaracchi, 1930), 1: 67ff.

political, François' case would hardly have been strengthened if questions about his theological orthodoxy had been circulating in Rome for the past seven years.[18]

Though it may have escaped formal condemnation, Foix de Candale's Hermetic masterpiece must have been a theological hot potato in Counter-Reformation Rome. Marin Mersenne's doubts, expressed some four decades later, surely indicate that reservations about the work's orthodoxy had been openly voiced in Catholic circles in France as well. Thanks to Antoine Lull's enlightening *censura* we now know what some of those reservations may have been.[19]

FREDERICK PURNELL, JR.

18. For the background to this event see Harrie, *François Foix*, 57–60.
19. Research embodied in the present article was supported in part by a Fellowship for Independent Study from the National Endowment for the Humanities and a PSC-BHE Research Award from the City University of New York.

APPENDIX

In preparing the following transcription I have expanded abbreviations and altered punctuation and capitalization to accord with modern usage.

Biblioteca Apostolica Vaticana, MS Vaticanus latinus 6207

f.80r: Censura Reverendi Domini Antonii Lulli Vicarii Bisuntini in Comentaria Episcopi Adurensis super Pimandrum Mercurii Trismegisti.

f.81r: Censura Reverendi Domini Antonii Lulli Vicarii Bisuntini in Commentaria Episcopi Adurensis super Pimandrum Mercurii Trismegisti. Ex litteris eiusdem Domini Antonii scriptis Illustrissimo et Reverendissimo Domino Cardinali Sanctae Severinae pridie Idus Martii, receptis prima Aprilis 1580.

Episcopus Adurensis in Aquitania, vir princeps e gente Flussa (de Foix), familia regum Navarrae, commentaria edidit hoc anno amplissima lingua Gallicana in Pimandrum Mercurii Trismegisti. In his veterem theologiam cum Christiana doctrina nititur componere, utiturque precipuo demonstrationum suarum fundamento, quod homo compositus sit ex tribus his: anima, corpore, et spiritu sancto deo, partibus inter se sic differentibus ut una sit deus realiter et vere mixtus cum materia, qui et contineatur tanquam in carcere subiectus arbitrio hominis, mensque nostra (Gallice, notre pensee) sit vere essentia dei aeterna nobis commissa, deducenda ad gloriam et obedientiam dei. Quae et imago dei est et similitudo, educta ex essentiis dei. Sicut infans ex matris educitur substantiis matri similis, sic deus in homine sit, et hominis mens aeterna, non temporalis, creatura. Ratio huius fundamenti datur: quoniam in rebus nihil inveniri potest deo simile nisi deus ipse, cum igitur deus imaginem suam homini dederit, aliud quam se ipsum dare non potuit. Et imago dei aliud non est quam praesentia dei, nec aliam habet deus imaginem quam suam praesentiam, applicatam sicut ipsi placet.

Cum haec ille confidenter asserat, et ex Irenaeo et locis nonnullis sacrae scripturae probare nitatur, mihi autem dogmata videantur sapere Gnosticorum et Manicheorum, cuperem audire quid sentiant doctiores. Viri amplitudo me terret; sed suspecta mihi valde est Aquitania. Sane Cyrillus et Basilius et alii quos afferebat Bessarion Cardinalis spiritum sanctum deum verum realiter et vere esse in hominibus iustificatis sensisse visi sunt, contradicentibus Ambrosio et Hieronymo / f.81v: / atque aliis communiter sentientibus. Et Magister Sententiarum censuram ea de re sustinuit. Sed quod mens hominis (sine intelligentia) sit spiritus sanctus et deus omnipotens, non nisi vetus tenuit theologia.

Suspecta mihi valde est, ut dixi, Aquitania. Nam et de sacramento eucharistiae, quod regenerationis alterum sacramentum et unicum remedium atque necessarium dicit post baptismum contra frequentia peccata, nulla facta mentione sacramenti confessionis, ita philosophatur ut per ideam tantum et spiritualiter sumi corpus Christi, non autem in re doceat. Errant, inquit, in fide huius sacramenti qui non putant aliter sumi quam corporaliter, cum potius sumatur in parte hominis incorporea et divina, quae est in homine, nempe cognitione, intelligentia, fide, non sensibus. Separat hic auctor essentiam corporis a corpore et substantiam ut quae pertineant ad res intelligibiles et divinas; corpus autem sit mutabile propter materiam. Cumque Christus (ut ait) sit compositus ex quatuor, videlicet secunda persona divinitatis, et anima, et corpore, et spiritu sancto, solum vero ex his corpus sit sensibile, reliqua intelligibilia, sequitur ut fiat corpus Christi in sacramento non sensibile, sed intelligibile tantum et incorporeum. Probationem elicit ex verbo illo substantivo quo usus est Dominus, Hoc est corpus meum. Per quod substantiam corporis intellexisse videtur, non materiam, veluti pedes, manus, brachia, ossa, et carnem cruentam, qualis esset in consideratione materiae, sed rem intelligibilem tantum, qualia sunt substantia et essentia rerum. Haec enim non sensibus corporis sed mente concipiuntur. Ex substantia tamen nomen suum accipit corpus, et effectus praesentiae suae ad paenitentem a quo sumitur, qui sic Christo coniungitur ut / f.82r: / idem fiat cum eo, qui inde idoneus fiat ut ascendat in caelum, quoniam idem factus est cum eo qui ascendit. Nam forma (inquit) dat esse rei. Ergo ubi forma est, ibi res est. Et rursum, ubi essentia seu substantia rei est, ibi forma rei est. Ergo licet substantia corporis Christi sit incorporea et iuncta formae, tamen ut praecipua pars corporis et iuncta formae, dat nomen et esse huic corpori. Quare ubi substantia corporis Christi est, ibi corpus Christi est, quia continetur ipsum esse in substantia, non autem materia, quae dimensionibus constituta est et qualitatibus materialibus, quae non possident ipsum esse subiecti.

Vides quam multa sibi permittit regius iste et realis philosophus. An non tota haec argumentatio eo tendit ut efficiat sumi corpus Christi per ideam et imaginationem tantum et fidem, non realiter nec vere? Aut certe ideas separatas subsistere in accidentibus sacramenti fateare, et ut substantias rerum sine rebus esse extra intelligentiam. Quas realitates si ponant Scotistae, non puto tamen eas posituros esse isto modo sub sacramento. Quantam licentiam obtinuit seculum hoc dogmatizandi!

FRA GIORDANO BRUNO'S
CATHOLIC PASSION

I

Introduction: The Heretic

La Chiesa poteva, doveva intervenire e intervenne; i documenti del processo dimostrano la legalità di esso e l'onestà con cui venne condotto.

> A. Mercati, *Il sommario,* 52.

It is one of the most extraordinary features of Bruno's outlook that he seems to have believed that his religion could somehow be incorporated within a Catholic framework.

> F. A. Yates, "Giordano Bruno,"
> *Dictionary of Scientific Biography,* 2: 540.

As Giordano Bruno's ashes cooled on February 17, 1600, in the Campo dei Fiori, there was relief that an obstinate heretic had been eliminated. The sentence read (February 8) and the execution carried out, Bruno's words and actions on these occasions seemed to indicate then, and have ever since, that he had had only scorn for his natal faith. Such seemed clear from the philosopher's remark when the sentence was read to him by the inquisitors: "Perhaps you feel more afraid in pronouncing this sentence than I do on hearing it."[1] Such seemed clear also from his scornful turning away from the proffered crucifix as the flames engulfed him. As Gaspar Scioppius, an eyewitness to the execution, said: "When they showed him the image of Christ, as he was on the verge of expiring, he turned his head away and rejected it with a scornful look. . . ."[2] No matter who has written about Bruno since that time, the memory of his condemnation and execution scenes has stood between the Nolan and his subsequent interpreter. "Fu bruciato!" Since February 17, 1600, Bruno's published works and his words at his trial have served only to confirm the terrible judgment carried out on that February morning.[3]

This continuous confirmation of the inquisitorial judgment has prevented complete understanding of Giordano Bruno's ideas and actions as a religious thinker. It would thus be well to read and view Bruno's words anew, trying as much as possible to escape the distorting lens of his condemnation and execution, and thus to view him just before the picture frame froze him forever beyond the pale of Catholic, indeed even Christian, thought and behavioral parameters. I believe that this fresh examination will be useful for several reasons. For one thing, work by Carlo Ginzburg,[4] whatever the final assessment of its methodology may be, has shown that inquisitors did not always easily or accurately comprehend or even taxonomize the responses given them by suspected heretics. This seems especially clear in Bruno's case for, as we shall see below, the inquisitors—as late as September, 1599—had not reached agreement on defining Bruno's heresies. And, indeed, as Hélène Védrine has rightly

1. V. Spampanato, *Documenti della vita di Giordano Bruno* (Florence, 1933), 202 (hereafter cited as *Documenti*): "Maiori forsan cum timore sententiam in me fertis quam ego accipiam."
2. *Ibid.*: "Hodie igitur ad rogum sive piram deductus, cum Salvatoris crucifixi imago ei iam morituro ostenderetur, torvo eam vultu aspernatus reiecit. . . ."
3. A. Mercati, *Il sommario del processo di Giordano Bruno* (Vatican City, 1942); Luigi Firpo, *Il processo di Giordano Bruno* (Naples, 1949); F. A. Yates, *Giordano Bruno and the Hermetic Tradition* (Chicago, 1964); idem, "Giordano Bruno," *Dictionary of Scientific Biography*, C. C. Gillispie, ed. 2 (New York, 1970): 539–544; and H. Védrine, *Censure et Pouvoir. Trois Procès: Savonarole, Bruno Galilée* (Paris/The Hague, 1976). Although these books differ in their interpretations of Bruno they are in general agreement that he had entirely rejected Catholicism and the Dominican Order
4. C. Ginzburg, *The Night Battles: Witchcraft and Agrarian Cults in the Sixteenth and Seventeenth Centuries*, trs. J. and A. Tedeschi (Baltimore, 1983).

pointed out,[5] the whole purpose of inquisitorial proceedings was biased, in the first place, and, in the second, was intent upon making the accused "see," "accept," and recant his "errors." We may argue, then, that Bruno's condemnation was *a fortiori* a prejudiced decision and that it could not help but shape all subsequent readings of the Nolan philosopher.

I propose in this paper, then, to survey Bruno's responses to the inquisitors and to try to assess their significance both in the light of related things he had previously written and in that of the problem of the internal consistency of his answers to the questions put to him by his judges. We cannot enter into a detailed accounting of Bruno's quotidial behavior and actions—what he did and said to those around him while he was a monk and while he was not a monk—for the evidence for such a brief does not exist, however lamentable that fact is. Thus we are left with scattered snapshots, as it were, of moments—many of them highly charged—in Giordano Bruno's life, and we must try to infer conclusions about that life from them. In so doing, we will be going through published material that is well known, as no new documents have been uncovered. I am, however, offering a fresh interpretation that is fully allowed by the evidence. By the time we reach the end of this analysis, we will have concluded that Bruno was probably not quite as "unchristian" and "Egyptian" in his religion as Frances Yates averred nor as morally flawed but, *au coeur*, Roman Catholic as Angelo Mercati argued. Fra Giordano rejected much of his Catholicism, but he continued to maintain some feeling for his monastic background and some longing for sacramental ceremonial. He might have been a Nicodemite, but his dislike of the Protestant doctrine of justification prevented, as we shall see, his being a proper Catholic Nicodemite.

---

5. Védrine, 93, for example.

II

The Truth of Words

Respondit (extollendo ambas manus et dicendo): Che cosa è questa?
. . . Io non ho mai detto tal cosa, nè mai mi passò per l'imaginazione
tal cosa. O Dio, che cosa è questa? Io vorrai esser più tosto morto
che mi fosse stato proposto questa cosa
                    V. Spampanato, *Documenti*, 111 [Venice, 2 June 1592].

The reader might question the sincerity of Bruno's response to the question of whether he had ever said that the miracles of Christ and the Apostles were not real but were done by magical art. The posture and words seem studied. Yet it could also signify genuine shock that such an outrageous thing could have been said about him. One could interpret the above-quoted statement either way. The former interpretation—that he was acting—is more consistent with the normative view of Bruno as a flamboyant individual whose public utterances tended to histrionics and perhaps even intellectual dishonesty.[6] Bruno's shock seems all the more implausible when one recalls Bruno's blasphemous aversion of his eyes from the crucifix in the last moments of his life. But this may be an overhasty conclusion. After all, given the fact that Bruno was finally condemned, as we shall see, despite the inquisitors' difficulty in reaching consensus on his crimes and despite his previous expression of contrition for any errors of thought and action he might have committed,[7] one can well understand that his state of mind on the morning of February 17 would not have induced him to turn toward the crucifix. The evidence against Bruno was in large part drawn from the testimony of his Venetian host-turned-betrayer, Zuan Mocenigo, and from that of his Venetian cellmate,

6. One thinks of Bruno's 1583 visit to and lecture at Oxford, when "he had more boldly than wisely got up into the highest place of our best & most renowned schoole, stripping up his sleeves like some Iugler, and telling us much of *chentrum* et *chirculus* et *circumferenchia* (after the pronunciation of his Country language) he undertooke . . . to set on foot the opinion of Copernicus. . . . When he had read his first lecture, a grave man,. . . repayring to his study, found both the former and the later Lecture, taken almost verbatim out of the works of *Marsilius Ficinus*. . . ." R. McNulty, "Bruno at Oxford," *Renaissance News*, 13 (1960): 300–305.

7. Firpo, 96–97. The inquisitors urged (Sept. 9, 1599) that Bruno be tortured again to elicit a clear confession of his errors. One of them, R.D. Julio Monterenzi, went so far as to say that Bruno "was not convicted," and that more torture was necessary in order to convict. Cf. also Védrine, 97. Already in Venice Bruno had admitted that he doubted the hypostatic union of Christ's humanity and divinity.

Fra Celestino da Verona. Neither man was unbiased. Mocenigo seems to have felt that Bruno had failed to teach him the art of memory that could have facilitated a brilliant career for the young nobleman, and Celestino may well have betrayed Bruno in a futile attempt to lighten his own sentence. When we survey the extant records of Bruno's trial, we are thus faced with the problem of Bruno's probity in the face of his questioners. The easy assumption is to conclude that Bruno, a brilliant intellectual fencer, ran circles around the inquisitors and generally lied to them. I do not believe that this assumption can be sustained. What seems clear from the testimony as well as from a comparison of the testimony with certain things that Bruno had written in *La Cena de le Ceneri*, *Lo Spaccio della bestia trionfante*, and *De l'infinito, universo, e mondi*, is that Bruno stayed close to the truth on those matters for which the inquisitors had close-to-hand evidence with which to assess his responses, and that he either stretched the truth of, or obfuscated, issues about which the judges were not likely to have contrary evidence. It was essential for Bruno to stretch the truth in this latter case in order not to reveal his deeper relations with Protestant churches or his Valois-appointed mission to bring about religious reunion. Such matters could not be revealed if Bruno held out any hope that his life be spared and that he be sufficiently reconciled with Rome to allow him active participation in the eucharistic ceremony. Ultimately, as we shall see, while Bruno may not have been orthodox, he saw himself as an apostle of the eucharist.

One of the best instances of Bruno's deliberate obscuring of the truth may be found in his response to a question directly relating to the point just made—whether he had ever written about an Ash Wednesday Supper:

I once wrote a *book* [my emphasis] titled *The Ash Wednesday Supper*. It is divided into five dialogues which deal with the motion of the earth; and because I engaged in this discussion in England with some physicians at a supper that took place on Ash Wednesday in the French ambassador's residence, I titled these dialogues *The Ash Wednesday Supper*, and dedicated them to the aforementioned ambassador. . . . My intent in the book was only to mock those doctors and their opinions on these matters.[8]

8. *Documenti*, p. 121: "Io ho composto un libro intitolato *La cena delle ceneri*, il quale è diviso in cinque dialoghi, quali trattano del moto della Terra; e perchè questa disputa io feci in Inghilterra in una cena che si fece il giorno delle ceneri, con alcuni medici, in casa dell' Ambasciator di

Bruno obviously wanted to avoid giving any religious significance to that Ash Wednesday Supper as he focused the inquisitors' attention on the safer—because then still neutral—ground of the Copernican theory and the comic aspects of the book. On the other hand, despite the care with which Bruno responded to this and other questions put to him, I do not believe we can assume that his responses are entirely devoid of truth value. Somehow it would seem out of character for Bruno to have been able to maintain a façade throughout his eight years of encounters with the inquisitors, notwithstanding the fact that on July 30, 1592 he confessed and begged pardon for all his errors and that, again, in September 1599 torture prompted him momentarily once again to recant, a type of confession that few today would really believe was sincere.[9] On December 21, 1599, Bruno reneged his recantation:

> He said that he ought not and did not wish to recant, that there was no subject about which to recant, and that he did not know about what he should recant.[10]

The modern psychological age might say that Bruno had a death wish. But, more likely, once the pain and memory of torture had abated, he once again realized that the case against him was a slender reed. As far as Bruno's credibility is concerned, credence can, I think, be given to many of his responses by dint of the fact that some were obviously liable to make trouble for him. Thus if he felt compelled to reply honestly concerning some questions, the answers to which threatened his safety, then why should we not assume that he consistently answered as honestly as he could, always trying to be true to his beliefs but yet showing their compatibility with orthodox Roman teaching? The evidence suggests that Bruno in some sense wanted to be reconciled with the Church, although not entirely on the latter's terms.

Francia, dove io stava, io intitolai queste dialoghi *La cena delle cenere*, e le dedicai al medesimo Ambasciator. . . . [E]d in questo libro la mia intenzione è stata solamente di burlarmi di quei medici e dell'opinion loro intorno a queste materie."

9. *Documenti*, 136; and Firpo, 98–99. See esp. *ibid.*, 99, note 6: ". . . quod [Frater Giordano] intendit recognoscere eius errores et facere totum et quicquid ei iniunctum fuerit a Sancta Ecclesia Catholica Romana. . . ."

10. *Documenti*, 183: "Dixit quod non debet nec vult rescipiscere, et non habet quid rescipiscat nec habet materiam rescipiscendi, et nescit super quo debet rescipisci."

III

The Habit, the Tonsure, and la Cène: *From Naples to Geneva*

Let us turn then to an examination of Bruno's testimony in the context of the chronology of his journey from Naples to Geneva (1576–1579). The confluence of the testimony with the chronology will enable us the better to reach some conclusions about Bruno's religious views and comportment.

Born in Nola in 1548, Filippo Bruno entered the Dominican monastery of San Domenico in Naples on June 15, 1565.[11] After a year, he completed his novitiate and became a Dominican friar, adopting the name "Giordano," in honor of the second leader of the Order.[12] He became a priest in 1572 and sang his first mass at the convent of San Bartolomeo in Campagna.[13] Not much is known of Bruno's activities as a friar over the next few years. By 1576, however, this period of relative calm ended and Bruno came to the attention of his monastic superiors. He had expressed some Arian-sounding ideas and was discovered to have read editions of Erasmus that had been prohibited. In addition, he seems to have taken to heart some of the latter's anti-ritualistic ideas, for Bruno "reformed" his own monastic cell:

At Naples, I had been brought to account two times: first, for having taken down certain figures and images of the saints, retaining only a crucifix, [and] thus I was thought to despise the images of saints.[14]

There is only fragmentary evidence of Bruno's doings after he had fled

---

11. *Documenti*, 7.
12. *Ibid.*, 7.
13. *Ibid.*, 80; D. Berti, *La vita di Giordano Bruno da Nola* (Florence, 1868), 50.
14. *Documenti*, 80. A. Corsano, *Il pensiero di Giordano Bruno nel suo svolgimento storico* (Florence, 1940/1948), 46, cites this as an example of Bruno's having acquired an Erasmian religious sensitivity and reformist bent. P.-H. Michel, *La cosmologie de Giordano Bruno* (Paris, 1962), 6, reports that Bruno had hidden the works of Erasmus in his privy. Berti, 56, says that when Bruno hurriedly left Naples in 1576, he left behind prohibited books of St. Jerome and St. John Chrysostom, as edited by Erasmus. D. W. Singer, *Giordano Bruno: His Life and Thought* (New York, 1950; repr. 1968), 12, goes too far when she suggests that his reading of Erasmus led Bruno (in 1576) "to examine the new [Lutheran] religion."

Naples, and then Rome, because of the charges of heresy brought against him. He travelled throughout Italy until he crossed the Alps and went to Geneva in 1579. Comments made at his trial indicate that he taught Sacrobosco's *Sphere* in Noli, along with grammar lessons to young boys.[15] He claimed to have published a book, *De' segni de' tempi,* in order to earn money while in Venice; however, its contents are unknown today.[16] Interestingly, at Bruno's request, the Dominican humanist Remigio Fiorentino authorized its publication, a fact that may indicate that the work contained nothing contrary to Catholic teachings.[17] When Bruno finally emerged from Italy, it was after he had once again donned the Dominican habit in Bergamo, having been urged to do so by Dominicans of his acquaintance whom he had met in Padua:

> Leaving Venice, I went to Padua where I met some Dominicans who knew me, [and] they persuaded me to put on the habit again, even should I not wish to return to the Order, as they were of the opinion that it was safer to go with the habit than without it; and with this thought I continued on to Bergamo. [There] I had a [Dominican] habit made out of cheap white cloth, and over it I put the scapular that I had kept with me when I left Rome. . . .[18]

Crossing the Alps, Bruno stayed for some time in the Dominican convent in Chambéry and continued to wear his Dominican robes:

> . . . and I continued to wear the habit as I proceeded in the direction of Lyons; and when I was at Chambéry, I lodged at the convent

15. *Documenti,* 81. He taught the *Sphere* again in Toulouse (*Ibid.,* 83).

16. *Ibid.,* 82. See also Singer, 204; and V. Salvestrini, *Bibliografia di Giordano Bruno (1582–1950),* 2nd ed. Luigi Firpo, ed. (Florence, 1958), no. 234.

17. One wonders if Bruno might not have approached Remigio Nannini (Fiorentino) because he was a humanist scholar whose interest in more speculative thought was minimal. The National Union Catalogue and the catalogues of the Bibliothèque Nationale, the British Library, and the UCLA Library indicate that Nannini was a commentator on Francesco Guicciardini's and Villani's histories, editor of Ovid, of Gerson's *On the Imitation of Christ,* and of a collection on the authority of the pope, residency of bishops and plurality of benefices, author of *rime,* and the editor of liturgical epistles and gospels. Kristeller, *Iter,* 1 and 2 does not indicate any manuscripts beyond the scope of the works just listed.

18. *Documenti,* 82: ". . . io andai a Padoa, dove trovando alcuni padri dell'ordine de S. Dominico mei conosenti, li quali me persuadettero a ripigliar l'abito, quando bene non avesse voluto tornar alla Religione, perendoli che era più conveniente andar con l'abito che senza; e con questo pensiero andai a Bergamo. E mi feci far una vesto di panno bianco di buon mercato, e sopra essa vi posi il scapulare, che io avevo conservato quando partii da Roma."

of the Order; and seeing that I was treated soberly, I discussed this with an Italian priest who was there. He said to me: "Be forewarned that you will not find courtesy of any kind in these parts [in convents], and the further you go [toward Lyons and into France] the less you will find."[19]

One interpretation of Bruno's life (shared in certain ways by Yates, Corsano, Védrine and Singer, among others) has it that Bruno was fully formed intellectually and, by implication, religiously, at the time of his flight from Naples. By further adducement, he is thought to have been already an "unchristian," a proponent of the Hermetic "Egyptian" religion, Lullism, and, perhaps, Copernicanism. However, none of the evidence presented here or, as far as I know, extant in the documents completely supports this line of interpretation. Rather, on the eve of Bruno's entrance into Geneva we have a picture of a thirty-one-year-old man, Dominican trained, whose somewhat iconoclastic and Erasmian tendencies had caused him to be alleged a heretic in the Kingdom and again in Rome. Understandably fearful, Bruno ran away and, by that act prompted by fear, he became apostate and thus a heretic.

Bruno is of course not the only monk or brother to have fled the cloister in the sixteenth century. Erasmus and Rabelais also did, to name only two of the most famous—and without the scandal that has hounded Bruno's reputation. Besides, unlike Erasmus and Rabelais, we are beginning to sense that Bruno had not completely broken with and distanced himself from the cloister. It is true that his readoption of the habit could have been purely for safety's sake. But why? How recognizable could Bruno have been as he wandered the streets of Padua and Bergamo? Why could he not have merged in with the other people on the crowded streets of these cities? Might it be the case that, having abandoned the Dominican habit when he fled Rome, he retained the tonsure? Nothing in the trial records or in any other source, as far as I know, speaks one way or the other about this matter. However, Bruno's own account of his arrival in Geneva, immediately after having left Chambéry, may indicate that he in fact did wear a tonsure:

19. *Ibid.*: ". . . e con questo abito me inviai alla volta de Lione; e quando fui a Chiamberi, andando a logiar al convento dell'Ordine e vedendomi trattato molto sobriamente e discorrendo sopra questo con un Padre italiano che era lí, me disse: Avertite che non trovarete in queste parti amorevolezza de sorte alcuna, e come piú andarete inanzi ne trovarete manco,"

> And [the Marchese of Vico] persuaded me . . . to get rid of my habit,
> [and] I took off those clothes and had a pair of breeches and other
> robes made; and the Marchese [and] other Italians gave me [a] sword,
> hat, cape, and other necessities for dressing myself.[20]

Perhaps Bruno's Genevan friends only wanted him to look the gentleman. But it is likely that, at the same time, they wanted him — whatever
his intentions vis-à-vis the Calvinist religion — to hide the tonsure from
Calvinist eyes.

It would not be surprising if Bruno had retained the tonsure ever since
leaving Rome in 1576, just ahead of the next step of the inquisitorial
process. Although he had fled the Inquisition and the Order, he may not
have thought of himself as a heretic, no matter how individual his ideas
had become or were becoming. Perhaps he kept the tonsure as a sign of
private religious commitment. This would explain better why his Dominican friends in Padua advised him to wear the habit — the rest of his body
ought to be garbed in line with his tonsure. Being tonsured, he was
easily recognizable as a lapsed brother. Since canon law forbade his putting aside the habit, he could have been prosecuted by Italian civil
authorities. And certainly, as he continued to wear the Dominican habit
even when he entered Geneva, he must have arrived there tonsured as
well.

That this maintenance of the tonsure — for I believe that this is what
he did, given the evidence that we have seen — and the putting on again
of the Dominican robes may well denote more than fear of discovery is
supported by the fact that Bruno had kept the Dominican scapular he had
worn in San Domenico and Rome. He had carried it with him until he
repositioned it over his readopted habit in Bergamo. This behavior betrays
more lingering commitment and attachment to the cloister and Church
than it would perhaps today for someone who, forsaking his religion entirely, might consign the object to the trash or to a soon-to-be-forgotten
spot in a drawer. Bruno had become a wanderer in 1576. Every object
he carried along with him must have meant something.

Bruno's residence in Geneva, however, confuses the matter of Bruno's

---

20. *Ibid.*, 83: "E persuadendomi in ogni caso a demetter quell'abito che io avevo, pigliai quei
panni e me feci far un paro di calce ed altre robbe; ed esso Marchese con altri italiani me diedero
spada, capello, cappa ed altre cose necessarie per vestirme."

religious feelings, especially since it seems to contradict what the evidence thus far implies: that Bruno retained certain attachments to Catholicism. For it is among the Genevan records that we find *prima facie* evidence that Bruno had entirely forsaken not only the Dominican Order but also the Roman Catholic Church. What else should one make of the fact that in Geneva he abandoned his religious name, "Giordano," and adopted his secular name, "Filippo"?[21] Not only this, but the municipal records found in Spampanato's *Documenti* show that Bruno desired a lifting of the ban that had, to use the Calvinist expression, "fenced him off" from the Lord's Supper in that city.

After his arrival in Geneva, Bruno had created a storm by attacking the Genevan Academy's leading philosopher, Anthoyne de la Faye, claiming that his lectures contained twenty errors. De la Faye brought suit against Bruno and his publisher, Jean Bergeron, and caused them to be imprisoned briefly.[22] Thereafter, we find that on Thursday, 13 August:

> Filippo Bruno appeared in Consistory to acknowledge his fault. . . .
> He was admonished to follow the true doctrine. He replied that he
> was prepared to accept censure . . ., [that] he has to acknowledge
> his fault, and that they had forbidden him the Supper in case he did
> not wish to confess his fault. . . .

And, on Thursday, 27 August, we learn of:

> Removal of the ban, with warnings. — Filippo Bruno, student, liv-
> ing in this city, appeared in Consistory. He asked that the ban on
> his taking the Supper be lifted.[23]

One final document, compiled and published in 1650, lists "Filippo Bruno

---

21. See *ibid.*, 33–35: "[6.VIII.1579] Philippe Jordan, dit Brunus . . ."; "[10.VIII.1579] Philippe Brunet, Italien . . ."; "[13.VIII.1579] Philippe Brun . . ."; "27.VIII.1579] Philippus Brunus Nolanus. . . ." The documents indicate that Bruno initiated the name change, as his signature in the *Livre du Recteur* (*Documenti*, 36) is an autograph: "Philippus Brunus Nolanus, sacrae theologiae professor."

22. Salvestrini, no. 235; *Documenti*, 33.

23. *Documenti*, 34–36: "Deffence de la cène. — Philippe Bruno a comparu en Concistoyre pour recognoistre sa faute. . . . A esté admonesté de suyvre la vraye doctrine. A dict qu'il est prest de recepvoyr censure. . . . [I]l aye à recognoistre sa faute, et que on luy deffende la cène en cas qu'il ne veullie recognoistre sa faute. . . . Absolution de la deffence avecq remonstrances. — A comparu en Concistoyre. Philippe Brun, estudiant, habitant en ceste cité, lequel recquiert la cène à luy deffendue luy estre remise. . . ."

of the Kingdom of Naples" as having been a member of the Italian Protestant church in Geneva.[24]

These shreds of evidence point to Bruno's conversion to Calvinism. He
had apparently become a member of the Italian congregation. Later, stung
by the furor over and the eucharistic consequences of his published attack
on Anthoyne de la Faye, Bruno was above all concerned to be readmitted
to the Calvinist Supper. These signs of change are confirmed, it would
seem, by his adoption of his secular name. Since the entry of his secular
name in the *Livre du Recteur* is an autograph signature, we know that
it was not simply the case of a Genevan Calvinist refusing to honor his
religious name; yet, registration in the university at most required an ac-
knowledgement of Christian doctrine as it was taught at Geneva, not a
confession of faith.[25]

Filippo Bruno the Calvinist? This is quite a different picture from the
one we have been sketching thus far. And it is quite a different picture
from the one Giordano Bruno painted for his inquisitors:

> [Having left Chambéry, I finally arrived in Geneva.] I went to lodge
> in an inn; soon thereafter, the Neapolitan Marchese of Vico, resident
> in that city, asked me who I was and whether I had gone there to
> settle and to profess the religion of that city. I gave an accounting
> of myself and the reason why I had left the religious state, [and then]
> I added that I did not intend to adopt the religion of Geneva, because
> I did not know what religion it was; and that I desired to stay there
> in order to be free and secure rather than for any other reason.[26]

24. *Ibid.*, 36.

25. See *Le Livre du Recteur de l'Académie de Genève (1559–1878)*, Vol. I: Le Texte, S. Stelling-
Michaud, ed., Trauvaux d'Humanisme et Renaissance, XXXIII,1 (Geneva, 1959), 14–15. (The
frontispiece of this edition is a plate of f. 68, exhibiting the signature of Philippo Bruno. One
wonders whether the choice of this folio and signature had any modern-day Calvinist ideological
import.) Up to 1576 students enrolling in the Academy of Geneva had to sign a Confession of
faith. In the period 1572–1576, students no longer enrolled or enrolled under false names, so as
not to be compelled in their beliefs. In 1576, the Venerable Company of Pastors substituted for
the Confession a "Summary of Christian doctrine taught at Geneva," whose recognition was no
longer required except from professors and regents. Bruno's Venetian testimony suggests he was
more an auditor of courses than a professor. Thus Bruno's adherence to Calvinism may not have
been complete, as it could well be the case that he never swore a Calvinist confession.

26. *Documenti*, 82–83: "Onde voltai alla volta de Genevre; ed arrivato là, andai ad allogiar al-
l'osteria; e pocco doppo il Marchese de Vico napolitano, che stava in quella città, me domandò
chi ero e che se era andato lí per fermarmi e professar la religione di quella città. Al quale doppo
che ebbi dato conto di me e della causa perché ero uscito dalla Religione, soggiunsi ch'io non

Which is the correct version: that contained in the municipal and university records of Geneva, or the one given by Bruno, that he merely wanted security and freedom in Geneva, not a new religion? The answer is that both reasons are correct. Bruno did become a Calvinist congregant for a brief period; and Bruno did want to find a place where he could live securely and without fear of inquisitorial prosecution. Above all, it is not to be wondered that Bruno did not want to confide to the inquisitors during his long trial in Venice and Rome that he had been a Calvinist congregant or a partaker of its communion. This was never admitted openly by Bruno at his trial, but we will be able to understand how he could hunger for both Protestant and Catholic communion when we understand *The Ash Wednesday Supper*. For the moment, we should simply realize that, as the rules obtaining at the time of his enrollment in the Academy of Geneva indicate, Bruno did not have to swear a Calvinist confession of faith before he signed his name in the *Livre du Recteur*. Thus, he did not have to commit himself publicly to Calvinist theology even though he seems to have—or at least have wanted to—take the Calvinist Supper.

IV

Paris, London, and the Eucharist

... e con littere dell'istesso Re andai in Inghilterra a star con l'Ambasciator di Sua Maestà...; in casa del qual non faceva altro, se non che stava per suo gentilomo. E me fermai in Inghilterra doi anni e mezo; né in questo tempo, ancora che si dicesse la messa in casa, non andavo [a casa] né fuori a messa, né a prediche, per la causa sudetta.

Spampanato, *Documenti*, 85

intendevo di professar quella di essa città, perché non sapevo che religione fosse; e che per ciò desideravo piú presto de star lí per viver in libertà e di esser sicuro, che per altro fine." The Marchese of Vico: Galeazzo Caracciolo (1517–1586), the only son of a noble Neapolitan family and the nephew of Paul IV; he came under the influence of Juan de Valdès and Peter Vermigli. He finally forsook his family and position in the royal service and fled to Geneva in 1551, becoming a citizen in 1555. Cf. Berti, 98; *The New Schoff-Herzog Encyclopedia*, S. M. Jackson, ed., 2 (New York and London, 1908), 411–412; B. Croce, *Vite di avventure di fede e di passione* (Bari, 1936), 179–281; and N. Balbani, *Historia della vita di Galeazzo Caracciolo* (Geneva, 1587; repr. Florence, 1875).

I have argued elsewhere that Bruno's long journey from Naples to Paris was intensely educational and that it was only in Paris that Bruno was finally introduced to Ramon Lull, the mystical philosopher who believed in the use of the art of memory to harmonize Muslims with Christians. Paris was where Bruno was introduced to the king who would send him to London to harmonize Anglicans with French Catholics, and where he began to get his first glimmerings of the Copernican Sun that would for Bruno become the sign and the motive engine of the Valois Henrican reform.[27] Sequestered in San Domenico and Naples, Bruno's knowledge of the Reformation and its controversies had probably been indirect and minimal. His only documented exposure was to the scholarly works of Erasmus (which, as I suggested above, either caused or reinforced a sensitive and somewhat reformist religious nature). But, after fleeing Naples and then Rome (out of fear of being prosecuted for having read the prohibited works of Erasmus),[28] his journey northward brought him an ever closer acquaintance with Reformation controversies. Once settled in Geneva, he found a religious community that had been, to some extent, influenced by Erasmian ideas.[29] Certainly Calvinist iconoclasm would have dovetailed with his own modest iconoclastic efforts in his Neapolitan monastic cell. In Geneva, too, he must finally have become aware of a quite different eucharistic feast than that to which he had been accustomed as a priest. This growing awareness was, I believe, the beginning of Bruno's belief that the crucial stumbling block of the Reformation debate, as far as religious reunion was concerned, was the question of Holy Com-

27. E. A. Gosselin, "Bruno's 'French Connection': A Historiographical Debate," forthcoming in A. G. Debus and I. Merkle, eds., *Essays in Memory of Frances Yates* (Washington, D. C., Folger Library Series). See also idem, " 'Doctor' Bruno's Solar Medicine," *The Sixteenth Century Journal*, 15 (1984): 209–224.

28. The charges brought against Bruno when he was arrested in 1592 in Venice are essentially the same as those on which he would have been tried in Naples or Rome in 1576: "libri proibiti e proposizioni ereticali." See the Index to the *Processi di Santo Uffizio (Veneziano)*, sub nom. "Bruno, Giordano." I have used the copy located in the Newberry Library. I wish to thank Mrs. Patricia Jobe for her help in locating and using this document.

29. Cf. H. R. Trevor-Roper, "Religion, the Reformation and Social Change," in his *The European Witch-Craze of the Sixteenth and Seventeenth Centuries and Other Essays* (New York, 1969), 26: ". . . the abuses of the Church drove its critics into extremity and the Erasmians . . . found themselves obliged either to surrender or to admit themselves heretics. For Calvin, far more than is generally admitted, was the heir of Erasmus. . . . And everywhere the Erasmian *bourgeoisie*, if it did not renounce its Erasmian views altogether, turned to Calvinism as the only form in which it could defend them."

munion, its definition, and its liturgy.[30] In Geneva, Bruno attended public
sermons by French and Italian preachers, including homilies on the Pauline Epistles and the Gospels given by Nicolò Balbani.[31] Perhaps thinking that he could find religious peace and communion in Geneva, he joined
the Church, but he soon ran afoul of the holy community because of his
attacks on de la Faye. (It may be that he already realized, as we will see
he did in London, that the Protestant doctrine of justification was anathema
to him.) In any case, Bruno did not remain long in Geneva. He betook
himself to Toulouse, which was, until the 1590s, a Calvinist town.[32]

In Toulouse, Bruno became affiliated with and taught at the university. Relative religious calm reigned in the city when Bruno arrived, so
the usual requirement that professors participate in the Protestant communion was not then enforced.[33] By 1581, Bruno had left Toulouse and
gone to Paris. There, he soon became known to court intellectuals and
to Henri III himself. The king offered Bruno an ordinary lectureship, but
the Nolan declined. Bruno's later remarks to the inquisitors explain why
he could accept the teaching position in Toulouse but not in Paris:

And then, because of the civil wars, I left [Toulouse] and went to
Paris where I gave an extraordinary lecture in order to make myself
known..., but when I was asked to give an ordinary lecture I refused, because full professors in Paris went to mass and other religious services as a matter of course. And I have always resisted this,
knowing that I was excommunicated for having fled the [convent
and] Order and for having discarded the habit; while in Toulouse
the ordinary lectureship did not require church attendance.[34]

30. See Bruno's comments to Guillaume Cotin, librarian of the Abbey of St. Victor in Paris
on 4 December 1585: "Il prise souverainement saint Thomas in *Summa contra gentiles* et in *Quaes-
tionibus disputatis*, aut earum saltem parte; contemnent les subtilitez des scholastiques, des Sacre-
ments et mesmement de l'Eucharistie, lesquelles il dit saint Pierre et saint Paul avoir ignorées,
mais seulement sçeu que *hoc est corpus meum*. Il dit que facilement les troubles en la religion seront
ostées, quand on ostera ces questions, et dit espérer que bien tost en sera la fin." (*Documenti*, 40.)
Bruno's sensitivity to the eucharistic controversy certainly modifies Singer's (pp. 14–15) comment
that "Bruno was in his incurable mental detachment in fact completely indifferent to the quarrels
between Catholic and Protestant, regarding them as irrelevant to the higher philosophic problems
that occupied his mind to the exclusion of all worldly wisdom and even of the commonest prudence."
31. *Documenti*, 83. Balbani authored the biography of the Marchese of Vico (see note 26, above).
32. *Documenti*, 83.
33. Singer, 16.
34. *Documenti*, 84: "E doppoi per le guerre civili me partii ed andai a Paris, dove me messi

One could read this statement to mean that Bruno refused to attend divine services because of disagreement with and repudiation of both (perhaps all) established religions. This interpretation stretches Bruno's words too far, however. One can more reliably infer that Bruno took his excommunication seriously, especially since— as we shall see—it was in Toulouse and Paris that Bruno was told he could not receive communion until he had received absolution in Rome and that, until such time, he could only pray in church. This reading is more likely, especially when his words here are considered in the light of his other comments about the eucharist.

One senses from Bruno's trial records as well as from *The Ash Wednesday Supper* that he had a special commitment or devotion to the eucharist. In reply to the inquisitors' question,[35] Bruno strenuously averred that he never spoke or wrote against the Roman Catholic doctrine of the eucharist:

> I have never spoken of the sacrifice of the mass, nor of transubstantiation, unless in the manner of the Holy Church; and I have always held and believed, as I now hold and believe, that transubstantiation changes the bread and wine into the body and blood of Christ, really and substantially, as the Church teaches.[36]

This reply is all the more striking when one recalls that Bruno quite calmly admitted that as a philosopher he had difficulty reconciling Christ's humanity with his divinity as well as understanding the hypostatic union of the Three Persons of the Trinity.[37] Indeed, even though Bruno admitted that

a legger straordinaria per farmi conoscer e far saggio di me; ... e doppoi essendo stato ricercato a pigliar una lezione ordinaria, restai e non volsi accettarla, perché li lettori publici di essa città vanno ordinariamente a messa ed alli altri divini offizii. Ed io ho sempre fugito questo, sapendo che ero scommunicato per esser uscito della Religione ed aver deposto l'abito; ché si bene in Tolosa ebbi quella lezione ordinaria, non però obligato a questo, come sarei stato in detta città de Paris, quando avesse accettato la detta lezion ordinaria." Ordinary lectures were those given by full or "ordinarius" professors. Extraordinary lectures were given by assistants (bachelors) or visitors, and were given either on feast days or in the afternoons.

35. *Ibid.*, 102: "Ei dictum: Avete raggionato mai intorno il sacrificio della santa messa e dell'ineffabile transubstanziazione del corpo e sangue di Cristo, che in quella si fa sotto spezie di pane e vino? e che cosa avete tenuto e creduto in questo proposito?"

36. *Ibid.*, 102: "Io non ho mai parlato del sacrificio della messa, né di questa transubstanziazione, se non nel modo che tiene la Santa Chiesa; ed ho sempre tenuto e creduto, come tengo e credo, che si faccia la transubstanziazione del pane e vino in corpo e sangue di Cristo realmente e substanzialmente, come tiene la Chiesa."

37. *Ibid.*, 94–95.

for many years [he] had known and associated with Calvinists, Luthe-
rans, and other sorts of heretics, [he] however did not doubt or argue against the transubstantiation of the sacrament of the Altar.[38]

Bruno's words are carefully chosen, but their artfulness does not, I think,
indicate complete falsification. Bruno seems to have valued the eucharist
and may privately have held to something that he did not think was completely incompatible with the orthodox doctrine. This inference becomes
possible when one reads Bruno's reply to the inquisitors' question concerning his view of the sacrament of penance:

> I know that the sacrament of penance was instituted to purge our
> sins. . . . It has been about sixteen years since I last went to confes-
> sion, except for two times: once in Toulouse [where I went to be
> confessed] by a Jesuit; and another time in Paris [where I tried to
> be confessed] by another Jesuit. . . . [Saying that my case had not
> been settled back home], they told me that they could not absolve
> me for being apostate, and I could not go to divine services [but
> could pray in church].[39]

It seems, then, that Bruno wanted to return to the Church, at least to
be allowed once again to receive the eucharist, and that it had been impossible for the two Jesuits to absolve him for being apostate; only higher
(Roman) authorities could do this. We might also note that Bruno does
not say that he himself wanted to perform the sacrifice of the mass, but
only that he wanted to partake of the communion following that sacrifice.
This sets some parameters upon what he meant by reconciliation with
Rome.

When one pieces together the various parts of Bruno's testimony, one
concludes that the Nolan longed for eucharistic communion, but that this

---

38. *Ibid.*, 102.

39. *Ibid.*, 104: "Sono da sedeci anni incirca che io non mi sono mai presentato al confessore,
eccetto due volte: una volta in Tolosa da un Iesuito; ed un'altra volta in Parisi a un altro Iesuito,
mentre trattavo, per mezo di Mons. Vescovo di Bergomo, allora nonzio in Paris e di don Ber-
nardin di Mendoza de ritornar nella religione, con intenzione di confessarmi. E loro me dissero
che non potevano assolverme per esser apostata, e che non potevo andar alli divini offizii. . . ."
Ibid., 133–134, Bruno again recounts his attempts to confess and to be absolved. He was told
that his censure could only be lifted by the pope (Sixtus V) and that, until such time, "non potevo
assister alli divini offizii, ma che potevo bene andar a udir le prediche e dir le mie orazioni in
chiesa."

desire was thwarted by his apostasy and by his conscientious understanding of the sacramental consequences of excommunication. We have seen that Bruno desired to partake of Holy Communion in Geneva. We also see that he did not want, according to his words, to go to divine service either in Protestant Toulouse or Catholic Paris.

Bruno's stories here do not seem to coincide with the real record, inasmuch as he denied going to communion in Geneva but yet we have seen him requesting to have the ban on the Supper lifted. Two answers to this contradiction are possible: either he was unable—given the short time he was in Geneva (during part of which he was under the ban)—to have an opportunity to take communion in that community where it was given only four times a year; or, probably more likely,[40] he simply did not want to admit to having taken communion in a non-Catholic land, especially since he had later been told he could not receive it in Catholic lands. Consequently, he consistently denied taking Protestant communion, and said he went to divine services only "out of curiosity," and that

... after the lesson or sermon, when they were about to distribute the bread in the manner of their Supper, I left, ... nor did I ever take their bread or observe their eucharistic rites.[41]

The evidence is ambiguous. However, whether or not Bruno did participate in the Calvinist liturgy, he ultimately found the Protestant sacrament loathsome. His attacks on Protestant doctrine and practice are based on theological principle and aesthetic judgment.

It is to *The Ash Wednesday Supper* that we must turn for guidance on Bruno's attitudes toward the eucharist and the Protestants.[42] In this work, Bruno exhibits a strong dislike for his English hosts. The *Supper* is replete with disparaging remarks about the English populace, whom Bruno describes as so many kicking and butting beasts, completely devoid of civility

40. Communion would have been given in Geneva quarterly and thus seasonally. We may expect, then, that Holy Communion was next scheduled for late September or early October. There generally was an effort to reform oneself in time to participate.

41. *Ibid.*, 116: "... anzi, che doppo la lezione o sermone, nell'ora che distribuivano il pane al modo della loro cena, ... né mai ho pigliato del suo pane né observato questi suoi riti."

42. Giordano Bruno, *The Ash Wednesday Supper*, E. A. Gosselin and L. S. Lerner, trs. & eds. (Hamden, Connecticut, 1977), hereafter cited as *AWS*; the Italian edition of *La Cena de le Ceneri* (London, 1584), hereafter cited as *Cena*, is found in its modern edition in Giordano Bruno, *Dialoghi italiani*, G. Gentile and G. Aquilecchia, eds. (Florence, 1972).

and humanity. Their barbarousness results, says Bruno, from the justification-by-faith-alone theology preached in Protestant England.[43] These statements lend credence to Bruno's reply to the inquisitors that

> Faith, hope, and charity [are necessary to salvation]. . . . I have always maintained that good works are necessary for salvation. [And in De l'infinito, universo, e mondi I said] "that type of religion which teaches people to trust in salvation without works . . . is more in need of being eradicated from the earth than are serpents, dragons, and other animals pernicious to human nature; because barbarous people become more barbarous through such confidence, and those who are naturally good become evil. . . ."[44]

Not only did Bruno find England's Protestant religion pernicious to human nature but he also disparaged the Protestant Supper, finding the Communion *sub utraque* repulsive in the extreme.

The second dialogue of *The Ash Wednesday Supper* recounts the Nolan's journey across London as he headed to the home of Sir Fulke Greville (*sic*; in reality, the dinner took place at the residence of the Marquis de Mauvissière, the French ambassador). He had originally been invited for dinner, but no one had come to the French embassy to escort him to Greville's. So, after having gone to visit some Italian friends, he returned to find John Florio, an Italian Protestant residing in England, and Matthew Gwynne waiting to take him to Greville's residence.[45] The dangerous journey along the Strand commenced, and Bruno and his friends encountered swinish passages, Avernus–like potholes, and the murderous "kicking and butting beasts" who worked in the streets and markets of London.[46] Such were the results of the Protestant economy of salvation.

When Bruno's *alter ego*, the Nolan, was finally delivered from this passion and had arrived at Greville's and was seated, Teofilo (Bruno's other *alter ego*, who recounts the story) "thanks God" that the "ceremony of the cup" did not take place. Nonetheless, Teofilo describes it in nauseating detail:

---

43. *AWS/Cena*, second dialogue, gives a scathing indictment of a society whose humanity is destroyed by the Protestant doctrine of salvation.

44. *Documenti*, 107–108. Bruno is paraphrasing the passage found in Bruno, *Dialoghi italiani*, 385. Similar sentiments are found also in *Lo spaccio della bestia trionfante*; see *Dialoghi italiani*, 623, 653–655, and 660–663.

45. On Bruno and Florio, see F. A. Yates, *John Florio* (Cambridge, 1934), 87–123.

46. *AWS/Cena*, 120–125/70–82.

Usually the goblet or chalice passes from hand to hand all round
the table ... with no order but that dictated by rough politeness
and courtesy. After the leader of this dance has detached his lips,
leaving a layer of grease which could easily be used as glue, another
drinks and leaves you a crumb of bread, another drinks and leaves
a bit of meat on the rim, still another drinks and deposits a hair
of his beard, and, in this way, with a great mess, no one is so ill-
mannered ... as to omit leaving you some favor of the relics stuck
to his moustache.... The meaning of all this is that, since all of
them come together to make themselves into a flesh–eating wolf to
eat as with one body the lamb or kid or Grunnio Corocotta; thus
by applying each one his mouth to the selfsame tankard, they come
to form themselves into one selfsame leech, in token of one community, one brotherhood, one plague, one heart, one stomach, one
gullet and one mouth.[47]

Teofilo goes on to say that this custom did not occur at this feast because
it had "remained only at the lowest tables, and has disappeared from these
others. . . ."[48]

This passage mocks the Communion *sub utraque*. For Bruno, what began as a sacral meal ends as a travesty of the sacrament, whereby religious
brotherhood transforms into illness and alimentary functions. While we
realize that many in the sixteenth century welcomed communion in both
kinds, it is all too easy to forget that this Protestant liturgical reform
could—as in the case of Bruno—have appeared as so much offal to the
minds of others who had also been raised and nourished in the Roman
faith. It seems unarguable that Bruno's sensitivities concerning eucharistic liturgy tended toward Roman Catholic rather than Protestant. There
is also a hint, in the passage just quoted, that the "gentlemen" gathered
at the Ash Wednesday Supper (except for Doctors Nundinio and Torquato whom the Nolan debates in the third and fourth dialogues of the
Supper) tended toward his views (or so he hoped), and that is why the
"ceremony of the cup" did not take place. Bruno was obviously appealing
in this book to English Protestants who would share his liturgical preferences for a more traditional, i.e., Roman Catholic, ceremonial—although

47. *Ibid.*, 126–127/82–84.
48. *Ibid.*, 127/84.

the significance given that ceremonial would transcend narrow confessional understandings.

This interpretation fits well with Bruno's later responses to the inquisitors concerning his beliefs on the eucharist. Bruno was probably telling them the truth, that the Supper took place at Mauvissière's official residence rather than at Greville's. We know that the ambassador accorded Bruno considerable publishing latitude while he lived with him as a visiting foreign gentleman. His residence in the embassy, his publishing enterprise in London, and his letters of introduction to Mauvissière from Henri III all indicate that Bruno operated in London under the aegis of the Most Christian King.

It is not irresponsible, then, to credit Bruno's assertion that the Ash Wednesday Supper took place in the French embassy. However, we have caught Bruno in a deception. He said, in the passage quoted at the head of this section, that he went neither to mass (either inside or outside the embassy) nor to Protestant services. We have also seen him tell the inquisitors that the Ash Wednesday Supper was only a gathering to debate the virtues of Copernicus' assertions about the motion of the earth. But we have just seen that the Ash Wednesday Supper and the book which commemorates it had to do with a sacramental Supper on Ash Wednesday. Why the prevarication? Bruno had to tread very carefully concerning his entire English experience, as he was involved in the middle of a French reunionist scheme. The reputation of Henri III in very orthodox Roman Catholic circles (e.g., among the Leaguers and, to some extent, in Rome) was badly tarnished, so Bruno was wise not to dilate upon his "mission" to England. Yet we can tell that something is awry in this part of his testimony, as he denies even having gone to hear Protestant preachers "just out of curiosity," which he did admit to having done in Geneva. Bruno might not have gone simply because he knew no English. In that case, however, he probably would have given that reason since the harm of wanting to hear Protestant preachers had already been done by his admissions in Geneva. No, he seems carefully to have distanced himself from all religious interests in his testimony about his sojourn in England, a lack of interest that is belied by the six *Dialoghi metafisici e morali* he published there. In a sense, seen in the light of his publications while in England, Bruno's very denial of interest in religion in that country—the only time he is so mute—shouts the opposite meaning to the modern reader of his

Italian dialogues and testimony. Bruno, a reformist and apostate Dominican, was the perfect French ploy by which to entice English candidates for conversion to a more moderate, because transcendent, Catholic understanding of the eucharist than that offered by the Holy See and its political allies, the Spaniards and French Guisards. It made perfect sense, then, to allow Bruno to participate in discussions about some kind of ecumenical celebration of the Lord's Supper on Ash Wednesday, February 14, 1584 — the beginning of the Lenten reform and a symbolic day for initiating a reformist and reunionist scheme sponsored by that strange Counter-Reformation figure, Henri III.[49]

To Bruno, the proponent of French Counter-Reformation policy, the transcendent, "Copernican" vision and understanding of the eucharist in no way outwardly contradicted either Roman Catholic or Protestant eucharistic doctrines, nor did it deny the inherent divine nature of the sacrament. Instead, it refocused how one viewed its divine nature. Not interested for this purpose in the issue of Christ's physical presence (though without, as he correctly told the inquisitors,[50] denying transubstantiation), Bruno honed in on the issue — dear to any mystically-inclined soul — of the reciprocal relationship between the Light of Divinity emanating from the central Sun and the spark of divinity inherent in the earth's inhabitants who ceaselessly circle about, to use the Hermetic expression quoted by Copernicus, that "visible God." A kind of Plotinian psychology governed Bruno's views on this matter.[51]

Accordingly, when Bruno was questioned about his views on the eucharist, he was able to say with some degree of truthfulness that his views were Catholic. Whether he had ever actually been a communicant (even

49. See Gosselin, "Bruno's 'French Connection' " (forthcoming; see note 27, above) for an analysis of Bruno's Parisian education in Lullism and introduction to Copernicanism, and how this fit in with Valois policy toward England. It is my contention in the article that, due to changes in Henri III's political fortunes in 1585, Bruno and his mission were unceremoniously jettisoned by the Valois faction at the disputation at the Collège de Cambrai (see Cotin's recounting of this event in *Documenti*, 44–46). I further suggest there that Bruno never learned this lesson, and that during his subsequent travels he continued to see himself "on mission" to propagate a (French) court Catholicism of latitudinarian dimensions.

50. *Documenti*, 102.

51. N. Copernicus, *De revolutionibus orbium caelestium* (Thorn, 1873), 30: "In medio vero omnium residet sol. . . . Siquidem non inepte quidam lucernam mundi, alii mentem, alii rectorem vocant. Trimegistus [*sic*] visibilem deum." On the Plotinian psychology at work in Bruno's understanding of the Copernican eucharist's efficacy, see my remarks in *AWS*, 36–37 (Introduction); and Gosselin, " 'Doctor' Bruno's Solar Medicine" (note 27, above).

though he wanted to be) at a Protestant Supper is unclear; in fact, however, he had been critical of the Protestant rite and of the doctrine of justification in his writings. Thus, Bruno's public views were not necessarily or outwardly incommensurate with Catholic teaching.

V

Bruno: The Catholic Nicodemite?

Certes, on n'a pas l'impression que ces théologiens [au procès] cherchent à comprendre les propos du Nolain. Animés par la volonté de poursuivre l'hérésie, ils ne cherchent pas ce qu'il peut y avoir de neuf et de révolutionnaire dans la *nolana filosofia*. Les oeillères de l'orthodoxie ferment la voie à toute discussion ouverte. Culpabiliser le prisonnier, tel est le but du procès.

H. Védrine, *Censure et pouvoir*, 93.

The title of this paper, "Fra Giordano Bruno's Catholic Passion," carries obvious multiple meanings. The record of Bruno's long trial paints a poignant picture of a God-lover fleeing his homeland and cloister for fear of prosecution for reformist ideas. This flight took him throughout Europe, treading paths that had probably once been soaked by the blood of one Christian killed by another in the cause of confessional truth. Bruno's search for security and for spiritual refreshment brought him finally back to Italy where he may have hoped to present his ideas to the pope himself in order that he be reconciled as he had tried to be in Toulouse and Paris and, before that, in another faith in Geneva. Before he could do this, however, Bruno was betrayed and turned over to the Inquisition. His trial makes difficult reading for anyone concerned for human dignity and freedom of ideas.[52] Yet we must always remember that these values were sadly lacking in the late sixteenth century. Nonetheless, the records of

52. As P. O. Kristeller pointedly noted in his review of Mercati's *Sommario* (*JHI* 8 [1947]: 240): "The editor, in trying to justify the Inquisition, fails to . . . discuss the question of principle whether the formulation of philosophical and religious opinions contrary to orthodoxy provides a sufficient basis for the prosecution, trial, sentencing, and execution of a thinker."

Bruno's trial help today to elucidate his views as a religious thinker and actor. Although the ambiguities concerning Bruno will probably never completely vanish, we can now dimly see the shadow (to use a favorite image of his) of a man who hoped to reconcile religious opposites and who hoped also to find a place where he, an "academician of no academy,"[53] could find rest. We do know now that the rest he sought had something to do with participation in the ceremonial of the eucharist, if not agreement with a doctrinal definition of its meaning. We also see that, for Bruno, human dignity was bound up with the action and choice of the human free will. We also know that, right up to the return to Italy in 1591, Bruno was able to become a member of the Lutheran community in Wittenberg and yet sign his religious name with a cross, in the manner of a Catholic priest,[54] and, two years later, to live in a Carmelite monastery in Frankfurt.[55] The pattern we have observed for the years between 1576 and 1585 persisted throughout his remaining years of freedom. Bruno could live as a Catholic or as a Protestant.

In a sense, some of the views and sentiments we have seen Bruno embrace are Roman Catholic. He was, as we have seen, more Catholic than Protestant in his sacramental views. But it would be an error, I think, to say, as did Angelo Mercati, that only his "vulgar" and "prideful" nature prevented his return to his original home and beliefs. Mercati has judged Bruno on the basis of Il Candelaio and has applied an inappropri-

---

53. Bruno so styled himself in Il Candelaio (Paris, 1582). See the modern edition, G. Squarotti, ed. (Turin, 1969), 1.2, 38.

54. The Enciclopedia italiana 7: 980, produces a photograph of Bruno's cross and signature, which follow these words written by Bruno:

> Salomon et Pythagoras
> Quid est quod est?
> Ipsum quod fuit.
> Quid est quod fuit?
> Ipsum quod est.
> Nihil sub sole novum.
>   Salus
>   ✝
> Jordanus Brunus Nolanus
> [Wittenberg] 18 Septembris [1588]

55. Iacobus Brictanus of Antwerp, testifying to the inquisitors on 26 May 1592 (Documenti, 73–76), said that "Il detto Iordano era là [a Francoforte] allogiato nel Convento de frati Carmelitani. . . ." The Carmelites followed Dominican practices, so this convent would have seemed familiar to Bruno.

ate, modern moral judgment on that work that, if applied to Rabelais, for example, would consign him to perdition, too.[56] It is more fruitful, I think, to view Bruno as a kind of Catholic Nicodemite. This is at best only a metaphor and cannot be strained, for Bruno—unlike a true Catholic Nicodemite—was unwilling to accept the Protestant doctrine of justification. Yet there is a similarity, in that both the Nicodemites and Bruno accepted the idea that outward religious form was trivial in comparison with inward belief.[57] Bruno also has similarities to the Familists of the late sixteenth century.[58] He believed in an overarching world harmony that could reconcile conflicting religions. Yet, Bruno did not cite or follow the guiding lights of the Family of Love, Niclaes and Barrefelt. He was, as he said above, an "academician of no academy" both in his philosophy and in his religion, and yet he strangely believed that he might be allowed to rejoin the Order but not live in it.[59] He belonged nowhere and everywhere. Perhaps this is what stirred Henry Cobham, English ambassador to France, to write to Sir Francis Walsingham (as Bruno was about to depart for London): "Doctor Jordano Bruno Nolano . . . intends to pass into England, whose religion I cannot commend."[60]

EDWARD A. GOSSELIN

56. See Mercati, 35–36 and 49, for his attack on Bruno's moral flaws that caused his irreparable fall into error.

57. On Nicodemism and justification, see D. Cantimori, "Submission and Conformity: 'Nicodemism' and the Expectations of a Conciliar Solution to the Religious Question," in *The Late Italian Renaissance*, E. Cochrane, ed. (New York, 1970), 262–263. On Nicodemism in general, see C. Ginzburg, *Il Nicodesimo* (Turin, 1970).

58. On the Family of Love and Familism, see A. Hamilton, *The Family of Love* (Cambridge, 1981); H. de la Fontaine-Verway, "Trois hérésiarques dans les Pays-Bas," *Bibliothèque d'Humanisme et Renaissance*, 16 (1954): 312–330; B. Rekers, *Benito Arias Montano* (London, 1972); and L. Voet, *The Golden Compasses: A History and Evaluation of the Printing and Publishing of the "Officiana Plantiniana"* (Amsterdam/London/New York, 1969).

59. Mercati, 107–108, contains items of testimony by Bruno's jailmates concerning what the Nolan intended to do "si cogetur reverti ad Religionem." See item 220 (p. 108), in particular.

60. *Calendar of State Papers, Foreign*, January-June 1583, 214.

CONRING

on

HISTORY

E ven though I do not believe that everyone can be bent to the circle of reason, and my efforts suffice to excite only better minds,
nevertheless I judge it to be my duty to inculcate again and again
what is to the advantage of the commonwealth.

Opinion is a sacred disease. But nothing rules this world as much
as it.[1]

FOR A LONG TIME the intellectual history of seventeenth-century Germany
has been neglected. The reasons why this should be so are not hard to
understand. With one generally acknowledged exception, namely Leib-
niz, famous thinkers like Luther, Kant, and Lessing seem to have avoided
life in the seventeenth century, and those who did not, like Descartes,
Hobbes, and Newton, preferred to be born outside of Germany. On the
face of it, the cultural landscape of Germany in the period between the

---

1. "Etsi . . . haud existimem posse omnes in rationis gyrum flecti, et vel illa mea sufficiant
meliori menti excitandae, nihilominus officii mei esse iudico itemtidem inculcare, quod reipublicae est commodum." 256.59–61. "Sacer scilicet morbus opinio est: mundus tamen hic nulla perinde
re quam hac ipsa regitur." 262.51. Unless otherwise indicated, references are to pages and lines
of volume 5 of J. W. Goebel, ed., *Hermanni Conringii . . . Opera*, 6 vols. and index volume (Braunschweig, 1730; repr. Aalen, 1970–1973). In quoting from Conring's writings, j has be replaced by i.

Reformation and the Enlightenment thus appears barren.[2] But there are reasons to doubt such an impression. The cultural efflorescence of the eighteenth century seems to presuppose a period of growth, subterranean growth perhaps, but nevertheless something different from the aridity usually ascribed to the terrain. Perhaps the presumed infertility of the seventeenth century is merely an optical illusion created by an unconscious but concerted effort of a later age to forget a debt it owed its forbears.

This is not the place to settle the question whether or not the prevailing opinion is correct. It has merely been brought up in order to establish the context in which the present study should be seen.[3] Its focus is narrow. It is limited to a single individual, to a particular aspect of his thought, and it makes no claim to treat even that aspect exhaustively. Still, there are good reasons to hope that it can make a contribution which at least by implication has more than limited significance.

Hermann Conring was born in 1606 and died in 1681. His professional life was spent teaching and writing at the University of Helmstedt, where he came to be the dominant figure. In its time, Helmstedt was a premier institution of higher learning in Protestant, perhaps in all of Germany. He thus takes a commanding place at the center of our subject, and it is reasonable to suppose that an understanding of his thought may shed light on the transformations which resulted in the Enlightenment.[4]

At present no such understanding exists. To be sure, there is a small body of scholarly literature devoted to him. But it is easy to show that his reputation is subject to a kind of illusion similar to the one alluded

2. For a typical view, see Hajo Holborn's assessment of the effects of the Thirty Years' War on German civilization in his *History of Modern Germany* (New York, 1964), 2:123.

3. The time for reexamining the seventeenth century from such a point of view seems to be ripe. In recent years scholars in growing numbers have devoted their attention to that part of the history of Germany. Since references to the secondary literature have been kept to an absolute minimum, the names of Michael Stolleis, Horst Dreitzel, Arno Seifert, and Notker Hammerstein, whose work is most closely related to the topic of this article, as well as those of James Vann, Marc Raeff, Robert Bireley, and the many publications sponsored by the Herzog-August Bibliothek in Wolfenbüttel may stand in place of a fuller bibliography. Much more guidance than the title suggests can be found in H. U. Scupin, U. Scheuner, eds. *Althusius–Bibliographie*, 2 vols. (Berlin, 1973). For more recent information, see the *Zeitschrift für Historische Forschung*, esp. H. Dreitzel, "Die Entwicklung der Historie zur Wissenschaft," *Zeitschrift für Historische Forschung*, 8 (1981): 257–84.

4. The article of D. Willoweit, "Hermann Conring," in *Staatsdenker im 17. und 18. Jahrhundert: Reichspublizistik, Politik, Naturrecht*, ed. M. Stolleis (Frankfurt, 1977) and the contributions to *Hermann Conring (1606–1681): Beiträge zu Leben und Werk*, ed. M. Stolleis (Berlin, 1983), cited as *Beiträge*, have recently established a new basis for all future work on Hermann Conring. The

to above. This is no slight on the historians concerned. It is rather a testimony to the power of tradition. Conring is best remembered for three
achievements: as a pathbreaking historian of German law, a political thinker
of note, and an early proponent of systematic *Quellenkritik*.[5] Memory is
right to point to those aspects of his work which have withstood the test
of time particularly well. Perhaps, for that reason, they are indeed the
most significant. But memory fails to give a faithful picture of his work
as a whole. Many of his writings were dedicated to medicine, natural
philosophy, theology, and moral theory, to mention only the broadest
possible categories in which his other interests can be organized.[6] By giving a place of honor to three particular achievements and forgetting the
rest, existing treatments of his thought cannot do it justice. They seem
rather to reflect the prejudices and specialized interests of later ages: the
eighteenth century's disdain for Aristotle, the nineteenth century's preoccupation with the history of laws and constitutions, and the specializa-
tion of the historiography of our own time.

There seems to be agreement among students of Conring's works today that no real understanding of the conceptual framework uniting his
thought exists and that this situation deserves to be remedied.[7] There is
less agreement about how to do it. Given the sheer mass of his writings,
amounting to more than 6000 folio pages in the standard edition, not
to mention his voluminous unpublished correspondence, it is obviously
necessary to build up understanding gradually. Yet to begin by studying
Conring's concept of history might seem to some a questionable proceeding.
Chronologically, and perhaps intellectually as well, Conring was a doctor
of medicine first. One needs merely to remember how important biology
is for an understanding of the thought of Aristotle—that physician's son
whose philosophy exercised so formative an influence on Conring's mind—
in order to suspect that Conring's medical writings hold important, possibly
the most important, clues. But the concept of history with which we
are here concerned was not what it is today. In the sense in which it is

---

older literature can be found through these works. N. Hammerstein, "Die Historie bei Conring,"
Beiträge, 217–36, approaches our subject in a different manner.

5. Cf. Willoweit, "Hermann Conring," 129.

6. See the bibliography of Conring's published writings in *Beiträge*, 535–67.

7. See for example D. Willoweit, "Hermann Conring," 129, and N. Hammerstein, "Die Historie
bei Conring," *Beiträge*, 217.

employed by the professor from Helmstedt, history, as will quickly become apparent, is central to a theory of all knowledge, and not only the knowledge of human affairs. A look at his thoughts about history may thus not be the only way to begin, but it does promise to lead to the comprehensive understanding we are seeking.

The best place to look for his definition of what history was, how it should be pursued, and what purposes it served are the three prefaces with which he introduced his editions of Tacitus' *Germania*.[8] The argument is set forth in full in the first of them, the preface to the edition of 1635. At the time he was but 29 years old, looking forward to more than four decades of prolific scholarly production. Fortunately for our enterprise, the later prefaces demonstrate that he continued to believe what he had written as a young man. To be sure, in the second preface, for the edition of 1652, he mentioned that parts of the first might deserve revision. But he decided against making any changes, not only because of the praise that he had received since 1635, as he was obviously proud to report, but also because "it may not be proper to balance the labors of youth on the scales of a more exacting age, and every blot that may be there should be left to its own times, so long as it does not bring on too much discredit. And thus there is no reason why I should alter anything."[9] This sentiment is subtle evidence for a remarkable sensitivity towards the autonomy of the past, one's own included. It also means that whatever changes he may have contemplated in 1652 can hardly have touched on the substance of his views.

The third and last preface was published in 1678, three years before his death. It contains the motto for this essay and thus confirms the continuity in his thought.[10] Far from considering the desirability of any

---

8. Goebel, *Opera*, 5:253–78. Cf. the judgment of N. Hammerstein, "Die Historie," 222f. Among the considerable literature on the reception of Tacitus, E.–L. Etter, *Tacitus in der Geistesgeschichte des 16. und 17. Jahrhunderts* (Basel, 1966), K. C. Schellhase, *Tacitus in Renaissance Political Thought* (Chicago, 1976), and J. Ridé's massive three volumes on *L'image du Germain dans la pensée et la littérature allemandes* (Paris, 1977) may be mentioned. See also the article on Tacitus by R. W. Ulery, Jr., in the *CTC*, 6 (1986): 87–174.

9. "Ipsemet ego nonnulla quidem paulo aliter scripta malim: sed fortassis haud fas est, iuvenilem laborem omnem exactioris aetatis trutina expendere, et singulis temporibus suus aliquis naevus relinquendus est, modo non nimium dedecoret: ac proinde non est cur quidquam mutem." 278.17–20.

10. The relevant text in full: "Finem denique huic libro imposuimus repetita editione nonnullorum, quae ipsemet de usu peritiae veteris Germaniae status iampridem fuimus commentati. Nec

changes, he rather underlined his commitment to the original preface with that characteristic shift to a slightly stubborn bluntness which is one of the privileges of age. The text also nicely illustrates the qualities that were blended in his personality: scholarship and service to the common good, reason and piety, a sense of lonely melancholy issuing from having to disagree with the majority of men, and pride in belonging to those of "better minds."

Conring begins his account of history with a eulogy of the pleasure it provides. "Whoever denies that the highest pleasure can be obtained from histories ... assuredly has either never read or heard of them, or he is utterly stupid and his mind not stirred by any pure and liberal emotions."[11] This is more than just a rhetorical topos[12] because there is a reason why history is so extraordinarily pleasurable:

> Apart from the fact that the common people know it only by experience, philosophers are not unaware of the cause of that delight. Seeing that we human beings are evidently born with a desire to know, a desire which may be either fulfilled by external instruments of the senses or by a hidden working of the mind, history is a wonderful compendium of someone else's knowledge, a guide to someone else, as it were.[13]

History thus pleases because it fulfills a natural desire for knowledge. The pleasure it yields is like that which is produced when one obtains

vero nos fugit, quam haec omnia a paucis suo pretio aestimentur, imo quam haec a plerisque soleant contemni. Etsi enim haud existimem posse omnes in rationis gyrum flecti, et vel illa mea sufficiant meliori menti excitandae, nihilominus officii mei esse iudico itemtidem inculcare, quod reipublicae est commodum. Perinde atque nunquam omitti debent seriae ad pietatis cultum invitationes, etsi pauci velint arctam illam semitam ambulare. In iis autem, quae iam ante hosce quadraginta tres annos fui praefatus, non hoc tantum docui, sed etiam de universae historiae usu, et cumprimis de notitia reipublicae imperii Germanici, undenam sit petenda, prolixius disserere fui coactus, quia vulgo tunc temporis plane alia erant persuasa magno cum publico damno." 256.57–257.4.

11. "Voluptatem summam ex historiis qui negat capi . . . nae ille aut numquam eas legit vel audivit, aut vero excors est nec sincero ac liberali quodam animi affectu commovetur." 257.25–27.

12. Cf. Hammerstein, "Die Historie," 220, note 6 with reference to E. R. Curtius, *Europäische Literatur und lateinisches Mittelalter* (Bern, 1948), 340.

13. "Praeterquam enim quod vulgus experimento id habeat cognitum, causam eius delectationis philosophi viri non ignorant. Quum nimirum hominibus nobis ingenitum sit sciendi desiderium, idque vel externis sensuum instrumentis vel arcana mentis agitatione expleatur, alterius notitiae mirum est compendium historia, alterius quasi manuductor." 257.31–34.

knowledge for oneself either through empirical observation or by rational contemplation. But it is also different, because it is "a wonderful compendium of someone else's knowledge." It enables seekers after knowledge to extend the limits which nature imposed on their desire. What one might therefore call its preternatural function is why it pleases so preeminently.

The significance of these opening remarks is not merely that they justify the praise of history which Conring had chosen in order to open his treatise in the properly rhetorical vein. It is rather that they establish a definition of history which fits squarely into a general theory of knowledge. He goes on to describe that theory more precisely:

> Beyond the one mentioned so far, there is another and nobler reason for history's charm. For all of the sciences and arts require as much experience of things as possible—excepting only the mathematical ones, which are called pure—and without such experience none of them can be acquired. History thus becomes a matter of the highest necessity inasmuch as it displays a broad grasp of every kind of experience. . . . History thus is a guide of the stricter sciences and yields as much delight as any of the sciences and arts bestow. But to reap this pleasure and this fruit of history is not for everyone. It is granted only to those who either know by their own ingenuity how to construct common laws and universal precepts from individual events, or at least have learned them from masters to the degree that nothing except experiments is required for an absolute knowledge of things in every detail.[14]

Conring thus affirms a fundamental distinction between experience on the one hand and "common laws and universal precepts" on the other. The latter are constructed out of the former. Knowledge properly speaking only exists where experience and rational principles are united. The

14. "Est vero praeter illam et alia nobiliorque amoenitatis istius causa. Quum enim scientiae atque artes omnes, solas si mathematicas, quas puras vocant, exceperis, experientia rerum ut quam maxime indigeant, neque sine hac ullam earum liceat assequi, hinc iam necessitas etiam summa historiae oritur, veluti quae exhibeat complexum aliquem experientiae cuiuslibet generis. . . . Manuductrix igitur severiorum scientiarum est historia, tantumque parit delectationis quantum scientiae atque artes quaelibet largiuntur. Sed hanc eius voluptatem atque hunc illius fructum percipere non est cuiusvis. Tantum enim iis id concessum est, qui communes leges atque praecepta universalia aut ipsimet suopte ingenio norunt construere ex singularibus eventis, aut vero a magistris hactenus ea didicerunt, ut ad absolutam omnibus numeris rerum scientiam nil praeter experimenta postuletur." 258.1–14.

term he prefers for such knowledge is *scientia*.[15] When it is necessary to distinguish it from subordinate kinds of knowledge, consisting of mere familiarity with the empirical data without rational understanding on the one hand, or pure awareness of rational principles without empirical confirmation on the other, he may also speak of *absoluta scientia*, or *absoluta eruditio*.[16] At any rate he never tires of pointing out that to know means to be able to explain the phenomena, and to be able to explain means to know the reasons and understand the causes behind them.[17] His favorite illustration is the example of a doctor. Unless he knows both the actual condition of Socrates' body and the science of medicine, he cannot properly be said to know whether Socrates is healthy or not.[18]

With a few words Conring has thus established a basic definition of history. History is a record of experience, any kind of experience. "For whatever the senses have perceived, whether things of nature or human affairs, history puts them all before [our] eyes."[19] It is one of the two basic ingredients in knowledge. Universal laws and principles are the other.

Three important consequences must be noted. First, the equation between history and experience gives the concept of history a much wider connotation than it has today. Its subject matter, in fact, is universal. It includes not only phenomena in the realm of human affairs but everything that is subject to empirical observation. One way of putting this is to

15. But note that for Conring, as for his teacher Aristotle, *ars* and *scientia* are both knowledge, the difference being only that *ars* is knowledge which can be used for practical purposes.

16. See the texts quoted in notes 14 and 42.

17. "Atque nobis quidem id paucis expeditum dare animus est; prius tamen in memoriam revocandum fuerit, ad eiusmodi aliquam scientiam non eventorum duntaxat aut aperte gestorum sed et causarum latentium notitiam pertinere. Habet videlicet et heic suum aliquem locum Aristotelis illud: *scire esse rem per causam cognoscere*." 264.30–33. Cf. 258.14–19; 259.13–15.

18. "Tum vero demum credimur medici naturam omnem nostri Socratis perspexisse, quum didicimus omne illud, quod in eo est sive sanum sive morbidum sive ambiguae inter haec conditionis: id quod est, nosse originem atque causas omnium illorum, quae ad valetudinem Socratis quoquo modo pertinent. Non enim satis est scire, quam ille naturam materno ex utero produxerit, aut quantum ab illa post recessum sit, quidque pristino etiamnum sese modo habeat: sed et causas affectuum omnium, sive illi secundum sive praeter naturam sese habeant, oportet notas esse: ut pateat, quidnam corrigi queat aut respuat medelam. Simili prorsus ratione igitur rerum imperii vere consultum decuerit non scire tantum quasnam in leges illud consenserit (quod pene geminum est conditioni nativae Socratis) aut vero, quantum iis hodierni mores vel adversentur vel congruant: sed et origo occasioque et legum latarum et eorum quae contra fiunt, intelligenda est." 263.10–20; cf. 258.48–49; 260.1–12; 262.61–263.10; 266.49–54.

19. "Quaecunque enim sensus percipiunt, sive illae res sint naturae sive negotia humana, isthaec omnia exponit oculis historia." 257.35–36.

say that there is not merely one history, but as many kinds of history as there are kinds of empirical data. "It is wonderful how much light that history which corresponds to each branch of learning brings to it, as natural history does to the natural philosopher, heavenly to the astronomer, political to the political thinker, medical to the doctor, and to each his own."[20] The only exceptions to this scheme, as was observed in the quotation above, are the "pure" sciences. Because they have nothing to do with empirical data at all they leave no room for history.

Second, even though the meaning of history is so wide, it does not extend to knowledge properly speaking. History is merely a prerequisite for knowledge. There may be a strong temptation to consider this as proof that Conring shared with modern historians the conviction that human affairs are not susceptible of scientific explanation. But unless one were to maintain that his concept of science was identical with the modern one, that would be a mistake. He certainly considered history "unscientific," but only because by definition it had to be distinguished from rational principles. That is no reason to believe that he denied the existence of rational principles by which experiences in the realm of human affairs could be "scientifically" explained.

It is, in fact, not difficult to show that he conceived of the study of human affairs as a science in precisely the same terms as those he had set forth for *absoluta scientia* in general. Its ingredients are explicitly discussed in his account of what is required for the study of the history of Germany.[21] On the one hand, there are the empirical data. They consist of "what has been done and decreed" and are found in the various kinds of histories.[22] Because of his overriding interest in the commonwealth, that is, the Empire, he usually concentrates on facts related to political history. But on occasion he stresses that there is more to human affairs than that. In the third preface he expressed a clear preference for documents describing "the lands, the customs, the commonwealth, and the differences between the various peoples," rather than tales of war and battle.[23]

20. "Igitur mirum est, quantum adferat lucis doctrinae cuilibet ea, quae illi respondet, historia: ceu naturali philosopho naturali, astronomo coelestis, civili civilis, medica medico, singulis sua." 258.7–9.
21. 264.26–265.17.
22. "Est autem hoc, scire quid actum aut decretum aliquando sit in reipublicae nostrae, adeoque imperii huius Romani, quod appellamus, negotiis." 265.9–11.
23. "Illa igitur duntaxat hic congesta sunt monumenta, quae terras, mores, rempublicam et

On the other hand, the study of the history of Germany also presupposes a knowledge of "common laws and universal precepts." They are taught by several disciplines, all of which belong in the sphere of practical philosophy. The most important among them is *civilis prudentia,* corresponding roughly to "political science," but best left untranslated and rendered as "civil prudence."[24] In addition to civil prudence, the historical scientist must also know natural law and morals.[25] In order to appreciate in full the kind of thinking which is here at issue, one must emphasize that this includes another kind of general principle. "Perhaps there are good grounds indeed to expect such an historian, or someone who is trying to walk this road towards history, to have a profound knowledge of revealed Christian doctrine."[26] The reason is that religion, along with natural law and morals, is the basis of all prudence. Conring insisted on the essential unity of these disciplines and deplored the didactic customs by which they were torn apart.[27]

Conring in other words had a well-developed concept of a science of human affairs, exactly parallel in its structure to science in general. It should be noted that there is a terminological difficulty in referring to it. "History" cannot really be used because it has already been defined as the record of empirical data of any kind. It is doubly confusing to use the same term to refer to a science, rather than to the facts it explains, and to restrict it to human affairs. But since no other term is available, confusion can hardly be avoided altogether. Conring himself clearly did not use history only in the strict sense which he gave to it in his systematic introduction. Thus the best one can do is to speak of "historical science," and defend

---

populorum varia discrimina recensent, suntque adeo reliquis omnibus hactenus praeferenda." 254.28–30.

24. 264.26–50.

25. "Praeter hanc vero, etiam morum iurisque naturalis prudentiam recte eumdem ob finem requiri, haud difficile iudicatu est. Intelligo autem illam scientiam quae, quemadmodum vitam suam homo cum erga semetipsum, tum erga alios, maxime vero erga Deum (nam et hoc iustitiae opus est) debeat gerere exponit; omnia enim haec artis unius sunt, si intra connata menti nostrae praecepta maneamus, licet hodie varias sit in partes docentium consuetudine discerpta. . . . Quur enim ita sentiamus, in promptu est docere. Quoniam nimirum sapientia civilis, quod alias probatur, fundamenti loco religionis, iuris, morumque omnium prudentiam habet, super quam sua magnam partem exstruat atque aedificet; eadem profecto necessitate ad hanc addiscendam astringitur historicae illius nostrae affectator scientiae, qua tenetur prudentiam civilem sibi comparare." 264.51–61.

26. "Quin imo haud inane fortassis fuerit, doctrinae Christianae revelatae non proletariam scientiam, ab illo historico aut eo, qui ad hanc historiam affectat viam poscere." 264.55–57.

27. See the text quoted above in note 25.

this combination by pointing out that, even though according to his own conceptual scheme this is almost an oxymoron, Conring himself used it at least once.[28]

This concept of a science of history also deserves to be stressed because of the gulf that has since come to separate history from science. It focuses attention, not only on Conring's view of the nature of the study of human affairs, but on his understanding of science in general. There can be no doubt that to give the distinction between an "unscientific" knowledge of human affairs and a "scientific" knowledge of the realm of nature the same importance it has in modern thought is to misrepresent his convictions. In the last analysis it may be necessary to qualify the basic pattern. But it first needs to be stressed that in his mind all of the "arts and sciences," including the study of human affairs, had an identical structure.

The third, and by far the most important, consequence derives from a prominent characteristic of history. History is after all not simply experience, but experience recorded by others. It can therefore not be taken at face value. "For there is no author whose truths are not injured by some area of error. Hence there is need for historical judgment, among the principal canons of which is that in history we should not be too credulous."[29] If one asks how lack of credulity is to be replaced by an ability to distinguish between the trustworthy and the not-so-trustworthy evidence, one gets a decided answer. The solution resides in those "common laws and universal precepts" mentioned above which are the other main ingredient in the formation of "absolute knowledge of things in all details."

A few passages may be quoted to support this observation. The strongest reason he adduces to show why the study of human affairs, like any other, cannot do without rational principles occurs in his description of the requirements for the study of German history:

> The third requirement, however, [in addition to a knowledge of the rational principles of civil prudence on the one hand, and of natural law, morals, and religion on the other] which must now be touched upon, is proper and native to German history. It is to know what has been done or decreed at any time in the affairs of our com-

28. He speaks of "historicae illius nostrae affectator scientiae" at 264.60.
29. "Nullus enim est autor, cuius veritates non aliquod erroris laesit confinium. Hinc iudicio historico opus, inter cuius principes est canones; ne in historia nimis simus creduli." 271.13–16.

monwealth, that is, of this so-called Roman Empire. For this now is the essence of our historical effort, *even though it cannot be accurately done without the help of those disciplines which we have mentioned.*[30]

Rational principles are thus considered necessary in order to assure the accuracy of the gathered data.

A slightly different problem is posed by gaps in the evidence. In the context of discussing the poor quality of the sources for early medieval German history, Conring makes a remarkable claim for the power of the same rational principles to produce knowledge even beyond what the data seem to warrant:

> For in the case of most events our ancestors' primitive ways of writing will not prevent a reader of this kind from grasping even purposes which were passed over in silence. Just as an experienced doctor easily realizes what is not mentioned in what uneducated people tell him and supplies what is missing from the narration with the help of his medical knowledge, while someone less learned would only understand it with considerable effort, so a reader who knows public matters and human life recognizes by slight indications what has not been said and exposes the concealed reasons of things openly, relying for assistance on the powers of his prudence and natural ability.[31]

An intelligent and well-trained reader, he says, that is, a reader who knows civil prudence, morals, etc., will at least in part be able to make up for the incompleteness of any given evidence. The parallel with medicine is important since it shows once again Conring's belief in the similarities between the study of human affairs and the study of nature.

There is another, still more basic difficulty which may be mentioned here because it, too, requires the use of rational principles in order to prepare the data for scientific explanation. It is the fact that the available evidence

---

30. "Tertium vero, quod nunc tangendum, Germanicae historiae proprium atque domesticum est. Est autem hoc, scire quid actum aut decretum aliquando sit in reipublicae nostrae, adeoque imperii huius Romani, quod appellamus, negotiis. Hoc enim ipsissimum iam opus nostrum historicum est: *etsi accurate fieri nequeat sine eorum quae diximus, adminiculo.*" 265.8–12. My italics.

31. "Nam ne rudis quidem illa maiorum scriptio obstat huiuscemodi lectori, quo minus in plerisque eventorum consilia silentio etiam praeterita ille adsequatur. Scilicet ut peritus medicus ex plebeia narratione facile intelligit et illa quae tacentur, supplente defectum narrationis medici peritia; quae tamen indoctior aliquis ne magno quidem nisu perceperit: Ita et reipublicae vitaeque humanae prudens lector, ex levibus indiciis cognoscit non dicta, abditasque rerum causas exponit in apricum, in subsidium prudentiae naturaeque viribus advocatis." 266.49–54.

is almost infinite. A rational criterion is needed in order to make a selection of data possible, even before the issue of their trustworthiness can be addressed. That in itself represents a task the magnitude of which he by no means underestimates. At one point, he criticizes the kind of knowledge which results when no other principle than pleasure governs the selection of the data. He grants that historians who adopt that standard will write interesting history, because in the absence of anything else to guide them they will seize on what is most pleasurable to relate. But he leaves no doubt as to his contempt for the result, which he calls *curiosa vanitas*.[32] Elsewhere, he considers the predicament of a novice who approaches the available literature for the first time and finds himself in danger of being overwhelmed by it. That danger can be avoided, thinks Conring, provided only that the reader is "prudent." He grows almost rapturous in describing the lightning speed with which the eye of a trained researcher is capable of sifting the relevant from the superfluous.[33]

In sum, there are two distinct problems, and perhaps more, which need to be solved even before the empirical data can be used for "scientific" explanation. The first is the impossibility of handling an infinite amount of data. That requires the definition of a criterion of selection. The second consists of the unreliability and incompleteness of the data. Canons of historical judgment and principles of interpretation must be formulated to remedy such defects in the evidence.

It may be obvious that such convictions have profound implications for Conring's concept of a historical science, and indeed for his concept of knowledge in general. They require the presence of rational principles before the evidence can be used. The theory of knowledge which has been discussed above, on the other hand, explicitly demands that rational principles are to be constructed out of the evidence. Conring thus finds himself

32. "Haec adeo causa est, quur multi nulla aeque re capiantur quam hoc studio: non quod fructum aliquem hinc ferant, sed quod animus incredibili voluptate semel illectus, suavissimo hoc pabulo nequeat saturari. Sed illorum hic labor fortassis non caret iusta reprehensione, etsi in illo soli liberalis ingenii homines occupentur, adeoque videri possit decere quemvis libera natum conditione. Facile quippe in iis, quae ad vitam aut necessaria non sunt aut non perinde utilia, non minus quam in aliis, intemperantia laboratur: desinitque tandem saepenumero haec diligentia in Appionis aut Dydimi curiosam quandam vanitatem. . . . Habet scilicet in huiusmodi rebus locum illud, quod de philosophia minus recte olim Neoptolemus Ennianus pronunciavit: *Philologandum est* (liceat ita nunc loqui) *sed paucis; nam omnino non placet*." 257.44–56. See also below, note 39. The quotation from Ennius on which Conring is punning can be found in Cicero, *Rep.* 1.18.

33. The problem and its solution are discussed at length at 266.26–267.28.

confronted with the problem nowadays referred to as the hermeneutical circle. Since the two elements of knowledge presuppose each other, it is impossible to see how he can escape from the circle. The neat conceptual scheme according to which knowledge consists of empirical data in conjunction with rational principles is thus exploded by a contradiction.

This contradiction between, on the one hand, the brief and systematic statement of the nature of historical knowledge which Conring gives in the opening paragraphs of his preface and, on the other, his detailed account of the difficulties inherent in the study of history, is the most important feature of the preface to the *Germania*. Nowhere does he address the issue as such. Perhaps that is a reason to deny him the status of a truly great thinker. But on the other hand, it is only fair to acknowledge that we have at this point encountered one of the central difficulties, perhaps the central difficulty, in the theory of knowledge which has occupied thinkers since ancient times. Moreover, even though Conring failed to turn his attention explicitly to it, his treatise contains numerous hints at possible alternatives. They make for most interesting reading and deserve to be studied with careful attention because they suggest that he himself was not quite satisifed with the state of affairs. Both the intrinsic difficulty of the subject and the short space available here make it impossible to give anything like a complete account of what he has to say about the matter and the implications of his position. But an outline of his views, schematic as it necessarily must be, is certainly worth the effort. It will suggest that a different theory of history is barely hidden beneath the surface of the text, a theory which takes on remarkably clear contours as soon as the contradiction in Conring's ideas is taken seriously.

Three ways can be imagined in principle to resolve the difficulty that rational principles are necessary to interpret the evidence out of which they are to be constructed. All three of them are in some fashion represented in the text. They shall be dealt with in order.

The first is to argue that at least a few rational principles are innate in the human mind and thus do not need to be taken from the evidence. At some points Conring seems to put his trust in that way out. He does believe that there are innate ideas. "About the life and morals of humanity and their relationship to mankind's true happiness, the best and greatest God has established many things in such a way that our mind itself immediately condemns everything opposed to them as iniquitous and dis-honorable."[34] In other words, there are universally valid ideas of right and wrong. That is undoubtedly why he considered religion to be the foundation of civil prudence. But he immediately disqualifies innate ideas of this kind as sufficient foundations for a knowledge of human affairs in general, much less of natural events. For he goes on to point out that politics are mostly concerned with a mere earthly felicity. "By far the greatest part of the matters which pertain to the commonwealth of our Empire is situated beyond the power of honor and dishonor. They are thus not controlled by such eternal laws of nature, but rather accept their laws and rights from those who have the arbitrary power of creating them."[35] What may have seemed a promising way out of the quandary must be discarded as a merely partial solution at best.

The second way out consists of accepting the contradiction as it stands and facing the necessary consequence: all hope of true knowledge must be abandoned. Occasionally it seems as though Conring felt an attraction to this kind of skepticism. In support, one might adduce the surprising ease with which he substitutes "faith" for "truth" as the cardinal virtue of the historian, as though there were no difference between statements merely believed and statements proved to be true.[36] "For it is not given to [those] born human beings to explore everything by themselves, but many things must be accepted on the considered testimony of others. What has already been attested to by the consent of better men, furthermore, only the impudent would call into doubt."[37] In the absence of any relia-ble standard by which to establish the value of "the consent of better men," it is hard to see what would distinguish faith in it from faith in the opin-ions of anyone at all. But on the other hand Conring vehemently con-

34. "De vita quidem moribusque omnis in universum humani generis, quatenus illa spectant veram omnibusque propriam beatitudinem, multa sic constituit ac sanxit Opt. Maxim. Deus, ut ipsa mens nostra ista quae contra fiunt iniquitatis statim atque inhonesti titulo infamet." 266.9–12.

35. "Ergo et eorum quae ad nostram pertinent imperii rempublicam longe maxima pars extra honesti atque inhonesti vim est sita, adeoque huiuscemodi aeternis naturae legibus non astringitur, sed leges atque iura sua ab iis accipit, quos penes ferendi ista arbitrium ac potestatis est." 266.16–19.

36. "Tres enim sunt historici virtutes: veritas, prudentia, atque eloquentia." 259.11–12. The parallel enumeration at 263.35 substitutes "fides" for "veritas." Cf. the use of *fides* in the text quoted in note 42 below.

37. "Neque vero datum est hominibus natis omnia per seipsos explorare, sed multa certis alio-rum testimoniis accipienda sunt; quae porro consensu meliorum iam sunt contestata, illa vocare in dubium non nisi impudentis fuerit." 257.5–7.

demned opinions as a "sacred illness."[38] Hence there is no doubt that he took the idea of absolute knowledge seriously and did not subscribe to pure relativism.

The reasons which permitted him to do so bring us to the third way. It consists of turning attention away from the theory of knowledge which was outlined above and towards the development of a critical method capable of accounting for the difficulties presented by it. If the analysis given so far is correct, a successful solution needs to do at least two things. It must provide a principle for selecting the evidence and it must establish criteria by which the evidence can be assessed. Elements of such a solution can be found scattered in several places in Conring's preface. Nowhere are they combined in any systematic way, and it may be thought foolhardy to do here what Conring did not do himself. But given the importance of the question, it is worth bringing ideas to the forefront which are undoubtedly there and bear directly on the issue, even though Conring himself did not explore their significance as far as one might have liked. But in order to avoid misrepresentation, one must insist on the hypothetical nature of this reconstruction.

To take up the principle of selection first, one may point out that, having just condemned the kind of history which results from unprincipled journeying through the data in search of nothing but entertainment, Conring turns to history that is governed by a consideration of the common good.[39] This suggests that the idea of the common good might supply the desired principle. There are two excellent and closely related reasons

38. Speaking of mistaken notions of Roman law: "Verum etsi nondum quidquam detrimenti attulisset haec opinio, quis tamen non videt quam in futurum fuerit noxium, si improvidae mentes aut rerum novarum cupidae huiuscemodi erroribus imbuantur? Sacer scilicet morbus opinio est: mundus tamen hic nulla perinde re quam hac ipsa regitur. Ita et futiles nonnunquam sententiae fascinant animos, et usque adeo iudicii aciem obfuscant, ut ne claro quidem meridie veritatis solem contemplemur." 262.48–53.

39. "Quum enim immensa quaedam historiae amplitudo sit, per omnes scilicet res mortalium porrecta, alii ad omnem feruntur sine discrimine, alii hanc aut illam sibi seorsim addiscendam sumunt, reliquam contemnentes. . . . Accuratius tamen rem omnem intuentibus facile apparet, si voluptatis solius gratia sit tractanda historia, perinde fortassis esse ad quamnam feraris dummodo delectet. Quamquam id valeat cumprimis ea quae et varia maxime est et res narrat multum a vulgari consuetudine remotas; talia enim iucunda sunt maxime. At qui per historiam ad prudentiam atque rempublicam affectant viam, iis liquet delectum aliquem observandum esse. Non enim quaevis pari ad illam ratione est utilis." 258.40–45. "Unde et ante omnia consequens est, historiam eius reipublicae, cui praeest quis sive auctoritate sive consilio, esse omnino necessariam in republica versanti homini, negligi certe haud posse sine publico detrimento." 258.62–64. Cf. above, note 18.

why this could be so. First, the common good is a practical idea, rather than a theoretical one, and thus does not need to be constructed out of the evidence. It is given by interests. Second, it has objective validity for all of the members of the community whose good is concerned. Because it poses questions interesting for everyone, attention to the common good permits a reasonable beginning in discriminating among pieces of evidence. Motives of this kind clearly shaped Conring's own particular path to history. As he points out, his study of the history of Germany and German law was provoked by his fear of the damage which might be done to the common good by those who argued that Germany was subject to the Roman law and thereby threatened public peace.[40]

The difficulty inherent in giving such a central role to the common good, however, cannot be ignored. Even if it could be allowed the function of providing the study of human affairs with an acceptable starting point, it is doubtful whether it could do so for natural science, too. It thus inevitably raises the question whether there is a fundamental difference between the study of nature and that of human affairs. It focuses attention on the relationship between practical and theoretical reason in the formation of knowledge. To insist on it would mean giving priority to practical reason. Such a conclusion may not be entirely unwarranted. It will be remembered that Conring's favorite example of the man of knowledge, the doctor, has also a practical concern in mind, namely the health of the patient. For now, however, it is impossible to go beyond the bare suggestion that the idea of the common good is a possible, but problematic, candidate to fill one of the two gaps in Conring's theory of knowledge.

To turn to the other question, namely, how to acquire knowledge in spite of the fact that those theoretical principles which must be presupposed to examine the data cannot be presupposed, it is necessary to recall that Conring describes not merely one, but two ways to arrive at absolute knowledge. The first is that of the masters, who by their natural ingenuity "know how to construct common laws and universal precepts from

---

40. "Interest enim pacis ac salutis publicae, vel nihil loqui in vulgus de statu publico, quod Platonis consilium est, vel certe non aliter de illo loqui quam sese res habet. Dubium autem nullum est, quin periculosae sunt illae quorundam sententiae: iustum esse ut secundum Romanas leges imperii respublica conformetur. Quum enim nostra haec longe sit diversissima maximeque ab illis remota, iniustitiae praesens status arguitur: quod motibus excitandis multum profecto valet." 261.6–11. Add the text quoted above, note 10.

individual events." The second is that of the disciples who "have previously learned [common laws and universal precepts] from their teachers, so that nothing except experiments is required for an absolute knowledge of things in every detail."[41] Conring himself describes the first way as difficult, but not impossible. He considers the natural gifts required to follow it as rare, but he seems to think that they do exist. The question is whether we may leave it at that. If it is true, as he says elsewhere, that no one can even begin to study the data if he does not already dispose of some general principles, then it is not merely difficult, but impossible for the masters to do what is asked of them. The fundamental contradiction from which Conring's thought suffers is nowhere more manifest than at this point.

If it is impossible to study the data without already having acquired a knowledge of general principles, then the principles inferred by the masters from the evidence can have no absolute validity. The difference between the masters and the disciples thus turns out to be merely superficial. The former, to be sure, derive their knowledge of general principles from direct observation, whereas the latter base it only on the authority of their teachers. But in either case such knowledge is provisional and requires some other means of confirmation. The way of the disciples supplies precisely such a means. Even though it might hitherto have seemed merely an insignificant elaboration of the way of the masters, it thus acquires far greater importance than Conring seems to be giving it.

A central text may be quoted to elucidate the matter:

> To judge the trustworthiness of what the masters pronounced in a more universal manner by comparing it with the historical evidence, which is the second step [after having first learned the universal principles from the masters], not only is free from great difficulty, but is also absolutely necessary for a perfect and exact knowledge of all things. . . . Or who would dare to declare that he knows with certainty what he has not yet grasped with the senses, but only been persuaded to accept by the master's authority? But it makes very little difference to its reliability whether one has seen the matter with one's own eyes or accepts it on the certain narration of others who have so seen it. For such a disciple, therefore, history is like a Lydian stone or a kind of ruler, inasmuch as it is a compendium of ex-

41. Cf. above, note 14.

perience against which anyone who pursues absolute erudition must test all laws, all precepts, and all universal propositions.[42]

A few remarks about this text are in order. First, it decisively shifts the emphasis in acquiring a "perfect and exact knowledge of all things" from the construction of universal precepts out of history to testing them against history. The crucial step is now the "experiment" by which a general statement is applied to the data. Conring thus decidedly prefers to argue from principles to the data, rather than the other way.[43] It would nevertheless be a mistake to infer that the role played by history in his thought is restricted to supplying examples by which to illustrate the principles of prudence. On the contrary, history continues to furnish the raw material out of which universal precepts are made, and thus remains "of the highest necessity because it embraces experience of every kind."[44] The point is merely that the grounds on which such precepts are accepted before they have been tested against the evidence are purely hypothetical. The reason then why he prefers the road from the general to the specific, rather than the reverse, is that in coming full circle the former completes a process begun by the latter.[45]

Second, history is now given another definition which has so far been purposely ignored. It is no longer merely a storehouse of empirical data, but also a "ruler" which makes it possible to test the validity of general

42. "Fidem autem eorum quae ab magistris ita universalius fuere pronunciata, exigere ad historiam, (quod secundum erat) id vero ut magna caret difficultate, ita ad perfectam exactamque notitiam rerum quarumcunque per est necessarium. . . . Vel quis ausit profiteri, certo sese id scire, quod hactenus nullis usurpatum sensibus, sola magistri auctoritate fuit persuasum? Parum vero interest ad fidem, tuisne oculis rem videris, an ab aliis visam certa acceperis narratione. Tali ergo discipulo historia quasi lapis est Lydius aut amussis quaedam: ut quae experientiae compendium sit, ad quam omnes leges omniaque praecepta ac pronunciata communia explorare quemvis absolutae erudituionis affectatorem oportet." 258.19–27. On Beatus Rheananus as the source for the "Lydian stone," see Hammerstein, "Die Historie," 222, note 15, 230, note 43.

43. "Caeterum quam expedita sit altera haec et posterior via, quae a prudentiae praeceptis ad historiam pergit, prae illa quae vulgo commendatur ab historiis ad praecepta ducens, quamque conveniat magis civilis sapientiae tyronibus, alias luculente ostendimus." 258.27–30.

44. "Nullum tamen est dubium quin historiarum peritia non dico utilis sit ad comparandam illam prudentiam, verum per etiam necessaria, quacunque tandem via grassari ad illam fuerit libitum." 258.30–32. Cf. the text quoted above, note 13. Hammerstein, "Die Historie," 225, seems to disagree: "Die Geschichte hat also immer nur illustrativen, beispielhaften Charakter, keinen eigenen Aussagewert!"

45. This reminds one of the method of resolution and composition familiar from the scientific works of Galileo and others. It does not seem necessary to pursue this issue further at this point, but it may be worth suggesting that differences are to be expected when this method is consciously applied to texts, as it is in Conring's case, rather than to sensory observations.

statements. This double function of history alone, as both raw material and instrument of criticism, makes the pursuit of knowledge possible. At the same time it should be clear that the result of arguing from general statements to the evidence may not only be to confirm or to refute the former. It may also serve the opposite purpose of interpreting the evidence or filling gaps in it.

Third, there is no reason to believe that this procedure can ever completely remove the element of faith inherent in it from the beginning. Those who adopt it must rather continue forever to repeat the steps of accepting untested evidence, constructing hypotheses out of it, or learning them from the masters, performing the experiment of testing the hypotheses against the evidence, accepting the result, and subjecting it to new tests. The road towards absolute knowledge thus takes the form of an infinite circle gradually spiraling around a center which it never reaches. But because the formulation of hypotheses makes the historian "prudent," such repetition is by no means futile. It rather enables him to search the evidence methodically for an answer to a clearly formulated question.

Fourth, it may now be possible to understand why Conring found it so easy to substitute faith for truth in his references to the historian's cardinal virtue. Faith comes at the beginning, and truth at the end of his search for knowledge. The difference is thus by no means abolished. But absolute knowledge resides in infinity, and therefore faith and truth coincide in practice.

Fifth, attention should be drawn to the astonishing declaration that "it makes very little difference for its reliability whether one has seen the matter with one's own eyes or accepts it on the certain narration of others who have so seen it." It is astonishing because it belittles the difference between one's own observations and observations reported by others.[46] It implies the conviction that no evidence, not even that of one's own eyes, can ever be totally relied upon, or, conversely, that all evidence requires

46. A. Seifert, *Cognitio Historica* (Berlin, 1976), 133f., on the contrary insists on the importance of this difference for Conring's thought. He quotes from Conring's *De civili prudentia*: "Quae ex historia itaque eiusmodi singularium rerum lecta vel audita proxime quidem oritur cognitio, itidem non diversa est ab ea quae per experientiam accipitur, nisi quod aliena fide narrantium illa nitatur, experientia autem ipse (!) propius sensu perceptis inhaereat." (Seifert's exclamation mark). But even though reliance on "aliena fides" makes for complications, the fundamental point of this text seems to be the similarity of direct observation and history.

interpretation. History thus becomes, not simply *a*, but *the* empirical prerequisite for science. The consequence is that, insofar as "it is not given to [those] born human beings to explore everything by themselves, but many things must be accepted on the considered testimony of others,"[47] the model discussed above may be applied to all sciences, and not just to the study of human affairs. That is not to deny the difference between actual and reported observations. But it is to say that the former, like the latter, have to be critically analyzed in order to serve as a basis for knowledge.

Sixth, and finally, a more than conventional reason can now be suggested why Conring insists that the historian needs the virtue of eloquence in addition to truthfulness and prudence.[48] He needs truthfulness, or faith, so that he will report the evidence without intentional distortion. He needs prudence so as to interpret it rationally. But, given the finitude of the human mind, rational explanation never succeeds in accounting for the data without remainder. An element of faith continues to be left over. Perhaps it is too bold to attribute a place of systematic theoretical importance to eloquence in his thought. But it is just possible that eloquence is necessary because it alone is capable of uniting truthfulness and prudence in such a way that the two will be completely fused.[49]

The effect of forcing the contradiction in Conring's views to the surface is thus to recognize a theory of knowledge quite different from the one initially proposed. It is founded on the realization that the human mind is not equipped with any absolute standard by which to ascertain the veracity of any given evidence. All knowledge begins instead with an element of faith, faith either in untested evidence or in the doctrines of the masters. The capacity of human beings for attaining truth, in other words, is severely limited. On the one hand, the radical distinction between masters and disciples is thus abolished, and the role of magisterial authority undermined. This may be considered to be one of the roots of the Enlightenment. On the other hand, as it is impossible to build knowledge on an unquestionably firm basis, faith in the authority of a magisterial tradition, "the consent of better minds," is certainly not the worst in-

47. Cf. above, note 37.
48. Cf. above, note 36.
49. On the similarly central role attributed to eloquence by earlier humanists, see J. E. Seigel, *Rhetoric and Philosophy in Renaissance Humanism: The Union of Eloquence and Wisdom, Petrarch to Valla* (Princeton, 1968), especially the chapter on Valla, pp. 137–69.

dication where to begin the pursuit of knowledge, and in most cases probably better than faith in one's own natural ingenuity. It may seem paradoxical that what has just been called an enlightened way of thinking should thus replace knowledge with faith in a tradition. But the paradox is only superficial. The point of course is that one need not stop here. On the contrary, it is not only possible, but necessary to go on and to subject that faith to what Conring significantly calls "experiments." Conring's explicit theory according to which knowledge consists of general principles which explain the empirical data is thus challenged by an implicit one according to which knowledge resides in the infinite process of subjecting opinions to critical examination.

In order to illustrate how Conring conceived the systematic relationship between the common good, prudence, and history, a brief example may now be instructive. In the preface to the *Germania,* he asks if the Holy Roman Empire is subject to Roman law. The question is posed by his fear of the damage done to the common good by those who argue for a positive answer. Prudential principles suggest three possible reasons which would support his opponents' case. First, Roman law may be a part of justice itself. Second, Germany may have voluntarily subjected itself to Roman law. Third, there may be someone else who has the right to demand obedience to Roman law from Germany. There is no need now to investigate whether Conring had developed these possible answers on his own or taken them from some tradition. The point is that they serve as hypotheses to guide his investigation. In order to test them, he asks whether any one of the three applies to the historical evidence. In the course of searching the record, further distinctions turn out to be necessary. For example, tacit must be distinguished from explicit consent to Roman law. In this way, the original hypotheses are modified. In the end, he establishes that Roman law is not part of natural law, that Germany did not consent to it, and that no one had a right to impose it on Germany. These statements may now be called facts. But it is clear that their truth is predicated on the unproven assumption that no further evidence needs to be considered and that no reasons why Roman law might be binding on the Holy Roman Empire have been ignored. They are therefore not beyond question.[50]

Our results may now be briefly summarized. The most important feature

---

50. The relevant text can be found at 261.5–262.39.

of the views presented by Conring in his preface to the *Germania* is the tension between a simple and explicit theory according to which knowledge consists in empirical data in conjunction with rational principles and the apparent impossibility of arriving at such knowledge. The tension is never explicitly recognized. But it is implicitly present in contradictory statements about the manner in which truth is discovered. More important, an attempt to resolve it is embedded in the text. It consists of a different theory of knowledge. Instead of deriving knowledge from a firm empirical basis, the pursuit of knowledge, built on a concern for the common good, begins with the formulation of hypotheses from questionable evidence and enters on a circular and infinite process of testing the hypotheses against the evidence, and the evidence against the hypotheses. It may thus be no accident that in the mottos chosen for this essay opinion is said to rule the world, and "the circle of reason" and "the advantage of the commonwealth" are mentioned in one breath. Perhaps it is precisely their combination which best characterizes the goal towards which Conring's thoughts were tending.

At this point, our study of Conring's concept of history, which has long ago changed into a study of his theory of knowledge in general, must come to an end. It leaves more questions open than it has answered—if it has answered any at all. Its conclusions, whatever their merit may eventually turn out to be, are as hypothetical as the basis they postulate for his thought. But since a hypothetical reconstruction is at the heart of this essay in any case, it may be fitting to end with a few equally speculative remarks about a possible place for Conring's thought in intellectual history. Here, too, the purpose is not to answer, but to raise questions.

As may have already become evident, the theory of knowledge with which he began is taken directly from Aristotle. The initial emphasis on the natural desire of human beings for knowledge, the distinction between mere experience and scientific knowledge, the preference for the example of the doctor, and even the choice of Socrates as the patient, all appear in the opening pages of Aristotle's *Metaphysics*. The primary role played by Aristotelian categories in Conring's thought is in fact too well known to need any further belaboring.[51] The other formative influence on his

---

51. A more important, but altogether different question is if Conring's Aristotle is the historical Aristotle.

mind, as is equally well known, is found in humanism, with which he became familiar during his student days at the University of Leiden. Humanist themes have not been insisted upon, but their ubiquity is obvious, obvious from the fact that the preface to the *Germania* itself is an introduction to an edition of a classical text, from Conring's insistence on good Latin style, and from his ideal of the *liber natus homo*. It is therefore extremely tempting to attribute the tension declared to have been fundamental for his thought to one between Aristotelianism and humanism.

One must be cautious not to misinterpret the nature of that tension. It is a mistake, as the scholar to whom this book of essays is dedicated has shown, to identify humanism with any particular doctrine. No such identification is here intended, nor is one necessary. Inveterate anti-Platonic empiricist that he may have been, Aristotle himself, after all, was forced to admit that the faculty of scientific understanding "enters [the body] from outside and is divine."[52] As has been pointed out above, reliance on innate ideas, or, in this case, the separate existence of *nous*, is one way of resolving the difficulty which Conring, like Aristotle, faced when asked how the phenomena can possibly be explained by principles which are yet to be derived from the phenomena. The contradiction in his thought thus exists in Aristotle's thought itself.

The point is rather that the difficulty, at least in the form in which it had been transmitted during the Middle Ages, was relatively comfortable to live with. Aristotle's model of knowledge was based on data conceived in terms of actual observations. At first sight, it seems so far-fetched to question the objective reality of what one has seen with one's own eyes that such data may continue to serve as a basis on which the whole building of scientific knowledge can be erected. The separate existence of the *nous* may almost seem an afterthought to an empiricist scheme which takes the data for granted.

Texts, on the other hand, are a kind of data whose reliability is not obvious. They have been created by human beings and may not be accepted without question. They can therefore not be incorporated in the Aristotelian model without raising the problem in an acute form. From this perspective, it may have been the most important effect of humanism's unprecedented attention to the study of texts to have lent new urgency

52. Aristotle, *Gen. Corr.*, 2.3, 736b27ff.

to a very old problem. A serious effort to derive knowledge from texts could only succeed if changes were made in the idea of knowledge. At the very least, it was necessary to add to Aristotle's views. But once it was recognized that the difficulties presented by texts were merely an exacerbated form of those raised by Aristotle himself, it became imperative to transform the theory of knowledge as a whole.

The achievement of Hermann Conring, and, perhaps, that of his seventeenth-century cohorts, may thus not only have been to have posed the problem in terms which forced a decision between abiding by the Aristotelian model or creating another one, but also to have adumbrated a view of reason that came to predominate in the following century. On the surface, Conring admittedly still conceived of knowledge in Aristotelian categories. But even though he had not yet made up his mind, he already had a remarkably clear idea of a different approach. Built on concepts developed for the study of texts, it abandoned the radical distinction between empirical data and rational principles in favor of a circular procedure which could be applied to all areas of knowledge.[53] It saw the pursuit of truth as founded on the critical examination of traditional opinions, collapsed the distinction between masters and disciples, and thus provided reasons to justify the enlightened assault on every form of authority. From there, it was not far to a philosophy which was explicitly founded on the certainty that all evidence includes an element of human creativity, which denied that there is any direct access to things in themselves, which concluded that criticism is the first task of those who desire knowledge, and which imposed stricter limits on theoretical than on practical reason. From there, in short, it was not far to the philosophy of Kant.

In general, the thought of Hermann Conring can thus be characterized as a response to the growth of written culture which humanism and printing had promoted. His humanist training and his familiarity with the difficulties inherent in searching texts for knowledge about the world forced an incipient recognition that the Aristotelian model could not be simply maintained. His response was neither fully developed nor was it the only possible one. One could have denied that what applied to texts also ap-

---

53. Cf. note 45 above. This view harmonizes with Dreitzel's characterization of Conring's achievement; see H. Dreitzel, "Die Entwicklung der Historie zur Wissenschaft," *Zeitschrift für Historische Forschung*, 8 (1981): 264–69. But if it is correct, the crisis of Aristotelianism, which Dreitzel dates circa 1700, *ibid.*, 272–74, may have been well advanced at a much earlier time.

plied to the study of nature. Here one may perhaps find a root of the modern distinction between science and history. One could also have built all knowledge on innate ideas. Perhaps it is possible to forge a link to Descartes in this way. Conring, however, tried a different way. His thought may not only help to understand why the German word *Wissenschaft* still covers all areas of knowledge, from history to natural science. It must also enter into an interpretation of the profound transformation of intellectual life which led to the German Enlightenment and the growing conviction that reason is historically conditioned.

CONSTANTIN FASOLT

SPINOZA
ON THE
POWER
AND
ETERNITY
OF THE
INTELLECT

IN THE FIRST THREE PARTS of the *Ethics*, Spinoza offers a systematic metaphysics, epistemology and psychology. This was required, he believed, as a foundation; a general understanding of the world and of human nature must provide a context before specifically ethical topics — the aim, after all, of the *Ethics* — can be intelligibly discussed. Finally, in Parts IV and V, Spinoza turns to ethics proper.

But there is an important difference in approach between the two parts. In Part IV, Spinoza emphasizes the limitations on human power and freedom. Such control as knowledge offers over the emotions comes about, in Part IV, only insofar as knowledge itself is an emotion. Knowledge, that is to say, counts as a modification which alters a person's power of action; as such it may interact causally with other modifications, resulting in a different emotional state. Someone might object that this does not require that knowledge exercise any power *as knowledge*, and Spinoza seems to agree:

> No emotion can be restrained by the true knowledge of good and evil insofar as it is true, but only insofar as it is considered as an emotion. (IV, 14)

A more positive role for knowledge in controlling the emotions is reserved for Part V, and the theories Spinoza offers there will be the central topic of this essay.[1]

Despite Spinoza's intention that his ethical doctrines should derive from his general philosophy, some readers have felt that the connection between Part V and the earlier parts is weak or inconsistent, and that Part V itself is obscure. I believe, on the contrary, that Part V is more intimately linked to Spinoza's metaphysics and philosophy of mind than these readers have recognized, and that evidence for this can be found in the text. Therefore, in presenting Spinoza's views I shall attempt to bring out some of the relationships that seem to me to have been generally overlooked.

Part V falls into two sections, the first concerned with control of the passive emotions, and the second, from Proposition 21 to the end, with genuine freedom and blessedness. I take up first the control of the emotions, then eternity of the mind.

I

Control of Emotion

Close to the beginning of Part V, Spinoza claims that

An emotion which is a passion ceases to be a passion as soon as we form a clear and distinct idea of it. (V, 3)[2]

1. Work on this project was supported by a fellowship from the National Endowment for the Humanities. I have treated some of the topics relating to Spinoza's views on the power of the mind at greater length elsewhere, and I have relied in this essay on those earlier discussions. See especially "Spinoza's Concept of Mind," *Journal of the History of Philosophy*, 17 (1979): 401–416; "Truth and Adequacy in Spinozistic Ideas," *Southwestern Journal of Philosophy*, 8 (1977): 11–34, reprinted in *Spinoza: New Perspectives*, ed. R. W. Shahan and J. I. Biro (Norman, Oklahoma, 1978), 11–34; and "Belief, Action and Knowledge in Spinoza," (forthcoming in the proceedings of a conference on the philosophy of Spinoza, Jewish Theological Seminary of America, New York, 1978).

In quoting from Spinoza's *Ethics* I have followed with occasional modifications the White-Stirling translation available in *"Ethics" Preceded by "On the Improvement of the Understanding,"* ed. J. Gutmann (New York, 1949). Latin texts follow the Gebhardt edition, *Spinoza Opera*, 4 vols. (Heidelberg, 1925). All quotations are identified in the text by part and proposition; thus, "IV,14" above refers to *Ethics*, Part IV, Proposition 14: "Vera boni, & mali cognitio, quatenus vera, nullum affectum coercere potest, sed tantum, quatenus ut affectus consideratur."

2. "Affectus, qui passio est, desinit esse passio, simulatque eius claram, & distinctam formamus ideam."

This is striking, for it appears to contradict such earlier doctrines as IV, 14, quoted above, as well as this one:

Nothing positive contained in a false idea is removed by the presence of the true insofar as it is true. (IV, 1)[3]

Moreover, V, 3 is intuitively implausible, besides seeming to contradict IV, 1. If I suffer from an emotion, why should understanding that I suffer, even understanding the exact nature of my suffering, bring the suffering to an end? On the contrary, it seems that we discover in ourselves many feelings which we recognize as undesirable yet continue to feel. What, then, can Spinoza have in mind?

In support of V, 3, Spinoza offers this demonstration:

An emotion which is a passion is a confused idea (by the general definition of the emotions). If, therefore, we form a clear and distinct idea of this emotion, the idea will not be distinguished—except by reason—from this emotion, insofar as the emotion is related to the mind alone (Proposition 21, pt. 2, with its note), and therefore (Prop. 3, pt. 3) the emotion will cease to be a passion. (V, 3, dem.)[4]

The crucial claim is that if we form an adequate idea of a confused idea (i.e., of an emotion), then this adequate idea will not be distinct from the confused idea—that is, from the emotion. It was shown in II, 21, that the idea of the mind is related to the mind in the same way as the mind is related to the body (that is, the mind is the *object* of the idea of the mind) and by II, 7, note, the mind and the body are one and the same thing; the idea of the mind and the mind, therefore, are *also* one and the same thing. Therefore, if the idea of the mind is *adequate*, that of which it is the idea—the passive emotion—must *also* be adequate; in other words, it must cease to be a passion. If we accept this argument, then it would seem that the only question remaining is whether the condition described in the proposition can ever be fulfilled—*can* we ever form a clear and distinct idea of a passive emotion? (Spinoza says in the immediately following proposition that it can be.)

3. "Nihil, quod idea falsa habet, tollitur praesentia veri, quatenus verum."
4. "Affectus, qui passio est, idea est confusa (per gener. Affect. Defin.). Si itaque ipsius claram, & distinctam formemus ideam, haec idea ab ipso affectu, quatenus ad solam Mentem refertur, non nisi ratione distinguetur (per Prop. 21. p. 2 cum eiusdem Schol.); adeoque (per Prop. 3. p. 3.) affectus desinet esse passio."

The appeal in the demonstration to II, 21, and through it to II, 7, note, is significant, for it shows that Spinoza's claim is not the one described as implausible a paragraph back—that a clear and distinct idea of the emotion causes the emotion to cease to be a passion because the idea is true. Instead, the idea has the effect claimed because it *is* the emotion; the appeal is to identity, not to truth. So there need be no contradiction of IV, 1, and by "form a clear and distinct idea of this emotion" Spinoza seems to mean not "form an idea which is a correct description of the emotion" but "form an idea which is clear and distinct and which is also identical with the emotion." But it is not evident that this helps much, for we seem merely to have substituted for one contradiction another, the suggestion that an emotion is a confused idea and yet is identical with a clear and distinct idea.

I take Spinoza's intent to be something like the following: If a confused idea can be apprehended in such a way that it is seen as following from a complete causal context—if we can grasp it so as to see its necessary connection with other things instead of seeing it in a merely fragmentary way—then this apprehending, which *includes* the emotion, counts as action instead of passion. Such apprehending might not be limited to considering just the changes that take place "in" the body; it might involve seeing those changes in relation to other things, so that the causal provenance of bodily changes could be apprehended. *This* is the apprehension that would be action, and in it the mind would be active instead of passive; it would feel joy instead of sorrow, since its power of thought would increase. The body, however, and its modifications would not be altered by the process. The body might continue, for instance, to be sick, even though the mind was active; understanding sickness as a necessary consequence of a system of causes does not remove the sickness. I take this to be the point of Spinoza's restriction in the demonstration; he says that the identity of the emotion and the clear and distinct idea of the emotion follows "insofar as the emotion is related to the mind alone;" it is this limited identity that he claims is shown by II, 21 (and ultimately, II, 7, note).

On this reading, the confused idea becomes a part of an adequate idea and thus is no longer a passion. This is consistent with the claim of IV, 1, that false ideas are not removed by the true insofar as it is true, for the claim is that the inadequate idea disappears insofar as it becomes part of an adequate context, not insofar as it is the object of an accurate or true description.

This reading helps to make sense of the claim in V, 4 that there is no modification of the body of which we cannot form some clear and distinct conception. Spinoza's demonstration of that proposition consists essentially in an appeal to II, 38, where he asserts that what is common to all cannot be inadequately conceived. From this it follows that a feature such as being a modification of extension, which all bodies have in common, must be adequately conceived, and I can form adequate ideas of the modifications of my body just insofar as my body exhibits properties that are shared by all other bodies. Now, we may object that this will not touch some of the bodily modifications that most concern us—toothache, for example. And it is true that understanding my body as a mode of extension will not help my toothache; nevertheless, it *is* action rather than passion of the mind, according to Spinoza, and to the extent that I can apprehend my toothache as a modification of extension, part of the natural order, my mind will be active, despite the pain. Cold comfort, we may think, but in Spinoza's view the only remedy available; moreover, *he* does not think it a poor one; properly understood, it can be recognized as true blessedness.

It is worth recalling here that joy and sorrow as originally defined in III, 11, note, pertain to the mind. When they are related to the body as well as the mind, Spinoza calls them "pleasurable excitement" (*titillatio* or *hilaritas*) and "pain" (*dolor* or *melancholia*). Here in Part V, Spinoza's claims relate to joy and sorrow, not to pleasurable excitement and pain.

But suppose we *could* adequately grasp the causes of the finite alteration of parts of the body, *then*, surely, we could overcome those modifications? We could overcome them, indeed, in the sense that they would then be our own actions, not things we "suffer." But we could not alter them in the sense of causing something else to happen in their place.

All this does not mean, however, that Spinoza thinks we have *no* control over finite modifications—that is, no way of bringing it about that we suffer less from them. He says in the note to V, 4, after showing that some clear and distinct conception can be formed of every bodily modification, that we should strive

that the emotion may be separated from the thought of an external cause and connected with true thought. Thus not only love, hatred,

> etc. will be destroyed (Prop. 2, pt. 5) but also the appetites or desire
> to which the emotion gives rise cannot be excessive. (V, 4, note)[5]

Thus, although we cannot understand the infinite chain of causes of our
bodily modifications, we *can* cease to link the emotion with the thought
of an external cause. In this way, the emotions such as love and hatred
that depend on association with an object will be destroyed, and the mind
left, to that extent, in a state of activity instead of passivity. For example,
if I receive a wound and hate the man who stabbed me, I feel both pain
and hatred. Pain can be mitigated so far as I can consider my wound as
part of the natural order of causes; this is activity of the mind, although
it does not cause the wound to heal. Hatred, however, can be *destroyed*
as soon as I detach my thought from its object, for hatred, by definition,
requires an object. This requires practice, since it involves forming appropriate associations for our images in place of the inappropriate (i.e.,
painful or "passion-producing") associations which they otherwise have.
To aid in this, Spinoza offers various "maxims" (*dogmata*) in the note to
V, 10, and summarizes them in the note to V, 20. These maxims for
daily life rest on the associationism of Part III — that is, on the theory of
imagination, and its relation to emotion. Sometimes the connection is explicit, as in V, 10n, which contains reference to the theory of imagination; at other times the connection is indirect. For example, one of the
maxims given in V, 10n, is that hatred is conquered by love or generosi-
ty, which Spinoza derives from IV, 46. But IV, 46 rests at several points
on the theory of association of images presented in Part III. It is noteworthy that here Spinoza describes the claim of IV, 46 as a "maxim" —
that is, as a precept like the other precepts in V, 10n and V, 20n which
have to do with control of passive emotions; moreover, IV, 46 is not unusual among propositions of Part IV in its dependence on Part III. The
dependence makes clear that although the bulk of Part IV has to do with
the life of reason, this is not "reason" in the sense of the life of genuine

---

5. ". . . Huic igitur rei praecipue danda est opera, ut unumquemque affectum, quantum fieri
potest, clare, & distincte cognoscamus, ut sic Mens ex affectu ad illa cogitandum determinetur,
quae clare, & distincte percipit, & in quibus plane acquiescit; atque adeo ut ipse affectus a cogita-
tione causae externae separetur, & veris iungatur cogitationibus; ex quo fiet, ut non tantum Amor,
Odium, etc. destruantur (per Prop. 2. huius), sed ut etiam appetitus, seu Cupiditates, quae ex
tali affectu oriri solent, excessum habere nequeant (per Prop. 61. p. 4.). . . ."

activity and blessedness; Spinoza does not develop in Part IV the advantages of the second and third kinds of knowledge. What he offers in Part IV is the life of reason in the sense of "what reason prescribes for control of the passive emotions" or, perhaps better, "how a man governed by reason would act in relation to men who are governed by their passions." How to become a man of reason, and how reason comes to have the effects described in Part IV, is saved for later. This characterization of Part IV is true in general, but there are a few exceptions, places where hints and anticipations of the life of true activity can be found; IV, 52, for example. But the highest kind of blessedness, knowledge of the third kind, is reserved for Part V.

Spinoza's program for control of the emotions is impersonal in the sense that it does not advocate coming to understand what is special to oneself as an individual. Unlike the forms of therapy that urge us to scrutinize our private feelings, our inner selves and unique personality, Spinoza demands a broader, not a more narrow point of view. In accord with the claims of Part III, that understanding the emotions lies in taking the third-person perspective instead of seeing the emotions from the point of view of the one who feels them, Spinoza claims in Part V that besides yielding understanding, the third-person point of view leads to power and mental health. His program differs also from those that urge people to seek the true objects of emotions on grounds that discovering one's hidden feelings makes one free to control or re-direct them. Spinoza talks not of re-direction but of removal, and he does not think that the key to therapy lies in discovering something previously hidden; unconscious guilts and loves and desires are, I believe, unintelligible for him. Control of the passive emotions, to the extent that it is possible, is a result of understanding, of taking the third-person perspective. A person controls passive emotions by gaining insight into their causes and exploiting the principles of association which Spinoza presents in Part III. No amount of phenomenology can provide the required knowledge; first-person awareness is not a source of truth, nor of power. "Exploiting," moreover, is not "manipulating." We do not change what happens, but when we understand things, then what happens counts more nearly as our own action. Spinoza complains in the preface to Part V that Descartes inclines to Stoical opinions; presumably, it is Descartes' claims for the faculty of will which link him for Spinoza with the Stoics who, he says, "thought that the emotions depend absolutely on our will." But despite Spinoza's vigorous rejection of the power of will, he himself seems close at times to Stoical opinions.

Now, Spinoza does resemble the Stoics in thinking that happiness is not to be achieved by attempting to alter the world so as to fit it to our desires. One reason for Spinoza to take this position is, of course, that alteration of the external world is in his opinion impossible, a limitation which has an analogue in Stoicism's denial of absolute control over physical objects. Faced with the limitations of human power, the Stoics conclude that the reasonable thing to do is to shape one's desires to what happens— this, they say, can be done, and once done there is no further possibility of frustrated desire, hence no unhappiness. Now, this position still regards happiness as satisfied desire, or, at least, lack of frustrated desire; also, it regards the external world (which we do not control) as the source of the things that may or may not satisfy desire. But *that* means, first, that there is an element of unfreedom in the attainment of happiness, since the objects of enjoyment are not products of one's own action. Second, it means that it makes no difference what objects one encounters; one set of objects could as well be the stuff of happiness as another. This second consequence has for most people been the principal objection to Stoicism; people insist that it does matter, in achieving happiness or its opposite, what objects one encounters and what experiences one has as a result. But it is the first consequence that is most telling for Spinoza. This is because freedom, in the sense of oneself being the source of one's action, is for Spinoza the very essence of happiness. This is not merely a matter of choosing one's attitude toward objects over which one has no control; for Spinoza the objects of enjoyment—that is, of the best kind of enjoyment, which is active love—must also be products of freedom, and the highest possible satisfaction lies in the contemplation of oneself as such an object. Stoicism seems paltry in comparison—an abandonment of self for the sake of a shallow tranquility. Spinoza, despite his recognition of the limitations of human power, does not endorse resignation or fatalism. He looks instead for understanding of the order of nature as a path, ultimately, to eternity.

II

Eternity of the Mind

At the end of the note to V, 20, Spinoza informs us that he has finished what he has to say concerning this present life, and announces his intention to consider "those matters which appertain to the duration of the mind without relation to the body." The ensuing discussion of eternity of the mind has been regarded by some readers as an ascent to the divine, by others as a descent to mysticism or impenetrable obscurity; some have found it incompatible with the rest of Spinoza's system. It is indeed true that this part of the *Ethics* departs in some ways from what has gone before, but what is new is the perspective or point of view, not the material. Scarcely any new concepts appear; that of intellectual love is the only important one which occurs here for the first time, and even it is derived from earlier definitions, not introduced by mere stipulation. Spinoza brings together topics which have previously been kept strictly separate, and offers a way of uniting the individual human mind with the divine. The last portion of the *Ethics* should be seen as an attempt at synthesis, not merely in the sense of tying up loose ends but in the stronger sense of reconciling doctrines that seem to be incompatible.

Let us begin by examining in some detail the propositions in which Spinoza demonstrates the eternity of the mind, beginning with Proposition 22 of Part V. The proposition and its demonstration are as follows:

> In God, nevertheless, there necessarily is given an idea which expresses the essence of this or that human body under the form of eternity.
> Demonstration: God is not only the cause of the existence of this or that human body, but also of its essence (Prop. 25, pt. 1), which therefore must necessarily be conceived through the essence of God itself (Ax. 4, pt. 1) and by a certain eternal necessity (Prop. 26, pt. 1). This conception, moreover, must necessarily be given in God (Prop. 3, pt. 2).[6]

---

6. "In Deo tamen datur necessario idea, quae huius, & illius Corporis humani essentiam sub aeternitatis specie exprimit.
Demonstratio.

Notice that Spinoza speaks of the essence of the human body, not its existence; he explicitly distinguishes essence and existence at the start of the demonstration, and then proceeds to talk about essence only. (Some English translations, such as the White-Stirling, use the word "exists" where Spinoza's word is *datur*; that Spinoza is not talking about existence is less evident in such translations than it should be.) Notice also that Spinoza's proof that there is in God an idea which expresses the essence of the human body under the form of eternity does not depend on any special features of the human body, or the human mind; the conclusion follows because there is an idea in God of the essence of *every* thing under the form of eternity; the claim rests on general metaphysics, not on the theory of human nature.

The expression "under the form of eternity" is not new; Spinoza introduced it in II, 44, cor. 2:

> It is of the nature of reason to perceive things under a certain form of eternity.[7]

He does not cite this corollary here in V, 22, although he does appeal to it later, in the note to V, 29. The demonstration of the corollary appeals to several important concepts — truth, the necessity of God's nature, and (*via* II, 41) the definitions of the second and third kinds of knowledge; these connections make it plausible to link perception under a certain form of eternity with knowledge of the third kind. The link is borne out by Spinoza's description of knowledge under the form of eternity in V, 29n, where he cites this corollary. Things conceived under the form of eternity are described as conceived

> to be contained in God and to follow from the necessity of the divine nature.[8]

Deus non tantum est causa huius, & illius Corporis humani existentiae, sed etiam essentiae (per Prop. 25. p. 1.), quae propterea per ipsam Dei essentiam necessario debet concipi (per Axiom. 4. p. 1.), idque aeterna quadam necessitate (per Prop. 16. p. 1.), qui quidem conceptus necessario in Deo dari debet (per Prop. 3. p. 2.)."

7. "De natura Rationis est res sub quadam aeternitatis specie percipere."

8. V, 29: "Quicquid Mens sub specie aeternitatis intelligit, id ex eo non intelligit, quod Corporis praesentem actualem existentiam concipit, sed ex eo, quod Corporis essentiam concipit sub specie aeternitatis. Scholium.

This is similar to the third kind of knowledge, which

> advances from an adequate idea of the formal essence of certain attributes of God to the adequate knowledge of the essence of things. (II, 40n2)[9]

It appears that conceiving under a form of eternity and knowing by the third kind of knowledge both consist in grasping things as contained in or following from the self-sufficient nature of God. Therefore, the claim of Proposition 22 that there is an idea which expresses the essence of this or that human body under the form of eternity amounts to the claim that the human body, like every other individual thing, can, in principle, be understood by the third kind of knowledge.

In Proposition 23, Spinoza asserts that

> [t]he human mind cannot be absolutely destroyed with the body, but something of it remains which is eternal. (V, 23)[10]

He demonstrates this by taking the idea in God which expresses the essence of the human body (i.e., the idea established in the previous proposition) and saying that this idea is "something which pertains to the essence of the human mind." Connecting this idea with the human mind is supported by II, 13. An immediate question is why Spinoza appeals here to Proposition 13 of Part II, instead of Proposition 11, which was, after all, the place where the human mind was introduced. Proposition 13 is required because it establishes that the object of the mind is a human body, not just an "individual thing"; only in 13 is it made explicit that humans are composed of just two attributes, Thought and Extension, and that if God has the idea of a human body, His idea must be (or "pertain to") the human mind. So Proposition 13 is required for the inference offered in V, 23; Proposition 11 would not do. (The argument is: if A is the

---

Res duobus modis a nobis ut actuales concipiuntur, vel quatenus easdem cum relatione ad certum tempus, & locum existere, vel quatenus ipsas in Deo contineri, & ex naturae divinae necessitate consequi concipimus. Quae autem hoc secundo modo ut verae, seu reales concipiuntur, eas sub aeternitatis specie concipimus, & earum ideae aeternam, & infinitam Dei essentiam involvunt, ut Propositione 45, Partis 2. ostendimus, cujus etiam Scholium vide."

9. ". . . hoc cognoscendi genus procedit ab adaequata idea essentiae formalis quorundam Dei attributorum ad adaequatam cognitionem essentiae rerum."

10. "Mens humana non potest cum Corpore absolute destrui; sed eius aliquid remanet, quod aeternum est."

idea of B, and if B = C, then someone who has the idea of C has A [or something "pertaining to A"]. But we can infer this only if we know that B = C, and this connection is provided by II, 13.)

The result of the two propositions, therefore, is that there is an idea which expresses the essence of the human body under the form of eternity (V, 22), and this idea, though not exactly identical to the human mind, does at least "pertain to" the human mind (V, 23). If we were right earlier in linking knowledge under the form of eternity with the third kind of knowledge, we can infer that the human mind, insofar as it is eternal, can be identified with knowing the body by the third kind of knowledge.

Relations between the mind and the body insofar as they are eternal are analogous in some important ways to relations between mind and body as described in Part II. First as regards the nature of the mind itself: the human mind is the idea of an individual human body actually existing, and similarly, the mind insofar as it is eternal is the idea of the essence of a human body under the form of eternity. In Part II, knowledge of the mind as a kind of subject or substance in which individual modifications inhere is derived from knowledge of the individual modifications; indeed, whatever the mind knows of itself, its body, or external things is known by means of bodily modifications (II, 19, 23, 26). Similarly, whatever the mind knows under the form of eternity is known by means of the body under the form of eternity:

> Everything which the mind understands under the form of eternity it understands . . . because it conceives the essence of the body under the form of eternity. (V, 29)[11]

I have argued in "Spinoza's Concept of Mind" that although the substantial mind is not directly perceived, conceiving the mind as a unified subject of action serves to unite the individual modifications, making them modifications of a single substance and providing the ground for a concept of a unified self. How far is this foundation for the self reflected in eternity? Not very far, seemingly, since perception by means of bodily modifications can hardly be eternal. But that raises the question what *is* the foundation for the individual self in eternity; is there, in fact, any room at all in Spinoza's system for eternity or immortality of the inidividual?

11. See note 8, above.

This question has been widely taken to amount to the question whether there can be separate ideas of individual bodies under the form of eternity. An argument against the possibility is that since the idea of each body under the form of eternity must involve the idea of all nature, the idea of one body under the form of eternity will be the same as the idea of any other body under the form of eternity; if the ideas cannot be distinguished there is no meaning to the claim of individual eternity. Now there are, in fact, several ways of arguing that for Spinoza there can be distinct ideas of different bodies under the form of eternity.

But this does not amount to showing the conceivability of individual immortality. Individual immortality, I take it, would have to include some sense of self. The question concerning individual immortality is not "is there in God an adequate idea of each individual body, different from the adequate ideas of other bodies?" but "could one be aware of oneself as eternal and also be aware of oneself as a distinct, unique self?" Showing that the answer to the first question is "yes" does not force an affirmative answer to the second. The idea of a given body under the form of eternity, whose reality is shown in V, 22, is an idea in God; the proposition does not show it to be an idea which the mind of that body possesses. Moreover, the theory of knowledge presented in Part II seems to require that the answer to the second question be "no."

It was shown in Part II that the human mind can have knowledge of finite physical objects only by means of modifications of the body. Ideas of bodily modifications are in addition the source of knowledge of the body itself and the mind itself as subjects of causal action, and it is this knowledge which provides the unification of the self. But ideas of bodily modifications are imaginations, and there can be no imagination except while the body exists:

> The mind can imagine nothing, nor can it recollect anything that is past, except while the body exists. (V, 21)[12]

It follows that knowing oneself as a separate subject of action would not be possible without supposing an existing body. A slightly different way to derive the same conclusion rests on observing that knowledge of one's own eternity is attainable not by imagination but only by understanding,

---

12. "Mens nihil imaginari potest, neque rerum praeteritarum recordari, nisi durante Corpore."

which is not personal or egocentric. Understanding concentrates on truths which do not depend on a unique or unsharable point of view and consequently do not pertain to one individual self exclusive of others. This is like saying that knowledge of its own eternity can be attained by the mind in the third person — as a conclusion of intellect — but not in the first person, not as an experience of the knowing self. Therefore, there can be no individual immortality in Spinoza's system.

But although the conclusion just reached seems to be required by his claims about knowledge and the mind, it is not Spinoza's position. He does wish to affirm a direct experience of eternity. To the proposition which shows the eternity of the human mind, he adds a note which reads in part:

> ... we feel and know by experience that we are eternal. For the mind is no less sensible of those things which it conceives through intelligence than of those which it remembers, for demonstrations are the eyes of the mind, by which it knows and observes things. (V, 23n)[13]

This is a startling claim, given the considerations adduced above against a sense of self as eternal. What can Spinoza intend? To understand his position we must distinguish more carefully the sources and types of the mind's knowledge of itself and its body. We shall find that the possibility of the mind's forming some sort of first-person apprehension of itself under the form of eternity (which is in effect what I have claimed individual immortality must consist in) does not depend for Spinoza on its forming an adequate idea of any individual finite body.

In so far as the mind's access to itself and its body rests on perception of individual bodily modifications, it can form no adequate ideas; this was shown in Part II. But perception of things under the form of eternity does not rest on perception of the modifications of an individual existing body:

> Everything which the mind understands under the form of eternity it understands not because it conceives the present actual existence

---

13. ". . . At nihilominus sentimus, experimurque, nos aeternos esse. Nam Mens non minus res illas sentit, quas intelligendo concipit, quam quas in memoria habet. Mentis enim oculi, quibus res videt, observatque, sunt ipsae demonstrationes. . . ."

of the body, but because it conceives the essence of the body under
the form of eternity. (V, 29)[14]

We saw above that to conceive things under the form of eternity is to
conceive them by the third kind of knowledge, which involves adequate
ideas. Now, we know from Part II that the things concerning the body
which the mind can adequately grasp are those which are "common to
everything . . . equally in the part and in the whole" (II, 38).[15] These
things were invoked also in the early propositions of Part V (4, 7) as the
foundation of that emotion which springs from reason. Obviously, things
common to every body cannot serve to separate one body from another;
therefore, so far as it has adequate knowledge, the mind does not perceive
its body as a unique entity, distinct from others. It follows that the mind
cannot grasp the idea of the individual body under the form of eternity,
even though there *is* such an idea in God (by V, 22); this conclusion,
in fact, repeats conclusions reached in Part II.

But it does not follow that the mind can form no idea of *itself* under
the form of eternity. On the contrary, it seems that whenever the mind
has an adequate idea, it necessarily has an idea of itself under the form
of eternity. Spinoza does not formulate this claim in quite the terms I
have just used, but I think we can see from V, 27 that this must be his
view. The proposition deals primarily with an issue that is not our immediate concern, namely the peace of mind which results from the third
kind of knowledge. But in the course of the demonstration Spinoza says
that someone who knows things by the third kind of knowledge has "the
idea of himself and his own virtue" and he supports this claim by appeal
to II, 43, which says that

He who has a true idea knows at the same time that he has a true
idea, nor can he doubt the truth of the thing. (II, 43)[16]

The use of this proposition to show that one who knows by the third
kind of knowledge has an idea of himself indicates that Spinoza does not
understand the proposition to mean merely that someone who has a true

---

14. See note 8, above.
15. "Illa, quae omnibus communia, quaeque aeque in parte, ac in toto sunt, non possunt concipi, nisi adaequate."
16. "Qui veram habet ideam, simul scit se veram habere ideam, nec de rei veritate potest dubitare."

idea knows that his idea agrees with its ideatum; the person also knows something about himself. We already know that an adequate idea exhibits the self-sufficient character of reality; now we can say that the person who knows that he has a true idea sees his own thought as an instantiation of self-sufficient being. In this way, the mind is aware of itself as subject, as something complete in itself through which other things can be understood. In slightly different terms, we can say that the mind here grasps its own nature as an active self. Some of these points are contained in V, 31:

> The third kind of knowledge depends upon the mind as its formal cause, in so far as the mind itself is eternal.[17]

To call the mind the "formal cause" of knowledge means that the mind is in reality ("formally") precisely the self-contained being revealed ("objectivity") in an adequate idea; apprehending something perfect is *being* perfect, and being perfect is construed here as an intrinsic (i.e. not a relational) property. It follows that possession of adequate ideas is quite literally a participation in the divine; the mind is united with God in the sense that it possesses God's formal characteristics. Spinoza expresses the same point this way:

> Our mind, in so far as it knows itself and the body under the form of eternity, necessarily has a knowledge of God, and knows that it is in God and is conceived through Him. (V, 30)[18]

From the preceding paragraphs, it is clear that we must separate two ways in which the mind may derive knowledge of itself. The first is by imagination, the second by adequate ideas. In addition, we must distinguish two sorts of knowledge: knowledge of oneself in one's uniqueness, as an individual distinct from others, and knowledge of oneself as a free agent, the source of one's own action. Proceeding by imagination one's knowledge is derived from awareness of bodily modifications; this gives knowledge of oneself as distinct from others, for it is the individual finite body which separates one person from another (as is clear in the demonstration of II,

---

17. "Tertium cognitionis genus pendet a Mente, tanquam a formali causa, quatenus Mens ipsa aeterna est."

18. "Mens nostra, quatenus se, & Corpus sub aeternitatis specie cognoscit, eatenus Dei cognitionem necessario habet, scitque se in Deo esse, & per Deum concipi."

13, discussed above). Imaginative awareness of bodily modifications is direct — 'inner" or first-person awareness — and it does presuppose or "point back to" a unified self, a sense of oneself as a substantial, or self-contained, source of modifications. But this self is beyond *direct* apprehension; the individual can know only *that* there is such an idea. The substantial unity underlying the imaginations — the adequate understanding of the individual finite body — is *God's* idea, which a human can grasp only as a conclusion of discursive reason, that is, in the third person.

Proceeding instead according to adequate ideas, concentrating on those aspects of his being that he can adequately understand, the individual again recognizes a center of causal activity underlying his adequate ideas, but in this case the center of causal activity is the completely adequate formal nature of God. The individual is aware of God as a source of his own nature in something like the way he was formerly aware of his individual self (that is, he grasps something standing as a substance to the objects immediately apprehended). But in this case the mind does directly apprehend the source; it sees the formal structure of its own apprehension as sufficient for what follows from it. Moreover, since this formal structure is precisely the self-containedness which defines substance, it is literally correct to say that one apprehends oneself as God. As a result, we can talk of adequate knowledge of self, or of self under the form of eternity, but the self knowable in this way is identified with the infinite intellect, not with a finite creature. The self which a human can know under the form of eternity is free and active, but it is not different from one individual to another; human knowledge of individual differences is erased along with the imaginative point of view. Knowledge of oneself as eternal is not a case of self-awareness in the sense of knowing one's own uniqueness, but in the sense, more important for Spinoza, of being aware of oneself as active and self-complete.

From this we can see that possession of the third kind of knowledge is a coming together of the third and the first person perspectives. That is, when the mind possesses knowledge of the third kind, it possesses both the immediacy of the first person perspective and the rational guarantee of the third. The uniting of these two perspectives becomes explicit in the propositions of Part V that we have been examining, but, armed with hindsight, we can see that the union was prepared in II, 43. This proposition has by now taken on the status of a sort of "master proposition" in Spinoza's theory of the mind; to quote it once again:

> He who has a true idea knows at the same time that he has a true
> idea, nor can he doubt the truth of the thing. (II, 43)[19]

There appear to be two separate claims here on behalf of the one who
has a true idea: first, that the idea is known to be true, and second, that
its possessor cannot doubt it. It would seem that the two must be distinct, since knowledge that an idea is true is an exercise of intellect, and
therefore rests on the third person perspective, whereas inability to doubt
derives from the psychological immediacy of the first. Nevertheless, it is
evident in the demonstration, and even more in the note, that Spinoza
does not regard the proposition as containing two independent assertions.
For him, recognizing a true idea and feeling certain are the *same* operation; if I have an idea which possesses the formal characteristics of a true
idea, then in grasping it I recognize myself as active, and know something about my own formal reality. The man who has true ideas not only
knows more but exhibits greater reality or perfection than the one who
does not. All this hinges on an idea's being an action, not a representa-
tional entity.[20] Spinoza sums up some of these points as follows:

> . . . no one who has a true idea is ignorant that a true idea involves
> the greatest certitude; to have a true idea signifying just this — to
> know a thing perfectly or as well as possible. No one, in fact, can
> doubt this unless he supposes an idea to be something dumb, like
> a picture on a tablet, instead of being a mode of thought, that is
> to say, the very act of understanding. (II, 43n)[21]

Spinoza is not always as explicit about the connections just described
as we might like, and sometimes takes them for granted, which can confuse twentieth-century readers who approach his philosophy armed with
quite different presuppositions. For example, in Proposition 28 of Part
IV, one of his claims is that the highest virtue (power, perfection) of the
mind is to know God, and to show this he writes:

---

19. See note 16, above.
20. I have argued this point in my "Truth and Adequacy in Spinozistic Ideas."
21. ". . . Nemo, qui veram habet ideam, ignorat veram ideam summam certitudinem involvere;
veram namque habere ideam, nihil aliud significat, quam perfecte, sive optime rem cognoscere;
nec sane aliquis de hac re dubitare potest, nisi putet, ideam quid mutum instar picturae in tabula,
& non modum cogitandi esse, nempe ipsum intelligere. . . ."

But the highest thing which the mind can understand is God . . .
and therefore the highest virtue of the mind is to understand or know
God. (IV, 28, dem.)[22]

To us, this appears to be simply a non-sequitur—saying that *I* am perfect
because what I understand is perfect. That Spinoza regards it as persua-
sive without any argument or citation (II, 43n could have been cited) indicates, I believe, the extent to which, for him, it is simply *evident* that
possession of adequate ideas involves recognition of one's own formal nature as complete and self-sustaining; the extent, that is, to which the views
presented above pervade his thought and color his descriptions.

A consequence of the views just discussed is that possession of the third
kind of knowledge can be described either in terms of the theory of emotions or the theory of action (as well, of course, as theory of knowledge).

In terms of the theory of action, possession of the third kind of
knowledge is action and not passion; the connection is summed up in
these two passages:

. . . he who knows by this kind of knowledge passes to the highest
human perfection. . . . (V, 27, dem.)[23]

The more perfection a thing possesses, the more it acts and the less
it suffers. . . . (V, 40)[24]

The connection between knowledge and action rests ultimately on the
points made above in discussing II, 43; II, 43 is cited by Spinoza in demonstrating V, 27.

In terms of the theory of emotions, possession of the third kind of
knowledge is a form of love:

We delight in whatever we understand by the third kind of
knowledge, and our delight is accompanied with the idea of God
as its cause. (V, 32)[25]

---

22. ". . . At summum, quod Mens intelligere potest, Deus est. . . : ergo Mentis summa virtus
est Deum intelligere, seu cognoscere."
23. ". . . Qui res hoc cognitionis genere cognoscit, is ad summam humanam perfectionem
transit. . . ."
24. "Quo unaquaeque res plus perfectionis habet, eo magis agit, & minus patitur. . . ."
25. "Quicquid intelligimus tertio cognitionis genere, eo delectamur, & quidem concomitante
idea Dei, tanquam causa."

This delight Spinoza calls "the intellectual love of God" (V, 32, cor.). Since the third kind of knowledge also involves knowledge of self, Spinoza could as well call it love of self as love of God, and, in fact, he comes close to describing it that way:

> The intellectual love of the mind toward God is the very love with which He loves Himself, not in so far as He is infinite, but in so far as He can be manifested through the essence of the human mind, considered under the form of eternity; that is to say, the intellectual love of the mind toward God is part of the infinite love with which God loves himself. (V, 36)[26]

In the demonstration, Spinoza calls this love

> an action by which the mind contemplates itself. . . . (V, 36, dem.)[27]

The fusing of the first and third person perspectives in Spinoza's theory of knowledge, which we have been describing above, has an analogue in his theory of action. The two perspectives are apparently incompatible; in the theory of action the analogous apparently incompatible theses are, on the one hand, the doctrine of universal causation, and on the other, the sense of oneself as an active subject. Universal causation is a conclusion of the intellect and thus of the third-person perspective; the sense of an active self rests once again on his theory of knowledge. We know that when it possesses adequate ideas the mind takes on the formal properties of self-sufficiency or perfection, and from V, 40 (quoted above) we know that this perfection counts as action of the mind. But in the note to Proposition 40, Spinoza says that from this

> taken together with Prop. 21, pt. 1, and other propositions, it is evident that our mind, in so far as it understands, is an eternal mode of thought which is determined by another eternal mode of thought, and this again by another, and so on *ad infinitum*. . . . (V, 40n)[28]

26. "Mentis Amor intellectualis erga Deum est ipse Dei Amor, quo Deus se ipsum amat, non quatenus infinitus est, sed quatenus per essentiam humanae Mentis, sub specie aeternitatis consideratam, explicari potest, hoc est, Mentis erga Deum Amor intellectualis pars est infiniti amoris, quo Deus se ipsum amat."

27. ". . . actio est, qua Mens se ipsum contemplatur. . . ."

28. ". . . ex quibus, & simul ex Prop. 21. p. 1. & aliis apparet, quod Mens nostra, quatenus intelligit, aeternus cogitandi modus sit, qui alio aeterno cogitandi modo determinatur, & hic iterum ab alio, & sic in infinitum. . . ."

Now, one "other proposition" that comes to mind at once is Proposition 28 of Part I, which asserts the infinite chain of causes among finite modes. But Spinoza is speaking here of infinite modes, and I suspect that the crucial "other proposition" is again II, 43. For if, as argued above, the claim that he who has a true idea knows that he has a true idea is to be understood as saying that the mind possesses the formal properties of adequacy and self-completeness when it understands and that this is a participation in the eternal as well as a recognition of it, then the claim is indeed equivalent to saying that "our mind, in so far as it understands, is an eternal mode of thought which is determined by another eternal mode of thought." From this we can form the notion of an infinite chain of causes among modes of thought, each of which is at the same time adequate and perfect in itself—in short, a reconciliation of the claims of universal causality with the demand for an active self.

We may conclude that in so far as the mind contemplates things under the form of eternity—that is, by means of adequate ideas or the third kind of knowledge—the three central topics of Parts II, III, and IV are combined; theory of knowledge, theory of the emotions, and theory of action all coalesce in the direct participation in the divine nature; we can regard this equally as a sharing of God's knowledge, His love, or His power.

* * *

I have spoken of a coming together of the first and third person perspectives as if this were an evidently intelligible possibility. In fact, I am by no means persuaded that it is intelligible; on the contrary, I very much doubt it, although the position I have described does seem to me to be Spinoza's. The difficulties do not stem from any topics newly-introduced in Part V; they have their origin in the epistemological claims of Part II, which we have seen to be the source of the doctrines we have been discussing. If the propositions on the eternity of the mind seem problematic—contradictory, even—it is not because Spinoza here strikes out in a new direction but because only here in Part V are we forced explicitly to confront the implications of Part II.

Spinoza's theory of the mind seems to be partly motivated by the conviction that, like everything else, the human body admits of being adequately apprehended—this yields the notion of a divine understanding presupposed in cases of adequate and inadequate ideas—and partly by the intuition that the individual person or ego should be identified at some level with this adequate apprehension of its own body. These two principles lead to the demand that there be *some* adequate understanding which is also personal; some knowledge which is simultaneously a salute and an embrace. To this demand Part V offers the solution that the third person and the first person perspectives come together "in eternity." Whether or not we accept such an answer for ourselves, we cannot but recognize that in this attempt at synthesis Spinoza's philosophy expresses—and attempts to satisfy—a human desire which has, historically, been widely felt; a desire, indeed, which may be among the initial motivations of philosophy itself.

THOMAS CARSON MARK

INDICES

INDEX OF MANUSCRIPTS
AND ARCHIVAL DOCUMENTS

GENERAL INDEX

mRts

medieval & renaissance texts & studies
is the publishing program of the
Center for Medieval and Early Renaissance Studies
State University of New York at Binghamton.

mRts emphasizes books that are needed —
texts, translations, and major research tools.

mRts aims to publish the highest quality scholarship
in attractive and durable format at modest cost.